WHERE
ARE THEY
BURIED?

Fitting Ends and Final Resting Places
of the Famous, Infamous, and Noteworthy

WHERE
ARE THEY
BURIED?

How Did They Die?

TOD BENOIT

BLACK DOG
& LEVENTHAL
PUBLISHERS
NEW YORK

Hardcover ISBN-10: 1-57912-287-6
Hardcover ISBN-13: 978-1-57912-287-4
PLC ISBN-10: 1-57912-678-2
PLC ISBN-13: 978-1-57912-678-0

Library of Congress Cataloging-in-Publication Data
on file at Black Dog & Leventhal Publishers, Inc.

Cover and interior design: Cindy LaBreacht

Photo credits:

All gravesite photographs copyright © 2003 by Tod Benoit

Photographs on the following pages are courtesy of Photofest:
Pages 22 (Chris "Notorious B.I.G." Wallace, Chris "Big Pun" Rios);
30; 33 (Brian Epstein, George Harrison, John Lennon); 54; 80; 112
(Lou Gehrig, Babe Ruth, Mickey Mantle, Roger Maris, Thurman
Munson, Joe DiMaggio); 156; 210; 277; 292; 364; 418; 437; 486
(Ray Kroc, Colonel Harland Sanders); and 517.

The remaining photograph credits are as follows:
Page 14: Ken Regan/Camera 5; page 22: Eric "Eazy-E" Wright
© Corbis; Tupac Shakur, AP/WIDE WORLD PHOTOS; page 33:
Stuart Sutcliffe © Bettmann/Corbis; page 112: Jim "Catfish" Hunter,
AP/WIDE WORLD PHOTOS; page 35: Sam Snead & Ben Hogan,
AP/WIDE WORLD PHOTOS; page 264: Gertrude Stein &
Alice B. Toklas © Bettmann/Corbis; page 394: Sid Vicious &
Nancy Spungen © Bettmann/Corbis; Bonnie Parker & Clyde Barrow,
AP/WIDE WORLD PHOTOS; page 486: Dave Thomas,
AP/WIDE WORLD PHOTOS; and page 548: Malcolm X &
Martin Luther King Jr., AP/WIDE WORLD PHOTOS.

Book manufactured in the U.S.A.

Published by
Black Dog & Leventhal Publishers, Inc.
151 West 19th Street
New York, New York 10011
www.blackdogandleventhal.com

Distributed by
Workman Publishing Company
225 Varick Street
New York, New York 10014

Hardcover: l k j i h
PLC: g f e d c b a

Dedication

This book is dedicated to the memory of Don Schellhammer, Sr., who died in November 2001 after a lengthy illness. At 58, Don was buried at St. Anne's Cemetery in Sturbridge, Massachusetts.

Appreciations

For their invaluable contributions, the author is sincerely grateful to the following folks: Brian Benoit for joining in the epic Seattle-to-San Diego run of 1996; Meryl Brodsky for her labors as research librarian extraordinaire and for untold largesse; Becky Koh for all of her generosities, including introducing my work to Black Dog & Leventhal; Cindi Inman for tracking down my final lost souls; Laura Ross, the discerning editor whose unflagging enthusiasm provided light at the end of the tunnel (and who will undoubtedly edit this sentence); Sid Roberts for mountaintop lodging; and Alisa Zinno for assorted personal kindnesses.

I'm also indebted to J.P. Leventhal and the staff and freelancers of Black Dog & Leventhal, including Cindy LaBreacht, Kylie Foxx, Michael Driscoll, Sara Cameron, Dara Lazar, Gregory Hurcomb, and True Sims. Their combined efforts have lent a quality to this work that I never could have envisioned.

Finally, kudos to the all of the nameless hundreds of people, from town clerks and funeral home directors to cemetery staff and priests, who've gone well out of their way to help this cause.

CONTENTS

INTRODUCTION

Tomorrow is the most important thing in life.
Comes into us at midnight very clean.
It's perfect when it arrives and it puts itself in our hands.
It hopes we've learned something from yesterday.
—JOHN WAYNE'S EPITAPH

⤜⟾◉⟾⤛

As I recall, the seasonably cool morning of December 9, 1980, became bitterly cold, for me anyway, right around ten o'-clock. I think that's when all this started, more or less.

I took my seat in an English class, nothing new there, and when the bell rang moments later, Chris Lozier bounced to her place directly in front of me. She was bright and cheerful, and in those days her arrival was a highlight.

"Can you believe that about John Lennon?" she asked.

"What, did he make a disco record or something?"

"No, he's dead. Someone shot him last night."

And so it was. The quick flash of a gun had claimed another victim. John Lennon hadn't been the first popular figure to pass on, and he wouldn't be the last, but the senselessness of his death, and the starkness of its brutality against the kindhearted way of his life, struck a particularly heartfelt chord. While a generation that had been raised to a Beatles soundtrack contemplated its own mortality, the world mourned. At school a few months later we were treated to a rendition of Lennon's "Imagine" by a most unlikely singer, a fellow student named John Wood. He sang it during an assembly and when he finished, the student body clapped reverentially. Though the pall of Lennon's death lingered, the pieces were picked up and everyone got over it. There was nothing else to be done.

During the mid-1980s, I attended university in Lowell, Massachusetts, swallowing whole the indoctrinations of the town's famous literary son, Jack Kerouac, an exhilarating drunk whose ruminating mind tended toward the exploration of society's underbelly. In an untimely fashion in 1969, Jack drank himself to death, and the buzz in some circles was that he was buried in a nearby cemetery. As friends and I had frequented his old barroom haunts, a pilgrimage to his grave seemed fitting.

The visit proved to be more complicated than I had anticipated. There are numerous cemeteries in Lowell and nobody seemed to know in which one Jack was buried. I finally learned the name of the cemetery by tracking down his obituary, but then had to figure out how to get there. Upon arriving, my plan was again confounded: The office was closed, there was no directory, and Jack's grave could be anywhere among the thousands of stones. After wandering the cemetery's rows for a few hours I gave up the search, but returned a few weeks later with John Macolini, a college roommate and fellow Kerouac devotee. Together we eventually located Jack's grave, but I knew there had to be an easier way to find such landmarks.

The locations of famous graves, and especially the puzzle of exactly how to find them, appealed to me as a kind of offbeat treasure hunt, but responsibilities beckoned and I put the matter on the back burner. Then, in 1992, the death of Sam Kinison, a sublimely deranged comedian, prompted me to pursue a quirky mental exercise: I began to compile a list of the famous deceased who mattered to me, or who might matter to someone else. Personalities like Babe Ruth and James Dean came to mind quickly and, once the most obvious individuals had been collected, I ferreted out additional notable folks from library reference sources. "Year in Review" issues of magazines were especially useful, and they yielded many more obscure or unconventional famous people, such as Dian Fossey, Jim Fixx, and Oskar Schindler. After compiling a list of several hundred famous deceased, I was the proud owner of an apparently worthless pile of information. Filing it away, I moved on.

But in 1994, I chanced upon a newspaper article concerning John Lennon's slaying. Across the street from the Dakota apartment building in New York City where he was shot, a section of Central Park had been dedicated to his memory and named "Strawberry Fields." More than a dozen years after John's death, a steady stream of visitors continued to arrive there in order to commune with John's spirit, their captivation showing no sign of abating. The article was a concise digest of this curious phenomenon, though, at its most fundamental level, the reporter didn't quite understand it. But I did.

Humans are unique in the cognizance of their own mortality. Though some may cling optimistically to the concept of a joyous hereafter, most acknowledge our granular contribution to the infinite beach of time and, by default, concede that the ultimate substance of our individual lives is largely irrelevant. But while we accept that all things must pass and nobody lives forever, we still strive to achieve a singularity, a legacy by which we might be remembered. This very human desire to "live on" is affirmed by the importance and elaborateness of our cemeteries, our penchant for visiting and caring for them, and the universally accepted notion of "respect for the dead." Every tombstone, a kind of waypoint between life and death, confirms individuality. "I was somebody," they seem to say.

Some 6,700 "somebodies" die in the United States every day, their passing mourned by survivors who keep the flame of their memory burning until joining them in ashes and dust. Though most passings are recognized by relatively small circles of family and friends, some deaths are more publicly mourned because, for better or worse, these people made a lasting imprint on the fabric of our society's culture. That culture includes all of us, and when John Lennon, or any famous or infamous person, is raised in memory, it's for the purpose of acknowledging and celebrating his or her unique and lasting stamp on our lives.

In the fall of 1994 I retrieved my list of famous deceased and the next step became obvious: It was time to find and document the resting places of our cultural heroes—and I was just the guy to do it. The project was ideally suited to my interests in history, travel, and research and, furthermore, I saw it as an opportunity to make the world just a little bit more fair. It somehow didn't seem equitable that some of our national icons, like John F. Kennedy and Elvis Presley, basked in the adoration of those who made the journey to the location of their well-documented monuments, while other worthy folks were relegated to the margins, cast off and all but forgotten.

I eventually cataloged the location of almost 700 famous graves, 450 of which are described in this book, and believe me, it was an enormous undertaking. There were multiple frustrations in locating many of the graves, and I pursued countless dead ends (no pun intended). However, that which did not kill me made me stronger, and I'm now grateful for my original ignorance: Had I comprehended the scheme's ultimate dimensions, I most certainly would have come up with a different hobby, and you'd be channel surfing right now.

Nonetheless, though there were innumerable disappointments and setbacks, it seemed that I was always rewarded for my persistence. Every blundering pitfall was supplanted by an equally elevating triumph. At a California cemetery, I suffered the wrath of some wasps whose nest I had inadvertently disturbed, but that misadventure resulted in a friendship with the groundskeeper. Later, I tapped out parts of this manuscript at his lofty Sierra Nevada mountain retreat. There were problems with rental cars: One particularly unlucky Taurus suffered a late-night collision with a near-sighted owl and, twenty minutes later, while I peeked through the new pattern of cracks in the windshield as we glided along a foggy stretch of Wisconsin blacktop, a suicidal skunk ambled into the car's path. The skunk never knew what hit him, but I'll bet the friendly Hertz staff in Minneapolis still cringes at the memory of that car's return. At another point, I accidentally deposited my vehicle's keys into a Long Island mailbox, but my idiocy was rewarded when it turned out that the mailman who arrived to retrieve them had known Mario Puzo personally. The helpful public servant showed me Mario's current digs and, with lukewarm Bud Lights retrieved from under the seat of his government-issue jeep, we saluted the progenitor of the fictitious Corleone crime family. In Texas, I lost a few pages of notes during a horrific windstorm but, a few days later in the lonely outpost of Picacho, New Mexico, I felt compensated when I was asked to serve as a sort of impromptu pallbearer for a forgotten pauper. I never knew what might be around the next bend in the road, and for that I'm thankful. It was an adventure.

I have one last anecdote to share. It's a little lengthy, but it's interesting, it's true, and it swings us full circle.

In October 1997 I was visiting famous graves in the Deep South, cutting a swath from Nashville to New Orleans when, on a dark stretch of Mississippi pavement, I came upon a traffic jam. There had been an accident and the road was temporarily closed to traffic in both directions. The midnight air was chilly so most people stayed in their idling vehicles, but I pulled to the side, slipped on my coat, and walked up to the crash site. It was gruesome, a pickup truck had clocked a bridge, and a dozen solemn bystanders gave the rescue team plenty of room. Unbelievably, I recognized the man who stood next to me in a dungaree shirt and cream-colored, flat-brimmed hat. I had to look twice, not quite trusting my eyes, but—sure enough—it was Bob Dylan. An hour earlier he had performed in concert at Mississippi State University, but he now stood anonymously in the shadows, exchanging short remarks with his personal bodyguard, a tough-looking Asian man nearly as thick as he was tall.

I casually sidled up to Dylan and offered commentary on the crash, but he was wary. His rugged sidekick eyed me suspiciously, no doubt concerned that his boss might end up like his old friend, John Lennon. My mind working at hyperspeed, I desperately sought a dialogue a notch above the typical tongue-tied, star-struck blather that Dylan most certainly detested. Knowing that he was a fan of boxing, I ventured to share a chuckle with him over the recent Mike Tyson ear-biting debacle, but the conversation quickly stalled. I dug deep. The previous day, in Montgomery, Alabama, I had visited the grave of Hank Williams and it just so happened that I knew that Dylan was a dyed-in-the-wool Hank fan. So I told him about it. And remarkably, he listened. For the first time, he looked at me while I spoke. There was something to this grave stuff after all.

The accident scene was almost cleared and the drivers that had been delayed grew anxious. Bystanders were now murmuring and pointing their fingers; Dylan had been recognized, and a state trooper interrupted us, asking for an autograph. The trooper went away satisfied, but the escort indicated that they should be returning to the tour bus. Dylan turned to leave and then paused. He asked me, "What was the name of that cemetery?"

I don't know that Bob Dylan ever paid a call to Hank Williams' grave, but I like to think that he did. In 1975 he had visited Jack Kerouac's grave in Lowell and, sitting cross-legged while Allen Ginsberg chanted along in double time, he strummed a guitar for the amusement of Jack's ghost. That was a fitting homage; such humble alms are precisely suited to the occasion of visiting a person's resting place, whether it's of someone famous or otherwise. My sojourns were never about being photographed in the presence of their notoriety or checking graves off in the style of a grocery list. I've conscientiously maintained a model of decorum and, should you choose to visit any of these sites, I trust you'll preserve the tradition.

In the grand scheme of things, I don't suppose that all of this talk about the deceased and their graves amounts to a hill of beans. Still, I choose to believe that keeping a flame of memory burning for them matters somehow, even if it's in some mystical way that we cannot fully grasp. For that reason, I uphold my end of that unspoken accord. Maybe now you will join me.

—TOD BENOIT

GEN-X
STANDOUTS

KURT COBAIN

FEBRUARY 20, 1967 – APRIL 5, 1994

With the 1991 groundbreaking release *Nevermind*, Kurt Cobain and his inventive band, Nirvana, produced in one deft stroke a new stepchild of rock and roll—alternative rock—and pulled rock away from the processed, synthetic and stale sounds of the 1980s back to something more sincere. *Nevermind's* signature song, "Smells Like Teen Spirit," was adopted by a disaffected generation as an anthem of discontent and cynicism, "grunge" was added to the national vocabulary, and thrift stores enjoyed a run on tattered flannel shirts.

But as an intense loner, superstardom never interested Kurt, and as the band skyrocketed, this reluctant guitar hero's personal life became a roller coaster. He was plagued by a chronic stomach condition that caused him a tremendous amount of pain and Kurt resorted to medicating himself with heroin. His 1991 marriage to Courtney Love, the brassy leader of the punkish group Hole, brought him some security but rumors of the couple's drug abuse were rampant; after a *Vanity Fair* article accused Love of using heroin while she was pregnant, child welfare authorities investigated and forbade the couple from being alone with their baby daughter for a month.

Just three years and three hit albums after Nirvana's breakthrough, Kurt's mental health had plunged and his already pronounced angst heightened. While on tour in Europe in March 1994, an overdose settled Kurt into a twenty-hour-long coma. Even though 50 doses of a Valium-like prescription drug called Rohypnol were found in his stomach, the couple called the overdose "an accident." They returned home to Seattle, but matters only worsened.

At the end of March, Courtney checked Kurt into a Los Angeles drug rehabilitation clinic and, while he worked on dislodging the monkey from his back, she settled into a hotel across town to work on an album. But Kurt sneaked away from the clinic and returned to their empty home. On April 5, Kurt barricaded himself inside a greenhouse above his garage, shot heroin one last time, then shot a shotgun one last time. Three days later, an electrician who had arrived to work on the home's security system discovered a very dead body. It was presumed to be Kurt, and he was ultimately identified through his fingerprints.

Kurt left a note, but therein lies a minor controversy. Kurt's suicide note reads like the draft of a speech announcing a retirement from the music business—only in the last four lines is there any allusion to the idea that he might also be retiring from life—and here's the kicker: The lines were added after his signature, and are written in a hand that's similar, but different. Of course, through a short leap of logic, some now believe that Kurt was murdered and that his ruthless killer, finding Kurt's retirement address, simply added a few lines to turn it into a suicide note.

But it's all pretty unlikely. It seems quite clear, instead (to this writer anyway), that the note may have been originally intended as a retirement speech but, when it came time to end his life, Kurt figured that the draft could serve as a serviceable suicide note as well. In his tormented state of mind just before killing himself, perhaps while strung out on smack, he scribbled a few personal lines to his family and was done with it.

The note is readily available on the Internet and you're free to draw your own conclusions. They never do just fade away, do they?

At 27, Kurt was cremated. It's since been reported that his ashes have been scattered, well, almost everywhere.

AALIYAH HAUGHTON

JANUARY 16, 1979 – AUGUST 25, 2001

In her short life, Aaliyah Haughton, known simply as Aaliyah, lived a modern fairy tale of stardom. The sultry and ethereal-voiced R&B singer hit the music scene young: At just eleven years, she performed on *Star Search* and with soul legend Gladys Knight. By age fourteen Aaliyah had earned a recording contract. The next year her debut album went platinum. During her senior year in high school, Aaliyah released a second hit album and was nominated for an Academy Award for her performance of the song "Journey to the Past" from the soundtrack of the animated movie *Anastasia*.

Movie deals and acting roles came next. In quick succession Aaliyah costarred in *Romeo Must Die*, garnered a starring role in the supernatural adventure film *Queen of the Damned*, and won coveted roles in two sequels to *The Matrix*.

There should have been many more chapters in this story, but it ended abruptly instead. While in the Bahamas shooting a music video, Aaliyah and her entourage were onboard a small charter airplane that crashed immediately after takeoff, killing all nine people aboard. It was later learned that the pilot did not have clearance to fly that particular airplane and, just twelve days earlier, had been in court on cocaine charges.

At age 21, Aaliyah was buried at Ferncliffe Mausoleum in Hartsdale, New York

CEMETERY DIRECTIONS: From I-87, take Exit 7 in Ardsley and follow Route 9A north for 1¼ miles. Then, at the traffic light, turn right onto Secor Road. Ferncliffe is a short distance on the left.

GRAVE DIRECTIONS: Enter Ferncliffe at the first entrance, bear right and park toward the right-hand side of the main mausoleum. Enter the mausoleum through the glass doors and take the elevator to the third floor. Turn right out of the elevator and, after about 75 feet, Aaliyah's crypt is on the left-hand wall.

SHANNON HOON

SEPTEMBER 26, 1967 – OCTOBER 22, 1995

Shannon Hoon wailed his way to stardom as frontman for the rock group Blind Melon. In 1992 the group's eponymous debut album went multi-platinum, primarily on the strength of its breezy hit single "No Rain." But Shannon's defining moment came during the 1994 Woodstock concert. Dressed up and emoting like a transgendered Janis Joplin, Shannon's plaintive laments of youth's desperation and uncertainty wove themselves easily into the weird nostalgic ironies of that revisited Woodstock. Shannon ignited the crowd when he sang, "I'll close my eyes and make you all go away." Sadly, he made good on the promise sooner than anyone expected.

Late in the summer of 1995, Blind Melon released its second album, *Soup*, and launched an extensive tour to promote the release. While killing time before a New Orleans show, Shannon shot up inside the band's tour bus and died of an accidental heroin overdose.

At 28, he was buried at Dayton Cemetery in his hometown of Dayton, Indiana.

CEMETERY DIRECTIONS: The cemetery is located on Route 38 just east of town.

GRAVE DIRECTIONS: Shannon's memorial is in the lower section, a few rows from the wire fence in back. If you happen upon his grandparents' markers, you're close—Shannon's grave is twenty feet behind you.

RIVER PHOENIX

AUGUST 23, 1970 – OCTOBER 31, 1993

Named for the river of life in Herman Hesse's counterculture novel, *Siddhartha*, River Phoenix was a heartthrob teen actor who was idolized and critically acclaimed for his openness and sensitivity.

The golden boy's early childhood was spent in Venezuela, where his parents worked as Children of God missionaries. Shortly after they moved to Los Angeles, ten-year-old River landed commercial roles that led to a television series *Seven Brides for Seven Brothers*, and eventually a movie career.

Star potential in the vegan, politically minded actor first showed in *Stand By Me*, and later roles could often be mined for flecks of autobiography: In *The Mosquito Coast* he played the son of a renegade idealist who sequesters his family in a Central American jungle; in *Running on Empty* he gave an Oscar-nominated performance as the son of fugitive radicals; and in *My Own Private Idaho*, River's character suffered narcoleptic convulsions.

As every generation faces the moment when the myth of its own immortality is shattered, so too did the Generation X'ers with River's untimely demise. It came outside Johnny Depp's hip Los Angeles club, the Viper Room, on Halloween in 1993. After seven or eight minutes of horrifying convulsions, with his sister Rain atop him in hysterics, trying desperately to somehow stop his spasms, River lay still and blue on the sidewalk when paramedics arrived.

He never regained consciousness, and River's death was attributed to accidental "acute multiple drug intoxication" involving lethal levels of cocaine and morphine.

River was cremated and his ashes scattered at his family's ranch near Gainesville, Florida.

SELENA

APRIL 16, 1971 – MARCH 31, 1995

With a pouting smile and suggestive clothing, singer Selena Quintanilla was the ruling diva of Tejano music—"La Reina De La Musica Tejana"—and for seven years in a row was voted its best female vocalist. Tejano's roots are in the bouncy and fast-paced polka rhythms that are popular in Texas, but Selena's added twists of salsa and merengue resulted in a new and irresistible form of Tejano that found overwhelming popularity.

Born and raised in Texas, Selena had an impressive fan base in her home state, but she was most popular south of the border, where she succeeded in becoming the first American to conquer the enormous Mexican and Latin American markets. In 1993, her eighth album, *Amor Prohibido*, spawned four number one Latin singles and sold millions. But despite her triumphs in the Latin markets, it became apparent that to gain true critical acceptance, Selena needed to develop a coast-to-coast fan base in the States, which required an album with lyrics sung in English. (Though English was her first language, Selena had always sung in Spanish.) Work on such a crossover album began and expectations were high, but Selena would never see its release.

Yolanda Saldivar was a rabid fan of Selena's who started a grass-roots Selena fan club. The club became the "official" fan organization and, due to her assertiveness, Yolanda soon gained access to Selena's inner circle. In 1993, when Selena introduced a clothing line and opened her own Selena Etc. boutiques, Yolanda's loyalty was rewarded and she was named manager of the fledgling San Antonio store. But it turned out that Yolanda had almost zero business acumen, and matters soured even further when Selena's father, through a casual audit of the business's receipts, discovered that Yolanda had been embezzling funds.

Yolanda steadfastly maintained her innocence, and she drove to Selena's hometown of Corpus Christi to meet with Selena, supposedly to present bank statements that would exonerate her. Yolanda checked into Room 158 at the Day's Inn at Interstate 37 and Navigation Boulevard and, on a Friday morning at around 11:45, Selena arrived. No one is exactly sure what happened at the motel, but somehow Selena was mortally wounded by a gunshot to the back. Staggering into the lobby, a terrified Selena fingered Yolanda as the shooter and collapsed. Though Selena was pronounced dead an hour later, for all intents, she died on the floor of the motel's lobby; when paramedics arrived there within minutes, she lay in a massive pool of blood with no pulse and no blood pressure.

In her red pickup truck, Yolanda kept police at bay for more than nine hours until she was taken without further shots fired. She was sentenced to life in prison and won't be eligible for parole until 2026.

Meanwhile, Selena's legacy lives on in her music, biographies, a movie, and her namesakes—in the five months following her murder, 619 Texas newborns were named Selena, a 600 percent increase over previous periods.

At 23, Selena was buried at Seaside Memorial Park in Corpus Christi, Texas.

CEMETERY DIRECTIONS: From I-37, take Route 358 east to the Airline Road exit, then follow Airline Road north for almost two miles. Turn left on Gaines Street and the cemetery is a short distance on the right.

GRAVE DIRECTIONS: Enter the cemetery and drive straight to the end of the drive. Turn right and, after 150 feet, you'll see Selena's grave.

YOUNG RAPPERS

Rap music originated during the 1970s as African American and Hispanic performers in New York City spoke rhyming words over an instrumental track composed of snatches of recorded music. In the mid-1980s, the rap group Run-DMC released a single with the hard-rock band Aerosmith that created a new audience for the young musical movement, and rap soon came charging into the mainstream. In the ensuing years, rap music accounted for a growing part of the recording industry's revenues, and its cultural impact on the urban style of dress, speech, and art has since become obvious.

But in the same way that rock and roll had been scorned by some as it gained popularity, rap too has had its opponents, and its social and musical merits are still debated. Since its inception, rap music has been called harsh and monotonous and has been criticized for lacking any traditional melodic qualities, while its lyrics have been lambasted for their vulgarity. On the other hand, defenders of rap music maintain that its lyrics, for all their rawness, are the poetry of the streets and constitute a straight-up social comment from the front lines of ghetto life.

In any event, as rap's audience grew exponentially, scores of releases from new artists were rushed into music stores and the careers of these fresh rappers were ignited. Unfortunately for a few of them, the success about which they had dreamed ignited a deadly fuse, and the violence and fatalism of their lyrics turned out to be tragically prophetic.

Eric 'Eazy-E' Wright
SEPTEMBER 7, 1963 – MARCH 26, 1995

Eric Wright grew up on the rough streets of Los Angeles where he dealt drugs for a living after dropping out of high school. In the mid-1980s he founded a rap record company, Ruthless Records. Shortly afterward, Eazy-E began his own rap group by

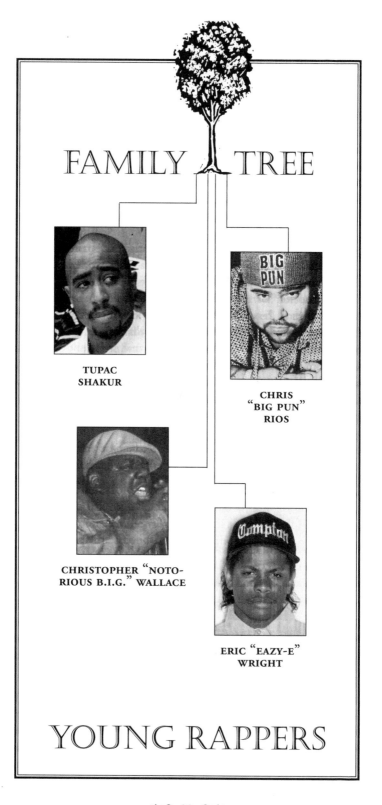

FAMILY TREE

TUPAC
SHAKUR

CHRIS
"BIG PUN"
RIOS

CHRISTOPHER "NOTO-
RIOUS B.I.G." WALLACE

ERIC "EAZY-E"
WRIGHT

YOUNG RAPPERS

forming NWA (Niggaz With Attitude), which featured Eazy-E's own high-pitched and whiny voice.

With raps and rhymes that celebrated urban violence, the denigration of women, and the glory of killing police officers, NWA became the most notorious group in rap. They are now considered the progenitors of the "gangsta rap" genre. Indeed, it was NWA that drew the ire of concerned citizens demanding that labels warning of explicit lyrics be required on these releases. Much to their dismay, the labels actually caused sales to increase, and gangsta rap became a commercial bonanza.

NWA split up in 1991 and Eazy-E embarked on a high-profile, full-time solo career. As he was still running Ruthless Records and producing new artists, Eazy-E's professional future looked bright. But in 1995, he discovered that he was dying of AIDS. Only a month after being diagnosed with the disease, at 31, he died of complications of the disease and was buried at Rose Hill Memorial Park in Whittier, California.

CEMETERY DIRECTIONS: From I-605, exit at Beverly Boulevard, head east, then turn north onto Workman Mill Boulevard (a.k.a. Norwalk Boulevard). Follow Workman for 1½ miles and enter the cemetery at Gate One on the right.

GRAVE DIRECTIONS: Proceed up the main road, turn left at the fifth drive, and the Lupine Lawn section will be on the right. After the hairpin turn around Lupine Lawn, the curb on the right is marked "2215." About fifty feet down the grass hill from this marking is Eazy-E's grave.

Tupac Shakur

JUNE 16, 1971 – SEPTEMBER 13, 1996

In the early 1990s Tupac Shakur joined the rap group Digital Underground, but he soon outgrew the group and went solo. His debut album, *2Pacalypse Now*, went gold, and a 1993 follow-up, *Strictly 4 My N.I.G.G.A.Z.* saw platinum. That same year, Tupac costarred in the popular movie *Poetic Justice*, which further fueled his celebrity.

The next couple years were turbulent, and the pages turned quickly. In late 1994 Tupac was in and out of court—and jail—on sexual assault charges. Then, during a robbery (to his credit, he was the victim and not the perpetrator), he was shot five times. In February of 1995 Tupac was sentenced to 4½ years in prison on sexual assault charges. While passing time behind bars, his third release debuted at number one. In October of 1995, while the case was on appeal, Tupac was released on bail, funded by Suge Knight, the owner of Death Row Records. Tupac's fourth release came in 1996 under Suge's label, and it raced up the charts.

On September 7, 1996, the whirlwind ended abruptly. Tupac was gunned down while in the passenger seat of Suge's BMW while stopped at a traffic light near the Las Vegas strip. Six days later Tupac died without ever regaining consciousness. He was cremated and his ashes scattered by family and friends.

Since Tupac's death, two others very closely related to his murder have themselves been murdered. Just two months later, Yafea Fula, a member of Tupac's entourage and an eyewitness to his murder, was gunned down in New Jersey. Next to meet a bloody end was Orlando Anderson, who happened to have had an assault suit pending against Tupac at the time of Tupac's murder. Further, just hours before Tupac was killed, he and his Crips gang brothers had rumbled with Tupac's entourage in a hotel lobby. Neither of those murders has been proven to be directly linked to Tupac's.

To date, Tupac's murder hasn't been solved, though not for lack of speculation about who might have had reason to commit it. Some of this speculation even spilled into a rival rapper's camp, which brings us to Notorious B.I.G.

Christopher 'Notorious B.I.G.' Wallace

MAY 21, 1972 – MARCH 9, 1997

Gangsta rapper Notorious B.I.G., a.k.a. Biggie Smalls, was born Christopher Wallace and grew up in New York's turbulent Bedford-Stuyvesant district. After an obligatory stint as a drug dealer and some jail time, B.I.G. turned to rapping. When Sean "Puffy" Combs heard his demo, B.I.G. was signed to Puffy's Bad Boy Records label and his 1994 debut, *Ready to Die*, quickly went platinum. B.I.G. won Billboard's Rapper of the Year award and basked in all of the perks that accompany rap stardom.

B.I.G.'s ascent to stardom took place simultaneously with Tupac's, and a feud developed between the two, despite the fact that they'd once been close associates. Tupac suspected B.I.G was behind the 1994 robbery that had left him with five bullet holes. Because B.I.G. was from the East Coast and Tupac from the West, what many viewed as a ridiculous animosity developed between their opposing camps over turf and record sales. Finally, Tupac claimed to have slept with B.I.G.'s wife and even bragged about it in a song.

On March 9, 1997, just six months after Tupac's murder, B.I.G. was gunned down in an eerily similar scene. In Los Angeles, after the Soul Train Awards, an unidentified assailant shot him to death as he sat in the passenger seat of a vehicle stopped at a red light. B.I.G.'s murder remains unsolved as well.

He was cremated and his ashes divided among three people—his mother, his wife, and his girlfriend (don't ask).

Chris 'Big Pun' Rios
NOVEMBER 10, 1971 – FEBRUARY 7, 2000

A Latino rapper and producer from the South Bronx, Chris Rios, or Big Punisher, released his debut album, *Capital Punishment*, in 1998. It became the first solo Latin rap album ever to go platinum. In 1999, he released another album of knockout rhymes with members of the group Terror Squad, and in early 2000 he anticipated the release of his second solo work.

But Big Pun didn't live to see that release. As an enormous man whose weight was reported as anywhere from 450 to 700 pounds, his heart failed on February 7, 2000, and he died at 28 years old.

Big Pun was cremated and his ashes were entrusted to his family.

Though Big Pun didn't live to see his second solo release hit the streets, it lingered on the charts for some months after his demise. This seems to be a common phenomenon among rappers. Indeed, something so insignificant as death is no longer an impediment to a continuing career in rap music—collectively, the four rappers profiled above released at least ten posthumous recordings.

BABY
BOOMER
ICONS

EDWARD ABBEY

JANUARY 29, 1927 – MARCH 14, 1989

The novelist and essayist Edward Abbey was a man mightily threatened by the encroachment of technocracy upon the individual and his environment. In his books and articles he profiled the West the way it once was, the way it is today, and the way he feared it would become unless the intrusions of civilization and industrialization were curbed. In his role as defender of the southwestern landscape, Abbey attained the status of a modern-day folk hero for ecological subversives everywhere.

Of his 21 books, the 1968 nonfiction work, *Desert Solitaire*, made his initial reputation, but seven years later Abbey eclipsed it with the riotous *Monkey Wrench Gang*. In it, he depicts a small gang of "monkey wrenchers," a term he seems to have coined, as they sabotage road builders and others who would develop the desert.

At 62, Ed died of complications brought on by hepatic hypertension.

As per his wishes, he was buried by family and friends in an old sleeping bag deep in the Cabeza Prieta Desert of southwestern Arizona. His body was transported in the bed of a pickup truck and there was no undertaker, embalming, or coffin. The exact location of his grave remains a secret known only by a select few of his survivors.

Until he was seventeen, Ed lived in the hamlet of Home, Pennsylvania, and in 1996 a private group erected a marker there to recognize him. You can see it on Route 119, about ten miles north of the town of Indiana.

ABBOTT & COSTELLO

Lou Costello

MARCH 6, 1906 – MARCH 3, 1959

William 'Bud' Abbott

OCTOBER 2, 1895 – APRIL 24, 1974

Through their cleverly crafted routines featuring an unlikely pair bantering back and forth in complete misunderstanding of each other, Bud Abbott and Lou Costello became one of the most successful comedy teams in Hollywood history. Abbott played the insulting, "I am not amused" straight man, while Costello was the boisterous "baaaaad boy" and buffoon—a short and round innocent who perpetually suffered his partner's berating and won the audiences' sympathies amid howls of laughter. The quick-tongued tandem found fame in vaudeville, radio, Broadway, television, and perhaps most famously, on the silver screen.

Their official teaming was in 1936, and the duo soon landed on radio's *The Kate Smith Hour*. It was on this program that their classic signature skit "Who's On First?" came to the national attention, and Abbott & Costello rocketed to fame. By 1939, they'd signed a movie deal with Universal Pictures. Their first few films, including *Buck Privates*, were smash hits, but the team's most popular films were yet to come. In 1948, the duo developed a comedy-horror genre with the hilarious *Abbott & Costello Meet Frankenstein* film, which ushered in the *Abbott & Costello Meet...* era. Over the next eight years the pair made a series of beloved films in which they "met" the Invisible Man, the Mummy, and Dr. Jekyll and Mr. Hyde, among others.

When Bud and Lou dissolved their partnership in 1956, the tabloids went into overdrive speculating about bad blood between the two comedians. But the truth seems to be that theirs was a completely amicable parting; at 60, Bud had grown noticeably weary of the spotlight, while Lou welcomed a change of pace and had other aspirations as a talk-show host and as a dramatic actor.

But just over two years later, any such inclinations of Lou's were put on permanent hold when he suffered a heart attack. Lou was ordered to go on bed rest, and he obliged, but a few days later the funny guy suffered a more massive coronary and died at 52.

Lou rests at Calvary Cemetery in Los Angeles.

CEMETERY DIRECTIONS: Whittier Boulevard is just north of the intersection of I-5 and I-710. The cemetery is at 4201 Whittier Blvd., a bit west of I-710.

GRAVE DIRECTIONS: Enter the cemetery, bear left, and drive to the big mausoleum on the hill. Inside the mausoleum is a chapel with three short halls that extend to the right. Lou's crypt is in the top row of the middle hall, and is marked with his given name, Louis Francis Cristillo.

In 1961, Bud suffered a sort of epileptic fit while aboard an airplane, and in 1965 he had a mild stroke. Bud was never quite the same after those calamities, but he did survive for nearly a decade,

ETERNAL COUPLE

ABBOTT & COSTELLO

and even provided the voice for his own character in the short-lived *Abbott & Costello Cartoon Show*. At 78, Bud died of cancer.

He was cremated and his ashes scattered in the Pacific Ocean.

THE BEATLES

When the Beatles made their U.S. debut on the *Ed Sullivan Show* in February 1964, playing their infectious new form of rock and roll, an entire generation realized that nothing would ever be the same again. And it wasn't. Over the next six years the Beatles— John and Paul, George and Ringo—dominated the culture and translated their style and music into new cultural trends in self-expression, appearance, attitude, and, of course, music. No group before or since has had a lasting effect on pop music and culture even approaching that of the Beatles.

John Lennon and, to a slightly lesser degree, Paul McCartney, were generally regarded as the group's backbone. Under their direction the Beatles tirelessly evolved and ignited revolutions at every new creative pinnacle. Each of their key albums—*Rubber Soul, Revolver, Sgt. Pepper's Lonely Hearts Club Band, Magical Mystery Tour, The White Album, Abbey Road*, was an increasingly honed masterpiece and introduced new areas of musical exploration and penetrating lyrical introspection. Public appearances by the band elicited a hysterical response that came to be known as Beatlemania. The hysteria became so tiring to the band members, and created such a barrier to any semblance of a "normal" performance, that the Beatles concert of August 1966 in San Francisco became their last, just 2 ½ years after their American debut on *Ed Sullivan*.

The band started to come apart after their manager, Brian Epstein, died in April 1967. They suffered a protracted, slow-motion breakup, and had totally disbanded by the autumn of 1970. John, Paul, George, and Ringo each pursued his own solo career with varying degrees of success, though none ever reached the popular heights enjoyed by the group as a whole.

Stuart Sutcliffe

JUNE 23, 1940 – APRIL 10, 1962

Stuart Sutcliffe was a friend and fellow art student of John Lennon at the Liverpool Art College when John suggested that Stu buy a bass guitar and join his band—never mind that he couldn't play.

Stu bought a bass and became a sort of pseudo-band member. (George, Paul, and drummer Pete Best were already in the band and Stu's services weren't absolutely essential.) Nonetheless, Stu played with them for about a year at a number of Liverpool engagements, during a brief May 1960 tour of Scotland, and at some nightclub gigs in Germany.

Stu is generally credited for naming the band; it was he who suggested "Beetles" as a play on Buddy Holly's Crickets. And Stu's girlfriend Astrid Kirchherr is generally credited for the Beatles "mop-top" hairstyles; she first cut Stu's and then George's hair in the distinctive style, and the other band members soon adopted it.

When the band went back to Liverpool after an extended 1961 booking at a nightspot in Hamburg, Stu stayed in Germany with Astrid, effectively bowing out of the Beatles. On April 10, 1962, the day before the Beatles were to arrive back in Hamburg for a round of shows, Stu died of a brain hemorrhage at 21. He was buried at Huyton Parish Church Cemetery on Stanley Road in Liverpool, England.

Brian Epstein
SEPTEMBER 19, 1934 – AUGUST 27, 1967

In the fall of 1961, while running his parents' North End Road Music Store on Whitechapel Street in Liverpool, Brian Epstein began getting an inordinate number of requests for records by the Beatles, a local band with just one single that had been released in Germany. His curiosity was piqued. Epstein went to see the band at a basement hall called the Cavern Club, and a month later Brian offered to manage them. Intrigued by Brian's straightforwardness, John agreed on the spot and on January 24, 1962, the Beatles and Brian signed a contract.

Brian's first order of business was to get the band a recording contract, and he used whatever clout he could muster from his family's small chain of Liverpool record stores to get meetings with British record companies. Brian and the band had plenty of rejections, but he finally secured them an agreement; in June 1962, two months after Stu Sutcliffe's death, George Martin signed them to Parlophone, a division of EMI. Martin later admitted that though he felt the Beatles had promise, he signed them in large part because of Brian's boundless enthusiasm.

John, Paul, and George next asked Brian to sack their drummer, Pete, and replace him with one Richard Starkey (who went by the

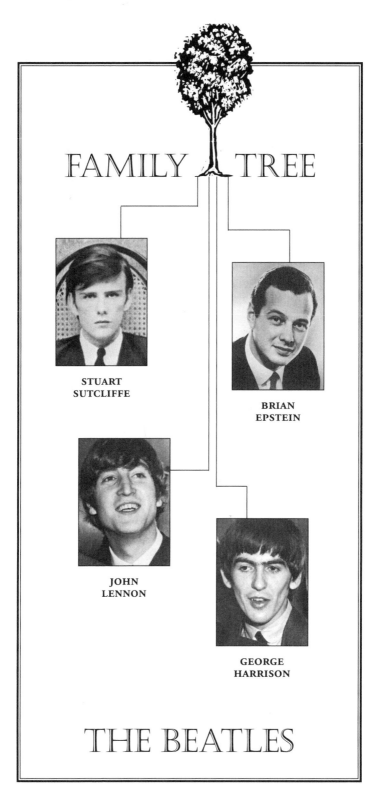

FAMILY TREE

STUART SUTCLIFFE

BRIAN EPSTEIN

JOHN LENNON

GEORGE HARRISON

THE BEATLES

name "Ringo Starr"), and that was accomplished by August 1962. Then Brian set to smartening up the Beatles' stage appearance. He put them in matching mohair suits and encouraged a rather theatrical synchronized bow at the conclusion of each song.

The Beatles were now complete, and during their almost six years with Brian as manager, they enjoyed the greatest success that any popular artists had ever achieved, and, it seemed, without a single reversal of fortune. Upon his death, however, they lost the one person who had been capable of resolving their differences and, after a tangle of artistic conflicts and personal jealousies, the Beatles broke up three years later.

Brian had suffered bouts of depression and he often took pills to help him sleep. On August 27, 1967, he died at 32 from what was ruled an accidental overdose of the sleeping pill Carbitol. He was buried at Kirkdale Jewish Cemetery on Long Lane in Liverpool, England.

John Lennon

OCTOBER 9, 1940 – DECEMBER 8, 1980

Through personnel and name changes during the 1950s and early '60s, John Lennon's band evolved from the Quarrymen, to Johnny and the Moondogs, to the Silver Beatles, before arriving at their final namesake, the Beatles. With co-helmsman Paul McCartney, John, the most blunt but thoughtful Beatle, steered the band that became a touchstone for their generation.

A year before the Beatles broke up, John married Yoko Ono and they began collaborating both creatively and as activists. He became an outspoken advocate of peace, even staging a flamboyant "Bed-In for Peace" protest with Yoko. In 1971, John again topped the music charts with his solo album *Imagine*, and through the decade he recorded with Yoko *Shaved Fish* and his final record, *Double Fantasy*.

On December 8, 1980, at around 5:00 p.m., John and Yoko left their apartment in the Dakota building in New York City and were approached by several autograph seekers. John obliged and among the autographs he signed was one on the cover of a *Double Fantasy* album for a Mark David Chapman.

The Lennons returned to the Dakota at about 10:50 p.m. When they exited their limousine, Chapman, who'd been waiting in the shadows, called out, "Mr. Lennon." He then fired four pistol shots, all striking John, who staggered to the concierge room, said, "I'm shot," and fell down. Police arrived within two minutes to a surreal scene. While John lay bleeding to death and a hysterical Yoko and passers-by helplessly comforted him, Chapman stood calmly where he had fired the shots, the gun on the ground at his feet. John was put in a police car, and as they raced to Roosevelt Hospital an officer asked, "Are you John Lennon?" The voice of a generation's final word was breathed in a soft moan: "Yeah."

At 40 years old, John was dead on arrival, and the medical examiner later announced that no one could have lived more than a few minutes with such injuries. As word of his death spread, horrified fans grappled with the seeming impossibility that their generation's idol was forever gone in the quick flash of a gun. Later that evening, a statement was issued on Yoko's behalf: "John loved and prayed for the human race. Please do the same for him."

After John's death, people from around the globe spontaneously gathered at the Dakota in a sort of communion and, naturally, they spilled into the lawns of Central Park across the street. This became *the* place to eternalize the singer and, in a 1985 ceremony, a particular two-acre patch was dedicated to his memory as "Strawberry Fields." Located at the intersection of 72nd Street and the west side of Central Park, the triangularly shaped garden's focal point is a beautiful circular mosaic of inlaid stones from countries the world over. The mosaic's center spells a simple plea: IMAGINE.

At every hour of every day, fans of John's music and message meander about Strawberry Fields and, on the anniversaries of his birth and death, impromptu services pay homage.

It's generally reported that John was cremated and his ashes given to Yoko Ono, who sprinkled some of them in John's hometown of Liverpool, England, and some at Strawberry Fields. However, the matter was confused when, in a 1990 interview, Yoko stated that John had actually been buried. She never expanded on the statement and didn't say where he was buried. And she has never retracted the statement or explained that she had been misunderstood. Instead, she simply has never talked about it again.

Chapman, a former security guard from Hawaii, pleaded guilty to John's murder and is serving a life term in prison in Attica, New York.

George Harrison
FEBRUARY 25, 1943 – NOVEMBER 29, 2001

A member of the Beatles since its very earliest Quarrymen days, George Harrison was the solid bassist known as "the quiet one." Though George's presence was generally overshadowed by the songwriting talents of John and Paul, and by Ringo's antics, he was certainly a remarkable musician in his own right, and contributed a number of songs to the Beatles' catalog. Interested in Eastern culture, he traveled to India in 1965 to study with musician Ravi Shankar and the influence is obvious on the following year's "Norwegian Wood." George later contributed "While My Guitar Gently Weeps" and "Here Comes the Sun," among other songs credited to him.

After the Beatles ceased working together, George released *All Things Must Pass* in 1971, a three-record work in which he demonstrated his affinity for mixing rock and religion. Later that year he organized concert fundraisers for Bangladeshi famine victims that featured himself and such artists as Eric Clapton and Bob Dylan, and the concerts resulted in another release, *The Concert for Bangladesh*. George's solo career seemed to peak then, and he later retreated from the public eye entirely.

In 1977 George got brief, though unwanted, attention when his marriage dissolved; his wife left him for his close friend Clapton, whom she would later marry. In 1987 George resurfaced as one of the all-star musicians in the Traveling Wilburys, and he followed that with *Cloud 9*, a solo work that included "When We Were Fab," a nostalgic tune recalling the Beatlemania heyday.

In a bizarre December 1999 episode, an intruder broke into his home wielding a knife. George said he shouted "Hare Krishna, Hare Krishna!" in an attempt to disorient him, but the crazed intruder attacked and plunged the knife four times into George, puncturing a lung. At that moment, George believed he'd been fatally wounded and a "personal memory" of a similar incident, perhaps Lennon's murder, flashed through his mind. George's wife beat the intruder with a brass poker and then a lamp, and moments later staff and police arrived.

Eighteen months later, reports trickled in that George was dying of cancer, though he vigorously denied them. But after a stay at a hospital on New York's Staten Island, where he underwent radiation treatment for a brain tumor, George succumbed to brain cancer on November 29, 2001, at the home of a friend in Los Angeles.

George was 58 at his death, and, in keeping with his Eastern faith, he was cremated and his ashes scattered on the River Yamuna in India, which runs through the area of his favorite spiritual retreat.

SALVATORE "SONNY" BONO

FEBRUARY 16, 1935 – JANUARY 5, 1998

Before he wed Cherilyn Sarkisian in 1964, Sonny Bono bumbled along as a songwriter, penning such hits as "Needles and Pins." But in 1965, the upbeat songs he cranked out became unexpected hits when he and his wife performed them as Sonny and Cher, topping the charts with "I Got You Babe" and "The Beat Goes On."

In 1971, Sonny shed his Depression-era roots and became a born-again flower child when he and Cher landed their own television show, *The Sonny and Cher Comedy Hour.* Donning suede-fringed vests and bell-bottoms, Sonny played the lovable goofball with a droopy mustache opposite his stunningly slender, sharp-tongued wife, Cher, who teased audiences in outrageous sequined outfits. Millions tuned in for their memorable on-stage bickering and the show proved to be a hit. But in 1974, as Sonny and Cher's marriage faltered, the show ended.

The couple was divorced in 1975 and, after a brief attempt to revive the show, it went off the air for good the next year. While Cher went on to a successful music and acting career, unpretentious Sonny took another direction and morphed into Citizen Bono. He opened two restaurants and, after a disagreement with City Hall over some building plans, Sonny ran for and was elected mayor of Palm Springs in 1988. In 1992 Sonny ran for the U.S. Senate, bottoming out in the primaries. But he waged another campaign in 1994, was elected to the House of Representatives and, in 1996, voters sent him right back to Washington. Sonny's humor, self-deprecating style, and homespun intelligence served him well on Capitol Hill, and he became an effective and popular lawmaker.

At Heavenly Ski Resort, Sonny enjoyed some vacation time with his wife, Mary, and their two children after the 1998 New Year. Around 2:00 p.m., while Mary tended to the kids after one of them fell, Sonny skied off alone, and that's the last time he was seen alive. Mary reported him missing when the resort closed, and at 7:00 p.m. Sonny was found dead of massive head injuries near an intermediate-level ski trail named Orion. As Sonny was wont to do, he had veered from the groomed trail in order to ski the deep powder of a wooded area, and was killed when he lost control and struck a tree. Though he was in an unmaintained area of the ski mountain, the section was not considered closed or off-limits to skiers.

An autopsy concluded Sonny was not under the influence of alcohol or drugs. On average, thirty people die in ski accidents annually, and Sonny just happened to be one of them.

At 52, Sonny was buried at Desert Memorial Park Cemetery in Cathedral City, California.

CEMETERY DIRECTIONS: From I-10, take the Ramon Road exit and proceed south for two miles to Da Vall Drive. Turn right and the cemetery entrance is immediately on the left.

GRAVE DIRECTIONS: Enter the cemetery, turn right, then follow the drive to the Fountain Court waterfall. Sonny's grave is right there in the grass, just ten feet from the base of the flagpole.

Three months after Sonny's death, a special election was held to fill his congressional vacancy. Sonny's widow, Mary, a waitress before they met, won the seat by a significant margin. In November 2000, she was overwhelmingly reelected to the post.

LENNY BRUCE

OCTOBER 13, 1925 – AUGUST 3, 1966

As a stand-up nightclub entertainer, Lenny Bruce's monologues on race relations, sexual mores, and organized religion are today admired for their trailblazing qualities—but in his heyday, from the late 1950s to his death in 1966, Lenny was more commonly denounced as a "sick comic." He was also one of America's most visible victims of censorship and was arrested five times on obscenity charges, though appeals courts overturned all of his convictions.

Before his legal problems began, Lenny was a fast-talking purveyor of biting political and social comedic commentary; afterwards he fell victim to his own cult of personality and validated himself, exulting, "I'm not a comedian, I'm Lenny Bruce." He became obsessed with his own arrests and grew more and more paranoid and less and less funny. His act often became just one long harangue, a recitation of court documents, or an endless stream of obscenities. Club owners refused to book him, Lenny's professional career spiraled sharply downward, and his personal life soon followed.

In 1964 Lenny woke up in a frenzy in the middle of the night and leaped, or fell, out of his San Francisco hotel window, breaking both ankles and a leg. After insisting that his casts be removed early, he was left partly crippled. With his body now wasted, he obsessed over his mortality, and began to lose his mind as well. Lenny became flabby and sickly, he secluded himself in his home, and injected more and more drugs to ease both his real and imagined pains.

Lenny contended that he most enjoyed shooting up while seated on the toilet. At 40, he was found lying dead in his bathroom, facedown and naked. His bathrobe's sash was cinched tightly above the tracks in his arm, a hypodermic needle was nearby on the tile floor, and the white throne from which he'd toppled stood as sole witness.

Today, Lenny lies at Eden Memorial Park in Mission Hills, California.

CEMETERY DIRECTIONS: Eden Memorial Park is at the intersection of Rinaldi Street and Sepulveda Boulevard. From I-405, this is just east of the Rinaldi Street exit.

GRAVE DIRECTIONS: Enter the park and start up the hill. After the mausoleum, make a right onto Mount of Olives Drive and stop at about the halfway point. Lenny's flat marker is on the right, six rows down the hill.

WILT CHAMBERLAIN
AUGUST 21, 1936 – OCTOBER 12, 1999

The 7-foot-1 Wilt Chamberlain so dominated the game of basketball that, in direct response to his abilities, the NBA changed some of its rules in order to give everyone else a fighting chance. The lane under the basket was widened, the offensive-goaltending rule was implemented, and regulations regarding inbounding and free throws were revised. Though the changes served their purpose to some degree, Wilt "the Stilt" continued to be a heavy presence. By the time of his 1973 retirement, he'd set a number of records, two of which will probably never be broken. First, Wilt never once fouled out through 1,205 games. Second, in 1962 he scored an astonishing 100 points in a single game.

In 1991 it came out that Wilt also held one other pseudo-record, though it was somewhat nefarious and hard to verify. In his autobiography, *A View from Above*, the lifelong bachelor devoted an entire chapter to sex and there made the revelation that, if he had to count his sexual encounters, he'd be closing in on 20,000 women. "Yes, that's correct, twenty thousand different ladies," he wrote. "At my age, that equals out to having sex with 1.2 women a day, every day since I was fifteen years old." Some fans recoiled at Wilt's macho accounting and roundly criticized him, while others contemplated that, even if he was exaggerating by a factor of ten…

At 63, Wilt died of congestive heart failure. He was cremated and his were ashes entrusted to his family.

ROBERTO CLEMENTE

AUGUST 18, 1934 – DECEMBER 31, 1972

It was a long journey to the Baseball Hall of Fame for Roberto Clemente, and sadly, the star outfielder and humanitarian never even witnessed his own induction ceremony. After learning the game on a muddy field in Puerto Rico where a tree branch was used for a bat, Roberto graduated to the Major Leagues in 1954, and, with the Pittsburgh Pirates, he became a cherished twelve-time All-Star who notched 3,000 hits and won eleven consecutive Gold Gloves.

But though his athleticism won him widespread admiration, Roberto's most genuine affection was earned well beyond the white lines of baseball diamonds. He sought to be an authentic role model, not merely a guy who could hit and catch a ball pretty well. To that end Roberto generously assisted charitable causes with hard cash, donated thousands of autographed pictures to juvenile facilities, and personally worked for the destitute during the off-season.

When a catastrophic earthquake hit Managua, Nicaragua, its neighbors and other organizations coordinated relief, but reports of Nicaraguan corruption resulting in the misdirection of supplies soon surfaced. Roberto was prompted to organize his own relief mission and, on the New Year's Eve of 1973, he boarded a donated DC-7 in San Juan, Puerto Rico, bound for Managua. Packed with five men and over 16,000 pounds of supplies, the airplane bobbed, bucked, and wheezed after takeoff. Moments later, an engine burst into flames and the plane took a nosedive into the ocean off Isla Verde beach.

Rescuers rushed to the scene but there was nothing to be done. There were no survivors, and Roberto's body was never found. He was 38.

JIMI HENDRIX
NOVEMBER 27, 1942 – SEPTEMBER 18, 1970

Jimi Hendrix's career and life were tragically brief, but his impact on music has spanned generations. The marriage of blues and rock that he initiated was a direct precursor to music as diverse as that of The Who and Prince, his guitar innovations set the stage for the heavy-metal movement, and he inspired guitarists from Jimmy Page to Eddie Van Halen.

Jimi was of mixed heritage, black and Cherokee Indian, and after a shy and quiet adolescence he quit school and served in the Army for three years as a paratrooper. In 1964 he moved to New York and formed a band called Jimmy James and the Blue Flames, and after two years of playing Greenwich Village coffeehouses, Chas Chandler, the former Animals bassist, recognized Jimi's talent and moved him to London.

There, in 1967, the Jimi Hendrix Experience was born. Within six months, aided by the release of their epochal debut album, *Are You Experienced?*, and a ferociously climactic performance at the Monterey Pop Festival, the band had become one of the biggest rock acts on either side of the Atlantic.

The next two years saw the release of two more albums, each as successful as the debut, but by that time Jimi's life had devolved into confusion as disagreements among managers and band mates created a revolving door of personnel. Some fans, not content to just let Jimi stand and play guitar, pressed him to take a political stance and make a public commitment to his roots.

In his mid-twenties, it was easy for Jimi to lose direction, and he did. Drinking and drugs became a normal part of his routine until, finally, his girlfriend woke to find him dead beside her in their London apartment. The cause of death was listed as the now-classic "suffocation due to inhalation of vomit during a heavily intoxicated sleep." Jimi was 27.

He was buried at Greenwood Memorial Park in Renton, Washington.

CEMETERY DIRECTIONS: From I-405, take the Bronson Way exit to Sunset Boulevard. Turn onto 3rd Street NE, go back under the interstate, and after four traffic lights the cemetery is on the right.

GRAVE DIRECTIONS: Enter the cemetery and go to the circular drive in the cemetery's southwest corner. You won't miss Jimi's 20-foot-high granite dome trimmed in rainbow marble.

TIMOTHY LEARY

OCTOBER 22, 1920 – MAY 31, 1996

Timothy Leary's name is synonymous with 1960s counter-culture as the key polarizer who extended the generational distance from a gap to a chasm. Disillusioned young people saw Timothy as a harbinger of social change, while their parents viewed the Harvard University psychologist as an antiestablishment corrupter of youth.

Until his Harvard days when he met Richard Alpert, Timothy's life was conventional, and he even attended West Point before entering the Army during World War II. In 1961, though, Timothy and Alpert (today known as Baba Ram Dass) began experimenting with lysergic acid diethylamide, or LSD. Timothy went one step further and publicly extolled the virtues of taking LSD as a vehicle for personal growth, and the "turn on, tune in, drop out" insurrection began.

By the time Timothy was fired from Harvard four years later, his psychopharmacological revolution, the Psychedelic Movement, was in full swing. At some point came the unspoken realization that LSD itself was not the key to spiritual or intellectual nirvana after all, and the psychedelic experience was then redirected into the Humanistic Revolution: an empowering ethereal movement emphasizing interpersonal relationships, multilevel personality assessments, group therapy, and body/mind interaction that ultimately fed into the enduring New Age movement.

While all of these revolutions and movements were finding their balance, Timothy was performing a balancing act of his own with the authorities. In January 1970, he was finally sentenced to up to twenty years on marijuana convictions. Nine months later, though, he escaped with help from the underground group, The Weathermen, and after joining Black Panther fugitives, eluded captivity for three years before being caught in Afghanistan.

In 1976 Timothy had a change of heart and was paroled after he cooperated with federal authorities; unbelievably, after having preached against the establishment all his adult life, he informed on the very Weathermen who had helped him bust out of jail.

He had survived the sixties, the drugs, and the busts, but after his release Timothy never again had quite the same impact on the world. In the following decades, as attitudes hardened toward recreational drugs, he maintained a legal income source from his many books, dabbled as a stand-up comedian and a software developer, consorted with Hollywood friends, and made sporadic talk-show appearances.

In 1995 he was diagnosed with inoperable prostate cancer and, ever preoccupied with being Timothy Leary, he managed to turn his protracted death into a media event. After announcing that his death was imminent, he spun this "most fascinating experience in life" into something about which he was "eager and enthusiastic." For a while, Timothy even contemplated committing suicide in real time; in this period when the Internet was not even yet a mainstream gadget, his idea was to develop a Web page wherein fans and well-wishers—or adversaries, for that matter—could watch as he set sail on a final and most profound, far-out trip.

In due time though, in private and in the still moments as the cancer began to assume control of his body, Timothy's enthusiasm for his death waned and his friends knew it was a trip he feared. Talking about taking one's own life and actually doing it are two very different things and, in the end, there was no last act of defiance.

Instead, at 75, Timothy died in his sleep at home. He died with dignity and he was not logged on or spaced out.

Space would have to wait just a little longer; Timothy still had one last "far-out trip" to experience. In April of 1997, about seven grams of the psychedelic cosmonaut's ashes, along with those of Gene Roddenberry and 22 other space enthusiasts were attached to the final booster stage of a rocket and blasted from the planet by a Texas-based company named Celestis, in the world's first space funeral. On May 20, 2002, after 28,132 orbits around the earth, the capsules of ashes reentered the atmosphere over New Guinea and burned up in a fiery finale.

JIM MORRISON
DECEMBER 8, 1943 – JULY 3, 1971

As lead singer and lyricist of the Doors, Jim Morrison's theatrical shock tactics and poetic (though sometimes disturbing) hyperbole came to symbolize the temptations and excesses of rock and roll. Full of himself, loaded with charisma and antics, Jim overshadowed the other members of the Doors. To their credit, however, they always seemed content to stand back and let Jim take center stage while they played the swirling and eclectic psychedelic rock music that was, in effect, the soundtrack of Jim's life.

Jim grew up the son of a strict and authoritarian Navy rear admiral, and this might have been a source of his outlandish rebellion. He would often falsely claim that both his parents were dead. Jim enrolled in UCLA's film and theater program in 1964, but found drugs, particularly LSD, more interesting than his studies. In 1965, he drifted from school and, together with classmate Ray Manzarek, formed the Doors.

In the summer of 1967 when their first album was released, Jim was still a slightly tentative frontman, but as the group rose to prominence and flower-power rockers pulsed to the hypnotizing rhythm of its "Light My Fire" single, Jim quickly worked himself into his role in grand fashion. Their next album, *Strange Days*, solidified the group's success, and Jim's throaty baritone and onstage persona became anything but shy, delivering keenly suggestive lyrics in alternate turns as a sullen poet and a fevered lunatic. His onstage behavior became increasingly erratic and exceedingly bizarre. After barrages of profanity at a show in New Haven, Connecticut, Jim was arrested on obscenity charges; in Miami, mimicking sex put Jim behind bars for lewd and lascivious behavior. Jim's indulgence in every hedonistic excess offstage and his off-the-wall behavior onstage put the band's very stability and survival at risk.

After the riotous concerts of 1969, the band went back to their songwriting roots and released two albums over the next two years; it seemed that perhaps Jim's spirit for good old rock and roll might be rejuvenated. When tours to promote the albums were announced, everyone hoped the over-the-top discord was in the past, but again, the shows were marked by controversy. Prompted by Jim's reputation, local police were a constant and intimidating presence, and the magic of the Doors live performances was lost. Fed up with the pressures from every direction, Jim withdrew and, in March 1971, went to Paris to unwind and write poetry with his companion, Pam Courson.

According to Pam, at 5:00 a.m. one morning, she found Jim lying in the bathtub of their apartment at 17 rue Beautreillis in Paris, dead as a doorknob. Oddly, only Dr. Max Vassille, who signed Jim's death certificate, and Pam actually saw Jim's corpse. No autopsy was done, but on the death certificate Vassille stated that Jim had died of a heart problem aggravated by the use of alcohol followed by an abrupt change of temperature. In short, while half in the bag, Jim plopped into his bath and the sudden temperature change prompted a heart attack. Yeah, the whole thing smells fishy to me, too.

Due to the mysterious circumstances surrounding Jim's demise and subsequent burial, theories ranging from accidental heroin overdose to murder have been trotted out as the "true" cause of his death. Some believe Jim never even died but merely staged it to escape the chains of stardom.

Jim, or at least his coffin, was interred at Paris's Père-Lachaise Cemetery. Drawing a million visitors per year, Jim's tomb is the fourth most popular tourist stop in Paris, which says reams about Jim, and Paris, for that matter.

CEMETERY DIRECTIONS: The easiest way to reach Père-Lachaise is by taking the Metro, and the line required is Nation-Porte Dauphine. Get off at the Phillipe-Auguste stop, take the steps leading to the Boulevard de Charonne, and the celebrated graveyard is marked by signs from there.

In a 1969 pagan ceremony, Jim and Pam were married by a practicing witch named Patricia Kennealy and, though they recognized the bond (more or less) it was not a legal marriage. Further complicating matters, about a year later, in June 1970, Jim and Patricia were themselves married in a Celtic ceremony. Still, Jim's one-page will was quite simple and clear: Everything was left to Pam. Less than three years after Jim's death though, Pam died of a heroin overdose in her Hollywood apartment. Like Jim, she was 27.

Pam was cremated and her ashes interred at Fairhaven Memorial Park in Santa Ana, California. Her nameplate is engraved "Pamela Susan Morrison" and there is no mention of her maiden name.

WALTER PAYTON

JULY 25, 1954 – NOVEMBER 1, 1999

In the years between Ernie Banks' retirement and Michael Jordan's emergence, Walter Payton took up the slack as sports-hungry Chicago's most beloved athletic hero. When the Chicago Bears picked him in the first round of the 1975 NFL draft, they had failed to compile a winning record for eight seasons, but with an aggressive running back destined for the Hall of Fame in their ranks, the Bears' fortunes changed quickly. After Walter's rookie year he posted the first of what would be ten consecutive 1,000-yard seasons, and by his third year in the league he won the first of two MVP awards.

In a 1977 match against Minnesota, he ran for 275 yards to set a single-game record that still stands. By the time of his 1987 retirement, Walter had played in 184 consecutive games and held the all-time rushing record with an incredible 16,726 yards—almost ten miles! But, of most importance to the city of Chicago, Walter led the once lowly Bears to a Super Bowl championship and gained them the status of respected adversary.

The team retired his number 34 uniform upon Walter's own retirement and he was elected to the Pro Football Hall of Fame in 1993.

In February of 1999, in an emotional press conference, Walter announced he was suffering from primary sclerosing cholangitis (PSC), a rare liver condition with no known cure but, if a suitable donor could be found, his life could probably be saved. While Walter languished with all the other waiting-list hopefuls, his liver condition deteriorated into a cancer, transplant became impossible, and he died at 45.

Walter was cremated and his ashes remain with his family.

ELVIS PRESLEY

JANUARY 8, 1935 – AUGUST 16, 1977

Born in Tupelo, Mississippi, Elvis Presley had a childhood that resembled those of all the other poor whites in the South. His father was a laborer who earned barely enough for the family to live on, and nowhere did there seem to be any hope for or indication of the kind of fame Elvis would later find. The family moved to Memphis and, after graduating high school, young Elvis got a job as a $41-per-week truck driver, a respectable enough career. That is, until Sam Phillips came along.

Under Sam's direction at Sun Studios in 1954, the budding superstar recorded his first single, "That's All Right Mama," and, with his sexy sneer, suggestive hip gyrations and breathy vocals, Elvis was an instant phenomenon. As the eye of a musical hurricane, he turned the establishment on its ear with one hit after another, eventually recording more than 700 songs. By the time of his death, he had sold some 600 million records. Now, more than 25 years after his death, the number is beyond counting.

But Elvis's appeal wasn't just limited to his swiveling hips and rockabilly sound. He had personal charm and bedroom eyes that Hollywood could hardly ignore. After a two-year stint in the Army, fostering a clean, all-American image, he married the daughter of a military officer and gave up live concerts with the intent of leading a quiet family life. But Elvis was soon persuaded to sign a movie contract and he made a series of films, some of which are almost painfully unwatchable. In Elvis' defense, though, his charisma made a few of them, such as *Jailhouse Rock* and *Viva Las Vegas*, genuinely entertaining.

In 1968, aware that his music career was foundering, Elvis went back on the road and jumpstarted the beginning of his tragic end with a period that bordered on self-parody as the burlesque "Las Vegas Elvis." In rhinestone jumpsuits topped with sequined capes, an overweight, drowsy-looking, mumbling, and sweaty incarnation of his former vibrant self held onstage court over swooning fans in more than a thousand performances. At the start of this period, his returns to the stage were often exciting, over-the-top productions, but eight years later, he wallowed in the depths as a sagging, 275-pound caricature of "Elvis the Pelvis," a pitiful reminder of the pitfalls of fame.

A new round of performances was scheduled for August 1977 and, as usual, they quickly sold out. In the week before the concerts began, Elvis hung around his Graceland mansion; he read his Bible, swam in the pool, played with his daughter, ate cheeseburgers, played racquetball and took his ungodly regimen of assorted pills. After a 10:00 p.m. visit to the dentist for two porcelain fillings, Elvis returned home and, unable to sleep, batted a racquetball around with his cousin, Billy Smith, until about 4:00 a.m. Elvis then joined his current girlfriend, Ginger Alden, in bed and reportedly read for a couple hours. She fell asleep around six and upon waking at nine, saw that Elvis still hadn't slept. In his best blue pajamas, he excused himself to the bathroom with the book *The Scientific Search for the Face of Jesus*, and that's the last time the 42-year-old King of Rock and Roll was seen alive. Around two that afternoon, Ginger found a bloated Elvis, with the book beside him, slumped in a fetal position on the brown shag carpet of his bathroom floor, and he wasn't breathing. Elvis had left the building.

A medical examiner declared that Elvis had died of cardiac arrhythmia—in layman's terms, he had a heart attack—and there was no indication of drug abuse of any kind. However, when the laboratory studies of his autopsy specimens were finally completed by toxicologists at the University of Utah in January 1978, eleven drugs, all consistent with medical treatment, were found to be present in the singer's system at the time of his death. Four of the drugs, all commonly known sedatives, painkillers, and depressants, were present in significant amounts. The remaining seven drugs were said to be present in insignificant amounts and one of them, morphine, has been trotted out as supposed proof that Elvis overdosed. However, toxicologists maintain that the trace amounts of morphine found in his system were solely a byproduct of the codeine sedatives; Elvis never actually ingested morphine. Well, not immediately prior to his death anyway.

Although there were a host of drugs in his system, Elvis actually died of heart disease. Though he would have been better off if he had laid off the drugs, Elvis had a weak cardiovascular system, and what he really needed was to lay off the cheeseburgers and play a lot more racquetball.

Dressed in a white suit, Elvis and his $3,600 copper casket were interred in a crypt at Forest Hills Cemetery for a short time. But in October 1977, two deranged fans attempted some manner of body snatching, and Elvis was removed from Forest Hills and buried at his fourteen-acre Graceland estate across town.

GRAVE DIRECTIONS: Just get yourself to Memphis and follow the tour buses to Elvis Presley Boulevard and Graceland. You won't miss it.

At Graceland, everything Elvis is on display. Every hour of every day, monotone-voiced tour guides march wide-eyed visitors through the property to see his costumes and cars, platinum records, horse pasture, and, yes, the infamous Jungle Room. But, if you can do without the memorabilia sideshow, admission is waived every morning for those who desire only to pay respects at the King's grave. To get in free, arrive before 9:00 a.m. and, later, take the twelve bucks you saved and treat yourself to an Elvis shot glass, potholder, thermometer, or plastic hatchet.

After Elvis's death, it was reported that a few particularly heart-broken fans committed suicide, which is about par for the course. Such reports are usually impossible to authenticate but, less than 48 hours after Elvis's death, there were two other explicit casualties of his passing. As mourners congregated outside Graceland, two inno-cent Louisiana teenagers, Alice Hovatar and Juanita Johnson, were mangled beyond recognition when a car driven by a very drunk Treatise Wheeler smashed into the crowd of Elvis mourners at 50 miles per hour. After avoiding being lynched on the spot, Wheeler spent nine years in prison for the deaths. Incidentally, both of Alice's parents had also been killed by a drunk driver back in 1965.

CHARLES SCHULZ
NOVEMBER 26, 1922 – FEBRUARY 12, 2000

Comic strip cartooning requires such a peculiar combination of talents that very few people are ever successful at it. Of those, Charles Schulz is in a league all his own. Reconfiguring and dominating the comic-strip landscape for fully half of its history, the importance of *Peanuts* to the genre, or even to popular culture, can hardly be overstated.

After seeing a "Do you like to draw?" advertisement, Charles took an art correspondence course, and from that dubious training created an indispensable cultural touchstone via a most unexpected medium: a comic strip called *Peanuts*. For 50 years, in an intensely personal effort, Charles himself wrote and sketched every one of the strip's panels; he even had a clause inserted into his contract preventing anyone else from releasing new *Peanuts* cartoons after his death.

The strip was introduced in 1950, at the height of the American post-war celebration, when being unhappy was considered an anti-social act rather than a personal emotion. *Peanuts* introduced to the world a group of children who told one another the truth. Charles dared to bring his own quirks, his lifelong sense of alienation, insecurity, and inferiority, into the strip—something new in a time when comics were dominated by action-adventure, melodrama, or slapstick gags.

His characters were contemplative, made smart observations, and broached with gentle humor and twinkling insight such previously taboo subjects as faith, depression, intolerance, loneliness, and despair. Charlie Brown became a real person with a real psyche and, when he first confessed, "I don't feel the way I'm supposed to feel," he spoke for people everywhere. Through the 1950s Charles provided unconventional commentary in the national margins, but in the next decade, *Peanuts* skyrocketed into a mainstream cultural powerhouse. As the politics of the 1960s intensified and nothing quite worked out, *Peanuts* became a refuge for people who were putting up with all they could take. With great deliberateness, the strip proved that you were not alone when you woke in the middle of the night, in the company of your failures, worrying that the world had gone mad.

In 1967, as the nation teetered, Charles soared to previously unknown heights of popularity when more than half the nation's television audience tuned in to his animated special, *A Charlie Brown Christmas*, the success of which confounded network executives. By then, the long-suffering Charlie Brown, high-spirited Snoopy, contemplative Linus, and domineering Lucy had already become revered international figures, but on that night, Charles reached a more diverse, and perhaps larger, audience than any other American artist in history.

Many of the *Peanuts* characters were based on real people in Charles' life. An uncontrollable childhood dog named Spike was

behind Snoopy, and the little red-haired girl, Charlie Brown's unrequited love, was based on a girlfriend who rejected Charles' 1950 marriage proposal. Charles maintained that Charlie Brown was born from a friendship he made through the art instruction correspondence school, but ultimately, it seems that Charles Schulz was Charlie Brown.

Despite his fantastic success, stoicism and insecurity became Charles' personal themes, and high anxiety dogged him all his life. Though the world begged him to move beyond gentle commentary to a role as a national observer, he had no itch to be a teacher or a guru. "I don't know the meaning of life," he once said, "and I don't know why we are here. I think life is full of anxieties and tears and it can be very grim. And I do not want to be the one who tries to tell somebody else what life is all about. To me it's a complete mystery." Instead, in his Santa Rosa studio at One Snoopy Place, everyday through the next three decades, he kept on drawing. He drew with the same old crow-quill pens dipped in ink and used the same drawing table; he liked to say he would remain at his desk until he wore a hole clean through it.

Though Charles took professional pride in the achievements of the strip, it did not automatically override his early disappointments, and he struggled to believe he was worthy of the admiration showered on him. "It is amazing that they think that what I do was that good," his voice quavered in a 1999 interview. "I just did the best I could."

By December 2001, a battle with colon cancer and a series of small strokes forced Charles to announce his retirement. Just hours before the final *Peanuts* installment appeared in newspapers around the world, a single-block Sunday strip featuring a reflective Snoopy typing Charles' farewell letter, Charles died in his sleep of a heart attack at home.

Charles was 77 at his death and was buried at Pleasant Hills Cemetery in Sebastopol, California.

CEMETERY DIRECTIONS: From Highway 101, follow Route 116 west for eight miles to the center of Sebastopol. At the traffic light, turn left onto Sebastopol Avenue, which will turn into Bodega Avenue after a short distance. After a mile, turn left onto Pleasant Hill Road and the cemetery is 1½ miles on the right.

GRAVE DIRECTIONS: Pull into the cemetery's first entrance and park at the triple fountains on the right. The stone bench near the top fountain marks Charles' grave.

Back when the strip peaked in popularity with 355 million regular readers, the branding of everything *Peanuts* became an enormous business. In fact, the strip almost single-handedly created that form of merchandising. Worldwide, more than a quarter million different products have been licensed based on the strip's characters and their carefree images can be found on everything from shoelaces to underwear, wind chimes to candles, and cookie jars to clocks. After tallying his hundreds of sources of income (don't forget advertising rights and even a Broadway production!), Charles' personal income rivaled that of the Beatles and Elvis Presley. Soon, his "lifetime" income will exceed a *billion* dollars. After all, he's posthumously making money—in 2001 alone, Charles' paychecks totaled an estimated $28 million.

PETER SELLERS
SEPTEMBER 8, 1925 – JULY 24, 1980

Peter Sellers' given name was actually Richard Henry Sellers, but his parents, eclectic vaudeville entertainers, always called him Peter in memory of his stillborn older brother. In any event, the child spent his youth traveling the vaudeville circuit, and by sixteen was touring as a jazz band's drummer. Immediately upon reaching legal age in 1943, he was drafted into the British Royal Air Force and spent the war years performing comedy sketches and playing in bands as an official RAF entertainer.

By war's end, Peter's comic and impressionist routines were fine-tuned, and he established himself as a sought-after radio personality. By 1951, he had his own radio comedy show called *The Goon Show,* which enjoyed an eight-year run in his native Britain. The show is now recognized as a significant influence on *Monty Python's Flying Circus.*

Peter also made his film debut in 1951, and his international reputation was firmly established with 1963's *Dr. Strangelove.* The following year brought the start of the *Pink Panther* film series, and during his years in the role of the bumbling and incompetent Inspector Clouseau, Peter's popularity was unrivalled. Five *Pink Panther* films hit pay dirt and, upon Peter's death, the studio was even able to cash in one last time with a posthumous release made with a collection of outtakes from the previous films combined with new footage of other cast members.

Peter's most accomplished role was probably in *Being There,* in which he played Chance, the television-watching, childlike gardener mistaken for a political guru. His controlled performance was astonishing and won him an Oscar nomination.

At 54, Peter died of a heart attack and was cremated. At Golders Green Crematorium in London, his ashes are buried under a rose-bush near the Chapel of Memory columbarium.

SENIOR
MEMORIES

ETERNAL COUPLE

FRED ASTAIRE &
GINGER ROGERS

FRED ASTAIRE & GINGER ROGERS

Fred Astaire

MAY 10, 1899 – JULY 22, 1987

Ginger Rogers

JULY 16, 1911 – APRIL 25, 1995

In the Depression era, Fred Astaire and Ginger Rogers were each relatively successful entertainers. Fred and his sister performed as a Broadway dance team while Ginger was well established in the American movie industry and had appeared in nineteen feature films. In 1933, Fred and Ginger partnered in the film *Flying Down to Rio* and something miraculous occurred: Ginger's down-to-earth brashness blended with Fred's airy, man-about-town sophistication. And when they danced, their pleasure in each other was palpable.

Due to the overwhelming and enthusiastic audience response, MGM Studios put them together again in *The Gay Divorcée* and film history was made. The film's story was flimsy, but the Astaire-Rogers dances were both sublime and revolutionary. Astaire lent the pair an emotional center and Ginger contributed an erotic charge. The couple never kissed on screen until years later, but they were clearly making love on the dance floor, and Astaire's light voice was the perfect instrument to express his ardor.

The duet evolved into the most beloved and celebrated dance team in the history of the American musical cinema. Ginger represented the down to earth while Fred was the elegant, European in grace. In ten dance musicals, they personified the idiosyncrasy of romance—two people who friends might never match up, but who are drawn together by an inexplicable attraction.

By 1939 though, it was clear that the magic expressed through their dances was waning, and the two amicably went their separate ways. In the decades following, both Ginger and Fred had enviable professional careers, but the charm, grace, and style of their years together would never be surpassed.

Fred died of pneumonia at 88 on July 22, 1987, and Ginger died at 83 on April 25, 1995, of congestive heart failure. They are both buried in Oakwood Memorial Park in Chatsworth, California.

CEMETERY DIRECTIONS: From Highway 118, follow Topanga Canyon Boulevard south to Lassen Street. Turn right on Lassen and, after ¾ mile, the park is in front of you.

DIRECTIONS TO FRED'S GRAVE: Enter the cemetery, turn at the second right and stop at the left-hand curb marked "G-79." Count seven markers down the hill and you'll find Fred's grave.

DIRECTIONS TO GINGER'S GRAVE: Enter the cemetery, turn immediately right and, after you pass two drives, stop at the left-hand curb marked "256 E." Count in fourteen markers and you'll find Ginger's grave.

JACK BENNY

FEBRUARY 14, 1894 – DECEMBER 26, 1974

Long characterized as "not one who said funny things, but one who said things funny," the comedian Jack Benny was originally a violinist for vaudeville companies and only happened to discover his talent for comedy at a U.S. Navy show during World War I. In a transition to comedy, he developed a mildly neurotic, self-important tightwad of a character who also happened to be a talentless violinist. Through the use of a very deliberate though leisurely paced delivery, he went on to become an American institution on the radio.

In a highly successful transition to television, Jack's character developed an effeminate walk and accompanying gestures, and endured insults from a regular supporting cast with a withering, long-suffering stare at the camera. Jack managed to successfully passage his radio personality to television, and he became revered as one of entertainment's old guard at celebrity roasts and galas with his buddies George Burns and Milton Berle.

At 80, Jack died of pancreatic cancer and now rests at Hillside Memorial Park in Los Angeles.

CEMETERY DIRECTIONS: The cemetery is just east of I-405 at the Centinella Avenue exit.

GRAVE DIRECTIONS: Enter the park, turn right and then left, and park at the mausoleum. Go in the main entrance, turn right and then left into the Corridor of Contentment. Jack's is the black tomb at the end.

In his will, Jack included a provision that one red rose be delivered to his wife everyday for the rest of her life.

MILTON BERLE

JULY 2, 1908 – MARCH 27, 2002

As Milton Berle's father was never able to provide for his family very well—they lived in an assortment of crummy flats and brownstones in the Bronx and upper Manhattan—his mother was determined to make one of their progeny a star. She chose Milton, apparently her cutest child. After scoring a tin cup at a Charlie Chaplin look-alike contest, Milton became the boy in the Buster Brown shoe ads. With the help of his mother, a tireless promoter, Milton was a veteran of vaudeville by sixteen and had appeared in several silent films.

Through the 1930s and '40s, Milton was a popular master of ceremonies, performed nightclub comedy routines, was heard on a few radio programs, and appeared 553 times in the Ziegfeld Follies. The radio shows weren't particularly successful for Milton; his style was too visual: the raised eyebrow, a turned head and a wink, a tap of the ever-present Cuban cigar. But in 1948 he received an offer to do the radio show *Texaco Star Theatre*, and Milton accepted the offer, though he really wanted to break into the new medium of television.

The show was a hit, and its success led Texaco to sponsor an hourlong television version that fall. While some of his radio competitors were reluctant to risk flopping on the tube, Milton jumped at the opportunity and was the first of the big-name comedians to get his feet wet in television.

The *Texaco Star Theatre* television show was finally renamed *The Milton Berle Show* in 1954. It was basically vaudeville on video (*vaudeo*, if you will) and it became immensely popular. For eight years the manic energy of "Uncle Miltie" permeated the Tuesday night airwaves with wacky skits and zany tunes, flying acrobats and full-bosomed showgirls and, of course, the no-holds-barred emcee Miltie, beaming with a Cheshire Cat-grin, dressed in drag and getting pies in the face.

Milton's success spawned many imitators, the show's ratings eventually waned, and in 1956 it was cancelled. Milton was all but washed-up as a major television personality, and for the remainder of his years was relegated to guest spots, limited comedy tours, and appearances on talk shows and award programs. With time on his hands, Milton also put his energies into the Friars Club, a high-profile, who's-who watering hole legendary for its honorary, good-natured "roasts." As Abbot of the Friars' Hollywood chapter, Milton presided over its jocular celebrity members for almost 30 years.

The position seemed to fit. "I think laughter is imperative and it's the important part of my life, making people laugh so they can forget their problems," Milton said. "A good laugh is better than anything."

After years of failing health, including colon cancer, Milton died in his living room at 93 while taking a nap. He was buried at Hillside Memorial Park in Culver City, California.

CEMETERY DIRECTIONS: This park borders the east side of I-405 at the Centinela Avenue exit, which is immediately north of the La Tijera Boulevard exit.

GRAVE DIRECTIONS: Drive straight into the park and loop almost all the way around the hill on which the big mausoleum is located. As you reapproach the park's entrance, on the left you'll see a mural of a rabbi officiating at a wedding. Uncle Miltie lies in a crypt immediately to the right of the mural, third row from the bottom.

HUMPHREY BOGART
DECEMBER 25, 1899 – JANUARY 14, 1957

While the images of other cinematic luminaries of Hollywood's bygone golden era have faded, the legend of Humphrey Bogart still looms large. With a trademark lisp, dangling cigarette and world-weary cynicism, Humphrey weaved his "Bogie" persona into an untouchable archetype of the reluctant but romantic anti-hero possessing a touching vulnerability.

As Sam Spade in *The Maltese Falcon,* he became a bankable action star, but it was his role opposite Ingrid Bergman in *Casablanca* that made him into a full-fledged leading man. In 1944 he married the twenty-year-old actress Lauren Bacall (it was his fourth marriage) and together they made such memorable features as *To Have and Have Not* and *Key Largo*. In 1951, Humphrey was showcased as an unkempt riverboat captain opposite Katherine Hepburn's strait-laced missionary role in the universally loved *African Queen.*

Humphrey made his final film in 1956, the gritty boxing drama *The Harder They Fall,* and shortly after its release he underwent surgery to remove a cancerous growth from his esophagus. A few months later in November, he went under the knife again to have some scar tissue in his throat removed, but Humphrey never quite recovered from that surgery. One afternoon, Lauren found him comatose in his wheelchair, and he died the next morning at 57.

Humphrey was cremated and his ashes interred at Forest Lawn Memorial Park in Glendale, California.

CEMETERY DIRECTIONS: From Highway 2, take the San Fernando Road exit and turn northwest. After a mile, make a right onto Glendale Avenue. The park's entrance is immediately on the right.

GRAVE DIRECTIONS: Get a map from the information booth and make your way up to the Gardens of Memory. Humphrey's ashes are in the Columbarium of Eternal Light, which is located within the Garden section just left of the statue of David. However, these gardens are locked and admittance "is restricted to those possessing a Golden Key of Memory, given to each owner at time of purchase." Still, sometimes you can get lucky and an owner will let you in.

If you're really determined to get into these gardens but don't want to hang around until a property owner with a key shows up and you don't want to jump the wall (which I do not condone, and which would constitute trespassing, besides), here's what you can do: Go to the park before it officially opens at eight o'clock and, though there may be placards in the driveway stating that it's closed, drive past them and proceed up to the Gardens of Memory like you own the place. (You'll need to have previously secured a park map.) This is the time of day when new guests are being interred and the maintenance staff is scurrying everywhere. The doors to the private sections are sometimes propped open by work crews or, if that's not the case, you'll at least have a good chance of persuading one of the maintenance people that you've forgotten your "Golden Key of Memory" and should be allowed entry.

GEORGE BURNS & GRACIE ALLEN

George Burns

JANUARY 20, 1896 – MARCH 9, 1996

Gracie Allen

JULY 26, 1902 – AUGUST 27, 1964

George Burns' early show biz attempts were not very successful. He played "lousy little theaters that played lousy little acts—and I was one of them," he said. Often the performances were so bad that he'd have to change the name of his act in order to be booked for a second engagement. "I was what you call a disappointment act," George later explained. "If an act got sick, I'd take their place."

But in 1923 George met a soft-spoken dancer, Gracie Allen, and, after a little coaxing, she agreed to team with him in a comedy act. They specialized in the humor of illogical logic; Gracie played the daffy but unflappable wife, while George was the unruffled but confused straight man whose simple questions elicited her nitwit answers. The combination was magical and for the next 35 years, including the twenty-year run with their *Burns and Allen* radio show, the first-class comedy pair delighted audiences with their hilarious homespun routines. George himself described their act as "having more plot than a variety show but not as much as a wrestling match."

In ill health, Gracie retired in 1958 and she died of a heart attack in her sleep six years later, at 62. George was devastated upon the death of his "Googie," the love of his life, and he retreated from the spotlight, never to remarry. He later allowed that he'd kept the light on at her side of the bed for three years and, for the remainder of his life, he visited her grave once a month. "I just talk to her and tell her what has happened. I don't know if Gracie can hear me, but it certainly does me a lot of good," he said.

Throughout the 1960s, George tried to revive his Burns and Allen act with Carol Channing and a few others, but the chemistry was never the same. George's career was finally revitalized when he replaced his ailing friend Jack Benny and costarred in *The Sunshine Boys*, winning an Academy Award in 1975. Soon, George was a fixture of television and film, and he adopted the role of raconteur, telling funny stories that he maintained were true but had been embellished over the years. Using his cigar for punctuation, George was a master of one-liners and sardonic wit: "Too bad all the people who know how to run the country are busy driving taxi cabs or cutting hair," he noted.

As George approached his 100th birthday, the media clamored around, asking the comic his secret to longevity. "Fall in love with what you do for a living," he said, taking a sip of a martini and a light puff of his cigar. "I don't care what it is. It works."

More than three decades after Gracie passed away, George curled up in their bed and died of natural causes at 100 years old.

According to his butler Daniel Dhoore, he was buried in a dark blue suit with a light blue shirt and a red tie. Dhoore continued, "We put three cigars in his pocket, put on his toupee, put on his watch that Gracie gave him and his ring. And, in his pocket, his keys and his wallet with ten hundred-dollar bills, a five, and three ones, so wherever he went to play bridge he'd have enough money."

In a companion crypt, George and Gracie lie together at Forest Lawn Memorial Park in Glendale, California.

CEMETERY DIRECTIONS: From Highway 2, take the San Fernando Road exit and turn northwest. After a mile, make a right onto Glendale Avenue. The park's entrance is immediately on the right.

GRAVE DIRECTIONS: Stop at the booth for a map of the cemetery's roads, then drive to the Freedom Mausoleum. Walk in the front entrance of the Freedom Mausoleum, proceed down the hall on the right, then turn left into the Sanctuary of Heritage. On the right at eye level is the companion crypt that George and his Googie share.

CHARLIE CHAPLIN
APRIL 16, 1889 – DECEMBER 25, 1977

Born in England, Charlie Chaplin built his career in America and made some 80 films in which, often as the legendary Little Tramp, he elevated popular slapstick to the realm of artistry and tickled the fancy of millions for half a century.

In 1915 *The Tramp* was released and film comedy was never the same. For the film, Charlie was told to wear something funny, and he assembled a grab-bag costume from other members of the company consisting of pants belonging to Fatty Arbuckle, size-fourteen shoes placed on the wrong feet, a tight coat, a derby, a prop cane, and a false, square mustache. On the spur of the moment he added a splayed, shuffling walk and with this combination found the comic means of expressing himself. Through the 1920s, he made a number of classic shorts and probably his most famous feature, *The Gold Rush*. But by the beginning of the next decade the silent film era had ended and "talkies" were the rage. Though Charlie ignored the new technology for ten more years, his releases managed to remain among the top grossing.

But moviegoers weren't the only ones to take an interest in Charlie. Proud to retain his British citizenship, he refused an offer of U.S. citizenship in 1924. That, coupled with his left-of-center political views in films like 1921's *The Idle Class*, brought him unwanted attention from paranoid federal officials who began compiling a file on the curious, baggy-pants actor. By the time Charlie had released *Modern Times*, a pointed commentary on the alienation of capitalism, and *The Great Dictator*, a satire of Hitler whose humor was lost on the sober and staid director of the FBI, J. Edgar Hoover, Charlie was a marked man and fingered by Hoover as a Hollywood "parlor Bolsheviki."

The feds accused Charlie of "un-American activities" and tried to remove his residency rights but, failing that, Hoover simply directed the INS to invalidate Charlie's reentry visa after he briefly left the United States to visit London in 1952. FBI documents that have since been made public show a concentrated effort to compile a deportation case against Charlie, but memos between agents reveal that there had been no evidence to support his visa's revocation should he have chosen to challenge the decision. In any event, a bitter Charlie decided not to pursue the matter and instead moved to neutral Switzerland.

Charlie got revenge, of sorts, with a satirical look at the House Committee on Un-American Activities in the 1957 film *The King in New York*, but he was still clearly broken by what he rightly perceived to be a snubbing by America. Charlie and America made brief and strained amends in 1972, when he returned to receive a special Academy Award for "the incalculable effect he has had in making motion pictures the art form of this century." In 1975, after many years of self-imposed exile from his native England, he was knighted Sir Charles Chaplin.

At 88, on Christmas day 1977, Charlie died of "old age" at his estate in Switzerland and was buried overlooking Lake Geneva. But not for very long.

Kidnapping is a risky business, and it can be difficult to keep the struggling victim from escaping while the ransom payment is arranged. In March 1978 two enterprising would-be criminal geniuses circumvented that quandary by kidnapping a dead victim: Charlie Chaplin. A few weeks after his coffin, with him in it, was dug up and spirited away, Charlie's widow, Oona, received a ransom demand of $600,000 for its safe return. She refused to consider the ransom but, with police at her side, bargained with the grave robbers over a tapped telephone. Two men, a Pole and a Bulgarian, were captured and charged with, among other things, "disturbing the peace of the dead." The Pole, regarded as the brains of the operation, was jailed for four years while the Bulgarian was given a suspended sentence.

Charlie, after being dug out of a cornfield ten miles away, was reinterred back in the small town cemetery of Corsier-Sur-Vevey, Switzerland, but, this time, in a concrete vault.

BETTE DAVIS

APRIL 5, 1908 – OCTOBER 6, 1989

In some 90 films, most of them unmemorable, Bette Davis played an unusually wide range of characters with a brassy but controlled edge, from drunks to glamour queens to retiring old maids and lunatics. Filmgoers loved her portrayals of these fiercely independent characters that usually suffered nobly but, in her real life, she acquired an often-justified reputation as bellicose and impossible to work with. Bette herself once said, "I adore playing bitches . . . there's a little bit of bitch in every woman, and a little bit of bitch in every man."

Bette's acting debut came in 1929, and three years later Warner Bros. signed her to a long-term contract. In 1935, the studio began giving her decent parts, and that year's release of *Dangerous* estab-

lished her, after 22 forgettable films, as a major actress. Bette won her first Academy Award and quipped that the statue's backside resembled her husband's, Oscar Nelson, which some say led to its nickname "Oscar."

By the end of the thirties, Bette was the industry's top-ranked female draw, but her popularity peaked in the early forties and began to sag under the weight of weak pictures by the end of the decade. By the fifties her career was seriously faltering, but in 1962, after a pairing with her nemesis Joan Crawford in *Whatever Happened to Baby Jane?*, Bette found a new audience and worked steadily thereafter on the big screen, as well as in theater and on television.

A survivor of four unhappy marriages, a heavy drinker, and a five-pack-a-day chain smoker, Bette suffered from numerous ailments in her later years and succumbed to cancer at 81 while in France.

In a large white crypt inscribed, "*Bette Davis—She did it the hard way,*" she rests at Forest Lawn Memorial Park in Hollywood Hills, California.

CEMETERY DIRECTIONS: From Highway 134, which is the connector between Highway 101 and I-210, take the Forest Lawn Drive exit. Proceed west for a mile and the park's entrance is on the left.

GRAVE DIRECTIONS: Stop at the booth and, after getting a park map, go to the Courts of Remembrance. In the grass on the front left is her resting place.

JIMMY DURANTE

FEBRUARY 10, 1893 – JANUARY 29, 1980

After an early career as a hot ragtime pianist, the gravelly voiced Jimmy Durante established himself as a lovable comedian and enjoyed a unique audience rapport that flowed from his compassion for "da little guy." His prominent proboscis earned him the nickname "Schnozzola," and he used it to comic advantage in a couple dozen movies and countless appearances on television variety shows. For a while, Jimmy even had his own show and, of course, children of all ages recognize him as the narrator of "Frosty the Snowman."

Jimmy is best remembered for the nonsense song "Inka Dinka Doo" and for his peculiar sign-off. Walking away from the camera in the spotlight, with his coat slung over his shoulder, Durante would turn back and say, in his wonderfully raspy voice, "Good night Mrs. Calabash, wherever you are."

The mystery of Mrs. Calabash was long the subject of speculation. After his death it emerged that she probably was a waitress, Lucy Coleman, of Calabash, North Carolina. In 1940, Lucy ran a restaurant in the town of Calabash, and Jimmy's touring entertainment troupe stopped in for dinner one evening. The always-gregarious Durante engaged Lucy in some lively chitchat and vowed, "I'm going to make you famous." Shortly afterward, Jimmy began signing off his radio shows with the message and he stuck with it to the end.

Following several years of ill health, Jimmy passed away at 86 and rests at Holy Cross Cemetery in Culver City, California.

CEMETERY DIRECTIONS: From I-405, take Slauson Avenue east for ½ mile. The cemetery is on the left at #5835.

GRAVE DIRECTIONS: Enter the cemetery, turn left, start up the hill and 100 yards to the left is the Grotto lawn and altar. Jimmy's grave is in Section F, which is the next patch of lawn, another level up and to the right of the altar. Just walk around the right side of the low rock wall and you'll find it there against the wall.

GEORGE &
IRA GERSHWIN

George Gershwin

SEPTEMBER 26 1898 – JULY 11, 1937

Ira Gershwin

DECEMBER 6, 1896 – AUGUST 17, 1983

In a career tragically cut short by a brain tumor, the composer George Gershwin, who bestrode the realms of both pop music and concert music, proved himself to be one of the great songwriters of his extremely rich era.

George left school in 1913 and, combining his classical piano training with the popular ragtime style, he became a major figure in the Tin Pan Alley tradition, composing for Broadway shows under the pseudonym Arthur Francis during his teens. At twenty came his first real hit, "Swanee," and the same year saw his first Broadway musical, *La, La, Lucille.* During the next eighteen years, George produced an impressive amount of music and, with lyrics written largely by his older brother Ira, their songs came to define the 1920s and '30s while musicals like *Strike Up the Band* and *Of Thee I Sing* delighted Broadway audiences.

In 1924 George composed his first classical piece, *Rhapsody in Blue*, as a piano concerto for a popular band, and its success made George contemplate the wide gap between Tin Pan Alley's simple arrangements and classical music's serious offerings. To him, that void represented an unrestricted frontier. By that simple abstraction, George strove to unite commercial and classical genres, and the result was historic jazz-oriented concert works such as *Rhapsody in Blue* and *An American in Paris*, as well as the folk opera *Porgy and Bess*. Almost every one of his concert works has entered the theater, and the American psyche, and people with no interest in opera hum parts of his pieces without knowing where the material came from or even that it's part of something larger.

In the mid-1930s George and Ira had a successful run in Hollywood writing for Fred Astaire and Ginger Rogers but, for some reason, the normally athletic and cheerful George grew less enchanted with the parties and womanizing he used to enjoy. In February 1937 his mind went blank during a performance, though a few moments later he continued without interruption. Two months after that, he had a similar blackout in a barbershop and, each time, George said the lapse was accompanied by the smell of burning rubber.

By June George was suffering painful headaches and was often confused, groggy, and irritable. Doctors could find nothing wrong with him and attributed his pains to stress. On July 9, George was too weak to get out of bed. He soon fell into a coma, and doctors finally diagnosed an inoperable brain tumor. George's condition deteriorated rapidly and he died two days later at 38.

Following George's death, Ira continued writing and made a successful living composing scores for films until his death from natural causes at 86.

Both George and Ira rest at Westchester Hills Cemetery in Hastings-on-Hudson, New York.

CEMETERY DIRECTIONS: From the Sawmill Parkway, turn east onto Jackson Street, then left at the traffic light. The cemetery is a half-mile ahead on the right.

GRAVE DIRECTIONS: Follow the main drive into the cemetery. The brothers are in the third mausoleum on the right. Though the mausoleum's primary marker is engraved "George Gershwin," Ira lies there as well.

BURL IVES

JUNE 14, 1909 – APRIL 14, 1995

Over the course of a long and diverse show-business career, the jovial balladeer Burl Ives was a memorable presence in 30 movies and a dozen Broadway productions, recorded over 100 albums, and gave countless radio and television performances.

As a child, he had performed in public for change, but his real start in the business came in 1929 when he dropped out of teachers' college to wander the country like a vagabond, playing banjo and singing to keep himself fed. His first professional roles came in theater—Burl's high-watermark there came later, though, in 1958,

when he originated the role of Big Daddy in *Cat on a Hot Tin Roof.* By 1940 Burl had moved into radio with his own show, *The Wayfarin' Stranger.*

At the same time, with his especially sweet and mournful method of singing folk ballads, Burl was putting his stamp on standards from *Jimmy Crack Corn* to *I Know an Old Lady (Who Swallowed a Fly)* as well as on such children's songs as *Frosty the Snowman* and *Rudolph the Red-Nosed Reindeer.* His role as the narrator in the TV version of that annual holiday classic has endeared him to several generations of young people.

Burl was an imposing figure who loved to smoke, eat, and drink. For most of his life, he carried more than 300 pounds on his frame. Despite his size, Burl lived to be 85, when he died of mouth cancer. He was buried at Mound Cemetery in Oblong, Illinois.

CEMETERY DIRECTIONS: From I-70, take Exit 119 and follow Route 130 south to Route 33. Follow Route 33 east for eight miles and turn north onto County Road 2100. After one mile, make a right onto County Road 1200 and the cemetery is a short distance on the left.

GRAVE DIRECTIONS: The Ives' plot is easy to find, just fifty feet behind the church.

AL JOLSON

MAY 26, 1886 – OCTOBER 23, 1950

Today, much of Al Jolson's material seems stilted because he worked in a genre, the blackface minstrel revue, that is now perceived as a vehicle for crude racial stereotyping. His distinctive vocal style, shaped by the necessity of projecting the voice to a large audience unaided by electric microphones, seems artificial to many modern ears. Consequently, few Americans are aware that he was the foremost popular singer of the beginning of the twentieth century, and most know him as little more than a name.

It was Al who starred in the first of the "talkies," *The Jazz Singer,* though his career had really flourished before the era of sound, in a spectacular ascent beginning with the vaudeville revues that were the backbone of popular music during that era. He first applied burnt cork to his face in 1904, and although Jolson went on to develop stock stage characters that fell clearly within the traditions of blackface minstrelsy, some critics are adamant that Al's blackface was an expression of racial prejudice.

By 1911, he was under extended contract at the prestigious Winter Garden Theatre in New York City, and over the next fifteen years he introduced most of the songs for which he remains famous: "California, Here I Come," "Rock-a-Bye Your Baby with a Dixie Melody," and George Gershwin's "Swanee."

By 1920, as the biggest star in the country, Al was eagerly sought by Hollywood's growing movie studios, and he made a few short silent films before agreeing to star in *The Jazz Singer* in 1927. The soundtrack of this first sound film featured Jolson—in blackface, as he would be in all except one of his subsequent dozen films —singing "My Mammy" and Irving Berlin's "Blue Skies." The movie concerned a Jewish singer's efforts to become a Broadway star despite his cantor father's disapproval, which paralleled events in Al's own life. *The Jazz Singer* was an unprecedented success and raised his star to its highest level.

Though he continued to make other movies, none of them was as well received as *The Jazz Singer*. By the 1930s Al's popularity began to wane. Jolson's forte had been performing to live audiences, but they were becoming increasingly fickle in this radio-dominated era.

At 64, shortly after returning from performances for U.S. military troops in Korea, he died of a heart attack while playing cards in a San Francisco hotel.

He was buried at Hillside Memorial Park in Los Angeles.

CEMETERY DIRECTIONS: This cemetery borders the east side of I-405 at the Centinela Avenue exit, which is immediately north of the La Tijera Boulevard exit.

GRAVE DIRECTIONS: Al's tomb is the magnificent centerpiece at the top of the waterfall. Al actually designed this tomb himself, and once you enter the park you cannot miss it.

LAUREL & HARDY
Oliver Hardy
JANUARY 18, 1892 – AUGUST 7, 1957

Stan Laurel
JUNE 16, 1890 – FEBRUARY 23, 1965

In 1919 Oliver Hardy, the fat one, began working as an all-purpose comic for the Hal Roach studio. In 1926 he was teamed with Stan Laurel, and a 30-year comedic partnership was initiated. In short time, the boys were hailed as the newest comedy sensation, and they eventually made more than 100 films. Their act was brilliantly simple: Hardy was an incapable buffoon, and Laurel was so exceedingly numb that, in his eyes, Hardy was a genius.

The pair easily made the transition to talkies, as there never was a lot of dialogue anyway, and in 1932 Laurel and Hardy won an Oscar for their short subject *The Music Box*. In that film, they struggled to deliver a piano to the top floor of a house on a hill only to have it topple down after they both let go of it to wipe their brows. A sort of film history was made when, instead of getting the laughs from the visual of a falling piano, the audience was treated to a prolonged close-up of their faces as they listened to the piano exaggeratedly crashing downward. Though the fare's premise seems painfully slight by the standards of today, film comedy had to start somewhere.

Oliver Hardy suffered a massive stroke in 1956 that left him partially paralyzed and never again able to speak. After a year in a bed, he died at 65. Oliver was cremated and his ashes interred at Valhalla Memorial Park in North Hollywood, California.

CEMETERY DIRECTIONS: This park is easy to find at 10621 Victory Blvd., just 2½ miles east of Highway 170.

GRAVE DIRECTIONS: Enter the cemetery, turn right and proceed toward the fountain. On the right, before you get to the fountain, there is a low, stone wall called the Garden of Hope. On the opposite side Oliver's ashes are interred, and there is a plaque dedicated to his memory attached to the wall.

STAN LAUREL
1890 – 1965
A MASTER OF COMEDY
HIS GENIUS IN THE ART OF
HUMOR BROUGHT GLADNESS
TO THE WORLD HE LOVED.

In 1965 Stan Laurel died at 74 after suffering a heart attack. It's reported that he was in bed and said to his nurse, "I wish I was skiing," and she asked, "Oh, Mr. Laurel, do you ski?" to which Stan replied, "No, but I'd rather be skiing than doing what I'm doing." And then he died.

Stan was cremated and his ashes buried at Forest Lawn Memorial Park in Hollywood Hills, California.

CEMETERY DIRECTIONS: From Highway 134, which is the connector between Highway 101 and I-210, take the Forest Lawn Drive exit. Proceed west for a mile and the park's entrance will be on the left.

GRAVE DIRECTIONS: Get a map from the information booth and drive to the Gardens of Heritage, which are across the drive from the Old North Church. Bolted to the second wall, two levels behind the statue of Washington, is a white plaque that marks Stan's resting place.

THE LINDBERGHS

Charles Lindbergh
FEBRUARY 4, 1902 – AUGUST 26, 1974

Anne Morrow Lindbergh
JUNE 22, 1906 – FEBRUARY 7, 2001

Charles Lindbergh, Jr.
JUNE 22, 1930 – MARCH 1, 1932

In 1926, Charles Lindbergh was flying a regular mail route between Chicago and St. Louis and, in those lonely hours, resolved to pursue the yet unclaimed $25,000 prize that had been offered in 1919 to the first aviator who flew nonstop between New York and Paris. Since its inception, the well-publicized challenge had been a sort of national obsession, and had captured the imagination of the American public. But, frustratingly, though there were plenty of front-page accounts glorifying the pioneers who set off to claim the prize, there had never been an exciting story of success. French aviators would fly out of Paris and crash-land in England, American fliers would be forced back to New York after encountering bad weather, and many pilots from both sides of the Atlantic simply took off and were never heard from again.

Charles had his own ideas about how to successfully cross the Atlantic. Unlike his contemporaries, he believed the passage should be flown alone, and he was also convinced that an airplane capable of crossing the Atlantic Ocean did not exist—it would have to be built. After enlisting the financial aid of a few St. Louis businessmen, he hired the Ryan Airplane company in San Diego to build a plane for the crossing, and when it was ready two months later, Charles flew it to New York in preparation for his Paris flight.

Charles' plane, the *Spirit of St. Louis*, was designed expressly to fly across the Atlantic. Described as a "two-ton flying gas tank," every possible accommodation was sacrificed for better fuel economy: There was no radio and no brakes, a small periscope replaced a forward-facing windshield, and Charles wore no parachute. For food, he brought five sandwiches. "If I get to Paris, I won't need any more and if I don't get to Paris, I won't need any more, either," he noted dryly. There was no room for error.

On May 21, 1927, after flying for twenty-eight hours, the Spirit of St. Louis landed in Paris. Charles' singular accomplishment electrified the world, and he immediately embarked on a goodwill tour of some two dozen countries. During a visit to Mexico he first met the aspiring writer Anne Morrow, daughter of Dwight M. Morrow, a former U.S. Senator and then-ambassador to Mexico. In 1929 the two were wed.

In 1932 the Lindberghs made headlines anew when their toddler son, Charles Jr., was snatched from his nursery at their Hopewell, New Jersey, home. A kidnapper left a note demanding $50,000 and after corresponding with the kidnapper through newspaper classifieds and an intermediary, the ransom money was delivered to a Bronx cemetery. But their baby was never returned. Instead he was found two months later, dead, near the Lindbergh home. Bruno Hauptmann was eventually arrested for the crime after he passed some of the ransom money at a gas station and, after a sensational trial, he was found guilty and went to the electric chair in 1936.

To escape media attention after the trial, the Lindberghs moved to England, and upon their return in 1939, Charles became spokesperson for the America First Committee, a group that opposed American entry into World War II. Charles' position put him at odds with President Roosevelt and ordinary Americans questioned his loyalty. They were particularly repelled by his vocal anti-Semitic stance. In response, Charles resigned his Air Corps commission, but then Pearl Harbor changed everything. In 1942 Charles asked to be reinstated into the Air Corps, but Roosevelt staunchly refused. Charles worked as an advisor at Henry Ford's B-24 bomber plant in Willow Run, instead. After the war, the public generally forgot about, or at least overlooked, Charles' pre-war shenanigans.

During their marriage, Anne had come into fame of her own. In the 1930s the couple had worked together as commercial air flight surveyors and, during a pioneering flight from Canada to China, she had served as Charles' copilot. A meticulous documentarian, Anne related the story of that adventure in her first book, *North to the Orient*, which became a bestseller, as did the other dozen titles she'd write. In 1954 Charles' book, *Spirit of St. Louis*, detailing his famous transatlantic flight and largely written by Anne, won a Pulitzer Prize. In 1956, Anne authored one of the landmark bestsellers of the century, *Gift From the Sea*, a reflection on women's lives and their struggle for identity. It spent 47 weeks as the best-selling book in the nation and, 45 years after its release, has never gone out of print.

In their twilight years, the Lindberghs continued to fly, though mostly for pleasure. Charles died of cancer at 72, on August 26, 1974, in their home on the Hawaiian island of Maui. After Charles' death, Anne began publishing her journals, letters and memoirs, in part to provide a historical record of aviation and also to end the many misconceptions and fallacies about herself and her husband. After suffering a series of strokes, Anne died at 94 in the company of her family at her daughter's Vermont home.

Today, Charles's *Spirit of St. Louis* airplane hangs in the atrium of the National Air and Space Museum in Washington D.C.

Before Charles died, he sketched a simple design for his coffin and grave. He was buried under the shade of a java plum tree at Palapala Ho'omao Congregational Church Cemetery in Kipahulu on the Hawaiian island of Maui. His epitaph, Psalm 139:9 – 10, reads, *"If I take the wings of the morning, and dwell in the uttermost parts of the sea."*

CEMETERY DIRECTIONS: Kipahulu is in a very remote area of Maui on the southeastern shore. From Kahului, follow Route 360 and, after passing through the town of Hana, start looking for the 41-mile marker. (Note that the markers are descending.) A tenth of a mile past the 41-mile marker, turn left onto a small drive alongside a meadow. Then, after another hundred yards, turn left again. The church and cemetery are a short distance along this drive.

GRAVE DIRECTIONS: Park in front of the church and walk over to the cemetery on the ocean side of the church. Charles's grave is located approximately in the cemetery center surrounded by a simple iron chain.

Anne was cremated, and, in accordance with her wishes, her ashes were "scattered over the places she loved."

Charles Lindbergh, Jr., who died at eighteen months, was cremated and his ashes scattered over the Atlantic Ocean.

GROUCHO MARX
OCTOBER 2, 1890 – AUGUST 19, 1977

After conquering Broadway in the 1920s, Groucho Marx and his four brothers moved to Hollywood and became a veritable comedy attack force, slinging a wild and anarchic style of humor at movie audiences, the likes of which had never been seen. With his trademark swallow-tailed coat, greasepaint moustache and rolling, leering, depraved eyes, the intensely verbal Groucho was the key to the brothers' success in a legendary series of movies highlighted by such pictures as *Animal Crackers* and *A Night at the Opera.*

After the brothers broke up in 1949, Groucho became host of the radio and TV series *You Bet Your Life* and he elevated his quick wit into an art form. On one occasion, he asked a contestant her age and she replied, "I'm approaching 40," to which Groucho shot back, "From which direction?" On another program, a contestant developed stage fright and was unable to utter a word, to which Groucho delivered the now infamous comment, "Either this man is dead, or my watch is stopped."

Groucho died of pneumonia at 86 and, after cremation, his ashes were interred at Eden Memorial Park in Mission Hills, California.

CEMETERY DIRECTIONS: This cemetery is at the corner of Rinaldi Street and Sepulveda Boulevard, just east of the Rinaldi Street exit off I-405.

GRAVE DIRECTIONS: Enter the park, turn at the first right and park your vehicle. Up the hill on your left is a large mausoleum that is divided into three sections. On the left-hand side of the middle section is the door to a columbarium and, inside at about eye-level, are Groucho's cremains.

His brothers Chico, Gummo, and Harpo are buried at Forest Lawn Memorial Park in Glendale, California. In 1979, death took the last surviving Marx brother, Zeppo, and he was cremated.

GLENN MILLER

MARCH 1, 1904 – DECEMBER 15, 1944

In the late 1920s, Glenn Miller began a sort of professional apprenticeship and spent several years playing and recording with the likes of the Dorsey Brothers and Benny Goodman. By 1935, he had secured an offer to record under his own name but, dishearteningly, the work received only a tepid response. Within just a few more years, though, and after countless engagements, Glenn and his orchestra were lauded in music circles for a new signature sound he had developed within the reed section of his orchestra. By applying that style to a careful mixture of swing and jazz, Glenn became one of the most celebrated big-band leaders of the day.

Record-breaking recordings of "Tuxedo Junction" and "Moonlight Serenade" confirmed the status of the Glenn Miller Orchestra, and in 1941 the band was off to Hollywood where it would make two movies, the first of which introduced the song "Chattanooga Choo Choo."

Soon, the United States entered World War II, and as men responded to the country's needs, the ranks of orchestras dwindled. In late summer of 1942, Glenn himself reported for induction and soon headed overseas to entertain and build the morale of fighting troops with his new 48-member Glenn Miller Army Air Force Band. While stationed in England, Glenn's band played some 300 concerts, as well as another 500 radio broadcasts, and along the way contributed to the modernization of military music as well.

In the fall of 1944, the band was scheduled for a six-week tour of Europe. Glenn needed to journey ahead of the band to make arrangements for its first appearance there and, just after lunchtime on a Friday, Glenn boarded a single-engine C-64 Norseman airplane bound for Paris. But somewhere over the English Channel, things went desperately wrong and neither Glenn, the pilot, or the other passenger aboard was ever seen again. No distress call was received, no oil slick or wreckage was ever found and, to this day, nobody knows what happened to the flight. It seems it just disappeared.

Nine days later, at 6:00 p.m. on Christmas Eve 1944, a press release announced to the world that Glenn was lost, and on the next day, the band played on. Without Glenn, the band performed their scheduled Christmas concert in Paris and continued to perform until July 1945, when they disbanded after a final engagement for President Truman.

Though his body lies in parts unknown, Glenn, gone at age 40, is honored with cenotaphs at three different locations.

Glenn's 418th AAFTC Orchestra and Marching Band was permanently stationed at Yale University in New Haven, Connecticut. At the Grove Street Cemetery, just east of campus, Glenn is recognized with a simple and tasteful black stone memorial.

On the Wall of the Missing, at the 305-acre Madingley Military Cemetery and Memorial, at Madingley, Cambridgeshire, England, Glenn's name is inscribed along with 5,124 similarly missing American servicemen. Madingley is located about an hour north of London, and sits just a few miles from Cambridge.

Finally, at his daughter's request in 1992, a stone was placed in Memorial Section H, Number 464-A, on Wilson Drive, at Arlington National Cemetery in Arlington, Virginia. On the west bank of the Potomac River, this cemetery is easy to find.

WILEY POST

NOVEMBER 22, 1898 – AUGUST 15, 1935

For as long as he could remember, Wiley Post was entranced by flying machines, and he came to be one of the most colorful figures in aviation.

After World War I, Wiley was a roughneck on an Oklahoma oil rig, but he turned to highway robbery and in 1921 was sentenced to ten years in the state penitentiary. Fortunate enough to be paroled the following year, Wiley eased into aviation as a parachutist and

worked for a flying circus, where he learned the rudiments of flying from show-pilot friends.

In 1926, Wiley returned to the oil rigs to earn enough money to buy his own plane but during his first day on the job he lost his left eye. He soon regarded this as a blessing because the $1,800 insurance settlement helped purchase his first airplane. The next few years found Wiley traveling to county fairs and carnivals in exhibitions of stunt flying, or barnstorming, as it was known, and in 1930 he achieved national prominence when he won the National Air Race Derby and its $7,500 prize. The following year, with navigator Harold Gatty, he set an around-the-world record, circumnavigating the globe in eight days and, in 1933, after adding an automatic pilot and a radio compass to his plane, Wiley bested the time by more than twenty hours and became the first solo flyer to circle the earth.

Wiley then turned to high-altitude experiments and, together with the BF Goodrich Company, built the first pressurized flying suit. In this suit, Wiley flew into the stratosphere and discovered the jet stream. He's regarded as one of space flight's pioneers, though he lived more than two decades before the establishment of a United States space program.

Back when he was working for the flying circus, Wiley met the famous humorist Will Rogers and through the years the two had become fast friends; while Wiley was employed as the personal pilot of a wealthy Oklahoma oilman he had the opportunity to borrow a plane, and he would sometimes shuttle Will between engagements. By 1935, Wiley had become interested in surveying a mail-and-passenger air route from Seattle to Russia, and the pair planned to scout the route together.

All went as planned until they became lost in bad weather near Point Barrow, Alaska, and were forced to land the pontoon-equipped plane in a lagoon. After asking directions, Wiley tried to take off again, but the engine stalled. The plane plunged into the water and both men were killed instantly.

At 36, Wiley was buried at Memorial Park in Edmond, Oklahoma.

CEMETERY DIRECTIONS: From Route 77, take the Memorial Road exit and you'll see the cemetery on the east side of Route 77.

GRAVE DIRECTIONS: Enter the cemetery, go around the office and proceed back to the flag and mirror pool. Make a right onto the drive after the pool, then stop after another hundred feet. On your left is an opening between two cedar trees, and there you'll find Wiley's plot, 30 feet from the drive.

THE RAT PACK

In the late 1950s, well before Las Vegas was a Corporate America theme park, Frank Sinatra summoned four cronies to the Sands Hotel and Casino. Its Copa Room was promptly the hippest place in the universe.

With crooning lover-boy Frank as nominal "chairman," "the Rat Pack," became a cult of personalities living the high life of booze, broads, and bright lights. The group consisted of the chairman, himself; the easygoing singer Dean Martin; the one-eyed, singing and dancing wonder-boy Sammy Davis Jr.; the upper-crust, British pretty-boy Peter Lawford; and the stiff-shouldered comic Joey Bishop. They were the new American gods, and Las Vegas was their Mount Olympus.

Their "summit" meetings became the ultimate nightclub act and, while Las Vegas matured in their shadow, the quintet held court at their anything-goes playground. With a confidence and arrogance secured by seemingly all the money in the world, Frank and his swingin' pals, the culmination of cool, roasted one another with one-liners and belted out the hits of the day, and of days past. Reveling in their heady, bourbon-filled presence, drop-dead gorgeous women squirmed in their midst while starstruck common folk basked in the privilege of proximity.

The Rat Pack even conquered celluloid in such films as the casino-heist caper *Ocean's Eleven*, so everyone could share in their obvious fun. One of the Pack, Peter Lawford, was married to a woman whose brother happened to be named John F. Kennedy and, after the boys staged concerts to raise money for his 1960 presidential bid, the Oval Office got in on the gambol, initiating the trendy association of politics and celebrity.

But the carefree days didn't last, and after a few glory years, the Rat Pack dissolved. Relations between Frank and Peter soured when the president frowned on their mob-associated fraternity, and Joey soon rightfully returned to his own lightweight gigs. By 1964, as the nation struggled with a presidential assassination, a looming war in Vietnam, and turbulence brought on by civil rights protests, the Rat Pack seemed hopelessly anachronous, and there was no longer room for their world without rules or consequences. The years of high living had taken their toll and the fun was done.

Peter Lawford

SEPTEMBER 7, 1923 – DECEMBER 24, 1984

Though he appeared in dozens of films, was the first to kiss Elizabeth Taylor on camera, and counted himself among Marilyn Monroe's playmates, the debonair Peter Lawford was never a real Hollywood player. His membership in the Rat Pack was among the most tenuous and, in the first place, his ticket into Frank's golden circle seems to have been predicated on his standing with the Kennedy family. In 1962, after a row over Kennedy's objections to alleged Mafia connections, the two men never spoke again.

Peter peaked with the Rat Pack and after, in quick sequence, Frank snubbed him, Marilyn overdosed, and JFK was assassinated, Peter's career went south. It was briefly rejuvenated when he teamed with Sammy Davis Jr. in 1968's *Salt and Pepper* and its 1970 *One More Time* sequel, but, by the end of his life, the jet-setting playboy was broke, divorced three times, and his health had been destroyed by years of vodka, painkillers and cocaine.

Peter was reduced to selling his life story to the tabloids and, at 61, he died of cardiac arrest complicated by kidney and liver failure. He was cremated and his ashes entombed but, three years later, it was learned that nobody had ever paid for the crypt maintenance. His children and wife at the time, Patricia Seaton, couldn't agree on who should pay the outstanding charges, so the tabloids were contacted again. In return for a photo spread of Peter's ashes being scattered at sea, *The National Enquirer* settled the balance with the cemetery.

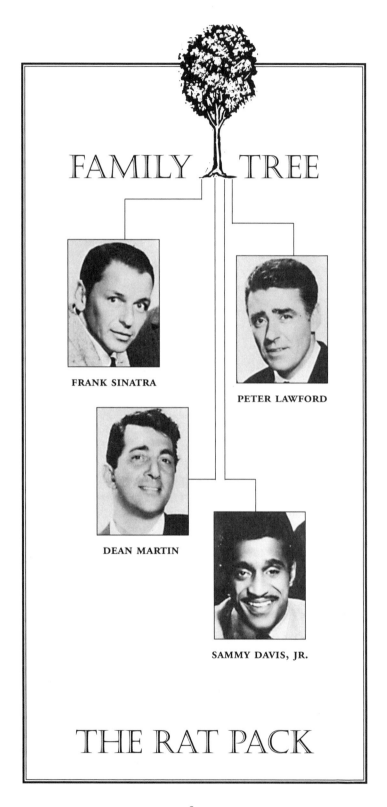

FAMILY TREE

FRANK SINATRA

PETER LAWFORD

DEAN MARTIN

SAMMY DAVIS, JR.

THE RAT PACK

Dean Martin

JUNE 7, 1917 – DECEMBER 25, 1995

Dino Paul Crocetti sweated in steel mills, boxed under the name Kid Crochet, and smuggled bootleg liquor before making a go as a crooner and mutating into Dean Martin. By 1946, he was kibitzing onstage with a nasal comedian named Jerry Lewis, and within two years, they had the industry in their hands. Thirteen hugely popular straight-man-Martin and manic-fool-Lewis comedy films followed, but while Jerry's comedic ambitions ballooned, Dean's musical spirit simmered, despite the 1953 hit "That's Amore." By 1956, tired of break-ups and make-ups prompted by Jerry's insecurities, Dean permanently dissolved the team. He never looked back and rarely even acknowledged Jerry's existence.

No one thought Dean would make it on his own, and he didn't. Instead the Rat Pack came calling and, in movies and Vegas nightclubs, Dean's persona was elevated to that of a most lovable and lecherous lush. Dean, with highball and cigarette firmly in hand, serenely floated above the fray, projecting a sense of utter detachment while audiences flocked to breathe the same rarefied air.

In 1964, Dean's deification was completed when "Everybody Loves Somebody" knocked the Beatles out of the number one spot. The next year saw the debut of the leering *Dean Martin Show*, but by the time of its cancellation nine seasons later, pop culture had inexorably shifted, and even Dean's workaday records no longer quite had a place. When playboy nihilism was finally shelved in the late 1970s, Dean's one-of-the-boys charisma made him seem absurdly passé and he loped through halfhearted singing gigs and celebrity roasts for the remainder of his life.

In 1987 his fighter-pilot son, Dino Jr., died in a plane crash and Dean completely removed himself from public life, spending his final quiet years haunting Hollywood restaurants alone. "I'm just waiting to die," he told Paul Anka one night.

On Christmas Day 1995, Dean's wait ended and he died of acute respiratory failure at 78.

He rests at Westwood Village Memorial Park in Santa Monica, California.

CEMETERY DIRECTIONS: This little cemetery holds numerous celebrities and is peculiarly located behind the office complex at 10850 Wilshire Blvd., just about a half-mile east of I-405.

GRAVE DIRECTIONS: As you stand in the cemetery yard and look toward the cemetery office, on your far left is a series of alcoves. Dean's crypt is in the Sanctuary of Love alcove, third row from the bottom. His nameplate reminds us that "Everybody Loves Somebody Sometime."

Sammy Davis, Jr.

DECEMBER 8, 1925 – MAY 16, 1990

Sammy got his showbiz start at age three as Silent Sam, the Dancing Midget, alongside his father and uncle in vaudeville productions. Consequently, though it never seemed to matter, he *never* went to any kind of school. Sammy's tap-dancing film debut came in 1932 and, after serving during World War II, he returned to his father's troupe. In 1946, at 21, he recorded "The Way You Look Tonight," which was named Record of the Year.

By the mid-1950s Sammy was riding high as a mime, comedian, drummer, actor, singer, and dancer, but he faced a sudden setback in 1954 when he lost his left eye in a near-fatal auto accident. During his hospital recovery, he converted to Judaism, causing a press-sponsored hullabaloo. Undaunted, Sammy soon returned to the stage, wearing an eye patch until he could be fitted with a prosthetic, and within a year he enjoyed new hit singles, including "That Old Black Magic" and "Love Me or Leave Me." The next year he made his Broadway debut in the musical "Mr. Wonderful," which ran for some 400 performances.

A friendship that would last a lifetime ignited between Sammy and Frank Sinatra in 1949 and, ten years later, Sammy counted himself as a charter member of Frank's Rat Pack. Barbed reproach was nothing new to Sammy and he was undaunted by criticism levied by many of his own race, who accused him of selling out as the token black in the white boys' pack. Those idle heckles paled against the public outcry and death threats that would follow his 1960 interracial marriage to Swedish actress May Britt.

But though he also later came under fire for his compulsive carousing and reckless gambling, and even for an admitted love for pornography and his 1972 support of Nixon, Sammy stuck to his art and rose above it all. Bedecked in heavy jewelry and clad in a snug jumpsuit or tuxedo, the slight showman with the crooked smile energized audiences and became one of America's most beloved entertainers.

By the late 1970s, though, after his chart-topping pop hit "Candy Man" and his own television variety show, Sammy's popularity waned, and he was primarily relegated to the casino circuit and second-rate films. With many from the entertainment world at his side, Sammy, a lifelong smoker, died in 1990 of throat cancer.

Wearing a pair of trademark Bojangles cuff links and a watch given him on his deathbed by Sinatra, at 64 Sammy was buried at Forest Lawn Memorial Park in Glendale, California.

CEMETERY DIRECTIONS: From Highway 2, take the San Fernando Road exit and turn northwest. After a mile, make a right onto Glendale Avenue. The park's entrance is immediately on the right.

GRAVE DIRECTIONS: Stop at the booth for a cemetery map, then drive to the Freedom Mausoleum. Walk into the courtyards in front of the Freedom Mausoleum and you'll see two closed sections, the Gardens of Honor. Within the Garden of Honor section closer to the Freedom Mausoleum, Sammy lies two rows in front of the white Davis family statue. However, these gardens are closed to the public and, "Admittance to these private gardens is restricted to those possessing a Golden Key of Memory, given to each owner at time of purchase." But if you want to get in there badly enough, there's always a way.

Frank Sinatra

DECEMBER 12, 1915 – MAY 14, 1998

Believe it or not, Frank Sinatra once aspired to be a journalist. He was a copyboy at the *Jersey Observer* newspaper and, after enrolling in secretarial school where he studied English, typing, and shorthand, he was promoted to cub sports reporter. But as a self-taught singer, Frank was also working for $25 a week at a country roadhouse as a maitre d', singer, and comedian. It was there that he was discovered by Harry James in 1939.

After touring with James' band, Frank rose to prominence recording more than 90 songs with Tommy Dorsey's orchestra. By 1943 he was a film star as well, debuting in *Higher and Higher*, and his live performances were disrupted by the hysterical commotion of "bobby soxer" fans. In 1949, though, Ol' Blue Eyes hit a soft spot; record sales stalled, concerts flopped due to his vocal cord hemorrhages, he was released from his film contract, and, on the personal front, an affair with Ava Gardner was an open scandal. At 34, the Voice seemed washed up.

Down but not out, Frank pulled himself out of the slump. With help from Ava, who was now his wife, Frank landed the role of the tough Italian, Angelo Maggio, in *From Here to Eternity* and, in 1953, he won an Academy Award for his efforts. A natural actor, Frank turned in top-notch performances in many more films, most notably *The Man With the Golden Arm* two years later and *The Manchurian Candidate* in 1962.

After his Academy win, Frank took off running once again. He overcame his vocal-cord afflictions and, armed with a new recording contract, Frank turned out a string of hits including "Young at Heart," "Hey Jealous Lover," and "All the Way." It was his own golden era. By the time he held court as chairman of the board over his Rat Pack brothers, Frank held all the cards and dealt them in inimitable style.

By the mid-1960s, a sea change came over Las Vegas and, as new money domesticated business, Frank had to make way for the newcomers. His popularity softened ever so slightly and, in 1971, as his famous voice began to waver, he announced his retirement. Over the next two decades Frank cut back on records and movies and only performed occasionally. His last public appearance came in 1994.

At 82, Frank died of heart failure and was buried at Desert Memorial Park Cemetery in Cathedral City, California.

CEMETERY DIRECTIONS: From I-10, take the Ramon Road exit and proceed south for two miles to Da Vall Drive. Turn right and the cemetery entrance is immediately on the left.

GRAVE DIRECTIONS: Enter the cemetery, turn left and follow the main drive around, but don't bear left toward the office. Once you've turned around the right-hand hairpin and Ramon Road is directly behind you, begin counting the trees on your right. Stop between the third and fourth trees, and count four markers in from the curb on the right to find Frank's grave.

NORMAN ROCKWELL
FEBRUARY 3, 1894 – NOVEMBER 8, 1978

In 1916 Norman Rockwell's spectacular career as America's favorite artist-illustrator was launched when the *Saturday Evening Post* first used one of his paintings on its cover. Thus began an association spanning 317 covers and 47 years. His warm and folksy paintings made Norman Rockwell a household name.

Painting eight hours a day, seven days a week, Norman took average America as his subject. Through wars, civil strife, and the Depression, Norman stuck to his easel and recorded the awkwardness of youth, the tribulations of romance, and the virtues of loyalty and compassion. His body of work yields an extraordinary visual history of the century, portrayed with benevolent affection.

In addition to his *Post* covers, Norman contributed to many other magazines, did 53 Boy Scout calendars, and his advertisements helped sell countless products. Norman illustrated the lives of Ben Franklin, Tom Sawyer, and Huckleberry Finn, and did portraits of all the presidential candidates from Eisenhower through Carter. In 1943 he painted his famous "Four Freedoms" series and reproductions were widely distributed by the War Department. When the originals went on tour, they helped sell $133 million in war bonds.

He left the *Post* in 1963, feeling that it had changed from a family-oriented periodical to one of "sophisticated muckraking," and his work changed dramatically. Norman left the role of chronicler of nostalgic America and became a crusader. Instead of painting gentler scenes of peace and prosperity, he showed a strong social conscience and delved into such issues as civil rights, poverty, the generation gap, and the war in Vietnam.

In a survey of Americans, his painting of a young boy standing on a chair inspecting the doctor's diploma while preparing to receive a vaccination in the behind was chosen by a majority as the favorite of his entire catalog. But Norman himself steadfastly maintained that he had no favorite painting. He once said, "Someone asked Picasso his favorite of all the pictures he ever painted and he replied, 'The next one.' I'll echo the master."

At 84, Norman died peacefully in his sleep and was buried at the town cemetery in Stockbridge, Massachusetts.

CEMETERY DIRECTIONS: From the center of Stockbridge, follow Route 102 west for a half-mile, then turn right onto Church Street. After a couple hundred yards, turn right again and enter the cemetery at the entrance between the stone pillars.

GRAVE DIRECTIONS: Proceed down the corridor of pine and hemlock trees and at the first drive, turn right and stop. The Rockwell plot is on the right, surrounded by a hedgerow.

While in Stockbridge, you'll certainly want to visit the warm atmosphere of the Norman Rockwell Museum, where a regular rotation of his paintings is on display. At any given time, the gallery is adorned with a few hundred of his works, but you'll have to return quite a few times before you've seen the approximately 4,000 that comprise Norman's catalog. The Four Freedoms series are the centerpiece of the museum and, when you look up to view them, the effect is a virtual cathedral to the American Dream.

To reach the museum, follow Church Street for another mile past the cemetery and watch for signs to the left.

WILL ROGERS
NOVEMBER 4, 1879 – AUGUST 15, 1935

Around the turn of the century, the part-Cherokee Oklahoman Will Rogers joined a traveling Wild West production as a trick roper; Will had especially keen lariat skills and developed a signature stunt of throwing three lassos at once, landing one around a running horse's neck, another around the rider, and the last under the horse to loop all four legs. He moved his routine along with a cracker-barrel wit, and before long, his folksy observations and homespun philosophies became more prized by audiences than his expert roping.

Americans adored his perceptive satire, which never crossed the line to mockery, and Will's persona became a pervasive cultural charm. He was a fixture and a favorite of the Ziegfeld Follies, appeared in dozens of movies and, in 1928, even ran for president on the Anti-Bunk ticket. Through some 4,000 syndicated newspaper columns and his own radio show, Will showcased an endless supply of sensibly sage, off-the-cuff quips and comments, like "I never met a man I didn't like," and "All I know is what I read in the papers." He remains a certified American folk hero.

Among Will's many friends and acquaintances was Wiley Post, a one-eyed record-setting aviator, who in 1935 was exploring a new air route between Seattle and Russia. The pair decided to scout the route together; Wiley needed to fly the course to determine whether it was practical, and Will was eager to document a trip with a maverick aviator to his faithful readers in newspaper columns banged out from faraway ports of call.

But a few days after leaving Seattle, the friends' adventure turned grim. With few landmarks to go by, Wiley had gotten his directions a little mixed up. After realizing he'd strayed from his planned course, he touched the pontoon-equipped plane down on an inlet near the tiny outpost of Point Barrow, Alaska. After getting their bearings from the locals, the pair was again on its way but, shortly after taking off from the water, the plane's engine quit. It fell straight down, and both Will and Wiley were killed.

Will was 55 at his death and is buried at his own Memorial and Museum in Claremore, Oklahoma.

GRAVE DIRECTIONS: From the center of Claremore, take Route 88 north and the Will Rogers complex will be on your right after one mile. Will's tomb, complete with a statue of a horse, is in the front overlooking the expansive lawn.

RUDOLPH VALENTINO
MAY 6, 1895 – AUGUST 23, 1926

Rudolph Valentino was the greatest Latin lover of the silent screen era. At eighteen he left Italy and, after arriving in New York aboard the steamer *S.S. Cleveland*, Rudolph was soon the star tango dancer at Maxim's, a high-class New York cabaret from which he moonlighted as a gigolo. After a particular married woman with whom he was having an affair killed her husband, Rudolph conveniently left town in 1916 with the Masked Model touring tango group and ended up in Hollywood.

Blessed with hypnotic eyes and a dashing charm, Rudolph was an instant star, mainly in the role of the romantic "Sheik" in a series of desert melodramas. From his days as a dancer, he had learned to move with a sort of grace and finesse unfamiliar to moviegoers of the day, and he enchanted audiences with his exotic appearance and unconventional mannerisms. In the seven years before his untimely death, Rudolph appeared in fourteen major films, including *The Four Horsemen of the Apocalypse* and *The Eagle*, and female moviegoers openly swooned over his extraordinary sex appeal.

By 1926, the Great Italian Lover's second marriage had collapsed and he set off newly single again. In the morning after an all-night party thrown in his honor, Rudolph went to the hospital with severe stomach pain. Doctors immediately performed surgery to repair a perforated ulcer and remove his ruptured appendix. However, uremic poisoning had already swept through his body and penetrated the wall of his heart. Six days later, Rudolph was dead.

Widespread hysteria among his idolizers ensued. At the Funeral Church at 67th Street and Broadway in New York, Rudolph was laid out in a silver-bronze coffin with a plate-glass barrier so fans could look at, but not touch, the man who had been the world's greatest lover. At one point, the frenzied throng broke through the church's front window and dozens of people were injured in the ensuing chaos. Eventually, some 80,000 people filed past the dead Sheik.

At 31, Rudolph was buried at Hollywood Forever in Hollywood, California.

CEMETERY DIRECTIONS: This cemetery is easy to find as it's just west of Highway 101 at 6000 Santa Monica Blvd.

GRAVE DIRECTIONS: Enter the cemetery, turn at the second left, drive straight through the next intersection, and park in front of the Hollywood Cathedral Mausoleum on the right. Walk in the mausoleum's main entrance, turn left at the second corridor, then right at the last corridor. Rudolph's crypt is on the left at the end.

Interestingly, this crypt was supposed to be his temporary resting place until a suitably grand monument could be built. However, plans for such a memorial never materialized, so Rudolph lies in this borrowed vault that belonged to his friend and agent, June Mathis.

For a period of years, a mysterious "Lady in Black" faithfully visited Rudolph's tomb on the anniversary of his death. Theories about her identity circulated endlessly until a movie house admitted to creating the event as a stunt intended to stoke interest in the Valentino mystique.

SPORTS
HEROES

THE ALLISONS

Clifford Allison
OCTOBER 20, 1964 – AUGUST 13, 1992

Davey Allison
FEBRUARY 25, 1961 – JULY 13, 1993

Clifford and Davey Allison were the driving forces behind the famed Alabama Gang, a squad of auto-racing legends that left its stamp at every track it raced since the Gang's father, Bobby Allison, their uncle Donnie Allison, and mentor, Red Farmer, first emerged as contenders in the 1950s.

During his racing career, Clifford traced his father's tire tracks all across Alabama's speedways. He raced the Late Model division, the ARCA series, and the NASCAR All-Pro series, winning the Montgomery International Raceway Championship in 1987. But in 1992 Clifford was killed at 27 in a single-car crash while running laps at Michigan International Raceway.

Clifford's older brother Davey made it to the Winston Cup tour and was considered a contender almost from the moment he arrived. He was the first rookie to ever line up on the front row for the Daytona 500, taking outside pole honors in 1987, and after two wins in that season he was named Rookie of the Year. Within eight years, Davey had collected nineteen Winston Cup wins and had pocketed more than six million dollars in prize money, but perhaps the most memorable moment of his career came when he finished second to his father at Daytona in 1988.

In 1993 Davey, a newly licensed helicopter pilot, drove his bird into the tarmac at Talladega Speedway and died of his injuries the following day. He was 32.

Both Clifford and Davey are buried at Highland Memorial Gardens in Brighton, Alabama.

CEMETERY DIRECTIONS: From I-20/59, take Exit 113. The cemetery is just a block west on 18th Avenue.

GRAVE DIRECTIONS: Enter the cemetery and turn right. Follow this drive and, after it bends to the left, you'll see a black granite bench dedicated to Davey on the right. Davey's grave is twenty feet behind the bench.

To see Clifford's grave, continue another 70 feet along the drive and stop at the next lawn area, which honors Our Lady of Lourdes. Clifford's flat, bronze marker is about twenty feet beyond the dogwood tree.

ANDRE THE GIANT
MAY 19, 1946 – JANUARY 27, 1993

Andre Rene Roussimoff, of French heritage and better known as Andre the Giant, was a professional wrestler afflicted with a genetic disorder resulting in gigantism. In 1973, he made his American debut at Madison Square Garden and, proving fantastically successful, wrestled more than 300 days a year for the next sixteen-odd years, becoming one of the world's most famous professional athletes.

Though he was advertised as seven feet, four inches tall, he was probably just under seven feet and tipped the scales at around 500 pounds. Andre's immense appetites for food and alcohol were legendary, and it was estimated he consumed 7,000 calories a day in alcohol alone.

In 1987, he played Fezzik, the gentle giant in the movie *The Princess Bride*, a role for which he was suited in both dimension and disposition, and it remained one of his most cherished achievements—he carried a video of the film with him when he traveled and held frequent screenings.

Unfortunately, as he grew older his size caused him frequent health problems and he became increasingly overweight and immobile.

At 46, Andre died of a heart attack and was cremated. His ashes were scattered at his horse ranch in Ellerbe, North Carolina.

ARTHUR ASHE
JULY 10, 1943 – FEBRUARY 6, 1993

Arthur Ashe was the first African American man to win tennis' most prestigious tournaments: the U.S. Open and Wimbledon. He first learned to play tennis on a segregated playground, then parlayed that into a twelve-year career that included 33 singles and 18 doubles titles. He later became president of the Association of Tennis Professionals and captain of the Davis Cup team, which won two championships under his direction.

Though the titles and ensuing endorsement contracts made Arthur a millionaire, wealth didn't distract him from the social issues of the day. He became a civil rights activist, fighting for all minorities that were victims of exclusionary practices. He also served as the national campaign chairman for the American Heart Association, edited several books, and contributed generously to African American programs everywhere.

After Arthur disclosed that he had AIDS in 1992, he devoted himself to becoming a role model in the fight against the disease, and began a $5 million fund-raising effort on behalf of his namesake foundation.

At 49 Ashe died of pneumonia, a complication brought on by AIDS, and was buried at Woodland Cemetery in Richmond, Virginia.

CEMETERY DIRECTIONS: From I-64 take Exit 192 to Route 360 east. Turn left immediately onto Magnolia Street, then, just before the underpass, turn right onto Magnolia Road. The cemetery is a short distance ahead on the left.

GRAVE DIRECTIONS: After entering at the cemetery's main entrance, turn at the first left and proceed for 100 yards. Arthur's grave is on the left.

Fans of Arthur's will also want to view the statue crafted in his honor that stands on Monument Avenue, the symbolic heart of the city of Richmond and the capital of the Confederacy. As a child, Arthur had not been allowed to play on Richmond's tennis courts because they were segregated. Today, his statue stands tall today alongside those of Robert E. Lee and Stonewall Jackson.

LEN BIAS
AUGUST 20, 1964 – JUNE 19,1986

Here's a trivia question: What professional sports team has retired the number of a player who never played a single game for them? Give up? The answer is the Boston Celtics, and the number is 30.

Just a day after he was drafted by the Celtics, Len Bias died suddenly of a cocaine-induced heart attack. In college, playing for the University of Maryland, he set a school record by scoring 2,149 points. Some speculate that if Len had lived he might have eclipsed even Larry Bird's career. But we'll never know.

Len was buried at Lincoln Memorial Cemetery in Suitland, Maryland.

CEMETERY DIRECTIONS: From I-495, take Exit 9 and follow Pennsylvania Avenue north for 2½ miles. Turn left onto Silver Hill Road. After a mile turn right onto Suitland Road, and follow the road for 1½ miles until you see the cemetery on the left.

GRAVE DIRECTIONS: Enter the cemetery, turn left around the office and proceed up the hill, staying left at the forks. Just before the top of the hill, 100 feet before the Bishop McCollough monument, stop. Forty feet off to the left is the flat stone that marks Len's grave.

TY COBB
DECEMBER 18, 1886 – JULY 16, 1961

As a daring base stealer, hustling outfielder, and powerhouse slugger, Ty Cobb, "the Georgia Peach," is considered to be among the best all-around players of baseball. He first lined up on a Major League diamond in 1905 and spent 24 seasons with the Detroit Tigers. Ty's lifetime batting average of .367 still stands as a record, though most of the others he held have since been broken (due largely to the longer schedule now played). But despite an unparalleled desire to excel and win, Ty never played on a World Series champion team.

For all of his on-field heroics, Ty was never adored by his fans; they admired his athletic prowess, but the love affair ended there. This has been alternately attributed to the fact that much of Ty's career occurred before Babe Ruth ushered in baseball's golden age, or that the Tigers were never a powerhouse team. But there's also a more accurate explanation: Ty Cobb was a self-centered, hot-tempered, overtly racist curmudgeon who seemed to delight in the controversy of contentious relations with other players, the press, and his own family.

In 1960, long after his playing days had ended, Ty contracted an up-and-coming sportswriter named Al Stump to write the "real story" of his life. Ty was dying, nobody gave a damn, and he now wished to counter for posterity what he felt was an inaccurate version of his life. Stump was happy to oblige but, soon enough, as Ty twisted the facts of every ugly incident to paint himself as the pitiful victim, it became clear to Stump that he was merely a hired gun; Ty, a bitter and unreasonable, cancer-ridden drunk who was deservedly lonely, was trying to use Stump as a shill to counter the "lies."

But Stump went along with it, writing Ty's biography the way Ty wanted it written, all the while secretly keeping notes about the real Ty on the side. In 1961, *My Life in Baseball: The True Record* told the story of Ty's life, and Ty went to his grave content that his "truths" had been established. Then in 1994, after a curious 33-year procrastination, Stump released *Cobb: The Life and Times of the Meanest Man Who Ever Played Baseball*, offering less antiseptic and sentimental insight into the baseball great.

Ty was shrewd off the field as well; he invested heavily in General Motors and Coca-Cola and, when he died, was worth millions. But his death was emblematic of his life. Instead of having friends and family at his side, a handgun and a fortune in stock certificates were on the nightstand next to his hospital bed. Only three former baseball colleagues attended his funeral, and there was no national mourning.

Not long before his death, when asked if he had any regrets, Ty replied, "If I had my life to live over again, I'd have done it a little different. I'd have more friends."

At 74 he was buried at the Royston Cemetery in Royston, Georgia.

CEMETERY DIRECTIONS: From the intersection of Routes 29 and 17 in the center of Royston, follow Route 17 south for about a mile and the cemetery is on the left.

GRAVE DIRECTIONS: The big mausoleum in the center of the cemetery is Ty's.

CUS D'AMATO

AUGUST 20, 1908 – NOVEMBER 4, 1985

Cus D'Amato was a pugnacious Bronx street tough who, in 1939, began managing his own boxing gym near Gramercy Park in Manhattan. He proved to be a master of ring technique. Cus shepherded both José Torres and Floyd Patterson to world championships during the 1950s and '60s.

After their careers ended, Cus toiled in relative obscurity for some years, surfacing briefly as Wilt Chamberlain's trainer when the basketball star toyed with boxing. But Cus later opened a gym in Hudson in upstate New York, and there he began working on his newest masterpiece. Cus learned of a boxing prodigy at a juvenile detention center in Johnstown, New York. After meeting the boy, Cus became his legal guardian and brought him back to his home in the Catskill Mountains. The young man's name was Mike Tyson and, after five years of mentoring under the weathered boxing sage, Tyson became the youngest world heavyweight-boxing champion ever at age twenty in 1986.

Unfortunately, Cus missed out on all the pomp. He died of pneumonia just months before Tyson's coronation.

At 77, Cus was buried at St. Patrick's Cemetery in Catskill, New York.

CEMETERY DIRECTIONS: From Route 9W, head west on Route 23B (Main Street) for a half-mile, turn right onto North Jefferson Avenue, and you'll see the cemetery after a short distance on the right.

GRAVE DIRECTIONS: Make a right turn into the cemetery, proceed to the flagpole, and turn right again. At the end of this drive, Cus's grave is on the left, eight rows back.

JAY "DIZZY" DEAN

JANUARY 16, 1911 – JULY 17, 1974

With a blazing Ozark fastball, Jay Hanna "Dizzy" Dean pitched himself right into the Baseball Hall of Fame. He did it by doing what came naturally, as he "was never taught to play baseball and never had to learn."

After his playing days, Dizzy became an announcer and was revered as a folk hero for his great turns of the English language in the booth. One player looked "mighty hitterish" to Dizzy, another "slud into third," and one team's problem was that "they ain't got enough spart." Pressed for an explanation of that locution, Dizzy replied, "Spart is pretty much the same as fight or gumption. Like the Spart of St. Louis, that plane Lindbergh flowed to Europe in."

At 63 he died of a heart attack, and was buried at Bond Cemetery in Bond, Mississippi.

CEMETERY DIRECTIONS: From the intersection of Routes 26 and 49 in Wiggins, follow Route 49 north for 2¾ miles, then turn right onto Pump Branch Road. Go over the railroad tracks and take the second right onto Proston Avenue, then make a quick left onto Second Street and then a right onto Cemetery Road.

GRAVE DIRECTIONS: Dizzy's grave is easy to find in the eleventh row from the road.

DALE EARNHARDT
APRIL 29, 1951 – FEBRUARY 18, 2001

Dale Earnhardt never had any doubt about what he would do with his life. As a boy his weekends were spent watching his father, Ralph Earnhardt, race stock cars, and he later summed up his commitment to the sport thusly: "I can't remember anything but racing. I didn't want to go to school or anywhere else, I just wanted to be racing."

Dale left school after the eighth grade, dreaming of making a living among cars. By eighteen he had succeeded; a service station attendant, he mounted tires and wielded wrenches to support himself and a young family. But that wasn't exactly the script he had dreamed of, and the aspiring, self-financed racer plugged away at his passion. In 1973 his father died of heart failure while working on his race car, and Dale resolved to make it big on the professional circuit for both of them.

The following year he competed in the NASCAR Sportsman Division and in 1975 made his Winston Cup debut at the World 600 in Charlotte, North Carolina. By 1978 Dale was a part-time member of Rod Osterlund's team and the next year the owner/manager took a chance on the 28-year-old and put him behind the wheel full-time. Dale's dream had come true and he didn't squander the opportunity, taking the 1979 Rookie of the Year award. The following year, Dale won the NASCAR Winston Cup Series title and became the only driver ever to win the rookie crown and the series' championship in consecutive seasons.

Midway through the 1981 season, Osterlund sold his team. After a few years of musical chairs, Dale migrated to RCR, Richard Childress Racing. His next championship came in 1986 and it marked the beginning of his storybook wonder years; in an incredible run, Dale captured six championship titles in nine seasons. He became one of NASCAR's winningest racers and claimed every major event at least once. He earned a total purse in excess of $40 million, and "the Intimidator" even promoted his own Dale Earnhardt team, which included his son, Dale Jr.

But Dale's fortunes changed at the 2001 Daytona 500 in Florida. On the last lap of the prestigious race, Dale was running in an "interference" position while his son and Michael Waltrip, another member of the Earnhardt team, held the top two spots. As long as Dale could hold onto his third-place standing, the team would enjoy a podium sweep. However, between the third and fourth turns of that final lap, just seconds from the finish, Dale inexplicably crashed his car into the wall at a speed approaching 200 miles per hour. Though it seems he was killed upon impact, Dale wasn't pronounced dead until arriving at the Halifax medical facility less than a mile away. His was the first driver fatality in the 43-year history of the Daytona 500.

It was later determined that Dale's seatbelt had failed which, of course, contributed to his death. But doctors also weighed in with their opinion that, had Dale been wearing a full-face helmet like that worn by virtually every other professional race-car driver, instead of the open-face helmet that his ego required, his injury pattern would've been different; Dale's chin struck the steering column in such a way as to fracture the base of his skull, and a full-face helmet may have saved his life.

At 49, Dale was buried on the grounds of his estate in Mooresville, North Carolina.

GRAVE DIRECTIONS: From I-77, take Exit 36 and follow Route 150 east for 2½ miles. Turn right on Route 136 and, after 4½ miles, you'll see a building that looks somewhat out of place on the left. (There is no sign.) That's the main workplace of Dale Earnhardt Incorporated, or DEI, as it's locally known.

In the front of this building are a small museum and a large gift shop wherein the public is cordially invited to shop for $24 coffee mugs and fashionably hideous $450 coats. That's as far as the public's invitation extends, however, and as a member of such, you'll not be allowed to cast your eyes upon Dale's resting place; he lies in a mausoleum within the confines of the estate behind the main DEI building.

The estate seems to be surrounded by a high, wrought-iron fence, but that's an illusion. Upon its descent into the woods, the iron fence is replaced by one that consists of a solitary wire. Still, I'm not recommending that anyone trespass; the Earnhardts are pretty serious about, and entitled to, their privacy. Besides, the estate spans 300 acres and you might be arrested—or shot—before you're able to locate Dale's large, blocky, porphyritic mausoleum emblazoned "Earnhardt" across the top, much less spend quality time with him. Sure, since his family continues to make more than a fair living from Dale's legion of fans ($20 million in 2001, by *Forbes'* count), it'd be nice if they'd share access with the public. But he is on private property (in fact, DEI employees won't even admit he's buried there), and that's apparently where he's going to stay.

GEORGE HALAS

FEBRUARY 2, 1895 – OCTOBER 31, 1983

George Halas was a University of Illinois star in both football and baseball and in 1919 even donned a Yankee uniform for a dozen games before being replaced by Babe Ruth. After the Yankees stint, George retreated to football and soon found himself both coaching and playing for the Decatur Staleys, one of eleven teams comprising a fledgling professional football league.

The next year, Staley Starch Works decided to abandon this football nonsense and dismantle the team. But George, chagrined that he would lose his livelihood, finagled a deal in which he became the team's owner while Staley, contributing just enough to keep the team solvent for one more year, maintained recognition as primary sponsor.

George immediately moved his team to Chicago and rented Wrigley Field for home games. In September 1921, he co-chaired a meeting at a Canton, Ohio, automobile agency, and a new football league was established, the National Football League. The next year, as a wordplay on the Cubs, Chicago's baseball team, George named his football team the Bears and, well, the rest is history.

George continued in his triple role of owner, coach, and player until 1929, when he retired from playing. He continued to coach for 31 of the next 54 seasons. However, George was never foolish enough to relinquish that most lucrative role, owner, and for his entire life he was sole holder of the Chicago Bears.

Upon his death at 83, George was eulogized for having had saved professional football from possible extinction and recognized for an incredible 324 coaching victories. Saluted as the game's original "Papa Bear," he rests at St. Adalbert Cemetery in Niles, Illinois.

CEMETERY DIRECTIONS: St. Adalbert is on Milwaukee Avenue about one mile south of the Route 43 intersection.

GRAVE DIRECTIONS: Enter the cemetery, take an immediate left and the second right, and you'll see the Halas mausoleum a short distance on the left.

JOHN HEISMAN
OCTOBER 23, 1869 – OCTOBER 3, 1936

For 36 years John Heisman coached college football, contributing numerous key innovations to the sport. He was responsible for legalizing the forward pass, he was the first coach to use the quarterback as safety on defense, and he promoted the division of the game into quarters and the scoreboard showing down, distance, time, and score. Heisman also introduced the center snap and the "hike" or "hep" count signals of the quarterback in starting play. Before that innovation, the center on an offensive line would roll the ball on the ground to the quarterback.

Between 1892 and 1927, he coached at eight different colleges including Clemson and Auburn, but it was his head coaching position at Georgia Tech that was most memorable. With the Yellow Jackets, Heisman introduced the "Heisman Shift," a feared offense used to compile an impressive 100-29-6 record over his sixteen-season tenure. In 1916, Heisman gave new dimension to the word "rout" when his Yellow Jackets stung Cumberland's Bulldogs, 222-0. That game, which has been called the Game of the Century, is still celebrated in Georgia Tech sports lore while Cumberland prefers to pretend it never happened.

After his death, the Downtown Athletic Club of New York City —of which John was the director—named its annual trophy in his honor. The Heisman Trophy is awarded each year to college football's outstanding player. Many of the trophy's past winners have gone on to lead illustrious professional football careers including such renowned players as Roger Staubach, Tony Dorsett and, of course, O.J. Simpson.

After a bout of pneumonia, John died at 66 and was buried at Forest Home Cemetery in Rhinelander, Wisconsin.

CEMETERY DIRECTIONS: Head east through Rhinelander on Business Route 8 and you'll notice the road makes a quick jog (a left, then a right). A few hundred yards after this jog, turn right onto Newell Street and the cemetery is a short distance on the left.

GRAVE DIRECTIONS: Enter the cemetery at the corner entrance, bear left, then stop just before the next paved road on the right. Follow the grass path on your right for about 80 feet to the Donaldson stone. This is John's wife's family plot, and here you'll find John's flat marker, as well.

GIL HODGES
APRIL 4, 1924 – APRIL 2, 1972

Former Brooklyn Dodger first baseman Gil Hodges endeared himself to fans to a degree not commonly seen in modern baseball. He was a steady workaday player who, following three seasons with the New York Mets, swatted 370 home runs, won three Gold Glove awards, and played in seven World Series. But Gil was also one of the most decent and humble men to draw a big-league check. He embraced Jackie Robinson, never used profanity, and never berated an umpire, even when his manager offered him 50 bucks to quit being so goodhearted and gentle. He surrendered two seasons to be a Marine on Okinawa, and it was three years before he mentioned to his wife that he'd won a medal for bravery. Gil is a beloved sports hero who, to the frustration of his fans, remains locked outside the Hall of Fame gates.

For all his success in the game, Gil's greatest accolades came after he retired from playing. In 1969, as manager of the lowly New York Mets, Gil engineered their "Impossible Dream" season. In an amazing turnaround, the 100-1 pre-season long shot "Miracle Mets" hovered near the top of their division all year, eventually blowing past the Chicago Cubs to claim the National League East division and finishing the season as World Series champs. That feat, by a team that only a few seasons before had been one of the most laughed at in baseball history, earned Hodges an eternal place in the hearts of sports fans.

But just two and a half years later, while in Florida for spring training, Gil suffered a heart attack and died after playing 27 holes of golf.

At 47, he was buried at Holy Cross Cemetery in Brooklyn, New York.

CEMETERY DIRECTIONS: From either Exit 11 off the Belt Parkway or Exit 28B off the Brooklyn-Queens Expressway (I-278), follow Flatbush Avenue to Clarendon Road. Turn east on Clarendon and follow it for almost a mile to Brooklyn Avenue. Turn north and, after a few hundred yards, the cemetery entrance is on the right.

GRAVE DIRECTIONS: Enter the cemetery, take the first left and the next left, and park in the circle at the end. Gil's is a brown stone at three o'clock on the circle, near the curb.

BEN HOGAN

AUGUST 13, 1912 – JULY 25, 1997

Ben Hogan started in golf as an eleven-year-old caddy and by nineteen was a professional player. In those Depression-era years, a career as a professional golfer wasn't nearly as lucrative as it is today, and tour pros pooled their monies and traveled together. The monetary reward for being a superior player wasn't at that time evident and diligence on the practice range was somewhat of an oddity. Upon reaching the professional ranks, many players were content to let their skills plateau.

Ben, however, was a pioneer at refining his game. While his competitors succumbed to other distractions, Ben, who called learning a "daylight-till-dark process," dedicated himself to developing a "repeating swing" that could stand up under the pressure of tournament play. True, in those early years, Ben was almost winless, so perhaps he needed the practice more than anyone else, but it seems, too, that through the rote discipline of perfecting his swing and other particulars, Ben was able to create a more solid base of golfing ability that stayed with him through the stress of competition.

His skills also stayed with him during his military service during World War II, when there wasn't a lot of time to play golf, or any game for that matter. Indeed, upon his discharge from the Army, Ben resumed his place on the tour and almost immediately dominated the competition, butting heads with rival Sam Snead in the process, and winning 62 USPGA events, including nine majors between 1946 and 1953. The tremendous run of athletic excellence came despite a horrific 1949 car accident from which he suffered, among other injuries, some loss of vision in his left eye.

Nearly unbeatable, Ben was asked how he'd learned his trade. "I dug it out of the ground," replied the master.

At 84, Ben died of heart failure and now rests at Greenwood Mausoleum in Fort Worth, Texas.

CEMETERY DIRECTIONS: From I-30, take Exit 12 and follow University Drive north for 1½ miles to White Settlement Road. Turn left and Greenwood is immediately on the right.

GRAVE DIRECTIONS: Pull into the drive after the funeral home, and the mausoleum is the low marbled building in front of you. Enter the mausoleum through the second door on the right side of the building (this would be the northeast entrance). Walk straight in, under the Yandell crypt, and twenty feet further, on the left is Ben Hogan.

FLO HYMAN
JULY 31, 1954 – JANUARY 24, 1986

While growing up in Inglewood, California, Flo Hyman began playing, and dominating, female volleyball during high school. After a playing career at the University of Houston, where she was a three-time NCAA All-American and the Collegiate Player of the Year in 1976, Flo became one of the original members of the U.S. Women's National Volleyball Team, which lived and trained full-time in Colorado Springs beginning in 1978.

The 6-foot-5 standout played a key role in establishing the United States' presence in volleyball and her team qualified for the 1980 Olympic Games in Moscow, but it did not compete because of that year's Olympic boycott. Four years later, the team, dominated by Flo, gained widespread recognition for winning a silver medal at the 1984 Games, defeating numerous supposedly superior teams during the showdown.

Since there was no professional volleyball in the States, after the Olympics Flo joined a league in Japan, where the sport is exceedingly popular. There Flo became a significant sports hero. But one evening at a match in the city of Matsue, while Flo sat on the bench during a routine substitution, she slowly and inexplicably slumped over, slid to the floor, and lay motionless. Flo was dead at 31.

An autopsy revealed that Flo's death was due to a rare congenital disorder known as Marfan syndrome that seems to particularly haunt the tall. The disorder had caused a dime-sized weak spot in Flo's aorta, the massive artery that carries the entire flow of blood leaving the heart, and there the artery had burst, exploding inside her chest as she sat on the sideline in Matsue.

Flo was buried at Inglewood Park Cemetery in Inglewood, California.

CEMETERY DIRECTIONS: From I-405, exit at La Tijera Boulevard and head east. After a half-mile, turn right onto Centinella Avenue and follow it to Florence Avenue. Turn left and the cemetery is another half-mile on the right at Number 720.

GRAVE DIRECTIONS: Enter the park and follow the white dotted road all the way to the back buildings. Turn left and the building on the right is the Manchester Garden Mausoleum. Park and walk to the mausoleum's front courtyard and there, on the left before the doors, is another courtyard—Manchester Court. Near the fountain in that court, in the second row from the bottom, is Flo's grave.

"SHOELESS" JOE JACKSON
JULY 16, 1887 – DECEMBER 5, 1951

By age nine, Joe Jackson was working twelve-hour days at a textile mill to help support his family. By twelve he was playing on the company's baseball team. In 1908, at eighteen, Joe joined the minor league Greenville Spinners. During one particular game, Joe wore a new pair of spiked baseball shoes, but they gave him blisters, so he finished the game in his stocking feet. Later, after belting a triple, he slid into third base and an opposing fan yelled "You shoeless son of a gun!" which led a sportswriter to dub him "Shoeless Joe."

Joe was soon promoted to the Major Leagues and after just two seasons with the Cleveland Indians he was revered as one of base-ball's best players, always a threat with the bat and a dependable fielder with a strong and accurate arm. In 1915 he was traded to the Chicago White Sox and over the next four seasons became the city's favorite sports hero, often leading the league in a variety of hitting statistics.

In 1919, Shoeless Joe and seven teammates, the Chicago Eight, were implicated in the so-called Black Sox scandal that charged they had received cash payments in return for playing below their ability and allowing the Cincinnati Reds to win that year's World Series. "Say it ain't so, Joe," soon became a tag line of fans that hoped that their heroes had not betrayed them or the game. The following year, the sports world wrung its hands in anxiety as the outcome of the eight players' trial for criminal fraud was anticipated.

As it turned out, the players were acquitted of fraud charges after a transcript of grand jury testimony was lost and the prosecu-tion's case crumbled. Nevertheless, after the 1920 baseball season the Chicago Eight were banned from baseball for life by Commis-sioner Kennesaw Landis. For the last 80 years, various baseball nuts have petitioned the league to reverse the ban against the players, and especially against Shoeless Joe, so that he might assume his place in Cooperstown.

To date, the ban has not been reversed, and for good reason, it seems. The "missing" transcript surfaced in 1923 and it demonstrates quite clearly that Shoeless Joe and three of the other players admitted to participating in the fix, albeit reluctantly. After being asked by the grand jury whether anyone paid him money to throw the series in favor of Cincinnati, Shoeless Joe replied, "They promised me $20,000 and paid me five [thousand]." Later, though, when asked whether he made any intentional errors on a particular day, Shoeless Joe replied, "No, sir, not during the whole Series." It appears that Shoeless Joe agreed to throw the game, then later had misgivings and played as well as he could, but his team lost anyway.

After their ban, none of the Chicago Eight played Major League baseball again, though a few may have surreptitiously played in other leagues, and Shoeless Joe retired to South Carolina, where he ran a liquor store and a pool hall.

Shoeless Joe died at 64 of a heart attack or, "coronary thrombosis caused by arteriosclerosis and cirrhosis of the liver," and he was buried at Woodlawn Memorial Park in Greenville, South Carolina.

CEMETERY DIRECTIONS: From I-385, take Exit 40 and follow Route 291 north for 1½ miles. Turn left on Edwards Road, then right on Wade Hampton Boulevard (Route 29), and the park is immediately on the left.

GRAVE DIRECTIONS: Enter the cemetery, turn at the first right, then bear left at the "Y." Stop 30 feet before the next intersection and look along the left-hand curb for the Landers plot in Section V. Shoeless Joe's grave is nine rows behind Landers. Joe's marker is just a flat one in the grass, but it's easy to find—just look for the spare baseballs and shoes left by previous visitors.

BOBBY JONES

MARCH 17, 1902 – DECEMBER 18, 1971

Bobby Jones, arguably the most talented golfer of all time, accomplished in 1930 what no one had ever done before—and no one has done since. He achieved a grand slam, that is, victories in the United States and British Opens and in the United States and British Amateur championships within a single season.

Then, at only 28 years old and at the pinnacle of his career, Bobby turned his back on the game. Promptly and decisively retiring from tournament golf, he established a successful career in law and made contributions to the game in other ways; he co-founded the Augusta National Golf Club and the Masters tournament.

A nation that idolized him for his athletic successes found a new respect for him and for his decision to treat golf as a game rather than a way of life. As for Bobby himself, he seemed never to regret his retirement decision. "Golf is like eating peanuts," he once said. "You don't want to have too much."

At only 47 years old, Bobby was diagnosed with syringomyelia, a progressive and incurable paralysis that caused him to use a cane, leg braces and, finally, a wheelchair.

He died at 69 and is buried at Oakland Cemetery in Atlanta, Georgia.

CEMETERY DIRECTIONS: From I-75/85, take Exit 94 and head east on Edgewood Avenue. At the first light, turn right onto Hilliard Street and proceed a half-mile to Martin Luther King Drive. Turn left and you'll see the cemetery a few hundred yards ahead.

GRAVE DIRECTIONS: Enter the cemetery and turn onto the first paved drive on the right. Go to the end of this drive and stop. On the left is a brick walk. One hundred feet down this walk, on the right against the brick wall, is Bobby's grave.

TOM LANDRY

SEPTEMBER II, 1924 – FEBRUARY I2, 2000

Tom Landry flew 30 combat missions and survived a crash landing as a bomber pilot in World War II. After the war, as professional football lurched forward, he became a star running back in the old-school, black-and-blue version of the game for New York teams. By 1956 he had moved away from playing and was the Giants defensive coach and, three years later, when Tom was offered the position of head coach for the new Dallas Cowboys expansion team back in his home state of Texas, he jumped on it.

The new outfit was awash in chaos and in that first year they were thoroughly trounced. But for one tie, they lost every single game. Dallas was the laughingstock of the league and it was seven long seasons before Tom fielded a winning team. But once he finally had one, he went ahead and had another and another, racking up twenty-straight winning seasons. While the dogged pattern of 270 victories took shape, the Dallas Cowboys became "America's Team," steamrolling over opponents with a startling array of playbook gadgetry, and showcasing a parade of football personalities, including

the eye-popping Cowboy cheerleaders who gyrated incongruously behind Tom, the proper Christian coach who stoically paced the sidelines in his trademark business suit and fedora.

Over 29 seasons with the Cowboys, Tom made his mark through stunning innovations, seemingly completely out of sync with his personality, which unleashed an unpredictable but controlled havoc on the field. Ushering in the efficient modern era of pro football, Tom uncorked a mathematical approach to the game by charting opposing offensive patterns, and he was the first to overhaul defensive schemes on the fly with signals from the sideline.

As expected, Tom's innovations were adopted by others, and by the late eighties, whispers suggested that perhaps Dallas didn't need Tom anymore. Indeed, Tom had begun to preach to his players that there were three important things in life: God, family, and football, and football had become an increasingly distant third on Tom's list. It was obvious that Tom didn't need the Cowboys, either. In 1989, he was sacked as head coach and settled into a citizen emeritus role in Texas, appearing on the nostalgia circuit at charity dinners and golf tournaments.

At 75, Tom died of leukemia and was buried at Sparkman Hillcrest Memorial Park in Dallas, Texas.

CEMETERY DIRECTIONS: Sparkman Hillcrest is on the Northwest Highway (Route 12) just a half-mile west of I-75.

GRAVE DIRECTIONS: Enter the cemetery, bear right around the funeral home, then bear left at the next opportunity. After a short distance, you'll see a sign on the right for the Garden of the Cross section. Stop here. On the left, directly across the drive from that sign, is a marker denoting the Crespi plot, behind which is the Landry plot.

VINCE LOMBARDI

JUNE 11, 1913 – SEPTEMBER 3, 1970

In 1949 Vince Lombardi left his $1,700-a-year high school teaching position to manage the defensive line of West Point's football team. Five years later Vince was in charge of offensive strategy for the New York Giants (Tom Landry handled the defensive responsibilities), channeling the talents of Frank Gifford from defense to offense and earning for himself a reputation as a steely-eyed visionary.

But by 1958, the 45-year-old Vince was tired of being an assistant and he jumped on an opportunity to prove himself, becoming head coach of football's perpetual losers, the sorriest team in the league, the Green Bay Packers. In 1959 he held the first of his notoriously intense training camps and made clear to his protégés that he expected obedience, dedication, and 110% effort from each man. "Dancing is a contact sport, football is a hitting sport," he told his Packers. "If you aren't fired with enthusiasm, you'll *be* fired with enthusiasm," he threatened. But Coach Lombardi also made his team a promise: If they obeyed his disciplines and observed his doctrines, they would be a championship team.

Three years later, the fiery coach's promise became a reality. At Lambeau Field in Green Bay on December 31, 1961, Vince watched proudly as his new Green Bay Packers defeated his old New York Giants 37-0 for the National Football League championship. When Vince retired as head coach in 1967, the Packers had put together nine phenomenal winning seasons and had dominated professional football, collecting five NFL championships and two Super Bowls (I and II), and acquiring a record of 98-30-4. The Packers had become the yardstick by which all other teams were measured.

Pacing the sidelines in his trademark wristwatch and button-down, short-sleeved white shirt, Vince had helped the men he coached live up to their innate abilities. He had commanded respect from his players; "When he says 'Sit down,' I don't even bother to look for a chair," one of them explained. Their efforts brought pride and victory. With the heavy-handed discipline of an all-knowing drill sergeant, he inspired complete trust. "Vince is fair. He treats us all the same—like dogs," said another player. Vince's legacy of perseverance had made his name synonymous with winning, and had turned him into an American icon that transcended his sport.

After retiring from the Packers, Vince soon realized that he still wanted to coach and accepted the head coaching position for the

Washington Redskins in 1969. During that season, Vince upheld the Lombardi tradition and led the Redskins to their first winning record in fourteen years.

But Vince would never lead another team to the Super Bowl. After one season with the Redskins he was diagnosed with intestinal cancer, and he died from the affliction at 57.

Vince was buried at Mount Olivet Cemetery in Red Bank, New Jersey.

CEMETERY DIRECTIONS: One mile north of the Navesink River bridge on Route 35, turn east onto Chapel Hill Road and the cemetery is a half-mile ahead on the right

GRAVE DIRECTIONS: Turn into the second entrance, stay straight for a bit, then bear right and take the next left. Proceed for the length of a football field, and then, on the left in Section 30 next to the road, is the Lombardi plot.

JOE LOUIS
MAY 13, 1914 – APRIL 12, 1981

In the opinion of many, Joe Louis, the plain, unobtrusive legendary Brown Bomber, was the best heavyweight fighter of all time. He held the world championship title for twelve years, defending it an amazing 25 times, including during a period of time beginning in December 1940 known as the "Bum of the Month" campaign, when he met challengers at the rate of one per month.

Many years after his career was over, Joe found himself in the public eye again when the IRS dogged him for more than a million dollars past due, which they eventually forgave as Joe was penniless and his earning days over. Despite all his money woes, Joe never considered himself broke. As his wife Martha described, "Joe is rich with friends. If he said he needed a dollar, a million people would send him a dollar and he'd be a millionaire."

At 66, just hours after attending a heavyweight championship fight at Caesar's Palace, Joe died of cardiac arrest and was buried at Arlington National Cemetery in Arlington, Virginia.

CEMETERY DIRECTIONS: Arlington National Cemetery is located on the west side of the Potomac River in Washington DC. From any of the major highways, you can easily follow the signs to the visitor parking lots.

GRAVE DIRECTIONS: Get a map at the information booth, then walk to Roosevelt Drive, which is in front of the Memorial Amphitheater. Standing on Roosevelt looking at the Tomb of the Unknown Soldier, there is a walkway on the far right that winds up the hill. Joe's grave is along this walkway in Section 7A, Stone #177.

ROCKY MARCIANO
SEPTEMBER 1, 1923 – AUGUST 31, 1969

Rocky Marciano was *the* world heavyweight boxing champion of the 1950s, and the crowning achievement in his brutal ring career is one that nobody else has yet matched: Rocky retired with a record of 49-0, the only world boxing champion to complete his professional career undefeated. To top it off, 43 of those wins were by knockout.

Rocky's boyhood was the typical sports-loving one and his professional athletic career actually started when he reported to the Chicago Cubs as a catcher. Released because of erratic throws to second base, Rocky then joined the Army where he discovered his real talents were in boxing.

He turned pro in 1947, and after strong victories over the heavy hitters of the day, Rocky earned the right to fight the heavyweight champion, Jersey Joe Walcott, in 1952. Marciano won by a knockout in the thirteenth round and over the next four years defended his title numerous times before retiring in 1956.

"No man can say what he will do in the future, but barring poverty, the ring has seen the last of me. I am comfortably fixed and I am not afraid of the future," Rocky said at his retirement. Indeed, he changed his focus, becoming very active in a wide range of charitable causes.

En route to a birthday party, Rocky and two others were killed when their Cessna Skyhawk airplane crashed into a wooded area as it approached the Newton Municipal Airport in Newton, Iowa.

At 45, Rocky was laid to rest at Lauderdale Memorial Gardens in Fort Lauderdale, Florida.

CEMETERY DIRECTIONS: From I-95, take Exit 29 and follow Broward Boulevard a half-mile west to NW 27th Avenue. Turn right on 27th and the cemetery is a short distance on the left.

GRAVE DIRECTIONS: Enter the cemetery and park at the semi-circular drive in front of the mausoleum. Enter the mausoleum, walk past the first reflecting pool, and continue to the second jaggedly shaped reflecting pool. Immediately before this pool, turn right and the Marciano crypt is on the right in the bottom row, the jagged pool pointing almost directly to it.

NEW YORK YANKEES

In professional sports, the generational staying power of the New York Yankees and the team's ability to somehow emerge consistently and, for some people, frustratingly, victorious is unmatched. Since 1903, when the franchise was purchased for $18,000 and moved from Baltimore, its roster of over 1,200 players has produced 24 World Series championships and 35 Pennants, and the team that baseball fans alternately adore and despise has boasted many of the game's most memorable and remarkable players.

George "Babe" Ruth
FEBRUARY 6, 1895 – AUGUST 16, 1948

There exist a dwindling number of people who have personally seen George "Babe" Ruth play. His speedy trot around the bases in old newsreels seems to belong to some faraway, distant time, yet Babe continues to exert an influence on our culture as his memory epitomizes the image of a larger-than-life sports hero.

George was the first of eight children, though only he and a sister survived to maturity. The family lived above his father's saloon in a dirty and crowded Baltimore neighborhood, but after the mischievous seven-year-old became too much of a bother, his parents signed custody of him over to an order of missionaries and he was sent to live at St. Mary's Industrial School for Boys.

St. Mary's was a combined juvenile detention center and orphanage, but George really belonged in neither type of facility, his parents just happened to be a couple of irresponsible drunks. George remained there for more than a decade and under its rigid structure he thrived, especially in athletics. At 19, he was offered a contract by the Baltimore Orioles, but because his parents had passed him to the missionaries he was bound to remain in their custody until the age of 21. To circumvent that legality, the manager of the Orioles actually assumed George's legal guardianship and it was then, as the youngest player on the team and the manager's adopted "baby," that the Babe nickname surfaced. The moniker stuck for the rest of his life—and then some.

After just a few months, though, in July of 1914, his contract was sold to the Boston Red Sox, where Babe developed into a feared southpaw pitcher. Six seasons later, the Sox set the fabled

"Curse of the Bambino" in motion by trading Babe to their New York Yankee rivals. At the time of the trade, the Yankees commanded zero respect and had never won a pennant. They didn't even have their own ballpark and instead rented space at the New York Giants' Polo Grounds. But after acquiring Babe from Boston they won seven pennants and four World Championships in thirteen seasons. Meanwhile the "Curse" relegated the Red Sox to a cycle of perpetual disappointment that continues to plague them even to this day, while the Yankees have gone on to become the most dominant franchise in all of sports.

Because of his demonstrated prowess on the mound, Babe's acquisition had cost the Yankees the then-fantastic sum of $100,000, but the Yankees management boldly chose to disregard his pitching skills and instead started Babe as an outfielder to exploit his diamond-in-the-rough batting ability. Babe hit 54 home runs during his first year with the Yankees and in short order he was baseball's preeminent player. With every mighty swing of the Sultan of Swat's bat, excitement for baseball was heightened and its new offense-orientation ushered in a Golden Age. The game forever became the quintessential American spectator sport. Fans packed ballparks in record numbers and the once-lowly New York Yankees built a tremendous new stadium, Yankee Stadium, which became known as "the House that Ruth Built." On its opening day in 1923, Babe slapped Yankee Stadium's first-ever home run.

To complement his on-field heroics, Babe led a hedonistic life, and off the field, some accuse him of being a loud-mouthed, overeating, headstrong lout. Too, he set the pace for endorsement contracts, shilling everything from underwear to shaving cream to shotguns. But Babe seemed never to forget his own childhood, and throughout his celebrity years, he was exceedingly philanthropic and kind to needy children.

By 1933, Babe's once-great talents began to diminish and he threatened to leave the Yankees unless given the opportunity to become a manager. The Yankees called his bluff and Babe left the following year to join the Boston Braves, who baited him with the promise of an eventual assistant-manager position. It shortly became obvious that the Braves wanted him only for his drawing power and had no intention of making him a manager, so Babe resigned from the team and made his last appearance as a player in May of 1935.

Upon his retirement he held 54 Major League records including two that were regarded as unbreakable: 60 home runs in a single season and 714 career home runs. In 1961 and in 1974, though, Roger Maris and Hank Aaron, respectively, broke Babe's records.

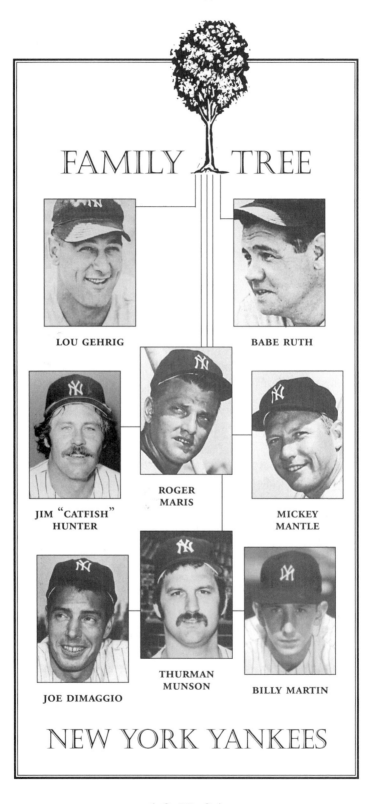

FAMILY TREE

LOU GEHRIG

BABE RUTH

JIM "CATFISH" HUNTER

ROGER MARIS

MICKEY MANTLE

JOE DIMAGGIO

THURMAN MUNSON

BILLY MARTIN

NEW YORK YANKEES

In 1946 Babe began suffering severe headaches and, in November, he finally checked into a hospital after the left side of his face became so swollen he couldn't swallow. Doctors removed a tumor in his throat but were unable to excise the source of the growth. After eighteen painful months, Babe died on August 16, 1948, of throat cancer at 53. For two days, his body lay in state at the main entrance to Yankee Stadium while thousands of people paid their last respects.

He was buried at Gate of Heaven Cemetery in Hawthorne, New York.

CEMETERY DIRECTIONS: From I-287, take Exit 4 and follow Route 100A north for 2½ miles (Route 100A will become Route 100 after 2 miles) to Lakeview Avenue, then turn right. Follow Lakeview Avenue to its intersection with the Taconic State Parkway, turn left and the Gate of Heaven Cemetery is a mile on the left. Turn left onto Stevens Avenue, go over the railroad tracks and make another left to enter.

GRAVE DIRECTIONS: Enter the cemetery, turn right and follow the main road up the hill. Turn right immediately before Section 25 and Babe's gravesite is 50 yards on the left.

Lou Gehrig
JUNE 19, 1903 – JUNE 2, 1941

In 1925, a husky and young Lou Gehrig faced another day as back-up first baseman on the New York Yankee bench. It was frustrating not starting because, in his entire life of baseball, playing from pockmarked New York City outfields to the fastidiously raked infield of Columbia University, he'd always been his teams' ace-in-the-hole. Lou yearned now to be back in the minors; at least he'd be playing.

A few weeks later, the team's starting first baseman was hit hard during batting practice and Lou was tapped to join the starting lineup. Trotting onto the field, the nervous but eager rookie promised himself he'd not blunder the opportunity, and he didn't; by game's end Lou had played rock-solid defense while posting three hits and an RBI.

On the strength of that performance, Lou earned the nod to start the next game, and the next, and the ... well, let's just say that, over the next fourteen years, for 2,130 consecutive games Lou Gehrig was the *only* Yankee to play first base.

He was part of the notorious Yankees' "Murderers' Row" lineup of powerhouse hitters, he was first in the league to hit four home runs in a single game, and he was a big part of five World Series triumphs. Yet Lou's unassuming demeanor and quiet home life never generated headlines, and he never experienced the adulation that defined his flashier teammates. Lou had become an authentic American working-class hero; it just so happened that his workplace was Yankee Stadium. Even to wife Eleanor, "Lou was just a square and honest guy."

But by 1938, it was clear that something was wrong with this Rock of Gibraltar; pitches that Lou should've homered became routine fly outs, and his sprints between bases deteriorated to slow-motion scrabbles. With the opening of the next season, it was clear that the off-season's pause had had little effect on his decline and, upon recognizing that his presence hindered the team more than it helped, Lou removed himself from the lineup and ended his celebrated consecutive-game streak.

Six weeks later, Lou was diagnosed with a degenerative and fatal condition of the nervous and muscular systems, amyotrophic lateral sclerosis, today known as Lou Gehrig's disease. On the 4th of July 1939, 60,000 fans turned out for a Lou Gehrig Appreciation Day and said goodbye to their "Iron Horse." After some prodding, Lou stepped to the microphone and in a simple but eloquent two-minute speech consigned himself to immortality: "Fans, for the past two weeks you have been reading about a bad break I got. Yet today I consider myself the luckiest man on the face of the earth …"

Lou died two years later at 37, and was buried at Kensico Cemetery in Valhalla, New York.

CEMETERY DIRECTIONS: From I-287, take Exit 4 and follow Route 100A north for 2½ miles (Route 100A will become Route 100 after 2 miles) to Lakeview Avenue and turn right. After a half-mile, turn right onto Commerce Street and enter the cemetery.

GRAVE DIRECTIONS: Proceed down Commerce Street, make a right turn onto Tecumseh Avenue, a left onto Cherokee Avenue, then a right onto Manitou Avenue. Go a little more than half way around the circle and there, behind the Winkhaus stone, is the Gehrig plot.

Joe DiMaggio
NOVEMBER 25, 1914 – MARCH 8, 1999

After Babe Ruth retired, the fabled Joe DiMaggio filled the Yankee lineup's void with grace and superlative play, and he was rewarded with the sweeping idolatry of sports fans everywhere during an American era when baseball reigned supreme. The son of an immigrant Italian fisherman, Joe learned baseball skills by hitting balls with a broken oar, beat the odds to rise to the summit of the sport, and was even married, briefly, to the most glamorous of movie stars, Marilyn Monroe.

Living the quintessential dream of the American boy, his allure reached far beyond the baseball diamond, and even those who cared not a lick for sports cherished Joe as a cultural icon. Though Joe's appeal depended largely on his exceptional on-field abilities, it was his off-field composure that clinched his universal intrigue; with impeccable dress and tailoring, he was always proud to be a great American sports hero and was committed to living up to the image by comporting himself with a self-assured style that was uniquely Joe DiMaggio.

It's important to note that most of Joe's years as an athlete were spent without the benefit of television. The successes of his life and career were widely reported in the print media and his games were broadcast on radio, but he retired before television became a common household fixture. Whereas television often demythologizes heroes through overexposure, radio and print served to make Joe famous but not *too* familiar, and heightened the DiMaggio mystique.

Joe played thirteen record-filled seasons with the Yankees, including the storied 1941 season, during which he hit safely in a still-unbroken streak of 56 consecutive games. At 37, with his game tapering slightly from the wonder years, Joe chose to leave baseball when it became obvious that, though the fans still adored him, he was failing to live up to the lofty New York expectations. Always elegant and inspiring, Joe retired in 1951, though he was offered enormous financial incentives to stay another year. Said DiMaggio's brother Dom, "He quit because he wasn't Joe DiMaggio anymore."

On March 8, 1999, Joe died of a lung infection at 84 and was buried at Holy Cross Cemetery in Colma, California.

CEMETERY DIRECTIONS: From I-380 follow El Camino Real (Route 82) north for 1½ mile and turn right onto Chestnut Avenue. At the second traffic light, turn left onto Mission Road and the cemetery is a mile on the right.

GRAVE DIRECTIONS: Enter the cemetery, drive up the hill, and go past the stop sign. Turn left at the next drive, go a little more than halfway around the circle, and stop before the Moynihan mausoleum on the right. There on the right under the trees is Joe's grave.

Mickey Mantle

OCTOBER 20, 1931 – AUGUST 13, 1995

Mickey Mantle's semi-pro baseball player father believed that the only way to excel in the Major Leagues was as a switch-hitter, and from a young age he taught his son to swing from both sides of the plate. The coaching paid off and, while still in high school, Mickey signed with the Yankees for the bargain price of $140 a week.

After two years in the minors, he earned a place on the team's 1951 big-league roster and, by the next year, became the primary focus of the New York media—Mickey had been the player chosen to replace the irreplaceable Joe DiMaggio. Mickey quickly adjusted to the majors and developed into a premier power hitter; one home run shot, later measured at 565 feet, might be the longest ever hit. Led by Mickey's talents, the Yankees again dominated baseball, and during his tenure, they won twelve pennants and seven World Series. Mickey himself was named MVP three times and in 1956 he won baseball's Triple Crown with a .353 batting average, 52 home runs, and 130 RBIs. Though he was frequently sidelined with a recurring injury, by the time of his 1969 retirement he had amassed 536 home runs, a record eighteen in World Series play.

Mickey's athleticism was impressive, but he was a flawed and reckless role model whose family life was marred by his alcoholism and well-publicized late-night pursuits. In the 1980s, Mickey became a sort of sports antihero and disgruntled many old fans by exploiting his fame in the burgeoning and tacky world of sports memorabilia shows.

In 1994 Mickey finally sought treatment for his alcoholism at the Betty Ford clinic. The following year, though, he learned that his irreparably damaged cirrhotic liver was on the verge of collapse, and that unless he received a transplant liver, he would soon die. Sympathy poured in, but Mickey's endgame was touched by controversy when, just 48 hours after his name went on a waiting list, he was chosen to receive a donated liver. Cynics criticized the apparent preferential treatment—Mickey had jumped ahead of more than 250 other Texans in the liver waiting line—but doctors maintained that he had received a liver so quickly because he was the sickest one on the list.

In any event, the transplant hardly benefited Mickey and he died of complications just two months later, at 63. He was buried at Sparkman Hillcrest Memorial Park in Dallas, Texas.

CEMETERY DIRECTIONS: Sparkman Hillcrest is on the Northwest Highway (Route 12), just a half-mile west of Exit 14 off of I-75.

GRAVE DIRECTIONS: Enter the cemetery, continue straight, and go all the way to the cemetery's rear, where the mausoleum is located. Park in the back of the mausoleum, enter through the rear door, and ahead 40 feet on the right, in the bottom row, is Mickey's crypt.

Roger Maris

SEPTEMBER 10, 1934 – DECEMBER 14, 1985

In 1953, fresh out of high school, Roger Maris signed with the Cleveland Indians farm team, and he finally made his Major League debut on opening day in 1957. Roger went 3-for-5 that day, and on the next, he hit his first big league home run, a grand slam that won the game. In 1960 he was traded to the Yankees and in his first game with them hit two home runs. With Mickey Mantle off the injured list, the team now had two solid sluggers in the lineup and the stage was set for the Yankees' return to dominance.

During the 1961 season, Roger and Mickey played out a drama for frenzied fans as they each swung for the heavens to claim the American League home run title. By mid-season it became obvious that they were both on pace to threaten Babe Ruth's "impossible to beat" record of 60 dingers in a season and their friendly competition took on a new intensity. Sports pages were filled with daily updates of the sluggers' duel and rabid fans argued over the possibility of either slugger breaking the record. (Babe had set his record when the season consisted of just 154 games, and the season had since then been expanded to 162 games.)

Mickey fell off the pace after suffering an injury in September but Roger pressed on and tied the home run record during the 159th game of the season. Finally, in the season's last game, Roger hit his 61st home run, breaking the Babe's 34-year-old record, establishing a new benchmark that would itself stand for the next 37 years.

Of course, not everyone was delighted with Roger's accomplishment. Many of baseball's old guard scoffed at his feat because Roger's record was established after 162 games. Besides, they said, nobody could be a better ballplayer than the legendary Babe Ruth. Roger felt the hostility and he later commented, "They acted as if I poisoned their record books or something. As a ballplayer, I would be delighted to do it again but as an individual, I doubt if I possibly could."

The Yankees capped that magical 1961 season with a world championship but the season also proved to be Roger's last great one. The next year he hit "only" 33 home runs and by 1966 he was traded away to the Cardinals. Two seasons later he retired to run a beer distributorship and, at 51, Roger died of lymphatic cancer. He was buried at Holy Cross Cemetery in Fargo, North Dakota.

Despite his accomplishments, Roger is not a member of baseball's Hall of Fame.

CEMETERY DIRECTIONS: Follow University Street north from town, turn left onto the dirt road of 32nd Avenue, and the cemetery is the third one on the left, near the end of the road.

GRAVE DIRECTIONS: Enter Holy Cross at the driveway after the metal garage, go down the hill, and Roger's black, diamond-shaped stone is on the left just before the road bends.

Billy Martin
MAY 16, 1928 – DECEMBER 25, 1989

Alfred Manuel Billy Martin grew up in Berkeley, California, a rough street kid who found an outlet for his aggression in baseball. After a couple seasons in the minors, Billy became a steady Yankee second baseman and got used to winning; in his seven seasons there, the Yankees won five World Series. Though Billy played with a scrappy ferocity, he really distinguished himself off the field, and his nefarious late-night carousing culminated at the infamous 1957 Copacabana melée, after which the Yankees, having had had enough of his drinking blowouts, traded him to Kansas City.

Billy bounced around among six teams in the next four seasons and retired from playing in 1961. Over the next dozen years he developed a reputation as a boy-wonder genius, a manager who could turn any team into a winner. In 1975, the despotic George Steinbrenner tapped Billy to pilot his ailing Yankee team.

Thus began an infamous Bronx psychodrama, the clash of outsized egos that pitted Billy the firecracker manager against the meddling owner Steinbrenner. Over the next ten years, Billy gained and lost his job managing the "Bronx Zoo" on five separate occasions. Though Billy's departures from the helm were the result of everything from vicious fistfights with marshmallow vendors, and even his own pitchers, to televised shouting altercations with Steinbrenner, Billy was always rehired because he really was a heck of a manager, perfecting a swashbuckling brand of baseball that came to be known as Billyball. Under his on-again, off-again tenure, the Yankees won two pennants and a World Series.

In 1986, Billy's beloved number 1 jersey was retired by the Yankees, and when Billy addressed the audience he told them, "I may not have been the greatest Yankee to put on the uniform, but I was the proudest."

In an interview, he once said, "As a manager, I demand only one thing of a player, hustle. It doesn't take any ability to hustle." Hustling home as a passenger in a pickup truck on a snowy road, Billy was killed on Christmas Day 1989, in a single-car crash in upstate Fenton, New York.

At 61, Billy was buried near Babe Ruth at the Gate of Heaven Cemetery in Hawthorne, New York.

GRAVE DIRECTIONS: Enter the cemetery, turn right and follow the main road up the hill. Turn right immediately after Section 25 and the Martin plot is 120 feet on the right.

Thurman Munson

JUNE 7, 1947 – AUGUST 2, 1979

After 99 minor-league games, Thurman Munson was called up to the Yankees, and as their starting catcher was named the 1970 Rookie of the Year. Despite a well-deserved reputation as a surly and irritable curmudgeon, Thurman was in 1976 named Yankee team captain—its first since Lou Gehrig—and he was a key element of the Yankees 1977 and 1978 World Series championships.

But on August 2, 1979, Thurman lost his life at the Akron-Canton airfield after crashing his Cessna Citation airplane 1,000 feet short of the runway while practicing touch-and-go landings. Upon hitting the ground, his plane burst into flames and, though his two passengers managed to extricate themselves, Thurman was paralyzed from the impact and died of asphyxiation. He was 32.

Following his death, the Yankees retired his number 15 uniform and dedicated a plaque to his memory on Yankee stadium's center-field wall. To this day, as a tribute, Thurman's locker remains unused.

He was buried at Sunset Hills Burial Park in Canton, Ohio.

CEMETERY DIRECTIONS: From I-77, take exit 109 and follow Everhard Road west for one mile. You'll then see the cemetery on the right.

GRAVE DIRECTIONS: Enter the cemetery at the last driveway, next to the office, and follow that drive to its end at a turnaround. On the left you'll see Thurman's grave marked with a grand memorial.

Jim "Catfish" Hunter

APRIL 8, 1946 – SEPTEMBER 9, 1999

Jim "Catfish" Hunter was a centerpiece of pitching staffs, first with the Oakland A's and then with the New York Yankees. In a fifteen-year career, he was the foundation of five World Series champion teams, including three straight in 1972-74 with the A's. He strung together five straight 20-victory seasons, and retired with 224 wins, one of which was a perfect game. Not surprisingly, Catfish landed in the Hall of Fame.

Catfish came up to the majors in 1965 with the A's and he was given his colorful nickname by the A's owner after he told him, in his inimitable country drawl, that he enjoyed "huntin'" and "fishin'." Catfish went along with the moniker and later even grew distinctive whiskers, completing the "Catfish" look.

But in 1974, after winning a third straight World Series with Oakland, Catfish was ready to become a baseball trailblazer. When the A's were late in paying a particular annuity clause in his contract, Catfish argued that he was no longer bound to the team and, after arbitration, he was declared a free agent. George Steinbrenner stepped to the plate with a landmark $3.75 million, five-year contract, and Catfish became a Yankee. In today's baseball economics, the contract was a small-change deal, but in 1974 it made him the highest-paid player in baseball history, and set the stage for full-scale free agency.

After signing on with the Yankees, Catfish became the team's workhorse. By 1977 they won the World Series championship for the first time since 1962 and the following year they won again. By 1979, though, after recurring arm trouble, Catfish finished his baseball career with the Yankees at just 33 and returned to his hometown farm.

In September 1998 Catfish learned he had, of all things, a disease most commonly known by the name of a fellow Yankee Hall

of Famer, whom it had killed almost 60 years before: Lou Gehrig's disease. The disease, for which a cure is unknown, attacks nerves in the spinal cord and brain that control muscle movement, causing progressive paralysis leading to death.

While battling the disease, Catfish reflected on his days as an ace pitcher. "I would trade all of that for good health," he said. "I'd be a groundskeeper and have nobody know me."

On September 9, 1999, Catfish died of the disease at 53 and was buried at Cedarwood Cemetery in Hertford, North Carolina, just a few hundred yards behind the high school he attended and where he learned to play the game.

CEMETERY DIRECTIONS: Follow Route 17 south from Elizabeth City and after about sixteen miles, turn right onto Business Route 17. Two miles later, after you've gone over the "S" Bridge, you'll be delivered into Hertford. Stay on Business 17 and, as you leave the other side of town, you'll see the high school on the left. Turn left immediately after the high school onto Jimmy Hunter Drive and follow the road into the cemetery.

GRAVE DIRECTIONS: You won't miss Catfish's grave on the right of the drive, opposite the flagpole.

On the way back from the cemetery, it's worth a stop in Hertford's tiny center; Catfish was a native son and the town is damn proud of him. On the lawn of the courthouse is a monument dedicated to his memory and, across the street, the Hertford Café displays Catfish memorabilia.

JESSE OWENS
SEPTEMBER 12, 1913 – MARCH 31, 1980

During the 1936 Olympic Games, Jesse Owens achieved the finest one-day showing in track history by winning an unprecedented four gold medals. What made his accomplishments even more memorable was that they unfolded directly in front of Adolf Hitler, in his own Nazi Germany capital, where it was expected that the Games would be a forum for his supposed Aryan supremacy. Instead, a black athlete named Jesse ruined Hitler's day by affirming that it was again only individual excellence, rather than race or national origin, that distinguishes one from another.

Upon his return to the States from that tremendous performance, Jesse was showered with accolades. But in those days athletes were not offered lucrative endorsement contracts, and Jesse needed to

support his young family. Taking a position as a playground director in Cleveland, Jesse took his first step toward a lifetime of working with underprivileged children, and for the remainder of his life, he was tirelessly and continuously involved in the promotion of youth guidance activities. In 1976, Jesse was recognized for his efforts with our nation's Medal of Freedom award, the highest civilian honor.

Seventy years ago, the detrimental effects of smoking weren't as well-known, and certainly not as well-publicized, as they are today. Many professional athletes smoked, and some even appeared in print ads advocating smoking because they had been led to believe that it helped open the lungs. Jesse was one of those misinformed athletes but, by the time the dangers of tobacco were widely publicized in the 1960s, it was too late for Jesse; he was hopelessly hooked on cigarettes.

Jesse died of lung cancer at 66 and was buried at Oak Woods Cemetery in Chicago, Illinois.

CEMETERY DIRECTIONS: Oak Woods is located on 67th Street, just east of I-94.

GRAVE DIRECTIONS: Enter the cemetery, turn right, then bear left at the "Y" onto Memorial Drive. After the lake, turn right and Jesse's grave is on the right.

STEVE PREFONTAINE
JANUARY 25, 1951 – MAY 30, 1975

At the University of Oregon, track specialist Steve Prefontaine won four consecutive NCAA titles in the 5,000-meter event and later held every national outdoor track distance record above 2,000 meters.

At the 1972 Olympics, he was a relatively young 21-year-old, but still managed a fourth-place finish in the 5,000. Always a crowd favorite for his talent as well as his exuberance—after a win Steve would often take not just one, but two or three victory laps while shaking his fists—he was well on his way to becoming perhaps the greatest American distance runner ever and it was generally expected that Steve would win gold in the 1976 Olympics.

But fate intervened, Steve's life was cut short and instead, his is a story of what might have been. Less than five hours after running the second fastest 5,000 meters in U.S. history, Steve died in a single-car crash in Eugene, Oregon. In his MG convertible, driving alone with a blood-alcohol level of 0.16, he lost control and the car flipped and pinned him underneath, where he suffocated.

Steve was only 24 when he was buried at Sunset Memorial Park in Coos Bay, Oregon.

CEMETERY DIRECTIONS: From the center of town, follow Route 101 south for 1½ miles. At the yellow flashing light, turn right onto Millington Frontage Road and drive up the hill to the cemetery.

GRAVE DIRECTIONS: Just 75 feet up the hill from the cemetery office, next to a small Alberta Spruce tree, is the flat stone marking Steve's grave.

BOBBY RIGGS
FEBRUARY 25, 1918 – OCTOBER 25, 1995

Bobby Riggs was one of the most resourceful and calculating tennis players the game ever saw. He had his best record, and the best in the world, in 1939 when he won nine of thirteen tournaments and went 54-5 in matches. It was that year that he also swept all three titles at Wimbledon, the only time he played there. An inveterate gambler, he said, "I scraped up every dime I could find," to take a London bookmaker's 200-1 odds against him winning the singles, doubles, and mixed-doubles titles. At tournament's end, Bobby pocketed $108,000. During the 1940s, he was one of the best players on the planet—he also won three U.S. Open titles—but his enduring legacy is surely his notorious "Battle of the Sexes" matches.

In 1973 Bobby seized center court by emerging from retirement claiming that any decent male player could defeat even the best female players. He challenged Margaret Smith Court, then the world's top-ranked female, to a winner-take-all Battle of the Sexes match on national television; Margaret accepted the challenge but lost.

After the match, Bobby declared, "I want Billie Jean King ... I want the women's lib leader." These were the early years of the women's movement, and Billie Jean King was an outspoken advocate and top-ranked player; such a match would transcend the boundaries of sport.

Like Margaret, Billie Jean gamely accepted the challenge and the contest attracted the attention of a broad spectrum of people. In a hyperbolic swell of promotion before the September 1973 event, Bobby brought sexist posturing to the level of self-parody, practicing in a "male chauvinist pig" tee shirt and vowing to jump off a bridge if he lost.

The "Libber versus the Lobber" match was broadcast live from the Houston Astrodome and in the circus atmosphere Bobby made his grand entrance in a gold-wheeled Chinese rickshaw pulled by six beautiful models, while Billie Jean was carried in on a red velvet-covered Cleopatra-style litter, held aloft by men clad in mini-togas. But once play began, the 29-year-old Billie Jean was all business, and she methodically overpowered the bespectacled Bobby, the pre-match favorite despite his 55 years, trouncing him in consecutive sets.

Bobby was humiliated before an estimated 40 million television viewers while Billie Jean was awarded the $100,000 prize, proving that female athletes could indeed excel in pressure-filled situations. The match, and especially Bobby's hype, inadvertently fueled an interest in women's tennis and helped make it the major spectator and money sport that it is today. Neither Bobby nor Billie Jean held any hard feelings and the two became good friends.

Bobby continued to enjoy the limelight as an over-the-hill hustler-player and, as women's tennis became popular, he softened, then abandoned his chauvinistic stance. In November 2002, at a tennis gala marking the match's 25th anniversary, Billie Jean said, "After the fact, he really understood he did make a difference. He'd be thrilled to be around for all these things this year. And I really want people to appreciate him for being one of the top ten players in history. I mean, he was number one at one time, and he won Wimbledon and the U.S. Open."

In 1988, long out of the spotlight, Bobby was diagnosed with prostate cancer. After battling the disease for six years, he made his condition public during the opening ceremony of the Bobby Riggs Tennis Museum Foundation in Encinitas, California. In the last year of his life, Bobby worked as a spokesperson to educate the public about the disease.

At 77, Bobby died of the cancer. He was cremated and, per his wishes, his ashes were sprinkled over a few of his favorite tennis courts.

JACKIE ROBINSON

JANUARY 31, 1919 ~ OCTOBER 24, 1972

BRANCH RICKEY

DECEMBER 20, 1881 ~ DECEMBER 9, 1965

On April 15, 1947, Jackie Robinson, grandson of a slave, crossed the white chalk line at Ebbets Field to play first base for the Brooklyn Dodgers and broke Major League Baseball's rigidly enforced color barrier. It's true that if not he, then some other black player would have integrated the national pastime eventually, but it was Jackie who did it, and because he did it so incredibly well, he became a near-mythic figure.

After a four-sport college career at UCLA and a stint as the top player in the Negro League, Jackie was asked by Branch Rickey, general manager of the Dodgers, to play for one of their farm teams. At first Jackie was disbelieving, not even interested, but Branch persisted and Jackie signed on. Many owners, sportswriters and fans were against the integration, claiming that it would destroy Major League Baseball, but Branch ignored his detractors, advanced Jackie through the ranks, and added him to the team's Major League roster. The Brooklyn Dodgers instantly became the favorite team of African Americans nationwide.

It's now been more than 50 springs since that day when Jackie first walked onto Ebbets Field and today it's difficult to appreciate

the full weight of the event; it would be eight years before Rosa Parks would refuse to move to the back of a Montgomery bus and no one had any idea who Martin Luther King, Jr. was.

While black fans huddled around radios and crowded together in the bleachers to delight in Jackie's achievement, Jackie himself suffered lonely indignities; pitchers took pleasure in picking him off, base runners tried to spike him, fans mocked him, and he was subjected to a steady stream of racial insults and hate mail. But Jackie let his playing do the talking. He was named Rookie of the Year and just two seasons later won the Most Valuable Player award. Renowned for his daring steals of home, Jackie came to be one of the sport's most exciting players, and baseball fans both black and white filled ballparks to see him in action. The Dodgers set new attendance records, he led them to the World Series six times, and by 1950 he was the highest paid player on the team.

He retired in 1957 and during his induction into the Baseball Hall of Fame five years later, Jackie asked Branch Rickey to stand with him on stage as he accepted the honor; time hadn't eroded his appreciation for the opportunity that Branch had afforded him and all others of his race.

For all of his strength and athletic prowess, Jackie's health deteriorated at a relatively young age and, nine days after throwing out the ball to open the second game of the 1972 World Series, he succumbed to complications from diabetes at 53.

Jackie was buried at Cypress Hills Cemetery in Brooklyn, New York. His epitaph reads: *A man's life is not important except in the impact it has on other lives.*

CEMETERY DIRECTIONS: From the Interboro Parkway, take Exit 3 and head south on Cypress Hill Street. (Watch the signs—it's not the same as the nearby Cypress Avenue.) At Jamaica Avenue turn left and the cemetery entrance is a short way on to the left.

GRAVE DIRECTIONS: Enter the cemetery, turn right, and drive past the office. After the road's left-hand bend, turn at the first right, then take the next left. Drive up the hill to Memorial Abbey and Jackie is buried across the drive from the abbey, next to the Sluter tomb.

Four years after bringing Jackie into the majors, Branch Rickey quit the Dodgers' front office and became general manager of the Pittsburgh Pirates. Concerned about players getting struck in the head by errant pitches, Branch presented the idea of a batting helmet to tinkerer Ralph Davia. In 1953 the Pirates' batters were obligated to don the new protective headgear and within three years batting helmets were a league-wide requirement. To meet demand, Branch formed the American Baseball Cap Company and today, headed by Branch's grandson, ABC thrives as a leading manufacturer for a variety of baseball equipment.

While addressing a meeting of businessmen, Branch suffered a heart attack at 83 and died a few days later.

He was buried at Rushtown Cemetery in Rushtown, Ohio.

CEMETERY DIRECTIONS: From Portsmouth, Ohio, follow Route 104 north for about six miles to the little village of Rushtown. A short distance beyond the railroad tracks, turn left onto McDermott Pond Creek Road. The cemetery is a short distance on the left.

GRAVE DIRECTIONS: Enter the cemetery at the entrance immediately after the little block building on the left, that entrance leading to the cemetery's middle road. In the first section on the left, at the top of the hill, is Branch's off-white stone.

WILMA RUDOLPH
JUNE 23, 1940 – NOVEMBER 12, 1994

With the cards stacked against her from birth, Wilma Rudolph was an unlikely Olympic hero. Besides being born with polio and wearing a steel leg brace until she was eleven, she was also stricken with double pneumonia and scarlet fever.

At fourteen, though, after years of intensive therapy began to affect her legs positively, she began participating in track meets and, incredibly, only two years later, at just sixteen, Wilma Rudolph was named to the 1956 Olympic team. That year, she failed to qualify for the 200-meter event but did run on the bronze-winning relay team. Four years later, at the 1960 Games in Rome, Wilma shocked the world by becoming the first American woman to win three gold medals at a single Olympics.

After her Olympics career ended, Wilma graduated from Tennessee State University and held a succession of positions as teacher, coach, and community service leader. In 1977, her autobiography was published, and it later became a television movie. Her story has served as an inspiration to handicapped youths ever since.

At 54, Wilma died of brain cancer and was buried at Foston Memorial Gardens in Clarksville, Tennessee.

CEMETERY DIRECTIONS: From I-24, take Exit 11, follow Route 76 west for three miles, then turn north onto Route 41A. Follow 41A

(Madison Street) for two miles, then make a left onto Golf Club Lane. After the golf course, turn left onto Thompkins Lane, and the cemetery is located after a short distance on the left at the Paradise Hill Road intersection.

GRAVE DIRECTIONS: Enter the cemetery between the brick pillars and Wilma's grave is in the center loop of the drive.

SAM SNEAD

MAY 27, 1912 – MAY 23, 2002

S am Snead was the son of a Virginian backwoods farmer and, though he caddied at the local resort to help his family, his dream was to become a football star. After a back injury put an end to his football dream, Sam chose to pursue golf, and by his early twenties he was a club pro. After working his way through local and regional tournaments, he pursued the tour full-time beginning in 1937 and at his second event, claimed his first professional victory.

In that rookie year, Sam went on to win four more events and, over the next 23 years, won at least one tournament every year on tour except one. His biggest season was in 1950, when he won eleven times. No one has won that many since. At age 52, he was the oldest player to win on the PGA Tour and he remained a threat well into his sixties. In 1979, at 67, Snead became the youngest player to shoot his age—and if that wasn't enough, he shot a 66 two days later. Though some players steeled themselves to win particularly prestigious events, Sam was never that fussy. "I don't give a damn what tournament it is," he said. "If you play it, you want to win it."

Despite 84 career victories on the American tour and another 80 worldwide, the U.S. Open always eluded him, though he was runner-up four times. But the Masters was a different story. It was his playground, and at Augusta Sam won three green jackets over a six-year stretch, finishing in the top five on six other occasions.

Beginning in 1983, Sam was the Masters Tournament honorary starter and he did it with style; wearing a straw hat and a cocky grin, he'd make a quick jaunt to the first tee and thunder a drive with his flawless swing, then retreat to the sidelines and tell golfing stories flavored with an inimitable brand of homespun humor and folksy wisdom. "The sun doesn't shine on the same dog's tail all the time," was a favorite Sam Snead maxim.

But in 2002, Sam had been ill before the Masters Tournament and, though lesser men might have politely bowed out of the engagement, Sam never considered passing on the tradition of hitting the first drive. Still, that Masters' appearance was more ceremonial than any ever before; someone else teed up Sam's ball and his shot flew into the gallery, striking a fan in the face and breaking his glasses.

Six weeks later, Sam died at home at 89, passing away in his bed while holding hands with his son and daughter-in-law.

Sam was buried at his estate in Hot Springs, Virginia.

GRAVE DIRECTIONS: The Snead estate is on the west side of Route 220, about thirteen miles north of the big paper mill in Covington. This estate though, is very private property. The Snead family still lives there, you can't see Sam's grave from the road, and I don't recommend showing up without an invitation.

WILLIE STARGELL
MARCH 6, 1940 – APRIL 9, 2001

Willie Stargell, known affectionately to Pittsburgh Pirates fans as "Pops," was a powerhouse hitter who crushed 475 soaring and majestic home run shots. Batting cleanup for most of his 21-season career, he rattled the confidence of pitchers by pinwheeling the bat in rhythm with their delivery and, once he connected, his sheer power was unmatched; Willie once held the record for the longest homer in nearly half of the National League parks and still remains the only person to have ever hit a ball out of Dodger Stadium. Later, as if to prove it was no fluke, he did it again.

Upon teammate Roberto Clemente's death in 1972, Willie stepped up to lead the team, and in 1979, he became the oldest player ever, at 39, to win the Most Valuable Player award. In 1988, he was elected into the Hall of Fame at Cooperstown in his first year of eligibility.

For the Pirates and their fans, opening day 2001 promised to be particularly memorable—the day would also mark the official opening of their brand-new PNC Park field, which had been built to replace the aged Three Rivers Stadium of Willie's glory days. But for all the pomp surrounding Pittsburgh's 2001 opening, the sunny April celebration turned out bittersweet. That morning, just hours before the first pitch was thrown, home run-king Willie died after a long battle with kidney disease. Fittingly, in a style of which Willie is assuredly proud, the very first hit at the new stadium was a home run.

At 61, he was interred at Oleander Memorial Gardens in Wilmington, North Carolina.

ETERNAL COUPLE

SAM SNEAD &
BEN HOGAN

CEMETERY DIRECTIONS: After a determined 2,600 mile run out of California, Interstate 40 unceremoniously ends in Wilmington when it merges into Route 132. After the merge, follow Route 132 for four more miles, then turn left onto Route 76 (Oleander Drive). After another three miles, make a right onto Bradley Drive, which in a short distance ends at the cemetery.

GRAVE DIRECTIONS: Enter the cemetery and immediately after the white, fenced bridge, turn left and drive up the hill to the mausoleum. At the mausoleum, Willie's crypt is on the right-hand wall, second row from the top.

JIM VALVANO
MARCH 10, 1946 – APRIL 28, 1993

The people and fans of North Carolina were simply not prepared for what hit them, and their ears, when Jim Valvano took over as head coach of the North Carolina State Wolfpack basketball team in 1980. The fast-talking coach made himself into the state's most audible character, appearing almost incessantly on a statewide radio hookup, accepting speaking engagements, and cheerfully promoting soft drinks and fast food.

But whatever misgivings his ubiquitous activities may have engendered were generally swept away by what happened at the end of the 1983 season. Finishing the regular season in a tie for third place in the Atlantic Coast Conference, the team did not lose again. They won a bid to the NCAA tournament and upset higher-ranked teams to reach the final.

Their opponent in the final was top-ranked Houston, which had won 26 straight and, for all its postseason flair, Jim's Wolfpack wasn't given a chance. But in that final game, Jim demonstrated his mastery as a coach, slowing the tempo of the game to frustrate Houston's charging style. In the final minute, with the Wolfpack trailing by a slim margin, he ordered his team to commit fouls to capitalize on their opponents' weak free-throw skills. The Wolfpack erased the deficit and after a few wild seconds of bedlam basketball at game's end, won 54-52, claiming the national championship in outlandish, Cinderella style. In the ensuing triumphant pandemonium, Jim Valvano lent himself to sports-reel immortality and defined the emotion of victory, leaping off the bench with a whoop and running madly down the court looking for someone to hug.

After being forced from his job six years later by a recruiting and admissions scandal, Jim started a career as a commentator, but in

1992, he was diagnosed with a cancer, adenocarcinoma, and given a year to live. Jim spent the remainder of his life establishing his own V Foundation as a money-raiser for the fight against cancer, which to date has awarded research grants totaling more than $4 million.

At 47 Jim was buried at Oakwood Cemetery in Raleigh, North Carolina.

CEMETERY DIRECTIONS: From the I-440 beltway that circles Raleigh, take either Exit 11 or Exit 298 and follow the signs on Route 401 to the Capitol Visitor Center. With many one-way streets and goofy intersections in the area, it's difficult to offer intelligible directions, but, once you locate the governor's mansion on Person Street, which is just east of the Visitor Center, you're almost to the cemetery. Oakwood Avenue is a block north of the Mansion and then, another four blocks east along Oakwood, is the cemetery entrance.

GRAVE DIRECTIONS: Enter the cemetery, turn right and go under the archway at the office. Then bear left twice, onto Elm and then Walnut Drive, proceed past the maintenance shed, and bear left onto Locust Drive. After a hundred feet, Jim's stone is near the curb on the left.

TED WILLIAMS
AUGUST 30, 1918 – JULY 5, 2002

When the Boston Red Sox brought Ted Williams up to the majors in 1939, he didn't exactly look like a home run hitter. But young Ted, "the Kid," smacked .327 with 31 homers during that rookie season and, most impressively, he drove in a mind-boggling 145 RBIs as well. In a nineteen-season career, he batted .344 and swatted 521 home runs, but his numbers could have been even higher if not for his Marine Corps service in World War II and the Korean War.

Throughout much of Ted's career, New York Yankee Joe DiMaggio was his archrival and when the Kid hit his fabled .406 in 1941, his feat was overshadowed by DiMaggio's 56-game hitting streak. That summer rightly belonged to both players and, in the 60 years since, no one has come within 12 games of DiMaggio's streak or 12 points of Ted's average. But, although Ted's career was longer (nineteen seasons to thirteen) and more productive (521 homers to 361), DiMaggio seemed to get more publicity, probably because he was a regular World Series champion. Like all Red Sox players since 1918, Ted never won a World Series ring.

Nonetheless, his statistics are undeniable, and they make a fair case that Ted achieved the goal he set for himself when he came up to the big leagues. He merely wanted, he said, people to look at him one day and say, "There goes the greatest hitter ever to play the game." But he had other qualities that made him a compelling figure and was an athlete who did not believe that the world owed him a living. Instead, he preferred a kind of isolation from the adulation of the crowd and the attentions of the media. His brother Danny had died of leukemia and, for over 50 years, Ted was willing to go anywhere and do anything that cancer funds asked him to do, as long as there were no cameras around to record him doing it. Ted was a perfectionist who measured himself by his own exacting standards. Like any artist, he let his work speak for him and had no tolerance for those less dedicated. Single-minded and stubborn, he was stoic and solitary in an age when ballplayers were becoming whiners and exhibitionists.

Considered by many to be the greatest hitter in baseball history, Ted fittingly ended his 19-year career in 1960 by smacking a homer in his final at bat. John Updike wrote about that moment: "He didn't tip his cap. He hid in the dugout. Gods do not answer letters." Nor, apparently, do they harbor any nostalgia; a few years after retiring Ted told a reporter, "I'm so grateful for baseball, and so grateful I'm the hell out of it."

In 1995, Boston dedicated a $2.3 billion tunnel bearing his name but, at the ceremony, Ted made it clear he didn't consider it a memorial. "Every place I go, they're waving at me, sending out a cheer, sending letters and notes," he said. "I've only seen that happen to somebody who's going to die. I'm a long ways from that."

After a series of strokes and congestive heart failure over several years, Ted died of cardiac arrest at 83.

After his death, Ted's body was taken to the Alcor Life Extension Foundation's cryogenic facility in Scottsdale, Arizona, though his will stated that he wanted to be cremated and have his ashes scattered at sea off the Florida coast. The change of plans came about when it was revealed that in November 2000, Ted, his son John Henry, and his daughter Claudia entered into a pact to freeze themselves after their deaths, according to a note that was filed in court. The handwritten pact, signed by all three parties, read "JHW, Claudia, and Dad all agree to be put in Bio-stasis after we die. This is what we want, to be able to be together in the future, even if it is only a chance."

The note was challenged in court by Ted's oldest daughter, Bobby Jo. She was left out of the pact and maintained that, since the note was made during a "tender moment before a surgery," it wasn't valid because Ted wasn't thinking straight. In December 2002, an accord was reached and Ted will hang indefinitely upside down in one of Alcor's liquid nitrogen-filled, cryonic suspension tanks at minus 325 degrees.

DENTON 'CY' YOUNG
MARCH 29, 1867 – NOVEMBER 4, 1955

His nickname arising from the shortened "Cyclone" moniker given him by a sportswriter, Denton "Cy" Young was an anatomical pitching marvel whose arm seemed never to tire. Over 22 seasons he started more than 800 games, finishing with more wins, more innings, and more complete games than any other hurler. Ninety years later, his records remain unchallenged.

Cy's Major League debut came in 1890 with Cleveland, where he stayed until 1898. After a two-year stint for St. Louis, he ended up in Boston and remained there until retirement. During that time, Cy pitched the first perfect game in American League history, threw three no-hitters and was honored to throw the first-ever pitch in a World Series. Finishing his career with 511 wins, Cy retired to his native Ohio in 1911.

At home, seated in his favorite armchair, Cy suffered a fatal heart attack at the age of 88 and was buried at the Church Cemetery in Peoli, Ohio.

CEMETERY DIRECTIONS: From the north, take Exit 65 off I-77 and follow Route 36 west for two miles to County Road 258. Turn left and follow CR 258 east for 11½ miles, at which point the cemetery will be on your right.

From the south, take Exit 54 off I-77, follow CR 541 east, then CR35 north, to CR 258. Make a right onto CR 258 and the cemetery is four miles ahead on the right.

GRAVE DIRECTIONS: Cy's plot is approximately in the center of this small cemetery. You'll see his stone about 50 feet to the left of the twin cedar trees.

Baseball didn't forget about Cy Young and in 1956, when an award program to recognize the outstanding pitcher of the Major Leagues was established, it was named the Cy Young Memorial Award. In 1967 the award was expanded to recognize two pitchers each year—one from each league—and today the award is the game's most-coveted pitching honor.

TELEVISION
& FILM
PERSONALITIES

STEVE ALLEN

DECEMBER 26, 1921 – OCTOBER 30, 2000

As a radio and talk-show host in the 1950s, Steve Allen caught the eye of network television producers working on a new program called *The Tonight Show*. It debuted in 1954 with Steve as its wisecracking host and, with his witty monologues, jocular ad-lib hijinks, comical skits, and engaging interviews with both celebrity guests and the "man in the street," he created the smashingly successful late-night TV formula. After laughing it up for two years, Steve handed the reins over to Jack Paar and hosted his own prime-time variety show, *The Steve Allen Show*, which ran until 1964 and launched the careers of a generation of comedians and personalities.

Though he is best remembered for his intelligent and informal comic style, Steve was also a gifted musician, seasoned author, and a part-time actor. An accomplished pianist who never learned to read music, he is listed in the *Guinness Book of World Records* as the most prolific composer of modern times, credited with some 7,000 tunes including such hits as "This Could Be the Start of Something Big" and "Impossible." He wrote newspaper columns and plays, published some 50 books on everything from poetry to social criticism to humor, and a dozen novels. Steve appeared in Broadway shows and on soap operas, and he even starred as the King of Swing in the 1956 movie *The Benny Goodman Story*.

When Steve died at his home at 78, newspapers dutifully reported that he'd suffered an apparent heart attack. However, most newspapers ignored the more interesting aspect of his death, which came to light with the release of his autopsy report two months later.

Steve had actually died due to a hemopericardium, a hole in the heart that leaked blood into the surrounding sac. On the day of his death, he had been in a minor traffic accident in which another driver backed his vehicle into Steve's car. The fender-bender bruised Steve's chest and ruptured tissue in his heart, which wasn't too healthy in the first place. The rupture caused a blood leakage and, when Steve dozed off after dinner, he simply never awoke.

He was cremated at 78 and his ashes remain with his family.

INGRID BERGMAN

AUGUST 29, 1915 – AUGUST 29, 1982

With luminous beauty, an intriguing accent and an effortless acting style, the Swedish-born actress Ingrid Bergman found a large and admiring American audience during the 1940s. After starring in *Casablanca* with Humphrey Bogart in 1942, she enjoyed unprecedented box-office appeal and nothing or no one, it seemed, could topple her from her throne.

Then, in 1950, Ingrid had an affair—and a baby—with Italian film director Roberto Rossellini, though both were married to other people. The affair did more than throw Bergman's personal life into turmoil. The public flames of indignation and outrage over her infidelity were fanned by the fact that her image had been particularly pure and wholesome. On the floor of the U.S. Senate, she was denounced and her affair prompted a proposal for a licensing system for foreign actors so they could be thrown out of the country on grounds of immorality.

Due to the scandal, Ingrid was unable to find work in Hollywood until 1956, when she starred in *Anastasia* and won an Academy Award. America's love affair with Ingrid Bergman was on again. In fact, over the ensuing decades, despite relatively few significant films, Ingrid became more adored and admired than ever because she survived the scandal with her dignity intact.

A couple of years before her death, she told an interviewer, "I've had a very rich life and there was never a dull moment. When I was very young in Sweden, I used to pray 'God, please don't let me have a dull life.' And He obviously heard me."

Ingrid died of cancer on her 67th birthday and she was cremated. Some of her ashes were scattered and the remainder were buried alongside her parents at Northern Cemetery in Stockholm, Sweden. They are in Section Kv11F, Grave 228-11573.

BILL BIXBY

JANUARY 22, 1934 – NOVEMBER 21, 1993

Bill Bixby was an accomplished actor with three long-running series to his credit. His first success was as the alien-plagued newspaper reporter in the comedy series *My Favorite Martian*, which began in 1963. He later starred as a single father coping with his young son's curiosities in *The Courtship of Eddie's Father*. Finally, from 1978 to 1982, Bill played Dr. David Banner, a fugitive scientist who, when angered, pumped up into a green and threatening (yet often helpful) monster in *The Incredible Hulk* television series.

But Bill's private life was at odds with his happy-go-lucky image. His son Christopher died at six in 1981 of a bacterial infection, and his distraught wife, actress Brenda Benet, committed suicide the following year. In the early 1990s, Bill attracted media attention and public respect for his courageous battle with prostate and bone cancer, undergoing several experimental treatments.

Bill married his second wife just seven weeks before his death from prostate cancer at 59.

He was cremated and his ashes scattered in Hana, Maui, Hawaii.

MEL BLANC

MAY 30, 1908 – JULY 10, 1989

Mel Blanc entered radio acting in 1933 and later gained fame as "the Man of 1,000 Voices," supplying the vocals for hundreds of popular and beloved animated cartoon characters, including Bugs Bunny, Woody Woodpecker, Daffy Duck, Porky Pig, and others.

Though Mel was virtually never seen on the silver screen during the golden era of *Merrie Melodies* cartoons, the myriad permutations of his acrobatic vocal cords have remained instantly recognizable by children of all ages around the globe for more than 50 years. Among the many lines he repeatedly uttered were "Eh . . . what's up, Doc?" through the wiseacre hare, Bugs Bunny; "I tawt I taw a putty tat," from the tart-tongued canary Tweety; and, of course, the stutter-strewn meanderings of Porky, the wistful pig.

"You know, my wife talks to me a lot about retiring," he once told an interviewer. "I say to her, 'What the hell for?' I never want to stop. When I kick off, well, I kick off." Or, as Porky said over those many years: "That's all folks!"

Mel died at 81 of heart disease and is buried at Hollywood Forever in Hollywood, California.

CEMETERY DIRECTIONS: The cemetery is easy to find at 6000 Santa Monica Blvd., just west of Highway 101.

GRAVE DIRECTIONS: Enter the cemetery, stay straight and then stop about 150 feet past the second drive on your left. There at the curb on your left is Mel's grave.

LLOYD BRIDGES

JANUARY 15, 1913 – MARCH 10, 1998

Known as one of Hollywood's hardest-working actors, Lloyd Bridges' film career began in 1941 when he made his debut in, of all things, a Three Stooges short called *They Stooge to Conga.* By the 1950s Lloyd's acting resume was heavy with roles in war flicks and Westerns, most notably alongside Gary Cooper in *High Noon,* but in 1957 Lloyd really hit his stride as Mike Nelson, the Navy frogman turned undersea investigator in *Sea Hunt.*

Lloyd worked almost exclusively in television through the 1960s and became one of the revered old guard of the entertainment industry. But in 1980 the craggy-faced veteran completely reinvented himself when he spoofed his own steely-eyed persona as a gruff but wacky air controller in *Airplane!* and its sequel. He followed up with other off-the-wall romps including *Joe Versus the Volcano,* and in 1998 Lloyd earned an Emmy nomination for his guest role on *Seinfield* as a combative (but nearly incapacitated) old trainer.

Lloyd died of natural causes at 85. He was cremated and his ashes remain with family.

JAMES CAGNEY

JULY 17, 1899 – MARCH 30, 1986

After ten years as an actor and dancer in vaudeville, in 1931 the raspy-voiced James Cagney became the talkies' first modern star and a favorite hoodlum for his role as Tom Powers opposite a bevy of floozies in *Public Enemy*. As Americans lionized the bootleggers of Prohibition and the gangsters of the Depression, Cagney played a string of antihero roles in such films as *The Roaring Twenties*, *The Frisco Kid*, and, later, *White Heat*.

Cagney was a rather plain looking man but his rapid-fire delivery and arrogant confidence made him a leading toughguy of the gangster genre. Still, he was not content to be pigeonholed and proved his range and versatility as patriotic showman George M. Cohan in the musical *Yankee Doodle Dandy*, for which he won an Oscar. He also took a Shakespearean turn as Bottom in *A Midsummer Night's Dream* and played the comically villainous Captain Powell in 1955's *Mister Roberts*.

Suffering from a number of health problems, Cagney retired in 1961 after playing a manic Coca-Cola executive in his 70th film, the Billy Wilder comedy *One, Two, Three*. He spent the next two decades on his 800-acre New York farm but emerged from retirement in 1981, as much for his own morale as for the sake of the art, to work with his old friend Pat O'Brien as a turn-of-the-century police chief in the film version of *Ragtime*.

It was his final film. On Easter Sunday 1986, Cagney finally succumbed to his diabetes and heart disease and he died at 86. Longtime friend and colleague President Ronald Reagan delivered his eulogy, and his survivors included his beloved Frances, who had married him 64 years earlier.

Cagney was buried at the Gate of Heaven Cemetery in Hawthorne, New York.

CEMETERY DIRECTIONS: From I-287, take Exit 4 and follow Route 100A north for 2½ miles (Route 100A will become Route 100 after 2 miles) to Lakeview Avenue and turn right. Follow Lakeview Avenue to its intersection with the Taconic State Parkway, turn left, and the Gate of Heaven Cemetery is a mile on the left. Turn left onto Stevens Avenue, go over the railroad tracks and make another left to enter.

GRAVE DIRECTIONS: Inside the cemetery is a large mausoleum laid out like the spokes around a wheel. Cagney's crypt is in the second bay of the spoke that is closest to the cemetery entrance.

JOHN CANDY

OCTOBER 31, 1950 — MARCH 4, 1994

John Candy joined the famed Chicago-based Second City improvisational comedy troupe in 1977 at Dan Aykroyd's urging, and from there success was just around the corner. In 1980 he appeared beside Aykroyd and his hilarious partner in crime, John Belushi, in the soon-to-be-famous film *The Blues Brothers*. That role led to plenty of others and John become an audience favorite for playing genial losers and big-hearted chumps with a touchingly human and genuine sincerity in such films as *Stripes, Uncle Buck,* and *Planes, Trains, and Automobiles*. John worked tirelessly and appeared in 34 movies during the 1980s, which allowed him to go from, as he put it, "macaroni and cheese to macaroni and lobster."

His exceptional girth was key to the Canadian-born comic's success, and though John often reacted to unexpected references to his size with self-deprecating jokes, he struggled behind the laughs with a succession of diets. Attending the Pritikin Longevity Center, John exercised on treadmills and stationary bicycles, but was never able to control his weight—or his cigarette addiction, for that matter.

By 1994, when John traveled to Durango, Mexico, to shoot the movie *Wagons East*, he was tipping the scales at 375 pounds. Eager to finish shooting as scheduled, they sometimes filmed for twelve hours in the stifling heat. On one particular morning, John's bodyguard rang him up but the phone went unanswered. A short while later, the guard let himself into John's accommodations and found John, dressed in a black and red checkered nightshirt, expired in his bed. He had died of a massive heart attack.

At 43, John was interred at Holy Cross Cemetery in Culver City, California.

CEMETERY DIRECTIONS: From I-405, follow Slauson Avenue east for a half-mile and the cemetery is on the left at #5835.

GRAVE DIRECTIONS: Enter the cemetery and drive to the mausoleum at the top of the hill. Walk through the front entrance and proceed down the hall on the right. On the right-hand side is Room 7, and in there John's crypt is on the right.

JACK CASSIDY
MARCH 5, 1927 – DECEMBER 12, 1976

Jack Cassidy's acting career took him from Broadway musicals to television and film, and he also recorded albums of songs from musicals in which he appeared. But at the time of his death, he was best known for his role on *The Partridge Family*, a popular feel-good show of the 1970s that showcased the limited singing and musical talents of his then-wife, Shirley Jones, and their son David Cassidy.

At 49 Jack dozed off while smoking a cigarette, which ignited the couch. The ensuing fire consumed the entire building. The charred remains of one person were found, but positive visual identification was impossible and family members desperately hoped that the remains weren't Jack's, as his car was missing from the garage. But it turned out that a friend had borrowed the car, and dental records later confirmed that the body was Jack's.

Jack's cremation was completed by professionals and his ashes scattered at sea.

IRON EYES CODY
APRIL 3, 1904 – JANUARY 4, 1999

In a public service announcement that aired on the first-ever Earth Day in 1971, Iron Eyes Cody paddled his canoe up a polluted stream past a belching smokestack and walked to the edge of a busy highway strewn with trash. As the camera moved in for a closeup, a single tear rolled down his cheek as a narrator said, "People start pollution, and people can stop it."

That tear proved to be more eloquent than any words, and viewers were moved to dedicate themselves to preserving the beauty of the American landscape. The ad is still remembered by millions and was recently named one of the best commercials of all time. For Iron Eyes, "the crying Indian," the spot proved to be a career zenith and it alone lent him more notoriety than did his 60 years of acting work in almost a hundred Westerns.

But as Iron Eyes gained celebrity and his brethren swarmed to champion his Native American roots, a petty issue nagged: Iron Eyes, it turned out, wasn't an Indian after all.

Instead, his true heritage lay in Kaplan, Louisiana, where records at Holy Rosary Catholic Church confirm he was baptized Espera DeCorti, the second son of Italian immigrants who toiled as replacements for freed slaves. Around 1925, Espera—or Oscar, as everyone called him—and two brothers struck out for California. They changed their surname to Cody, and Oscar "turned 100 percent Indian," as his half-sister May Abshire put it. "He had his mind all the time on the movies." Even as a youth, she recalled, Oscar would dress up as an Indian and lead neighborhood boys in outdoor games. "He always said he wanted to be an Indian. If he could find something that looked Indian, he'd put it on."

The Iron Eyes Indian guise became a comfortable escape from his unsettling past and proved to be a ticket to Hollywood fame besides. But his was not a short-lived masquerade, or one that was donned and doffed whenever expedient. As Iron Eyes Cody, he seldom left home without his beaded moccasins, buckskin jacket and braided wig; he married an Indian woman, Bertha Parker, and adopted two Indian boys. He spoke of how his Cree Indian mother and Cherokee father raised him in Oklahoma and he generously pledged time and money to Native American causes.

For their part, the Native American community accepted the plain evidence that Iron Eyes was not an Indian, but they continued to honor him, pointing out that his charitable deeds trumped his non-Indian heritage. But Iron Eyes never made apologies. "You can't prove it," he said. "All I know is that I'm just another Indian."

After a series of strokes, he died at 94 and rests at Hollywood Forever in Hollywood, California.

CEMETERY DIRECTIONS: This cemetery is easy to find at 6000 Santa Monica Blvd., just west of Highway 101.

GRAVE DIRECTIONS: There are a number of famous people residing at Hollywood Forever, and the cemetery encourages visitors. They sell a guidebook in the flower shop, and even just a simple map of the grounds will set you back a sawbuck. But you won't need those.

Enter the cemetery, turn right after the information booth, then make a left and stop in front of the Hollywood Forever Mausoleum (sometimes referred to as the Abbey of Psalms), which is the huge building on your right. Walk into the mausoleum and turn right into the Sanctuary of Memories hallway. Iron Eyes is three-fourths of the way down this hall, on the left-hand side in the third row from the floor, at number 3301.

NICK COLASANTO

JANUARY 19, 1924 – FEBRUARY 12, 1985

Were it not for his last role, Nick Colasanto's passing would have gone virtually unnoticed by the American public. But as "Coach" on the television comedy series *Cheers*, Nick endeared himself as the loveably slow-witted, befuddled but good-hearted bartender.

Nick's acting credits also include Broadway plays and motion pictures, most notably *Raging Bull*, and when he died after a heart attack at 61 his demise tugged the heartstrings of millions.

Nick was buried at St. Ann's Cemetery in Cranston, Rhode Island.

CEMETERY DIRECTIONS: From I-95, take Exit 22 and follow Route 10 west for 2½ miles to the Cranston Street exit. Turn right off the exit, then left at the traffic light. Then make a right at the fifth light (this is still Cranston Street) and the cemetery is a half-mile on the right.

GRAVE DIRECTIONS: Enter the cemetery through the drive between the two churches and turn right. Continue in this direction—past the white cement block office—until you get to the sign for Section 32. (There are a couple jogs in the road but continue in the same general direction.) At the Section 32 sign, turn left and then, after another block, Section 31 is on the right. In Section 31, locate the Troppoli stone next to the road and twenty feet further in is Nick's flat stone.

GARY COOPER

MAY 7, 1901 – MAY 13, 1961

Gary Cooper was raised on a sprawling Montana ranch and worked as a newspaper political cartoonist before he made use of his masterful horsemanship skills as a stuntman in the cowboy movies of the era. He parlayed that opportunity into leading-man roles, and over a 30-year career the handsome and rangy actor came to embody the ideal male sex symbol for legions of women, and the quintessential strong, silent American hero to men.

The early forties marked the pinnacle of Gary's career, as he stepped into a series of unforgettable roles: He played a stewbum who makes good in the sentimental *Meet John Doe*; he won his first Oscar in the title role of *Sergeant York*; his exceptional portrayal of

Lou Gehrig in *The Pride of the Yankees* invited an Oscar nomination; and he received yet another Academy nod for his lead work in *For Whom the Bell Tolls.* Perhaps the most commanding performance of his career came in 1952's *High Noon,* considered one of the great westerns of all time.

Gary died of cancer at 60 and was buried at Sacred Hearts of Jesus and Mary Cemetery in Southampton, Long Island, New York.

CEMETERY DIRECTIONS: The cemetery is west of town along the north side of Route 27.

GRAVE DIRECTIONS: The cemetery entrance is at a break in the hedges along Route 27. Enter and make an immediate left, then stop just before the road turns to the right. Forty feet to the right, under a large boulder, is Gary's grave.

BOB CRANE

JULY 13, 1928 – JUNE 29, 1978

From 1965 to 1971, Bob Crane played Colonel Hogan on *Hogan's Heroes,* an improbably popular television comedy set in a Nazi prisoner-of-war camp. It featured a wily group of World War II prisoners who each week outsmarted their German captors, Colonel Klink and Sergeant Schultz.

Before *Hogan's Heroes,* Bob had been a drummer with the Connecticut Symphony Orchestra and a radio disc jockey, but after the show's cancellation he turned to dinner theater. His new travel schedule enabled him to pursue his desperate sexual compulsion on a more or less full-time basis, and Bob slept with hundreds of women, recording the encounters in still photography and then, once the technology was available, on videotape. That extravagantly promiscuous and meticulously documented sex life seems to have, at the least, been a contributing factor to his death, and his subsequent tabloid notoriety has eclipsed his rerun celebrity.

At 49, Bob was found savagely beaten to death in his apartment. Though his swinging video-technician friend, John Carpenter, was a prime suspect, the police were never able to assemble a solid case. In 1994, realizing that the passage of time was jeopardizing their already tenuous case, the authorities decided to proceed with the circumstantial evidence and Carpenter was charged with Bob's murder. But Carpenter was acquitted and Bob's murder remains unsolved.

Bob was originally interred at Oakwood Memorial Park in Chatsworth, California, his grave marked by a small, flat stone.

But, twenty years after his death, the Crane family removed their beloved Bob and deposited him into an unmarked grave at Westwood Memorial Park in Santa Monica.

CEMETERY DIRECTIONS: Follow Wilshire Boulevard a half-mile east from I-405, then turn right onto Glendon Avenue. The cemetery is immediately on the left. Or, you may want to park your car along Wilshire and walk to the cemetery behind the office complex at 10850 Wilshire Blvd.

GRAVE DIRECTIONS: Bob lies somewhere in the middle of the lawn, not too far from Natalie Wood's stone.

JOAN CRAWFORD

MARCH 23, 1908 – MAY 10, 1977

Joan Crawford was a Broadway chorus-line dancer and progressed to Hollywood, where she found success in silent films. In 1928 she starred in *Our Dancing Daughters* as a flapper—that liberated, devil-may-care, flirtatious, high-society creature of the period—and the role catapulted her to major stardom.

She easily made the transition to "talkies" and the next two decades brought Joan a string of successes playing socialites and rags-to-riches shopgirls opposite many of the biggest male leads of the day. Her personal life mirrored her roles in some ways; Joan's love affairs and public break-ups with the likes of Douglas Fairbanks, Jr. and Clark Gable made gossip headlines. Perhaps her most brazen and scandalous tryst was with Franchot Tone, an involvement that found her in a love triangle with Bette Davis. Both women fancied themselves the sole object of Tone's affections, yet Joan emerged victorious and married him. Marked by two miscarriages and frequent beatings, the marriage lasted just four years, with Joan finally divorcing Tone after she caught him and a young starlet in a compromising position.

Through the fifties, Joan's career slowed and she was relegated to more menial roles, until 1962 when she starred with her arch-rival Bette Davis as a pair of nutty sisters, showbiz has-beens living in a decaying Hollywood mansion, in *Whatever Happened to Baby Jane?* The popular black comedy brought brief new life to each of their waning careers, afforded gossip journalists a field day, and reignited their old feud as well, prompting a remark from Joan that Davis had "slept with every male star at MGM except Lassie."

The last years of Joan's life were devoted to Christian Science and vodka, and she died of cancer at 69.

She is interred at Ferncliffe Mausoleum in Hartsdale, New York.

CEMETERY DIRECTIONS: From I-87, take Exit 7 in Ardsley and follow Route 9A north for 1¼ miles. Turn right onto Secor Road at the traffic light, and the Ferncliffe Cemetery is a short distance on the left.

GRAVE DIRECTIONS: Enter Ferncliffe at the first entrance, bear left and park toward the left-hand side of the main mausoleum. Enter the mausoleum through the front bronze doors and turn left, right, left, left, and right. Joan is in Alcove E on the right in the Steele crypt, which was the name of her last husband.

JAMES DEAN
FEBRUARY 8, 1931 – SEPTEMBER 30, 1955

The handsome and brooding actor James Dean had one of the most spectacularly brief careers of any screen star. In just more than a year and in only three films, James created a sensation and became an instantly recognizable image with his blue jeans, dangling cigarette, and characteristic slouch, personifying the restless American spirit of 1950s youth. Immortalized through at least a dozen biographies and songs, fan clubs, and a postage stamp, he's deeply etched into American pop culture.

After growing up in Indiana's farm country, James relocated with his father and stepmother to California in 1949 and attended Santa Monica City College, majoring in pre-law. But the only class in which James shined was drama, and he left after two semesters to live precariously as a parking-lot attendant, chasing auditions wherever they were available. After a few television commercials and bit film roles, young James took the advice of an actor's workshop and in 1951 moved to New York in pursuit of a career. While earning a living as a busboy, he appeared in several television shows and landed parts in two Broadway plays.

The New York exposure paid off. In 1954, James won the role of troubled adolescent Cal Trask in the screen adaptation of John Steinbeck's *East of Eden,* which shortly led to the swaggering James being cast in a new but similar role as the angst-ridden Jim Stark in 1955's *Rebel Without a Cause.*

In March 1955, James celebrated the universal praise he was enjoying for his *East of Eden* role by purchasing his first Porsche, a

356 Super Speedster convertible. By June, he was an aspiring race-car driver, with three amateur road race events under his belt. When *Rebel* finished up that month, he met up in Texas with fellow cast members Elizabeth Taylor and Rock Hudson to shoot his third film, *Giant*. Again, James was directed to be charming but restless, this time as the tough, half-genius ranch hand, Jett Rink.

After filming was completed in September, James bought another Porsche, a silver 550 Spyder, and had the nickname he had earned on the set of *Giant*, "Little Bastard," hand painted on its back end. Now with a bit of free time on his hands, James anticipated racing his new car and, at the end of the month, he and his mechanic, Rolf Wutherich, jumped in the Porsche and headed from Los Angeles to a race in Salinas.

But they never got there. James delighted in his new vehicle and along the way, he intermittently goosed the high-performance car up to its speed comfort zone. At 3:30 p.m., his driving caught the attention of a patrol officer who pulled the star over for driving in excess of 80 m.p.h. and warned him to slow down. But 2½ hours later, when James was traveling west on Route 466 just before the city of Cholame, he was speeding again when a Ford Tudor driving in the opposite direction with Donald Turnupseed at the wheel made a left turn onto Route 41 in front of him. The impact was direct and the Porsche was demolished. Rolf suffered serious injury and Donald walked away with only superficial harm, but James was dead on arrival at Paso Robles Memorial Hospital.

Less than a month later, *Rebel Without a Cause* opened in New York City and the James Dean legend was born.

At just 24, James was buried at Park Cemetery in Fairmount, Indiana.

CEMETERY DIRECTIONS: From I-69, take Exit 55 and follow Route 26 west for five miles. Make a right turn onto Main Street and the cemetery is a half-mile on the left.

GRAVE DIRECTIONS: Enter the cemetery at the entrance after the culvert, bear right at the fork and take the next right. At the crest of the hill, James's grave is on the right.

Rolf Wutherich died in another traffic accident in 1981. Donald Turnupseed passed away of cancer in 1995.

WALT DISNEY

DECEMBER 5, 1901 – DECEMBER 15, 1966

From his fertile imagination and factory of drawing boards, Walt Disney, himself only a mediocre artist, turned animation into an art form and in Mickey Mouse and Donald Duck fashioned the most popular stars ever to come out of Hollywood. His film company became *the* provider of family entertainment, and from the base that Walt built, Disney Studios has grown into one of the most successful film companies in the world.

Walt first scored big in 1928 when he and long-time associate Ub Iwerks developed Mickey Mouse. The first two Mickey shorts were silent and for the third, which featured sound, Walt himself provided Mickey's squeaky voice. With *The Three Little Pigs* he was the first to gamble on Technicolor's expensive new three-color system and, after testing animation's appeal in a full-length format with *Snow White and the Seven Dwarfs,* he quickly followed with *Pinnochio, Dumbo,* and *Bambi.* Every film required the creation of new, lovable, and unsophisticated cartoon characters and Walt created nearly all of them.

In the fifties, Walt diversified from animation and produced live-action films like *Treasure Island* and *Old Yeller.* Later, his visionary and wildly successful amusement parks perpetuated the Disney magic.

In November 1966, Walt's cancer-ridden left lung was removed but, within a month, at 65 he succumbed to the disease anyway. Walt rarely attended funerals and no announcement was made for his own, which was attended only by relatives. The secrecy initiated a rumor that Walt, instead of being buried, was encased in a deep-freeze cryogenic vault to await a cure for his lung cancer, at which time he'd be thawed and resume living. But such stories are pure fantasy. Walt was cremated and his ashes interred at ground temperature at Forest Lawn Memorial Park in Glendale, California.

CEMETERY DIRECTIONS: From Highway 2, take the San Fernando Road exit and turn northwest. After a mile, make a right onto Glendale Avenue and the park's entrance is immediately on the right.

GRAVE DIRECTIONS: Stop at the booth for a map of the cemetery's roads, then drive to the Freedom Mausoleum. Walt's plot is in the garden just to the left of the Freedom Mausoleum's main entrance. His marker, you'll see, is quite cleverly positioned and visible only when you're standing on the mausoleum's front steps.

DIVINE

OCTOBER 19, 1945 – MARCH 6, 1988

Harris Glenn Milstead, better known by his stage name and alter ego, Divine, was a drag queen and a high-profile character in the overwrought gay culture of the sixties and seventies. With Divine as the star and neighborhood pal John Waters directing, a series of films that crossed every taboo and charted an exceedingly bizarre course of self-expression bred a distinctly new genre that, even by underground standards, was intensely offbeat.

Dreamland Studios, the production company that Waters operated out of a basement, churned out about a dozen shorts and features that quickly enjoyed the status of cult classics. Perhaps their crowning achievement was 1972's *Pink Flamingoes*, the premise of which is that Divine, as Babs Johnson, is in a competition of sorts to prove she is the dirtiest person alive. Film history is made in the final scene when Divine eats dog feces on camera—straight from the dog, without any edits.

By 1988 Divine and Waters had toned their work down a few notches and the mainstream release, *Hairspray*, won critical acclaim. Divine, however, failed to enjoy this breakthrough as he died in his room at the Regency Hotel in Los Angeles of an enlarged heart caused by obesity.

At 42, Divine was buried at Prospect Hill Cemetery in Towson, Maryland.

CEMETERY DIRECTIONS: From I-695, take Exit 26A and follow Route 45 (York Road) south for a mile. The cemetery is on the left. The entrance comes up quick as you crest a steep hill and be careful turning into it.

GRAVE DIRECTIONS: Follow the drive to the lower area of the cemetery and stop when you see on your left an old set of stairs that lead back to the upper area. Opposite those stairs, in the lawn on the right and about 30 feet off the pavement, is Divine's grave.

FAMILY AFFAIR

Television sitcoms seem to have an affinity for single-parent households and, if that's the recipe for comedy, then *Family Affair*, which lifted the one-parent theme to the next stratum, should have been hilarious.

The show's premise was that six-year-old twins Buffy and Jody, (Anissa Jones and Johnny Whitaker), along with their sixteen-year-old sister Cissy (Kathy Garver) were orphaned when their parents were killed in a car wreck. Their Uncle Bill (Brian Keith), a wealthy and swinging bachelor, had a bombshell dropped on him when the children showed up on the doorstep of his luxurious Fifth Avenue pad needing a place to live. Although reluctant at first, the gruff-but-lovable Uncle Bill and his fastidious butler, Mr. French (Sebastian Cabot), acquiesced and the show's storylines followed the new family's predictably sweet and tame crises.

After five seasons, when the "six-year-olds" looked as if they might be soon driving their own cars to the set, everybody involved with the program, especially the viewers, seemed to have had enough. The show was cancelled in 1971.

Anissa Jones

MARCH 11, 1958 – AUGUST 28, 1976

Anissa Jones was thirteen when *Family Affair* ended and, after unsuccessfully auditioning for the part of Regan MacNeil, the possessed head-spinner in *The Exorcist,* she promptly quit show business and enrolled in public high school. Her parents had divorced acrimoniously years earlier and they still wrangled over Anissa's custody. Eventually, she began rebelling against both of them through drugs and alcohol. Anissa moved in with a friend at sixteen and, at eighteen, she finally was able to tap into a $75,000 trust fund that had been set up during her acting days. She spent some of the money on long-pending bills, but the remainder of it financed cars and apartments and, especially, partying supplies for herself and her friends. Sadly, within just a few months the money was gone and Anissa resorted to working at a donut shop. After a day of partying in Oceanside, California, Anissa died alone, only five months after turning eighteen. Her death from an overdose of drugs was ruled accidental, though the coroner stated that Anissa's was the most massive overdose he'd ever seen.

Anissa had no funeral but was cremated and her ashes scattered over the Pacific Ocean.

Sebastian Cabot

JULY 6, 1918 – AUGUST 23, 1977

The very English Sebastian Cabot got his start as an actor in British stage and films in the late 1930s. Older folks recall him as the criminologist on the 1960s TV drama *Checkmate*, while the younger generation recognizes his voice as the narrator of Disney's *Winnie the Pooh* cartoons. At 59, Sebastian died of a stroke. He was cremated and his ashes interred at Westwood Memorial Park in Santa Monica, California.

CEMETERY DIRECTIONS: Just about a half-mile east of I-405, this tiny cemetery is peculiarly located behind the office complex at 10850 Wilshire Blvd.

GRAVE DIRECTIONS: Across the drive from the park office is a cluster of small markers for cremains. In the top row, you can find Sebastian's marker.

Brian Keith

NOVEMBER 14, 1921 – JUNE 24, 1997

During World War II Brian Keith was a Marine fighter-pilot hero, and after the war he played secondary roles in a few dozen films. It appeared his acting career might peak with *Family Affair*, but Brian was able to parlay his popularity as Uncle Bill into many other roles, including three seasons as the cranky Judge Milton "Hardcase" Hardcastle in the somewhat popular action series *Hardcastle and McCormick* during the mid-1980s.

By 75, Brian was suffering from lung cancer and emphysema, and was overwhelmingly distraught by the gunshot suicide of his daughter, Daisy. Two months after her death, Brian shot himself to death inside his home. After cremation, his ashes were interred with Daisy's at Westwood Memorial Park in Santa Monica, California, the final residence of his old friend Sebastian Cabot.

GRAVE DIRECTIONS: Enter the cemetery, turn left at the office and, after the chapel, walk down the ramp into the new Garden of Serenity section. Turn left before the triple fountain and, fifteen feet along the wall on the left, in the top row, are Brian and Daisy's remains.

Johnny Whitaker today runs a talent agency with his sister. Their company, Whitaker Entertainment, counted former child star Dana Plato as a client until her untimely 1999 death.

ERROL FLYNN

JUNE 20, 1909 – OCTOBER 14, 1959

The charming actor Errol Flynn was a well-to-do Tasmanian who, after being expelled from several fine schools in Australia and England, had his share of adventures before making Hollywood his playground. A natural athlete and a rugged outdoorsman, Errol managed a New Guinea tobacco plantation, sailed the Southern seas for months, took a turn as a gold prospector and, for a gold-mining company, he "recruited" unwilling natives to toil in the depths as slaves.

After rave performances on English stages, the gallant Errol and his irresistible accent headed for Hollywood in 1935. In his first film, *The Case of the Curious Bride*, he played a corpse, but in the more than twenty movies following, Errol usually starred as a swashbuckling, quick-witted, romantic hero. Women were instantly attracted to his virility and dashing good looks, while male moviegoers admired his vigor, devil-may-care attitude, and witticisms. There was a native intelligence behind his affable, sometimes even self-deprecating disposition, and Errol parlayed his unusual appeal into a spectacular Tinseltown success story. His crowning achievement came in 1938 with the stupendous hit *The Adventures of Robin Hood*. When Westerns became the rage in the 1940s, Errol looked rather silly outfitted as a cowboy, but audiences didn't seem to mind and continued to flock to his films.

By the 1950s, though, Errol's off-screen life began to take a physical toll. That which made him a lovable, drink-sloshing knave on film transformed him into a bloated drunk in real life. The same passion with which he embraced assorted celluloid bombshells enflamed his fiery off-screen affairs. Barely fifteen years after capturing movie audiences with his dashing portrayal in *Captain Blood*, his best swashbuckling days were behind him. Errol tried more dramatic roles with little success until 1957, when he was cast as an aging alcoholic in Hemingway's *The Sun Also Rises*, in a bit of real-life typecasting that hit its mark.

Worn out at 50, Errol died in Canada under dubious circumstances, supposedly while having sex with a teenaged lover.

Before Errol was buried at Forest Lawn Memorial Park in Glendale, California, friends slipped a bottle of whiskey into his coffin.

CEMETERY DIRECTIONS: From Highway 2, take the San Fernando Road exit and turn northwest. After a mile, make a right onto Glendale Avenue and the park's entrance is immediately on the right.

GRAVE DIRECTIONS: Stop at the booth, get a map, drive to the Freedom Mausoleum and walk up to the courts. Errol's grave is in the Garden of Everlasting Peace, opposite the garden's entrance, in the grass near the wall.

REDD FOXX

DECEMBER 9, 1922 – OCTOBER 11, 1991

The cantankerous Redd Foxx is best remembered as the irascible junk dealer Fred Sanford in the 1970s television series *Sanford and Son*. Before he made it on television, though, Fred had a long career as a very "blue" stand-up comedian. In the tell-it-like-it-is style that hallmarked his personality, he was one of the first to broach the taboo topics of sex, race, and religion on more than 50 of his own "party records"—spoken comedy with no music—a genre he originated in 1956.

As Fred Sanford he often feigned heart attacks, so when he collapsed of a real heart attack while filming a new series, the people on the set initially thought he was joking. It was no joke—Redd was dead at 68 and is buried at Palm Memorial Park in Las Vegas, Nevada.

CEMETERY DIRECTIONS: From I-515, take Exit 73, follow Eastern Avenue south for 8½ miles. The cemetery is on the left.

GRAVE DIRECTIONS: Enter the cemetery and immediately on your left will be an island, a drive, and a lawn area, the Garden of Devotion. From the drive, count nineteen rows into the lawn and there, 50 yards from Eastern Avenue, is Redd's grave.

CLARK GABLE &
CAROLE LOMBARD

Clark Gable

FEBRUARY 1, 1901 – NOVEMBER 16, 1960

Carole Lombard

OCTOBER 6, 1908 – JANUARY 16, 1942

Clark Gable and Carole Lombard epitomized that most allegorical picture of marital bliss, two famously gorgeous people sharing the world as their oyster in the fullest and most fortuitous time of their lives.

Carole's start in show business came when she was twelve; a natural rough-and-tumble tomboy, she played a mischievous spitfire in a 1921 silent film. By sixteen, she had seven credits on her silent film resume but after suffering extensive facial injuries in a near-fatal 1926 automobile accident, her film contract was cancelled. Within two years, scar tissue on her face had lightened considerably and, with a lot of camouflaging makeup, she returned to the big screen.

Meanwhile, across town lived Clark Gable, a struggling actor with big ears and little visible talent who for a dozen years had honed his craft in minor roles, dreaming of the day he'd make it big. After working together briefly in 1932 on the set of *No Man of Her Own*, Clark and Carole began a friendly and eventually romantic offscreen relationship while, during those Depression-era years, both of their careers raced for the stratosphere.

Clark found his springboard to superstardom in 1934 with an Oscar-winning role in a comedy opposite Claudette Colbert, *It Happened One Night*. Carole, a more natural and steady talent, earned her fan base through a long string of solid performances. In March 1939, Clark and Carole were wed during a break in the filming of Clark's latest movie, *Gone with the Wind*.

The newlyweds settled in the relatively rural San Fernando Valley and balanced high-profile public appearances with a country-style personal life. Following the entrance of the United States into World War II, Clark was made chairman of the Hollywood Victory Committee and he arranged for Carole to headline a War Bond rally. But on January 16, 1942, the 33-year-old Carole, her mother

ETERNAL COUPLE

CLARK GABLE &
CAROLE LOMBARD

Elizabeth, and 21 others were killed when their airplane crashed into Mount Potosi, 30 miles outside of Las Vegas. Clark drove to the crash site and, after a search for his beloved's body, Carole and Elizabeth were interred at Forest Lawn Memorial Park in Glendale, California.

Clark was devastated and felt absolute responsibility for Carole's death as he had arranged the tour. Perhaps to blunt his grief and guilt, he enlisted in the Army Air Corps and served out his time as a tail-gunner. After the war, he returned to Hollywood to make a number of undistinguished films and in 1960, Clark signed on to the making of a "modern Western," *The Misfits*. During filming, he performed several grueling stunt scenes with wild horses that perhaps proved too much; on November 16, 1960, just two days after completing the film, Clark died of a heart attack. At 59, he was interred alongside Carole and her mother.

CEMETERY DIRECTIONS: From Highway 2, take the San Fernando Road exit and turn northwest. After a mile, make a right onto Glendale Avenue, and the park's entrance is immediately on the right.

GRAVE DIRECTIONS: Get a map at the information booth and make your way to the Great Mausoleum. Except for a small area where the public is invited inside to view a slide show, this enormous mausoleum is closed to the public. But as it turns out, that inch of invitation yields just enough of a toehold for you to see where Clark, Carole, and Elizabeth lie.

Walk into the mausoleum, tell the woman at the booth that you'd like to see the Last Supper slide show that's offered at regular intervals throughout the day, and she'll direct you to the area where it's shown. Once there, you'll see an entrance on the right that leads into the Columbarium of Prayer. If you look in there you can see the Sanctuary of Trust. There will be a sign in the entrance that states the area is restricted to property owners so at this point, you're on your own. Clark, Carole, and Elizabeth are in that Sanctuary of Trust, on the left wall at waist height about halfway into the first room.

Remember, this is private property and there are cameras around (in fact the woman in the booth has surveillance monitors at her disposal). Really, it's not worth it to trespass and there's not much to see anyway, just three plain nameplates.

GRETA GARBO

SEPTEMBER 18, 1905 – APRIL 15, 1990

The photophobic and reclusive Greta Garbo began her career as a model for a department store, then moved into film during its silent era, in her native Sweden. In 1925, Mauritz Stiller, an acclaimed director who had been mentoring Garbo, was offered a Hollywood contract by MGM that he accepted on the condition that the unproven and inexperienced Garbo be offered a contract as well, so taken was he with her talent. MGM agreed and at just nineteen Garbo came to the States.

In 1925 Garbo began shooting her first MGM film, *The Torrent*, and with breathtaking incandescence, revealed to the studio's executives the exciting qualities that Stiller had recognized. The camera loved her from any angle, and she projected an intoxicating eroticism. Stiller, though, was finished. MGM replaced him and he returned to Sweden, where he died two years later.

After a few more silent films, Garbo debuted in a "talkie" in 1930, *Anna Christie*, for which she was nominated for an Academy Award. She was thrilled that she'd successfully made the transition to sound in a language not even her own. During the next several years, Garbo's work was distinguished by increasingly intense performances and in 1935 she gave the performance of her life in *Anne Karenina*, playing the title role of a woman torn between her lover and her son.

Never a publicity hound, Garbo defied Hollywood convention by refusing to sign autographs or grant interviews. In fact, she would not even attend her own premieres and her studio never managed to obtain her telephone number. Never married (she once stood up John Gilbert at the altar), her sexual orientation was ambiguous and Garbo herself may have deliberately fed the rumor mill by juxtaposing torrid affairs with her leading men with whispered liaisons involving beauties of her own gender. Of course, the more reclusive the actress became, the more her public wanted to know about her private life—but Greta was unyielding.

By 1941 though, it was all over. Greta's last film was *Two-Faced Woman*, a domestic comedy that flopped. The Swedish Sphinx gradually withdrew into an isolated retirement. In virtual seclusion for the next 50 years, she painted, gardened, wrote poetry, followed a daily exercise routine, and most determinedly, perpetuated the Garbo mystique from her Manhattan home. Appearance and interview requests never let up, but Garbo never wavered.

At 84, Garbo died of natural causes and was cremated. For almost ten years, her ashes remained in an urn entrusted to her sole heir, but in 1999, they were buried at Woodland Cemetery (Skogskyr-kogarden) in Sweden, which is on the southern city limits of Stockholm. Marked by a beautiful and elegant, sandstone-like slab simply inscribed, "Greta Garbo," her ashes are now eternally along-side her parents.

AVA GARDNER

DECEMBER 24, 1922 – JANUARY 25, 1990

The dark and sultry Ava Gardner was a popular actress of the 1950s and '60s and her catalog includes memorable roles in 61 classic movies including *Mogambo*, for which she was nominated for an Academy Award, *The Sun Also Rises*, and *Showboat*.

But despite her accomplishments as an actress, Ava was better known for her offscreen whirlwind marriages and high-profile romances with the days' most coveted men, not all of them single. At just nineteen she wed Mickey Rooney, but they divorced within a year. Two years later, Ava and bandleader Artie Shaw went to the altar, but with Artie as with Mickey, a year together proved to be plenty and the couple split up. Ava's next romance made for wonderful tabloid fodder as whisperings of a torrid affair with the then-married Frank Sinatra eventually proved true. Sinatra divorced his wife and married Ava, but after three years of tumult and three years of separation, this union also ended.

Ava moved to Madrid in 1958. She had discovered Spain's allures while filming *The Barefoot Contessa* in 1954, and at her new retreat she dated high-profile playboys and matadors. Ava's last major film was *The Night of the Iguana* in 1964, and in 1968, Ava moved to London. She lived the remainder of her life there, only occasionally returning to the U.S. to act in one minor role or another. A notable but short-lived role of that era was as Ruth Galveston, the manipulative matron on *Knot's Landing*, a popular 1980s nighttime soap opera.

Ava suffered a stroke in 1989, and the next year died of pneumonia at 67.

She was buried at her family's plot at Sunset Memorial Park in her hometown of Smithfield, North Carolina.

CEMETERY DIRECTIONS: From I-95, take Exit 95 and follow Business Route 70 west for 2¼ miles, at which point Sunset Memorial Park will be on the left.

GRAVE DIRECTIONS: Enter the cemetery and at the "T" make a left turn and stop. On the right is a cement walk, and at the end of this walk is Ava's plot.

JACKIE GLEASON

FEBRUARY 26, 1916 – JUNE 25, 1987

Growing up in a downtrodden Brooklyn neighborhood, Jackie Gleason hung with the Nomads, an "athletic club" one knife fight away from being a street gang, and there he developed a keen flair for rough verbal play, sharp dress, and virtuoso pool playing. Upon being orphaned at sixteen, during the Depression, those street smarts were his sole asset, and he used them to finagle himself a position as master of ceremonies at a vaudeville house. That gig led to others, and for the better part of the next twenty years Jackie jumped from one opportunity to another in a continuous search for a berth that might perfectly suit his professional persona. He worked as an emcee, a carnival barker, and a bouncer; he was a house comic and a disc jockey; he landed bit roles on Broadway and minor parts in Hollywood films; but by 1950 he'd plateaued and was at a crossroads.

Jackie was in his mid-30s and just when he needed a stroke of fortune, he got one: he was signed as host of the *Cavalcade of Stars*, a comedy-variety television program that perfectly suited his talents; the show's format required that the host be able to move seamlessly between sketches and Jackie's years of emceeing had made him a master of the segue. Television close-ups captured the extravagant mugging and grandiose gestures that were often lost when he worked on stage.

Jackie was so successful that within two years he headlined his own show, *The Jackie Gleason Show*, over which he was given full authorial control and a lavish budget. There, he honed the formula that had worked so well for him and developed his signature opening routine. Asking the bandleader for "a little travelin' music," Jackie danced wildly across the screen and froze stage right to announce, "And awa-a-ay we go," which led viewers into an hour of sketch comedy and guest appearances by top musical acts.

The Honeymooners was the show's most popular sketch and the pairing of Jackie as a nervous and quick-tempered Ralph with his dim-witted upstairs neighbor Ed Norton (Art Carney) yielded one of television's first great original comedy teams. During the 1955-56 season, Jackie repackaged the sketch into a filmed half-hour situation comedy of 39 episodes, and they became one of the most successful commercial properties in show-business history. Unlike other popular series, those 39 episodes of *The Honeymooners* were all that were ever made, and they have run countless times each, gathering new generations of fans. Jackie explained that "the excellence of the material could not be maintained, and I had too much fondness for the show to cheapen it."

Perhaps the most remarkable and little-known aspect of Jackie's showbiz career was in the record business. He composed many songs, including the theme songs for both *The Honeymooners* and *The Jackie Gleason Show*. Because he could not read a note of music, Jackie would hum the melodies for transcribers. He also recorded what he called "pure vanilla music," popular songs with moody, string-laden orchestrations. In 1955 he assembled an orchestra and, personally wielding the baton, recorded his own lush arrangements of old standards. That first release, *Music for Lovers Only*, sold more than half a million copies and Jackie followed with 36 more.

Now a television superstar, Jackie's services were in high demand for feature movies, too. In 1961, he was cast opposite Paul Newman in the film *The Hustler* as the legendary pool player Minnesota Fats and performed his own pool shots; the role earned him an Academy Award nomination. In the 1970s he played the cantankerous, drawling redneck lawman Buford T. Justice in the *Smokey*

and the Bandit series, and in 1985 he reunited with Art Carney for the television movie *Izzy and Moe.*

"Life ain't bad, pal," Jackie once told an interviewer. "Everything I've wanted to do I've had a chance to do."

Jackie died of colon and liver cancer at 71 and is buried at Our Lady of Mercy Catholic Cemetery in Miami, Florida.

CEMETERY DIRECTIONS: From the Florida Turnpike (Route 821), take Exit 26 and follow Route 836 east for ¼ mile to 107th Avenue. Turn north on 107th and, after one mile, make a left onto 25th Street. The cemetery is a half-mile on the right.

GRAVE DIRECTIONS: Enter the cemetery and proceed to the "T" at the flagpole. Make a left and park at the circle at the end of this drive. On your right, 150 yards across the lawn, you won't miss the large white memorial that marks Jackie's plot.

CARY GRANT

JANUARY 18, 1904 – NOVEMBER 29, 1986

Originally, Cary Grant's specialty was stilt walking, and he actually broke into show business while performing in his native England as an acrobatic dancer. He arrived in the United States in 1920, and for three years he sang, danced, and juggled for a meager living. Eventually he dropped his real name, Archie Leach, earned a contract with Paramount Pictures, and went on to become one of Hollywood's greatest stars.

Cary's enduring style had some quirks, including a cosmopolitan manner of speaking and a flair for managing to be irresistible to a heroine while exhibiting little more than indifference toward her. Unafraid to typecast himself, he cultivated a distinctive screen persona that became the central figure in a broad range of movies.

It was in Cary's first film that vamp Mae West silkily breathed her famous line, "Why don't you come up and see me sometime?" and through the 1930s he gained a reputation as a star of sophisticated comedies. During World War II he entertained the armed forces, and in the 1950s starred in several Alfred Hitchcock films, among others. After 72 films he retired in 1965, and despite repeated inducements to return to acting, he never did.

Cary died of a stroke at 82 and in accordance with his wishes there was no funeral service of any kind.

He was cremated and his ashes entrusted to his widow and fifth wife, Barbara.

FRED GWYNNE

JULY 10, 1926 – JULY 2, 1993

The lumbering six-foot, five-inch tall Fred Gwynne followed a complicated path to his destined role as the fumbling and sweet-tempered Herman Munster.

The son of a successful stockbroker, Fred was packed off early to a prestigious Massachusetts preparatory school and, after graduation, he enlisted in the Navy and served on a World War II sub chaser. Later, Fred spent a year at a design school developing his dormant drawing talents and then entered Harvard University on the G.I. Bill. At Harvard, he presided over and contributed cartoons to *The Harvard Lampoon* and after a few performances in the Hasty Pudding Club's farcical productions, Fred decided that his future was on stage.

Most casting directors found Fred too tall or unattractive, but he did manage to appear in a few Broadway plays and even had a bit part in *On the Waterfront*, though work as a commercial artist was really paying the bills. Finally, in 1961, he was hired to co-star in the TV sitcom about two hapless cops, *Car 54, Where Are You?* and upon its cancellation three years later, Fred finally found a tailor-made role in *The Munsters* as Herman Munster. Actually, Fred wasn't completely perfect for the part—he had to wear five-inch-high platform soles—but he was right at home as a lovable Frankenstein, and audiences adored him.

The Munsters flashed only briefly and after its demise Fred found to his chagrin that the Herman role had typecast him for life. But eventually, as his hair thinned and his facial features became patriarchal, he returned to Broadway and film, usually as a booming, authoritative character. Fred's career took on new zest in 1992 when he played an autocratic Southern judge in the comedy film *My Cousin Vinny*.

But Fred decided to go out while he was still on top and, even as the accolades for *My Cousin Vinny* poured in, he withdrew and purchased a farm in rural Maryland. After just a short period of tranquility, Fred was diagnosed with pancreatic cancer. Surgery and chemotherapy followed, but the cancer continued to spread. He died at 66.

Fred was buried at Sandymount United Methodist Church in Sandyville, Maryland.

CEMETERY DIRECTIONS: Follow I-795 to its northern terminus, then follow Route 140 another four miles north. Turn left on

Sandymount Road and once you reach the stop sign, you'll be able to see Sandymount Church across the street to your left.

GRAVE DIRECTIONS: Walk into the cemetery behind the church and near the back is a distinctive brown Shannon stone. About twenty feet in front and to the left of the Shannon stone, Fred is buried in a grave that, but for the grass covering it, has no marking of any kind.

JIM HENSON
SEPTEMBER 24, 1936 – MAY 16, 1990

As a child, Jim Henson was fascinated by television, and in the summer of 1954 he learned that a local station needed someone to perform with puppets on a children's show. Jim wasn't particularly interested in puppets, but he did want to get on TV, so he and a friend made a couple of puppets, and they were hired. That show ended quickly but, within a few months, Jim landed a new program on a local NBC-affiliate station and called it *Sam and Friends*.

Having realized that it was necessary for television puppets to have "life and sensitivity," Jim's proto-Muppets on *Sam and Friends* were much different from traditional puppets. Kermit the Frog was there right from the start, and he looked and sounded much as he always would (until his death, Jim provided the voice and animation of Kermit); even at this early time he had a face that was pliable, he could move his mouth in synchronization with his speech and could gesticulate in ways that were impossible for a marionette.

Throughout the early 1960s, Jim's creations made appearances on variety and talk shows, but it was on Sesame Street, the public television program for preschoolers that first aired in 1969, that his Muppet crew won the hearts of a generation. With wit that also appealed to adults, Oscar the Grouch, innocent Big Bird, considerate Bert, fun-loving Ernie, and the rest of the lovable gang helped youngsters learn about everything from numbers and the alphabet to birth and death.

But despite the Muppets' success on *Sesame Street* and their demonstrated appeal to adults as well as children, no U.S. network would give Jim a show of his own. Finally in 1976, after a British producer offered Jim the necessary financing, *The Muppet Show* was born. It ran until 1981, when Jim decided to end it lest its quality begin to decline. Later, Jim turned to the big screen and produced three box-office hit Muppet films.

At 53, Jim died suddenly of an especially aggressive bacterial infection known as streptococcus pneumonia. He arrived at a New

York hospital suffering from an inability to breathe and was immediately treated with high doses of antibiotics but, despite the aggressive regimen, the infection overwhelmed his body. Within twenty hours of walking into the hospital, Jim died of uncontrollable bleeding into his lungs. Before contracting the illness, Jim had been in excellent health and had never even had a personal physician.

He was cremated and his ashes were scattered at his ranch outside Santa Fe, New Mexico.

AUDREY HEPBURN
MAY 4, 1929 – JANUARY 20, 1993

Although she was the daughter of a Dutch baroness and a wealthy English banker, the elegant Audrey Hepburn, born Edda van Heemstra Hepburn-Ruston, had a difficult childhood. During the Nazis' occupation of the Netherlands, Audrey and her family fairly starved, some family members were executed, and Audrey herself suffered from anemia and edema.

After the occupation Audrey earned a ballet scholarship in London and her big break came when she was cast in the title role of a stage adaptation of the novel *Gigi*. The Broadway hit paved the way for her first starring film role, as an errant princess in 1953's *Roman Holiday* for which she earned a best actress Oscar. Through 1967 the waif-like Audrey more than held her own against the abundantly endowed screen sirens of the age and among her most memorable performances were *Funny Face, Love in the Afternoon, Breakfast at Tiffany's,* and *My Fair Lady*. The disturbing 1967 film noir *Wait Until Dark*, in which she portrayed a blind woman trapped in her apartment with a killer, was a landmark for the actress, marking a departure from her trademark heroines and earning her her fifth, and final, Oscar nomination.

After 1967, Audrey almost entirely abandoned filmmaking and concentrated her efforts instead on her personal life. In 1986 she was appointed the official Goodwill Ambassador for the United Nations International Children's Emergency Fund (UNICEF) and, apart from a memorable turn as an angel in the film *Always*, Audrey devoted the last years of her life to working tirelessly on behalf of sick and destitute children. When she was selected to be the recipient of the Jean Hersholt Humanitarian Award, to be presented at the 1993 Oscar ceremonies, Audrey taped her acceptance of the award in advance, knowing that she had reached the terminal stage in her fight with colon cancer.

At 63, Audrey died of cancer at her chalet in Tolochenaz, Switzerland. In this bucolic hamlet, an old schoolhouse has been converted into a quaint museum dedicated to her memory and, within walking distance, Audrey's grave is at the village cemetery.

BENNY HILL

JANUARY 21, 1925 – APRIL 20, 1992

The British comedian Benny Hill worked as a radio performer during the 1940s and for the next two decades appeared on a variety of programs in that medium as well as on television. In 1969, writing nearly all of his own material, Benny began making a series of sketch comedies for Thames Television and, when 111 half-hour long compilations of the sketches debuted on American television as *The Benny Hill Show* in 1979, he achieved international cult status.

Benny was a master of the double-entendre, and his sketches featured skimpily clad women, sight gags, a lot of cross-dressing, and a healthy dose of *The Three Stooges*. With his own uniquely comic twist, he turned ordinary slapstick into something entirely new. A typical Benny skit might find Benny and a pretty young woman walking arm in arm along a path when they come to a puddle. Like a gentleman, Benny removes his coat and lays it over the water so his lady might cross without wetting her feet. But, of course, the water is deeper than expected and the woman is immersed up to her neck.

Critics said his humor too often crossed the line from good fun into sexism but Benny was never bothered by the complaints. "I use a pretty girl the way Henny Youngman uses his violin—as a bridge between one laugh and the next," explained Benny. Bemoaning the treatment he received at the hands of feminists, Benny answered them by pointing out that he had never chased a woman on screen in his life—they had always chased him.

On Benny's fiftieth birthday he told his small, bald sidekick, Henry McGee, that he had had a very good life, that he'd been lucky, and that he would not mind if he died the next day. However, even with the astounding success that Benny would enjoy in the subsequent decade, it is hard to see his life as anything other than sad and lonely.

Benny lacked confidence in the medical profession as a whole and, in a case of life imitating art, he entrusted his health to a gynecologist with a pathological obsession with pinching women's bottoms. Despite his wealth, he shied from the responsibility he associated with property ownership, and instead lived in a series of rented flats, each one sparsely furnished and scattered with cardboard boxes. Rejected by both women to whom he'd proposed, Benny never married and, it seems, may have died a virgin.

In the spring of 1992, Benny's neighbors sensed a particularly pungent odor emanating from Benny's apartment and, realizing they hadn't seen the funnyman for a few days, called the police. Their fears were soon realized; Benny had died very much as he had lived his life, alone. In front of his television, he was slumped on the couch, surrounded by cardboard boxes, unwashed crockery, empty glasses, and piles of videotapes.

At his death of heart failure at 67, Benny left no survivors and was buried at Hollybrook Cemetery in Shirley, Southampton, England.

CEMETERY DIRECTIONS: Shirley is about 120 miles northwest of London and the cemetery itself is on the high ground along Chilworth Road, two miles north of the Southampton West railway station.

GRAVE DIRECTIONS: From the main gate, turn left at the chapel and Benny's black marble tomb is the first grave in the seventh row.

After Benny' death, his will was contested by a few parties and, since Benny wasn't particularly trusting of traditional financial vehicles, the actual disposition of some of his fortune was unclear. (It became rumored that some had been buried with him.) In October 1992, grave robbers unearthed Benny, but only they know whether or not his coffin hid anything; when officials peered into his open grave the next day, there was no treasure to behold. Since then, a solid slab of granite has been laid across the top of his grave.

ALFRED HITCHCOCK
AUGUST 13, 1899 – APRIL 29, 1980

In 1919 Alfred Hitchcock joined London's Paramount studio as a lowly title designer, but he quickly moved up the ranks. Within six years he was directing and, over the course of the next 50 years, Alfred spun a remarkably consistent thread of suspense-thrillers, a genre he virtually invented. He deftly wove sex and humor into his stories in a steady demonstration of the eternal symmetry of good and evil and, as a brilliant technician, he developed a stock of subtle techniques and clever camera tricks that inspired his contemporaries and all who came after.

Just a year after his 1925 directorial debut, he launched his breakthrough film, *The Lodger,* a prototypical example of the classic Hitchcock plot: An innocent protagonist is falsely accused of a crime and becomes involved in a web of intrigue. This was also the first film in which he appeared as an extra. Such cameo roles would later become another of his trademarks, and spotting him would become a passion among fans. In his first "talkie," *Blackmail,* in 1929, he introduced a "selective sound" technique; a young woman's anxiety was emphasized by gradually distorting all but the word "knife" in a scene with her neighbor. In *Murder!,* released the following year, he first made explicit the link between sex and violence. Through the remainder of the 1930s, Alfred was the leading director in Britain and garnered international acclaim as well for a series of spy thrillers, including *The Man Who Knew Too Much.*

In 1939, he moved to Hollywood where he continued his prodigious output: *Notorious, Shadow of a Doubt, Spellbound* and *Lifeboat* exemplify his work of the next decade. The 1950s however, turned out to be Hitchcock's decade of personal inspiration and his three masterpieces of that period, *Rear Window, Vertigo,* and *North by Northwest,* lifted the typical manifestations of evil to a new plane. Employing subtle male-female relationships, witty symbolism, and dramatic film techniques and scores, he expanded classic Hitchcock to something sleeker and faster-paced and, ultimately, more entertaining. By contrast, 1960's *Psycho,* which has been held aloft as a classic of shot selection and editing, may have, in the end, only served to inspire the slasher genre.

Though Alfred seems to have had a few favorite actors—Cary Grant, Grace Kelly, James Stewart—he was also famous for his general disregard for the acting profession, and when his celebrated comment, "Actors are cattle," stirred up protest, he issued a correction and said, "I have been misquoted, what I really said is: Actors should be treated as cattle." Not surprisingly, performers weren't very enamored with him either. His meticulous planning of every shot and complete refusal to improvise or deviate from his shooting schedule ruffled plenty of feathers, but complaints to studio heads always fell on deaf ears; the strength of Hitchcock's directorial feats and his popularity guaranteed him the last word.

Though he was nominated for an Academy Award on six different occasions, he never won one. Instead, in a gesture that seemed prompted by the common knowledge that his time was drawing near, Hitchcock received a Lifetime Achievement award six months before his death.

Severely arthritic and suffering from kidney failure for a year, Alfred expired of heart failure at 80.

He was cremated and his ashes were scattered, though no one seems to know where.

ROCK HUDSON

NOVEMBER 17, 1925 – OCTOBER 2, 1985

After a stint in the Navy during World War II, Roy Harold Scherer, Jr., worked as a vacuum cleaner salesman and a truckdriver in Hollywood while awaiting his big break. It arrived in 1948 when he was offered a role in the film *Fighter Squadron*, and Roy, never one to squander an opportunity, delivered his one line flawlessly after just 38 takes. His effort went uncredited.

After his agent persuaded him to have his teeth capped and change his name to Rock Hudson, he appeared in dozens of films during the 1950s, most notably alongside James Dean and Elizabeth Taylor in *Giant*, but Rock's defining role came opposite Doris Day in the following decade. The pair starred in a series of comedies with suggestive titles like *Pillow Talk* and *Lover Come Back*, Rock epitomizing the comely and charismatic, perpetually aroused ladies' man, while Doris flustered as a professional virgin. In 1966 he starred in *Seconds*, a psychological thriller that was panned at the time but has since become a cult classic.

For decades, females fawned over Rock's rock-solid good looks, fabulous physique, and imperial grace, but Rock obliged only one time, marrying his agent's secretary in 1955 and divorcing her three years later. He afterwards engaged only in the most private of trysts and, in 1984, Rock seemed to confirm 30-year-old suspicions that he was a homosexual when he announced he was dying of AIDS, a disease that, up to that point, was mostly limited to the gay community.

The following year, at his death at 59, Rock became the first public casualty of the disease. He had no immediate survivors, but a lover, Marc Christian, successfully sued his estate for $14.5 million in actual damages on the grounds that Rock had kept his AIDS diagnosis a secret and caused him "enhanced fear" that he might contract AIDS. In 1989, Christian, who was never diagnosed with the disease, was awarded an additional $14.5 million in punitive damages.

Rock was cremated and his ashes scattered along the Pacific Coast, but ten years later friends honored his memory by having his name inscribed in the Tower of Memories at the Palm Springs Mortuary and Mausoleum in Cathedral City, California.

CEMETERY DIRECTIONS: From I-10, take the Ramon Road exit and proceed south for two miles to Da Vall Drive. Turn left, make a quick right into Palm Springs Mortuary, and park in the office lot on the left.

GRAVE DIRECTIONS: Walk back across the lane that you just drove in on, proceed past the fountain, and on the right is the Tower of Memories, just before the rest rooms. There's a checkerboard pattern of tiles on this wall and Rock's name is engraved on the tile that's third from the top and third from the left.

I LOVE LUCY

Desi Arnaz and Lucille Ball created the situation comedy *I Love Lucy* in 1951 and the show quickly achieved unprecedented popularity. The program featured Lucille's antics as Lucy, the wacky, high-spirited wife of a struggling Cuban bandleader named Ricky Ricardo, played by Desi. Meanwhile, their good-natured landlords and best friends, Fred and Ethel Mertz, played by William Frawley and Vivian Vance, came along for the laughs. Every Monday night during its six-year run, millions of people across America gathered in front of what was usually the first television set in the house to watch their continuing comedic adventures.

Desi and Lucy weren't just a couple onscreen, they were married in real life as well. In 1953 when Lucy Ricardo was seen going to the hospital to give birth to "Little Ricky" (who was actually Lucille's real son, Desi Arnaz, Jr.), it was a sort of national occasion. Nonetheless, all things must pass and, after illuminating the direction for years of future television programs, *I Love Lucy* ended its run in 1957, only to begin a new run of worldwide syndication that shows no sign of ending anytime soon.

Desi Arnaz

MARCH 2, 1917 – DECEMBER 2, 1986

Lucille Ball

AUGUST 6, 1911 – APRIL 26, 1989

Though married just twenty years, the lives of Desi Arnaz and Lucille Ball are inextricably linked. After marrying in 1940, they continued their own careers; Lucy was in radio and "B" movies, while Desi was a touring big-band musician. With Desi constantly on the road, the marriage was problematic from the beginning and when CBS proposed that Lucy take her popular radio program, *My Favorite Husband,* to the new medium of television, she saw a chance to save their failing marriage and agreed to the program on the condition that Desi play her husband.

CBS agreed but balked at their next demand: Lucy and Desi proposed filming their show and then beaming it to audiences at a later time. In 1951, before the perfection of videotape, nearly all television shows were live productions, fed from the East Coast because of time-zone differences. CBS agreed to their proposal on the condition they take salary cuts to cover the increased expenses, and Lucy and Desi granted that concession providing Desilu, a company they'd created, would own the programs after the initial broadcast. A few years later, the couple sold the films back to CBS for more than four million dollars, a sum that provided the economic base for building what became the powerful Desilu production empire.

The couple divorced three years after *I Love Lucy* ended and, after Lucy bought Desi's half of Desilu for three million dollars, he soon retired to gambling and alcohol and only rarely made public appearances again. But Lucy wasted no time: She reformatted the old show into a new series called *The Lucy Show* and later, *Here's Lucy,* which ran on prime time through 1974.

In 1986, at 69, Desi Arnaz died of lung cancer at his home in Del Mar, California. He was cremated, his ashes reportedly scattered.

A week after undergoing open-heart surgery in 1989, Lucy suffered a ruptured aorta and died at 77. She was cremated and her ashes are interred at Lakeview Cemetery in Jamestown, New York.

CEMETERY DIRECTIONS: From I-86, take Exit 12 and follow Route 60 south for a half-mile to Buffalo Street. Turn left onto Buffalo, and the cemetery is immediately on the left.

GRAVE DIRECTIONS: Drive straight into the cemetery and after a couple hundred yards, turn right and go up the hill. Across the drive from the grand Sheldon monument, Lucille's grave is in the grass at the tree shaded Hunt plot. At the time of this writing she has no marker of her own, but she's planted right next to her father, Henry Ball.

William Frawley

FEBRUARY 26, 1887 – MARCH 3, 1966

Originally a vaudeville and then Broadway stage actor, William Frawley was later known for playing supporting roles, usually as a gruff but likeable character, in over 100 films. Because of a reputation as a hard drinker, his contract with *I Love Lucy* stipulated that he'd be fired if he had more than three days of unexplained absence or if he ever showed up drunk. Bill agreed to the stipulation and for $350 a week joined the cast as landlord Fred Mertz.

Offscreen, Bill made no bones about his dislike for Vivian Vance, who played his on-screen wife, Ethel, once remarking, "She's one of the finest gals to come out of Kansas, and I often wish she'd go back there." Likewise, Vivian often expressed her disgust at having to play opposite a curmudgeon who was 25 years her senior.

After *I Love Lucy* went off the air, Bill appeared as Bub the housekeeper on *My Three Sons*. In 1966, he suffered a heart attack while walking down Hollywood Boulevard and, a few minutes later, died in the lobby of a nearby hotel.

At 79, Bill was buried at San Fernando Mission Cemetery in Mission Hills, California.

CEMETERY DIRECTIONS: Just south of where I-405 splits from I-5, take the Rinaldi Street exit off of I-405 to Sepulveda Boulevard south. You'll immediately see the cemetery. The entrance is accessed by making the left onto Stranwood Avenue.

GRAVE DIRECTIONS: Enter the cemetery, turn left and stop where you see a statue of Jesus on the lawn to the right. Here, five rows from the curb, is Bill's grave.

Vivian Vance

JULY 26, 1912 – AUGUST 17, 1979

In the summer of 1951 Vivian Vance was a stage actress at the La Jolla Playhouse. At the urging of *I Love Lucy*'s director, Desi went to see her performance and, after the show, she was cast as

Ethel Mertz, the Ricardos' landlady and Lucy's best friend. After *I Love Lucy*, she joined Lucy as Vivian, not Ethel, on *The Lucy Show* for three seasons and later retired to Connecticut.

In 1979 Vivian succumbed to bone cancer at 67. She was cremated and her ashes scattered by family and friends.

BORIS KARLOFF

NOVEMBER 23, 1887 – FEBRUARY 2, 1969

Born the son of a wealthy British diplomat, Boris Karloff enjoyed the privileges customary to the family of an agent of the Crown in late Victorian England. His childhood included private schooling, exposure to art and theater, extensive travel and, finally, enrollment at London University in preparation of a career in his country's foreign service. But at 21, Boris promptly abandoned the aristocracy and eloped with the first of his five wives to Canada.

To support himself, Boris worked as a farm laborer in Ontario and joined a touring theater company. Though he became known as a skilled character actor, often donning heavy makeup and playing men many years older, he was divorced and penniless at 30 and left to find work in Hollywood. Boris had fantastic success working in Hollywood—in a dozen years he made eighty film appearances—but the quantity of work dwarfed both his monetary compensation and critical recognition for all the effort.

Finally, in 1931 Bela Lugosi refused to take a role in which he would have his face hidden by makeup and have no lines, the role of the creature in *Frankenstein*, and so the part went to Boris, who had no vanity or misgivings about his work in the horror genre. The picture became a classic and 70 years later, Boris's is the only name readily associated with it, though he was not even credited in the original release, receiving just a question mark.

Over the next 25 years Boris reigned as the King of Horror and made countless movies in that vein—in his career he had more than 200 film credits—but by the late 1950s he abandoned the hectic pace as his health faltered. Still, he didn't give up making movies entirely and, in the last decade of his life, though he suffered from severe emphysema and was forced to use a wheelchair and an oxygen mask between scenes, his appearance remained familiar to television viewers and moviegoers.

At 81, Boris died at his home from complications of his emphysema. He was cremated and his ashes buried in the Garden of Remembrance at Mount Cemetery, which sits high on a hill above

Guildford, England. Guildford is a quaint borough located about 45 minutes southwest of London.

ANDY KAUFMAN

JANUARY 17, 1949 – MAY 16, 1984

After scoring a zero on the draft board's psychology test, resulting in a 4-F deferment, Andy Kaufman pursued a career as a comedian of the most unorthodox variety. His act tested the audience's discomfort threshold and during performances he alternately read passages from *The Great Gatsby*, ate potatoes, sang religious songs, and even took an extended onstage nap. Nonetheless, Andy's mainstream potential became evident in 1975 when his "foreign guy" character was showcased on *Saturday Night Live*'s inaugural broadcast. The heavily accented, nonsensical character was the genesis of Latka Gravas, a goofy Latvian mechanic, and beginning in 1978 Andy played him to the hilt during the hit television show *Taxi*'s five-year run.

Andy was a frequent guest player on *Saturday Night Live* but his bizarre offstage antics eventually alienated fans and in a November 1982 phone-in poll, he was voted off the show by viewers, 195,544 to 169,186. The conflict had arisen after Andy took the show's humorous Inter-Gender Wrestling Champion role to a bizarre extreme and turned it into his own alter-ego on the professional wrestling circuit. In the guise, Andy lobbed insults at the audience and baited women with a $1,000 prize if one were able to pin him. More than 60 accepted the challenge, and Andy won all the bouts, but the dirty fights garnered him few allies. In this time spent out of his element, Andy somehow developed a weird vendetta against pro-wrestler Jerry Lawler, and the whole grotesque affair promptly ended after Jerry pile-drove Andy into the hospital with a damaged cervical vertebrae.

In November 1983 Andy developed a nagging and hacking cough. After it persisted, then worsened, he was subjected to a battery of medical tests and it was finally determined that he had a rare, large-cell carcinoma in his lungs. The cancer was in its advanced stages, inoperable and incurable. Andy had never smoked and he was a strict health-food fanatic, so when this news became public, many believed that the whole thing was another cleverly crafted performance piece. The news was all too real for Andy, though, and in a search for a magic cure, he even traveled to the Philippines for help from shamans.

But Andy eventually succumbed to the cancer and, because faking his own death seemed to be the apotheosis of his bad taste, some arrived at his funeral expecting a reception from him in one or another of his personas. But instead, they found Andy's lifeless body and, hoping that this was his strangest put-on of all, many poked him when they thought no one was looking to be certain that he really was gone.

At 35, Andy was buried at Beth David Cemetery in Elmont, New York.

CEMETERY DIRECTIONS: Elmont is on the very western edge of Long Island, just east of Queens. From the Belt Parkway, take Exit 26B and follow Route 24 east for a mile. Turn south on Elmont Road and the cemetery is a half-mile on the left.

GRAVE DIRECTIONS: Enter the cemetery and go past the office. Make a right onto Lincoln Avenue, then turn left onto Brandeis Avenue. At Autumn Avenue turn right and stop at its end. The Kaufman plot is just to the left.

SAM KINISON

DECEMBER 8, 1953 – APRIL 10, 1992

Sam Kinison was a high-flying, patently outrageous performer who was simultaneously loved and hated from the time he found success as a comedian in 1985 with an appearance in Rodney Dangerfield's *Back to School* until his death seven years later. On one side of the fence, gays, feminists, and conservatives howled in protest against Sam's poisonously rude and bitter jokes, while an adoring legion of equally vocal fans thrilled at his shocking, high-decibel outbursts. Often appearing in a trademark beret and over-coat, the former Pentecostal preacher's pitch-black routines, delivered in loud-mouthed, wildman style, were surpassed only by his real-life offstage excesses. An avid substance abuser, Sam lived a reckless life filled with drugs, alcohol, women, and controversy.

By 1992 though, Sam had revamped his comedy act to direct it toward a more lucrative mainstream television audience. He made frequent appearances on *Saturday Night Live, In Living Color,* and even played a starring role as Charlie Hoover on the short-lived sit-com of the same name. It was ironic then that, after years of hard partying followed by a renewed commitment to cleaning up his abusive habits, Sam was killed—while sober—in a traffic collision caused by a driver who had been drinking.

Having just returned from their Hawaii honeymoon, Sam and his new wife, Malika Souiri, a Las Vegas dancer, were traveling in Sam's new Pontiac Viper to a sold-out Friday evening show in Laughlin, Nevada. Meanwhile, in the other direction, two teenagers in a pickup truck littered with beer cans swerved into oncoming traffic near Needles, California. In the ensuing head-on impact, Sam met his demise. In the moments after the horrific crash, Sam seemed to be fine, according to his brother Bill, who witnessed the tragedy from his own car following behind. With relatively minor cuts on his face and forehead, Sam wrenched himself free of his mangled vehicle, but then lay down by the side of the road.

Sam's face had no color and he kept saying, "I don't want to die, I don't want to die." Bill cradled Sam's bleeding head in his arms while Sam had what seemed to be a conversation with somebody else. "But why?" Sam asked. It was like he was talking to somebody upstairs. "Then I heard him say, 'Okay okay, okay,' and the last 'okay' was so soft and at peace like whatever voice was talking to him gave him the right answer, and he just relaxed with it. He said it so sweet, like he was talking to someone he loved," Bill related.

Sam hadn't been wearing his seatbelt and an autopsy revealed that when Sam's body struck the steering wheel, his internals had decelerated so quickly that his aorta had been ripped from his heart. On the side of Highway 95, while his older brother comforted him helplessly, Sam died of a broken heart at 38.

Sam was buried in his family's plot at Memorial Park Gardens in Tulsa, Oklahoma.

CEMETERY DIRECTIONS: From I-44, take Exit 232 and follow Memorial Drive (Route 64) south for two miles to 51st Street. At this intersection you'll see the cemetery on your left.

GRAVE DIRECTIONS: Enter the cemetery and follow the yellow line that's painted on the main drive to the chapel. Once at the chapel, you'll see the Lakeside Mausoleum off to your right, in front of which is Section 28, Garden of the Apostles, where Sam is buried.

Section 28 is divided into quadrants by four walkways, and the Kinison plot is in the southeast quadrant. (When standing in Section 28 and looking at the mausoleum, north is to your left, so the southeast is to your right front). Within the southeast quadrant, Sam's grave is seven rows east of the walk and about two-thirds of the way north.

The grave location sounds confusing (there are few landmarks to use for orientation), but once at Section 28, the directions will be clearer.

CHARLES KURALT
SEPTEMBER 10, 1934 – JULY 4, 1997

At 25, Charles Kuralt was CBS's youngest-ever correspondent, and during the 1960s he cut his teeth on such choice assignments as Vietnam and Latin America, covering stories for which most hard-nosed reporters yearned. But, weary of hawks and doves, after just eight years Charles turned his attention to his own country and took to the road in a quest to tell the story of Smalltown, U.S.A. Eventually his poetic storytelling and curiosity led to the creation of "On the Road," a leisurely TV news magazine that followed his travels.

As television's Everyman, he was gifted with the ability to see poetry where others saw the prosaic, ferreting out the stories from a motor home and logging up to 50,000 miles a year. Charles got the ideas for his quirky vignettes from viewers, or he found the items himself in snippets buried in rural newspapers. He was genuinely interested in the people he profiled, even the kookiest, and spoke with them without the slightest hint of condescension.

The balding and pudgy reporter was anything but intimidating and the persona helped him get to the heart of such stories as a high school basketball team that lost 127 straight games and a gas station that doubled as a poetry factory. Charles interviewed a country-song-singing dentist, a 93-year-old bricklayer, and a paraplegic auto mechanic. From unicyclists and professional wrestlers to lumberjacks, whittlers, and horse traders, Charles' stories celebrated America and its everyday people.

Too, Charles' patriotic love of America was readily apparent and, when he passed away at 62 of complications of lupus, it was fitting that he departed on the Fourth of July.

But after Charles' death, it emerged that the best oddball story might have been one he never told. For 29 years while his wife remained at their home in the concrete canyons of New York City, Charles maintained a second family in the wild canyons of Montana. He had met Patricia Shannon, the woman of his dreams, just a year after starting his *On the Road* travels, and he visited for two or three days every few weeks. He bought Shannon a $50,000 cottage in Ireland, put her children through college, gave her $400,000 to start a London business, and together they purchased acreage and a cabin along the Big Hole River and backpacked in the neighboring mountains.

Charles' infidelity came to light when Shannon instigated a court action against Charles' legal wife, Suzanna Kuralt, claiming that Charles had intended for her to keep a second Montana property. Suzanna died in October 1999 (and is faithfully buried alongside Charles) but Charles' daughters continued the court battle, which they lost in December 2000. Adding insult to injury, a judge ruled in 2002 that the daughters were required to pay the estate taxes on the second Shannon property, even though it was ultimately awarded to Shannon.

Charles, dead at 62, and Suzanna are buried at the Old Chapel Hill Cemetery, on the campus of the University of North Carolina in Chapel Hill, North Carolina.

CEMETERY DIRECTIONS: From I-40, take Exit 266 and follow Route 86 south. After 4½ miles the road will divide into two one-way streets. At this point, turn left onto Cameron Avenue and then make a right onto Raleigh Street. At the next intersection, turn left onto South Road and the cemetery is a short distance on the left.

GRAVE DIRECTIONS: Enter the cemetery at the third entrance and walk 50 yards up the path. You'll see the Kuralt plot on the left.

BRUCE &
BRANDON LEE

Bruce Lee

NOVEMBER 27, 1940 – JULY 20, 1973

Brandon Lee

FEBRUARY 1, 1965 – MARCH 31, 1993

While his parents were visiting the States, Li Jun Fan was born in San Francisco and, after claiming his American birth certificate, the happy family returned to Hong Kong. Obsessed with martial arts and bodybuilding, Li spent his adolescence turning his small body into a weapon and he appeared as a child actor in twenty movies. As he approached eighteen, his mother shipped him back stateside to keep him from fraternizing with his violent gang buddies and, after taking the name Bruce Lee, he got a job teaching the Wing Chun style of martial arts in Seattle. In 1964, at the first major American demonstration of kung fu, Bruce, an unknown, decimated his competitors and recast the martial arts culture.

After landing a role as Kato in the television series *The Green Hornet*, he attracted students like Steve McQueen and Kareem Abdul-Jabbar. By 1968 he had become the patron saint for the era's cult-of-the-body devotees; Bruce took vitamins and steroids, tortured himself with isometrics, experimented with electrical muscle stimulation, brewed ginseng teas, ate raw eggs, and drank beef blood. But despite his readiness to promote and embrace all that was American, Hollywood wouldn't embrace him, and Bruce soon returned to Hong Kong to make films.

By 1973 Bruce had made three kung fu flicks, *The Big Boss*, *Fists of Fury*, and *Way of the Dragon*, which, played back-to-back, can almost be mistaken for a single, eternally long exhibition of spin-kicks and flying leaps. On this side of the Pacific the films were roundly panned. One critic wrote that they make "the worst Italian western look like the most noble achievement of cinema," but they set box-office records in Asia, and Hollywood approached Bruce for a strictly American version.

Lest the producers change their minds Bruce cobbled together *Enter the Dragon* in a couple of months featuring the same tired sequences; a few dozen enemies attacked Bruce only to die as soon as he karate-chopped them. But three weeks before the film opened, Bruce died in Hong Kong at the apartment of actress Betty Ting Pei, who had a role in his next movie, *Game of Death*, which they were then filming. Bruce was at her apartment "discussing the script," as the story was later spun, and after he complained of a headache, Betty gave him a prescription painkiller, Equagesic. Bruce went to lie down in the bedroom, Betty was later unable to rouse him, and he died at the hospital later that night.

The coroner determined that Bruce had died of a "cerebral edema," a brain aneurysm, possibly prompted by an allergic reaction to the Equagesic. But of course Bruce's fans would have none of this. It was impossible for superhumans of Bruce's ilk to drop dead from a mere allergic reaction, or even an aneurysm, for that matter, and it was obvious, to them anyway, that his death was the result of some conspiracy. A choice motive was that Bruce had been murdered for flouting his traditional ancestors and giving away ancient fighting secrets to Westerners. For this, Bruce had been killed either by an undetectable Oriental poison or, by "the vibrating hand," a mysterious death touch that kills two years after it's applied.

In any event, at 32, Bruce was buried at Lakeview Cemetery in Seattle, Washington and, 25 years later, his son Brandon met his own peculiar end.

Following in his father's footsteps, Brandon became a player in martial arts films, though by the time Brandon surfaced the genre had matured into a form that even viewers who weren't karate-chop aficionados could enjoy. His first role was in 1986's *Kung Fu: The Movie* and, after a handful of similar roles, filming for *The Crow* began in 1993.

A particular scene in that movie called for Brandon to be shot. The scene began and actor Michael Masee fired a gun containing a dummy bullet at Brandon, who collapsed to the floor exactly as the scene specified. But as the other actors continued playing out the remainder of the scene, it became apparent that Brandon's writhing on the floor was more than an act. Brandon really had been shot and he died of his wound the next day.

After an investigation, the accident was determined to have unfolded this way: For an earlier close-up scene that required the gun to be filmed being loaded, the gun was loaded with a dummy bullet. That is, the bullet had a slug (a projectile) for visual effect, but the bullet's casing had no gunpowder. However, when that dummy was taken out of the gun, its slug was dislodged from its casing, and the slug remained unnoticed within the gun's firing chamber. Next, a different kind of dummy bullet, the exact opposite of the previous dummy, was put into the firing chamber. This dummy bullet consisted only of a casing holding gunpowder for sound effect—it had no slug. The gunpowder of the second dummy bullet propelled the slug left behind by the first dummy bullet and, in effect, the two dummies conspired to produce one very smart, lethal bullet.

At 28, Brandon was buried alongside his father in Seattle.

CEMETERY DIRECTIONS: From I-5, take Exit 165 to Madison Street and head east for a mile to 15th Avenue. Turn left on 15th and the cemetery is 1½ miles on the left.

GRAVE DIRECTIONS: Enter the cemetery and go to the top of the hill, where there is a circular road. Near this road's curb, on the side closer to the entrance, is the Lee plot.

VIVIEN LEIGH
NOVEMBER 5, 1913 – JULY 7, 1967

In 1937 producer David Selznick began searching for an actress to play the part of the impetuous Southern belle, Scarlett O'Hara, in the film adaptation of Margaret Mitchell's epic love story, *Gone With the Wind.* After passing on hundreds of starry hopefuls, including Katharine Hepburn, Bette Davis, and Joan Crawford, Selznick became so frustrated that he started filming without a Scarlett. At the same time, the doe-eyed, British sweetheart Vivien Leigh was campaigning across town for the role of Cathy in *Wuthering Heights,* opposite leading man Laurence Olivier, with whom she was carrying on an affair. But Vivien was turned down for the role because she was unknown in America at the time. It became the ultimate irony that Vivien was instead cast as Scarlett O'Hara in *Gone With the Wind,* which premiered alongside *Wuthering Heights,* and completely eclipsed it at the Academy Awards for 1939. Upon *GWTW*'s premiere in January 1940, Vivien became America's newest darling and captured the Academy Award for Best Actress.

It was also in 1940 that Vivien and Laurence married, after they left their respective spouses. The couple acted together on stage and film but, after miscarrying in 1944 and battling tuberculosis in 1945, Vivien became manic-depressive and their marriage became strained. As was customary for those times, Vivien underwent electroshock therapy to ease her depression, but the treatment seemed only to worsen her condition.

Because of her illnesses, Vivien appeared in only a handful of film and stage productions after *Gone With the Wind*. In 1951 she appeared on Broadway as Cleopatra in two separate shows, alternating nightly (Shakespeare's *Antony and Cleopatra* and George Bernard Shaw's *Caesar and Cleopatra*). But Vivien's best-received work was in film, particularly *A Streetcar Named Desire*, in which she played another Southern belle, the aging Blanche DuBois, a touching role in light of Vivien's own deteriorating mental health. For this she earned a second Academy Award.

Vivien never really shook the tuberculosis, and it plagued her repeatedly, recurring to varying degrees for the remainder of her life. By 1960, when Laurence was long gone, her condition had substantially worsened and she developed a persistent, hacking cough. But even then, perhaps due to the breakup of her marriage, Vivien tried to rejuvenate her stage career. Her illness, however, changed her from the Scarlett O'Hara audiences expected to see, and her coughing prompted numerous absences. In May 1967, Vivien suddenly began to lose weight and cough up blood. Her tuberculosis had advanced considerably and she was ordered on bed rest. Finally, Vivien was found on her bedroom floor, dead of the disease that had drowned her lungs in fluid.

At 53, Vivien was cremated and her ashes scattered over the waters of the mill pond at her estate, Tickerage, outside of London in Blackboys, England.

JACK LEMMON

FEBRUARY 8, 1925 – JUNE 27, 2001

John Uhler Lemmon III was born in an elevator; his mother went into labor during a bridge match and the closest she got to the delivery room was the hospital lift. Jack's father had high hopes that his anxious progeny would follow him into the doughnut business, but Jack was more interested in "the theayatuh," as he called it.

After a stint in the Navy, he graduated from Harvard University in 1947, and immediately took off for the bright lights of New York, where he supported himself mainly by playing piano in a local saloon. Seven years later Jack nabbed his first Hollywood role in *It Should Happen to You* and, after an exceedingly steep learning curve, he played the anxious-to-please Frank Pulver in *Mister Roberts* the next year and won the Oscar, firmly establishing his career. Next came a string of fifteen comedies, including *Some Like It Hot* and *The Apartment*, but Jack ached to show what he could really do and, in 1962, he did; after his harrowing portrayal of an anguished, alcoholic husband in 1962's *Days of Wine and Roses*, roles were Jack's to pick and choose.

Though fans still seemed to love him most in comedic romps as one or another neurotic in anxious conflict with his better instinct, Jack's style matured and he particularly found his center in 1973 when he portrayed the desperately cornered garment maker, Harry Stoner, in *Save the Tiger*. After Jack played the lead in *The China Syndrome* in 1979, he was universally admired. After he nailed the part of the washed-up real-estate hotshot Shelly "The Machine" Levine in the brilliantly dark *Glengarry Glen Ross*, he became a vivid and permanent part of American pop culture.

Jack's vulnerability and wounded grace mirrored an uneasy generation's passage from eager upward mobility to embittered confusion borne of age and social upheaval. His public identified with his dubious characters that crossed the line, and it's hard to find anyone who flatly disliked him. His biographer summed it up nicely: "Everybody likes Jack. Attacking him would be like pulling a chair out from under your mother."

Of complications from cancer, Jack died at 76 in the company of his family.

He was buried at Westwood Memorial Park in Santa Monica, California.

CEMETERY DIRECTIONS: This little cemetery holds numerous celebrities and is peculiarly located behind the office complex at 10850 Wilshire Blvd., just about a half-mile east of I-405.

GRAVE DIRECTIONS: Enter the cemetery, turn left at the office and, just after the chapel on the right, you'll see Jack's stone along the drive.

THE LONE RANGER
& TONTO

Clayton Moore

SEPTEMBER 14, 1914 – DECEMBER 28, 1999

Jay Silverheels

MAY 26, 1918 – MARCH 5, 1980

Clayton Moore and Jay Silverheels are infinitely better-known by their on-screen names: the Lone Ranger and Tonto from the long-running television series, *The Lone Ranger*. The show debuted in 1949 as a descendant of a hit radio program of the same name, and it was one of the first shows to be filmed exclusively for television. Its premise was that the Lone Ranger was the sole Texas Ranger to survive an ambush by the vicious Hole-in-the-Wall gang. With his identity protected by a mask and his loyal American-Indian sidekick Tonto by his side, the Lone Ranger exhibited unparalleled integrity and bravery as a maverick ridding the Old West of its outlaws.

Clayton hailed from Illinois and was offered the lead role after a stint as a high-flying aerialist in a circus troupe and working his way through the acting ranks into afternoon serials. Jay also had an athletic background; the full-blooded Mohawk Indian from Ontario had been a runner-up Golden Gloves boxing champion and played on the Canadian national lacrosse team. Upon landing in Hollywood in 1938, he secured work as a stuntman and extra, most of his roles earning him credit solely as "Indian."

The Lone Ranger ran for eight years and after its 1957 cancellation, Jay made occasional film appearances until he died of a heart attack in 1980, at 61. He was cremated and his ashes spread over the Six Nations of the Grand River Reserve near Brantford, Ontario.

Clayton never really gave up the role of the Lone Ranger when the series was cancelled. For the rest of his days, Clayton thrived on a self-made Lone Ranger cottage industry, making countless appearances in the famous black mask championing the TV character's merits. In 1975, Jack Wrather, who actually owned the Lone Ranger rights, sued to prevent Clayton from making such personal appearances because a new Lone Ranger feature movie was in the works and Clayton no longer personified the youthful hero. In a court compromise, Clayton was forbidden from wearing the mask and he instead resorted to equally ridiculous mask-like sunglasses. The movie bombed and ten years later, Clayton went back to wearing the real trademark mask.

In 1999, Clayton died of a heart attack at 85 and was buried at Forest Lawn Memorial Park in Glendale, California.

CEMETERY DIRECTIONS: From Highway 2, take the San Fernando Road exit and turn northwest. After a mile, make a right onto Glendale Avenue and the park's entrance is immediately on the right.

GRAVE DIRECTIONS: Get a map at the information booth and proceed to the area of the Freedom Mausoleum. In front of the mausoleum is the walled Garden of Everlasting Peace. Walk into this garden and you'll find Clayton's grave in the top row of the big grass area in front of the Morgenroth statue.

BELA LUGOSI
OCTOBER 20, 1882 – AUGUST 16, 1956

Bela Lugosi was a serious and successful stage actor in his native Hungary for almost two decades before he moved to America in pursuit of a silent film career. In 1927, Bela garnered the lead in the Broadway production of *Dracula*, and three years later, Universal Pictures bought the rights. As the first huge horror hit of the sound era, the film *Dracula* was an instant sensation and the role made Bela, with his black cape, dark menacing eyes, and velvet voice, a star.

The next year Bela passed up an offer to play the lead role in *Frankenstein* and, unwittingly, gave Boris Karloff his big chance. From then on, the two actors were rivals for the public's attention as heir to the horror genre throne that had been vacated with the passing of Lon Chaney. Over the next twenty years, Bela appeared in dozens of horror films, from *White Zombie* to *Abbott and Costello Meet Frankenstein*. While plenty of them had very questionable scripts, others were just downright awful.

In the mid-1950s, when Bela's morphine addiction had kicked into overdrive and Hollywood wanted nothing to do with the 70-something-year-old has-been, he met up with the transvestite schlock director Edward D. Wood, Jr., who today is ignobly known as the worst director of all time. Bela appeared in several of Wood's films, including 1955's *Bride of the Monster*, but after Bela's death, Wood cobbled together miscellaneous footage and made the worst film of all time, *Plan 9 from Outer Space*. For scenes in which Wood was unable to find pertinent footage of Bela, he employed his wife as Bela's double, her face completely obscured by the ridiculous cape.

In his later years, Bela had become increasingly strange and began taking his horror image rather seriously. He often gave interviews while lying in a coffin. In April 1955 Bela committed himself to a hospital to kick his morphine addiction and left in August, supposedly clean as a whistle. But Bela's days were numbered anyway and, just a few months after marrying his fifth wife, he died of a heart attack—a wooden stake or silver bullet wasn't necessary after all.

Bela was buried at Holy Cross Cemetery in Culver City, California and, as he requested, he's wearing his Dracula cape. Not surprisingly, he died a pauper, but, supposedly, Frank Sinatra wrote a check to provide him a decent burial.

CEMETERY DIRECTIONS: From I-405, follow Slauson Avenue east for a half-mile and the cemetery is on the left at #5835.

GRAVE DIRECTIONS: Enter the cemetery, turn left and start up the hill. A hundred yards on the left is the Grotto lawn and altar and, four rows from the altar, is Bela's grave.

JAYNE MANSFIELD
APRIL 19, 1933 – JUNE 29, 1967

Jayne Mansfield took her place in Hollywood as a caricature of the blonde stereotype starlet. Though a married mother at just seventeen, she parlayed her 40-22-34 curves into bit television parts, but superstardom on the order of Marilyn Monroe was her real goal and much of her career was an unending campaign of self-promotion.

During one memorable ploy, Jayne was "stranded" on a desert island. But her most successful gimmick was a carefully designed scheme that unfolded at a press junket to promote a new Jane Russell film, *Underwater*. On that day she "fell" into the pool while sunbathing, causing her bathing suit strap to break. Upon coming up for air her endowment was captured by the scrambling press. "I worried about becoming famous first, then an actress," Jayne later confessed in an interview.

Though her stunts were successful to a degree—she eventually secured a contract with Warner Brothers—moviegoers never really went for Jayne's limited acting ability, and her resume is fleshed out with a string of flops. Her striking looks did help sell merchandise, however, and she promoted an array of products ranging from maple syrup to nylon sweaters to electric switches. Her ample proportions were not lost on *Playboy* magazine either, and Jayne was one of the first stars to take it off for the monthly.

Jayne later toured the country with a burlesque nightclub act that featured show tunes and comedic skits and climaxed with a striptease routine. In the early morning hours after she'd performed the act at the Gus Stevens Supper Club in Biloxi, Mississippi, Jayne and three of her children, plus her boyfriend and a driver, glided along a narrow country road (now Highway 90) on the way to New Orleans. The road became obscured by the white haze of a mosquito fogger and, unable to discern its presence, the twenty-year-old driver slammed the Buick Electra into and under the slow-moving truck. The three adults in the front seat were killed instantly, but Jayne's three children asleep in the back were spared serious injury.

After a blonde bouffant wig was photographed lying on the ground at the accident scene, it became contemporary lore that Jayne had been decapitated but, for the record, though her death was gruesome, she was not actually beheaded. Her death certificate notes

a "crushed skull with avulsion (forcible detachment) of cranium and brain," which in layman's terms means that her skull was cracked open and a piece of it and her brain were separated. Her "death car" has been exhibited in several far-flung museum collections.

At only 34, Jayne was buried at Fairview Cemetery in Pen Argyl, Pennsylvania.

CEMETERY DIRECTIONS: From Route 33, take Route 512 north to Pen Argyl. At the third light, turn right onto South Main Street and the cemetery is a short distance past the town garage.

GRAVE DIRECTIONS: Enter the cemetery at the second entrance and go around the U-shaped drive. Two hundred feet before the stone pillared exit, you'll see Jayne's heart-shaped grave on the right.

WALTER MATTHAU
OCTOBER 1, 1920 – JULY 1, 2000

Graduating from high school during the Depression, Walter Matuchanskavasky took a series of government jobs—as a forester in Montana, a gym instructor for the WPA, a boxing coach for policemen—before enlisting in the Army Air Corps and serving as a radio cryptographer during World War II. One of the senior officers on the base was none other than Jimmy Stewart and, after sneaking in to watch Jimmy do a morning briefing, Walter decided that he wanted to become an actor.

After the war, Walter took some acting lessons and, after a stint on Broadway, by 1955 was sharing film credits with some of the great stars of the day including Burt Lancaster in *The Kentuckian* and Kirk Douglas in *Lonely Are the Brave.* But Walter really hit his stride in 1966 as an unscrupulous lawyer trying to win an insurance settlement opposite Jack Lemmon in *The Fortune Cookie,* for which he won an Oscar for best supporting actor.

That collaboration also marked the first of many memorable teamings with Lemmon. The duo, whose banter was as playful off-screen as on, worked together on some of Hollywood's funniest flicks, usually featuring Walter's character mercilessly tormenting Lemmon's. In addition to *Fortune Cookie,* the duo appeared in 1974's *The Front Page,* 1981's *Buddy, Buddy* and 1993's *Grumpy Old Men.* But their most memorable face-off was in the 1968 movie version of Neil Simon's classic *The Odd Couple,* with Walter playing the disheveled sportswriter Oscar Madison to Lemmon's anal-retentive Felix Unger.

"Every actor looks all his life for a part that will combine his talents with his personality," Walter once said. "*The Odd Couple* was mine. That was the plutonium I needed. It all started happening after that."

Despite professional triumphs, Walter faced trials in his personal life. He publicly admitted that his struggle with compulsive gambling had cost him an estimated $5 million over the years and he agreed with physicians that the strain of his gambling and heavy smoking had contributed to a heart attack suffered while filming *The Fortune Cookie* in 1966. Though he gave up his three-packs-per-day smoking habit, coronary bypass surgery came in 1976, he was hospitalized with double pneumonia in 1993, and in 1995 he underwent surgery to remove a non-malignant colon tumor. In typical form, Walter attributed his maladies to his bad eating habits: "If you eat only celery and lettuce, you won't get sick. ... I like celery and lettuce, but I like them with pickles, relish, corned beef, potatoes, peas. And I like Eskimo Pies."

Despite health issues, Walter continued to work steadily, playing his trademark codger, an irritable ailing father, in his final film, 2000's *Hanging Up*.

Following a heart attack, America's favorite grumpy old man died at 79.

He was buried at Westwood Memorial Park, Santa Monica, California.

CEMETERY DIRECTIONS: This little cemetery holds numerous celebrities and is peculiarly located behind the office complex at 10850 Wilshire Blvd., just about a half-mile east of I-405.

GRAVE DIRECTIONS: Enter the cemetery and turn left at the office. Pass the chapel, pass Jack Lemmon's grave and, on the right after a few more plots, you'll see Walter's stone along the drive.

SAL MINEO

JANUARY 10, 1939 – FEBRUARY 12, 1976

Sal Mineo became a teen idol after his breakout role in 1956's *Rebel Without a Cause*. By playing Plato, the switchblade-wielding juvenile delinquent cloaked in an aura of smoldering boyishness, Sal was transformed from a Bronx gang member and parochial-school dropout to an Academy Award nominee who received some 4,000 letters a week from adoring fans.

The next few years were lucrative for Sal; he had plenty of offers and appeared in numerous films, most notably *Exodus*, for which he was nominated for another Oscar. But once he matured from teen idol status, his best film offers were behind him and Sal was relegated to scraping out a living on stages in Los Angeles.

Late one evening after parking his car in the carport outside of his West Hollywood apartment, Sal was stabbed in the heart and, at 37, died on the sidewalk before the paramedics even arrived. With the absence of any apparent motive, the slaying went unsolved for two years until an inmate in a Michigan prison bragged that he'd killed Sal and that "it had been easy." In 1979 Lionel Williams was convicted and sentenced to fifty-one years.

Despite a barrage of tabloid theories that the motive for Sal's murder was everything from a bad drug deal to a homosexual lovers' quarrel, the reason behind the killing has never been established, and now it's generally believed Sal was just the victim of a robbery gone wrong.

Sal is buried at the Gate of Heaven Cemetery in Hawthorne, New York.

CEMETERY DIRECTIONS: From I-287, take Exit 4 and follow Route 100A north for 2½ miles (Route 100A will become Route 100 after 2 miles) to Lakeview Avenue and turn right. Follow Lakeview Avenue to its intersection with the Taconic State Parkway, turn left, and the Gate of Heaven Cemetery is a mile ahead on the left. Turn left onto Stevens Avenue, go over the railroad tracks, and make another left to enter.

GRAVE DIRECTIONS: Enter the cemetery, turn right and follow the main road up the hill. Bear left at the fork, make a right just before section two (toward the stone tower), then turn right again at the next drive. A couple hundred feet on the right, Sal's grave is marked with a flat stone in front of the Donofrio mausoleum.

MARILYN MONROE
JUNE 1, 1926 – AUGUST 5, 1962

The movies have lent a millennial shelf life to Marilyn Monroe's most perishable qualities of youth and beauty. Had she been born before the cameras rolled, she may have existed as only a Helen of Troy legend but, thanks to celluloid, her bumping and cooing will be here to greet the Second Coming. Media stars live forever, and Marilyn is their torchbearer.

Marilyn came into this life named Norma Jean, the daughter of a film cutter who flirted with insanity. Due to her mother's assorted delusions, Norma Jean spent most of her childhood in foster homes. At 16, when her then foster family planned to move and could not take her with them, they arranged for her to marry a family friend, the 21-year-old James Dougherty. Before James left to serve during World War II, he secured Norma Jean a job at Lockheed and she became part of the home-front war effort, working in a division that made target planes.

At some point, a magazine team visited the plant to take inspiring propaganda shots and a bright-eyed, curly haired, brunette named Norma Jean Dougherty soon found herself on the magazine's cover. She quit her job, had corrective dental work, went on a diet, and had her dark, wool-tight curls straightened and platinumed. She divorced her husband, who had been absent for almost the entirety of their marriage, and Norma Jean became a popular photographer's model, her likeness gracing pin-up posters, advertisements, and pulp magazine covers.

Encouraged by success, Norma Jean aimed for a career in motion pictures. Despite her lack of acting experience, she found work and bounced from studio to studio, filling out the visual landscape of lightweight comedic romps as the fresh-faced Marilyn Monroe. After nude calendar photos of her emerged, Marilyn's star-appeal soared and she participated full-bore in the promotion of her sex-symbol image. In 1953, she secured a place in media history when she graced the premier issue of *Playboy* magazine. That sensation propelled Marilyn to the stratosphere.

Marilyn laid bare her life and begged the public to love her, and they did. Movie studios competed for Hollywood's newest sex kitten, and the deals came in fast sequence. Predictably, Marilyn most often played the hopelessly irresistible home-wrecker or the warm-hearted floozy in a series of romantic farces whose titles, *The Seven-Year Itch, Gentlemen Prefer Blondes,* predicated the storylines. But, because she wasn't a trained actress, the improbabilities of her movies' plots perfectly complemented her provocative bravado. In other films, particularly 1959's acclaimed *Some Like It Hot,* in which she played the lovelorn singer Sugar Kane, Marilyn's patent grandiosity and inimitable breathy singing style made an indelible mark.

In contrast to her successful professional career, Marilyn's affairs were unsteady, to say the least. Three heavily flashbulbed marriages and divorces, including those to Yankee Clipper Joe DiMaggio and literary icon Arthur Miller, left her personal life a shambles, while tabloid tell-alls burst with abortions and off-duty trysts involving Frank Sinatra and multiple Kennedys. After her last two film releases flopped, a 30-something Marilyn must have wondered how much longer her sex-kitten status would last and, perhaps, she decided that stardom had become too much of a burden.

By August 1962, Marilyn was increasingly dependent on medication and was getting prescriptions from at least two doctors. Her housekeeper, Eunice Murray, had been sleeping at Marilyn's Brentwood home at the request of Marilyn's psychiatrist and, one evening, Eunice found Marilyn dead in bed. Though the coroner declared her death a suicide from ingestion of nearly fifty Nembutal sleeping pills, as well as a quantity of another sleeping potion, chloral hydrate, Marilyn's death has since been otherwise variously attributed to accidental overdose, political necessity, and a mob hit.

After more than 300 biographies, countless documentaries, and a postage stamp, the debate over the "real" Marilyn and her untimely death has yet to be resolved. Meanwhile, adoring fans cling to the memory of the beloved actress who may have gotten some of what she wanted but not all of what she needed.

Marilyn was laid to rest at Westwood Village Memorial Park in Santa Monica, California.

CEMETERY DIRECTIONS: This little cemetery holds numerous celebrities and is peculiarly located behind the office complex at 10850 Wilshire Blvd., just about a half-mile east of I-405.

GRAVE DIRECTIONS: As you stand in the cemetery yard and look toward the cemetery office, on your far left is a series of small rooms with crypts. Marilyn's crypt is several yards to the left of the Room of Prayer.

DUDLEY MOORE
APRIL 19, 1935 – MARCH 27, 2002

After leaving Oxford University in 1958, Dudley Moore performed as a cabaret pianist and toured widely before founding the Beyond The Fringe comedy revue with partner Peter Cook. The troupe's antics opened the door to television, which, in turn, led to a screen debut in *The Wrong Box* in 1966. Dudley wrote, starred in, and composed the score for his next film, *30 Is a Dangerous Age*, two years later.

In 1979 Dudley found a wider audience when he played a composer grappling with a midlife crisis in the hit movie *10* and, with his diminutive stature, he became one of Hollywood's most unlikely stars. Afterward he appeared in a string of comedies and is best remembered as the lovable, drunken playboy in the 1981 box-office smash, *Arthur*. Prompted by some fans to consider more serious fare, "Cuddly Dudley" once remarked, "I would love to do serious roles, but I'm just not built that way."

In the early 1990s Dudley seemed to become unreliable and began having trouble remembering lines. It was widely believed that he was spiraling downward due to alcoholism or a drug problem and in 1995, fed up with his inconsistency, Barbra Streisand fired him from the movie *The Mirror Has Two Faces*.

In 1997 Dudley had an extended hospital stay after a stroke and open-heart surgery, and it was then discovered that his erratic behavior didn't stem from substance abuse after all. Instead it had been caused by a rare and incurable condition called Progressive Supranuclear Palsy (PSP), similar to Parkinson's disease. In the last years of his life, the disease slowly robbed Dudley of his faculties; his vision became hazy, his motor control was impaired, and his speech slurred. Eventually, even swallowing became difficult.

At 66 Dudley died of pneumonia, a complication of PSP, and was buried at Hillside Cemetery in Scotch Plains, New Jersey.

CEMETERY DIRECTIONS: From I-78, take Exit 40 and follow Route 531 south for three miles to its intersection with Route 22. Turn east on Route 22 and, after three more miles, make a right onto Terrill Road. After a half-mile turn right onto South Avenue. After another half-mile make a left onto Woodland Avenue and then, two miles later, the cemetery is on the left.

GRAVE DIRECTIONS: Enter the cemetery and follow the signs to the office. Pass the office and bear left and shortly you'll see Section D-3 on your left. Drive to the end of this section and stop where you see the Wodrich stone. Dudley's grave is behind the Wodrich plot in what at the time of this writing is an unmarked plot.

AUDIE MURPHY
JUNE 20, 1924 – MAY 28, 1971

Audie Murphy was the most decorated American combat soldier of World War II. He received 28 medals, including the Medal of Honor and three Purple Hearts, and later parlayed his war-hero status into a Hollywood career.

But in deference to the untold millions who also dedicated themselves to that war, it's important to point out that Audie Murphy wasn't the bravest or most courageous—he was the most decorated.

He was exactly like everyone else who gallantly fought for his country but he lived to tell about it, unlike many of his fellow patriots, and he even gained celebrity from it. By that measure, then, we should say that Audie Murphy was a brave and courageous soldier, but if we wish to apply a superlative, then perhaps we should say only that he was the luckiest.

After the war, *Life* magazine ran a cover story on Audie's exploits and actor James Cagney became convinced that Audie's looks and persona, as well as his status as a war hero, could make him a star. Audie was invited to Hollywood and, after a few lean years, Cagney's hunch proved right and Audie's career took off. He eventually appeared in some 40 films. His earliest films were war movies but by the 1950s he moved from the genre, barely, and the majority of his roles were in Westerns.

Critics generally agree that Audie's best film performance was in Stephen Crane's Civil War epic, *The Red Badge of Courage*, but the most popular of his 44 films was his autobiographical *To Hell and Back*. The movie was so popular in fact, that after its release by Universal Pictures in 1955, that studio did not have a higher-grossing picture until 1975's blockbuster film *Jaws*.

With varying success, Audie branched into other arenas as well. Horse racing gained his attention, especially its gambling aspects, and he eventually became a racehorse owner and breeder. Remarkably, Audie also had a talent for songwriting, and his songs have been recorded by such renowned performers as Dean Martin, Charley Pride, and Roy Clark.

Plagued with insomnia and depression, Audie suffered from what is now called Post Traumatic Stress Disorder. The condition was then known as "battle fatigue," which implied that its effects would wear off with time and rest. But decades after WWII had ended, many veterans, including Audie, could find no respite. In his celebrity, Audie was candid about his battle-fatigue problems and made a public call for the United States government to study the emotional impact of war and to address its effects.

At 46, Audie and five others died when their plane crashed into the side of a mountain near Blacksburg, Virginia. Contrary to popular belief, Audie was not the pilot of that plane. Although he did hold a pilot's license and once owned his own plane, on that tragic day he was merely a passenger on a chartered flight.

Audie was buried at Arlington National Cemetery in Arlington, Virginia.

CEMETERY DIRECTIONS: Arlington National Cemetery is located on the west side of the Potomac River in Washington D.C. From any of the major highways, you can easily follow the signs to the visitor parking lots.

GRAVE DIRECTIONS: Get a map at the information booth and then walk to Memorial Drive. With the Tomb of the Unknown Soldier behind you, Audie's grave is in front of you in Section 13.

THE NELSONS

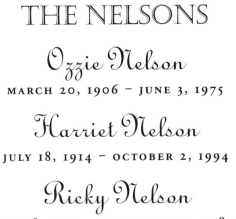

Ozzie Nelson
MARCH 20, 1906 – JUNE 3, 1975

Harriet Nelson
JULY 18, 1914 – OCTOBER 2, 1994

Ricky Nelson
MAY 8, 1940 – DECEMBER 31, 1985

In 1952 the eight-year-old radio program *The Adventures of Ozzie and Harriet* debuted as a television show and over the next fourteen seasons and 435 episodes, the Nelsons became America's ideal nuclear family. The most remarkable aspect of the slow-paced, light comedy was that the on-screen Nelson household was portrayed by the real-life Nelson family, which comprised the husband-and-wife team of Ozzie and Harriet, and their two sons, Ricky and David. Viewers especially took to the boys, who, before the viewers' very eyes, bloomed through pubescence, dated lucky teenage girls, and eventually married and had children of their own, all while the cameras kept rolling.

From his first appearance, the wisecracking kid brother, Ricky, was the show's most popular character, and his trademark line, "I don't mess around, boy," became a catch phrase. On a 1957 telecast, Ricky sang the popular Fats Domino hit "I'm Walkin'," which became a real-life million-seller, and Ricky began a new chapter of his career as America's first "teen idol," the phrase coined by *Life* magazine.

Ricky's new popularity was, of course, engendered by the show, but it turned out that he actually was possessed of some genuine talent. Over the next half-dozen years he had a number of teen-angst, rockabilly-flavored pop hits, including "Travelin' Man," "Lonesome Town," and "Hello, Mary Lou," but the Beatles soon stole Ricky's fans, and his career ebbed during the mid-sixties. Moving into a smoother form of country rock, in October 1971 he gigged a bill at Madison Square Garden with a number of other 1950s acts. But he was booed practically off the stage by a crowd that wanted to hear oldies; they didn't pay to see a longhaired, rockin' Ricky Nelson in bell-bottoms. Devastated, he reflected on the experience with a new track, "(I Went to a) Garden Party," which became a top-ten hit. Ricky's talents were ultimately legitimized in 1987 when he was inducted into the Rock 'n' Roll Hall of Fame, albeit posthumously.

In 1983 Ricky purchased a vintage DC-3 that had been previously owned by Jerry Lee Lewis, and was dubbed the "flying bus" because of its sluggishness and its propensity for mechanical failure. After leaving Alabama for a New Year's Eve concert in Dallas, Ricky, age 45, and his new fiancée (unfortunately for viewers, Ricky's divorce from his first wife had occurred after the TV series was cancelled) and four members of the Stone Canyon Band were killed when the plane caught fire and was forced to crash-land in DeKalb, Texas. Upon landing, the passengers were trapped by a fire that raced through the cabin, and they all perished in its flames, though the pilot and copilot managed to escape through the cockpit window. Early press reports suggested that drug usage, specifically the free-basing of cocaine, might have played a role in the airplane's fire, but the National Transportation Safety Board conclusively determined that the fire was caused by a malfunctioning gas heater.

After *The Adventures of Ozzie and Harriet* ended its run in 1966, Ozzie and Harriet retreated from the limelight and made only occasional benefit appearances. At 69, Ozzie died after a bout with cancer, and Harriet passed away at 80 of congestive heart failure.

Ozzie, Harriet, and Ricky are all buried at Forest Lawn Memorial Park in Hollywood Hills, California.

CEMETERY DIRECTIONS: From Highway 134, which is the connector between Highway 101 and I-210, take the Forest Lawn Drive exit. Proceed west for a mile and the park's entrance is on the left.

GRAVE DIRECTIONS: Get a map from the information booth and drive to the Revelation section. Across from where Crystal Lane intersects Evergreen Drive, walk up the grass hill and count thirteen rows to find Ozzie's and Harriet's markers. Ricky's marker is two rows further up the hill and it's engraved with his given name, Eric Hilliard Nelson.

CARROLL O'CONNOR

AUGUST 2, 1924 – JUNE 21, 2001

HUGH O'CONNOR

APRIL 7, 1962 – MARCH 28, 1995

In his early years, Carroll O'Connor slogged through stage acting roles and appeared in thirty films playing indistinguishable roles. In 1968 Carroll's break came when he was offered the lead role in an adaptation of the popular British program *'Til Death Do Us Part.* When the sitcom finally aired in 1971 as *All in the Family,* Carroll's portrayal of its intolerant, word-mangling, bigoted star helped change not only American television, but possibly America itself.

All in the Family marked a sharp departure from the bland comedies that the viewing public had been force-fed, and when it premiered, audiences did not quite know what to make of it. Carroll starred as the working-class ignoramus Archie Bunker who lived in Queens and was constantly at odds with his daffy but wise wife, Edith, his feminist daughter, Gloria, and her overeducated, chronically unemployed, outspoken husband, whom Archie called "Meathead." It might sound like typical television fare, but the storylines and content surely were not.

In the post-civil rights era, the series became a forum for social commentary and unabashedly confronted subject matter that had formerly been taboo. For the first time on American television, controversial topics of the day—racism and feminism, intolerance and bigotry, affirmative action and integration—were addressed through the eyes of Archie Bunker, a befuddled but strong-willed, somehow-likable, blue-collar guy who was trying his best to get along in a world that was changing way too fast.

The show ran for eight seasons and in that time, anyone who was even peripherally involved with the program received piles of awards. When it was over, both Archie's and Edith's prized living-room chairs were installed in the Smithsonian Institution.

Carroll later starred in the *Archie Bunker's Place* spin-off, and for six seasons, beginning in 1988, starred as Chief Bill Gillespie on the well-received *In the Heat of the Night* series, frequently alongside his only child, Hugh O'Connor, who was a regular on the show. Carroll adopted Hugh in 1962 during the filming of *Cleopatra* in Italy. However, Hugh endured a long battle with drugs, and his addictions culminated in suicide at 32. Hugh was cremated and his ashes interred at a private crypt in Rome.

After Hugh's death, Carroll became a teary public advocate urging parents to help their children abstain from drugs. He died of a heart attack brought on by diabetic complications at 76 and was buried at Westwood Memorial Park in Santa Monica, California.

CEMETERY DIRECTIONS: This little cemetery holds numerous celebrities and is peculiarly located behind the office complex at 10850 Wilshire Blvd., about a half-mile east of I-405.

GRAVE DIRECTIONS: Enter the cemetery, turn left at the office, and the first grave past the chapel on the right is Jack Lemmon's. The next stone is Carroll's which, as of this writing, remains unmarked.

DANA PLATO
NOVEMBER 7, 1964 – MAY 8, 1999

At thirteen years old, Dana Plato won the role of Kimberly Drummond, the daughter of a wealthy New York businessman who takes in two disadvantaged boys on the sitcom *Diff'rent Strokes*. Written out of the program six years later when she became pregnant, Dana hoped to return after giving birth, but the show was cancelled before she was able to make her comeback.

Having sampled fame, Dana wanted more and was dismayed that she was unable to find new acting work. Dana spent the next fifteen years chasing an ever-elusive dream, and the tragedy of her life was the self-destructive path she took in her quest to get back to her fame. After *Diff'rent Strokes*, Dana appeared in low-budget films like *Bikini Beach Race*, and to shed what she felt was her teenage girl image, shed her clothes for *Playboy* magazine in 1989. By 1991, battling alcohol and drug problems, Dana was handed a five-year probation sentence after an armed robbery of a Las Vegas video store; the following year she was arrested again for forging Valium prescriptions.

The truth is, Dana was never a very good actress, and once her arrests and substance-abuse problems became tabloid fodder, an acting career was highly unlikely. Everyone seemed to know that except for Dana, and she continued to languish on the fringes, always seeking a reentry point. Finally, after she starred in a lesbian soft-porn movie in 1997, any hopes of a legitimate acting career were gone, and, soon, so was her life.

In 1999 Dana and her fiancé, Robert Menchaca, were living in a Florida RV park when Dana, still hoping for an acting comeback, secured an appearance on Howard Stern's radio program. After that, she flew to Robert's parents' home in Oklahoma, where Robert was waiting for her with the Winnebago. The next evening, Robert, seemingly distraught, called 911 to report that Dana had retired to the Winnebago to take a nap but was now unresponsive. Paramedics arrived but it was too late. Dana was dead at 34.

In an odd twist it was learned that Robert had actually taken pictures of Dana as she lay dying because he thought she was "snoring funny." Family members requested that Dana be autopsied to find out if perhaps foul play was involved—after all, it didn't seem that someone's death rattle could be mistaken for an odd snore. An autopsy and an investigation were conducted but authorities found no evidence of foul play.

Dana's death was ultimately ruled a suicide by multi-drug intoxication.

She was cremated and her ashes scattered in the Pacific Ocean.

FREDDIE PRINZE

JUNE 22, 1954 – JANUARY 29, 1981

Coming from one of New York City's worst neighborhoods, the Hungarian-Puerto Rican comedian Freddie Prinze began performing stand-up at Manhattan's Improv comedy club in 1972. Within four years, at just 22, Freddie was costarring in the popular *Chico and the Man* television series as the carefree Chico, was a millionaire with a wife and son, and had legions of adoring fans.

Although the series stayed in the top of the ratings, the bottom began to fall from Freddie's personal life, and a latent weakness for drugs was invigorated by the new influx of cash. Quaaludes and cocaine washed down with wine became favorite intoxicants and, after Freddie was arrested for driving under their influence, his wife petitioned for a divorce.

In January 1977, Freddie moved into a cushy Los Angeles hotel and adhered to a rigorous shooting schedule for his television series, while performing his stand-up routine as well. He was attending therapy to relieve the strain but the only thing that seemed to help were the Quaaludes and cocaine, and Freddie began to tell friends "life isn't worth living."

On January 27 he received a restraining order from his wife and the next night Freddie made a series of disturbingly emotional phone calls to family and friends. In a short while, Freddie's manager, Martin "Dusty" Snyder, arrived and Freddie handed him a note that read, "I cannot go on any longer," while proceeding to make his phone calls. Panicked, Dusty went into another room and called Freddie's therapist, who assured him that Freddie was only crying out for attention.

Snyder returned to the room and, moments later, Freddie pulled a .38-caliber revolver from under the sofa cushion and held it to his head. Snyder desperately tried talking the actor out of taking his life, and Freddie, seemingly coming to his senses, took the gun from his head and held it loosely at his side. As Dusty stepped toward the sofa to retrieve the gun, Freddie swept the gun up to his temple and fired. For the next 33 hours, Freddie lay brain-dead at UCLA Medical Center, then he expired.

The note he left behind read: "I must end it, there's no hope left. I'll be at peace. No one had anything to do with this. My decision totally—Freddie Prinze P.S. I'm sorry. Forgive me. Dusty's here. He's innocent. He cared."

At 26, Freddie was laid to rest at Forest Lawn Memorial Park in Hollywood Hills, California.

CEMETERY DIRECTIONS: From Highway 134, which is the connector between Highway 101 and I-210, take the Forest Lawn Drive exit. Proceed west for a mile and the park's entrance will be on the left.

GRAVE DIRECTIONS: Stop at the booth at the entrance and get a park map. Then drive up to the Courts of Remembrance and walk into the courtyards. After the second courtyard, turn right into the Sanctuary of Light corridor. Freddie's crypt is on the right wall.

HARRY REASONER

APRIL 17, 1923 – AUGUST 6, 1991

After a stint as a reporter for the now-defunct *Minneapolis Times*, the perpetually silver-haired Harry Reasoner switched to radio in 1948, and four years later debuted as a television commentator and special news narrator for CBS. By 1961 Harry was co-hosting a morning news show called *Calendar* and in 1968, with Mike Wallace, he initiated the *60 Minutes* series, a gutsy news program that forever changed broadcast journalism and spawned a stream of copycat investigative newsmagazine shows.

Harry left the show after just two years and became an ABC network anchor. He then returned to the ticking stopwatch of *60 Minutes* in 1979 and stayed there until his death in 1991.

Harry, who was also suffering from pneumonia, died of complications after a blood clot was removed from his brain, and at 68 was buried near his parents at Union Cemetery in Humboldt, Iowa.

CEMETERY DIRECTIONS: From the junction of Routes 169 and Route 3, follow Route 3 west past the hospital, then turn right onto 19th Street at the Hogslat sign. At the top of the hill, turn left at the "T," then make a right into the cemetery at the main gate between the stone pillars.

GRAVE DIRECTIONS: Harry's grave tablet is easy to find, just three rows north and six rows east of the Soldier's Monument.

ROBERT REED

OCTOBER 19, 1932 – MAY 12, 1992

Robert Reed was a classically trained actor whose early credits included starring roles in a number of Broadway productions, most notably *Barefoot in the Park*. His TV acting debut came in 1961, playing a young attorney in the courtroom drama *The Defenders*.

As part of Paramount's stable of contract players, in 1969 Robert was cast as the quintessential family man, Mike Brady, in the sitcom *The Brady Bunch*. But as a dramatic actor, he often lacked enthusiasm for the role and wasn't always comfortable with the show's gags and gimmicks. Still, *The Brady Bunch* and its syrupy, albeit charming, view of suburban family life enjoyed a successful, five-year run. It was cancelled when the Brady child actors physically outgrew their roles but since then, through endless syndication, the popularity of the series has swelled to a phenomenal level.

Few were aware of it but, as loving husband Mike Brady, Robert was a bit out of his element. "I'm not a family man," he once confessed.

Indeed. When Robert died of colon cancer at 59, television's tawdry sleuth Geraldo Rivera obtained a copy of his death certificate and learned that AIDS had been a "significant condition contributing to (Robert's) death." Geraldo tracked down a few of Robert's long-time confidants, including a bartender who waited on Robert for 30 years at a gay nightspot and, on his *Now It Can be Told* tabloid television show, Geraldo announced that Robert had been gay. Some called Geraldo's tactics unconscionable and others made comments that can't be reprinted here, but the point is, everyone listened. Finally, it all made sense.

Convinced that his career would be ruined if it became known that he was gay, Robert had lived a lonely life of one-night stands with sex-for-hire partners. Remote and standoffish, he became an expert at small talk and effortlessly deflected innocent inquiries about his personal life. Robert so effectively kept his homosexuality a secret that even most *Brady* cast members were blindsided by the development.

At 59, Robert was buried at Memorial Park Cemetery in Skokie, Illinois.

CEMETERY DIRECTIONS: From I-94, take Exit 37B and follow Dempster Street (Route 58) east to the first traffic light. Turn left onto Gross Point Road and the cemetery is ahead about two miles on the left.

GRAVE DIRECTIONS: Enter the cemetery, turn left after the office and follow this drive for several hundred yards. On the right you'll see the Memento Mori Chapel and then, on the left, is a sign marking the "1-9 Annex" section. Turn left just before this section and look for the Ayersman stone on your right. Robert's grave is nine rows behind the Ayersman plot.

GEORGE REEVES
JANUARY 5, 1914 – JUNE 16, 1959

Though George Reeves was an accomplished film and play actor, he's certainly best known for his role as the original Superman during the six-season run of the 1950s television series. But unlike the invincible hero he portrayed, George was mortal and, at 45 years old, just three days before he was to be wed to fiancée Lenore Lemmon, he was killed by a single gunshot wound to the head. His death has been the subject of endless speculation because, though police have always considered his demise a suicide, there are a number of puzzling factors.

On the evening of his death, George was entertaining his fiancée and a few friends in his lavish Hollywood home when he reportedly felt tired and went upstairs by himself to his bedroom. After about 30 minutes, the guests heard a gunshot and George was found dead, sprawled nude on his bed with a bullet hole in his right temple. The death was ruled a suicide because the houseguests could provide no other explanation, and there was no sign of an intruder or forced entry.

However, no suicide note was found and, when George was lifted from the bed by authorities, the bullet's shell casing was found to be *under* him. Furthermore, the gun was found on the floor between his feet, and no fingerprints were found on it. There were no powder burns on his head wound, implying that the gun was held at least several inches from his head at the time it was fired, which is unusual for a suicide, and the police were not called for at least a half an hour after the death.

George was cremated and his ashes interred at Mountain View Cemetery in Altadena, California.

CEMETERY DIRECTIONS: From I-210, take the Fair Oaks Avenue exit, proceed north for 2½ miles and the cemetery is on the right.

GRAVE DIRECTIONS: Enter the cemetery, bear right and, at the first opportunity, turn right again. Park in the lot and walk into the Pasadena Mausoleum, then turn immediately left into the columbarium. George's ashes rest in the seventh niche on the right, at about waist height.

GENE RODDENBERRY

AUGUST 19, 1921 – OCTOBER 24, 1991

As a decorated B-17 pilot who flew 89 combat missions during World War II, Gene Roddenberry's stories and essays written during spare moments in the South Pacific were published in newspapers and magazines. After the war, Gene studied literature at Columbia University and became a commercial airline pilot for Pan Am. But in 1948, after an engine fire forced Gene to crashland into the Syrian desert, killing 38 of the craft's 46 passengers, he decided to pursue writing full-time. Gene moved to Los Angeles and, supplementing his initially meager income by working for the LAPD as department spokesman, Gene eventually attracted interest in his screenplays.

By 1953, Gene had left the LAPD and was writing full-time. He sold scripts for numerous television productions, including *Dragnet* and *Goodyear Theater* and, as head writer for *Have Gun Will Travel,* Gene won an Emmy. For four years beginning in 1960, Gene produced *The Lieutenant,* which spawned the wildly popular boy's doll, G.I. Joe. Despite all these accomplishments, though, Gene will be forever remembered for taking generations of viewers on a journey into "space, the final frontier" as creator and producer of the television series, *Star Trek.*

As a science-fiction devotee, Gene saw similarities between space explorers and American pioneers, and he envisioned a science-fiction television series that would feature continuing characters just as the popular *Wagon Train* Western series had. In 1966, Gene presented his idea of a "wagon train to the stars" to a culture whose schoolchildren practiced nuclear attack drills and whose World's Doomsday Clock was set at just twelve minutes to midnight. *Star Trek* initiated the notion that anything was possible, fearsome technologies had righteous worth, man was inherently noble, the future was full of hope, and both the horizon and our destiny were infinite.

Star Trek's optimistic view of the future found an adoring mainstream audience while it's fanatical cult faction took on a life all its own. Aboard the *Starship Enterprise*, the dauntless Captain Kirk and his pointy-eared comrade Mr. Spock became cultural icons that spawned a major entertainment industry. Legions of zealots known as Trekkies inspired a cottage industry, flocking to conventions dressed as out-of-this-world travelers to socialize with other intergalactic pilgrims and debate the merits of such futuristic hardware as "transporter beams" and "phaser guns."

The magnitude of the *Star Trek* phenomenon surprised everyone. And today, after three sequel television series, numerous feature films, dozens of books, and countless other forms of merchandising, it shows no signs of slowing. Even Gene never imagined such a future. Instead, he wished merely to "demonstrate that television need not be violent to be exciting. Neither promiscuity, greed, or jealousy have a place in *Star Trek*."

Gene died of a massive blood clot and heart attack at 70.

He was cremated and, in April of 1997, a bit of his ashes, along with those of Timothy Leary and 22 other space enthusiasts, were blasted into space from Vandenberg Air Force Base in the world's first space funeral. Celestis, a Texas-based company, organizes such ventures and piggybacks the ashes, sealed in lipstick-sized capsules, aboard commercial satellites. On May 20, 2002, after 28,132 orbits around the earth, the capsules reentered the atmosphere over Papua, New Guinea, and burned up in a fiery finale.

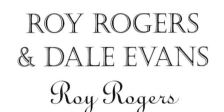

ROY ROGERS
& DALE EVANS

Roy Rogers

NOVEMBER 5, 1911 – JULY 6, 1998

Dale Evans

OCTOBER 31, 1912 – FEBRUARY 7, 2001

During the 1940s, '50s, and '60s, the Roy Rogers and Dale Evans husband-and-wife, cowboy-cowgirl entertainment team was the most recognized anywhere. They made some 400 recordings and 27 films together, had a hit television program, and their personas were immortalized on everything from western wear to lunch pails. But even before their union, both Roy and Dale had separately enjoyed their own successes.

As Leonard Franklin Slye, Roy got started in the music business by playing at square dances with his cousin Stanley. In 1937 he became Roy Rogers and his big break came the following year when he was cast to replace Gene Autry in a film following a contract dispute. With his trusty palomino Trigger under him and his dog Bullet at their side, Roy made scores of films and gained an enormous following for his gallant exploits in the then-popular musical-Western genre that romanticized the Old West.

As Frances Smith, Dale took a more indirect route to showbiz, but ultimately her singing and songwriting abilities were recognized. Pregnant at 14, she eloped with an older schoolmate and, after their son's birth, took a secretarial position at a Memphis radio station. Upon discovering she could sing, the station manager put her on the air and she eventually ended up as Dale Evans, a jazz singer in Chicago supper clubs during the music's heyday.

After a stint as a USO trouper, she found herself a California agent and repackaged the Dale Evans persona for the Hollywood publicity machine. Seven years were shaved off her age, she no longer wore a wedding band, and her selfless devotion to her teenaged brother Tommy was extolled. (He was, of course, actually the son she'd had at 14.)

In 1944 Dale was offered a role alongside Roy in *The Yellow Rose of Texas*, and the Western film showcased an irresistible chemistry between them. The on-screen chemistry quickly spilled over to an off-screen friendship and romance and, after Dale divorced her third husband and Roy's wife Arlene died following complications from childbirth, the two were married on New Year's Eve 1946.

As the "King and Queen of the Cowboys," Roy and Dale became emblematic of all-American family values and domestic solidarity and found great success in film and records. *The Roy Rogers Show* aired in 1951. It ran until 1957 and was then revamped and reintroduced in 1962 as *The Roy Rogers and Dale Evans Show.* Dale was an especially prolific songwriter—she claimed more than 200 credits in her lifetime—and she penned the show's theme song, "Happy Trails."

In contrast to the couple's blissful professional life, their family life was marked by tragedy; the only child they had together died from complications of Down Syndrome before her second birthday and though they eventually adopted four other children, one died in a 1964 church bus accident, and the following year another choked to death.

As an active Evangelical lay minister, the tragedies inspired Dale to write moving motivational books, and her first, *Angel Unaware,* was applauded for raising acceptance of retarded children in an era when most were institutionalized their entire lives. She wrote a total of twenty inspirational and religious-themed books and they led to a Christian program, *A Date With Dale,* that she hosted until her death.

Roy died of congestive heart failure at 86 in 1998, and Dale died of heart failure three years later at the age of 88.

They are buried at Sunset Hills Memorial Park in Apple Valley, California.

CEMETERY DIRECTIONS: From I-15, follow Happy Trails Highway (Route 18) east for 5½ miles, then turn left onto Dale Evans Parkway. Two miles later, turn right at the "T" and follow Waalew Road for four miles. You'll find the cemetery on the left.

GRAVE DIRECTIONS: Enter the cemetery and Roy and Dale's plot is immediately on the left beside the reflecting pools.

Also, in the nearby town of Victorville, is the Roy Rogers and Dale Evans Museum, which is filled with Roy and Dale memorabilia, as well as some of their costars: their horses, Trigger (who died at 33) and Buttermilk, as well as their faithful dog, Bullet. They were stuffed and mounted for posterity after their natural deaths. Take the Roy Rogers Drive exit off I-15, turn west, then turn left onto Civic Drive. The museum will be right there in front of you.

SATURDAY NIGHT LIVE

The freewheeling television program originally titled *NBC's Saturday Night* first aired October 11, 1975, showcasing zany comedy sketches by the "Not Ready for Primetime Players." The program represented a bold leap for television and was an immediate hit; within two years, its name by then changed to *Saturday Night Live*, it was the highest-rated late-night show in America and since then, *Saturday Night Live* has hardly looked back.

Over the years, regular players have come and gone while the show's main elements have remained the same: a celebrity host and a musical guest, comedy sketches, commercial parodies, and a news segment. *Saturday Night Live* has proved to be a springboard for the careers of many previously unknown talents including, to name just a few, Bill Murray, Eddie Murphy, Julia Louis-Dreyfuss, Billy Crystal, Dana Carvey, Mike Myers, Chris Rock and, of course, the four entertainers profiled here.

Gilda Radner
JUNE 28, 1946 – MAY 20, 1989

As a child, Gilda Radner was severely overweight, had a speech impediment, and few friends, and she later attributed her keen sense of humor to these setbacks. After majoring in drama at the University of Michigan, she landed a job playing a clown on a Canadian children's television show, and in 1973 began performing with an improvisational troupe at Toronto's Second City comedy club. The following year Gilda joined Dan Aykroyd and John Belushi (both also Second City alumni) on the *National Lampoon Radio Hour* in New York. In October 1975, after answering Lorne Michaels' call for actors and comedians, the three debuted as regular cast players on the new program that would come to be known as *Saturday Night Live*.

Gilda frequently eclipsed her female costars on the show and she developed a number of memorably beloved and zany characters, many of which contributed catch phrases to the slang lexicon. There was, "It just goes to show you, it's always something," from the prickly mock-news commentaries of squinty-eyed, fright-wigged Roseanne Roseannadanna. The near-deaf, inept, spinsterly media analyst Emily Litella ended her tangents with "Never mind," and schoolgirl geek Lisa Lupner coined "That was so funny I almost forgot to laugh."

Gilda left *Saturday Night Live* in 1979 and moved on to Broadway, starring in a one-woman show that she co-wrote, *Gilda Radner: Live From New York,* and the next year she married *SNL* guitarist G.E. Smith. By 1982 things seemed to be going great for Gilda, but privately, she was suffering from nervous exhaustion, her marriage was crumbling, and she was battling bulimia, which she had overcome once before. Nonetheless, Gilda teamed with Gene Wilder in the comedic adventure *Hanky Panky* that year and, during filming, the two became romantically involved. They were married two years later.

In 1985 Gilda suffered chronic fatigue and mysterious bouts of unexplained illness and pains that her doctors dismissed as the flu or overwork, but the following year she collapsed and was found to have been suffering from advanced ovarian cancer. Through nearly three years of treatment, Gilda retained her sense of humor and when she lost her hair during radiation therapy, she opted to wear her gravity-defying Roseanne Roseannadanna wig. Gilda appeared for the last time, as herself, on *It's Garry Shandling's Show* in 1988. Her last able days were spent penning her memoir, *It's Always Something,* and bolstering the spirits of other cancer patients with impromptu visits.

While her own spirits never seemed to fail, the physical toll finally became too great and, with Gene at her side, Gilda died in Los Angeles in 1989.

In the wake of her death, Gene and her family and friends worked to found Gilda's Club, a nonprofit psychological- and social-support organization for cancer patients whose flagship center in New York has since spawned branches all over the world. The clubs offer free workshops and counseling, and a special program for children called "Noogieland," so-named because of the noogies Gilda was often forced to endure while playing her character Lisa Lupner.

At 42, Gilda was buried at Long Ridge Cemetery in Stamford, Connecticut.

CEMETERY DIRECTIONS: From the center of Stamford, follow Route 104 north for five miles. Turn left on Erskine Road and the cemetery is a short distance ahead on the left.

GRAVE DIRECTIONS: Along the road, about two-thirds of the way down the cemetery's length, you'll see a few old stairs that lead into the cemetery. Just about 50 feet directly behind these stairs, near a small bench, Gilda's grave is marked with a flat stone.

John Belushi

JANUARY 24, 1949 – MARCH 4, 1982

John Belushi was another original member of the *Saturday Night Live* troupe, and he quickly became an audience favorite for his maniacal style, luxuriating in a comedic netherworld a tick away from categorical insanity. For six years, John delighted in his uniquely manic and belligerent characters on the show, portraying everything from a Samurai warrior to a Greek luncheonette hamburger-slinger.

John quickly parlayed his popularity into a spate of comedy films. His biggest hit was 1978's crowd-pleaser for the college set, *Animal House*. In it, he starred as the classic crude, flunking, frat-house drunk, Bluto, who bashed beer bottles over his head and incited riots. Later, John and his partner in crime, Dan Aykroyd, developed personas as the Blues Brothers, decked-in-black blues singers who caused havoc everywhere they went. Their portrayals became the basis of a movie of the same name.

In March 1982, John was staying in Bungalow Number 3 at the Chateau Marmont on the Sunset Strip in Los Angeles. After partying it up at the nightclub On The Rox, John returned home where, for a short time, a few friends, including Robert DeNiro and Robin Williams, joined him. When everyone left, John, always needing a little more action, had his friend Cathy Evelyn Smith shoot him up with a drug concoction called a speedball, a mixture of heroin and cocaine.

After John had seemingly passed out, Cathy left the room. A few hours later it was discovered by another of John's friends that he was no longer just passed out, but was quite dead. The cause of death was classified as a drug overdose and, after Cathy related her story to a tabloid, she was arrested for supplying the drugs and served thirty months in prison.

Atop his motorcycle, Dan Aykroyd led the funeral procession to Abel's Hill Cemetery in Chilmark, Massachusetts, where John was buried at 33. However, the story doesn't end there.

Weary of fans tramping around the cemetery's grounds looking for John's grave, a large boulder simply marked "Belushi" was installed at the cemetery's entrance in 1985. This monument helps to minimize foot traffic in the cemetery and, surrounded by a split-rail fence, the picturesque patch offers dignified sanctuary. But, almost surely, John is not actually buried beneath.

It's believed that John's body was never moved to the new monument. Instead, the original "Here Lies Buried The Body of John

FAMILY TREE

JOHN BELUSHI

PHIL HARTMAN

GILDA RADNER

CHRIS FARLEY

SATURDAY NIGHT LIVE

Belushi" gravestone that marked his plot in the rear of the cemetery was removed and, while gawkers flock to the new boulder at the cemetery's entrance, John enjoys some peace and quiet a few hundred feet away.

But we're not done yet. It's also been reported that even before the new monument was installed, John's family, fearing that drunken pranksters might try to dig him up some night, had John moved to a new grave just fifteen feet from his original grave to thwart such an attempt. So far, that makes three possible gravesites.

Finally, after John's widow remarried in 1996, John's name was engraved on his family's stone in Illinois. Possibly, since John's tenuous ties to Martha's Vineyard were effectively broken once Judith remarried, his family decided to inter him in the family plot alongside his deceased parents. Cemetery officials at Elmwood Cemetery in Illinois, where the Belushi plot is located, unequivocally maintain that although John's name was added to the family memorial, his body was not interred there. But celebrity graves have often been hidden by diversionary fibs and outright lies.

So, where is John? To their credit, John's family pulled a fast one and only they, along with the few people who actually moved, or didn't move, John's body really know for sure.

DIRECTIONS TO ABEL'S HILL CEMETERY IN CHILMARK, MASSACHUSETTS: This is the cemetery where John was definitely buried in March 1982. He may be under the big "Belushi" boulder at the entrance, or he may be in an unmarked grave near the back row of the cemetery. To get to the cemetery, you first must first travel from the mainland to the island of Martha's Vineyard. Ferries to the Vineyard are available from a few mainland towns, but the one that docks at Wood's Hole is the only one open year-round. If you plan on taking your car across, reservations are required during the high season. From the Oak Bluffs ferry landing on Martha's Vineyard, follow the main road toward Chilmark and, after ten miles, you'll see Abel's Hill Cemetery on the right.

DIRECTIONS TO ELMWOOD MEMORIAL CEMETERY IN RIVER GROVE, ILLINOIS: This is the cemetery where the Belushi family has a plot and, though John's name has been inscribed on the family stone since 1996, cemetery officials say his body was never interred there. To get there take Exit 48B off of I-90/94 and follow Route 64 west for eight miles. Turn north on Route 171 and the cemetery is 1¼ miles ahead on the right.

DIRECTIONS TO BELUSHI FAMILY PLOT AT ELMWOOD: Enter the cemetery and continue straight until you see the Manof mausoleum. Make a right there, then a left at the "T," then take the next right. After the road winds a little bit, you'll see Section 7 on the right, and the Belushi plot is there near the drive.

Phil Hartman

SEPTEMBER 24, 1948 – MAY 28, 1998

Phil Hartman came into comedy by way of an improv troupe, The Groudlings. After co-writing *Pee-Wee's Big Adventure* with fellow troupe-member Paul "Pee-Wee Herman" Reubens, he joined *Saturday Night Live* in 1986 and remained on the show for eight seasons. Phil excelled at playing treacherous and weaselly characters, which he nailed with his insincere grin and comically smug demeanor. But he was probably best known though for his over-the-top impersonations, dozens of them, including Frank Sinatra, Ted Kennedy, and Bill Clinton.

Phil left *SNL* in 1994 and got himself a new job as the arrogant, egotistical, news anchor Bill McNeal on the sitcom *News Radio*. Phil also lent his memorable baritone to a number of characters on The Simpsons, including attorney Lionel Hutz and spokesman Troy McClure.

One night in May 1998, Phil's wife, Brynn, who had a history of substance abuse and instability, went out partying with a few friends. For reasons known only to Brynn, upon returning home around 2:00 a.m. she executed Phil while he lay sleeping in their bed, shooting him in the head, neck, and arm.

In a panic she fled the house, leaving the couple's two school-aged children sleeping in their beds, and went to a friend's house. Brynn told her friend, "I shot Phil," but because she was so wired and her story so outlandish, he didn't believe her. Later, while Brynn dozed, he found and confiscated a revolver from her purse. Together they went back to the Hartman residence but, upon arriving, Brynn grabbed a second gun and locked herself in the master bedroom with Phil's body.

The friend called 911 just after 6:00 a.m., and police were escorting the couple's children, who'd slept through everything, from the house when another shot rang out. As Phil lay dead beside her, Brynn had put the gun's barrel into her mouth and pulled the trigger while officers struggled to break in through one of the bedroom windows.

At 49, Phil was cremated and his ashes scattered around Emerald Bay at Catalina Island, California.

An autopsy confirmed that Brynn had consumed alcohol and cocaine as well as the antidepressant Zoloft. Brynn's family brought a wrongful death suit against Zoloft and it was settled out of court.

Chris Farley

FEBRUARY 15, 1964 – DECEMBER 1, 1997

After graduating from Marquette University, Chris Farley studied at the Improv Olympic theater school and was performing at Chicago's Second City when he was discovered by *Saturday Night Live* producer Lorne Michaels in 1989. The next year Chris became a regular *SNL* player and his boisterous, fat-guy schtick quickly won him wide appeal.

One of Chris's most hilarious characters was a giddy and flabby Chippendale's strip-club dancer who competed in an audition against Patrick Swayze, his jiggling gut spilling over his waistband. But his signature bit was the sweaty, tightly-wound, motivational speaker Matt Foley whose identity was predicated on Chris's foghorn voice and whose vein-popping speeches invariably ended with him smashing through the furniture in a froth, his polyester leisure suit bursting at the seams.

After he left *SNL* in 1995, Chris hammed his way through a string of starring roles as the same kind of lovable, bumbling slob in such movies as *Tommy Boy* and *Beverly Hills Ninja*. But though Chris's hilarious onscreen routines garnered him professional triumph, his offscreen lifestyle propelled him toward disaster. For years Chris had battled against compulsions to overeat and over-indulge in drugs and alcohol, and by 1997, those forces had conspired in a manner that was anything but funny.

It troubled the 300-pound, 5-foot-8 comic that he'd never had any meaningful girlfriends, and he often indulged in prostitutes to help ease the pain. Chris bought an apartment on the 60th floor of Chicago's John Hancock tower and after a December day spent doing hard drugs with a call girl named Heidi, they ended up at his place. Around 3:00 a.m., Heidi went to depart when Chris collapsed onto the floor, wheezing, "Don't leave me." Ten hours later, Chris's brother found him still lying on the floor, but no longer wheezing.

In an interview Chris had once confessed that he "dreamed of being John Belushi. I wanted to follow him," but unfortunately, he never realized how far he would follow him. Just like his idol, Chris died at 33 of an accidental overdose of heroin and cocaine.

Chris was laid to rest at Resurrection Cemetery and Mausoleum in Madison, Wisconsin.

CEMETERY DIRECTIONS: Resurrection Cemetery is at 2705 Regent St., a sizable Madison road that begins just southwest of the Capitol building. From either the north or the south, follow Route 151 to its intersection with Regent Street, turn west and, within a mile, you'll see the cemetery. Just before the cemetery, bear right at the "Y" and enter at the main drive on the left.

GRAVE DIRECTIONS: Immediately in front of you is the chapel and mausoleum. Walk into the chapel and you'll find Chris's crypt on the top left, just behind the altar.

TELLY SAVALAS

JANUARY 21, 1924 – JANUARY 22, 1994

Over the course of his 30-plus-year acting career, Telly Aristotle Savalas appeared in dozens of movies, from *The Greatest Story Ever Told* to *The Dirty Dozen* to the James Bond flick *On Her Majesty's Secret Service*. But it was his personification of the tough-talking but big-hearted Lieutenant Theo Kojak in the *Kojak* television series that brought real celebrity to Telly. Fans adored him as the lollipop-addicted detective with a shiny, shaved head and trademark line, "Who loves ya, baby?" and the show enjoyed a six-season, award-winning run.

Reflecting on the recognition that the *Kojak* role brought him, Telly said, "Before *Kojak,* I made 60 movies with some of the biggest names in the business and people would still say 'There goes what's-his-name.'"

Telly died of prostate cancer at 70 and is buried at Forest Lawn Memorial Park in Hollywood Hills, California.

Either Telly or his survivors attempted to incorporate the writings of Aristotle (Telly's middle namesake) into his epitaph but, embarrassingly, the chosen quote actually contains the last words of Socrates, as recorded by Plato.

> *The hour of departure has arrived,*
> *and we go our ways.*
> *I to die and you to live.*
> *Which is the better God only knows.*

CEMETERY DIRECTIONS: From Highway 134, which is the connector between Highway 101 and I-210, take the Forest Lawn Drive exit. Proceed west for a mile and the park's entrance is on the left.

GRAVE DIRECTIONS: Get a map from the information booth and drive to the Gardens of Heritage, which are across the drive from the Old North Church. Enter the Gardens at the stairs that are to the left of the statue of Washington, walk up four short flights, then turn left. Telly lies 40 feet to the left, around the side of the Chu plot.

JESSICA SAVITCH

FEBRUARY 1, 1947 – OCTOBER 23, 1983

Young Jessica Savitch was a diligent Philadelphia newscaster whose big break came when she got national exposure during coverage of the 1975 Ford/Carter presidential debate. Within a year, she held the Senate news beat for NBC, and while old-school broadcasters were unimpressed with Jessica's starlet style and follow-up remarks that sometimes displayed a lack of background knowledge, viewers loved her and she parlayed that into becoming one of the most prominent women in network news.

But as her professional career zoomed, Jessica's personal travails became tabloid fodder. There were reports of the usual celebrity problems—screaming off-camera rants, cocaine binges, and promiscuous weekends—but other peculiar gossips surfaced as well. Jessica married the wealthy socialite Mel Korn, 30 years her senior, and after a quick divorce she then married her gynecologist, Donald Payne. During the marriage to Donald, Jessica carried on an affair with reporter Ron Kershaw (who reportedly beat her resulting in bruises that makeup artists weren't always able to conceal), and a distraught Donald hung himself in her basement with the leash of her dog, Chewy.

By 1983, Jessica's on-camera persona had become increasingly unreliable and her popularity waned. As other bright newswomen emerged, the competition for a finite number of anchor positions intensified and Jessica's on-screen time was reduced. In one of her final spots, she humiliated herself with a slurred and confused newsbreak delivery.

After dinner at Odette's Restaurant in New Hope, Pennsylvania, with Martin Fischbein, vice president of the *New York Post*, Jessica and Martin (and her infamous dog, Chewy) drowned after Martin accidentally drove the car into a canal bordering the restaurant's parking area. In poor visibility due to an evening downpour, Martin had drifted left off of the pavement and once the driver's side wheels went over the edge, the whole car plunged upside down into the canal. Though the canal held just four feet of water, knee-deep mud sealed the doors shut and the two were trapped inside. Nobody had seen the accident and it was about four hours before the car was found. By that time, Jessica and Martin were long dead. Neither drugs nor alcohol were determined to have been a factor in the accident.

At 36, Jessica was cremated together with her dog Chewy and their ashes were scattered in the ocean surf near Atlantic City, New Jersey.

ROD SERLING

DECEMBER 25, 1924 – JUNE 28, 1975

On the day he graduated from high school, Rod Serling enlisted in the Army. During the invasion of the Philippines he was wounded by shrapnel and awarded the Purple Heart and, when Rod was discharged from the Army, he was "bitter about everything and at loose ends." For the remainder of his life, in flashbacks and nightmares, Rod was troubled by the hypocritical experiences of the war and by the ultimate dimensions of mankind's assault on its own humanity.

After the war, while attending Antioch College on the G.I. Bill, Rod began writing and acting for a local radio station and, by 1952, he was writing for television fulltime. Rod won three Emmys during television's golden age: for *Patterns* in 1955, *Requiem for a Heavyweight* in 1956, and *The Comedian* in 1957. Though he was very successful, many scripts Rod wrote contained social commentary or touched on weighty issues, and corporate sponsors in 1950s America were unwilling to underwrite anything that might clash with the time's apple-pie outlook.

But Rod also realized that advertisers might approve scripts with potentially controversial material as long as they took place in a fictitious world. ("I found that it was all right to have Martians saying things Democrats and Republicans could never say.") From this awareness came *The Twilight Zone* in 1959 and, with its instantly recognizable opening theme music and Rod as the charismatic host, the program achieved a permanent place in American popular culture as well as, it seems, permanent syndication. And, much to Rod's gratification, its out-of-this-world vignette format lent him license to skewer dozens of formerly untouchable social issues including bigotry, religious zealotry, capital punishment, aging, and sexism.

After production of *The Twilight Zone* ended in 1964, leaving Rod "tired and frustrated," he began to concentrate on movie scripts; his most acclaimed screenplay was the adaptation he co-wrote with Michael Wilson of Pierre Boulle's book, *The Planet of the Apes*. Later, Rod was enticed back to television, writing episodes of the 1970s anthology series *Rod Serling's Night Gallery*, a kind of *Twilight Zone* stepchild. During the 1970s, Rod showed another side of his personality, that of a liberal and concerned American who spoke frankly about social reform and the nation's policies concerning Vietnam.

A lifelong smoker, Rod died at 50 of complications after a coronary bypass operation. He was buried at Lakeview Cemetery in Interlaken, New York.

CEMETERY DIRECTIONS: North of town on Route 96, turn east onto County Road 150 and the cemetery is a short distance ahead on the left.

GRAVE DIRECTIONS: Enter the cemetery and bear right at the first two forks. Go past the concrete holding house on the left, turn right at the four corners, and stop at the twin cedar trees on the left. A hundred feet further left is the flat stone that marks Rod's grave.

JIMMY STEWART
MAY 20, 1908 – JULY 2, 1997

In 1932, upon graduating with a degree in architecture from Princeton University, where he had served on the cheerleading squad, the stammering, "aw-shucks" actor Jimmy Stewart promptly got into theater. After some summer stock and barnstorming stage work, he headed to Hollywood and for a few years languished as a bit player in everything from murder mysteries to musicals. But in 1938 Jimmy scored in the romantic comedy *You Can't Take It With You*, and the next year he received an Oscar nomination for *Mr. Smith Goes to Washington*. In 1940, Jimmy won an Oscar for his performance as a smitten reporter in *The Philadelphia Story*.

In his 50-year career, Jimmy often played the earnest and bashful hero, slow to anger but possessed with bottomless reserves of perseverance. In an age of elegant, handsome matinee idols, lanky Jimmy was more the average-looking guy next door who embodied the small-town values of decency and moral courage, both on the screen and off. While he served in the Air Force as a bomber pilot he refused all the publicity the military tried to pour on him, insisting instead on being treated like any other serviceman. He continued as a reservist after the war, retiring as a brigadier general in

1968. Jimmy sometimes returned to help his family's small-town Pennsylvania hardware store where, his best actor Oscar was displayed in the window for twenty years. Jimmy was married just once, for 45 years, and he and his wife lived quietly, generally avoiding the Hollywood social whirl.

Of course, he's best known for his role as a suicidal businessman who finds redemption in the 1946 Christmas classic *It's a Wonderful Life*, but Jimmy also starred in the great Alfred Hitchcock films *Vertigo* and *Rear Window*. In these roles Jimmy set a precedent that actors profit from today. Trading his flat salary for a percentage of the movie profits, he benefited handsomely when the films went on to become box-office hits. But Jimmy even refuted credit for that idea, saying, "There's too much praise for small things. I won't let it get me, but too much praise can turn a fellow's head if he doesn't watch his step."

Suffering respiratory problems and mourning the recent death of his wife, Gloria, he died of cardiac arrest at his home in 1997. Jimmy's last words were, "I'm going to be with Gloria now."

At 89, he was buried at Forest Lawn Memorial Park in Glendale, California.

CEMETERY DIRECTIONS: From Highway 2, take the San Fernando Road exit and turn northwest. After a mile, make a right onto Glendale Avenue and the park's entrance is immediately on the right.

GRAVE DIRECTIONS: Enter the park, start driving up the hill and turn at the first left. As the road winds around in a wide, right-hand curve, on the right is the Taylor memorial, which is a statue of a crouching archer. Stop here, walk up the hill and orient yourself so that the archer is aiming directly at you. Then, six rows from the memorial's base, you can find Jimmy's grave.

ED SULLIVAN
SEPTEMBER 28, 1901 – OCTOBER 13, 1974

Straight out of high school, Ed Sullivan became a stringer reporter and sports columnist for New York's Hearst-owned newspapers, and in 1932 seized an opportunity to replace rival reporter Walter Winchell as the reporter for the *New York Daily News* Broadway gossip column, "Little Old New York." As a leading entertainment columnist for the next 42 years, he was wooed by celebrities from all walks of media and his access to the glamorous world of stars made him a luminary himself.

Frequently exploiting his column contacts to enlist celebrity guests for charity galas and parties, Ed finally took full advantage of his unique situation in 1948 and debuted his *Toast of the Town* variety show on CBS. The network gave Ed just $375 to secure his guest lineup for the opening show, and even with that paltry budget he was able to produce a half-dozen acts, including the little-known comedy team of Dean Martin and Jerry Lewis.

As a host, Ed Sullivan had a strange drawl, awkward mannerisms, and a deadpan delivery style—but whatever he lacked in stage presence, he compensated for in his outstanding eye for talent. Temperamental and controlling, he choreographed each act's staging and edited their material, but as the popularity of the show grew, it was understood that Sullivan was a certified star maker and few argued with his demands, lest they be denied their "big break." From Elvis Presley and the Beatles to Sammy Davis, Jr. and Phyllis Diller, the show was a hit. After being renamed *The Ed Sullivan Show* in 1955, it ran until 1971 for a total of 1,087 shows, and Ed continued his tenure as newspaper gossip columnist throughout.

Ed died of heart failure at 73 and is interred at the Ferncliffe Mausoleum in Hartsdale, New York.

CEMETERY DIRECTIONS: From I-87, take Exit 7 in Ardsley and follow Route 9A North for 1¼ miles. Then, at the traffic light, turn right onto Secor Road and Ferncliffe is a short distance ahead on the left.

GRAVE DIRECTIONS: Enter Ferncliffe at the first entrance, bear left and park toward the left-hand side of the main mausoleum. Enter the mausoleum through the front bronze doors and turn left, right, left, left, and right. Then go to the end of the last hall and Ed's crypt is along the wall near the elevator.

SHARON TATE
JANUARY 24, 1943 – AUGUST 9, 1969

Sharon Tate was a Texas homecoming queen who aspired to be a movie actress. After a number of insignificant appearances in film and television, Sharon landed the more visible role of Jennifer North in 1967's *Valley of the Dolls* and gave a breakthrough performance. By the time of her marriage to the director Roman Polanski the following year, Sharon's star was on the rise.

At her Los Angeles estate one warm summer evening, while Roman was away finishing a project in London, an eight-months pregnant Sharon and her four houseguests, Abigail Folger, Wojciech

Frykowski, Steve Parent, and Jay Sebring, were stabbed, shot, beaten, and strangled to death by unknown assailants. The murder scene was particularly gruesome: Cryptic expressions had been written on the walls in the victims' blood, and a rope fastened around Sharon's neck snaked through the bloody pools.

Not surprisingly, the murders made headlines but, before authorities were able to even to catch their balance, the killers struck again the following night, slaughtering grocer Leno LaBianca and his wife, Rosemary, in equally grisly fashion. Hysteria gripped Los Angeles, sales of guard dogs and home alarms boomed, and, though a number of theories for the seven apparently motiveless murders were put forward, it later turned out that the actual motive was even more grotesque than, perhaps, the murders themselves.

Charles Manson was a deranged, self-styled guru who presided over a gaggle of equally troubled disciples at his squatters' manor, an isolated and abandoned movie ranch in the desert mountains. Through some perverse twist of illogic, Manson came to believe that a kind of apocalyptic racial war in which black men would prevail and oversee the demise of every white was imminent. While the conflict raged, however, Manson and his "family" would be living safely inside the earth, only to emerge and seize power from "the black man" to rule the world.

Manson was obsessed with this vision. The only other thing that intrigued him equally was the Beatles because, as Manson considered himself the fifth angel, Jesus Christ, the Beatles were the other four angels. In 1969 the Beatles released what became known as the *White Album*. (How much of a clearer signal could they send Manson?) The recording was interpreted by Manson as a message from his angels that the time for the race war was nigh, and he adopted the title of one of its feature songs, *Helter Skelter,* as the name for his imagined Armageddon. In his mind, the Helter Skelter war was to be initiated by indiscriminate killings of whites by blacks, but when the blacks failed to act, Manson became frustrated and decided it was his responsibility to get things moving.

To that end, Manson handpicked a few of his apostles and instructed them to select a house within a distinctive neighborhood and massacre its white occupants, while making it somehow look like the crime was committed by blacks.

Manson and four of his followers were convicted of the murders and sentenced to death. When California abolished its death penalty, their sentences were changed to life terms. Every few years they are each eligible to apply for parole, though to date they've been repeatedly denied it.

As for Sharon, she was 26 at her death and now resides at Holy Cross Cemetery in Culver City, California.

CEMETERY DIRECTIONS: From I-405, take Slauson Avenue east for ½ mile. The cemetery is on the left at #5835.

GRAVE DIRECTIONS: Enter the cemetery, turn left and start up the hill. One hundred yards on the left is the Grotto Lawn and an altar and to the left of the altar is another level, St. Ann's Garden. Sharon's grave is in that garden, third row from the top.

DANNY THOMAS
JANUARY 6, 1914 – FEBRUARY 6, 1991

Beginning his life as Muzyad Yakhoob, Danny Thomas was an enduring television entertainer whose comedic talents were surpassed only by his shrewd production activities and his well-known philanthropy. He began his career as the stand-up comic Amos Jacobs, developing his storytelling shtick into a familiar routine of lengthy narratives peppered with a blend of Irish, Yiddish, and Italian witticisms. Quite often these routines tended toward sentimentality, only to be rescued in the end by what he called the "treacle cutter," a one-liner designed to undercut the mushy sentiments with irony.

After a USO tour with Marlene Dietrich, Danny was cast in his first film, *The Unfinished Dance*. He refused to surgically alter his trademark nose, a decision that may have contributed to the short-lived nature of his film career, but he performed to good reviews for his appearance in 1951's *The Jazz Singer*, and a costarring role in *I'll See You in My Dreams*.

Meanwhile, Danny anxiously pursued a television series. He soon got one, *Four Star Review*, but its fast-paced sketches were ill suited to his expository style. In 1953 Danny came up with the autobiographical premise of *Make Room for Daddy*, which revolved around the absentee-father dilemmas of a traveling singer-comic named Danny Williams. The show was a domestic comedy that incorporated Danny's singing and storytelling talents and it became one of television's most successful comedies, remaining on the air until its cast left to pursue new avenues in 1964.

Danny had an enormous impact upon the growing medium of television; he invented the concept of a "spinoff" series and his off-camera stand-up routines for the studio audience were imitated and institutionalized as the now commonplace "warm-up." While starring on *Make Room for Daddy*, Danny met Sheldon Leonard and together they established Thomas-Leonard Productions. The powerhouse production company became responsible for a multitude of successful series including *The Andy Griffith Show*, *The Dick van Dyke Show*, *Gomer Pyle* and, in 1965, *The Danny Thomas Hour*.

In the 1970s, semiretirement from television production allowed time for live appearances, and Danny traveled the globe to perform in front of longtime fans. He formed an act with Milton Berle and Sid Caesar appropriately called "The Legends of Comedy" and, in 1990, they filmed a movie, *Side By Side*.

And of course, Danny was renowned the world over for his humanitarianism. While his television career skyrocketed in the 1950s, Danny assembled fund-raisers and benefits for a new children's hospital that would become his legacy. In February 1962, the St. Jude Children's Research Hospital opened in Memphis, and Danny told the crowd that had gathered for the dedication, "If I were to die this moment, I'd know why I was born." For the remainder of his life, he organized and performed at fund-raising events for St. Jude, a world leader in research and treatment of childhood disease and, in 1984, was presented the Congressional Medal of Honor for his efforts.

Danny died of a heart attack at 77 and now rests in his own Memorial Garden at his beloved St. Jude Children's Research Hospital in Memphis, Tennessee.

GRAVE DIRECTIONS: From I-40, take Exit 1B and follow the signs on Danny Thomas Boulevard to the hospital. Just inside the gate, on the left past the guard shack, is the beautiful courtyard that contains his tomb.

THE THREE STOOGES

The act that was to become television's *The Three Stooges* started in 1922 as a vaudeville act. In 1930 came the trio's big-screen debut in *Soup to Nuts* and, four years later, the Stooges were offered a contract by Columbia to make their knockabout-style, slapstick comedy shorts. They made about 200 in all, setting a record for the longest-running comedy series in Hollywood. Their humor, tasteless and repetitive, was punctuated by pokes, grunts, screeches, and various bits of bedlam, and it was also liberatingly funny. Moe was atingly funny. Moe was the know-nothing, know-it-all leader who committed cheerful acts of mayhem against his partners that magically never seemed to harm them; Larry was the innocent with a porcupine hairdo who just wanted to get along; and Curly was the bald, round, wacky, "nyuck-nyuck," wildman with a hilarious habit of reducing to rubble everything he touched.

The team, with four different Curlys over the years, enjoyed a quarter-century of success before finally being released by Columbia in 1958. But shortly afterwards, a whole new generation discovered the trio and, in the twilight of their lives, the Stooges were hotter than they had ever been. A cult of sorts was spawned, complete with marathon film festivals, fan clubs, lunch boxes, and coffee mugs, and the Stooges cashed in with personal appearances and a few feature films. Failing health finally shut down their act but the shows are in endless syndication on television.

Though the most familiar incarnation of the trio consists of Larry Fine, Moe Howard, and his brother Jerome Howard as Curly, the part of Curly was also played by Moe's older brother, Shemp, by Joe Besser, and finally, by Joe DeRita.

Moe Howard

JUNE 19, 1897 – MAY 4, 1975

In 1922, Moe, his brother Shemp, and friend Ted Healy ad-libbed a hilarious stage act that was, though they didn't know it, the first incarnation of the Three Stooges. Moe later sold real estate for a time (would you buy a house from this man?) and, as the only Stooge with any business experience, he handled all of the business particulars for the group.

After completing his memoirs in May of 1975, Moe succumbed to lung cancer at 77. He's lying quite peacefully at Hillside Memorial Park in Los Angeles.

DIRECTIONS TO CEMETERY OF MOE: This cemetery borders the east side of I-405 at the Centinela Avenue exit, which is immediately north of the La Tijera Boulevard exit.

DIRECTIONS TO MOE'S GRAVE: Enter the park, make a left after the flagpole, then drive about 100 yards and stop. Walk down the stairs of the Court of Love, which is on your left. Across the court is the Alcove of Love where Moe rests in Crypt C-233.

Larry Fine

OCTOBER 5, 1902 – JANUARY 24, 1975

Before becoming the happy-go-lucky Stooge, Larry was a professional violinist. Keeping a low profile, always trying to keep the peace, and almost never delivering funny lines, he was considered insignificant by some fans, but it's doubtful the show would have gone anywhere as *The Two Stooges*. When Larry suffered a stroke in 1970, the Stooges' act finally ended forever.

Larry died five years later at 72 from complications of his stroke, and he lies at Forest Lawn Memorial Park in Glendale, California.

DIRECTIONS TO CEMETERY OF LARRY: From Highway 2, take the San Fernando Road exit and turn northwest. After a mile, make a right onto Glendale Avenue and the park's entrance is immediately to the right.

DIRECTIONS TO GRAVE OF LARRY: Stop at the booth, get a map, and drive up to the Freedom Mausoleum. Walk in the front entrance, make a left, and go down the stairs. At the bottom of the stairs, turn right and then right again. The last hall on the right is the Sanctuary of Liberation. It's where you'll find Larry's crypt.

Jerome Howard

OCTOBER 22, 1903 – JANUARY 18, 1952

Replacing his brother Shemp in 1932, Jerome shaved his head for the mundane purpose of looking starkly different from Moe and Larry, and he became the first Curly with that look. He constantly forgot his lines and his "woo-woo-woo-woo" trademark was originally an improvisation for when he was stuck for words. It stuck.

During the filming of the Stooges' 97th short in May 1946, Jerome suffered a stroke while on the set. He recovered enough to get married again and have a daughter but he didn't return to acting. After a few more strokes, he died in 1952. At 48, Jerome was buried at Home of Peace Memorial Park in Los Angeles.

DIRECTIONS TO CEMETERY OF JEROME AND SHEMP: Just west of the intersection of I-5 and I-710, Home of Peace is at 4334 Whittier Blvd.

DIRECTIONS TO JEROME'S GRAVE: Enter the park, bear right, take the next right and the next left. Stop on this drive about 100 feet before it makes an abrupt left. On the curb to the right are markings for the Western Jewish Institute. Jerome's stone can be found five rows back.

Shemp Howard
MARCH 17, 1895 – NOVEMBER 3, 1955

Shemp was the original Curly and seems to be the favorite of many Stooge aficionados, if there could even be such a thing. He was there at the beginning of their run, but in 1932 he left the act to pursue a solo career, only to return in 1946 after Jerome suffered a stroke. Over the next nine years Shemp made 73 shorts with the Stooges but his run came to a quick end in 1955 when he suffered a fatal heart attack while riding in a car with friends. At 60, Shemp was interred at Home of Peace Memorial Park in Los Angeles, like his brother Jerome, though they are in completely different areas of the cemetery.

DIRECTIONS TO SHEMP'S GRAVE: Enter the park, bear right, then turn left and park in front of the mausoleum. Walk inside through the pews and turn left at the Corridor of Benevolence. Then turn right at the Corridor of Eternal Life and Shemp's crypt is on the right, second row from the bottom.

Joe Besser
AUGUST 12, 1907 – MARCH 1, 1988

Joe was named as Shemp's replacement in 1956 and he certainly had his own style; he was the only Stooge who dared to hit Moe back with any regularity. But after only sixteen comedies, Columbia cancelled *The Three Stooges* and Joe was cast back into the real world.

At 80, Joe died of heart failure and, like Larry, he lies at Forest Lawn Memorial Park in Glendale, California.

DIRECTIONS TO GRAVE OF JOE BESSER: Stop at the booth, get a map, and drive up to the Freedom Mausoleum. Joe is buried in the grass outside of the mausoleum, across the drive in the Dedication section. His grave is directly across from the Williamson plaque and nine rows down the hill from the curb.

Joe DeRita

JULY 12, 1909 – JULY 3, 1993

After the Stooges comedies were released to television in 1958, their new-found popularity provided opportunities to make films, but the fact that Joe Besser had to care for his ailing wife left them one Stooge short. That's when Joe DeRita stepped in, helping them make six feature films during the 1960s including, *It's a Mad, Mad, Mad, Mad World.*

You'd think that out of the six different comics that made up the Stooges, at least one of them would have had an interesting or funny parting from this world. But it seems that relatively pedestrian passings are the theme here. When Joe died of pneumonia at 83 in 1993, an era ended: His passing marked the demise of last Stooge.

Joe was buried at Valhalla Memorial Park in North Hollywood, California.

DIRECTIONS TO CEMETERY OF JOE DERITA: This park is easy to find at 10621 Victory Blvd., just 2½ miles east of Highway 170.

DIRECTIONS TO GRAVE OF JOE DERITA: Drive through the gate, turn right and stop 50 feet after the road bends to the left. Joe is buried in the grass on the right, close to the road.

HERVE VILLECHAIZE
APRIL 23, 1943 – SEPTEMBER 4, 1993

The three-foot, nine-inch actor Herve Villechaize was best known for his TV role as Ricardo Montalban's sidekick, Tattoo, on the popular *Fantasy Island* program. Every episode opened with a planeload of guests arriving at the island to realize their fondest dreams, and in his role Herve would excitedly exclaim, "Boss! De plane! De plane!"

Over a salary dispute, Herve quit *Fantasy Island* the year before it was retired in 1984, and perhaps his absence hastened its cancellation, but the show seemed to have crested a few seasons earlier, anyway. Herve's next project was a lengthy unemployment streak broken only by an appearance in a doughnut commercial where he resurrected his infamous line in the context of his pastry preference: "De plain! De plain!" That's show business.

Born with undersized lungs and suffering from ulcers and a spastic colon, of all things, Herve's despondency over his health problems, and other personal issues, too, culminated in his suicide. He shot himself to death behind his garage at age 50.

Herve was cremated and his ashes scattered off Point Fermin in California.

JOHN WAYNE
MAY 26, 1907 – JUNE 11, 1979

After attending the University of Southern California on a football scholarship, Marion Morrison appeared in over 50 feature films and serials, mostly Westerns, during the 1930s. At some point in that early career, an executive did him the favor of a lifetime by unceremoniously changing his name to John Wayne, simply because he didn't like his real name. Nonetheless, John Wayne appeared to be doomed to a role as a leading player in low-budget films.

But in 1939, John was cast in the lead role of John Ford's *Stagecoach* and the film proved to be a turning point in his career. Although it took time for him to develop his rugged, American image, within a decade John was a top box-office draw and even today, he is one of the most popular actors of all time. Though the majority of his roles in the next 75 films were as an archetypal, no-nonsense hero in classic Westerns such as *The Searchers* and *The*

Man Who Shot Liberty Valance, John also personified the hard-as-nails patriot in war films like *Sands of Iwo Jima* and *The Green Berets*.

After four decades of Hollywood stardom, John and his fans suspected that the 1978 film *The Shootist* would be his last hurrah. John had lost a lung to cancer back in 1964 and, after studio press agents tried to conceal the nature of the illness, he'd gone before the public and shown that the disease was no match for John Wayne. But now the disease had invaded his internal organs and everyone, especially John, was cognizant of the awful, impending reality; the selfless hero onscreen was being done in by a selfish villain offscreen. When he died in the final shootout scene, everybody knew they'd seen the last of both John Waynes, the real and the imaginary.

John died of stomach cancer at 72 and was buried at Pacific View Memorial Park in Corona del Mar, California.

CEMETERY DIRECTIONS: From Route 1, turn east onto Marguerite Avenue where it intersects the highway a couple miles south of Newport Bay. Follow Marguerite Avenue for a mile to the "T," then turn right onto Pacific View Drive and you'll be led directly into the park.

GRAVE DIRECTIONS: Enter the park, bear left, and go up the hill toward the Lagunita Hill mausoleums. Across the drive from the mausoleums, find the "578" curb marking and John's grave is six rows down the hill.

LAWRENCE WELK

MARCH 11, 1903 – MAY 17, 1992

Who could ever have imagined that an uneducated, heavily accented, dirt-poor farm boy from North Dakota would preside over one of the longest-running shows in television history? Lawrence Welk attained that distinction by blending his folksy charm and his orchestra's easy-listening music with such traditional entertainment forms as tap and ballroom dancing, ragtime piano, jazz accordion, and mellow singing acts.

After a quarter-century of crisscrossing the country and leading his band everywhere from Yankton, South Dakota, to Newport, Oregon, to Hackensack, New Jersey, Lawrence scored a television show in 1955. *The Lawrence Welk Show* was an immediate success and it popularized his "champagne music," a term coined by a Pittsburgh radio announcer that succinctly characterized his sparkling and light, middle-of-the-road sound.

As the years wore on and the day's popular music continually reinvented itself, Lawrence stayed true to his muse; he made no pretense of being even remotely hip, and he refused to vary his basic recipe: Play what the people understand, keep it simple so the audience feels like they participate and, when in doubt, return to a composition that puts the girl back in the boy's arms. The show's banality became the butt of jokes, and detractors considered it tinkly Mickey Mouse music dispensed to geriatrics, but legions of fans adored the sentimentality as a reassuring time capsule of a simpler and happier time. And Lawrence continued to be popular long after his contemporaries faded, suggesting that perhaps he was onto something after all.

In 1971, *The Lawrence Welk Show* was cancelled, but Lawrence shrewdly signed up some 250 independent television stations and kept the program going for another eleven seasons. In sum, there were 1,542 "wunnerful, wunnerful," Lawrence Welk-hosted, champagne music broadcasts. Even today, at the Welk Resort Centers and Museums in Escondido, California, and in Branson, Missouri, additional productions continue in one form or another.

At 89, Lawrence Welk died of pneumonia at his Santa Monica beachfront condo.

He was buried at Holy Cross Cemetery in Culver City, California.

CEMETERY DIRECTIONS: From I-405, take Slauson Avenue east for a half-mile and the cemetery is on the left at #5835.

GRAVE DIRECTIONS: Enter the cemetery, drive up to the mausoleum on the hill, and to the right of the mausoleum you'll see a flower shop. Lawrence's grave is about 175 yards diagonally behind and to the left of the flower shop in Plot 110-T9.

Due to Lawrence's accent and his affinity for polkas, most folks thought he was Polish. In fact, he was born in the U.S. His parents had emigrated from Russia eight years earlier.

ORSON WELLES
MAY 6, 1915 – OCTOBER 10, 1985

A lthough he worked on the stage for more than 50 years, gave countless radio performances, starred in more than 60 films—many of which he both wrote and directed—and had a hand in another hundred or so motion pictures, Orson Welles' fame rests primarily on two projects he completed before he was barely 25 years old. By Orson's own admission, he "started at the top and worked my way down."

The public became aware of Orson with his chillingly realistic 1938 radio dramatization of *War of the Worlds*, complete with news bulletins and field reports of a supposed Martian landing and invasion in New Jersey. The radio play caused a panic among thousands of listeners; some even armed themselves and fled for the hills.

Orson was also the boy genius that co-wrote, directed, and starred in the film *Citizen Kane*, an extraordinary epic that some consider to be the greatest movie ever made. The film won Orson accolades and Academy Awards as well as numerous offers to direct many other films. After *Citizen Kane,* though, Orson's directorial work was inconsistent and he was eventually unable to find work as a director. Orson resorted to acting, just for the money it seems, as his primary ambition was to acquire necessary financing for a number of his other dream projects. The next decades of his life were a cycle of bad movies, grandiose projects that inevitably failed, and then more acting work to acquire more funds. After years of acting in truly terrible films (with the exceptions of *Jane Eyre* and *A Man for All Seasons*), and decades of relentless panning by critics, Orson had fallen from grace in Hollywood.

In the twilight of his life, Orson enjoyed a new acceptance within the show-business mainstream and, even though he still could not attract the funding to direct motion pictures, he became a frequent talk-show guest and commercial pitchman. And in 1975, the American Film Institute presented him with its Lifetime Achievement Award.

In his latter years, Orson was obese and suffered a number of weight-related ailments. Seated at his typewriter working on the next day's script changes for his movie, *The Other Side of the Wind*, Orson suffered a heart attack and died at 70.

He was cremated and his ashes shipped to the retired bullfighter, Antonio Ordóñez, an old friend in Ronda, Spain. Orson's cremains were placed into an old brick well at Ordonez's country house, which was then sealed and, per Orson's request, no designation of any kind marks the spot.

MAE WEST

AUGUST 17, 1892 – NOVEMBER 22, 1980

Mae West left formal education behind at age twelve to join a professional stock company, and by fourteen was consistently drawing crowds to the vaudeville stage. With tight-fitting clothing and provocative comments delivered in a throaty voice, Mae soon gained a bawdy reputation and, throughout her career, never squandered an opportunity to heighten this risqué allure or, better yet, use it to advantage.

In 1926 she wrote a play entitled *Sex*. It was popular on Broadway, but after 41 weeks of performances the entire cast was arrested and Mae was found guilty of corrupting the morals of youth. Later plays, *The Drag, Pleasure Man,* and *Constant Sinner* also became the targets of censors and some were forced to close after just one performance.

Tired of censorship struggles, Mae moved to Hollywood in 1931, confident that a career in film would afford more artistic freedom. Already popular on stage, she immediately won a contract with Paramount and enjoyed an enormous streak of success at the box office. Opposite many of the biggest actors of the day, Mae played diverse roles, from lion tamers to gangsters' girlfriends, with the haughty sexuality that had become her trademark.

By the 1940s though, Mae's age began to show and as her allure slipped, so did her popularity. Mae attempted to return to the stage but, beyond writing and starring in the risqué play, *Catherine Was Great*, her revival was not well received. In the early 1950s Mae tried again to revive her career, this time creating a nightclub act, complete with bodybuilders in loincloths, that portrayed her as a sultry siren, though she was now over 60.

Apparently, Mae never heard the word "quit," because in the 1960s she was back again—this time with an album that featured her singing Bob Dylan and Beatles songs. In 1977, at 84, Mae made one last movie, *Sextette*, which even her die-hard fans agree was her worst ever.

In her final years, Mae became increasingly interested in para-normal events and insisted she was in contact with a pet monkey who had died. Mae herself expired at 88 after suffering a stroke and lies at Cypress Hills Cemetery in Brooklyn, New York.

CEMETERY DIRECTIONS: From the Interboro Parkway, take Exit 3 and head south on Cypress Hill Street (not the same as the nearby Cypress Avenue). At Jamaica Avenue turn left, and the cemetery entrance is a short way beyond to the left.

GRAVE DIRECTIONS: Enter the cemetery, turn right and go past the office. After the road's left-hand bend, turn at the first right and then the next left. Go up the hill and Memorial Abbey will be in front of you. In this Abbey, which is generally locked, is the West family tomb.

FLIP WILSON

DECEMBER 8, 1933 – NOVEMBER 25, 1998

One of eighteen children born to a poor New Jersey household, Clerow "Flip" Wilson lied about his age and joined the Air Force at sixteen. With a lively sense of humor, he excelled in the service and it was his fellow servicemen who branded him "Flip," for his "flipped-out" personality. After leaving the Air Force at 21, Flip worked as a bellhop and moonlighted as a stand-up comedian. In 1965 he was invited to appear on *The Tonight Show*, and after that exposure, his star rose meteorically. Within a few years he had his own television show, *The Flip Wilson Show*.

The variety comedy show received only a tepid response at first, but wide-eyed Flip quickly drove the show to the top of the ratings with his keen wit and a collection of stock characters to which he brought comedic life with his hysterical body fluidity: Geraldine Jones was the sassy and swinging liberate who "don't take no stuff." There was the lecherous and slightly less-than-honest Reverend LeRoy of the Church of What's Happening, and Sonny the White House janitor was the "wisest man in Washington."

In 1974, after four award-winning seasons, the show's time was up and, strangely enough, so was Flip's. Though he'd exhibited that he could draw audiences, his career immediately lost its momentum and, except for an occasional guest spot, Flip vanished from show business.

At 64, Flip died after surgery to remove a malignant tumor on his liver. He was cremated and his ashes given to his family.

THE WIZARD OF OZ

If *The Wizard of Oz* had been released in almost any other year but 1939, it more than likely would have swept the Academy Awards. However, 1939 was one of the greatest years in movie history and *Oz* competed against such acclaimed films as *Mr. Smith Goes to Washington, Of Mice and Men, Wuthering Heights,* and *Gone With the Wind.* Opposite such strong competition, *Oz* won just two "Ozcars."

It did establish a new Hollywood benchmark of excellence for family musicals, but *The Wizard of Oz* didn't receive its deserved recognition until it debuted on television, almost twenty years later, to an audience that was very different from the Depression-era movie patrons who had celebrated its first release.

In 1956 MGM sold the *Wizard of Oz* rights to CBS. It debuted on television in November of that year and, because their agreement stipulated that *Oz* could only be aired once a year, CBS presented the film with all the pomp and circumstance afforded a precious jewel, causing a substantial lifting of the film's cultural status in the opinion of viewers. For the next 30 years, the annual showing of the *Wizard of Oz* was a can't-miss event for children of all ages because, if you did miss it, there was a one-year-long wait until Dorothy would again click her heels together. As a result, though *The Wizard of Oz* is certainly secure on its own merits as one of the best films ever made, the pageantry that surrounded its airings has indelibly branded *Oz* into the psyche of Baby Boomers who link it to the warmth and security of an innocent time long gone. Indeed, there's no place like home.

Judy Garland

JUNE 10, 1922 – JUNE 22, 1969

With her overambitious stage mother prodding her along, thirteen-year-old Judy Garland reported to MGM as a contract player in 1935 for $100 a week. Judy attended school on the studio lot with other future stars Ava Gardner and Mickey Rooney and, except for appearing in a handful of unremarkable movies, Judy was more or less just another teenager until 1939, when she lost herself and found Dorothy Gale, the forever-young, celluloid image of magnetic warmth blessed with a beautifully strong, tremulous singing voice. Later, when Dorothy became more than just a film personality to Judy's fans, the innocent teenager named Judy disappeared forever.

In the decade after *Oz*, superstar Judy was a moneymaking machine for MGM and she made films at a breakneck pace. Judy married twice, began smoking heavily, and rode the roller coaster of drug and alcohol abuse. When the pace became unbearable in 1950, Judy escalated her troubles by slitting her own neck with a piece of glass. Within a few years, though, life for Judy turned more agreeable; MGM cancelled her contract, her domineering mother died, and she married Sid Luft. It was Sid's idea that she sing in concerts and the 1950s turned out to be some of Judy's best years. While dazzling sellout crowds with concerts that invariably included her lifelong theme song: "Over the Rainbow," Judy also returned to the silver screen and gave a knockout performance in *A Star is Born*.

But by the early sixties, the screw had again turned and she accelerated toward her tragic destiny. As an honorary member of the Rat Pack, her drinking problem was exacerbated and *The Judy Garland Show* was cancelled after she appeared on it drunk and disoriented once too often. Although she was brilliant in *Judgment at Nuremberg*, she was fired from other movies. Her personal life was again a shambles; she lived in hotels, was constantly in and out of hospitals for substance-related illnesses and, not surprisingly, her fourth marriage was disintegrating. By the late 1960s the prematurely aged Judy was performing on stage again, but her voice was shot, and she would often slur her way through her concerts.

In 1969 Judy was living in London with her fifth husband, Mickey Deans. He awoke one morning to a phone call for Judy and, seeing that she wasn't in bed, called for her in the bathroom. Getting no answer and finding the door locked, Mickey climbed onto the roof to look in the bathroom window and, there on the toilet, he saw Judy slumped over dead at 47.

The coroner determined she had died "of an incautious self-overdosage of sleeping pills," though others saw her death in less clinical terms. Ray Bolger, the Scarecrow, said, "Judy didn't die of anything except wearing out. She just plain wore out."

In the silver lamé gown she'd worn at her most recent wedding, Judy was interred in a crypt at the Ferncliffe Mausoleum in Hartsdale, New York.

CEMETERY DIRECTIONS: From I-87, take Exit 7 in Ardsley and follow Route 9A north for 1¼ miles. Turn right onto Secor Road at the traffic light, and the Ferncliffe Cemetery is a short distance on the left.

GRAVE DIRECTIONS: Enter Ferncliff at the first entrance, bear left and park toward the left-hand side of the main mausoleum. Enter the mausoleum through the front bronze doors and go up the stairs on the left. At the top of the stairs turn left, go to the end of the hall, and turn left again. Then make the next right, walk up the four stairs, and turn at the next right. Judy is in Alcove HH on the left bottom wall.

L. Frank Baum

MAY 15, 1856 – MAY 6, 1919

Originally from a wealthy family in the castor oil business, Lyman Frank Baum took turns as a small-town journalist, a chicken breeder, and an actor before failing as the proprietor of a South Dakota general store. Finally, at 40, Frank settled into writing and in the course of his remaining days turned out 30 books, from fairy-tale collections to window-dressing manuals. But, of course, Frank's most celebrated book is *The Wonderful Wizard of Oz.*

The book was immediately popular upon its release in 1900 and two years later, it became a musical stage production. Soon Frank's life revolved around everything *Oz;* he wrote thirteen *Oz* sequels, published a periodical, *The Ozmopolitan,* and built a home in California that he called "Ozcot." But for all his enthusiasm for his progeny, Frank would not live to enjoy its greatest celebrity.

At 62, twenty years before his *Wizard of Oz* appeared in Technicolor, Frank died of a congenital heart defect. He directed his last words to his wife, saying, "Now we can cross the shifting sands," a reference to the boundary that separates this world from the Land of Oz.

Frank was buried at Forest Lawn Memorial Park in Glendale, California.

CEMETERY DIRECTIONS: From Highway 2, take the San Fernando Road exit and turn northwest. After a mile, make a right onto Glendale Avenue. The park's entrance is immediately on the right.

GRAVE DIRECTIONS: Get a map at the information booth and drive over to Section G, which is in a maze of lawns behind the funeral home. In the middle of the section you'll see the white Peters stone, and just twenty feet left is the big and blocky Baum stone.

Clara Blandick

JUNE 4, 1881 - APRIL 15, 1962

Clara Blandick enjoyed a 40-year career as a stage and film actress but, as Auntie Em on the film that would immortalize her, she worked for just one week. And she's almost forgotten there; for some reason, Clara's name doesn't appear in the film's opening credits and she is billed last in the closing credits, right below Pat Walshe, who was the chief winged monkey. Perhaps MGM felt that the $750 Clara received for her appearance was payment enough.

After *The Wizard of Oz,* Clara continued acting and most often appeared as an archetypal maternal character or kindly spinster until her retirement in 1950.

In 1962, after years of surviving as a near-blind arthritic, Clara had had enough. Following a Palm Sunday service, Clara returned to her room at the Hollywood Roosevelt Hotel, dressed in her finest clothes, and penned a suicide note that began, "I am now about to take the great adventure . . ." Clara then ingested a number of sleeping pills, secured a plastic bag around her head, and died.

At 80, Clara was cremated and her ashes interred at Forest Lawn Memorial Park in Glendale, California.

CEMETERY DIRECTIONS: From Highway 2, take the San Fernando Road exit and turn northwest. After a mile, make a right onto Glendale Avenue and the park's entrance is immediately on the right.

GRAVE DIRECTIONS: If you'd like, you can stop at the booth, get a map of the grounds, and make your way over to the Great Mausoleum where Clara's remains are interred, but it probably won't do you any good. The Great Mausoleum is open only to property owners and there's a gatekeeper at its entrance that keeps everyone honest. But if you do manage to schmooze your way in, Clara's niche is Number 17230 in the Columbarium of Security.

Ray Bolger

JANUARY 10, 1904 - JANUARY 15, 1987

While Ray Bolger's portrayal of the Scarecrow made him one of the most beloved characters in *The Wizard of Oz,* Ray seemed to love *Oz* fans just as much. He was one of the few *Oz* actors who lived long enough to enjoy the movie's success after it became a television phenomenon, and he faithfully made *Oz*-related appearances, signed autographs, and sat for interviews.

Starting in vaudeville, Ray Bolger was half of a dance team called Sanford and Bolger. By 1936 Ray had secured a contract with MGM and when casting began for *The Wizard of Oz*, he was delighted to be included, then horrified to find out that he had been cast as the Tin Man. Knowing his dance style was better suited to the rubbery-legged straw man, he fought for the Scarecrow role and eventually wore down studio executives, who agreed to a switch.

The slow pace of moviemaking took its toll on high-energy Ray and, a month after finishing *The Wizard of Oz*, he asked to be released from his MGM contract. Ray then returned to his comfort zone on Broadway stages, though he reunited with Judy Garland in *The Harvey Girls* in 1946 and with Margaret Hamilton in *The Daydreamer* in 1966. He had his own television sitcom in 1953, *The Ray Bolger Show*, and later made the rounds on talk shows. In 1985, Ray took an affectionate look back at his 50-year career in a *That's Dancing* film extravaganza that was sentimentally co-hosted by Judy's daughter, Liza Minnelli, and directed by her ex-husband Jack Haley, Jr., who was the son of the Tin Man from *Oz*, Jack Haley.

Three years later, Ray died of bladder cancer and he bequeathed a $2.5 million trust in his name to the UCLA School of Theater, Film, and Television.

At 83, Ray was laid to rest at Holy Cross Cemetery in Culver City, California.

CEMETERY DIRECTIONS: From I-405, take Slauson Avenue east for a half-mile. The cemetery is on the left at #5835.

GRAVE DIRECTIONS: Enter the cemetery, drive to the mausoleum at the top of the hill and enter it through the front door. Proceed straight into the chapel and you'll see Ray's crypt alongside the pews, the sixth one on the bottom left.

Billie Burke

AUGUST 7, 1884 – MAY 14, 1970

Billie Burke, the delightful redhead cast as Glinda the Good Witch in *The Wizard of Oz*, was named after her father, Billy Burke, a Barnum and Bailey circus clown.

After establishing herself as a stage actress in London, where she spent her formative years, Billie moved to the States in 1908 and duplicated that success in the New York theater. In 1919 Billie married Florenz Ziegfeld, the producer whose dazzling Ziegfeld Follies revues featuring glitzy costumes and lavish sets epitomized the theatrical excesses of the Roaring Twenties. With money no longer an issue, Billie retired from show business to have a family, but the stock market crash of 1929 financially devastated their household and Billie was forced to return to work. Three years later, Florenz died of a stress-related heart attack.

Billie was 55 when she was cast as Glinda in 1939 and, as she was under contract to MGM, she didn't receive any more compensation for the blockbuster movie than her regular paycheck. By the time she played her last role in 1960, Billie had appeared in almost 70 films, usually as a daffy and scatterbrained lady of society. Highlights include *Dinner at Eight*, *Father of the Bride*, and *Merrily We Live*, the last of which earned her an Oscar nomination.

Ten years after she retired for good, natural causes sent Billie over the rainbow at 85.

She rests alongside husband Florenz at Kensico Cemetery in Valhalla, New York.

CEMETERY DIRECTIONS: From I-287, take Exit 4 and follow Route 100A north for 2½ miles. (Route 100A will become Route 100 after 2 miles.) Turn right on Lakeview Avenue, and after another half-mile, turn right onto Commerce Street and enter the cemetery.

GRAVE DIRECTIONS: Proceed down Commerce Street, make a right turn onto Tecumseh Avenue, a left onto Cherokee Avenue and, when you get to the "T," turn right onto Powhattan Avenue. Drive up to the circle and 75 feet behind the Roth mausoleum is the plot.

Victor Fleming
FEBRUARY 23, 1883 – JANUARY 6, 1949

Starting in Hollywood as a chauffeur, Victor Fleming eventually finagled a position as an assistant cameraman. Later, as President Woodrow Wilson's official cameraman, he filmed the signing of the Treaty of Versailles, which marked the end of World War I. Armed with those credentials, Victor returned to Hollywood in 1919 and made his directorial debut, launching a three-decades-long career with MGM Studios.

Victor had a talent for spectacular action movies but, though *The Wizard of Oz* may have been a bit of a departure from his usual directorial duties, the film certainly doesn't seem to have suffered. Remarkably, *Oz* wasn't the only blockbuster that Victor directed in 1939; when George Cukor quit as director of *Gone With the Wind*, Victor took over the job and, for two months until the shooting for

Oz finished, he directed them simultaneously. When Academy Awards were passed out in February 1940, it was no surprise that a frazzled Victor walked out with the award for best director, though it was for his *Gone With the Wind* work.

At 65, Victor died of a heart attack and now lies at Hollywood Forever in Hollywood, California.

CEMETERY DIRECTIONS: This cemetery is easy to find at 6000 Santa Monica Blvd., just west of Highway 101.

GRAVE DIRECTIONS: Enter the cemetery, turn right after the information booth, then make a left and stop in front of the Hollywood Forever Mausoleum (formerly called the Abbey of Psalms) which is the huge building on your right. Victor is inside this mausoleum in the Sanctuary of Refuge. Walk inside, turn left and, about halfway down this hall, on the right-hand side and second row from the floor, is Victor's crypt at number 2081.

Charlie Grapewin
DECEMBER 20, 1869 – FEBRUARY 2, 1956

By the time Charlie Grapewin was offered the role of kindly old Uncle Henry in *The Wizard of Oz*, he'd already spent nearly 40 years in the movie business and was thinking about getting out of it for good. But when casting began for the movie, Charlie was the first choice to fill the role, in no small part because he appeared in the original *Wizard of Oz* stage musical back in 1902. For old times' sake, he postponed his retirement and accepted the role.

Apparently, Charlie enjoyed his one week of filming because he forgot his retirement plans and appeared in another two dozen movies after *Oz*, most notably as Grandpa Joad in *The Grapes of Wrath*.

At 86 Charlie died of natural causes. He was cremated and his ashes interred at Forest Lawn Cemetery in Glendale, California.

For directions, see Clara Blandick's profile above. Her ashes happen to be interred in the same mausoleum as Charlie's, though his are kept at Niche 14639 in the Columbarium of Inspiration.

Jack Haley
AUGUST 10, 1899 – JUNE 6, 1979

Jack Haley, the Tin Man who wanted a heart, used to say that the first five years of his life were a waste because he didn't yet know what he would do with his life but, at six, he attended a play and resolved to become a dancer. After a run in vaudeville, Jack became a contract player at Fox and he appeared with Judy Garland in her very first feature film, *Pigskin Parade*, in 1936. But like the rest of the cast, it was his *Oz* role that brought Jack immortality.

Buddy Ebsen was MGM's original choice for the Tin Man, but after he suffered a nearly fatal allergic reaction to the makeup, Fox lent Jack out for the role. Jack later recalled that his days on the *Oz* set were among his most miserable because of the costume. Two hours a day were spent in the makeup chair, and once he had his costume on, he could not sit or lie down.

In 1974, an oddly personal bond was forged between Judy Garland and Jack; the Tin Man's real-life son, Jack Haley, Jr., married Dorothy's real-life daughter, Liza Minnelli.

Ironically, after wanting for a heart in *Oz*, it turned out that Jack's real-life ticker failed him. At 79, he died of a heart attack and was buried at Holy Cross Cemetery in Culver City, California.

CEMETERY DIRECTIONS: From I-405, follow Slauson Avenue east for a half-mile. The cemetery is on the left at #5835.

GRAVE DIRECTIONS: Enter the cemetery, turn left and start up the hill. A hundred yards on the left is the Grotto lawn and altar and six rows down the hill from the altar is Jack's grave.

Margaret Hamilton
DECEMBER 9, 1902 – MAY 16, 1985

Margaret Hamilton, who was a kindergarten teacher before landing her first movie role in 1933, played the cackling Wicked Witch of the West. And, like Jack Haley, the Tin Man, Margaret wasn't the studio's original choice for the role of the Wicked Witch.

The producers originally wanted the Wicked Witch of the West to be slinky and glamorous, like the wicked queen in Disney's *Snow White*, and they cast star actress Gale Sondergaard, envisioning her in a tight-fitting black sequined dress. But when it was decided that the witch would instead be ugly and hateful, Sondergaard backed out of the film and Margaret got the nod.

When Margaret Hamilton stepped onto the set she was already experienced in the role, having played it twice in community theater productions. After suffering through the makeup routine, Margaret's withering scowl and screeching chortle further enhanced the char-

---

acter's identity and audiences believed her to be very old. But in fact, Margaret was just 36, while Billie Burke, as Glinda the Good Witch, was 55.

After *Oz*, Margaret continued to act in a variety of media and in the 1970s she appeared in commercials as Cora, the shopkeeper who sold only Maxwell House coffee.

At 82, Margaret died of a heart attack. She was cremated and her ashes remain with her family.

Bert Lahr

AUGUST 13, 1895 – DECEMBER 3, 1967

Like most of his *Oz* costars, Bert Lahr, the Cowardly Lion, got his start in burlesque theatre and vaudeville. He met his wife, Mercedes Delpino, on the circuit and by 1925 they were listed as a Keith-Albee All-Star Act. By the 1930s, Bert's career was firing on all cylinders but Mercedes' mental health was deteriorating and she was soon committed to a sanitarium. Bert spent the next years mugging and gagging his way through film roles but, personally, he anguished over Mercedes.

Within a few years it was apparent that Mercedes' situation was hopeless, and Bert became involved with another woman, Mildred. But Bert was unable to annul his marriage to Mercedes and, in the meantime, Mildred married someone else. By the time filming for *The Wizard of Oz* began, Bert was beside himself, constantly anxious, unable to sleep, and suffering from a variety of imagined illnesses— just like the Cowardly Lion.

The boundless energy that made Bert the perfect lion made him difficult to cast in other films and after *Oz*, Bert retreated back to the stage. Bert was finally offered a role in the nostalgic 1967 film, *The Night They Raided Minsky's*. But unfortunately, he died of a hemorrhage resulting from cancer complications during the film's production, forcing the producers to finish the film with a different actor in several scenes.

At 72, Bert was buried at the Union Field Cemetery of Congregation Rodeph Sholom in Ridgewood, Queens, New York.

CEMETERY DIRECTIONS: From the Jackie Robinson Parkway, take Exit 3 and turn west along Cypress Avenue. The cemetery is a short distance ahead on the right.

GRAVE DIRECTIONS: Proceed down the road that's directly behind the office. After it bends to the left, watch for path markings on the curb and stop at number 5 on the right. A short way down this path, Bert is buried on the right-hand side.

Frank Morgan

JULY 1, 1890 – SEPTEMBER 18, 1949

When casting began for *The Wizard of Oz*, MGM executives searched for a famous comedian to fill the title role. But their first choice, W.C. Fields, wanted too much money and Ed Wynn turned down the part because he felt it was too small.

Finally, one of the studio's own character actors who already had an Academy nomination under his belt, Frank Morgan, auditioned for the part of the befuddled Wizard. He was perfect. In fact, Frank landed not just one part but five: Frank also played Professor Marvel, the Emerald City gatekeeper, a cabby, and a soldier.

After *The Wizard of Oz*, Frank continued acting and earned another Oscar nomination for *Tortilla Flat* in 1942. Away from Hollywood, he tended to his 550-acre California farm.

At 59, Frank died in his sleep and was buried at Greenwood Cemetery in Brooklyn, New York.

CEMETERY DIRECTIONS: The main entrance to Greenwood is at the intersection of 5th Avenue and 25th Street. It's easy to reach by exiting the Prospect Expressway at either Exit 2 or Exit 3.

GRAVE DIRECTIONS: Enter through the cemetery's elaborate gates, bear left up Battle Avenue, and drive up the hill. Turn left onto Border Avenue, keeping the city street and fence to your left, until you reach Sassafras Avenue. Turn right, then make a left onto Grape Avenue and, immediately before Lychnis Path, you'll see the Wupperman plot on the left. (Wupperman was Frank's given surname.)

Toto

1932 – 1945

Contrary to popular belief, the little Cairn terrier who played Toto in *The Wizard of Oz* was not named Toto, until *Oz* became so popular that almost everyone forgot what her original name was. Like all of the other cast members, she had a character name, Toto, and a real name, Terry. She may have been the best player on the set too, because, without even the benefit of makeup or a costume, Terry the girl dog played Toto the boy dog.

Terry's owner and trainer, a guy named Carl Spitz who ran the Hollywood Dog Training School, adopted her in 1933 but had no plans for little Terry to become a movie star. Her original owner had left her to be trained but never returned. Later, when the casting director put out a call for a dog that looked like the one in the illustrations in *The Wonderful Wizard of Oz*, Carl knew right away that they needed a Cairn terrier, and he brought Terry to the studio.

Terry was hired on the spot and she immediately began living the high life, which meant two weeks at Judy Garland's house and a $125-a-week salary. But life in the spotlight wasn't always glamorous. Terry didn't like being in the basket, she cowered when the set's wind machines were switched on, and she suffered a sprained foot after being stepped on accidentally by one of the Witch's guards. But Terry recuperated, and she returned a few weeks later to film the Munchkinland scenes, as good as new.

After *Oz*, Terry's name was officially changed to Toto and she appeared in another half-dozen films. In 1945, Toto died at thirteen (that's 91 in dog years) and was buried somewhere in Carl's backyard, somewhere in Hollywood, California.

NATALIE WOOD

JULY 20, 1938 – NOVEMBER 29, 1981

Natalie Wood was only four years old when she began her Hollywood career, and this little darling became one of the very few child actors who made a successful transition to adult stardom. Born Natasha Gurdin to Russian parents, Natalie made her mark as a nine-year-old costar in *Miracle on 34th Street*. After struggling through adolescence on a television series called *Pride of the Family*, she broke out for good as a young adult opposite James Dean in *Rebel Without a Cause*.

In 1961, the success of *West Side Story* vaulted petite and doe-eyed Natalie to superstar status and so began an insatiable public appetite for Natalie. The reports of her flamboyant lifestyle, huge salaries, and romantic escapades, her mansions and yachts, midnight swims, motorcycle rides, celebrity parties, and night life, fueled the aura surrounding Natalie Wood. Heightening the mystique further, many of her films' titles during this era were suggestive and controversial and, even though most were not critical successes, her films were consistent box office hits because of her star power.

Natalie was wed three times, including twice to the same guy, actor Robert Wagner. At 19, she married him for five years and then, at 30, she married British producer Richard Gregson with whom she stayed for four years and had a daughter. In 1973, when she was 35, Natalie and Robert married for the second time, but several years later the marriage again began to crumble.

One night in November 1981, after a swordfish dinner and a lot of wine at a posh restaurant on California's Catalina Island, Natalie and Robert, along with actor Christopher Walken, returned to the couple's yacht, anchored offshore. Walken had been romantically linked to Natalie and he was costarring with her in *Brainstorm*, a science-fiction film that would be released posthumously. Around midnight, Natalie excused herself and went to bed while the two drunken men carried on, sometimes arguing.

Unable to sleep because the dinghy kept bumping into the vessel, it seems that she went out on the deck to tie it more securely but, inebriated from the night's refreshments, she accidentally slipped into the water. Wearing bed socks, a short tartan nightie, and wrapped in a waterlogged red duvet, the Coast Guard found Natalie in the morning, floating face down in the water offshore from Catalina's lava caves.

Robert and Walken, as well as the yacht's captain, who had been sleeping in his cabin, were separately interrogated, and their testimony was found to be fairly consistent. Bruises found on Natalie's arms and hands were believed to have been a result of her struggles to climb back aboard the vessel, and her death was ruled an accidental drowning.

Robert had named their yacht *Splendor* after the 1961 movie *Splendor in the Grass*, for which Natalie was nominated for an Oscar. It was an odd gesture since, during its filming, Natalie had fallen for the routine seductions of costar Warren Beatty, which led to the breakup of her first marriage with Robert. Even more ironic, in *Splendor in the Grass* Natalie played a girl who tried to drown herself.

Natalie was 43 and was buried at Westwood Memorial Park in Los Angeles.

CEMETERY DIRECTIONS: This little cemetery holds numerous celebrities and is peculiarly located behind the office complex at 10850 Wilshire Blvd., which is just about a half-mile east of I-405.

GRAVE DIRECTIONS: Natalie's marker is in the central lawn of the cemetery. Counting from the drive bordering the top of the lawn, it's in the fifth row, approximately in the middle.

ORIGINAL
WOMEN

ERMA BOMBECK

FEBRUARY 21, 1927 – APRIL 22, 1996

As America's first lady of household humor, Erma Bombeck turned her views of daily life in the suburbs into satirical newspaper columns and fourteen best-selling books, including *I Lost Everything in the Post-Natal Depression* and *The Grass Is Always Greener Over the Septic Tank.*

Erma began a career in journalism but left the profession in 1953 to start a family. At 37 she realized she was, "too old for a paper route, too young for Social Security and too tired for an affair," and started writing a weekly column for a local paper. The column, "At Wit's End," was a showcase for her repartee and observations on such drudgery as dirty laundry, uncooperative pets, nosy neighbors, and her blossoming, know-it-all children. She was master of precise witticisms, to wit: "No one ever died from sleeping in an unmade bed;" "Never go to a doctor whose office plants have died;" and "It goes without saying that you should never have more children than you have car windows." Erma's banter raised the spirits of housewives and, within a year, her column was syndicated, eventually appearing in more than 600 papers.

In 1991 Erma was diagnosed with breast cancer and underwent a mastectomy shortly thereafter. Two years later she began a daily routine of dialysis as polycistic kidney disease took hold and, in April 1996, Erma received a kidney transplant. For the first time, Erma discussed her disease in a column to her readers, writing about illness and compassion, and her faithful, adoring readers responded by the thousands with moving sympathy for their adored spokeswoman.

Three weeks after the operation, Erma died of complications from the transplant at 69.

At her funeral service, one eulogist reminded mourners of a final Erma quotation: "When I stand before God at the end of my life, I would hope that I would not have a single bit of talent left and could say, 'I used everything you gave me.'"

She was buried at Woodlawn Cemetery in Dayton, Ohio.

CEMETERY DIRECTIONS: From I-75, take Exit 52 and follow Route 35 east to the Jefferson Street exit. Turn south on Jefferson Street, which will become Warren Street and then Brown Street. (Brown Street is now also known as Erma Bombeck Way.) After about a half-mile, turn left onto Woodland Avenue, and the cemetery is a short distance ahead.

GRAVE DIRECTIONS: Enter the cemetery and, after about 150 yards, to the left you'll see a bench with two derby hats sculpted into it (dedicated to the Wright Brothers). Behind this bench is a boulder, and just behind this stone lies Erma. Her grave is otherwise unmarked.

RACHEL CARSON
MAY 27, 1907 – APRIL 14, 1964

Ecologist and author Rachel Carson is considered the mother of the modern environmental movement. After studying at Johns Hopkins University and working at the Woods Hole Oceanographic Institution, Rachel began working for the United States Fish and Wildlife Service in 1936 as a writer of conservation and natural resource pamphlets. Several years later she was named editor in chief for all of the Service's publications. Rachel also wrote natural history articles for the *Baltimore Sun* and gained a devoted following for her instigation of the notion that humans hold a vitally unique responsibility for nature: As the only species that could ruin the state of natural world, it's the duty of humans to police themselves and act as environmental stewards.

In 1941, Rachel released *Under the Sea Wind*, a best-selling narration of marine life written in clear and nontechnical prose for the layperson. Its follow-ups, *The Sea Around Us* and *The Edge of the Sea,* came in the next decade and these works together constituted a biography of the ocean.

After receiving a Guggenheim Foundation fellowship in 1951, Rachel changed her focus from the oceans to the land and in 1962 released her damningly influential, best-selling book, *Silent Spring.* In carefully worded and measured prose she challenged agricultural scientists, the government, and especially the chemical industry, for their profligate use of synthetic chemical pesticides and called for their banning. Not surprisingly, Rachel was labeled an alarmist, but the proverbial cat was out of the bag and a presidential commission endorsed her findings. *Silent Spring* came to be a socially influential book; it spurred an environmental consciousness among Americans, lent a scientific respectability to the environmental movement, and is credited with prompting the creation of the Environmental Protection Agency.

Unfortunately, Rachel never got to see the effects of her work. After a long battle against breast cancer, she died at 56. Rachel was cremated and her ashes buried at Parklawn Memorial Park in Rockville, Maryland.

CEMETERY DIRECTIONS: Take Exit 6 off of I-270, turn east and proceed straight through a series of lights and intersections. The road will change from Montgomery Avenue to Jefferson Street to Veirs Mill Road, but continue straight. After four miles the cemetery is on the right.

GRAVE DIRECTIONS: Enter the cemetery and follow the yellow-dashed drive. Stop immediately after you cross the fifth bridge, and near the curb on the right is a marker for Cynthia Tompkins. Rachel is just a few yards further up the hill behind Cynthia.

DIANA, PRINCESS OF WALES

JULY 1, 1961 – AUGUST 31, 1997

Daughter of an earl in one of the most aristocratic British families, Diana Frances Spencer was the perfect candidate to marry Prince Charles, heir to the throne. Their courtship began after her older sister Sarah's nine-month relationship with Charles ended and, at nineteen, Lady Diana Spencer had become an object of fixation for the national media. She soon cultivated a bashful but charming smile for the cameras that earned her the nickname "Shy Di."

In February 1981, Charles proposed to Diana, and the couple appeared together in public for the first time at the official engagement announcement. They were married in the wedding of the century on July 29, 1981, at St. Paul's Cathedral. The couple smiled blissfully from the balcony at Buckingham Palace and kissed dutifully. To the adoring public, Diana and Charles appeared to be the perfect royal couple, especially when they produced William and Harry, an "heir and a spare."

Reports that their marriage was steadily unraveling leaked from the palace in the late 1980s and the relentless press speculated that both Charles and Diana were having extramarital affairs. Indeed, Charles had resumed a liaison with a darling from his bachelorhood, Camilla Parker-Bowles, while Diana carried on with a cavalry officer, James Hewitt. In December 1992 it was announced that Charles and Diana were separating and a year later, Charles admitted in a television interview that he'd had an adulterous relationship with Camilla. Diana responded with her own admission of adultery during a 1995 televised interview and expressed her desire to be "queen of people's hearts."

In a February 1996 letter, Queen Elizabeth II urged the couple to divorce and by the end of the year their decree was officially granted. Under the terms of the divorce agreement, Diana shared custody of William and Harry, received a lump-sum payment of $26.5 million, and was allowed to remain in a five-bedroom apartment in Kensington Palace. Diana was also stripped of her honorific "Her Royal Highness" and would instead be known simply as Diana, Princess of Wales.

Though Diana maintained a hectic schedule of appearances, especially those for her favorite charity causes—AIDS, breast cancer, child abuse, and land mines—as a divorcée, she began finally to live on her own terms. Unencumbered by stodgy royal protocols, she lived and socialized more freely. By the summer of 1997, Diana splashed into a romance with the debonair Emad (Dodi) al-Fayed, an Egyptian-born businessman and movie producer. Though she'd been rumored to have been involved with a number of men since her marriage disintegrated, her romance with Dodi was her first serious attachment.

Only five weeks into their whirlwind relationship, Diana and Dodi were killed in a car crash in a tunnel along the Seine River in Paris. News of Diana's death shocked the world and precipitated an outpouring of condolences that no one could have predicted. Anger was directed toward the paparazzi, which supposedly had been pursuing the fleeing Diana and her entourage, indirectly causing the crash. (It was later determined by a French court that the driver of their car, Henri Paul, who was also killed, was legally drunk and on prescription drugs at the time of the crash.) The court's report further stated that both Diana and Dodi would have survived the crash had they been wearing seatbelts.

Donations flooded the newly established Diana, Princess of Wales Fund, which was set up to serve her favorite charities, and Elton John earmarked future royalties from his song "Candle in the Wind," which he'd reworked to eulogize Diana, to the trust. After an extravagant service at Westminster Abbey, Diana was laid to rest on a leafy island in the center of a tranquil ornamental lake known as the Oval at the Spencer family's Althorp estate. The estate is 70 miles north of London and just about 6 miles west of the town of Northampton, and it's open to the public during the summer months for a small admission fee. But if you wish to see Diana's grave, save your money. Access anywhere near her resting place is restricted.

DIAN FOSSEY

JANUARY 16, 1932 – DECEMBER 27, 1985

In 1967, Dian Fossey established the Karisoke Research Center in Rwanda's Volcano National Park, and from this primitive and isolated rainforest camp, she studied mountain gorillas for almost twenty years. Dian's methodology was not to study the apes from afar, but rather to ingratiate herself into their society as a peripheral quasi-member. Thus, she put together a firsthand chronicle of the elusive apes' world.

By the 1970s, though, poachers had uncovered markets wherein gorilla babies could be sold for exhibition, and they were also able to command high black-market prices for the trophy heads, hands, and feet of adults. The appendages were made into ashtrays, of all things. Recognizing the threat posed to the gorillas' fragile population, Dian fought against the poachers. Rwandan authorities, however, did not consider poaching a priority, nor did they have adequate resources to control it.

Fears for the safety of her own gorilla "family" were justified in 1978 when her most darling gorilla, Digit, was killed. His hands and feet had been hacked off and other members of his family killed, too. Dian buried the massacred gorillas in a cemetery she built by her camp and steeled herself to become a vigilante of sorts, engaging in an all-consuming, unconventional war against the poachers. Circulating stories that she was a sorceress who could curse her enemies, she played the role of a witch around suspected poachers and fueled the notion that she had the power to damn them. She organized antipoaching patrols and placed bounties on poachers' heads. On one occasion, she abducted the child of a local woman suspected of stealing a gorilla baby and offered to exchange hostages. Meanwhile, her Western colleagues wondered if Dian had gone bananas.

Animosity between Dian and the poachers reached a boiling point and finally, at age 53, Dian was found dead at her tent compound, her body hacked to death by machete. No arrests were ever made, but conventional wisdom suggests that the killer or killers likely came from the poachers' ranks.

Fittingly, she was buried in her own Gorilla Graveyard near her beloved friend, Digit.

Dian's headstone summarizes her life:

> *Dian Fossey 1932-1985*
> *No one loved gorillas more . . .*

Deep within Africa's Virunga Mountains, the Karisoke Research Center and its Gorilla Graveyard lie in Rwanda, south of the base of Mount Visoke and Volcanoes National Park, two miles from the border with the Democratic Republic of the Congo (formerly Zaire).

The Center is still supported by the Dian Fossey Gorilla Fund International and functions as an important base for international research but, in 2001, less than 300 people were allowed to visit due to the dangers posed by Hutu rebels. In June 1997, the area was closed due to the Rwandan genocide and, when it reopened in July 1999, a number of mountain gorillas were missing or dead. Today there are believed to be about 620 gorillas remaining.

SUSAN HAYWARD

JUNE 30, 1919 – MARCH 14, 1975

In more than fifty films, Susan Hayward's inspirational roles made her a favorite of female movie fans, and during the 1950s she was one of the most sought-after stars in Hollywood.

Beginning her life as Edith Marrener, Susan created an indelible impression of brassy charm, pert sexiness, and a spirit that met tragedy with defiance in movies like *I Want to Live!* and *Smash-Up: The Story of a Woman*. Her greatest impact was playing real women who dealt with heartbreak and struggle, and endured.

Susan's personal life mirrored her movies, with many ups and downs: a modeling career started with a lucky break—she walked in the door of an agency just as it received a call for a redhead; a director who saw her picture in a magazine offered her a screen test; she was rejected as costar in *Gone with the Wind*; a bicycle accident cast her onto the lawn of an agent who created her lasting stage name. A gutsy appeal to a convention of film distributors set her career rolling, and she enjoyed public triumph, stardom, and an Oscar. But then, personal tragedy struck: an ugly divorce, a custody battle for her twin sons, and an attempted suicide. Finally, a happy marriage ended tragically when Susan was widowed.

In a final twist, it was discovered in 1973 that Susan had a brain tumor, the same affliction that befell her character in *The Stolen Hours*, and at 55 she died of the ailment.

Susan was buried at the Cemetery of Our Lady of Perpetual Help Catholic Church in Carrollton, Georgia.

CEMETERY DIRECTIONS: From I-20, take Exit 4 and follow Route 113 south for four miles to Center Point Road. Turn right, and the church and cemetery are a short distance on the left.

GRAVE DIRECTIONS: You won't miss Susan's grave in the Chalkey plot with the elaborate stone curved headwall.

BILLIE HOLIDAY
APRIL 7, 1915 – JULY 17, 1959

Billie Holiday was born in the Baltimore ghetto and at age six, when perhaps she should've been in school, she was instead working at Alice Dean's brothel, running errands and scrubbing floors for a living. At ten, she was raped by a neighbor and for that "offense" was sent to a home for wayward girls. By thirteen Billie had surfaced in Harlem and was working as a part-time prostitute.

Fortunately, at around sixteen, it was discovered that she was a bit of a jazz singer, and Billie went from selling her physical talents to her musical ones. She became a fixture of the nightclub scene and in 1932, Columbia talent scout John Hammond (who years later discovered both Bob Dylan and Bruce Springsteen) heard Billie's wailings and arranged for her to record a few titles with Benny Goodman's orchestra.

After recording with Goodman and touring with a number of other popular orchestras over the next few years, Billie had elevated her technique and, despite never having received any technical training, her delicately wavering voice made her the outstanding jazz singer of her day. Billie came to be known as Lady Day, and between 1933 and 1944, she recorded over 200 "sides," though, egregiously, she never received royalties for any of them.

From 1944 to 1950, Billie recorded with Decca and, with trademark white gardenias fastened in her hair, she turned second-rate love songs into jazz classics. During the mid-1940s, though her demon was knocking at the door, Billie was at an artistic peak. "Singing songs like the 'The Man I Love' or 'Porgy' is no more work than sitting down and eating Chinese roast duck, and I love roast duck," she wrote in a 1956 autobiography.

The demon that Billie was dueling was of a familiar variety: She was addicted to heroin and spent much of 1947 in a federal women's prison in West Virginia for heroin possession. Furthermore, for years after her release, she was refused a New York cabaret license, which she needed in order to sing at the popular clubs that were the fundamental venues of her career.

By 1959, Billie was a physical wreck. She collapsed during a Greenwich Village performance after just two songs and was admitted to a city hospital in Harlem, suffering from cirrhosis and heart trouble. In those sad last days, she was arrested again for heroin possession, on her gurney, after a nurse said she found a foil package of the white powder near her bed. At 44, Billie's lungs became congested and her heart gave out. When she was removed from the bed, fifteen $50 bills were found taped to one of her legs, an advance for some autobiographical articles.

Wearing her favorite pink lace stage gown and pink gloves, Billie was buried at St. Raymond's Cemetery in the Bronx, New York.

CEMETERY DIRECTIONS: St. Raymond's is located just north of the Throggs Neck bridge. From I-295, take Exit 9, then follow 177th Street in a northwest direction to Lafayette Street. You'll see the cemetery on the left at 177th and Lafayette Street.

GRAVE DIRECTIONS: Enter the cemetery and, shortly ahead on the right, not far from the main office, is the St. Paul section. Billie is buried there at Range 56, Plot 29. In this cemetery's parlance, the notation means Billie's grave is in the 56th row (every 15th row is marked), and her stone is the 29th from the road.

JANIS JOPLIN

JANUARY 19, 1943 – OCTOBER 4, 1970

Janis Joplin grew up in a relatively comfortable family and, though her siblings did not challenge their traditional way of life, Janis abhorred it. She left her Texas home at seventeen and, after a few years as a country-and-western singer around Houston, hitchhiked to her destiny in San Francisco.

Soon she joined a new group called Big Brother and the Holding Company and everything fell into place. Until Big Brother, Janis hadn't done much rock singing but she found it to be a perfect outlet for her pent-up frustrations, while the band's exuberant and jagged sound complemented her raw vocals. Janis became a vibrating, explosive part of the songs, and with soaring screams and wails and almost animalistic abandon, she sang to sellout audiences up and down the West Coast.

Janis so overshadowed the group that it was only a matter of time before she went solo, and shortly after the band released *Cheap Thrills* in 1968, she struck out on her own. It turned out to be a miscalculation on her part. She assembled two different bands over the next two years but, though each was musically adept, there was little feel for Janis's undisciplined style, and the raucous excitement of her work with Big Brother was missing.

In the fall of 1970 Janis was working on a new album while staying in room 105 of the Landmark Hotel (now the Highland Gardens Hotel) in Hollywood. On a Saturday afternoon, she called City Hall to inquire about getting a marriage license with her latest boyfriend and that night, recorded until about eleven o'clock. Janis next visited a bar with a couple of friends and, upon returning to her room, shot up with heroin.

When her guitarist wondered why she hadn't emerged from her room all day, she was found dead in bed. Though some still believe Janis committed suicide, the coroner ruled the 27-year-old's death accidental.

In accordance with her wishes, Janis was cremated and her ashes scattered from an airplane over the coastline of California's Marin County.

Janis had a will (evidence for those who speculate she committed suicide) that included the following bequests: $2,500 for two memorial gatherings for her friends in New York and in California; all rights and royalties for her work to be divided equally among her parents, her brother, and sister.

After her death, Janis's album *Pearl*, which includes her raspy rendition of Kris Kristofferson's "Me and Bobby McGee," was released and went gold.

FLORENCE JOYNER
DECEMBER 21, 1959 – SEPTEMBER 21, 1998

While growing up in the Watts ghetto of Los Angeles, Florence Joyner took up running through a local youth foundation. She later attended UCLA on a track scholarship and, the year after graduation, earned a Silver Medal in the 200-meter event at the 1984 Olympic Games. After the Olympics, Flo worked as a bank service representative during the day and as a hair stylist at night and, at one point, added almost 60 pounds to her previously superbly athletic physique.

But by 1987, in a resolve to return to competition and qualify for the 1988 Games, Flo began training anew with her husband, Al Joyner, and her sister in-law, Jackie Joyner-Kersee, who had each already won their own gold medals. By the time of the Olympic Trials, Flo's comeback was on track and she shaved an astonishing 2.7 seconds from the women's 100-meter dash, a record that stands today.

At the games in Seoul, Flo's comeback was complete. Flashy and confident, she stunned the world's track community by claiming three gold medals for the 100-, 200-, and 400-meter races, as well as a silver medal for the 1600-meter relay. During that summer of spectacular performances, Flo (or Flo-Jo, as she came to be known) also teased audiences by showing off her perfectly toned physique in signature one-legged racing outfits with low-cut tops. She made a further fashion statement with her lengthy and elaborately painted fingernails

Not surprisingly, on the heels of her Olympic knockout performance, rumors swirled that Flo had been taking performance-enhancing substances. She always denied the accusations and never failed a drug test. She soon announced her retirement and lived comfortably on her endorsements of athletic gear and fingernail products. Later, Flo established the Florence Griffith Youth Foundation, a nonprofit program for disadvantaged youth.

On a September morning in 1998, Al Joyner awoke to find Flo unresponsive and not breathing. She had died during the night. A preliminary investigation suggested that she suffered some kind of cardiac problem, and the public's immediate assumption was that Flo had died of a heart attack instigated by the excessive use of steroids. However, an autopsy revealed that Flo had died of "positional asphyxia due to epileptiform seizure" caused by a brain abnormality known as "cavernous angioma." In layman's terms, a deviation in her brain had caused an epileptic seizure, though not of the common convulsing variety, and Flo had simply suffocated in her pillow. The Orange County coroner added that he knew of no connection between that condition and steroid use.

But the story wasn't over. Another of Flo's endorsements was for milk and she had appeared in print advertisements wearing a "milk moustache" in a familiar Milk Council campaign. There is in milk a particular protein called casein that can produce a violent histological reaction in some people, especially in African Americans who happen to be more commonly lactose allergic. There is now a small movement afoot, initiated by folks who are adamant that humans have no business drinking cows' milk in the first place. They suggest that Flo's death was triggered by an allergic reaction to a dairy product, but that the information is being suppressed for fear of damaging the dairy industry.

At 38, Flo was buried at El Toro Memorial Park in Lake Forest, California.

CEMETERY DIRECTIONS: Lake Forest is a village that doesn't appear on all California maps. It's about ten miles south of Santa Ana on I-5. Take the Lake Forest Drive exit and follow it east for 2½ miles to Trabuco Road. Turn right and the cemetery is ahead one half-mile on the left.

GRAVE DIRECTIONS: Drive straight into the cemetery and park on the right in front of the Zaki Abujudeh bench, just before the "Park Rules" signboard. Follow the concrete path so that all of the columbarium niches are on your left and, at the end of the path, walk into the grass on the right. There you'll find Flo's grave in front of the white Duncan bench.

CHRISTA McAULIFFE

SEPTEMBER 2, 1948 – JANUARY 28, 1986

In 1985, Christa McAuliffe, a New Hampshire fifth-grade social studies teacher, was chosen by NASA to be the first "ordinary person" to fly into space. In the months leading up to the celebrated six-day mission, American classrooms around the nation tuned in to follow her experience and Christa endeared herself to the public at large. She was comfortable in front of a camera, well-spoken, and likable, and her "Reach for the Stars" history-making space shuttle mission was proving to be a public relations bonanza for NASA.

On January 28, 1986, Christa and her fellow astronauts Greg Jarvis, Ron McNair, Ellison Onizuka, Judy Resnick, Dick Scobee, and Michael Smith boarded the space shuttle *Challenger* and a spellbound nation watched with high expectations as their craft

lifted cleanly off the launch pad at 11:38 a.m., leaving its typical trail, a blazing geyser of fire and smoke. But 73 seconds into the flight, as the majestic spacecraft soared 13 miles into the deep blue sky above Florida, *Challenger* exploded in a ferocious fireball whose power was later described by NASA scientists as comparable to a "small nuclear weapon."

For a lingering moment there was stunned silence. As the pieces of wreckage traced slow-motion arcs out of the sky, the 1,200 well-wishers who had gathered around a giant television screen in Concord, New Hampshire, prayed in hushed disbelief. At Cape Canaveral's VIP viewing room, families of the seven astronauts who'd perished before their eyes shared an inconsolable grief.

After being bombarded by countless scientific and not-so-scientific explanations, conspiracy allegations, and talk-show elucidations, the official cause of the accident was presented through the Report of the Presidential Commission on the Space Shuttle Challenger Accident in June 1986. The report concluded that there was a failure of an O-ring seal in one of the craft's solid rocket motors. The seal failed due to a sensitive design that was degraded by external factors including temperature and reuse.

It was assumed by the general public that all those aboard *Challenger* died the moment the external fuel tank blew up. Of course, NASA was initially careful not to disturb this opinion, but the agency later concurred with scientists and engineers who insisted that not everyone, and probably no one, aboard the Challenger died the second the tank exploded.

If the cabin depressurized immediately, the crew would only have lived for perhaps 15 seconds after the blast. But if the cabin remained pressurized, which is possible, they might have survived for the full 2 minutes and 45 seconds it took to fall 65,000 feet back to Earth. However, they could not have survived the crushing 207 m.p.h. impact into the Atlantic Ocean, which refutes the wilder tabloid stories that had them alive for hours, or even days, waiting under the sea for rescuers who failed to reach them in time.

Possibly the best clue to solving the mystery of how long the doomed crew survived lies in the four emergency air packs that were recovered. Three had been manually activated, which demonstrated that at least some of the crew realized something was amiss, but the remaining inactivated packs indicate that loss of consciousness was also occurring at the same time.

A complete understanding of exactly what transpired is elusive because NASA remains highly secretive about the specifics of the tragedy. Furthermore, the agency may not themselves know exactly what befell the crew members as the wreckage and bodies spent up to six weeks in the sea before being recovered. Even then, much of the debris was never found.

At 38, Christa's remains were buried at Calvary Cemetery in Concord, New Hampshire.

CEMETERY DIRECTIONS: From I-93 take Exit 15W. At the second light turn right onto North State Street, and the cemetery is a mile ahead on the left.

GRAVE DIRECTIONS: Enter the cemetery at the third entrance (the one with the granite archway). Bear right after the archway, take the next left, then go all the way to the back. Christa's gravesite is marked with a black headstone on the left.

Unfortunately, the identity of all the recovered remains could not be established and, in a private ceremony on May 20, 1986, the unidentified remains were placed in a single, common grave at Arlington National Cemetery in Arlington, Virginia. The site in Section 46 is marked with a single tablet dedicated to the memory of the seven *Challenger* astronauts.

GEORGIA O'KEEFFE
NOVEMBER 15, 1887 – MARCH 6, 1986

Georgia O'Keeffe's catalog is an embodiment of boldly original paintings encompassing a wide vision, from sensuous evocations of flowers to dramatic cityscapes to bleached bones stranded in the high desert. She settled in New York City with the internationally known photographer and art impresario Alfred Stieglitz after he discovered her professionally. They wed in 1924, and the couple was the centerpiece of New York's burgeoning modern-art scene for three decades. After Alfred's death in 1946, Georgia moved west into an old adobe house on what came to be known as her Ghost Ranch, in New Mexico north of Santa Fe.

In the following four decades, Georgia painted an ambitiously vivid narrative of the region featuring multicolored desert particularities against strident skies in hues designed to startle the senses. The territory's dramatic mesas and desiccated terrain, as well as its ancient Spanish architecture, became her constant themes, and she only occasionally departed to interpret details of her home's doors and windows or romanticize large-scale patterns of clouds and landscapes seen from the air.

Although she had a major retrospective at the Art Institute of Chicago and an exhibit at the Museum of Modern Art, Georgia had almost completely withdrawn from the public during her New Mexico years. By 1973, she abandoned painting entirely when her eyesight began to fail, but she soon had a new outlet for her vision of the world when she took in a 27-year-old potter who had an uncanny resemblance to the young Alfred Stieglitz. She started Juan Hamilton off pruning hedges, but he soon helped her complete her well-received 1976 autobiography. When she died, Hamilton became the sole heir to her $70 million estate—an inheritance reduced after it was contested by a niece and nephew.

Before her death of natural causes at 98, a reflection on that destiny confirmed her unflagging spirit: "When I think of death, I only regret that I will not be able to see this beautiful country anymore … unless the Indians are right and my spirit will walk here after I'm gone."

Georgia was cremated and her ashes scattered at Pedernal Mountain, 30 miles north of Santa Fe near Abiquiu, New Mexico.

In 1997, the Georgia O'Keeffe Museum opened in Santa Fe.

SYLVIA PLATH

OCTOBER 27, 1932 – FEBRUARY 11, 1963

Sylvia Plath was writing complete poems by the age of five and, at eight, she had one of her works published in the *Boston Herald* newspaper. By seventeen she was an experienced writer and her short stories appeared in teen magazines. As a scholarship student at Smith College, she won a magazine fiction contest and was awarded two Smith poetry prizes.

Sylvia was sensitive, intelligent, and a perfectionist. Under the perfect surface though, was grave personal turmoil, and after having returned from a stint as a guest editor at *Mademoiselle* magazine while still a student, Sylvia made her first suicide attempt. After electroshock and psychotherapy treatments, Sylvia resumed her pursuit of academic and literary excellence, graduated from Smith *summa cum laude* in 1955, and went on to Newnham College, Cambridge, England, on a Fulbright fellowship.

In 1956, Sylvia and the poet Ted Hughes married and, though Sylvia had committed herself to an honest run at happiness, Ted was not the ideal husband she imagined; he was moody and slovenly, flirtatious and adulterous, while Sylvia was blindly faithful. After two years in Massachusetts, where Sylvia taught literature at her alma mater, the couple moved back to England and by 1962 had two children. But their marriage was coming apart at the seams. Sylvia's suspicions of Ted's adultery were soon proven correct and he abandoned her for another woman.

Sylvia kept writing throughout these tribulations. Her talent was keenly displayed in 1960 in her book of poems, *The Colossus*, and again in 1963 in her loosely autobiographical novel, *The Bell Jar*. But the formal precision of these works only hinted at what was fermenting as her relationship with Ted disintegrated.

The winter of 1963 was furiously cold in London and, while Ted cavorted in Spain with his new maiden, Sylvia battled the flu with her children in a cold and dark London flat, mustering the courage to execute her final plan. Late one night, Sylvia left a little food and milk in the bedroom of her sleeping children, cracked open their window, and sealed their door with towels and tape. Downstairs in the kitchen, Sylvia ingested a handful of sleeping pills, sat on the floor and rested her head inside the oven, its gas taps turned on full.

Sylvia's nurse found her in the morning. At her side, a suicide note read simply, "Please call Dr. Horder."

After Sylvia's death at 30, the poems over which she had toiled during the last chapter of her life were collected and released in three volumes: *Ariel, Crossing the Water,* and *Winter Trees*, each of which astonished the literary world. In these confessional poems Sylvia abandoned the restraints and conventions of her earlier work and unleashed graphically macabre verse full of ironic wit and hallucinogenic imagery.

"Dying is an art like everything else. I do it exceptionally well," she wrote in "Lady Lazarus."

"I am terrified of this dark thing that sleeps in me," read a passage in the poem "Elm."

It is upon these poems that Sylvia's literary reputation mainly rests and, because her divorce from Ted was never finalized, he won control of all their rights. In 1981, after Ted assembled some of them into *The Collected Poems*, Sylvia was honored with a posthumous Pulitzer Prize.

She was buried in the new cemetery adjoining the Church of St. Thomas Becket in Heptonstall, a small hilltop village above the town of Hebden Bridge in West Yorkshire, England. To find her grave, enter the cemetery from the entrance nearest the church and walk to the left along the second row of graves. Sylvia's unassuming stone is about two-thirds of the way down the row.

On her gravestone there is an inscription, from "Monkey," a story written by Wu Ch'eng-en about 1560: "Even amidst fierce flames the golden lotus can be planted."

MARGARET SANGER

SEPTEMBER 14, 1879 – SEPTEMBER 6, 1966

In 1912 Margaret Sanger was a public health nurse serving New York's poverty-stricken Lower East Side tenement families whose misery was mostly the result of unchecked childbirth. Her duties brought her into contact with many prematurely old and tired women, their bodies weakened by far too many pregnancies, and who, in panic at the thought of another child, customarily resorted to a self-induced or back-street abortion that oftentimes ended in death from blood poisoning. Others simply chose suicide directly. When women begged doctors for information on how to prevent future pregnancies, they were flippantly advised to "have their husbands sleep on the roof." Margaret attributed her own mother's premature death to her eighteen pregnancies and, from all this despair, she launched a revolution that discarded age-old birth-control taboos and made it acceptable not only to the medical profession, but to the public at large.

Of course, Margaret faced obstacles in her fight to make birth control information available. One was ignorance: Not even the medical community knew much about contraception. Another was

public opinion: Many people considered family planning immoral and perverted, and even the discussion of it unthinkable. But the main obstacle was the Comstock law, a federal statute that classified all contraceptive information as pornography and provided hefty fines and prison sentences of up to 45 years for its violators.

In 1914 Margaret established a newspaper, *The Woman Rebel*. In this radical monthly, the term "birth control" was coined and, though the newspaper contained no specific how-to information, Margaret was charged with violating federal law. Wanting the case against her to rest on something more fundamental than the generalized offenses of which she was accused, Margaret hurriedly assembled and distributed a pamphlet entitled *Family Limitation*, which included the forbidden contraceptive information, then fled overseas to avoid prosecution. For the next year she studied birth control in the more-liberal European countries, particularly the Netherlands, where the first clinics operated. Now fully prepared to face the charges against her, Margaret returned to the United States, but was disappointed when the government backed down, reluctant to grant her a public forum or try a case that might lead to changes in the law.

In October 1916 Margaret mounted a more direct challenge to Comstockian censorship and, with her sister Ethyl Byrne, opened America's first birth-control clinic in a desperately poor Brooklyn neighborhood. They were arrested ten days later, and the clinic was declared a public nuisance and shuttered. The defiant sisters were sentenced to jail for 30 days and the publicity made birth control a new matter of public debate. But, far more importantly, she won a clarification of a New York law that forbade distribution of birth-control information, and this change opened the door for doctor-staffed birth-control clinics.

Despite continuing legal harassment and strident opposition from religious groups who called her, among other things, "a lascivious murdering monster," Margaret pressed on. In 1923 she opened another New York clinic, this time staffed by a physician who offered contraceptive counseling and instruction not only to neighborhood women but also to other doctors. Police stormed the clinic six years later, but this time physicians sprang to its defense, claiming that the privacy of the doctor-patient relationship had been violated, and all charges were dismissed.

Margaret formed the American Birth Control League, forerunner of the Planned Parenthood Federation, a national lobbying group that spearheaded action on the legislative front and served as a clearinghouse for information on birth-control research, education, and services. The league slowly chipped away at various legislative restrictions, and in 1936 the Comstock law crumbled. Margaret expanded the scope of her movement worldwide and presided at conferences on birth and population control and, by the 1940s, the birth-control movement had been accepted by the medical profession and increasing numbers of the American public.

After four years in a Tucson nursing home, Margaret died of congestive heart failure at 86. Shortly before her death, she said that she hoped to be remembered for helping women because women take care of culture and tradition, they preserve what is good, and they are the strength of the future.

Margaret was buried at Fishkill Rural Cemetery in Fishkill, New York.

CEMETERY DIRECTIONS: Take Exit 13 from I-84, follow Route 9 north for a mile, and the cemetery is on the left.

GRAVE DIRECTIONS: Enter the cemetery, go past the office, and stay on the paved drive after the bridge. Turn right between Sections G and R, turn right again at the "T" in the road, then stop after 30 feet. A dozen yards to the left is the Slee plot, belonging to her husband's family, and there Margaret is buried.

GERTRUDE STEIN & ALICE B. TOKLAS
Gertrude Stein
FEBRUARY 3, 1874 – JULY 29, 1946

Alice B. Toklas
APRIL 30, 1877 – MARCH 7, 1967

After her formative years in San Francisco, Gertrude Stein became disillusioned while studying psychology at Johns Hopkins University and, in 1903, moved to Paris, where she would stay for the rest of her life. There, Gertrude soon established herself as a leading patron of avant-garde art and opened a salon with her brother Leo, who was himself an art critic and painter. As a result of Gertrude's notoriously sharp wit and formidable literary and artistic

ETERNAL COUPLE

GERTRUDE STEIN
& ALICE B. TOKLAS

judgment, the salon became a gathering place for developing artists and writers including Henri Matisse, Ezra Pound, Pablo Picasso, F. Scott Fitzgerald, and Ernest Hemingway. It was Gertrude who coined the phrase, adopted by Hemingway, "the lost generation," to describe the expatriate writers living abroad between the wars.

In 1907 Gertrude met Alice B. Toklas. In addition to their many mutual interests, they shared a strong personal attraction, and they eventually settled into life as partners. Gertrude wrote while Alice juggled all the domestic chores, proofreading and typing Gertrude's manuscripts besides. Since Gertrude fulfilled herself while Alice took care of her, some scholars have since criticized their relationship as mimicking the worst heterosexual marriage. Still, both women expressed contentment in their roles and were devoted to each other.

Never one to underplay her intellectual ability, the strong-willed Gertrude referred to herself as "the creative literary mind of the century," but her writing style, which mirrored the fragmented and abstract Cubist art style, was not commercially well-received. Her first two books, *Three Lives* and *Tender Buttons*, found favor with only a small, discerning audience and, during this time, Gertrude and Alice lived almost solely off their modest inheritances. Later came the more influential works *The Making of Americans* and *How to Write* and, finally, in 1933, Gertrude came to real prominence for *The Autobiography of Alice B. Toklas*. (The work is actually a biography of Gertrude, written by Gertrude, told from Alice's perspective.) Further confusing the matter was the popular film *I Love You, Alice B. Toklas*, which was released in 1968 and had absolutely nothing to do with the book, Gertrude, or Alice.

After surviving the Nazi occupation of France, Gertrude contracted cancer. Before undergoing surgery, she turned to a worried Alice and asked, "What is the answer?" Alice was silent and Gertrude continued, "In that case, what is the question?" These were among her last words; she died during the surgery at 72.

Alice lived another 21 years and tried her own hand at writing, contributing articles on cooking to magazines and compiling her memoirs in *What Is Remembered*. A reviewer called her "a woman who all her life has looked in a mirror and seen someone else."

When Alice died at 89, she was buried with Gertrude in a joint plot at the Père-Lachaise Cemetery in Paris.

MOTHER TERESA

AUGUST 26, 1910 – SEPTEMBER 5, 1997

In 1928 Agnes Gonxha Bojaxhiu, Mother Teresa, arrived in India by way of Ireland and Turkey, and for twenty years taught at a relatively wealthy Christian girls' school in India. After a spiritual second calling, the Vatican granted her permission to begin a new kind of work, and in 1950 her Missions of Charity order, where the most abjectly poor and terminally ill would be served, received official status.

Mother Teresa needed immediately to secure a place where she could care for these desperate people and, remarkably, the first location offered to her for this Christian work was an empty "dormashalah"—a place on the grounds of a sacred Hindu Kali Temple where pilgrims rested after their holy journeys. There, the sisters rallied against the squalor and worked to fill the last days of the loneliest destitute with dignity. Their order's distinguishing garment —a simple white sari with sapphire blue bands—soon became a familiar identifier of the caretakers of Calcutta's most impoverished.

In 1953 Mother Teresa's first orphanage opened and four years later her mission began working with lepers. In 1959 the order expanded outside of Calcutta and today there are more than 500 Missions of Charity worldwide, all dedicated to service of the most indigent.

By popular consensus and in the wake of her 1979 Nobel Peace Prize, Mother Teresa was lionized by the public but nonetheless continued to strike an apolitical pose, refusing to take a stand on anything other than strictly religious matters. Never a social critic, she did not attack the economic or political structures of the cultures that were producing the people she served. Her role was only to provide constant love.

At 87, Mother Teresa left her physical body and was buried in the back courtyard of the Mother House of the Sisters of the Missionaries of Charity in Calcutta, India, on the street of Acharya Jagadish Chandra Bose.

In normal circumstances the canonization of a potential saint does not begin until five years after his or her death. But Pope John Paul II, who has declared more saints than his predecessors in the last four centuries combined, signaled his great affection for Mother Teresa by allowing work to begin on the beatification of the diminutive missionary just two years after death.

In December 2002, he formally recognized a miracle attributed to her, and she is now set to be deemed a saint once a second miracle is credited.

GREATS OF
LITERATURE,
PHILOSOPHY
& THE ARTS

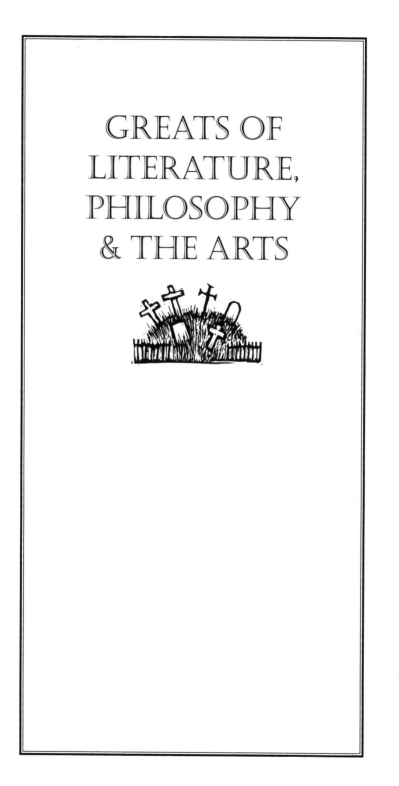

ANSEL ADAMS

FEBRUARY 20, 1902 – APRIL 22, 1984

The man responsible for the most majestic black-and-white landscapes of the American West liked to credit his photographs to luck, saying, "I get to places just as God is ready to have someone click the shutter." In reality, each of Ansel Adams' finished prints was the result of a painstaking effort to achieve an artistic result.

In 1916 Ansel's family vacationed in Yosemite and, from that visit until his death, he maintained a love affair with the land and became an advocate for its conservation. The visit also marked the beginning of his involvement with photography. Armed with his father's Kodak Brownie box camera and with one of the country's most beautiful landscapes before him, young Ansel began taking photographs, and he simply never stopped.

Though he worked as a concert pianist during his twenties, Ansel's photography hobby eventually overwhelmed his musical aspirations and he began to articulate his ideas about photography as an art form. In 1927, with *Monolith, the Face of Half Dome*, Ansel first developed his unique photographic style, using a red filter to dramatically darken the sky while leaving the famous granite formation in clear and sharp focus. He opened a studio in San Francisco, gave an exhibition in New York, and, by the time of World War II, was training the military's photographer historians.

Over the next decades Ansel produced most of the finest examples of the country's glorious and epic vistas. He received fellowships to record the national parks, was director of the Sierra Club for 37 years, and, by the 1970s, his prints accounted for half of the total dollar value of commercial photographic art sales in the United States. He was awarded the Presidential Medal of Freedom, the nation's highest civilian honor, and the humble visionary graced the cover of magazines. Indeed, Ansel always stressed the importance of vision, as distinct from gadgetry. "A picture," he said, "is only a collection of brightnesses and there is nothing worse than a brilliant image of a fuzzy concept."

Ansel died of heart disease at 82. In a fitting tribute, Congress passed legislation designating more than 200,000 acres near Yosemite National Park as the Ansel Adams Wilderness Area. Later, his ashes were scattered on Mount Ansel Adams, an 11,760-foot mountain within the wilderness area that was named in his honor.

DOUGLAS ADAMS

MARCH 11, 1952 – MAY 11, 2001

During a hitchhiking trip around Europe, British teenager Douglas Adams was lying in a field, a little bit drunk, thumbing a copy of *A Hitchhiker's Guide to Europe*, when it occurred to him that somebody should write a similar guide to the galaxy. As it happened, that "somebody" was Doug himself, and in 1979 his *The Hitchhiker's Guide to the Galaxy* was published, though it actually began life the previous year as a BBC radio series.

The cult science-fiction comedy is a picaresque account of mild-mannered suburbanite Arthur Dent's travels through space with his friend Ford Prefect after the Earth is destroyed to make way for an intergalactic highway. The book blends Doug's witty philosophy with memorably named characters like Zaphod Beeblebrox and Marvin the Paranoid Android, and is a repository for all knowledge, including the answer to "the ultimate question of life, the universe and everything" which, as it turns out, is 42.

Spawning best-selling sequels including *The Restaurant at the End of the Universe* and *So Long, and Thanks For All the Fish*, as well as hit television and stage shows, the *Guide* became a huge success, and one for which Doug always claimed he was quite unprepared. "It was like being helicoptered to the top of Mount Everest," he said, "or having an orgasm without the foreplay."

Doug died of a heart attack at 49 while working out at a gym near his home in Santa Barbara. He was cremated and his ashes entrusted to his family.

AUTHORS' RIDGE

Most Americans have heard of Concord, Massachusetts, and are aware of its historical significance during the Revolutionary War. Depending on one's interest level, anywhere from a few hours to a few days can be spent enjoying the area's historical landmarks and, if it's your inclination, be sure to include a visit to Sleepy Hollow Cemetery. The cemetery holds numerous Revolutionary-era heroes and, at the area of the cemetery known as Author's Ridge, the four authors profiled below rest peacefully beside one another.

Louisa Mae Alcott

NOVEMBER 29, 1832 – MARCH 6, 1888

Louisa Mae Alcott began writing a series of popular melodramatic short stories under the pseudonym A. M. Barnard in the late 1840s, but the turning point of her career came with the publication of *Little Women* in 1869. Though the work now seems somewhat dated and moralizing, *Little Women* and its four sequels document 1800s New England life with touching accuracy. They were instrumental in changing the focus of juvenile literature to include more sensitive and realistic portrayals of young adults, they have undergone several film adaptations, and adolescents continue to flock to the works today.

After spending the last decades of her life working for women's suffrage, Louisa Mae died at 55 of the long-term effects of mercury in her system. At the time, mercury was a common treatment for the effects of typhoid fever, to which she'd been exposed as a child.

Ralph Waldo Emerson

MAY 25, 1803 – APRIL 27, 1882

After graduating from Harvard in 1825, poet Ralph Waldo Emerson entered the ministry. He soon became an unwilling preacher, however, and, unable in good conscience to administer sacraments to his deceased nineteen-year-old wife, he resigned his pastorate in 1831. Soon he had settled in Concord, and in 1836 Emerson's ideas were collected in a volume of essays entitled *Nature*. The work prompted him to be considered, along with his contemporary Henry David Thoreau, as a chief proponent of the new Transcendentalist philosophy and literature movement, a reaction against scientific rationalism. The central tenet was that everything in our world is a microcosm of the universe, "an infinitude of the private man." Transcendentalists tended to disregard external authority and to rely instead on direct experience. Emerson's motto, "Trust thyself," became the movement's watchword.

For the remainder of his life, through a series of essays, poems, and lectures, Emerson preached these recurring themes, encouraging his audience to trust instinct and use their potential talents for authentic self-discovery to create a new American culture.

At 78, Emerson died of pneumonia.

Nathaniel Hawthorne

JULY 4, 1804 – MAY 19, 1864

In 1842 Nathaniel Hawthorne settled in Concord and, though he fraternized with the Transcendentalist crowd, he didn't share in their intellectual idealism. Instead, Nathaniel concentrated on the Puritan origins of American history, and on creating a distinctive literary style in two of the first truly great works of American literature, *The Scarlet Letter* in 1850 and its companion, *The House of the Seven Gables,* in the year following.

When Franklin Pierce became President in 1853, he appointed his old college buddy to an ambassadorship in England, and there Nathaniel wrote his last major work, *The Marble Faun.* In 1864 the two friends reunited for a pleasure trip to the White Mountains of New Hampshire, where Nathaniel quietly expired in his sleep at 59.

Henry David Thoreau

JULY 12, 1817 – MAY 6, 1862

Although he lived in relative obscurity, the rugged individualist Henry David Thoreau has come to be considered one of the central figures of American thought. He celebrated Independence Day 1845 on his own terms by beginning a two-year, self-imposed exile at a hut near Walden Pond, a period he later described in his most famous work, *Walden; or, Life in the Woods.* The book is an unfulfilled plea for simplicity and deliberateness in everyday life and continues to haunt those who are cognizant of the distance between their ideals and our materially driven culture.

(The use of the word "exile," by the way, is not wholly accurate. In actuality, Thoreau made frequent trips to Concord, welcomed occasional visitors, and entertained dinner guests. During this time, he even went to jail for refusing on principle to pay a poll tax and that one-night imprisonment was the catalyst for one of his most important political essays, "Civil Disobedience." In it, Thoreau exalts the law of conscience over civil law and implores citizens to nonviolent protest: "Unjust laws exist; shall we be content to obey them, or shall we endeavor to amend them, and obey them until we have succeeded, or shall we transgress them at once?" he wrote.

Finally, Thoreau is embraced by conservationists for his essay *Walking,* in which he celebrates the joys of the amble and pleads for conservation of the world's wild places. Published a month after his

death, the work is recognized as one of the pioneering documents in the conservation and national park movement in America.

After suffering a prolonged case of tuberculosis, Thoreau died at 44.

If you journey to Concord, you may also want to see Thoreau's house—the yellow one at 255 Main St. It's now a private home, but I'm sure the residents are used to gawkers. Thoreau lived in its attic during the last third of his life and, in the parlor just to the right of the front door, he died.

CEMETERY DIRECTIONS: From Boston, follow Route 2 west toward Concord. Once you get close, follow the signs to the center of town. From there, take Route 62 east, and Sleepy Hollow Cemetery is a short distance ahead on the left.

GRAVE DIRECTIONS: Once in the cemetery, look for the stone signs that direct you to the parking area for Author's Ridge. A walk up a small knoll delivers you to the ridge, and there you'll find the graves of Alcott, Emerson, Hawthorne, and Thoreau, each within a short distance of the others.

THE BEATS

The Beats were a group of carefree writers who emerged out of the strait-laced, post-World War II era to shake up the literary scene forever. Their refreshingly original approach advanced a reckless stance against the establishment, and their styles challenged the very notion of what constituted "literature," uprooting entrenched norms.

The word "beat" was itself a common localism for society's underbelly and was never meant to be elevating at all. It meant just the opposite, in fact—to be exhausted by existence. The word acquired historical resonance when Jack Kerouac, who would become the most cherished of the Beat writers, remarked to John Clellon Holmes, "I guess you might say we're a beat generation." Appropriating this conversation, Holmes brought the word into the mainstream in a November 1952 article, "This is the Beat Generation," in which he described it as "a feeling of being reduced to the bedrock of consciousness."

Writers soon began to invest the viewpoint of the defeated with a mystical perspective. Allen Ginsberg wrote, "the point of Beat is that you get beat down to a certain nakedness where you actually are able to see the world in a visionary way, which is the old classical understanding of what happens in the dark night of the soul." Through its literature, the Beat Generation outlived its historical moment, it survived its notoriety and the ensuing media blitz, and its works still inspire passionate ideals.

Jack Kerouac

MARCH 12, 1922 – OCTOBER 21, 1969

If there's a father of the Beat generation, his name is certainly Jack Kerouac. He came out of a broken-down New England mill town during the Depression and, as the star back on his high school team, won a football scholarship to Columbia University, from which he hoped to bring new prosperity to his blue-collar family. But things went wrong at Columbia and Jack dropped out. After being discharged from the Navy for having "an indifferent character," he ended up sailing with the merchant marines in 1942 and, when Jack wasn't sailing, he hung around New York with a new crowd of friends: a libertine Columbia student, Allen Ginsberg; a brilliantly bizarre literary inspiration, William S. Burroughs; and Neal Cassady, a joyful street cowboy from Denver.

Jack was already an author, but in 1951 he created something different. During a twenty-day binge, Jack wrote a "stream of consciousness" manuscript on a continuous, 128-foot scroll of tracing paper that became his *On The Road* masterpiece. With a sharp edge of social comment, it's an autobiographical story of two friends, Sal Paradise (Jack) and Dean Moriarty (Neal), who spontaneously and exuberantly reject middle-class conventions and wander through America in search of respite from mundane conformity. Jack, who also incorporated his sometime-mentor Allen into the book as Carlo Marx, spent years trying to get the work published, carrying it around in a rucksack wherever he went, until finally it was released in 1957. The work was an immediate success, but was mostly panned by literary critics, who objected to its fast and mad style. (Truman Capote famously complained, "That's not writing, that's typing.") But it's now a basic text for disenchanted youths whose lives have become claustrophobic and oppressive. More important, the book was a catalyst for the unfettered Beat lifestyle.

But Jack didn't react well to his sudden celebrity. Trying to live up to the image he'd presented in *On The Road*, his penchant for drink considerably worsened. He pursued Zen Buddhism and moved to California, but his brightness dimmed and he aged prematurely. In the half-dozen years after *On The Road*, Jack published many similar books, including *The Dharma Bums* and *The Subterraneans*, but most had actually been written years earlier. He lost his momentum as a writer, though he continued to be an involuntary celebrity through the 1960s. But mostly, Jack drank.

Defeated and disconnected, in 1961 Jack moved in with his mother, watching television, playing solitaire, and retreating into an alcohol-induced mania. In 1967 he married Stella Sampas, a maternalistic childhood friend, and the remainder of his life was spent sharing a home with both women. At 47, Jack died of an abdominal hemorrhage—he had drunk himself to death.

He was buried at Edison Cemetery in Lowell, Massachusetts.

At his death Jack was destitute, but in 2001, his original *On The Road* manuscript was sold at auction for $2.43 million.

CEMETERY DIRECTIONS: From either I-495 or Route 3, follow the Lowell Connector to Exit 5A and turn onto Route 3A south toward Billerica. After a mile you'll see the cemetery on your right. Enter at the main entrance, which is on the right just after Route 3A breaks into a "Y."

GRAVE DIRECTIONS: The main road inside the cemetery is 3rd Avenue. Follow it to Lincoln Avenue, turn left, then stop 30 feet after Seventh Avenue. Forty feet into the lawn on the right, in the Sampas family plot, is the flat stone that marks Jack's grave.

Neal Cassady

FEBRUARY 8, 1926 – FEBRUARY 3, 1968

Raised by an alcoholic father in skid-row hotels, Neal Cassady was a car thief who developed the suave instincts of a charming con artist—though he never seemed to want to con anybody out of much more than a ten-dollar bill or a roll in the hay. He became one of the most vibrant members of the Beat movement and ultimately influenced Kerouac, Ginsberg, Ken Kesey, Tom Wolfe, and the Grateful Dead, among others.

Neal met Jack and Allen Ginsberg in New York in 1946. Allen, a homosexual, immediately fell in love with him, and Neal, ever the hustler, began a sexual relationship with Allen, balancing it with his numerous heterosexual liaisons. But Neal and Jack soon left New York and began racing aimlessly around the country on adventures that would become *On The Road.* Jack wrote about their exploits even as they unfolded, but Jack grew frustrated, unable to find a style that fit the content. Later, a series of letters from Neal gave Jack the idea of documenting the trips exactly as they had happened, without pausing to fictionalize or even think, and to write the book the way Neal talked, in a rush of mad, unpretentious ecstasy. This spontaneous approach worked, and *On The Road* became a sensation by replicating Neal's unconstrained voice.

Neal was in tune with America and he resonated along the same frequency as the currents that were giving rise to the hippies and their "flower power." In 1964 Neal met Ken Kesey and before long, Ken's work was also showing the influence of Neal's optimistic ideals. Neal swayed the scene at Ken's "acid tests" while the Grateful Dead provided the soundtrack. Later, while his old friend Jack withdrew into alcoholism and early middle age, Neal began an entirely new series of road adventures as one of Ken's Merry Pranksters. A natural highwayman, he was the driver slinging abstractions in double time behind the wheel of their psychedelic bus, Furthur.

In San Miguel, Mexico, twenty months before Jack died, Neal wandered away from a Mexican wedding and, with a belly full of drinks and assorted recreational drugs, he decided to walk the fifteen miles to the next town. Neal slipped into the chilly desert night wearing only a t-shirt and jeans, and the next morning was found comatose alongside a stretch of railroad tracks. He died later that day at 41.

Neal was cremated, and his ashes are kept by his son in an ornate box. On a scrap of paper stapled to the box's side are the fading, typewritten words: *Contiene Cenizas Del Sr. Neal Cassady Jr.*

Allen Ginsberg

JUNE 3, 1926 – APRIL 5, 1997

Allen Ginsberg and Jack Kerouac greatly influenced each other's work. From Jack, Allen learned to write instinctively and impulsively and, in Allen, Jack found a tireless promoter for his labors. But during the 1960s their paths diverged. While Jack withdrew, Allen became more visible. In 1955, while television's married couples slept in separate beds, he released his declamation against the hypocrisy and silence of society's elders in his poem "Howl." But, unlike Jack, Allen stood publicly in defiant contrast to every kind of conformity.

Allen's detractors saw him as a drugged-up, blissed-out, left-wing pederast (which, of course, he was), but they failed to recognize that his relentless bombardment of the excesses of America's consumer-crazed culture was right on the money. The whole confused mish-mash of the nation's changing scene needed a point man, and Allen, never one to ignore any sloppy mainstream contradiction, gladly volunteered.

Away from poetry, he was a ringleader at be-ins and antiwar demonstrations and, in one particularly politically charged stunt, he even "exorcised" the Pentagon. He was at the acid tests, he was with the Dead and the Hell's Angels, and he supported Abbie Hoffman's hijinks at the 1968 Democratic Convention. Long before "coming out" was defined, Allen proudly pronounced his homosexuality. In music, he championed Bob Dylan as the electronic poet laureate and, later, songwriters from Patti Smith to Beck systematically took Allen's lyrical models to heart. He coined the term "flower power" and extolled the virtues of Buddhism, along with just about every inebriant or psychedelic drug that came his way. Wherever something "happened," it seemed, Allen Ginsberg was there.

At 70, surrounded by 40 family members and friends, Allen died of a heart attack related to his terminal liver cancer.

He was buried at B'nai Israel Cemetery in Newark, New Jersey.

CEMETERY DIRECTIONS: Take Exit 13A off of the New Jersey Turnpike (I-95) and follow Routes 1 and 9 north for a mile to McClellan Street. Turn west on McClellan Street and, after a half-mile, make a right turn onto Mt. Olivet Avenue. Banai Israel is the last cemetery on the left, though there is no sign.

GRAVE DIRECTIONS: Park at the gate next to the brick shed and walk into the cemetery along the paved drive. From the circle, the Ginsberg family plot is 30 feet to the right.

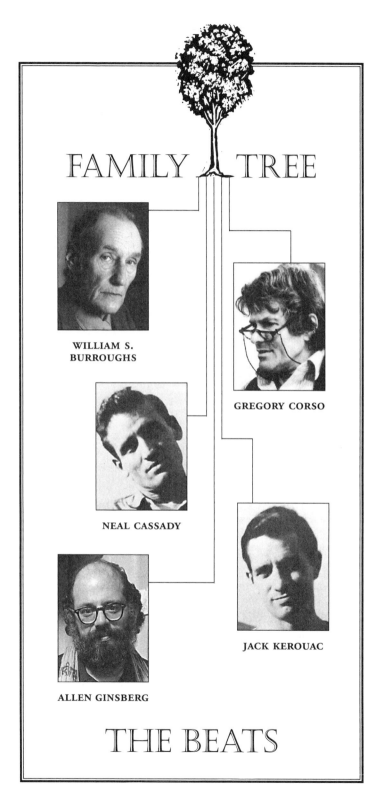

FAMILY TREE

**WILLIAM S.
BURROUGHS**

GREGORY CORSO

NEAL CASSADY

JACK KEROUAC

ALLEN GINSBERG

THE BEATS

The self-penned epitaph gracing his stone reads:

Father Breath once more farewell,
Birth you gave was no thing ill,
My heart is still as time will tell.

William S. Burroughs

FEBRUARY 5, 1914 – AUGUST 2, 1997

In 1945 Jack and Allen shared a Greenwich Village apartment with William S. Burroughs, who, as the elder, published sage, introduced his juniors to the esoterics of literature and the lowlife haunts of the big city. William was the most colorful and curious of any would-be Beat. As the grandson and namesake of the inventor of the adding machine, he had turned his back on a life of privileged respectability to sample drugs and pass his life in an outrageous, self-destructive fashion.

At thirteen, William's short essay, "Personal Magnetism," debunking control, was published. Two years later he somehow "learned to hate horses" at a New Mexico boys school. After graduating from Harvard University in 1936, he lopped off his left little finger and presented it to his analyst. By 1942, William was working as a New York City exterminator because "he knew where all the roaches were," but in 1946 William left the city after he and Jack were arrested for failing to report the murder of a quasi-friend. Although William, Jack, and Allen never again lived in proximity, Jack followed William to his various expatriate enclaves around the globe, and Allen later bluntly assessed William's impact on his writing by saying, "He showed me the world."

William got married and, after being a no-show for a New Orleans court appointment where he was to answer charges of drug possession, he and his wife, Joan, moved to Mexico City where William shot Joan dead in 1951 while trying to reenact the story of William Tell. He left Mexico before the incident could be investigated and, for the next twenty years, flitted about the globe more or less on the lam. Though he was spiraling into drug addiction, he was also writing again and, after Jack visited him in Morocco and helped him organize his "routines," *Naked Lunch* was published in 1959.

Though William's style mirrored that of his Beat buddies, the content of *Naked Lunch* came from some other distant netherworld. It's a torrent of nightmarish descriptions of bodily functions, sex acts, and grotesque medical procedures told under the influence of hallucinogenic addiction. It was praised as "a daring assault on conformity" by some quarters, while others dismissed it as "gibberish masquerading as social commentary." But, not surprisingly, it achieved cult status and William rode that success back to New York in 1974. Later, William began to write more conventional narratives, including *Place of the Dead Roads,* and with the renewed interest in the Beat movement during the materialistic 1990s, its stone-faced godfather gained new popularity as an avant-garde pioneer.

At 83, William died after suffering a heart attack and was buried at Bellefontaine Cemetery in St. Louis, Missouri.

CEMETERY DIRECTIONS: From I-70, take Exit 245B, follow West Florissant Avenue north for a half-mile. Enter the cemetery at the Willow Gate entrance on the right.

GRAVE DIRECTIONS: Inside the cemetery, make an immediate right after the office, which is Fountain Avenue. The drive winds around a bit, up and down a hill, then becomes Lake Avenue. Turn left when you get to the "Y," and the Burroughs plot is immediately on the right, marked with a big, white, granite obelisk.

There are a half-dozen Burroughs family members buried in this plot and none has his or her own stone; there's only the single obelisk. The William that most interests us is in Grave Number 7, which is the top grave all the way to the right as you look at the plot from the road. His grandfather William, inventor of the adding machine, is two plots to the left. The executor of William's estate planned to install individual grave markers for every plot, as well as a pair of decorative benches but, as William has been dead five years now, that proposal seems to have lost its momentum.

Gregory Corso
MARCH 26, 1930 – JANUARY 17, 2001

After being released from prison in 1950, the troubled Gregory Corso met Allen Ginsberg, who introduced him to his circle of bohemians and their experimental poetry. Gregory forged friendships and work alliances within the group, and even seduced Jack's girlfriend, which won him a role in Jack's *The Subterraneans* as the character Yuri Gregorovic. He was soon spouting words to huddled masses in street corner cafes. By 1958, when his *Gasoline* was issued, Gregory had become an emblematic character of the Beat movement, due in part to his bad-boy, jailhouse background.

During his career, Gregory published twenty volumes of poetry, plays, and fiction, notably *The Happy Birthday of Death, Long Live Man*, and *Elegiac Feelings American*, which was a requiem for Jack. To the literary world, Gregory's "wiseguy, artless diction" effected intimate expressions a notch below his contemporaries, though, at times, he could be more shocking than any of them. Aside from championing Lawrence Ferlinghetti's eclectic City Lights Bookstore in San Francisco (which also had a small press that published the works of Ferlinghetti's Beat pals), Gregory faded from the spotlight in later years. He surfaced when Allen Ginsberg died in 1997 and, attending a tribute to his old friend, he took the stage and uttered a one-word poem to him. "Toodle-oo," he said.

After a battle with prostate cancer, Gregory died at 70, and his passing marked an era; he was the last of the Beats to go. At his funeral, punk-rocker Patti Smith sang a hymn to the accompaniment of a pipe organ.

Gregory was cremated and, per his wishes, his ashes were buried at the Cimitero Acattolico, a non-Catholic (and non-Protestant) cemetery in Rome, Italy. This historical cemetery on Via Ostiensis, adjacent to the Pyramid of Cestii, also contains the remains of Gregory's spiritual mentors, John Keats and Percy Bysshe Shelley.

WILLIAM BLAKE
NOVEMBER 18, 1757 – AUGUST 12, 1827

Though he's today seen as a mystic revolutionary, during his lifetime William Blake was viewed as an eccentric, even insane, would-be poet and artist. To keep from starving he worked as an illustrator and, until he was rediscovered decades later, it was believed that his only meaningful contribution was the development of a significantly new method of engraving. In this process, which Blake dubbed "illuminated printing," both words and decorations were drawn on a copper plate. After the copper was etched with acid, the text and designs were left in relief and could be printed in any color.

Beginning in 1788 with *Natural Religion*, Blake published his own beautifully illustrated works in this fashion. His 1789 *Songs of Innocence* offered a unique ideological perspective of life, while *Songs of Experience* offered just the opposite. Released in 1794, it contained poems with some of the same titles as those in *Songs of Innocence* but from darker, more visceral perspectives. In *The French Revolution, America: A Prophecy*, and *Visions of the Daughters of Albion*, Blake combined his political beliefs and his visionary ebullience into a call for revolt against authority; he was a very free thinker with ideas that might be seen as radical even by today's standards.

The books sold slowly, for a few shillings each. Broke and disheartened by a lack of attention to his life's work, Blake died at 69 from some ailment, possibly gallstones. Today, a Blake original can fetch tens of thousands of dollars.

He was buried in London in an unmarked common grave that was then known as the Dissenters Burial Ground, though the area is today more pleasantly referred to as Bunhill Fields. It's a popular lunchtime spot for office workers and easy to find at the intersection of City Road and Bunhill Row in the north-central part of the city. Blake's marker, erected in 1927, sits smack-dab in the center of a walkway and states, "Nearby lie the remains of the poet-painter William Blake."

PEARL S. BUCK

JUNE 26, 1892 – MARCH 5, 1973

Born to Southern Presbyterian missionaries, Pearl S. Buck was taken to China at the age of three months and lived there for 40 years. She became intimately familiar with the daily lives of China's poorest inhabitants, and the village where she lived provided the primary setting for her first stories, including her novel *The Good Earth*. Loved by millions of readers since its publication in 1931, it was one of the most popular novels of the twentieth century, won a Pulitzer Prize, and was made into an Oscar-winning film.

But Pearl's ambitions weren't sated by mere success as a best-selling author. Upon her return to the United States, she was compelled to write and speak out on behalf of various humanitarian concerns and was active in campaigns for civil rights, the equal rights amendment, a nuclear test ban, and the improvement of international relations. She also worked on the problems of handicapped children and orphans, and raised millions of dollars for medical relief in China. Pearl established herself as one of the most influential women of the twentieth century and left a legacy far larger than her writings.

At 80 she died of cancer and was buried at her Green Hills Farm Estate in Dublin, Pennsylvania.

CEMETERY DIRECTIONS: Green Hills Farm is located on Dublin Avenue, the country road that runs for three miles between Dublin and Hillside, Pennsylvania. Along the road is a narrow stone bridge, and the farm is located just south of this bridge.

GRAVE DIRECTIONS: Enter the farm's main driveway and after about a hundred yards is a small paved pullout on the right. Stop and park here. Across the drive, follow the paved walk a short distance to Pearl's grave under an ash tree. She chose the grave site herself and her tombstone, which she designed, does not record her name in English; instead, the Chinese characters representing the name Pearl Sydenstricker are inscribed.

Green Hills Farm is now a National Historic Landmark and houses the international offices of the Pearl S. Buck Foundation. The work of the privately sponsored foundation is to assist Amerasian children in their native countries, particularly abandoned offspring fathered by American servicemen stationed overseas.

MICHELANGELO BUONARROTTI

MARCH 6, 1475 – FEBRUARY 18, 1564

As a sculptor, architect, and painter, Michelangelo was one of the most inspired creators in the history of art. He was the most potent force of the Italian High Renaissance, and his expressive use of the idealized human form had a tremendous impact on subsequent Western art.

Though Michelangelo spent the greater part of his adulthood employed by the popes in Rome, he was a Florentine art prodigy who, by fifteen, was living in the ruling Medici palace, with Lorenzo de Medici acting as his sole patron. Lorenzo died in 1492, and when the French invaded under Charles VII two years later, Michelangelo fled Florence and eventually landed in Rome.

There, Michelangelo quickly returned to his art and by 1498 his reputation was cemented with the completion of a magnificently sculpted Pietà (a representation of Mary's mourning over Christ's body), which now stands in Saint Peter's Cathedral. Word of his talent spread and Michelangelo returned to Florence in 1501 to sculpt the marble *David* that now flanks the entrance to the Palazzo Vecchio. Upon *David*'s completion, Pope Julius II summoned Michelangelo again to Rome to begin work on his tomb, which the master considered to be the low point of his career; by fits and starts, a scaled-down version of the colossally egoistic original was completed 40 years later.

While the tomb was in its early stages, Julius also commissioned Michelangelo to decorate the ceiling of the chief Vatican chapel, the Sistine. This would prove to be his masterpiece. Michelangelo and perhaps a half-dozen subordinates began the work in 1508 but, almost immediately, dissatisfied with his assistants' inability to meet his evolving demands, he sent them away and completed the monumental task single-handedly over the next four years. In a 1510 sonnet entitled "On Painting the Sistine Chapel Ceiling," Michelangelo offered a poignant account of his grueling task, painting while bent over backwards: "My belly's pushed by force beneath my chin, My beard toward Heaven, I feel the back of my brain."

By 1516, Florence was again under Medici power and Michelangelo again returned, working there intermittently on a number of projects until 1534, when he left Florence for the last time, settling in Rome. The first five years back in Rome were largely spent on the huge *Last Judgment* altarpiece painting for the Sistine Chapel, and over the next five years he finally finished the tomb of Julius II (who, by then, had been dead some 30 years).

Next, Pope Paul III appointed Michelangelo to take over the architectural design of Saint Peter's Cathedral, an enormous church with a huge central dome surrounded by a series of secondary structures. By the time Michelangelo died, a considerable part of Saint Peter's had been built, and it stands today as testimony to his grand vision. He died at 89, and though the Pope desired his body to be buried in Saint Peter's, Michelangelo had left instructions that he rest in Florence. His body was interred there, in the church of Santa Croce, and may be visited whenever the church is open.

ALBERT CAMUS

NOVEMBER 7, 1913 – JANUARY 4, 1960

In 1938 the selective thinker and writer Albert Camus relocated from his Algerian homeland to France. History there overtook him, and he joined the resistance movement against Nazi occupation as a standout underground journalist. In the midst of the carnage that ravaged France in 1942, Camus put out his enigmatic novella *The Stranger*, his most hard-boiled work and the one for which he was awarded the Nobel Prize for Literature fifteen years later. In this product of a five-year effort, Camus rendered his doctrine that the inevitability of death renders human life ultimately meaningless. Further, the individual cannot make rational sense of his life experience and is an insignificant victim of the absurd orthodoxy of habit.

In 1947, concluding that his journalistic activities were a response to the demands of the time, he retired from newspapers to concentrate on his fiction and essays. For the most part, Camus' later works were a continuation of his stringent search for moral order, and he expounded upon his philosophies most notably in *The Plague* and *The Rebel*. In 1970 the unfinished novel *La Mort Heureuse* was published posthumously, in which Camus succinctly announced, "All that matters really, is the will to happiness, a kind of enormous, ever-present consciousness. The rest is nothing but excuses."

In the winter of 1960, Camus was traveling to Paris in the front seat of a Facel-Vega sports car driven by his publisher, Michel Gallimard, whose wife and daughter were in the back. Thirty miles south of Paris, near a village named Petit Villemomble, the car slid off the wet road and hit a tree. Camus' neck was broken and he died instantly.

At 46, he was buried at Lourmarin Cemetery in Lourmarin, France, 30 miles north of Marseilles.

TRUMAN CAPOTE

SEPTEMBER 30, 1924 – AUGUST 25, 1984

THE CLUTTER FAMILY

DIED NOVEMBER 15, 1959

Born Truman Streckfus Persons to a sixteen-year-old beauty queen, Truman Capote was to become one of America's most controversial authors, partly due to his literary works, but perhaps even more as a result of his flair for publicity, his hunger for malicious gossip, and interest in his flamboyant lifestyle.

As a child, Truman was shuttled among a variety of relatives and, for a time, lived in Monroeville, Alabama. A close childhood friend there was none other than fair-haired tomboy Harper Lee, who in 1961 would become the Pulitzer Prize-winning novelist of *To Kill a Mockingbird*. Truman and Harper were inseparable—the entrepreneurial Truman charged other neighborhood children a nickel to use Harper's swimming pool—and she later modeled one of *Mockingbird*'s central characters, Dill Harris, on Truman.

After a stint with the *New Yorker* magazine, Truman established himself as a serious author for his frank discussion of homosexuality in *Other Voices, Other Rooms*, and the provocative picture of himself on its cover stirred the gay community. In the 1950s, Truman's literary works lifted him to celebrity status, and he was the newest wonder boy of the jet set, a fixture of chic parties, and a notorious philanderer. For this, Truman was accused of frivolity, and his stock response—"I'm researching my next book"—was supported in 1958 by the release of *Breakfast at Tiffany's*, a sensational account of high society. The overwhelming success enjoyed by the book, as well as its celebrated 1961 film adaptation, assured Truman's position in the upper crust.

But Truman wasn't done yet. He became intrigued with the idea of writing a new kind of book, one that would blend journalism and fictional techniques to a previously untested degree and, in fact, Truman was looking toward a new art form—the "nonfiction novel." In November 1959, he read a small news item about the deaths of the Clutters, a Kansas family who were systematically and savagely murdered by point-blank shotgun blasts to the head, and decided he had found his ideal subject. Just three days after the murders, he traveled to Kansas and began a six-year, all-consuming writing project about the case. His intensive research included hours of interviews with the two killers, who were tried, convicted, and eventually executed.

Upon its release, the chilling masterpiece *In Cold Blood* was an instant success and won Truman glowing reviews, a good deal of money, a swarm of imitators, and an even greater measure of celebrity. He swiftly moved to his next novel, *Answered Prayers*, which was to be a bitingly honest portrayal of his high-flying world but, in 1975, when its first few chapters were released in *Esquire* magazine, a major scandal erupted. Truman had been too honest. He did "what people always tell writers to do, but [he] didn't wait till they were dead to do it."

The result was that Truman became ostracized from the world in which he was both working and living. He quickly declined into drug abuse and alcoholism, and the book was never finished. Shortly before his death Truman offered an apology of sorts by saying, "I am not a saint. I am an alcoholic, I am a drug addict, and I am a homosexual. But I am a genius."

The health of his liver compromised by hard living, Truman died of heart failure at 59 and today lies at Westwood Village Memorial Park in Los Angeles.

CEMETERY DIRECTIONS: Follow Wilshire Boulevard a half-mile east from I-405, then turn right onto Glendon Avenue, and the cemetery is immediately on the left. Or you may want to park your car along Wilshire Boulevard and walk to the cemetery behind the office complex at 10850 Wilshire Blvd.

GRAVE DIRECTIONS: Enter the cemetery and turn left. On the wall just left of the Sanctuary of Tenderness is Truman's crypt.

The subjects of *In Cold Blood*—Herbert, Bonnie, Nancy and Kenyon Clutter—are buried at Valley View Cemetery in Garden City, Kansas.

CEMETERY DIRECTIONS: Valley View is on Third Street on the north side of town. From Route 50, turn north at the Third Street intersection (there's a tall water tank there) and the cemetery is ahead a short distance on the left.

GRAVE DIRECTIONS: Enter the cemetery and drive to the rear northwest corner, where you'll see a maintenance garage. The Clutter stones are in the sixth row of the section diagonally opposite the garage.

LEWIS CARROLL
JANUARY 27, 1832 – JANUARY 14, 1898

Charles Lutwidge Dodgson was the scholarly son of a vicar who at eighteen entered Christ Church College at Oxford University and, in one capacity or another, stayed there until his death some 50 years later. A student of mathematics, he later wrote a number of weighty academic texts on the subject, but Charles is more commonly remembered, of course, for the children's stories he wrote under the pseudonym Lewis Carroll.

Lewis had personal issues that many historians neglect. He purported to be called to answer holy orders his entire life but, though he was ordained as a deacon in 1861, Lewis avoided the priesthood and sermonizing, probably because of his lifelong stuttering affliction. An exceedingly undemonstrative introvert who kept his hands hidden inside black gloves, he was uncomfortable around adults and never dated or married. All of his close friendships were instead with children, especially young girls, for whom he performed marionette shows and created puzzles and word games. Lewis was able to acquire a camera by 24 (no petty feat in 1856), and photography of children became his preferred pastime. Some of these pictures were undeniably erotic and featured young girls in stages of undress.

A particular muse of Lewis's was Alice Liddell, the eleven-year-old young daughter of the Christ Church College dean. During a rowboat excursion with Alice and two of her school-aged friends, Lewis wove for them a whimsical tale about a girl who went down a rabbit hole in search of a rabbit that was late for a tea party. He later expanded the story into a full manuscript and presented it as a gift to Alice entitled, *A Christmas Gift to a Dear Child in Memory of a Summer Day*. He also suggested to Alice's parents that he was interested in courting their daughter. By order of the Liddell parents, Lewis was forbidden from further association with Alice.

But they had to admit that he'd written quite a story, and they encouraged him to publish it. In 1865 Lewis self-published the story after renaming it *Alice's Adventures in Wonderland* and, seven years later, its *Through the Looking Glass* sequel came into print. *Alice's Adventures in Wonderland* has become one of the most widely translated and beloved children's stories ever written and, after nearly 140 years, has never gone out of print.

At 65, Lewis died of a bronchial infection at the Chestnut, the estate in Guildford, Surrey, England, that he inherited from his family. In Guildford, 40 miles southwest of London, Lewis's grave is marked by a marble cross under a pine tree at Mount Cemetery.

Many years after Lewis fantasized about his real-life Alice, there came a new interest in the storybook Alice from an unlikely quarter, the acid-test counterculture. In 1967 the Jefferson Airplane rock band's hit song "White Rabbit" graced the airwaves, and its lyrics revealed perceived drug allegories within the *Wonderland* story. That Alice's "trip"—in which she ingests potions that change her consciousness and lead to encounters with a cast of strange characters, including a Mad Hatter and a hookah-smoking caterpillar—might have been Lewis' allusions to an opium trip was not a new idea and had long been debated in literary circles. But the Jefferson Airplane song placed the debate squarely into the popular forum and, in short order, college students lined up for midnight showings of Disney's animated version of *Alice in Wonderland*. Meanwhile, in panicked libraries across the nation, the children's storybook began appearing on lists of banned books.

AGATHA CHRISTIE
SEPTEMBER 15, 1890 – JANUARY 12, 1976

The 90-plus novels and two dozen or so collections of short stories produced by mystery-writer Agatha Christie stagger even the most insatiable detective-fiction addict. More impressive yet, her works have been translated into dozens of languages, selling well over a billion copies in total. Only the Bible and Shakespeare's works have sold more, but even the Bard has little on her; thirty years after one of Agatha's dozen plays, *The Mousetrap*, opened in London in 1952, it became the longest continuously running play in theatrical history.

Agatha introduced her eccentric Belgian detective, Hercule Poirot, in her first detective novel, 1920's *The Mysterious Affair at Styles*. In 40 books, the comic and amiable master-sleuth astutely observed a mountain of details that invariably led him, and the reader, to the identity of the murderer. Agatha later introduced another fictitious criminologist, the shrewdly inquisitive Miss Jane Marple, who was no less sensible than Poirot but relied more heavily on her feminine sensitivity and empathy to solve crimes. In fact, the perceptive methodologies of these characters were the key to Agatha's success. Readers were mesmerized by the unexpected twists that peppered her deliciously intricate plots until, in the end, they were surprised to find that they'd blindly ignored a vital clue that had been casually introduced hundreds of pages earlier. Her knack for consistently fooling her would-be detective readers in such works as *Murder on the Orient Express* and *Death on the Nile* earned Agatha her fans' allegiance.

In 1971 Agatha was made an honorary Dame of the British Empire.

Just a year after Agatha killed off Poirot in *Curtain: Hercule Poirot's Last Case* (which earned him a front-page obituary in the *New York Times*), Agatha herself died, though merely of natural causes.

At 85 she was buried at the Saint Mary Churchyard in Cholsey, Oxfordshire, England, 45 miles west of London. Her grave is marked by a tall headstone and the 25 trees that were planted in the churchyard in 1990 to mark the centenary of her birth.

SALVADOR DALI

MAY 11, 1904 – JANUARY 23, 1989

The 1930s European surrealists were influenced by the cubism of Picasso and Freud's controversial writings on the unconscious, dreams, and sexuality. Incorporating these concepts into their work, they aimed to break the constraints of realist representation and reach the fantasies and dreams that constitute inner life. Salvador Dali emerged as the leader of that Surrealist movement, and his *Persistence of Memory* (the painting with the droopy clocks) is perhaps the most widely recognized surrealist painting.

Realistic and disturbing depictions of nightmarish images on vast and uninviting landscapes became his trademark. Dali claimed his work was a product of a "paranoiac critical method," a sort of self-hypnosis that allowed him to hallucinate freely, and that he himself was surprised by what appeared on his canvases.

Dali's reputation swelled worldwide and was based as much on his flamboyance and flair for publicity as on his prodigious output. He worked in several media, and his legacy includes poetry, fiction, and a controversial autobiography. His works in film includes credit for the dream sequence in Alfred Hitchcock's *Spellbound.*

By the late 1960s Dali's work was hampered by Parkinson's disease, but his personality had so captured the public's imagination that he continued to exert influence, if only as a source of ideas. In 1974 he championed the opening of his own museum, but the decade also found Dali mired in financial and strategic scandals, the worst of which was his reported signing of thousands of sheets of blank paper, falsely rendering anything later added to the paper a Dali lithograph. It was eventually estimated that collectors had been bilked for at least $750 million on phony Dali prints.

Dali's health, both physical and mental, deteriorated sharply after his wife's death in 1982, and the remainder of his life was spent in almost total seclusion.

He died at 84 of heart failure and respiratory complications, and is entombed in the basement of his own museum, Teatro Museo Dali, in Figueras, Spain, 70 miles northeast of Barcelona.

CHARLES DICKENS

FEBRUARY 7, 1812 – JUNE 9, 1870

In 1824 Charles Dickens' father and family were imprisoned for debt, while the twelve-year-old Charles was put to work at a factory. This experience and his childhood of poverty and adversity haunted him for the remainder of his life, but also proved to be a source for his novels. His writings frequently delved into themes of alienation and betrayal, compassion for the lower classes, and Industrial Revolution-era social reform.

At 22, Charles joined a London newspaper and shortly thereafter began publishing monthly stories and sketches, the seeds of what would later become his novels. After the initial success of these stories, Charles embarked on a full-time career as a novelist and produced works of increasing complexity at an incredible rate, all the while continuing his journalistic activities.

In his novels—*Oliver Twist, A Christmas Carol, David Copperfield, A Tale of Two Cities* and *Great Expectations*, to name a few—he created a Shakespearean gallery of characters, many of which later found life in film and theater, and all of which continue to enthrall the reading public today.

At 58, Charles died of a stroke and it was his wish to be buried in the graveyard of Rochester Castle Moat with "no scarf, cloak, black bow, long hat band or any other revolting absurdity." Instead, he was buried in the heart of London, in the Poet's Corner of Westminster Abbey opposite the Houses of Parliament.

An hour southeast of London, Dickens lived in the village of Rochester for most of his life. There are numerous places in town associated with him, and he's honored with an annual festival. At the graveyard, a simple plaque says: "Charles Dickens wished to be buried here."

F. SCOTT & ZELDA FITZGERALD

F. Scott Fitzgerald

SEPTEMBER 24, 1896 – DECEMBER 21, 1940

Zelda Fitzgerald

JULY 24, 1900 – MARCH 10, 1948

The early lives of the author F. Scott Fitzgerald and his wife Zelda epitomized the triumphs of the Roaring Twenties in affluence, accomplishment, and melodramatic love. Unfortunately, their fable reflected both sides of the dream, and they later suffered the common tragedies of intemperance.

Upon publication of his first novel, *This Side of Paradise*, Scott married Zelda in an extravagant ceremony. They rode the crest of success and enjoyed the fame that his novel brought. Their exploits, recounted in newspapers and popular magazines, included jumping into the Plaza Hotel's fountain fully clothed, riding in an open car through the city streets, and reveling at glamorous parties. They led the privileged lives of aspiring socialites.

Their life together though, lacked any semblance of order, and their wealth was something of an illusion. Scott, the overnight sensation, in fact earned very little for his work, and wrote for mass-circulation magazines to supplement his income. Though he endeavored to further his literary reputation, he was gaining common recognition only as an extravagant drunk. Meanwhile, Zelda struggled to maintain an identity, and her formerly charming, unconventional behavior became eccentric and bizarre.

After endless revision, *The Great Gatsby* was finally released in 1925 to critical praise, but even these sales proved disappointing, and the Fitzgeralds continued to live far beyond their means. As debts mounted, Scott plunged into alcoholism, and domestic rows triggered by drinking were frequent. Increasingly unstable, Zelda was institutionalized in 1930 and eventually diagnosed with schizophrenia. She would spend the rest of her life in and out of psychiatric hospitals.

After 1934 they would never live together again and soon Scott, hopelessly in debt, in poor physical health, and often incapacitated by excessive drinking, had what he described as his own "crack-up."

ETERNAL COUPLE

F. SCOTT & ZELDA
FITZGERALD

In 1937, almost in spite of himself, he won a contract as a screen-writer for MGM, fell in love with another woman and, after finding new spark in his writing, quit drinking altogether.

In 1940, Scott was living in Hollywood and working on a new novel, *The Last Tycoon*. In November he suffered a mild heart attack and was ordered to bed rest. He continued to work on his novel and, a month later, collapsed of a massive attack as he rose from a living room chair. At the time of his death at 44, all of his novels were out of print and he believed himself a failure. But by the 1960s, a Fitzgerald resurrection had occurred, and he's since achieved a secure place among America's acclaimed writers.

Zelda continued her unsteady course after Scott's death. In March 1948 she was staying at Highland Hospital in Asheville, North Carolina, in a room on the top floor, when a fire broke out in the middle of the night. She and eight others were killed, trapped behind the mental institution's locked doors.

At 47, Zelda was laid to rest alongside Scott at Saint Mary's Catholic Church Cemetery in Rockville, Maryland.

CEMETERY DIRECTIONS: From I-270, take Exit 6 and follow Route 28 east for two miles. Immediately after crossing Route 355, turn left into the church and school grounds.

GRAVE DIRECTIONS: Their graves are in the eighth row from the church, just a few rows behind the two old tombstones surrounded by an iron fence.

IAN FLEMING
MAY 28, 1908 – AUGUST 11, 1964

In almost every way, Ian Fleming's life mirrored that of his best-known fictitious progeny, the dashing man of intrigue and British secret agent, James Bond 007.

Ian hailed from an extremely wealthy Scottish family. His father was a military hero and member of British Parliament, and after a childhood of privilege and exclusive schooling, Ian sought a career in the foreign service. But he was rejected as an operative and turned to journalism instead, working for Reuters for a year before gaining an esteemed banking position in London. There he enjoyed the life of a playboy, entertained by high-stakes bridge games, elaborate meals, and carefree romances.

As Hitler's war machine steamrolled on in 1939, Ian was unexpectedly sent to Moscow to report on a trade mission for the *Lon-*

don Times but, surreptitiously, he followed an ongoing espionage trial. Next, Ian was recruited by British Naval Intelligence to work with the super-secretive Ultra network, which, among other things, cracked the Nazi's Enigma code and ultimately changed the course of the war. But it wasn't until ten years after his death that the extent of Ian's wartime intelligence work emerged and, even now, it's unclear exactly when he began working as an operative. Was it when he was in Moscow with the *Times*, or did his service begin while he was living as a banking playboy in London? It's now believed that Ian was never rejected as an operative in the first place and, from the time he went to work for Reuters, he was slyly working to establish an everyman guise.

At war's end, Ian built his Goldeneye estate on Jamaica's north coast, and he traveled there each winter to lounge in paradise and chase divorcées. However, one particular conquest turned out to be married, and after she ended up pregnant with his child, Ian decided it was high time he made some coin. In seven weeks he wrote *Casino Royale*, a spy thriller set in the tropics with a debonair, womanizing British secret agent named James Bond as its central character. Ian had woven his own elite existence, arrogance, and acid wit into the character and the resulting book, published in 1952, was a smashing success. Ian penned eleven more Bond novels, including *Goldfinger*, *Dr. No*, and *From Russia with Love*, and the Bond hero with vodka martinis "shaken, not stirred," became immortalized in celluloid and, ultimately, in popular culture.

In 1961, Ian suffered a heart attack and, recognizing that perhaps his time was near, put to paper an entirely different kind of story, a tale of a flying car with a bubbly personality, a story he had been carrying around in his head for years. Based on bedtime stories he used to tell his son, the children's classic, *Chitty Chitty Bang Bang*, was published just a few months before Ian's August 1964 death, at the age of 56, to heart failure. A year later, his final Bond thriller, *The Man with the Golden Gun*, was released, it's last few chapters completed by a writer who still remains anonymous.

Ian was buried near the stone church at St. Andrews Churchyard in Sevenhampton, England, a picturesque village 60 miles west of London.

His monument, a simple, four-foot-tall obelisk, contains the Latin inscription, "*omnia perfunctus vitai praemia marces*," from Lucretius, an Roman who wrote the words around 50 B.C., in his third book, *de rerum naturae*, (*On the Nature of Things*). Translated, it means: "After enjoying the gifts of life, you lack ambition."

ROBERT FROST

MARCH 26, 1874 – JANUARY 29, 1963

As one of America's most widely read and critically acclaimed poets, Robert Frost was a master at using the natural rhythm of informal American speech to portray ordinary people in realistic situations. As is usually the case with grand success though, Robert's prosperity didn't come easily, and his career as a poet languished for the first half of his life when publishers showed little interest. At 40, he'd not published a single book of poems, and his work had been seen in just a handful of magazines. To support his family, Robert ran a chicken farm in New Hampshire.

But in middle age he made a daring decision to sell the farm and use the proceeds to make a new start in London, where publishers might be more receptive to his talents. He was almost immediately successful; within a year, *A Boy's Will* was published and it was quickly followed by *North of Boston*. In London, Frost was in vogue within literary circles, and the sensation soon crossed over to America.

In 1915, the Frosts returned to the States, an edition of the "new" poet's work became a bestseller, and Robert never looked back. He embarked upon a long writing career and, in the remainder of his life, received an unprecedented quantity of honors for his work, including four Pulitzer Prizes. Never before had an American poet achieved such rapid fame after such long delay.

In the twilight of his life, his political conservatism caused him to lose favor among literary critics, but his reputation as a major poet remains secure. He succeeded in realizing his life's ambition to write "a few poems it will be hard to get rid of."

Robert was a chronic sufferer of cystitis and he died of a pulmonary edema. At 88, and was buried at the Old Bennington Cemetery in Bennington, Vermont.

CEMETERY DIRECTIONS: From the junction of Routes 7 and 9, follow Route 9 west for 3/4 mile and you'll see the cemetery on the left. But go past the cemetery to the top of the hill and park in front of the Old First Church.

GRAVE DIRECTIONS: Follow the path on the left of the church into the cemetery. There, on the far right-hand side of the cemetery, about 100 yards behind the church, is the Frost plot.

ZANE GREY

JANUARY 31, 1872 – OCTOBER 23, 1939

Pearl Zane Grey attended the University of Pennsylvania on a baseball scholarship and after graduation, set up a dental practice in New York City while retreating to the Delaware River region on weekends. After meeting his future wife Dolly there, his first piece of writing, *A Day on the Delaware*, which Dolly had encouraged, edited, and presented to publishers, found publication in 1902. Three years later Zane and Dolly married and settled in the river valley, leaving dentistry behind as Zane pursued a full-time writing career financed by Dolly.

In 1906 the couple took a late honeymoon to Arizona and California and, during that trip, Zane's imagination was stimulated. Upon his return, he pioneered the new Western literary genre and, from his *Riders of the Purple Sage* to *The Last Round-Up*, he reinvented the public's conception of the West, presenting it as a moral battleground where the desperados and the righteous were alternately destroyed and redeemed.

Zane sold some 17 million copies of over 100 different books, and his works became the basis for almost 100 Western films. But even the most dedicated admirers of Zane's work admit to his character-development limitations. Still, there is a consensus that Zane deserves recognition as a custodian of the West's history, as a sort of proto-environmentalist, and as an interpreter of the outdoors.

Zane expired quietly in his sleep at 67 and, after Dolly died at 73 almost two decades later, the ashes of both were interred at Union Cemetery in Lackawaxen, Pennsylvania, fulfilling their wish to rest together at the edge of the Delaware River.

CEMETERY DIRECTIONS: From I-84, take either Exit 34 or Exit 46 and proceed north to the intersection of Routes 6 and 434. From this intersection, head north on Route 434 for two miles, then turn left on Route 590, following it almost five miles to Beisel Road, where you'll turn right. After passing under the railroad tracks, the cemetery is a short distance on the right.

GRAVE DIRECTIONS: In this small cemetery, the Grey plot is easy to find on the right-hand side about three-fourths of the way to the rear.

Just before the cemetery, the Zane Grey Museum on the right is open seasonally.

JOHN GUNTHER, JR.
& JOHN GUNTHER, SR.

John Gunther, Jr.
NOVEMBER 4, 1929 – JUNE 30, 1947

John Gunther, Sr.
AUGUST 30, 1901 – MAY 29, 1970

At the time of his death, seventeen-year-old John Gunther, Jr. was just another young and nameless victim of cancer. But afterward, his father, John, Sr., who happened to be a journalist and author, compiled a timeless and inspirational chronicle from his son's personal diaries, and that work, *Death Be Not Proud,* has stood alone for more than 50 years as the definitive and poignant account of a life cut short.

"A primitive to-the-death struggle of reason against violence, reason against disruption, reason against brute unthinking force—this was what went on in Johnny's head. What he was fighting against was the ruthless assault of chaos. What he was fighting for was, as it were, the life of the human mind."

John, Sr. chose not to profit from his son's death and donated all proceeds from the book to charity.

John, Jr. died at 17 and, after cremation, his ashes were interred at the Ferncliffe Mausoleum in Hartsdale, New York.

CEMETERY DIRECTIONS: From I-87, take Exit 7 in Ardsley and follow Route 9A North for 1¼ miles. Then, at the traffic light, turn right onto Secor Road. Ferncliffe is a short distance ahead on the left.

GRAVE DIRECTIONS: Enter Ferncliffe at the first entrance, bear left, and park toward the left-hand side of the main mausoleum. Enter the mausoleum through the front bronze doors and go up the stairs to the left. At the top of the stairs turn left, turn left at the end of the hall, then right and right again. Go up the three stairs, turn left at the next hall and John's ashes are in a niche on the left wall. They're five rows from the bottom, just before Alcove CC.

John, Sr. died at 68 and was buried at a town cemetery in Greensboro, Vermont.

CEMETERY DIRECTIONS: From I-91, take Exit 21 and follow Route 2 west for 9½ miles to Route 15. Turn right onto 15 and, after another ten miles, turn right onto Route 16. After 1¾ miles make a left onto Main Street, follow it through the village of East Hardwick and, after a few more miles, you'll arrive at a four corners with Breezy Center Road. Proceed straight through the four corners and follow Lake Shore Drive to the cemetery two miles ahead on the right.

GRAVE DIRECTIONS: John's plain white stone is about halfway to the cemetery's rear, in front of a spruce tree.

ALEX HALEY

AUGUST 11, 1921 – FEBRUARY 10, 1992

While serving with the Coast Guard during the Second World War, Alex Haley, a voracious reader, ran out of things to read, which prompted him to start writing. Alex toiled over his short stories for several years, suffering hundreds of rejections until one was finally accepted by a magazine in 1947. By 1952, the service had taken notice of their budding author and created for Alex the new rating of chief journalist, and he began writing for the United States Coast Guard's public relations office. In 1959, after twenty years of military service, Alex retired from the Coast Guard and launched a new career as a freelance writer.

Alex wrote for *Reader's Digest* and then moved on to *Playboy*, where he initiated the magazine's trademark in-depth interview feature. One of the personalities he interviewed was Malcolm X, a meeting that inspired Alex's first book, 1965's *The Autobiography of Malcolm X.*

His hundreds of hours of intriguing conversation with Malcolm prompted Alex to search out his own genealogy, an endeavor that proved to be an exhaustive, eleven-year odyssey. As Alex searched further and further back in time, he eventually landed in the village of Juffure in Gambia, West Africa, where a native oral historian, a *griot*, recounted to Alex seven generations of Mandinka tribal history. In the griot's account, Alex's early ancestor, sixteen-year-old Kunta Kinte, was wrested from the forest while searching for wood to make a drum, then sold into slavery.

Alex painstakingly chronicled his ancestors' passage from slavery to freedom and, in 1976, his acclaimed book, *Roots: The Saga of an American Family*, jolted America's conscience with its powerful affirmation of black history and shattering view of slavery. *Roots* became a phenomenon. The book became a number-one national bestseller, the twelve-hour television miniseries broke ratings records, lesson plans based on *Roots* were used in schools, and a new interest in African American genealogy was stimulated. Alex was awarded a special Pulitzer Prize, received honorary degrees, was lauded with a resolution by the U.S. Senate, and labeled a "folk hero" by *Time* magazine. *Roots* was indeed a cultural milestone, bringing the issues of slavery and racism to the forefront of American consciousness. It was groundbreaking and monumental but, unfortunately, it was also fiction.

In 1977 Harold Courlander filed a suit charging that *Roots* plagiarized his novel, *The African*. In fact the history of Kunta Kinte closely resembled that of a character named Hwesuhunu as chronicled in Courlander's work, and several passages in *Roots* were copied almost verbatim from *The African*. After a threat of perjury from a trial judge, Alex settled out of court for $650,000.

And there were even more unsettling discoveries. Subsequent investigation of tapes in Alex's own archives revealed that Kunta Kinte was a historical imposter invented with the full cooperation of Gambian government officials. From a review of Alex's private papers, virtually every genealogical claim in Alex's story has been shown to be false. Even his attempt to recreate the Middle Passage experience of enslaved Africans by sleeping on a "rough board between bales of raw rubber in the hold" of a transatlantic ship is fundamentally inaccurate; he sailed the Red Star from Dakar to Florida in 1973, but never stayed in the hold, according to the ship's first mate, Frank Ewers. "I had the keys to the hold and Haley never went down there at night. He would have died from the cocoa fumes."

In 1980 Alex wrote a television series called *Palmerstown, USA*, in 1988 published *A Different Kind of Christmas*, and *Queen: The Story of an American Family* was released posthumously. Unfortunately, none of these works had the impact of *Roots*. On its own merits, *Roots* is an astounding piece of culturally significant fiction, and if Alex had released it as such, with appropriate bibliographic footnotes, his reputation would be untarnished and permanent. As it is, his place in literary history stands under a shadow.

At 70, Alex died of a heart attack and was buried at his boyhood home in Henning, Tennessee.

GRAVE DIRECTIONS: Henning is located 40 miles northeast of Memphis. From the center of Henning (Routes 87 and 209) follow Haley Avenue one-third of a mile to its intersection with Church Street. The Haley home is on the corner, and Alex's marker is in the front yard.

Upon Alex's death, his literary and royalty rights went to his widow, Myran Haley, who filed for bankruptcy in 2001. In August 2002, John Palumbo of Jacksonville, Florida, an investor who buys "unusual" assets, purchased them from an Arizona bankruptcy court trustee for what would seem to be an impossibly low price of $10,400.

ERNEST HEMINGWAY
JULY 21, 1899 – JULY 2, 1961

MARGAUX HEMINGWAY
FEBRUARY 16, 1954 – JULY 1, 1996

While World War I raged, young Ernest Hemingway tried to enlist in the Army but was rejected due to a vision problem in one eye. Eager for action, he instead took a job driving an ambulance for the Red Cross, and in that capacity found himself under fire on the Italian front. After being severely wounded by a mortar blast, then two machine gun rounds as he was being carried away on a stretcher, Ernest the war hero recovered at an Italian hospital and fostered a relationship there with a nurse. These experiences would provide the groundwork for one of his greatest novels, *A Farewell to Arms*, written ten years later.

Ernest married during a short stay in the U.S. and, in 1921, the couple moved to Paris, flitting into an intellectual circle of expatriate authors and artists that included F. Scott Fitzgerald, Ezra Pound, and Gertrude Stein, who, at some level, Ernest accepted as a mentor. This "lost generation," a term that Stein coined but Ernest made popular in the epigraph of 1929's *The Sun Also Rises*, characterized a postwar generation that decried the false ideals that led naïve soldiers marching to their dooms for the gratification of carnal elders. This book was the first to bring widespread recognition to Ernest.

After Paris, Ernest traveled extensively for both work and pleasure, hunting in Africa and witnessing bullfights in Spain, where he returned in the late 1930s as a correspondent covering its Civil War. Again drawing from personal experience, Ernest wrote *The Snows of Kilimanjaro, Death in the Afternoon*, and his most ambitious novel, *For Whom the Bell Tolls*. In this period, he gained international acclaim for simple, straightforward prose sprinkled with unemotional but realistic dialogue.

During the Second World War, Ernest volunteered as a Caribbean submarine spotter using his own fishing boat, and it was then that he discovered the allure of Cuba, to which he's now inextricably linked. By 1950, the literary clique was whispering that "Papa" was finished, as for the last decade Ernest had been living in a small Cuban village, making no waves. But in 1952 Ernest unexpectedly set readers on their heads again with what many consider his most significant short work, *The Old Man and the Sea*, for which he was awarded the Pulitzer Prize.

After Fidel Castro's revolutionary movement triumphed in 1960, Ernest again relocated, this time to Idaho. By then, his physical health had begun to decline, partly as a result of internal injuries he'd suffered in an airplane crash during an African safari, and he was repeatedly hospitalized for uncontrolled high blood pressure and hepatitis. Increasingly confined to his home and complaining that he was unable to write, Ernest suffered anxiety attacks and depression, and his mental stability spiraled downward.

His wife, Mary, found him one morning holding a shotgun and staring out a window, and Ernest spent the next two months under heavy sedation at the Mayo Clinic. Upon his return home, Mary locked all the guns in the basement, but Ernest remembered where to find the keys. Two days later, while Mary slept, he chose a favorite shotgun he'd used many times to hunt birds and, with the magnificent view of the Sawtooth Mountains at his foyer's bay window, Ernest put the gun to his forehead and pulled the triggers of both barrels.

At 61, Ernest was buried at Ketchum Cemetery in Ketchum, Idaho.

CEMETERY DIRECTIONS: From the center of town, follow Route 75 a half-mile north and the cemetery is on the right.

GRAVE DIRECTIONS: Enter the cemetery, bear right and proceed about 100 yards. On the right is a stand of three evergreen trees, under which is the marble tablet marking Ernest's grave.

The Hemingway family seemed to have an uncanny predilection for suicide. Ernest's father, Dr. Clarence Hemingway, shot himself to death with a revolver in 1928. In 1966, Ernest's sister Ursula did herself in with a deliberate drug overdose, and in 1982, his brother Leicester killed himself with a pistol. More than one wag has suggested that perhaps the Hemingway family's NRA membership should be revoked.

And of course, who could forget about Margaux? She was the fresh-faced granddaughter of Ernest who burst onto the modeling scene in the early 1970s. Some maintained, probably correctly, that Margaux's ascent was solely due to the Hemingway mystique but, in any event, she leveraged her popularity and moved to acting. Her star soon dimmed though, and her roles became increasingly marginalized as she appeared in one lackluster film after another. If any were notable, perhaps it was her first, the decidedly dreary 1976 drama, *Lipstick*.

By 1980 Margaux's life was a slow-motion train wreck. Middle-child syndrome left her feeling unloved, dyslexia hindered the memorization of scripts, bulimia left her weak, depression encumbered ambition.

In 1987 Margaux admitted herself to the Betty Ford Clinic for alcoholism treatment, in 1990 came a last-ditch effort to jump-start her career by posing for *Playboy*, and in 1991 she filed for bankruptcy. In 1994 it seemed her troubles might finally be worked out with the Dalai Lama's spiritual guidance. But after returning from a visit with him, Margaux experienced difficulty separating fantasy from reality. She was hearing voices, and soon checked into an Idaho mental hospital for several weeks. In 1995 she hit rock bottom, filming infomercials for the Psychic Friends Hotline.

After Margaux hadn't been seen for a few days in June of 1996, concerned friends asked the handyman of her Santa Monica apartment building to check her quarters. Upon entering, he was overwhelmed by a horrible odor; Margaux had been dead a few days. She was found covered up in her bed, wearing only a white T-shirt. On a coffee table was an altar of sorts, complete with salt at each corner, an arrangement of candles, a variety of pendants lined up alongside burned incense, a white horseman chess piece, and pieces of paper arranged in a heart-shape. On the papers, in Margaux's hand-writing, was written, "Love, healing, protection for Margot forever."

An autopsy found Phenobarbital in Margaux's system at many times the recommended dosage, and it was concluded that she died of a suicidal overdose, in the Hemingway family style, at 42.

After cremation, Margaux's ashes were buried at Ketchum Cemetery alongside her grandfather. Her epitaph reads, "Free Spirit Freed."

Ever since entering show business, her name had been alternately spelled "Margaux" or "Margeaux," which differed from her given spelling, "Margot." But on her altar note, as described above, and on her gravestone, she reverted to her given spelling.

WASHINGTON IRVING
APRIL 3, 1783 – NOVEMBER 28, 1859

Washington Irving studied law haphazardly and amused himself by writing essays on New York society and theater under a variety of pseudonyms, including Diedrich Knickerbocker. (The surname was a colloquialism for Dutch settlers but, after being used by Irving, it became slang for "New Yorker.") In 1809 he published *A History of New York*, which purported to be a scholarly account of the occupation of the New World but was really a satire. Today it is regarded as the first great American book of comic literature.

Washington traveled to Europe on three different occasions that, considering the period in which he lived, ranked him very highly within that elite category of the well traveled. His first two trips were in service of his family's durables business and, after the enterprise soured, Washington refocused his concerns. He arranged a collection of his stories and essays into *The Sketch Book*, publishing it in 1819 under the name Geoffrey Crayon. Within this compilation were two widely loved tales that would immortalize the Washington Irving name—"Rip Van Winkle" and "The Legend of Sleepy Hollow"—and their enthusiastic reception immediately promoted him to the status of best-known living figure in American literature.

By 1826, Washington had parlayed his credentials into an appointment as a diplomatic attaché at the American embassy in Madrid, and there he produced a number of other narratives and sketches, though none as popular as his previous work. Upon his final return from Spain, where he served as Ambassador, Irving labored on a comprehensive, five-volume biography of George Washington, which he completed just before his death at 76.

For 137 years, Washington was buried in the village of North Tarrytown, New York, but, in November 1996, without ever having been moved, he was at once buried in the village of Sleepy Hollow. By referendum, the residents of the village honored their deceased son and legally changed the village's name to Sleepy Hollow. He's buried there at the Old Dutch Burying Ground.

CEMETERY DIRECTIONS: From I-287, take Exit 9 and turn north onto Route 9. Drive through town and the cemetery is 1½ miles ahead on the right.

GRAVE DIRECTIONS: Turn in at the main gate before the church, bear left at the "Y" and take the next left onto Crane Way. Surrounded by hedges, 100 yards on the right is the Irving plot.

KEN KESEY

SEPTEMBER 17, 1935 – NOVEMBER 10, 2001

Ken Kesey was raised in a religious fire-and-brimstone household, in high school was an Oregon champion wrestler and voted "Most Likely to Succeed," and upon graduation married his high-school sweetheart. While Ken studied for a Speech and Communications degree at Stanford University, he worked to support his family, which had suddenly developed into a three-baby affair, yet he still managed to impress the faculty so that he was awarded a Woodrow Wilson Fellowship to pursue his writing interests.

While at Stanford, though, Ken's progress toward Young Republican of the Month changed course after he participated in experiments in the psychology department to earn extra money. The studies included the ingestion of chemicals, and the chemicals included lysergic acid diethylamide or, more commonly, LSD. The acid experiences certainly had an effect on Ken, well beyond any temporary color-hearing or psychedelic, out-of-body experience. His life's focus was altered, and though he never strayed too far from his familial responsibilities, Ken's crowd of friends shifted and he tuned in to the burgeoning San Francisco scene.

Around this time, Ken was also working as an orderly in the psychiatric ward of the Menlo Park Veteran's Administration hospital. In 1962, he released his first novel, which clearly showed the influences of his experiences, the critically and popularly successful *One Flew Over the Cuckoo's Nest.* In 1974, Ken would sell its movie rights for just $5,000, and a film version would sweep the Academy Awards. In 1964, his *Sometimes a Great Notion* was published and, though it was well received, the book never approached *Cuckoo's* success.

As the 1960s blossomed, Ken was at the forefront of the counterculture. He threw "acid test" parties around Palo Alto's bohemian community and became a patron of a local band called the Warlocks, later known as the Grateful Dead. In 1964 his band of proto-hippie friends, dubbed "the Merry Pranksters," loaded onto an LSD-fueled, Day-Glo colored school bus nicknamed "Furthur" and, with Neal Cassady at the wheel (the real-life Dean Moriarty of Jack Kerouac's *On the Road*), Ken orchestrated the ultimate cross-country road trip. The journey immortalized the psychedelic sixties and was later chronicled in Tom Wolfe's *Electric Kool-Aid Acid Test*.

After a short jail term on marijuana charges in 1965, Ken moved to Oregon. He raised beef cattle, served on the school board, and coached high-school wrestling while Furthur rusted away in a boggy pasture. Though he continued to write short fiction and the occasional magazine article, he found that it had become harder to write since he became famous. "Fame isn't good for a writer. You don't observe well when you're being observed," he said. His last major novel, *Sailor Song,* was published in 1992.

Before undergoing surgery for a spot of cancer on his liver, Ken sensed the end was at hand and penned a goodbye note to his fans that was released after his passing. Closing the message, he wrote, "Meanwhile, I've still lots of forms to fill out and they're looking for a bigger halo but durned if I'm going to play that harp. I'm holding out for the thunder machine. See you around. Kesey."

At 66, Ken died of complications after the surgery. After a public memorial service in Eugene, his tie-dyed coffin was brought back to his Pleasant Hill estate and, there on the privacy of his farm, Ken was buried next to his son Jed, who'd perished in a 1984 van crash. There are no visiting hours.

LOUIS L'AMOUR
MARCH 22, 1908 – JUNE 10, 1988

In 1923 the LaMoore family was uprooted from its native North Dakota after a series of bank crises and, over the next 25 years, Louis wandered the world over. He skinned cattle in west Texas, sailed the world's seas as a merchant seaman, lumberjacked the great Northwest forests, hobo'd to New Orleans, biked across India, mined for silver in Nevada and, after attending Tank Destroyer school, commanded a platoon of fuel-supply vehicles in Europe during World War II. As if that weren't enough, during many of those years Louis complemented his erratic income by boxing on professional fight cards.

After the war, he concentrated on writing and nearly starved as he struggled to find a suitable genre, moving from adventure tales to detective yarns to sports stories. In 1950 Louis was hired to write Hopalong Cassidy novels as Tex Burns and there, in the sage brush and box canyons, he found his home as a writer of Westerns. In 1952 Louis pitched his *Gift of Cochise* short story to Bantam Books and, though they were not enamored of his new surname (spelled as "L'Amour," which insinuated it'd be a "Western written in lipstick"), Louis was signed to a long-term contract. The next year *Gift of Cochise* was made into the feature film *Hondo,* starring John Wayne, and Louis' career skyrocketed.

Over the next three decades his historically accurate novels sold an astounding 200 million copies, confounding critics who denounced his work as pulp fodder with haphazard composition and stilted dialogue. Meanwhile, Louis remained unapologetic for any shortcomings, maintaining shortly before his death that, "I don't give a damn what anyone else thinks. I know it's literature and I know it'll be read a hundred years from now." Indeed, he's on track—in the fifteen years since his passing, another 60 million L'Amour sagas have been sold.

After being diagnosed with inoperable lung cancer, Louis began his long-postponed memoir, *Education of a Wandering Man,* and was editing the book the afternoon that he died.

At 80, he was buried at Forest Lawn Memorial Park in Glendale, California.

CEMETERY DIRECTIONS: From Highway 2, take the San Fernando Road exit and turn northwest. After a mile, make a right onto Glendale Avenue and the park's entrance is immediately on the right.

GRAVE DIRECTIONS: Get a map at the information booth and make your way to the Great Mausoleum. But don't go inside—Louis is buried outside near the mausoleum's Memorial Terrace entrance. His grave is against the wall on the right, just beside the white statue of Jesus Christ seated with children.

JACK LONDON
JANUARY 12, 1876 – NOVEMBER 22, 1916

Jack London dropped out of Berkeley to join the Alaskan Klondike gold rush in 1897, and of his brutal experiences there, and later at sea, he wrote vigorous tales of men and animals at odds with one another. Upon his return to San Francisco the following year, he published his first collection of stories, *The Son of the Wolf*, but it was his next adventure story, *The Call of the Wild*, in 1903, that turned him into the most successful and best-known writer in America in the early 1900s.

Over the remainder of his life, Jack wrote another 45 books of fiction and nonfiction. Most of his work was in the adventure genre, but he occasionally strayed, most notably in the philosophical and politically tinged *The Sea Wolf*, and *The People of the Abyss*.

Always a heavy drinker, Jack probably died of physical ailments related to alcoholism, but some scholars believe he committed suicide.

In any event, after his death at 40, he was buried on the grounds of his estate, which is now the Jack London State Historical Park, in Glen Ellen, California.

GRAVE DIRECTIONS: The park is located just a few miles north of Sonoma and is signed from Route 12. Though you can get a map at the park ranger's booth and use it to find Jack's grave easily, directions are also included here so you may visit Jack when the park isn't open, if you wish. After the ranger's booth, turn left and park in the lot. On the right, just beyond the gate marking the lot's entrance, is a service road that is closed to vehicles. Walk about 500 yards down that road and you'll come to a small field. On the left of the field is a path, which, after another 100 yards, ends at Jack's grave.

KARL MARX
MAY 5, 1818 – MARCH 14, 1883

Expelled from Germany, France, and Belgium for radicalism, renowned socialist thinker Karl Marx lived most of his adult life in "a long, sleepless night of exile" as a stateless and penniless London journalist in poor health. In a crusade of "merciless criticism of everything existing," he published hundreds of articles and essays promoting revolutionary reformist ideas, but his reputation primarily rests with two works: *Das Kapital* (Capital) and *Manifest der kommunistischen Partei (Communist Manifesto)*.

Marx's central tenet is that the materialistic conception of history involves two basic notions: First, the economic system at any given time determines the prevailing ideas; and second, history is an ongoing process predetermined by economic institutions and evolving in regular stages of thesis, antithesis, and synthesis. Thesis corresponds to the precapitalist period when there were no classes or exploitation. Antithesis corresponds to the era of capitalism and labor exploitation. Synthesis, or communism, would be the final product under which capital would be owned in common and exploitation could not exist.

To Marx, then, capitalism is the last stage of historical development before communism, and the proletariat is the last historical class. The two are fated to be in conflict until the proletariat inevitably establishes a transitional order into communism, or a classless society. In Marxism, the complete collapse of industrial capitalism and its replacement by communism is inevitable.

Based on these ideas, Marx was a revolutionary who sought to effect social change and, indeed, his mission in life was to contribute, in his own peaceable and intellectual way, to the overthrow of capitalist society. His most famous treatises, his copious militant pamphlets, his work in underground organizations in Paris, Brussels, and London and, finally, crowning all, his founding of the International Working Men's Association in 1864 stand as testimony to his purpose.

Though Marx's analysis of capitalist economy and his theories of historical materialism, the class struggle, and surplus value have greatly contributed to an almost scientific understanding of social divisions, Marx's influence during his life was not great. But after his death, his ideas and theories gained more prominence as Marxism was adopted by the labor movement.

Marx's theories on the nature of the capitalist state and the road to power were of critical importance with respect to subsequent historical epochs. During the twentieth century a radical incarnation of Marx's doctrines became the core of Bolshevik theory and, under the mercilessly brutal hand of Vladimir Ilich Lenin, communist Russia was born. However, it should be made clear that the totalitarian, police-state style of Communist governments that led to the misery of millions in places like the Soviet Union and North Korea bears little resemblance to the social form that Karl Marx idealistically proposed.

In the last two decades of his life, Marx was tormented by a mounting succession of ailments. In January 1883, it became tremendously difficult for him to swallow after a tumor developed in his throat. Two months later, he died in his armchair at 64.

Marx was buried in London's Highgate Cemetery. This elegant Victorian cemetery is at the top of Highgate Hill on the north side of town, near Hampstead Heath, off of Swain's Lane.

Marx's grand monument is surrounded by a black iron fence and topped by his intimidating, bearded bust.

CARSON McCULLERS
FEBRUARY 19, 1917 – SEPTEMBER 29, 1967

After suffering a near-fatal attack of rheumatic fever at fifteen, the Georgia-born Lula Carson Smith was plagued with exceedingly poor health throughout life, her frailties prompting her to try her hand as a writer instead of a pianist. In 1937 Carson married Reeves McCullers, but the newlyweds separated from their stormy union after just three years, she engaging in lesbian dalliances while he moved in with a boyfriend.

Around the same time, when Carson was still just 23, her first novel, *The Heart Is a Lonely Hunter*, found immediate success and she moved to New York, where she was welcomed into the literary scene as its newest prodigy. Carson quickly leveraged her success and completed the similarly acclaimed *Reflections in a Golden Eye* and *The Member of the Wedding*. Her works offered glimpses of autobiography written with a certain adolescent spirit, and her ballad-like stories resonated with the alienation and dislocation of characters that haunted society's margins.

By 1945 Carson had reconciled with Reeves and the turmoil of her life was rekindled. A few years later, her already tenuous physical health was further compromised when she suffered a series of strokes and, by her early 30s, Carson was left without the use of her left hand. Meanwhile, Reeves, the love-hate companion of her life, committed suicide in 1953, a feat she had herself attempted in 1948. Carson continued writing despite her tribulations and, after her last significant work, a novella, *The Ballad of the Sad Café*, was published in 1951, she confessed, "Writing, for me, is a search for God."

After a mastectomy, Carson suffered one last massive stroke and died of the resultant cerebral hemorrhage at 50.

She was buried at Oak Hill Cemetery in Nyack, New York.

CEMETERY DIRECTIONS: From I-287, take Exit 11 to Route 9W. Follow Route 9W north and the cemetery is one-quarter mile ahead on the left.

GRAVE DIRECTIONS: Go two-thirds of the way up the back hill and, on the drive that sweeps across the hill along the big mausoleums, orient yourself so that the mausoleums are on your right. In front of you, at the end of that drive, is a short lawn that extends up to the woods. Walk straight up that lawn and you'll find Carson's stone three rows from the back.

JAMES MICHENER

FEBRUARY 3, 1907 – OCTOBER 16, 1997

Abandoned by his parents shortly after birth, young James was adopted by a Quaker widow, Mabel Michener. In his memoir, *The World Is My Home*, he wrote that his wanderlust sprouted upon realizing that the road outside their home continued forever, to strange lands and adventures he could not even imagine. He went on lengthy hitchhiking trips before he was old enough to drive and, ultimately, James came to be the consummate traveler.

But it wasn't until he was in his 30s, when the Navy sent him to the primitive South Pacific islands to gather wartime information, that he found his calling as a writer. The visits later provided the backdrop for some of his most memorable novels, which were invariably laden with geographical and historical details. James himself once admitted that he wasn't a "stylist" and wasn't very good at composing dialogue, but he also knew he could "put a good narrative together." Perhaps because he never knew his own roots, foreign backgrounds intrigued him. "I feel myself the inheritor of a great background of people," he said. "I could be Jewish, part Negro, probably not Oriental, but almost anything else, so I can't afford to be scornful about anyone."

On his first try as a published author he won the Pulitzer Prize for his 1948 collection of short stories, *Tales of the South Pacific*. These were later adapted into *South Pacific*, a long-running Broadway musical and motion picture. For the next five decades James took readers on obsessively detailed journeys across time to the far corners of the planet. Many of his 44 works had simple, one-word titles like *Hawaii, Sayonara*, and *Poland* and, often for 600 pages, the epics entertained while arguing James' universal ideals: religious and racial tolerance, hard work, and self-reliance.

Beginning in 1993, James waged a battle against kidney failure and, three times a week in three-hour-long sessions, his blood was pumped out, cleansed, and pumped back into his body by a dialysis machine. His once wide world was reduced to only the city of

Austin, which he lamented as "my prison." He never quit working, saying, "as long as the old brain keeps functioning, I know the desire will always be there," but life eventually became too much of a burden. "For the first time I understand how a person could say 'the hell with it,'" he confided.

Finally, the globetrotter refused to undergo anymore life-sustaining dialysis treatments, and he died of kidney failure two weeks later.

At 90, James was cremated and his ashes buried at Austin Memorial Park in Austin, Texas.

CEMETERY DIRECTIONS: From Highway 1, the Mopac Expressway, take the 45th Street exit and head east for a short distance to Bull Creek Road, where you'll turn left. After a half-mile, Bull Creek ends at a "T" with Hancock Drive, and the cemetery is across the intersection to the left.

GRAVE DIRECTIONS: Enter the cemetery, turn at the first drive on the right, and follow it up the hill. The last section on the right is Section 11, and there next to the curb is the reddish-colored Michener monument.

MARGARET MITCHELL
NOVEMBER 8, 1900 – AUGUST 16, 1949

While growing up, Margaret Mitchell was regaled with stories of Confederate Atlanta by her father, who was president of Atlanta's Historical Society. By the time Margaret was 27, she had written over a hundred feature stories for the *Atlanta Journal* newspaper but, once she was confined to her home after breaking her ankle, her second husband encouraged her to change gears and pursue her fiction-writing aspirations. Night and day, Margaret labored over her Remington typewriter and, after three years, she had completed a draft of *Gone with the Wind*, a fictitious epic featuring the experiences of a beautiful and manipulative Southern Belle, Scarlett O'Hara, and describing the secession, Civil War, and Reconstruction periods from the seldom-heard Southern point of view.

The next half-dozen years were spent perfecting the book's historical accuracy and, once it was finally published in 1936, Margaret's 1,037-page novel immediately broke all previous records, selling two million copies within a year. Many critics panned it for being "overly Southern" but, nonetheless, *Gone with the Wind* was awarded the Pulitzer Prize the next year, and Margaret soon sold the film rights for $50,000. In 1939, its archetypal celluloid adaptation starring Clark Gable and Vivien Leigh premiered. This too was a smash. The film broke box-office records and the catch phrases it spawned—"Frankly, my dear, I don't give a damn," and "Tomorrow is another day" (Margaret's original title for the book)—haven't fallen from favor some 60 years since.

Remarkably, Margaret never wrote again. *Gone with the Wind* was the only book she ever authored and she was very adamant that, as the story could stand on its own, no sequel was necessary. Though it brought her fame and fortune, the book seems to have yielded her little joy. Chased by the press and public, Margaret and her husband lived modestly and traveled rarely.

On a hot Atlanta night in 1949, Margaret and her husband decided to go downtown to see a movie. After parking the car across the street from the theater, the couple hurried across Peachtree Street arm-in-arm when a car suddenly sped toward them. In a panic, Margaret ran without her husband back to the curb, but the car skidded and struck her, breaking her pelvis and fracturing her skull. She never fully regained consciousness, and, at 48, she died five days later. The driver, who had 23 prior traffic violations, was later convicted of involuntary manslaughter and served ten months in prison.

In her will, Margaret instructed her secretary to burn all of her letters and the original *Gone with the Wind* manuscript, save for a few pages preserved to prove her authorship. And so, shortly after her death, her secretary and the custodian of the apartment building in which Margaret had been living burned nearly all of her documents in the building's boiler.

Margaret was buried at Oakland Cemetery in Atlanta, Georgia.

CEMETERY DIRECTIONS: From I-75/85, take Exit 94 and head east on Edgewood Avenue. At the first light, turn right onto Hilliard Street and proceed a half-mile to Martin Luther King Drive. Turn left and you'll see the cemetery a couple hundred yards ahead.

GRAVE DIRECTIONS: Enter the cemetery and turn left at the first paved drive. Just after crossing another paved drive, as the road bends to the right, stop. On the left is a brick walk that extends in the direction from which you were just driving. Follow this walk and then, at the second walk, turn left. A short distance on the left, behind the Peel mausoleum, is Margaret's grave.

FLANNERY O'CONNOR

MARCH 25, 1925 – AUGUST 3, 1964

Focusing on the decaying South and the rhythms of a darkly comic people, writer Flannery O'Connor's small body of work was profoundly shaped by the spiritual heritage of her home region. She preferred not to approach the subject of religion directly, but instead paid attention to the contradictions and hypocrisies that can result from wholesale religious indoctrination, and the dramas that emerge when spiritually charged individuals lock horns with the secular world.

In 1952, Flannery's first novel, *Wise Blood*, was published and, for this tale of a man who tries to start a church without Christ, she immediately gained recognition as a blossoming author in the Southern tradition. The book had been written in New York, where Flannery had moved in order to indulge in the company of other writers. But around the same time, Flannery began suffering from disseminated lupus, a debilitating blood disease, and was forced to return home to her family's Georgia farm. Cortisone injections slowed the disease's progress, but the medication also weakened her bones, and by 1955, Flannery was relegated to the crutches upon which she remained dependent for the rest of her life.

When Flannery died of lupus before her 40th birthday, her career was cruelly cut short; she had completed one other novel, *The Violent Bear It Away*, and 31 imaginative short stories including "A Good Man Is Hard to Find." When her stories were collected in *The Complete Stories of Flannery O'Connor* in 1971, her prestige in the modern literary hierarchy was cemented and Flannery was posthumously awarded the National Book Award.

Flannery was buried at Memory Hill Cemetery in her hometown of Milledgeville, Georgia.

CEMETERY DIRECTIONS: From either Route 22 or 49, turn south onto Clarke Street. Follow Clarke to its intersection with West Franklin Street, and the cemetery is on the corner.

GRAVE DIRECTIONS: Enter the cemetery, turn left and proceed along this drive for about 200 feet, stopping at the large stone on the left that marks the Stembridge plot. Beside the Stembridge stone, but nearer the fence and surrounded with white landscaping stones, is Flannery's grave.

GEORGE ORWELL

JUNE 25, 1903 – JANUARY 21, 1950

The British author George Orwell achieved prominence in the late 1940s as the author of two brilliant satires that attacked totalitarianism. He established himself as one of the most influential voices of the century.

His first important work, *Animal Farm*, was a fantasy novella, a mocking allegory of the Russian Revolution played out by sentient animals, some of who were declared "more equal than others." Later, in a prophecy of a world laid waste by warring dictators, *1984* offered a bitter protest against the nightmarish direction in which Orwell believed the modern world was moving, complete with Thought Police and professional History Revisionists. At their core, both works are concise illustrations of the manner in which the degradation of language and the suppression of free speech precede all other oppressions. These powerful works are required reading at many schools of higher learning.

Just four months after the publication of *1984*, Orwell died at 46 of complications arising from a chronic tuberculosis condition.

He was buried in the yard of the All Saints Church in Sutton Courtenay, England. The large village is just a few miles south of Oxford, while this early fourteenth-century church is at the north end of the town square. Orwell is buried under his own name, Eric Arthur Blair, and there is nothing on his headstone to indicate his achievements.

PABLO PICASSO

OCTOBER 25, 1881 – APRIL 8, 1973

Pablo Picasso is considered by many to be the most influential artist of the twentieth century, and he almost single-handedly created modern art. He was the first artist to enjoy the obsessive attention of the mass media. No artist, not even Michelangelo, has ever been as famous as Picasso in his own lifetime, and it is quite possible that none ever will be again, now that the mandate to set forth social meaning and generate memorable images has been largely transferred to the electronic media. Picasso's audience, meaning people who'd heard of him or who knew of his work, was possibly in the hundreds of millions, and his efforts were the subject of unending analysis, receiving both criticism and adoration.

Picasso is best known for his invention of revolutionary art styles and for his experimentation on a range of themes. In fact, one of the more remarkable qualities of his career was the rapidity and ease with which he evolved. Picasso's most important contributions include pioneering the Cubism movement, and using collage and assemblage as artistic techniques.

In 1907, after his Blue and Red periods (so named for the dominant use of each color in his paintings), Picasso worked on the simplification of art and shocked the masses with his distortion of the human form in his Cubist works: a demonstrative style of pictorial dissection that creates an abstract, multi-angled representation.

Around 1912 Picasso and his contemporary, Georges Braque, began experimenting with new techniques: Using *papier collé*—a type of paper glued onto canvases with various other materials— they created a new form known as *collage*. Later, with the advent of the Surrealist movement in the 1920s, Picasso's work turned to the grotesque, and he created figures endowed with several heads, displaced noses and mouths, and enlarged limbs. One of Picasso's most historically significant works, *Guernica*, painted in 1937, expressed Picasso's horror at the fascist brutality of the Spanish Civil War. *Guernica* remains one of the most powerful political images in modern art. Deemed a masterpiece, its completion marked the final major turning point in Picasso's career.

The last period of Picasso's life was itself a tapestry, a torrentially productive era whose infuriating laxity of quality control incited controversy and criticism. Beginning in the 1950s, Picasso confronted his predicament; as an old man, he wallowed in unprecedented adoration as an artist and "national monument," but was himself unfulfilled by his body of work. But he still yearned to indulge in his celebrity.

Having no need for the approval of others, Picasso chose in his final years to do exactly as he pleased; he took advantage of his own achievements, fanning a vulgar, cynical image of himself and became a King Midas of art—everything he touched turned to gold. Over the next two decades, Picasso's prodigious output, some of which was certainly meritorious, was nonetheless marred by his deliberate embellishment of his own reputation; shoddy "signed" lithographs by the thousands and even throwaway doodles on restaurant napkins were gobbled by "collectors" who yearned for any piece of the restless experimental artist that Picasso had once been.

Picasso once told a visitor who admired his vigor, "A painter never finishes. Whenever you stop, it's only because you've started again." By some terms, the manic and obsessive quality of those words, and his productions, almost imply that he expected the creative act to forestall his death, though it did not.

At 91, Picasso died of a pulmonary edema.

His grave, adorned with his own "Woman with the Vase" sculpture, is located on the terrace leading to the front entrance of his castle in Vauvenargues, France. You're welcome to visit this bucolic village in the rural wine-producing region of Provence but Picasso's castle, its grounds, and his grave are closed to visitors.

EDGAR ALLAN POE

JANUARY 19, 1809 – OCTOBER 7, 1849

Edgar Allan Poe created the narrative mystery-thriller genre and, more than any other writer, deserves credit for elevating short stories from a disrespected anecdotal form to an honorable artistic genre.

Both of Edgar's parents died before he was three and, after being taken into the home of the wealthy Allan family of Richmond, he was baptized Edgar Allan Poe. At 17, he entered the University of Virginia to concentrate on classical languages, but after running up a $2,000 gambling debt that his stepfather refused to cover, Edgar left school and enlisted in the Army, eventually landing at West Point. While there, his first book, *Tamerlane and Other Poems*, was published, and Edgar, uninterested in a cadet future now that his writing talent had been validated, neglected his responsibilities until he was dismissed for "gross neglect of duty."

Edgar took up residence in Baltimore with his aunt, Maria Clemm, and her daughter Virginia, his first cousin, whom he married in 1836 when she was thirteen. He became editor of the *Southern Literary Messenger* and there published much of his own fiction, most notably "Berenice," but beyond his own contributions, his editorial attention was scant. As Edgar's only other focus seemed to be alcohol, he was soon asked to resign.

The pattern of Edgar's career now seemed prescribed, and his experience at the *Southern Literary Messenger* was mirrored at a variety of other publications in Philadelphia and New York over the next decade. Edgar contributed his best flawlessly constructed fiction, including "The Fall of the House of Usher" and "The Tell-Tale Heart," to an assortment of literary periodicals, but his endless literary feuding, his alcoholism, and his inability to get along with people irritated employers, ensuring that his various tenures were invariably short.

In 1845, after releasing "The Raven" to popular acclaim, Edgar was pleased to find he could generate on-the-spot income by reciting the verse to paying audiences. His household's financial situation improved to its best level ever, but just as it seemed that Edgar's star might finally be rising, his young wife Virginia died in 1847, and Edgar retreated to hard drinking.

On a trip from Richmond to New York, Edgar's steamboat made a stop in Baltimore and, six days later, in the middle of the day, he was found deliriously ill, lying half-conscious in the street by a printer who knew him. He was wearing clothes that probably were not his own and, in a delirious state, kept calling for a polar explorer of the day named Reynolds. Taken to a hospital, Edgar drifted in and out of consciousness for the next four days until he uttered his final words: "Lord help my poor soul," and passed on at 40. The cause of death was presumed to be related to his alcoholism, and his brief obituary reported that he had died of "congestion of the brain." Today, however, historians speculate that he may have been suffering from some other condition of which doctors of that day were unaware. As the literary community did not particularly like Edgar, his obituaries weren't very kind and one stated simply, "We hope he has found his rest, for he needed it."

Edgar was buried the next day in an unmarked grave at Baltimore's Westminster Presbyterian Church Cemetery. Eventually, the literary world came around and a particular group of admirers organized a drive to purchase a suitable grave monument for the neglected poet. In 1875 Edgar and his wife Virginia, who had been buried in New York, were exhumed and reburied at a prominent site within the

Westminster Cemetery. Aunt Maria was buried with them upon her death in 1885, and the struggling family was reunited for eternity.

Since 1949, on the night of the anniversary of Edgar's birth, a mysterious stranger known as the Poe Toaster has left a half-empty bottle of cognac and three roses at the Poe monument. The significance of cognac is uncertain, as it does not figure in Poe's works, but it's presumed that the three roses are for the three persons whose remains lie beneath. At Baltimore's Poe House and Museum, several of the bottles of cognac from prior years are on display.

CEMETERY DIRECTIONS: At the southern end of I-83 in central Baltimore, turn right onto Fayette Street and follow it for a mile to Greene Street, where you'll see the church and cemetery on the left corner.

GRAVE DIRECTIONS: Walk into the churchyard and the Poe plot is immediately to the right.

To reach the Poe House and Museum, continue on Fayette Street and, after a half-mile, turn right on Amity Street, where the Poe House is number 203.

MARIO PUZO

OCTOBER 15, 1920 – JULY 2, 1999

For 48 years Mario Puzo basked in relative middle-class obscurity; he served in the Air Force during World War II and, through a variety of jobs, barely supported a wife and five children over the next couple of decades. In 1955 Mario's income was augmented by monies earned through the sale of a novel, *The Dark Arena,* and nine years later an autobiographical chronicle of the experience of Italian American immigrants, *The Fortunate Pilgrim.* Both works were only moderately successful and Mario continued writing freelance book reviews, stories, and articles for newspapers and magazines.

But Mario's fortunes changed after he secured a $5,000 advance for a book about a different group of Italian American immigrants. In 1969 he published a fictitious account of the Sicilian Corleone crime family, *The Godfather.* An instant smash hit, it has sold at least twenty million copies and became one of the best-selling books of all time.

The Godfather and its sequels were of course also adapted for the screen, and Mario wrote the screenplays as well. Today *The Godfather* films, directed by Francis Ford Coppola, are recognized as masterpieces, and are responsible for adding such phrases to the pop-culture lexicon as "Make him an offer he can't refuse," and "It's not personal … it's strictly business."

Later, it was speculated that Mario himself must have been in the Mafia to have the depth of knowledge of its workings that is displayed in his books, but the author vehemently denied the allegation. "Where would I have had time to be in the Mafia? I starved before the success of *The Godfather*," he once said in an interview. "If I was in the Mafia, I would have made enough money so I wouldn't have to write."

In 1996, he continued his best-selling traditions with *The Last Don* and, in 2000, Mario's final installment in the mob soap-opera genre came in *Omerta*, which was published a year after his death.

Mario doesn't "sleep with the fishes." Instead, at 78, he was buried at North Babylon Cemetery in West Babylon, New York.

CEMETERY DIRECTIONS: From the Southern State Parkway, take exit 37S and follow Belmont Avenue a half-mile south to Hubbards Path. Bear left and, after three-fourths of a mile and beyond the underpass, take another left onto the Sunrise Service Road, then a right onto Livingston Avenue.

GRAVE DIRECTIONS: Mario is in the section of cemetery to your right. As you enter the drive you'll see the big Christopher stone in front of you, and four rows behind is the Puzo plot.

AYN RAND

FEBRUARY 2, 1905 – MARCH 6, 1982

Born Alyssa Rosenbaum, the celebrated author Ayn Rand lived through the Bolshevik Revolution and learned to hate her Russian homeland, a country she later described as "an accidental cesspool of civilization." Early on, she planned to escape to the United States and, after studying philosophy and history at the University of Petrograd, her opportunity came in 1926 when she was allowed to briefly visit relatives in America. She never returned.

Speaking little English and virtually penniless, the 21-year-old stayed with relatives in Chicago before changing her name and moving to Hollywood, where she eventually found work as a script evaluator at Cecil B. DeMille's studio. By tripping him on purpose, Ayn met the tall, handsome actor Frank O'Connor, and they married in 1929.

Ayn later became a screenwriter and, having developed into a passionate, communist-hating capitalist, she spent years laboring over an ambitious novel. Rejected countless times for being "too intellectual," *The Fountainhead* was published in 1943 and fourteen years later, *Atlas Shrugged* followed. These two 1,000-plus-page bestsellers reflect Ayn's deep belief in a philosophy she termed "objectivism," which glorifies the pursuit of unbridled self-interest as the right thing to do from an economic standpoint, and a moral one as well. That is, she believed that unrestrained, even arrogant, capitalist pursuit does far more to lift the world's standard of living than does an altruistic life of self-sacrifice.

Critics consider *The Fountainhead* to be the better work, but *Atlas Shrugged* more pointedly propagates Ayn's philosophy. It reads like a mystery, but its premise is that innovators become so fed up with those who regulate and tax and otherwise feed off of achievers that the achievers withdraw their talents from the world and threaten to send us all back to the Dark Ages. After its 1957 publication, Ayn spent the remainder of her life espousing the objectivist philosophy through lectures.

In 1979, Ayn underwent surgery for a spot of cancer on a lung, and the remainder of her life was plagued by poor health. Five days after being released from the hospital for pneumonia, she died of heart failure in her New York City apartment. At her funeral, Ayn was laid out in a coffin next to a six-foot-tall dollar sign.

At 77, she was buried at Kensico Cemetery in Valhalla, New York.

CEMETERY DIRECTIONS: From I-287, take Exit 4 and follow Route 100A north for 2½ miles (Route 100A will become Route 100 after 2 miles) to Lakeview Avenue and turn right. After a half-mile, turn right onto Commerce Street and enter the cemetery.

GRAVE DIRECTIONS: Proceed down Commerce Street, make a right turn onto Tecumseh Avenue, then a left onto Cherokee Avenue. Where Manitou Avenue on your right intersects Cherokee Avenue, stop. There on the left, 30 feet from the drive, are the graves of Ayn and her husband, Frank.

DR. SEUSS
MARCH 2, 1904 – SEPTEMBER 24, 1991

Returning from Europe by boat in 1936, Theodor Geisel amused himself during the long voyage by putting together a nonsense poem to the rhythm of the ship's motion. He later drew pictures to illustrate the rhyme, and after being rejected by either 23 or 28 or 38 publishers, depending on whom you ask, the resulting children's book, *And to Think That I Saw It on Mulberry Street,* made it into print the following year. Ted released the book under the name Dr.

Seuss—a pseudonym he arrived at by inserting a "Dr." in front of his middle name—because he intended to keep his surname for more serious work. But when he later got around to doing a grown-up book, *The Seven Lady Godivas,* in 1939, he found that adults did not seem to care for his humor. So he went back to writing for children, and became famous and wealthy in the process.

For a time Seuss toiled as a freelance magazine cartoonist, and sold humorous prose after dropping out of an Oxford University English literature Ph.D. program in 1926 because his studies seemed "astonishingly irrelevant." The rollicking verse of *Mulberry Street,* his first children's book, was the prototype for his style of outlandish, whimsically illustrated stories, and its success heralded Seuss as an important new children's writer.

The outbreak of World War II forced Seuss to devote his talents to the war effort and, working with the Information and Education Division of the Army, he made documentary films for American soldiers. His film *Hitler Lives* won an Academy Award, a feat Seuss repeated with *Design for Death,* a documentary about the Japanese war effort.

In 1954, a magazine article argued that children were having trouble learning to read because their Dick and Jane primers were pallid and idiotic. The charge inspired Seuss's publisher to challenge him to write a book using no more than 250 words derived from a scholastically approved vocabulary list, which was the publisher's idea of how many words a first grader could absorb at one time.

Seuss responded with the zany classic, *The Cat in the Hat,* an iconoclastic story in rhyme that presented an impelling incentive to read. Using just 223 words and considerable repetition, its short, choppy sentences reassured beginning readers and provided a lively alternative to the wooden dullness of the "See Spot run" learners. Its enthusiastic reception cemented Seuss's reputation, and led him to found Beginner Books, a publishing company specializing in easy-to-read books for children. A whole line of ridiculously logical storybooks was launched—all written by Seuss, and for the most part illustrated by him, as well—that forever changed the world of children's books.

Seuss created modern classics from *Green Eggs and Ham,* which managed in a vocabulary of just 50 words to explain the need to try new experiences, and *Fox in Socks,* a series of increasingly boisterous tongue twisters, to *The Lorax,* about environmental preservation. Though some adults developed an occasional aversion to Seuss's books by reading them aloud one too many times, admirers were drawn to the unflagging momentum and breathless pace of his highly inventive vocabulary, and the way in which he championed virtue and goodness, while still managing to keep things lively. Seuss was one of the few authors of children's books who could get away with moralizing.

Dr. Seuss claimed his ideas started with doodles. "I'll doodle a couple of animals and if they bite each other, it's going to be a good book." Certainly those doodles aided his phantasmagoric imagination in the creation of persnickety Loraxes and fractious Sneetches, not to mention indescribable Zubble-wumps and ooey-gooey green Ooblecks. And Sam, of course.

At 87, Dr. Seuss quietly expired in his sleep at his home in La Jolla, California; at the time of death his 46 children's books had sold more than 200 million copies and been translated into twenty languages and Braille.

He was cremated and his ashes remain with his family.

WILLIAM SHAKESPEARE
APRIL 23, 1564 – APRIL 23, 1616

Relatively little is known about William Shakespeare's life and, though his works, considered the greatest in the English language, have been meticulously examined for flecks of autobiography, interpretations have fallen short. In any event, we know that words came easily to the playwright and that he had an incalculable influence on literature. "The Bard" converted the hitherto stiff verse meter into an instrument capable of expressing every facet of human emotion and intellect. And, through a brilliant array of characters, he explored the nature of man through astounding dramas that have never been equaled.

It's believed that Shakespeare spent the years 1580–82 as a teacher, then moved to London to become an actor. When the theaters were closed in 1592 due to plague, he turned to writing and, by the time the theaters opened again in 1594, Shakespeare had emerged as a rising playwright. He became a charter member of the Lord Chamberlain's Men, a group of actors who later changed their name to the King's Men when they gained the sponsorship of King James I. Around 1598 Shakespeare became "principal comedian" of the troupe and it was during this time that he penned comedies such as *A Midsummer Night's Dream*. Likewise, when he became "principal tragedian" around 1603, works such as *Hamlet, Macbeth*, and *King Lear* were the result. Later came the romances, *Romeo and Juliet* among them.

Though the profession of playwright was not particularly noble or well paying, successful and prosperous actors were relatively respected and Shakespeare was able to live well as such. In 1596 he applied for a coat of arms for his family, in effect making himself into an aristocrat. Around 1610, he returned to his hometown where he had a house built and lived out the remainder of his years as a country gentleman.

Shakespeare died at 56 and was buried in the sanctuary of the Collegiate Church of Holy Trinity in Stratford-on-Avon, Warwickshire, England, about 80 miles northwest of London.

It seems ludicrous to question the authorship of the works of William Shakespeare but, in the centuries since his death, his legacy has indeed been debated. A number of respected books, particularly the 1908 work by George Greenwood, *The Shakespeare Problem Restated*, suggest that credit has been given to the wrong man and that someone other than the man we know as William Shakespeare is the author of his credited volumes. According to *Shakespeare Problem* proponents, there isn't a shred of hard evidence to prove that he wrote even one of his dramas. To the contrary, they argue, there is considerable evidence that he couldn't possibly have been the true Bard. Some who share this conviction regard Francis Bacon as the "real" author, while others champion Christopher Marlowe.

One of the lesser reasons that *Shakespeare Problem* partisans disregard him is that, in contrast to the passing of other distinguished literary folk of the era, Shakespeare's death was not an event. In fact, they say, "as far as anyone can know and can prove," Shakespeare wrote only one poem during his life, and his authorship of it stands undisputed. That one poem is the epitaph that he commanded be engraved upon his tomb. He was obeyed, and it remains there to this day. It reads:

> *Good friend, for Jesus' sake forbeare,*
> *To digg the dust enclosed heare!*
> *Blese be ye man yt spares these stones.*
> *And curst be he yt moves my bones.*

MARY SHELLEY

AUGUST 30, 1797 – FEBRUARY 1, 1851

Given her family legacy (both her parents were influential authors and propagandists), it seemed inevitable that Mary Shelley was to make a significant contribution to literature. Her mother, Mary Wollstonecraft, was an early (*very* early) feminist who authored the radical tome, *A Vindication of the Rights of Women,* which is still read today. Mary's father, William Godwin, was a celebrated liberalist whose goal was to translate France's Enlightenment into an English context, though his once voguish radicalism fell out of favor after the bloody excesses of the French Revolution.

The Godwin-Wollstonecraft relationship was intellectually based; the two even kept separate households until just before Mary's birth on the principle that women had the right to independence. When her mother died days after her birth, Mary was left to be reared by her father, an undemonstrative, self-absorbed, and cerebral man.

By the time she was ten, Mary was a student of her mother's oeuvre, and often retreated to the tranquil comfort provided by her mother's grave for study. At 16 she eloped with poet Percy Bysshe Shelley, a peer of her father's. As Mary was by now herself a writer, the couple immersed themselves in their own brainy relationship and enjoyed impulsive poetically inspired European jaunts.

In July 1816, they visited Lord Byron's Villa Diodati home near Geneva and fell to reading each other ghost tales. After being joined by Gothic author John Polidori, the talent in the Villa superseded the stories being read and Byron suggested a kind of contest to see which of them could write the best supernatural tale; 18-year-old Mary's effort became *Frankenstein: or, the Modern Prometheus.*

In more than 40 *Frankenstein* film adaptations, the general spirit of the story has been significantly shifted to the shallow horror of a grunting, bolt-headed monster and his mad-scientist creator. But in fact, the *Frankenstein* story is largely a sympathetic narrative of a creature embittered after being unloved and deserted by his creator, and it reflects the net effect of Mary Shelley's life: a motherless child with a distant father. In any event, though she wrote five more novels, Mary's reputation rests with her "hideous progeny," the Creature created by Dr. Victor Frankenstein.

Mary Shelley died in her sleep at 53 and is buried alongside her parents at Saint Peter's Churchyard on Hinton Road in Bournemouth, England.

Prior to her death, Mary's poet husband Percy drowned off the coast of Italy in 1822, and his body was burned there in a beachfront funeral pyre. During the immolation, his friend Edward Trelawny retrieved Percy's heart from his body and later presented it to the newly widowed Mary, who must have been delighted by his thoughtfulness. Until her own death she kept it pressed flat in a copy of his poem "Adonais," at which time both the poem and heart were buried with her.

Percy's ashes were later buried at the Cimitero Acattolico in Rome, Italy. This historical cemetery is adjacent to the Pyramid of Cestii on Via Ostiensis.

JOHN STEINBECK
FEBRUARY 27, 1902 – DECEMBER 20, 1968

The fact that John Steinbeck spent his formative years in California—where migrant fruit pickers of the San Joaquin valley toiled the hard land while shiftless and carefree drifters camped together in shanties along Monterey Bay—was extremely influential on the budding writer.

After a short stay at Stanford University, a couple of lost years in New York, and two undistinguished novellas, Steinbeck refocused his writing efforts and in 1935 released *Tortilla Flat*, a sometimes-comical but affectionate story of rootless Mexican-American drifters. It was Steinbeck's first popularly successful work and it was followed quickly by the similarly acclaimed *The Red Pony* and *Of Mice and Men*.

In 1936 Steinbeck began hanging around the camps of farming refugees who had been stripped of their Midwestern livelihoods and displaced to California by the Dust Bowl hardships. Three years later Steinbeck released *The Grapes of Wrath*, the saga of one Okie family's struggle along Route 66 on the way to the promised land, and the family's subsequent pains at the hands of exploitive farm owners. It was an American masterpiece.

As is usually the case, not everyone was ecstatic about the work, and Oklahoma's governor characterized it as "a lie, a black, infernal creation of a twisted and distorted mind." But the following year, Steinbeck was redeemed when he received the Pulitzer Prize.

Steinbeck spent 1941 collecting marine life in Mexico with his marine-biologist friend Edward F. Ricketts, and the two men collaborated in writing *Sea of Cortez*, a study of the fauna of the Gulf of California. During World War II he took various war-correspondent assignments abroad and, after the war, etched more sentimental novels like *Cannery Row* and *The Pearl* while contributing the story for Alfred Hitchcock's film *Lifeboat*. Steinbeck's last work was *Travels with Charley*, a 1962 chronicle of his tour around America in a camper with his wife's poodle.

At 66, John died peacefully in bed at his home in Sag Harbor, New York.

After his funeral, at which Henry Fonda read a eulogy, John was cremated. A few days later, along a stretch of very rugged coastline

several miles south of Monterey, John's family scattered some of his ashes at a place overlooking Whalers Bay while sea otters played in the surf below. The remaining ashes were buried at the Garden of Memories Cemetery in Salinas, California.

CEMETERY DIRECTIONS: From the north, exit Highway 101 at John Street, turn west and, after a short distance, turn left onto Abbott Street. After three-fourths of a mile, turn right onto Memory Drive and enter the cemetery.

From the south, exit Highway 101 at Abbott Street (it's a left-hand lane exit) and follow Abbott north for five miles to Memory Drive on your left. (To access Memory Drive, you'll need to go past it and make a U-turn at East Romie Lane).

GRAVE DIRECTIONS: Enter the cemetery, turn right at the flagpole, and go past the mausoleum. Turn at the next right and, halfway down this drive, you'll see a "Steinbeck" sign and an arrow pointing left. John's ashes are interred 100 feet across that lawn in front of the Hamilton stone.

ROBERT LOUIS STEVENSON

NOVEMBER 13, 1850 – DECEMBER 3, 1894

In 1867, Robert Louis Stevenson entered Edinburgh University with the tacit understanding that he'd follow his father and become a civil engineer. But Robert enjoyed a more romantic nature, and he instead spent his time studying literature and history. As a compromise, he switched to law and, though he was called to the Scottish bar in 1875, Robert never actually practiced. Instead he devoted himself to writing travel sketches and short stories for magazines.

Suffering from tuberculosis since childhood, Robert took advantage of his newfound adult freedom and jockeyed from place to place with the seasons to ease his respiratory discomforts. His rambles soon blossomed into wanderlust. "I travel for travel's sake," he wrote, "The great affair is to move," and the wanderlust, in turn, rendered inspiration for romantic adventure novels.

In 1878, his first book, *An Inland Voyage*, was published, and by 1883 he was held in high regard for *Treasure Island*. In 1886, after writing *The Strange Case of Dr. Jekyll and Mr. Hyde*, which was based on a dream and written and printed in a ten-week blizzard of activity, and *Kidnapped*, which recounted the tale of his ancestor David Balfour, Robert looked up from his notebooks to find he'd became the most popular author of the day.

Dogged by his flagging health, Robert and his family set sail for the South Pacific in 1888, and the following year he bought an estate in Samoa where he hoped to live happily ever after. The climate suited his respiration, the people were neighborly, and, more importantly, the island had a reasonably functional postal system. The Stevenson estate boasted a dozen Samoan servants who called Robert "Tusitala" ("the teller of tales") and in his time there he pounded out an impressive number of works, though none rivaled the popularity of his earlier successes.

But Robert's blissful experience on Samoa was short-lived. One evening while chatting with his wife, he suffered a cerebral hemorrhage. At 44, he was buried atop Mount Vaea on his own 300-acre Vailima estate in Apia, Samoa.

Robert's grave marker is graced by his own words:

> *Here he lies where he longed to be;*
> *Home is the sailor, home from the sea,*
> *And the hunter home from the hill.*

J.R.R. TOLKIEN

JANUARY 3, 1892 – SEPTEMBER 2, 1973

Upon his 1915 graduation from Exeter College, John Ronald Reuel Tolkien immediately took up a commission as a second lieutenant on the front lines of the raging Great War. In time, though, he was sent back to England to recover from a case of trench fever and he joined the English Dictionary staff (writing entries in the w's) at Oxford University. Around this time, Tolkien's enthusiasm for the myths and languages of northern Europe caught fire through his membership at a literature club, and the groundwork for his stories about Middle-earth was laid.

Tolkien conceived of a Middle-earth fantasy world as the setting for his visionary tales, and its creation occupied him for twenty years. The details of the realm were derived from Celtic and Germanic sources whose common traditions were reworked to reflect Tolkien's belief in the importance and perfectibility of man. Though its most striking creatures are the elves and dwarves, goblins and dragons, and wizards and demons, the most important race in Middle-earth is men and, free to choose their own destinies, they run the gamut from goblin-like evil and depravity to elf-like purity and integrity.

Tolkien also composed stories for his own children and, about 1930, began one with the idle sentence, "In a hole in the ground there lived a hobbit." As the story evolved, it became clear to Tolkien that this adventure of one Bilbo Baggins took place in the same Middle-earth, though at a much later time. In 1937, this story, *The Hobbit*, was published as a children's book to critical and popular acclaim.

Bolstered by his success, Tolkien immediately began work on his next book, *The Lord of the Rings*, a longer, intense and more intricately themed adult version of *The Hobbit* and, after years of painstaking revision, it was published in 1954. The work secured him a standing as an unequaled writer of imaginative literature, and Tolkien spent the rest of his life polishing and refining his vision. Leaving the original stories relatively untouched, he embellished their context with genealogical tables, historical speculations, and theological explications, all designed to clarify the meaning of his creation.

At 81, Tolkien died of a chest infection and was buried at Wolvercote Cemetery in Wolvercote, England.

Wolvercote is a picturesque parish of Oxford, 40 miles northwest of London that overlooks the Thames River. The cemetery is off of Five Mile Drive, and the Tolkien grave is fairly elaborate. The main headstone is flanked by two smaller headstones for Tolkien and his wife, Edith, and they are engraved with flower patterns based upon those found in a posthumous work, *The Silmarillion*.

LEO TOLSTOY

AUGUST 28, 1828 – NOVEMBER 20, 1910

The Russian author Leo Tolstoy was of a noble family dating back to the fourteenth century. His father, Count Nikolay, had a passion for gambling and, though he exhausted the family wealth, he was able to recover by marrying an heiress of the Volkonsky fortune that included 800 serfs and a 4,000-acre estate, Yasnaya Polyana, where Leo was born.

As man of the house in his 20s, Leo contracted heavy gambling debts himself, and he lost the estate's 42-room mansion to a man named Gorokhov, who dismantled the structure as payment. After losing the main house, the family moved into one of the mansion's remaining wings, while Leo and his brother meandered to the southern Caucasus Mountains, volunteering for service in the Crimean War. Drawing material from his self-lacerating diary entries, he began to write during the long lulls between fighting, and by 1857 had published the trilogy *Childhood, Boyhood,* and *Youth.*

Leo once said, "The one thing that is necessary, in life as in art, is to tell the truth." An entry in his wife's diary for October 1863, reads: "Story about 1812, he is very involved with it," and indeed, Tolstoy was intent upon telling his truth through the historically accurate masterpiece *War and Peace.* Tolstoy was convinced that philosophical principles could only be understood in their concrete expression in history, and in his vast canvas of five families against the background of Napoleon's invasion of Russia, Tolstoy espoused that all is predestined, that we cannot live unless we imagine that we have free will. In his attention to the social matrix and psychological truth of his characters, Tolstoy reached the apogee of world literature.

No sooner did Tolstoy complete one masterpiece than he started another, and in 1877 he finished *Anna Karenina.* In this work he juxtaposed the crises of family with the quest for love. Tolstoy considered *Anna Karenina* his magnum opus. He later renounced all his earlier works, confessing, "I wrote everything into *Anna Karenina.*"

The idolization that Tolstoy enjoyed during the 1880s caused him to see himself as a moral prophet, and the ethical quest that tormented him drove him to abandon all else in order to seek meaning. As Tolstoy took up cobbling and obsessed over Chinese philosophies, his family relations became increasingly strained, especially as he played with the idea of giving all his wealth to charity. But in 1884 he compromised with his wife Sonya and assigned her the estate and all copyrights. Still, he continued to write and especially noteworthy is his powerful 1886 story, "The Death of Ivan Ilyich," which affirmed his belief in the primacy of individual conscience over group-collective morality. But at various times throughout the remainder of his life, Tolstoy tried to live as a wandering ascetic, returning home only to leave again on extended pilgrimages. After a quarrel with Sonya, Tolstoy set out on his last pilgrimage in November 1910 and soon died of pneumonia at the remote railway junction of Astapovo.

At 82, he was returned and buried at the place of his birth, Yasnaya Polyana estate near Tula, Russia.

Years after his death Sonya remarked, "I lived with Leo for 48 years, but I never really learned what kind of man he was."

Yasnaya Polyana is located in western Russia, about 120 miles directly south of Moscow. Though there is nothing grandiose on the property—no ostentatious architecture or fancy gardens—its tree-lined lanes and tranquil ponds offer a bright spot in the otherwise drab and run-down industrial region of Tula. Tolstoy's peaceful grave is on a leafy overlook above a ravine.

MARK TWAIN
NOVEMBER 30, 1835 – APRIL 21, 1910

Samuel Langhorne Clemens, better known by his pseudonym, Mark Twain, so hated school as a boy that he stopped attending at twelve and became an apprentice printer at *The Hannibal Journal* in Missouri. Immersed in the newspaper business, he was soon contributing short essays of frontier humor and jokes to the paper and, at eighteen, he left home to work as a journalist in Philadelphia and New York.

A few years later he jumped from the news business when an opportunity to work steamboats on the Mississippi River arose, and by 23, he was a licensed river pilot. From that experience came the pen name he'd later employ, which related to the distance between the steamboat's bottom and the riverbed; when a depth of two fathoms was detected, the leadsman sounded an alert: "By the maaaark, twain!"

Steamboat traffic dried up with the commencement of the Civil War's river blockade in 1861, and Mark, whose sympathies in those days were with the South, hurried to Hannibal and enlisted with a company of rangers. But, after a few cheerless weeks, and with no one yet to fight, Mark deserted and, along with thousands of others avoiding the War, moved west. Landing in San Francisco, Mark returned to journalism for the duration of the war.

By 1866, he was in New York City working as a correspondent aboard the Quaker City steamer, which was departing for a voyage to Europe, Russia, and the Middle East. Before he left, he compiled his writings from his western days and arranged for the publication of his first book, *The Celebrated Jumping Frog of Calaveras County and Other Sketches*. Mark returned from the eight-month trip to find that *Calaveras* had been a success, and the next year he published a book of his travel letters from the Quaker City voyage, *Innocents Abroad*.

Between 1873 and 1889, Mark settled in Hartford for a period of concentrated writing. These were his most productive years and he completed seven novels, including the childhood classics *The Adventures of Tom Sawyer, Life On the Mississippi,* and his masterpiece, *Adventures of Huckleberry Finn.* In these novels, in which he wove colloquial language through socially intimate storylines, Mark Twain captured the era's rhythms and by 1890, stood among the greatest character writers in the literary world.

For most of his final decade, having outlived his wife and three children, Mark resided in New York City in the company of dignitaries, usually appearing in his trademark white linen suit. Though he continued to write for the remainder of his life, none of his subsequent works ever approached the popularity of his Tom Sawyer and Huck Finn tales.

Mark had been born with Halley's Comet clearly visible in the heavens, and he predicted he'd "go out with the comet." While it streaked through the skies almost 75 years later, Mark slipped into a coma and died of angina pectoris. He was buried at Woodlawn Cemetery in Elmira, New York.

CEMETERY DIRECTIONS: From I-17, take Exit 56 and follow Church Street 1 3/4 miles to Walnut Street. Turn right and, after about a mile, Walnut Street ends at the cemetery.

GRAVE DIRECTIONS: Enter the cemetery and turn at the second right. Then turn at the second left and stop. The Twain plot is on the right.

VINCENT VAN GOGH

MARCH 30, 1853 – JULY 29, 1890

Though painter Vincent van Gogh's work became an important bridge for modern painting between the nineteenth and twentieth centuries, he was almost wholly unknown during his brief lifetime and, of his more than 1,500 paintings and drawings, he sold just one of them.

The son of a Protestant minister, Vincent alternately worked at his uncle's art dealership, clerked at a bookshop, studied theology at the University of Amsterdam, and served as a lay missionary until he was 27. Then, in 1880, Vincent attended a Brussels school and chose art as a vocation, which he considered to be his spiritual calling.

Interested in the poor and dispossessed, Vincent concentrated on depicting miners and peasants in his so-called Dutch period, between 1880 and 1886. But, except for one picture, *The Potato Eaters,* his works from that period display few hints of the talent that was growing within.

By 1886 Vincent was drawn to the bohemian life and artistic activity of Paris and went to live there with his brother, Theo, who directed a small gallery in the city. Through contacts provided by Theo, he met the leaders of impressionism—Monet, Pissarro, and Gauguin. Under their influence, Vincent was persuaded to adopt more brilliant hues and change his subject matter to more typical impressionist themes such as the cafés and cityscapes reflected in works like *Restaurant de la Sirene at Asnieres.*

Vincent painted in Paris for almost two years and, though his palette was liberated, he wearied of the city's frenetic energy and its long months of winter, and he left for southern France. In Arles, Vincent worked feverishly to capture the rustic life of the Provence region; he applied colors in simplified, highly saturated masses, and his images became more virile and incisive than ever before. Among the masterpieces of his Arles period are *Still Life with Sunflowers* and *Night Café.*

In the fall of 1888, Gauguin moved to Arles in an effort to work more closely with Vincent. But by this time Vincent had begun to experience maddening blackouts and seizures, which historians today speculate may have been caused by epilepsy or syphilis. Whatever van Gogh's affliction, he and Gauguin often fell into violent quarrels. Finally, in an irrational fit of anger, Vincent mutilated the lower portion of his left ear with a razor and brought the severed lobe to a brothel, where he presented it to a woman there. Gauguin left immediately for Paris and the two never met again.

By May 1889, some of the citizens of Arles had become alarmed by Vincent's increasingly bizarre behavior and after a group petitioned their concerns to the city's board, Vincent volunteered to have himself confined. At the St. Remy asylum, Vincent soon resumed painting at his feverish pace and in this period was drawn to natural objects under stress, such as whirling suns and twisted cypress trees. His colors lost their intensity, his lines became restless, and he applied the paint more thickly and violently, as in one of his best-known works, *Starry Night,* an obsessively beautiful exercise in circularity.

A year after being admitted to St. Remy, Vincent left to live near Theo again, this time in Auvers. Here he produced his last painting, *Wheat Field with Crows,* a disturbing struggle of savage brush strokes supercharged with crows, a universal symbol of death. A few days after its completion, Vincent set out his easel and painting materials in a wheat field and shot himself in the chest. The bullet did not kill him, however, and he staggered back to his room and collapsed in bed. Two days later, Vincent died in Theo's arms.

Vincent and Theo were very close, even for brothers, and corresponded constantly through letters. These letters form a uniquely human biographical record, and the 700 of them authored by Vincent provide a vivid historical account of his hopes and disappointments as his physical and mental states fluctuated. Six months after Vincent's death at 37, Theo, the grief-stricken brother, died at 33.

Now, you may well be wondering where did the brothers then Gogh? Theo was buried in Utrecht in the Netherlands, but, almost 25 years later, his wife had him reinterred alongside Vincent. They now both rest at the cemetery of Auvers-sur-Oise, France, a sleepy little town on the banks of the Oise, one of the tributaries of the Seine, just north of Paris.

ANDY WARHOL

AUGUST 6, 1928 – FEBRUARY 22, 1987

Andy Warhol is considered the creator of Pop Art. His paintings and prints of presidents, movie stars, and other American icons—coupled with a keen talent for attracting publicity—earned him a following that still regards him as one of the most important artists of the modern era. Indeed, that his art could even maintain the interest of a notoriously fickle public for all these years is testimony to his dominion.

Throughout the fifties, Warhol worked as a commercial artist in New York City, but by the early sixties he hung up his brush and turned exclusively to hard-edged images made in the medium of silkscreen print (which he pioneered). The results were the depersonalized images that would become his trademark. Producing a portrait of cans of Campbell's Soup wasn't his only radical act; he also adapted a means of producing the images en masse; a new consumer art had effectively mimicked both the process and look of consumer culture.

Although himself shy and quiet, Andy attracted dozens of disciples who were anything but introverted, and their energy combined with his genius to produce a number of notorious events throughout his career. His Manhattan studio, the Factory, became a chic hangout for like-minded artists, musicians, fashion mavens and movie stars, as well as the usual hangers-on and groupies who flocked to the new jet-set scene. Andy also produced underground films, some of which attempted to redefine our ideas of boredom and repetition; one showed 33 minutes of someone having his hair cut and another featured a follower, Edie Sedgwick, talking about herself through out-of-focus frames. Later, a rejected disciple shot Andy, who was momentarily declared dead, but Andy the survivor recuperated and thrived for two more decades.

At 58, Andy died of complications after a relatively routine gallbladder operation and was buried at Saint John the Baptist Catholic Cemetery in Castle Shannon, Pennsylvania.

CEMETERY DIRECTIONS: In this village seven miles south of Pittsburgh, this cemetery is easy to find at the corner of Route 88 and Connor Road. If you proceed south along Route 88, you won't miss it on the right.

GRAVE DIRECTIONS: Directly behind the office, up the grassy hill and six rows from the chain-link fence, is the Warhol plot. (Incidentally, Andy's given family name was Warhola, but in 1949 a magazine crediting his work misspelled his name. He decided to make the change permanent.)

E.B. WHITE
JULY 11, 1899 – OCTOBER 1, 1985

Known more commonly by his initials than by his given first name, literary stylist Elwyn Brooks White graduated from Cornell University in 1921 and soon joined the staff of the newly established *New Yorker* magazine. In a crisp and graceful style, E.B. churned out hundreds of essays advocating respect for nature and a simple life, detailing the complexities and failures of technological society, questioning the merits of organized religion, and celebrating internationalism. He married the magazine's literary editor, Kathryn Sergeant Angell, and continued to contribute to the publication for the remainder of his life.

E.B. first gained wide fame in 1929 when he copublished *Is Sex Necessary?* with colleague James Thurber. But it was the children's books that he wrote that brought him the most accolades. In 1945 he depicted an independent mouse child in *Stuart Little*. A few years later came *Charlotte's Web* and its barnyard friendships. And in 1970 a mute swan found his voice in *The Trumpet of the Swan*.

In 1939 E.B. moved to a farm in Maine and continued writing without the responsibilities of a regular job. He never stopped loving New York, calling it "a riddle in steel and stone," but he also foresaw the vulnerability of the city when he wrote in 1949's *Here is New York*, "A single flight of planes no bigger than a wedge of geese can quickly end this island fantasy, burn the towers, crumble the bridges, turn the underground passages into lethal chambers, cremate millions. Of all targets New York has a certain clear priority in the mind of whatever perverted dreamer might loose the lightning."

In 1978 E.B. was awarded a special Pulitzer citation for his body of work and he died from complications of Alzheimer's disease a few years later. At 86, he was buried at the Brooklin Cemetery in Brooklin, Maine.

CEMETERY DIRECTIONS: From Highway 1, take Route 15 and then Route 175 into Brooklin. Just before the center of town you'll see the cemetery on the left.

GRAVE DIRECTIONS: Side by side under twin gray tombstones you can find the graves of E.B. and Kathryn. They're all the way in the back, under the oak tree near the maintenance sheds.

WALT WHITMAN
MAY 31, 1819 ~ MARCH 26, 1892

Born to an undistinguished Long Island family, Walt Whitman had almost no formal education but, by self-teaching through immersion in Shakespeare and Dante, he became a schoolteacher at seventeen. By his early 20s Walt moved into journalism and, though he published some of his writings, by his 30s he had still not displayed the slightest hint of any unique talent or vision.

It's difficult, then, to account for Walt's sudden transformation from hack writer into revolutionary poet. But, somehow, at 36,

Walt distinguished himself when he self-published a slim volume of poetry, *Leaves of Grass*, in 1855. The twelve poems in his first edition were plain and simple celebrations of the explosive joy of living, and they seemed to have come from nowhere. Their style was connected to nothing else being written at that time or any other; Walt had turned his back on literary models of the past and virtually ignored meter and rhyme. Stressing the rhythms of native American speech, Walt delighted in colloquial and slang expressions. His ideas were as sexually frank as diary entries.

Walt received little attention and even less money for his groundbreaking *Leaves of Grass*. But by the time he added twenty more poems for its second issue, and an additional 146 that appeared in his "new Bible" third printing, he had created controversy for readers, whose attentions had by then turned to the Civil War's battlefields. Walt was enormously impacted by the Civil War, and he published his reminiscences in a publication he called *Drum-Taps*. With aesthetic simplicity, these poems captured the horror and anguish of the war, and they too were later folded into *Leaves of Grass*, which by the end of Walt's life had been issued in nine different editions.

In his last years Walt received the homage due a great literary figure. *Leaves of Grass* has been widely translated, and his reputation is worldwide. His emphasis on native idiom, his frank approach to muses hitherto thought unsuitable to poetry, and his divergence from approved structural precepts have all contributed to his reputation as having had a profound influence on modern poetry.

> *I believe a leaf of grass is no less than the journeywork of the stars,*
> *And the pismire is equally perfect, and a grain of sand, and the*
> *egg of a wren.*

At 54 Walt suffered a paralytic stroke and thereafter devoted much of his time to putting *Leaves of Grass* into final order; by the time he was 60, the collection's final arrangement was settled. A sunstroke at 64 and another paralytic stroke made him increasingly dependent on others, and Walt died of complications at 72.

Walt was buried at Harleigh Cemetery in Collingswood, New Jersey.

CEMETERY DIRECTIONS: From the center of town follow Haddon Avenue north for about a mile and the cemetery is on the right, immediately beyond the underpass of routes 30 and 130.

GRAVE DIRECTIONS: Enter the cemetery at the second gate, turn left in front of the office, then take the next right. After a short distance you'll see Walt's tomb on the left, before the pond.

LAURA INGALLS WILDER

FEBRUARY 7, 1867 – FEBRUARY 10, 1957

Enticed by the free land offered to homesteaders during the 1870s, the family of Laura Ingalls Wilder moved west from Wisconsin when she was a child and settled in what is now South Dakota. From those earliest childhood days, and all through adulthood, Laura persevered through a simple but arduous life on the American frontier. She was alternately a teacher and a farmhand and occasionally submitted small pieces to newspapers through those difficult days. By her 40s, Laura secured a position at the *Missouri Ruralist* newspaper, eventually becoming its editor.

At 60 years old, Laura began to write her memoirs in a manuscript entitled *Pioneer Girl.* The concept of this book, which was essentially the entire series in one, led to the start of the *Little House* string of books, which featured stories drawn from her family's experiences as pioneers in the mid-1800s. Written with a folksy common sense, the books celebrated a peculiarly American spirit and good humor, and the eight-part series became children's classics. Later, the books enjoyed a revival as the basis for the *Little House on the Prairie* television series.

As Laura's family moved frequently, a number of enterprising wind-swept towns have managed to turn her assorted homesteads into a bit of a cottage industry. There are no less than six different Wilder museums and historic sites scattered among the states of the Midwest and Great Plains.

Laura died in her sleep at 90 and was buried at Mansfield Cemetery in Mansfield, Missouri.

CEMETERY DIRECTIONS: From Highway 60, take Business Route 60 south into the center of Mansfield. At the town center, make a right and stay on BR 60 for another half-mile, then turn right onto Lincoln Street. The Mansfield Cemetery is a short distance ahead on the left.

GRAVE DIRECTIONS: Enter the cemetery at the second drive and stop after 100 feet. About 30 feet away, on the right, you'll see the Wilder plot.

TENNESSEE WILLIAMS
MARCH 26, 1911 – FEBRUARY 25, 1983

By showcasing the Old South's gentility by way of tormented and unforgettable stage characters, Thomas "Tennessee" Williams created a series of powerful portraits of the human condition, earning respect as one of the greatest playwrights in the history of American drama. His emphasis on the irrational and desperate nature of individuals in many ways mirrored his personal experience and, indeed, Tennessee confessed, "If I did not write, I'd go mad."

Though he hailed from a prestigious Tennessee family that boasted the state's first governor and senator, his immediate family was a bit less distinguished; Tennessee's distant and abusive father traveled for business, his anomalous mother was never quite accepted by the genteel society she pursued, and his sister spent most of her life in mental institutions. After attending three different universities and working briefly alongside his father at a shoe company (an experience Tennessee called "a living death"), he moved to New Orleans in 1938.

In the Big Easy, he seemed to reinvent himself, starting with his name, which he legally changed to Tennessee. Having struggled with his sexuality all through his youth, Tennessee embraced the city's liberal attitude and, with a new name, a new home, and his developing talent, fully entered gay life. After struggling for a few years, Tennessee began to write about what he knew and, after mining his past for inspiration, the pristine tenderness of *The Glass Menagerie* propelled it into a Broadway hit, making 1945 a turning point for Tennessee. The next fifteen years were his most productive: *A Rose Tattoo, Baby Doll,* and *Night of the Iguana* were well received by critics and popular with audiences. But it was two other works in that period, both Pulitzer Prize-winners, that sealed Tennessee's reputation as a supreme dramatist: *A Streetcar Named Desire* traced the decline of a sensitive woman at the hands of her brother-in-law; while *Cat on a Hot Tin Roof* tracked the moral decay of a Southern family, its Big Daddy character modeled after Tennessee's own father.

But the '60s and '70s were less kind and, after his longtime companion and steadying influence, Frank Merlo, died in 1961, Tennessee began a long downward spiral. Suffering from depression, he lived in fear that he would go insane like his sister. He became dependent on drugs, especially alcohol and, though he owned homes in New Orleans and Key West, he often lived as a sort of wealthy gypsy, moving frequently among hotels. Tennessee was terribly insecure and, as the quality of his work declined as a result of his personal difficulties, he got caught in a desperate and vicious circle of self-pity and violent jealousy of younger playwrights.

A monumental hypochondriac, Tennessee was obsessed with sickness and death. He worried that his heart would inexplicably stop beating and, in desperation, took pills that he didn't need. His death at 71 came in a way he probably never expected; after a night of heavy drinking, Tennessee choked to death on a bottle cap at the luxurious midtown Hotel Elysée in New York City.

Tennessee was buried at Calvary Cemetery in St. Louis, Missouri.

CEMETERY DIRECTIONS: Calvary Cemetery is located at 5279 W. Florrisant Ave. It's easily found by taking Exit 29 off I-270 and traveling south for six miles. Or, you can take Exit 245B off I-70, from which point the cemetery is a mile north. (Go past Belle-fontaine Cemetery first.)

GRAVE DIRECTIONS: The grounds of Calvary are very large and the roads within are numerous and mazelike, so you should stop at the office and get a map. Tennessee is buried in Section 15 and, though Section 15 comprises three smaller sections, his plot is easy to find in the northernmost area. It is the pink-tinted stone near the road.

FRANK LLOYD WRIGHT
JUNE 8, 1867 – APRIL 9, 1959

Frank Lloyd Wright is considered one of the great figures in twentieth-century architecture. After just a few years of apprenticeship, he started his own Chicago firm in 1893, and from there espoused his philosophy of "organic architecture" whose central principle—"form and function are one"—demands that a structure be developed out of its natural surroundings.

Frank's Prairie House residential concepts were distinguished by low-pitched rooflines, deep overhangs, and uninterrupted walls of windows merging the horizontal home into the landscape. The interior space was maximized by eliminating attics, rooms flowed into one another with half-walls, and centralized stone fireplaces, translucent ceilings, and garden areas provided environmental oneness. His 1937 Kaufmann House (now known as Fallingwater and open to the public in Pennsylvania) is a later example of Frank's residential style.

But he was also a bold revolutionary in industrial design and departed from the lifeless arrangements favored by his contemporaries. He introduced numerous innovations, such as steel-reinforced concrete, all-glass revolving doors, indirect lighting, air conditioning, and even metal furniture. One of Frank's more remarkable engineering developments was an earthquake-proof design that featured a cantilever construction atop a floating foundation. With a shape reminiscent of a snail's shell, New York City's Guggenheim Museum is an example of a Wright work that mimics a design found in nature.

In Wisconsin, Frank converted his own Taliesin home into a school and workshop for apprentice visionaries, but in 1914, tragedy struck. One night while Frank was away on business, an employee of the school went berserk and burned Taliesin to the ground. Worse, before setting the complex ablaze, he nailed the exterior doors shut except for the lower half of a Dutch door. By the time the inferno was extinguished, seven people were dead, five of whom had been bludgeoned with an ax by the deranged employee as they tried to escape through the bottom of the Dutch door. Frank's wife and two stepchildren were among the victims.

Frank rebuilt Taliesin and later remarried. In 1938, he built Taliesin West, a winter home and school situated atop a central Arizona mesa. The 37,000-square-foot country estate includes living quarters, offices, and farm buildings that are subtly distinguished from their environment. The 600-acre complex still functions as the winter campus for the Frank Lloyd Wright School of Architecture.

At 91, Frank died at Taliesin West after complications arose following an operation for an intestinal obstruction. Per his instructions, he was buried at the original Taliesin in Spring Green, Wisconsin, alongside the confessed love of his life, his first wife Mameh, who had been killed on that terrible night in 1914. However, it seems that Frank's last wife, Olgivanna, had her own idea about how Frank should spend eternity. Upon Olgivanna's death in 1983, her will stipulated that Frank be exhumed and cremated, his cremains mixed with her own, and the combined remains kept in an urn at Taliesin West.

Olgivanna's wishes were fulfilled and the urn holding their ashes is kept in Scottsdale. At the moment the urn is not available for public viewing, and is instead tucked safely away "in storage."

HEROES OF ROCK & BLUES MUSIC

DUANE ALLMAN

NOVEMBER 20, 1946 – OCTOBER 29, 1971

On their 1969 self-titled debut, the Allman Brothers introduced a new sound that fell somewhere between earthy American blues and the untrained incandescence of British rock. On their next three classic recordings, *Idlewild South, At the Fillmore East,* and *Eat a Peach,* the band perfected this sound on such tunes as "Blue Sky," "Melissa," and "Midnight Rider," and established itself as the premier act for this new "Southern rock." Younger brother Gregg's brawly but articulate vocals positioned him as leader of the group, but it was Duane's slide guitar, played in a distillation of everything from classic wailings to eloquent phrasings and riffs, that moved the band in its trademark lengthy solos. Over the years a host of bands have drawn on their model, and though they've often been imitated, 30-plus years later the Allman Brothers' efforts have not been duplicated.

At the end of October 1971, the band took a break from the road and returned to their hometown of Macon, Georgia. At the time, the band's base of operations was at "the Big House," at 2321 Vineville Ave. (now a part-time Allman Brothers museum). On his motorcycle, Duane left the house and, traveling west on Hillcrest Street, laid his bike down on its side to avoid colliding with a truck pulling out of Bartlett Street. Duane instead struck a parked vehicle, suffered extensive internal injuries, and died a few hours later at Middle Georgia Hospital without ever regaining consciousness. He was 24.

At Duane's funeral, while his guitar leaned on his casket, the remaining Allman Brothers played "The Sky is Crying" and "Stormy Monday" for their fallen brother.

Just about a year later and only a few blocks from where Duane lost his life, the band's bass player, 24-year-old Berry Oakley, was killed when he drove his motorcycle into the side of a bus.

Today, the band mates rest side by side at Macon's historic Rose Hill Cemetery.

CEMETERY DIRECTIONS: From I-16, take Exit 2 and follow Spring Street south. Go over the Ocmulgee River bridge, and at the traffic light turn right onto Riverside Drive. After a third of a mile, turn right and proceed up the hill to the cemetery.

GRAVE DIRECTIONS: Enter the cemetery and proceed straight down the cement drive to its end. Turn right, going parallel to the train tracks, and at the next paved drive on the right turn and go up the hill. (Don't take the hardest right—just the 90-degree turn). Off to the left and halfway up the hill are the twin polished tombs of Duane and Berry.

Oddly enough, Rose Hill Cemetery is also a place where the Allmans sometimes hung out and practiced during their early years. Later, one of their jams was labeled with a name borrowed from a gravestone, and the free-spirited tune, "In Memory of Elizabeth Reed," is now familiar to classic-rock radio listeners everywhere. Contrary to popular belief, Elizabeth Reed wasn't a friend of the band or anyone the Allmans knew. Instead, she was a Macon resident who died in 1935 at the age of 89, long before the Allmans' time. As it happened that her grave was among the Allmans' old session quarters, a song was dedicated to her memory.

You can see Elizabeth Reed's grave here, too. About 100 feet after taking the right-hand turn that puts you parallel to the train tracks when you're on the way to the rockers' graves, look on the right for a plot with two terraced levels. The grave on the lower level with a concrete urn atop is Elizabeth's.

THE BAND
Richard Manuel
APRIL 3, 1943 – MARCH 4, 1986

Rick Danko
DECEMBER 9, 1942 – DECEMBER 10, 1999

Beginning around 1960, a quintet of Toronto-area musicians slowly came together as the Hawks to supply the backing sound for American rockabilly singer Ronnie Hawkins. Their music wove the old sounds of country blues with the new spirit of rock and roll, and the result was a distinctly new, listenable, and catchy style. By 1965, the Hawks had outgrown the roadhouse circuit and were touring with Bob Dylan on the infamous, boo-filled world tour that marked the former folkie's "going electric."

By the next year they were calling themselves the Band and had holed up near Woodstock, New York, in a crash pad they affectionately dubbed Big Pink. In the basement of Big Pink, guitarist and chief-songwriter Robbie Robertson, bassist Rick Danko, pianist

Richard Manuel, organist Garth Hudson, and drummer Levon Helm honed their unique lyrical and pastoral style, mentored by Dylan, who dropped by after crashing his motorcycle. Their harmony-filled debut album, *Music From Big Pink*, was released in 1968 and became the fulcrum for country rock.

A succession of albums and tours followed and the Band became a firm fixture in the rock aristocracy. But less than a decade later they had had enough and the Band officially called it quits with a celebratory final concert at San Francisco's Winterland Ballroom on Thanksgiving Day, 1976. The concert featured an unprecedented all-star lineup including the likes of Muddy Waters, Neil Diamond, Eric Clapton, and Van Morrison, and was documented by Martin Scorsese in his film, *The Last Waltz*. Many consider it the finest concert film of all time.

The rich baritone and lonesome falsetto of pianist Richard Manuel helped the Band's rise to success, but by the time the band mates regrouped in 1983, an unexplained weariness and despondency had settled over Richard. After a sold-out reunion show in Winter Park, Florida, Richard hanged himself in a motel bathroom while his wife lay sleeping.

At 42, Richard was buried at Avondale Cemetery in Stratford, Ontario, Canada.

CEMETERY DIRECTIONS: Stratford is about 1½ hours west of Toronto. Once you get into town, turn northwest onto Route 8, which is Huron Street. After Saint Joseph's Church, turn left onto Avondale Avenue, follow it to its end, and the cemetery will be in front of you.

GRAVE DIRECTIONS: Enter the cemetery, turn right, and proceed down this drive to where it bends hard to the left. After the hard left, count three more roadways on your left, then stop. On your left is Range 23A, and Richard is buried in this lawn at plot number 193.

After *The Last Waltz*, bassist and part-time lead singer Rick Danko continued his musical pursuits and was a mainstay of the tour circuit for the remainder of his life. His talent shone in his 1978 debut solo album, *Rick Danko*, and in the late 1980s he toured as part of Ringo Starr's All-Starr Band. In 1993 Rick spearheaded the release of a long-awaited new album by the Band, the acclaimed *Jericho*. In 1994 he and the Band were inducted into the Rock 'n' Roll Hall of Fame.

At 57, Rick died in his sleep of a heart attack and was buried at Woodstock Cemetery in Woodstock, New York.

CEMETERY DIRECTIONS: From I-87, take Exit 19 and follow Route 28 west for six miles. Turn right onto Route 375 and turn left at its intersection with Route 212. After a half-mile, turn right onto Rock City Road and the cemetery is a short distance ahead on the right.

GRAVE DIRECTIONS: Drive all the way to the cemetery's rear and, along the back road, you'll find a reddish, double heart-shaped stone for the Cooks. Two rows behind this stone, Rick lies in a grave that, as of this writing, is unmarked.

THE BEACH BOYS

Dennis Wilson

DECEMBER 4, 1944 – DECEMBER 28, 1983

Carl Wilson

DECEMBER 21, 1946 – FEBRUARY 6, 1998

In 1961, Brian Wilson, with brothers Carl and Dennis, cousin Mike Love, and friend Alan Jardine, formed the Beach Boys. Though they only knew how to play three songs at their first concert, endless airplay of their feel-good pop tunes—"Surfin' USA," "Good Vibrations," and "Fun, Fun, Fun," among dozens of others— later lifted the Beach Boys, and each band member individually, to esteem as the epitome of California's carefree spirit.

The Beach Boys also elevated surfing itself, and the arcane pastime soon became a preoccupation among teenagers who lived far from any ocean. Their thickly layered wall of sound was best when it stayed within the bounds of that "surfing sound," but Brian, the group's visionary, contrived a new direction for his musical vision, and in 1966 *Pet Sounds* was released. The album's complex composition of harmonies and instruments raised the bar for musical artistry and inspired the Beatles to weave their own masterpiece the following year with *Sgt. Pepper's Lonely Hearts Club Band.*

The Beach Boys were later eclipsed by groups with harder sounds and rougher images and, though they pressed on over the next decades in various incarnations (and continue today), they ceased to be a consistent rock music force after the 1960s.

Dennis was the only surfer of the bunch. Always at the beach instead of practicing, his mother had to later advocate for his inclusion in the band, which led to Dennis being the drummer by default. Though regarded as the least talented of the brothers, Dennis was a musician in his own right; he contributed a few songs to the Beach Boys' albums and in 1977 had an acclaimed solo release, *Pacific Ocean Blue.* Prompted by that success, Dennis returned to the studio and began a follow-up, tentatively entitled *Bamboo,* but substance abuse slowed his creative momentum and the project stalled.

By 1983 Dennis was nearly broke, a victim of excess. A few days after Christmas, while friends watched from the dock, he repeatedly dove into the chilly waters of the empty slip that once held his boat, the *Harmony,* in Marina del Ray, California. Each time Dennis emerged from the depths, he proudly displayed mud-clad treasures that had been tossed or dropped from his boat in the years before: drinking tumblers, a framed photo of him and his wife Karen. Back to the bottom he went again and again, until at last he failed to resurface. After a frenzied search, the 39-year old Dennis was found an hour later, drowned in the depths where he'd spent his last moments happily searching for his own sunken treasures.

The Heart and Voice of an Angel

♥ CARL DEAN WILSON ♥

DEC. 21, 1946 - FEB. 6, 1998

The World is a Far Lesser Place Without You

Dennis's widow insisted that a burial at sea had been his desire but, as such a burial is reserved for deceased naval personnel, a special dispensation permit had to be requested from the U.S. government. The permit was granted and Dennis was so interred.

After Brian drifted into seclusion from the Beach Boys (and the world) and Dennis died, brother Carl became the last active Wilson in the band. Carl had always been overshadowed by his brothers' attention-grabbing lifestyles, and his lead guitar, which drove the band's concert sound, was consistently underrated. But with the departures of Brian and Dennis, Carl earned his deserved prestige. With his guitar, his melodic anchoring vocals, and his diplomatic presence, he led the band through an endless parade of sun-and-surf Beach Boy nostalgia tours during the eighties and nineties.

In February 1998, Carl died of lung cancer at age 51, and was buried at Westwood Memorial Park in Santa Monica, California.

CEMETERY DIRECTIONS: This little cemetery holds numerous celebrities and is peculiarly located behind the office complex at 10850 Wilshire Blvd., just about a half-mile east of I-405.

GRAVE DIRECTIONS: Enter the cemetery, turn left at the office and, after about 50 feet, you'll find Carl's marker five rows into the grass on the left.

Today, Mike Love fronts a band billed as the *Beach Boys* while Alan Jardine heads up another touring group called *The Beach Boys Friends and Family*. Many still line up for the opportunity to see the last vestiges of the Beach Boys perform as through they were still the 1960s rock and roll juggernaut.

MARC BOLAN
SEPTEMBER 30, 1947 – SEPTEMBER 16, 1977

Marc Bolan and his band T. Rex were an important part of the glitter-rock scene that in many ways prefigured punk rock. Inspired by the work of J.R.R. Tolkien—unicorns and gnomes figured prominently in their song lyrics—the band was originally a hippie acoustic duo with percussionist Steve Took and Marc on guitar. But in 1970, the band expanded to a quartet and went electric, and success beyond their wildest dreams ensued. T. Rex became huge in England, logging eleven consecutive top-ten hits, most of them from the albums *The Slider* and *Electric Warrior*.

Later, as the mania surrounding T. Rex ebbed, the band struggled through a few incarnations and, though Marc became disillusioned at times, he remained committed to the band even as he developed other interests; by the mid-seventies he was writing a weekly column for an English music magazine and hosting his own TV talk-variety show as well.

One evening, Marc and his girlfriend Gloria Jones went out for dinner and a few rounds of assorted adult refreshments. When it was finally time to head home around 3:30 a.m., they jumped into her purple Mini 1275 GT (Marc had never learned to drive) for what should have been an unremarkable drive. But along the way, Gloria lost control of the car, its passenger side was smashed into a sycamore tree, and Marc was killed instantly. He was 29.

Marc was cremated at Golders Green Crematorium in London and is remembered there with a rose bush and a bronze plaque. He shares the site with his parents, under the Feld name (his legal surname) and you can find it at the Keats Rosebed, plot number 46087.

By the way, Steve Took, T. Rex's first drummer, choked to death on a cherry pit in 1980, and is buried nearby in Kensal Green Cemetery.

JOHN BONHAM
MAY 31, 1948 – SEPTEMBER 25, 1980

Bonzo, as John Bonham was affectionately known, was an icon of the 1970s rock and roll scene, known for his thundering drumming in the hard-rock band Led Zeppelin.

Led Zeppelin itself had come together after the Yardbirds' rapid breakup left guitar-hero Jimmy Page in a bind; he was contractually obliged to perform ten concerts, but he no longer had a band. So Page called a few friends together—drummer John, frontman Robert Plant, and bassist John Paul Jones. The ten gigs were quite well received and the foursome decided to stick together. After a half-dozen smash albums and a few hit singles, including the rock anthem "Stairway to Heaven," Led Zeppelin was the hottest rock act anywhere. But it wouldn't last.

Besides being renowned for his drumming talents, John was also known as an avid consumer of daunting quantities of alcohol, and this proved his undoing. During a night of heavy partying at Page's home in Windsor, England, legend has it that John consumed some forty shots (!) of vodka, then passed out. In his extravagantly inebriated state, John failed to rouse even as his stomach ejected its contents. Consequently, in the plainest terms, John choked to death on his own vomit.

John was buried at the bucolic Saint Michael's Church Cemetery in Rushock, England, which is about 120 miles northwest of London. He was 32.

HARRY CHAPIN
DECEMBER 7, 1942 – JULY 17, 1981

Harry Chapin was one of America's best-loved troubadours, and he wove poignant tales of common people, lost opportunities, and life's cruel ironies and hypocrisies. He had only two pop hits, "Taxi" and "Cat's in the Cradle." Both were in his self-described "story song" style, a narrative form of songwriting similar to talking blues.

Though widespread commercial success always eluded him, it doesn't seem that he was ever in it for the money anyway. A charitable performer who pioneered the idea of benefit concerts—half of his shows were for charitable causes—Harry's principal commitment was to end world hunger.

While driving near Exit 40 on the Long Island Expressway one summer day in 1981, Harry turned on his emergency flashers and was slowing and changing lanes when his car was struck from behind by a tractor-trailer rig. The collision set his Volkswagen on fire and, though the truck's driver dragged an incapacitated Harry from the flaming wreckage to safety, Harry was pronounced dead at a hospital a short time later. Though it was generally reported that Harry died of his burns or other injuries suffered in the collision, his burns were superficial and his injuries may not have been life threatening. Instead, Harry actually died of a heart attack, and it's now believed that this is what prompted him to slow his car and attempt to pull to the side of the highway.

At 38, he was buried at Huntington Rural Cemetery in Huntington, New York.

CEMETERY DIRECTIONS: The cemetery in Huntington is on Route 110, on the left if you're heading north, five miles from the Northern State Parkway.

GRAVE DIRECTIONS: Enter the cemetery, bear right at the office, continue straight through the four corners, then go left up the hill. Turn at the next two lefts, then stop when the road bends to the right. On the right is Section 6L and Harry's grave, marked with a large boulder, is in the middle of this section. This boulder was transported from Harry's boyhood home where, in his youth, he learned to play guitar while sitting on it, or so the legend goes.

Incidentally, Harry's causes have not been forgotten, and the Harry Chapin Foundation has since raised millions for the many anti-hunger groups and other charities he supported. In a gesture of gratitude, the open-air theater in East Meadow, New York, where he was to have performed a benefit on the day he died was renamed the Harry Chapin Lakeside Theater.

EDDIE COCHRAN & GENE VINCENT

Eddie Cochran

OCTOBER 3, 1938 – APRIL 17, 1960

Gene Vincent

FEBRUARY 11, 1935 – OCTOBER 12, 1971

No one person "invented" rock and roll. Rather, over the years it worked its way out of the blues, and in the 1950s its development accelerated due to the imagination and innovation of about fifteen pioneers. Eddie Cochran and Gene Vincent were two such pioneers; they recognized rock's potential and, for a while, anyway, helped develop the foundations of a new cultural phenomenon. Though Eddie only had a couple of hits, most notably "Summertime Blues" in 1958, his influence was considerable in terms of musical arrangements, the role of the drums, and, indeed, the very deliberate and wild sound and attitude that he lent to rock music. Gene's sole hit was "Be-Bop-a-Lula," but it added fuel to the fiery excitement of the time, and his frenzied and energetic performing style was copied by his contemporaries.

For the first few months of 1960, Eddie teamed with Gene for a tour of England, where Gene had been living since 1958, successfully pacing the rock and roll mania that gripped the country's youth. After their last show at the Hippodrome Theatre in Bristol, Eddie, now a budding star, his girlfriend Sharon Steely, and headliner Gene caught a taxi back to London from where Eddie and Sharon planned to catch a plane. Zooming through the night along winding country roads, the taxi driver lost control at Rowden Hill in the village of Chittenham, and the Ford MKII was destroyed as it slammed into a lamp pole. Gene suffered a few broken bones and

Sharon's pelvis was shattered, but Eddie went through the windshield and died of massive head injuries ten hours later.

At 21, Eddie was buried at Forest Lawn Memorial Park in Cypress, California.

CEMETERY DIRECTIONS: From Highway 91, take Carmenita Road south, turn west onto Lincoln Avenue, and the park is a mile ahead on the right.

GRAVE DIRECTIONS: Drive past the gates and stop after about a hundred yards. Eddie's big, flat stone is on the left, fifteen rows back.

By promoting his rebel image, Gene had become one of Britain's biggest draws by the time of his tour with Eddie. But by 1964 he'd lost favor with English audiences who were instead flocking to their homegrown bands, the Beatles and the Rolling Stones. He returned to the States but failed to stage a comeback. In 1971 Gene's alcoholism spurred a bleeding ulcer, and he died in his mother's arms at 36.

Gene was buried at Eternal Valley Memorial Park in Santa Clarita, California.

CEMETERY DIRECTIONS: Follow Highway 14 north from I-5 and exit at San Fernando Road, which is also Route 126. Proceed west, turn left at the traffic light onto Sierra Highway, and the park is a short distance ahead on the right.

GRAVE DIRECTIONS: Enter the cemetery and make an immediate left up the hill. Stop on the left after about 50 yards, perhaps 30 feet past the yellow water spigot. In the grass along the curb, find Lilard Rainbolt's marker and Gene's grave is just two rows further into the lawn.

JIM CROCE
JANUARY 10, 1943 – SEPTEMBER 20, 1973

You know his songs—everybody does. You sing along with "Bad, Bad Leroy Brown" in your car and hum along to the Muzak recording of "Time in a Bottle" in elevators. But few actually remember Jim Croce, a mustachioed and cigar-smoking, working-class folk artist who struggled for years to break into the mainstream.

In 1969, with his wife Ingrid, he cut an album titled *Ingrid and Jim Croce* and they remained on the New York City coffeehouse circuit for a couple of years before eventually tiring of city life. Moving a little west to Pennsylvania, Ingrid learned to bake bread and can vegetables while Jim worked low-paying odd jobs, pursuing music more as a hobby than a profession. But by 1972 Jim had penned a number of catchier pop ballads and that year he put out a solo album, *You Don't Mess Around With Jim*, which was an instant success. As his songs played on radios and turntables across America, Jim became a club and concert headliner.

After an appearance at Northwestern State University in Natchitoches, Louisiana, Jim and the four members of his band boarded a small, chartered airplane. On takeoff, the plane clipped a pecan tree at the end of the runway and went down, killing all on board. After Jim's death, sales of his music tripled and his signature songs became mainstays of classic-rock stations. The lesser tragedy is that Jim never lived to enjoy this broad popularity, and we can only hope that he's somehow basking in it now.

At 30, Jim was buried at Haym Salomon Memorial Park in Frazer, Pennsylvania.

CEMETERY DIRECTIONS: From Route 30, turn north onto Planebrook Road and the park is one mile ahead on the right.

GRAVE DIRECTIONS: Jim rests about 50 yards to the right, almost in front of the office. His is a flat stone shaded by a pine tree.

In San Diego's historic Gaslamp Quarter, Ingrid now operates Croce's, an award-winning restaurant featuring live local and national R&B acts nightly.

THE DAY THE MUSIC DIED

Buddy Holly

SEPTEMBER 7, 1936 – FEBRUARY 3, 1959

Ritchie Valens

MAY 13, 1941 – FEBRUARY 3, 1959

J.P. 'Big Bopper' Richardson

OCTOBER 24, 1930 – FEBRUARY 3, 1959

Buddy Holley played violin and piano as a child, and at thirteen adopted his signature guitar. By the time he teamed up with the Crickets at just 20, he'd already released a few records with Decca (the label accidentally dropped the "e" in his last name), and last name), and had introduced a unique songwriting style characterized by a blues-heavy lyricism.

In these very early days of rock and roll, Buddy Holly and the Crickets began recording at a New Mexico studio, and by May 1957 had nailed "That'll Be The Day," its title lifted from a line uttered by John Wayne in *The Searchers*. The song raced up the charts and they went on tour in its support, and by November "Peggy Sue" and "Not Fade Away" had joined the first hit. With the Crickets, Buddy appeared on *The Ed Sullivan Show* twice in those few short months and the limelight inspired a decidedly cosmopolitan shift in Buddy's appearance and manners; he began to wear stylish New York suits and donned the thick, black eyeglasses that he became known for.

In autumn of 1958, because of managerial and royalty disagreements, Buddy parted from the Crickets and their manager. He shortly assembled a new backing band, including future country-star Waylon Jennings on bass, and joined the Winter Dance Party tour, an assemblage of acts that would tour the upper Midwest.

The acts included Ritchie Valens, a hot, young artist known for his rock and roll version of the old Mexican standard "La Bamba," and Jiles P. "Big Bopper" Richardson, a Texas deejay-turned-rocker who found success with the song "Chantilly Lace." Buddy would headline, and Dion and the Belmonts rounded out the list of performers.

The 24-stop tour hit its eleventh stop at the Surf Ballroom in Clearwater, Iowa, and the performers arrived cold, tired, and disgusted. Since they'd set out ten days earlier they had been traveling between venues in the bitter cold of a Midwest winter on a bus with a spotty heater. Dreading the 400-mile trip to Fargo, North Dakota, Buddy asked Carroll Anderson, manager of the Surf Ballroom, to arrange a charter flight instead. Carroll found a plane, a three-passenger Beechcraft from Dwyer Flying Service, and Buddy informed band mates Waylon Jennings and Tommy Allsup that they wouldn't have to ride on the bus to Fargo after all.

However, during the concert at the Surf, Waylon Jennings gave his seat on the plane to the Big Bopper, whose stocky frame was a poor fit in the bus's narrow and uncomfortable seats, and who was suffering from the flu, to boot. After the switch, Ritchie Valens began begging Tommy Allsup to give up his plane seat, too. Tommy finally agreed to let a coin toss settle it; Ritchie called "heads," winning the toss and a seat on the plane. After the concert, Carroll drove Buddy, J.P., and Ritchie to the airport in nearby Mason City and bid them goodbye. With his wife and son, Carroll watched the plane take off and circle around as it took up its course. Nothing appeared out of the ordinary, and Carroll and his family went home.

By the next morning though, it was clear to Jerry Dwyer, the plane's owner, that something was wrong. He hadn't yet heard from the pilot, Roger Peterson. After checking for Peterson by telephone at airports along the way to Fargo, Dwyer went on an aerial search and soon spotted the plane's wreckage in a stubbled cornfield 5½ miles from the Mason City airport. Except for a solitary wing that was relatively undamaged, the plane was hardly distinguishable. Its three passengers were scattered around the field and the pilot was still trapped inside the wreckage; all four were dead.

Authorities could never find a reason for the crash; the pilot was experienced and competent, the navigational equipment was functioning properly and set for a course to Fargo, the aircraft was properly maintained and in good condition, and, contrary to some reports, the weather was favorable for flying; the night had been clear with just trace amounts of snow in the air. All appearances are that, for some unexplained reason, perhaps disorientation or inattention, the pilot flew the plane into the ground.

For teenagers of the period the crash was certainly devastating, but for the general public the news was not terribly significant. Buddy's clean-cut image and scandal-free life, coupled with the young ages of the three rockers, made the story all the more poignant. But rock and roll was new and not taken very seriously in those days, and Buddy Holly became a largely forgotten figure.

Then, in 1971, a little-known singer-songwriter named Don McLean released a seven-plus minute song called "American Pie." Its narrative is a rhyming allegorical history of rock and roll structured around the hook "the day the music died," a direct reference to Buddy's first hit "That'll Be The Day." Since then, Buddy has gotten his deserved credit and recognition, and in 1986 he was inducted into the Rock 'n' Roll Hall of Fame.

Buddy was 22 at his death and was buried at the City of Lubbock Cemetery in Lubbock, Texas.

CEMETERY DIRECTIONS: From I-27, take Exit 3 and follow Route 62 east for 1½ mile to Martin Luther King Jr. Boulevard. Turn right (south) on MLK, and after a mile turn left onto 31st Street, which will bring you into the cemetery.

GRAVE DIRECTIONS: Enter the cemetery and turn right. After about 100 yards there are two silver posts on the left side of the road. Another 30 feet beyond these posts, alongside the curb, is Buddy's grave.

Ritchie Valens was just 17 when he died in the plane crash, and he was buried at San Fernando Mission Cemetery in Mission Hills, California.

CEMETERY DIRECTIONS: From I-405, exit at Rinaldi Street, follow Sepulveda Boulevard south for a half-mile, then turn left onto Stranwood Avenue. The cemetery is immediately to the left.

GRAVE DIRECTIONS: Enter the cemetery and park in front of the flower shop. Ritchie is buried across from the flower shop between curb numbers 235 and 247 in the third row from the drive.

At his death, Jiles P. "Big Bopper" Richardson was 28. He was buried at Forest Lawn Memorial Park in Beaumont, Texas.

CEMETERY DIRECTIONS: Take Exit 855A off of I-10, follow Pine Street north for 1½ miles, turn left onto East Lucas Drive and the cemetery entrance is immediately to the right.

GRAVE DIRECTIONS: After entering the cemetery, the Lilypool Garden lawn is immediately to the left. Near the curb in Lot 31 the grave of J.P., "the Big Bopper."

Waylon Jennings, who gave his plane seat to J.P., enjoyed a very successful career in country music. He died in 2002 and is profiled within these pages, as well. Years after losing the coin toss for his plane seat to Ritchie Valens, Tommy Allsup opened Tommy's "Head's Up" Saloon in Dallas, Texas.

CLARENCE LEO FENDER
AUGUST 10, 1909 – MARCH 21, 1991

In the 1930s, musical instruments functioned much as they had for years: drums provided the beat, horns performed the melody, and, because they couldn't be heard very well, string instruments were relegated to the background. But then a new invention changed modern music—and popular culture, as well—the electric guitar.

By rudimentary physics, a vibrating metal object—a guitar string, for instance—moving in a magnetic field creates a signal that can be picked up by a wire coil. In 1931 an inventor named George Beauchamp applied this principle to his guitar hobby and, on his dining room table, built a crude version of the world's first electric guitar.

For the first time, a guitar could hold its own against the horn section, and guitarists could pick out melody lines instead of just strumming the rhythm. Beauchamp finally got a patent in 1937, but by then the electric guitar had been introduced to the jazz world, was redefining swing orchestra ensembles, and several companies were making their own electric guitars. After a few technical headaches were overcome and some stylistic changes were advanced by Les Paul and other pioneers, radio-repairman Leo Fender jumped onto the scene in 1945.

Leo advanced a solid-body guitar with a better pickup and tone controls but, most important, within a few years, his guitar was cheap. Leo revolutionized the scene by mass-producing the instrument, beginning with his 1948 Broadcaster, a guitar for the masses. The tools of the revolution that would soon become rock music were now in the hands of America's youth, and the culture would never be the same.

Leo died at 81 after a battle with Parkinson's disease and was buried at Fairhaven Memorial Park in Santa Ana, California.

CEMETERY DIRECTIONS: From I-5, take Route 22 east and exit at Grand Avenue south. Make an immediate left onto Fairhaven Avenue and the park is a half-mile ahead on the right.

GRAVE DIRECTIONS: Enter the cemetery, turn left after the office, and from that point stay as parallel as you can with Fairhaven Avenue. Turn right when you finally reach a pronounced "T," then stop after twenty feet. In the grass on the right, Section J, count eleven rows to find Leo's grave.

And later on, check your attic. Though Leo offered his 1948 Broadcaster for $75, such an early original can today fetch $30,000.

TOM FOGERTY

NOVEMBER 9, 1941 – SEPTEMBER 6, 1990

The economical style of rock and roll promoted by Creedence Clearwater Revival was a long way from rock's mainstream in the late 1960s, but these guys hit it big anyway. With a consistent recipe of three-minute songs, Creedence earned eight gold singles. Featuring the growling vocals and rhythmic guitars of brothers Tom and John Fogerty, the band seemed destined for greatness. But conflicts arose because of John's totalitarian attitude, and Tom left the band in 1971 to pursue a solo career.

In December of 1980, the original band reunited onstage for the first time in nine years during Tom's wedding, but this proved to be their last performance together. Tom released eight solo albums but never found much commercial success, and at 48 died of respiratory failure due to tuberculosis.

He was cremated and his ashes scattered in Hawaii and around California's Half Moon Bay.

Tom and John never fully reconciled and remained estranged even as Tom lay dying. The animosity between John and the other band members continues and, when Creedence was inducted into the Rock 'n' Roll Hall of Fame in 1993, John declined to play with his ex-band mates.

ALAN FREED

DECEMBER 21, 1921 – JANUARY 20, 1965

Disc jockey Alan "Moondog" Freed is widely credited with coining the term "rock and roll" in 1951 to describe the up-tempo black R&B records he was playing on his program, the Moondog Rock 'n' Roll Party. A tirelessly enthusiastic advocate of the music, Alan kept time to the records by beating his hands on a phone book. He called it rock and roll because "it seemed to suggest the rolling, surging beat of the music." When his Moondog Coronation Ball was held at the Cleveland Arena in March of 1952, more than 20,000 fans showed up to crash the gates, prompting the event's cancellation. Though this Moondog Ball never actually took place, it's considered to be the first rock concert.

For all the contributions that Alan Freed made to our music, it's unfortunate that his name is inextricably associated with the "payola" scandals of the late fifties. During the witch hunt for disc jockeys that were being bribed by record companies to play certain artists, Alan steadfastly maintained that he never played a record he didn't like. In December of 1962, though, he pleaded guilty to two counts of bribery, was fined $300, and was fired from his radio program.

Essentially blackballed from the business, he began drinking heavily, and at 43 died of uremia. Those closest to him, however, swear he died of a broken heart.

Alan was cremated and his ashes interred at the Ferncliffe Mausoleum in Hartsdale, New York.

CEMETERY DIRECTIONS: From I-87, take Exit 7 in Ardsley and follow Route 9A north for 1¼ miles. At the traffic light, turn right onto Secor Road, and Ferncliffe is a short distance ahead on the left.

GRAVE DIRECTIONS: Enter Ferncliffe at the first entrance, bear left, then park toward the left-hand side of the main mausoleum. Enter the mausoleum through the bronze doors and turn left. Then turn right, left, left, right, and right again. There, take the elevator to the basement. Make a right, then a left out of the elevator, and in the last room on the left (Room S-T) are Alan's cremains. They are in the back, about six feet up.

MARVIN GAYE
APRIL 2, 1939 – APRIL 1, 1984

Marvin Gaye was a charter member of that generation of soul artists that skyrocketed to fame under the Motown label, and his songs, unique blends of soul music and old-time gospel, cut a wide swath from torrid sexual abandon to impassioned social rectitude.

He'd grown up in Washington D.C., the son of an iron-fisted Pentecostal minister, Marvin Gay, Sr. (For show business, Marvin, Jr. added an "e" to his surname.) While he was still quite young it became obvious to anyone within earshot that Marvin, Sr.'s son could *really* sing and the boy became a church fixture, leading the congregation through hymns between his father's sermons. Eventually, the protracted religious discourses and his father's inflexibility induced an animosity that worsened through Marvin's teens. Still, though Marvin's lifestyle later drifted light-years away from the strictures of Pentecostalism, he was always quick to credit his father for instilling in him the faith he felt was central to his success.

At eighteen, Marvin enlisted in the Air Force but, by mutual agreement, was discharged honorably before his duty was up. Next, he played with a few different vocal groups, performances that led to a solo Motown recording contract. In 1964, Marvin hit real pay dirt: a duet with Mary Wells on "My Guy" was the smash that opened the floodgates. For the remainder of the decade, both Marvin and Motown Records cashed in.

After a string of hits, including "Can I Get a Witness?" and "How Sweet It Is to be Loved by You," Marvin released 1971's *What's Going On?*, an album filled with outspoken social commentary that surprised fans who'd come to expect danceable love songs. Still, the album was a Motown milestone, and it demonstrated that its popular artists were not mere dance-steppers.

Later in the 1970s, Marvin struggled with substance abuse, his marriage disintegrated, and he fell deeply into debt. Marvin fled his demons rather than face them, but after a three-year, self-imposed European exile, he seemed to have a new vitality and went back to the studio. His 1982 release *Midnight Love,* a modern quilt of electronic sounds woven through an oblique reggae beat, was hailed as a masterful comeback. Marvin won two Grammys for his efforts and the singles "Let's Get It On" and "Sexual Healing" became radio standards.

Though Marvin's professional life seemed to be back on track, his personal life was a runaway train; the IRS dogged him for back taxes, he succumbed to cocaine addiction, romantic relationships imploded, and he was becoming ridiculously paranoid. After a tempestuous tour following the *Midnight Love* album, Marvin retreated to the Los Angeles home that he'd bought for his parents. But Marvin and his father had never addressed their 25-year-old animosities, and now, living together but apart (Marvin spent his days alone in his room), their conflicted relationship worsened.

On April 1, 1984, after an argument and an altercation concerning Marvin, Sr.'s inability to locate a letter from an insurance agency, the string finally broke. Without saying a word, Marvin, Sr. entered his son's room and shot him while he sat on his bed. Marvin, Jr. slumped to the floor, his father fired again, and his mother Alberta screamed to the heavens for her son. Marvin, Sr. then went outside, threw the gun onto the front lawn, and waited on the porch for the police. Later that afternoon, on the day before his 45th birthday, Marvin Gaye, Jr. was pronounced dead.

After a service at which Stevie Wonder sang, Smokey Robinson spoke, and 10,000 people passed by his open casket, Marvin was cremated and his ashes scattered in the Pacific Ocean.

Marvin Gay, Sr. was arrested and stood trial for his son's death, and Alberta promptly divorced him. At trial, photographs of Marvin, Sr.'s body demonstrated that he'd been abused by his son and, after a no-contest plea of voluntary manslaughter, Marvin, Sr. was sentenced to five years' probation. Alberta died in 1987 of bone cancer. Marvin, Sr. died of a stroke in 1998.

BILL GRAHAM

JANUARY 8, 1931 – OCTOBER 25, 1991

While most of his family members died at the hands of the Nazis, Wolfgang Grajonca was able to escape their grasp, and at twelve he landed in New York City. At the onset of the Korean War he was drafted into the Army and there he changed his name, Bill coming from the English equivalent of Wolfgang, and Graham being closest to Grajonca in the phonebook. Bill served until 1953 and, after being awarded a Bronze Star for valor, was awarded United States citizenship.

After his discharge, Bill organized gigs for theater troupes, but when the members of one group were arrested for performing in a public park without a permit, Bill discovered his true organizational calling. In 1965 he arranged a benefit to raise the troupe's bail money and, sensing a larger business opportunity, set to work organizing larger and more elaborate community events. Bill raced to provide legitimate venues for the performers in San Francisco's strange, new counterculture scene. He eventually bought the Fillmore Auditorium and the hall quickly became the entertainment nexus for the burgeoning music scene. Charging nominal fees, Bill presented artists as varied as Miles Davis and Frank Zappa, and supported the entire culture by presenting performance artists, "acid tests," and "love-ins."

In 1968 Bill opened the Fillmore's spin-off in New York City, the Fillmore East, and, with his bookend auditoriums, became the leading promoter of rock music, hosting hundreds of turbulent performances. A stickler for quality and detail, Bill invested heavily in sound and lighting, and the revolutionary music shows he presented became a yardstick against which all his competitors were measured.

As rock music's popularity steamrolled worldwide, Bill led the movement with his shrewd business acumen. His production company, Bill Graham Presents, pioneered the rock concert as a social statement with events for charitable causes; he directed monster-sized tours for super-sized groups, and he was the catalyst for the industry's

booming merchandise business. In short, Bill amassed an untold fortune from the flower power phenomenon and its progeny.

At 60, Bill died when the helicopter that was returning him from a Huey Lewis concert he'd promoted hit electrical lines and crashed near Vallejo, California. A week later, his company put on a massive free concert in his honor at the Polo Field in San Francisco, a site of many past benefit concerts Bill had organized. The concert featured many acts that Bill had nurtured over the years and, in remembering him, Neil Young commented, "He always made all of us look good."

Bill's will specified that, upon his death, Bill Graham Presents was to be sold to fifteen of his long-term employees, and the promotion company still thrives today.

Bill was buried at Eternal Home Cemetery in Colma, California.

CEMETERY DIRECTIONS: Eternal Home Cemetery is on the east side of El Camino Real, which is also Route 82. From I-380, it's about four miles north or, from I-280, it's about 1½ miles south. There are at least six cemeteries adjacent to one another in this area and Eternal Home seems to have budgeted the bare minimum for their sign, meaning it can be quite difficult to distinguish. Instead, look for Greenlawn Memorial Park. Eternal Home Cemetery is within the walled-in area across the street.

GRAVE DIRECTIONS: Enter the cemetery, turn left, and park at the second circle. Bill's grave is six rows from Route 82 and a dozen stones from the north wall.

GRATEFUL DEAD

In 1963, Jerry Garcia formed his first band, Mother McCree's Uptown Jug Champions, with some friends including guitarist Bob Weir and keyboardist Ron "Pigpen" McKernan. Neither Jerry nor anyone else could ever imagine the ultimate outcome of that modest inauguration. By 1965 bassist Phil Lesh and drummer Bill Kreutzmann had joined in the fun and, along with lyricist Robert Hunter, they took to calling themselves the Grateful Dead, a moniker based upon an old English fable Jerry had stumbled across in the dictionary about a reluctant corpse.

Just as the poets at coffee houses gave way to rock bands at dance halls, the Dead invented a spacy, extended performance style that made for perfect background music for the burgeoning, hippie counterculture of "acid tests" and free love. The band members soon moved into a communal house at 710 Ashbury St. in San Francisco and rose to the top of the heap of psychedelic bands. Though 1967 saw the release of their debut album, *The Grateful Dead*, it was on their fifth and sixth albums, both released in 1970, that the band really hit full stride. On *Workingman's Dead* and *American Beauty*, the Grateful Dead created a watershed in rock music history. The songs on these albums, most notably "Truckin'" and "Casey Jones," exposed the band out to a much wider audience, while cuts like "Ripple," "Uncle John's Band," and "Friend of the Devil" became cornerstones of the band's performance-based career, inspiring a supremely "deadicated" cult following.

Despite tempting fate with both its name and its lifestyle, the band somehow managed, for the most part, to avoid the type of ugly incidents that plagued many of their rock and roll contemporaries. For the next quarter-century, with only occasional changes in the lineup, the group concentrated on their music and toured endlessly. In a sea of tie-dyed attire, enchanted "Deadhead" fans dutifully followed the band around the world, from Japan to Vermont to the pyramids in Egypt, though most ordinary folks who were out of the loop never quite understood all the hubbub. Jerry tried to sum it up for them in 1981, saying, "Our audience is like people who like licorice. Not everybody likes licorice, but the people who like licorice, really like licorice."

Ron 'Pigpen' McKernan

MAY 7, 1946 – MARCH 8, 1973

Bedecked in a leather jacket and bandana, Ron "Pigpen" McKernan was beside Jerry from the very beginning. It was through his persistence that their jug band became an electric rock and roll band, and it was his dusty voice that handled the lead in those earliest days. Pigpen later mostly stuck to the keyboards and harmonica, only occasionally fronting during live shows, and even less often in the studio. Pigpen also developed an intensive audience-interactive rap session that became a highlight of Dead shows.

By 1968, Pigpen had become unreliable due to severe health problems resulting from his intoxicating vices, and the band added another keyboardist, Tom Constantine, to help take up some of the slack. In the summer of 1971 Pigpen was diagnosed with cirrhosis of the liver and, after detox, he never drank again. But the change did not come soon enough. Too ill to maintain the pace of touring, Pigpen retreated shortly after the Dead's 1972 tour of Europe. His general health continued to decline, and finally Pigpen died of a gastrointestinal hemorrhage.

At 26, Pigpen was buried at Alto Mesa Cemetery in Palo Alto, California.

CEMETERY DIRECTIONS: From Highway 101, take the exit for San Antonio Road south and, after a quarter mile, turn right onto East Charleston Street. Stay on this road—you'll notice after 1½ miles that its name changes to Arastradero Road—then, after another ¾ of a mile, the cemetery is on the left.

GRAVE DIRECTIONS: Enter the cemetery and bear left after the office. Then make a hard right at the second opportunity and stop about three-quarters of the way down this drive. Ron's flat marker is on the left, third row from the curb.

Keith Godchaux

JULY 19, 1948 – JULY 23, 1980

In October of 1971, keyboardist Keith Godchaux joined the Dead after Pigpen's original replacement, Tom Costantine, left. Two months later, Keith's wife, Donna, joined the band as a vocalist. Though they remained aboard for more than seven years, which happened to be some of the band's weakest years musically, they

FAMILY TREE

KEITH
GODCHAUX

BRENT
MYDLAND

RON "PIGPEN"
MCKERNAN

JERRY GARCIA

GRATEFUL DEAD

never quite seemed to fit. In February 1979 they agreed with the band that it might be best if they left, and they did.

Keith and Donna assembled a new act called the Heart of Gold but, after just a single concert, Keith was killed in a California car accident. At 32, Keith was cremated and his ashes scattered off the coast of Marin County.

Brent Mydland
OCTOBER 21, 1952 – JULY 26, 1990

Picking up where Pigpen and Keith left off in the revolving-door keyboard spot, Brent Mydland joined up in 1979 and remained with the Dead through the '80s. In this period when the band became a full-blown cultural institution, Brent initially seemed a little overwhelmed, but he gained confidence after studio releases included some of his own songs, among them "Just a Little Light" and "Hell in a Bucket," which he co-wrote with Bob Weir. Eventually Brent was singing lead and trading verses on a number of songs.

But during a break in the 1990 summer tour, Brent was found dead at his home of an overdose of cocaine and morphine.

At 37 he was buried at Oakmont Memorial Park in Pleasant Hills, California.

CEMETERY DIRECTIONS: From Highway 24, take the Pleasant Hill Road exit and follow it north for a mile to Reliez Valley Road. Turn left and, after three miles, Oakmont is on the left.

GRAVE DIRECTIONS: Enter the cemetery, drive up the hill past the office, then, at the top of the hill, loop left around the Lesher mausoleum before the Garden of Meditation. Turn at the next right, go straight through the next intersection (the Garden of Hope will be in front of you), then bear left. After another hundred yards, stop at the "Always In Our Hearts" bench on the left in the Garden of Remembrance. Brent's grave is in the row above this bench, eighteen markers to the left.

Jerry Garcia
AUGUST 1, 1942 – AUGUST 15, 1995

In the spring of 1960, after just nine months of association, the Army and Jerry Garcia had had enough of each other, and the two parted ways. An aspiring musician, Jerry embarked on a hand-to-mouth existence with future Dead lyricist Robert Hunter, and the two lived out of their broken-down cars, which were stranded next to each other in a Palo Alto parking lot. To make ends meet in the barest way, Jerry was filling in at a music store and giving guitar lessons whenever he could find a willing victim. Eventually, however, after a few lean years that included gigs at pizza parlors, things started to fall together. By 1965 Jerry was frontman of his Grateful Dead progeny and, as the house band for the "acid tests" of Ken Kesey's "Merry Pranksters" (later documented in a book by Tom Wolfe, *The Electric Kool-Aid Acid Test*), the band played what would be the soundtrack for everything '60s, while Jerry himself came to be known as "Captain Trips," the personification of all that was groovy.

As his band steamrolled through the 1970s, Jerry also pursued an array of side projects, including the bluegrass group Old And In The Way, guest spots with a number of popular artists, solo efforts, and touring with his own Jerry Garcia Band in the lulls between Dead tours. In the next decade though, Jerry's solo output slowed as he battled heroin addiction and, in 1986, Deadheads were spooked when Jerry went into a diabetic coma, from which he emerged seemingly unscathed five days later.

By the time the 1990s rolled around, the Dead was a cultural powerhouse and a concert phenomenon that couldn't misstep; even a line of Jerry-designed ties netted a few million dollars. But Jerry had sunk back into heroin addiction. In the summer of 1995 he entered Serenity Knolls, a drug-rehabilitation facility in the hills north of San Francisco and, while struggling to overcome his chemical dependency there, Captain Trips died of a heart attack. He was found dead during a routine bed check, expiring in a very Spartan room that contained little more than a dresser and a closet. Witnesses said, "it looked like he just went to sleep."

At 53, Jerry was cremated. Some of his ashes were scattered in the Pacific Ocean and others were placed in the Ganges River near the town of Rishikesh, India.

While Jerry's death spelled the end of the Dead as a continuing creative entity, the story was far from over, and the band's merchandising arm went into overdrive. In addition to *Dick's Picks*, a series of archival releases of classic live material, licensed products ranging from Dead tee shirts to sporting goods flooded the market. Plans were even announced for Terrapin Station, an interactive museum site.

In December 1995, the remaining band members announced that the Grateful Dead was officially disbanding. But in 2002, the Dead rose, coming together for shows billed as "a Grateful Dead Family Reunion."

WOODY GUTHRIE

JULY 14, 1912 – OCTOBER 3, 1967

Borne of Oklahoma hardscrabble people, Woody Guthrie had almost no formal education, his father died drunk, and his mother killed his only sister in an insane rage. But out of that heartache and adversity, and as a caustic witness to the impasses that mark the psyche of America's everyman—oil field busts, labor union lockouts, Depression and Dust Bowl despair, World War horror and Cold War paranoia—Woody bequeathed his inimitable folk songs and colloquial prose.

At 18, long after his family had broken up, the oil prosperity of Woody's hometown went bust, and he began a journey that he never entirely abandoned (that is, until he was institutionalized for the last dozen years of his life). By 1933, he was married with three children and living in Texas but, while the Great Depression had made it hard to scrape together an existence, the Dust Bowl that hit in 1935 made it nearly impossible. Leaving his family behind, Woody and his guitar embarked on a Steinbeck-ian odyssey, joining the mass migration of Okie refugees who plodded westward in search of opportunity.

By the time he arrived, hungry and broke, in California in 1937, Woody had suffered the scorn of the outsider, a badge he wore the rest of his life. After walking into a Los Angeles radio station, he became a regular, performing his corpus of "people's songs": "I Ain't Got No Home," "Talking Dust Bowl Blues," and "Hard Travelin'," among dozens of others. The radio gig provided Woody a pulpit for commentary on everything from unionists to legislators, from Jesus Christ to John Dillinger. Not surprisingly, he railed against the establishment; he even abdicated his own rights in a songbook of lyrics: "This song is copyrighted for a period of 28 years, and anybody caught singin' it without our permission will be mighty good friends of ourn, cause we don't give a dern. Publish it. Write it. Sing it. Swing to it. Yodel it. We wrote it, that's all we wanted to do. W.G."

Never comfortable in one place for too long, Woody hitchhiked east in 1940 and, along the way, wrote, "This Land is Your Land," inspired by Irving Berlin's "God Bless America." In New York, Woody was embraced for his "authenticity," and cultural anthropologist Alan Lomax recorded him in a series of conversations and songs that are today's folk music touchstones. Then, in what seemed to be a departure from his philosophies, Woody accepted an obligation from the Bonneville Power Commission to write songs for a film promoting the development of the Columbia River and its newly constructed Grand Coulee Dam. The resulting *Columbia River Songs* was yet another remarkable collection.

Amidst all this activity, Woody remarried and, in a period of relative domestic stability, completed a semi-autobiographical account of the Dust Bowl, *Bound for Glory*. While World War II raged, he had four children with this second wife, but even they were not enough to exempt him from the draft, and he served until 1946.

Returning home to Coney Island, Woody formed the Weavers with Pete Seeger, which became the most successful folk group of its era. But after just a few years, restless and disillusioned with New York's "sissified and nervous rules of censorship," he rolled out again and, in California, married a third time. Around this time, Woody's behavior became unpredictable and his guitar-playing erratic. Confused about his condition, he took the only reasonable course of action and hit the road yet again, eventually tracing a path back to New York.

After being mistakenly diagnosed with everything from alcoholism to schizophrenia, in 1954 Woody admitted himself to a New Jersey hospital. It was later learned that he suffered from Huntington's Chorea, a degenerative disease of the nervous system that would slowly steal from him every physical and mental capacity. Upon learning that the affliction is inherited maternally, Woody realized that it had also been responsible for his little sister's death.

For the next dozen years, Woody deteriorated in a shuffle among various infirmaries, while his hundreds of songs were made popular by the newest folk revival. Finally unable to sit up or even speak, Woody died at 55 at a hospital in Queens, New York.

Woody was cremated and family members, including his son, Arlo (also a folk singer), threw his container of ashes into the ocean. Waves soon tossed it back onto the beach, so for a second attempt, the container was opened to prevent floating and, while the wind whipped some of the ash back into their faces, the ghost of Woody Guthrie slipped beneath the Atlantic surf.

BILL HALEY

JULY 6, 1925 – FEBRUARY 9, 1981

Bill Haley led country-and-western bands around the Philadelphia area beginning in 1942, but by the early 1950s, he had morphed the style of his band, the Comets, into a new sound that would eventually become rock and roll.

In fact, it can be fairly argued that Bill is the true father of rock music, which he bore at around 4:30 p.m. on April 12, 1954, in a Manhattan sound studio. From the moment when the studio's silence was broken by drummer Billy Gussak's two sharp rim shots, music would never again be the same. After the drum opening, Bill Haley shouted out the inspired and immortal words, "One-two-three o'clock, four o'clock ROCK!" and the song "Rock Around the Clock" became the international anthem of rock music. The song was perfect and, though it's since been covered by hundreds of artists, none has ever captured the special magic of Bill Haley and the Comets on that spring day in New York City.

"Rock Around the Clock" went to the stratosphere, the song proved to be Bill's highwater mark and, throughout the remainder of his life, he was content to release just the occasional recording and tour with various rock and roll revival shows.

At 55, Bill died in his sleep of a heart attack at home in Harlingen, Texas. He was cremated and his ashes remain with his family.

JOHN LEE HOOKER

AUGUST 22, 1917 – JUNE 21, 2001

John Lee Hooker was the son of a sharecropping Baptist minister who discouraged his child's musical bent, but John's stepfather later taught him to play guitar, and by the time he was a teenager, John was performing at local fish fries and dances. In 1945 he moved north to find work and, after landing in Detroit three years later, he recorded his first hit, a stomping guitar boogie called "Boogie Chillen'."

John soon quit his janitorial job to pursue music full-time. He melded the country blues of his native Mississippi Delta with electric guitar and his hypnotic, one-chord jams—which often included no intelligible words, just a discord of humming and mumbling in a mysterious, stream-of-consciousness growl—became John's hallmark. Over the next five decades, his foot-stomping songs, including "I'm In The Mood" and "Crawling King Snake," cemented his reputation as a key shaper of the modern blues and, by default, rock music.

Interestingly, as much as John was the quintessential Mississippi bluesman, he didn't succumb to the ills that often plagued his peers. He never had serious bouts with alcohol, drugs, or the law, and he didn't die broke. In his later years, John enjoyed his success by tooling around in his fleet of expensive cars and, occasionally, dropping in unannounced to tear through his catalog of hits at smoky music joints.

Toward the end of his life, when his legacy was sealed as a grand-father of music, John remained confounded by his success and confessed, "People say I'm a genius but I don't know about what."

At 83, John died of natural causes at home in his sleep, and now rests at the Chapel of Chimes Mausoleum in Oakland, California.

CEMETERY DIRECTIONS: Take the 51st Street exit from Highway 24 and follow it south for one mile. (Its name will change to Pleasant Valley Avenue along the way.) Turn left onto Piedmont Avenue and the mausoleum is a short distance ahead on the left at Number 4499.

GRAVE DIRECTIONS: Enter the building through the glass doors to-ward the rear of the parking lot. Go to the end of the hall, turn left and then right, then take the elevator to the third floor. Out of the elevator, turn left and then right, and John's crypt is on the left, on the bottom after the French doors.

ROBERT JOHNSON
MAY 8, 1911 – AUGUST 16, 1938

It's generally accepted that the blues were born out of the hard times and suffering endured by Mississippi Delta blacks at the start of the twentieth century, and they've been called "a solo recitation of misery." Robert Johnson, were he alive today, would probably agree, as his songs certainly sprang from a life of poverty and squalor.

Born into the large family of a sharecropper, he learned to play the harmonica and guitar in the conventional "country blues" style, but it was his later development of guitar techniques that earned him the respect of modern musicians. Robert, it seems, was the first to play a guitar in the "finger-picking" style, a complex melody technique that allows one guitar to do the work of two by placing a treble-string melody over a constant bass-string accompaniment. And, though he didn't invent the bottleneck style in which a bottle is placed on the little finger of the fretting hand to yield that distinctive metallic *glissando* effect that's commonly heard in Hawaiian music, he cer-tainly popularized and perfected it. Later, the bottleneck, or slide effect, as it's more commonly called, figured prominently in the works of artists such as Duane Allman and Jimi Hendrix.

Though Robert's lyrics were simple and colloquial, touching on the common themes of a longing to be somewhere else or of fleet-ing love, his compositions were fully developed and the language

articulate. This was a significant departure from the traditional oral improvisation common to his day's music. Further, he defined a song structure—instrumental, several verses, instrumental, verse, and end—that is used in rock music almost without variation today.

Robert Johnson recorded only 32 songs (his most famous being "Crossroads") and never received a cent in royalties. In true blues fashion, his demise was dramatic: He was poisoned with strychnine-laced whiskey provided by a jealous husband. After three days of torturous agony, lolling madly on a makeshift cot amid the relentless humidity of a Mississippi summer, Robert died of his poisoning at 27.

He was buried at Mount Zion Baptist Church Cemetery in Morgan City, Mississippi.

CEMETERY DIRECTIONS: From the intersection of routes 7 and 82 near Greenwood, follow Route 7 south for just about ten miles, then turn left on Matthew's Brake Road. The church and cemetery are a short distance ahead on the left.

GRAVE DIRECTIONS: You won't miss Robert's grave marker next to the road.

BRIAN JONES

FEBRUARY 28, 1942 – JULY 3, 1969

If Brian Jones couldn't achieve rock immortality through the musical talent that burst from his seams, it seems he resolved to attain notoriety by virtue of the four different palimony suits that hung over him by age 24. But in the end, Brian was prematurely martyred as another rock-music casualty.

In 1960 Brian was a multitalented blues and jazz musician, but after picking up guitar, his style began increasingly to favor the new rock sounds. By the end of 1962 Brian had formed his own band, the Rolling Stones, its lineup highlighted by guitarist Keith Richards and frontman Mick Jagger, while Charlie Watts thudded out the drum beats and Bill Wyman plucked bass lines. Through 1966, Brian was the leader of the band, nurturing them from ragtag anonymity to regal pop stars with a series of hit singles including "Ruby Tuesday," "Time is on My Side," and "Heart of Stone."

By 1967 though, manager Andrew Oldham was increasingly developing the Jagger-Richards songwriting partnership to more effectively compete with their Lennon-McCartney rivals, and Brian, who had become the group's most substantial consumer of assorted recreational pharmaceuticals, was relegated to its margins. By the time of the *Beggar's Banquet* recording sessions in 1968, Brian's contributions were almost nil, and in June 1969 he officially departed the band citing musical differences.

All but forgotten a month later, Brian's status skyrocketed after newspaper headlines screamed he'd been found at the bottom of his swimming pool, dead at 27. A postmortem revealed that both his heart and liver were grossly enlarged due to long-term alcohol abuse, and traces of "an amphetamine-like substance" were found in his urine. However, no appreciable quantity of any other drugs was found in Brian's system and the final analysis handed down by the coroner declared his death was "by misadventure, cause of death drowning."

None of the witness statements given by the three people present at Brian's estate when he drowned never quite tallied, and questions lingered about who was doing what while Brian went for his fateful midnight swim. Especially questionable were the whereabouts of Frank Thorogood, a laborer at the estate, who maintained in his statement that while Brian was in the pool he had "popped indoors" for a cigarette. (*Indoors* for a cigarette?) In 1994 a recording of a deathbed confession by Thorogood surfaced, but after a brief investigation it was found to be fraudulent. Then in 1999, Anna Wohlin, Brian's girlfriend, who had found him dead in the pool, wrote a tell-all, alleging that Thorogood had indeed killed Brian in a row over money. It's not clear why she waited 30 years to come forward but, because she offered the information via a pricey book instead of in a free-of-charge police report, cynics pointed out the obvious motive while the rest of the world hardly noticed.

A horse-drawn hearse carried Brian to his resting place in Prestbury, Gloucestershire, England. After a two-hour drive out of London on the M40 heading northwest, you can find his neatly groomed grave at Priory Road Cemetery, along the lane near the chapel.

HUDDIE "LEADBELLY" LEDBETTER

NOVEMBER 20, 1885 – DECEMBER 6, 1949

Huddie "Leadbelly" Ledbetter personified the Delta bluesman. He was born on a Louisiana plantation and during his early adult years survived as an itinerant musician and sometime farm laborer. In 1918 Leadbelly received a 7-to-30-year prison sentence after pleading guilty to shooting a man to death in Texas, and it's been endlessly romanticized that he was pardoned after the governor heard a song of his in which he pleaded for release. Though Leadbelly did write such a song, it's clear that he was let out for good behavior after serving the minimum time.

In any event, Leadbelly was back behind bars by 1930. A white man had insisted to Leadbelly that "niggers is supposed to walk in the road" instead of on the sidewalk and, though he may have been guilty of assault after a scuffle ensued, the prosecution added that Leadbelly had "intended to murder," and he received six to ten years of hard labor.

While on a 1933 tour of the South to document Negro work songs for the Library of Congress archives, John Lomax recorded Leadbelly in a Louisiana prison. Lomax returned the next year and Leadbelly, who sincerely believed that his Texas prison release came about because of that earlier ballad, convinced Lomax to put a similar ballad on the flip side of a recording of one of his favorite songs, "Goodnight Irene." Lomax personally delivered the record to Louisiana's governor and this time, the song may indeed have been instrumental in gaining Leadbelly's release, though Lomax's elucidation of the trumped-up charges upon which Leadbelly had been convicted didn't hurt.

In 1935 Leadbelly followed Lomax to New York and recorded the majority of his work there, including "Midnight Special" and "Gallow's Pole," over the next dozen years. While his legend preceded him, Leadbelly performed tirelessly and played the part of a subservient Southern black that curious white audiences expected to see. Passing the hat after appearances in which he always played his "pardon songs," Leadbelly became the cajoling dark minstrel: "Bless Gawd, dat's a dime! Where is all de quarters? Thank you, boss! Thank you, missy, thank you!"

During a series of performances in Europe, Leadbelly's extremities grew numb and he died six months later, penniless at 64, from what was believed to be a particularly aggressive form of Lou Gehrig's Disease.

Leadbelly was buried at Shiloh Baptist Church Cemetery in Mooringsport, Louisiana.

CEMETERY DIRECTIONS: From I-220 in Shreveport, take Exit 7A and follow Route 71 north for 1½ miles to its intersection with Highway 1. Follow Highway 1 a short distance north, then reverse your direction in order to access Pine Hill Road on the west side of the highway. After 13 miles on Pine Hill Road (which at some point becomes Blanchard-Latex Road), the church and its cemetery are on the left.

GRAVE DIRECTIONS: Leadbelly's grave is in the middle of the cemetery surrounded by a black iron fence.

LYNYRD SKYNYRD

Ronnie Van Zant

JANUARY 15, 1948 – OCTOBER 20, 1977

Cassie Gaines

JULY 5, 1948 – OCTOBER 20, 1977

Steve Gaines

SEPTEMBER 14, 1949 – OCTOBER 20, 1977

Allen Collins

JULY 19, 1952 – JANUARY 23, 1990

Leon Wilkeson

APRIL 2, 1952 – JULY 27, 2001

In the summer of 1964 Ronnie Van Zant and four friends formed a band called the Noble Five, and that December they played their first paying gig at an auto-parts store's Christmas party. At the end of the night they were handed a single, crisp, $10 bill and, after chipping in for gasoline, they strutted home with $1.75 each.

With nowhere to go but up, the band mates practiced incessantly. Their band's name evolved into the peculiar Lynyrd Skynyrd, a play on the name of a gym teacher, Leonard Skinner, who they particularly disliked for his dutiful enforcement of the school dress code prohibiting sideburns and long hair. By 1973 the Southern-style, rebel-rock band had gained a tremendous following throughout Florida, landed a deal with MCI Records, and seen their debut album, *Pronounced Leh-Nerd Skin-Nerd*, released. After they were tapped to be the opening act for the Who's U.S. tour later that year, they never looked back. By 1975, with two more best-selling albums under their belts, Lynyrd Skynyrd was one of America's hottest and hardest-working rock and roll acts.

Predictably, the temptations of the road took their toll, and Lynyrd Skynyrd picked up a well-deserved reputation as a collection of hellbent, redneck, rock-star drunks. Despite the hard partying, they remained true to their music and churned out a string of irrepressible and incendiary guitar-driven singles, "Gimme Three Steps," "Sweet Home Alabama," and "Saturday Night Special," to name a few. In 1976 the band made personnel changes in order to fine-tune its sound, the most critical being the addition of guitarist Steve Gaines and a female backup vocal group, the Honkettes, of which Steve's sister Cassie was a member. By 1977, the band was at an all-time high and its new lineup hit the road in support of the album, *Street Survivors*.

In Greenville, South Carolina, after the fourth concert of a planned 80-concert tour, the band and its twelve-person entourage boarded their leased Convair 240 and headed for their next gig in Baton Rouge, Louisiana. At 6:42 p.m. on October 20, 1977, the pilot radioed from 6,000 feet over McComb, Mississippi, that his craft was dangerously low on fuel and, less than ten minutes later, the plane clipped the tops of branches over a swamp, then cut an 800-foot path through the trees until it lurched to a halt within the dense thicket. Because the plane had run out of fuel, it didn't burst into flames, and eighteen people emerged from the wreckage with assorted injuries, some more serious than others. Not everyone survived, however, and among those killed were the new guitarist, Steve Gaines, and his sister Cassie, as well as the frontman and founder Ronnie Van Zant, without whom the real Lynyrd Skynyrd band ceased to exist. Who else could ever justly imitate his introduction of the song "Freebird": "What song is it you want to hear?"

At 29, Ronnie was laid to rest wearing his trademark, black Texas Hatters cowboy hat. His favorite fishing pole was placed inside his coffin. Though Steve, 28, and Cassie, 29, were from Oklahoma, they were buried alongside Ronnie at the Jacksonville Memory Gardens in Florida. In 1999 someone defaced their graves and, shortly thereafter, they were exhumed and moved to a location that this author chooses to not disclose.

On the tenth anniversary of the plane crash, most of the surviving original members of Lynyrd Skynyrd reunited for the Tribute tour in which lead vocals were provided by Ronnie's younger brother, Johnny. Besides those killed in the crash, a former band member glaringly absent from the lineup was Allen Collins, who had been in the original incarnation of the Noble Five and who had distinguished himself and the band as lead guitarist. But Allen had also been one of the band's most notorious substance abusers both before and after the plane crash.

In 1986 Allen lost control of his car while driving under the influence of alcohol. The ensuing crash killed his girlfriend and left him paralyzed from the waist down, with only limited use of his upper body and arms. Allen later pleaded no contest to DUI manslaughter. Part of his sentence required that, as a celebrity, he make public service announcements warning others of the consequences of drunk driving. Allen served as musical director during the 1987 Tribute tour but remained wheelchair-bound on the sidelines while his band took center stage. Before each concert, Allen would be rolled up to the microphone to explain to his fans that he wouldn't be playing guitar because, on another night long ago, he had chosen to drive drunk.

As a result of decreased lung capacity from his paralysis, Allen developed pneumonia, from which he died at 37.

Allen Collins was buried at Riverside Memorial Gardens in Jacksonville, Florida.

CEMETERY DIRECTIONS: From I-295, take Exit 7 onto Normandy Boulevard. Head east and the cemetery is immediately to the left.

GRAVE DIRECTIONS: Enter the cemetery and drive past the fountain. Stop after about 75 yards and you'll see on the left a cement walk leading into the Garden of Cross. Eighty feet down this walk is a stone bench inscribed "Collins-John." (John is the maiden name of Allen's wife, Kathy, who died in 1980 from complications after a pregnancy.) Opposite the bench are the graves of both Allen and Kathy.

The Tribute tour was such a success that Lynyrd Skynyrd reunited for good and since then, they've released five albums and become a staple of summer concert tours. Unlike Allen, bass player Leon Wilkeson rejoined his old friends on stage and, with the two other original members, keyboardist Billy Powell and guitarist Gary Rossington, teased the prying eyes of fans who longed for the Lynyrd Skynyrd of yesteryear.

After more than a decade of thumping along in the band's new incarnation, Leon died in his sleep in a Florida hotel room during a brief break between shows. A medical examination found that he'd suffered from diseases of the liver and lungs and, after toxicology tests came back negative, it was ruled that he died of natural causes at just 49.

Leon was buried at Riverside Memorial Park Cemetery in Jacksonville, the same park as Allen.

GRAVE DIRECTIONS: Leon's stone is along the main drive, near the fountain on the left.

THE MAMAS
& THE PAPAS

'Mama' Cass Elliot

SEPTEMBER 19, 1943 – JULY 29, 1974

'Papa' John Phillips

AUGUST 30, 1935 – MARCH 18, 2001

During the 1960s the Mamas and the Papas burst out of the Southern California pop scene and bombarded the Top Forty with lushly harmonized folk-pop songs. The group was formed by John Phillips, who was also the creative talent and hit-writing machine of the foursome, after he pulled up stakes and left New York as the folk music scene went electric. The group's other three members—alto Cass Elliot, John's long-time collaborator Denny Doherty, and John's second wife, Michelle Phillips—contributed to the radiant blended sound, while session musicians provided the bulk of the instrumentation.

Projecting diversity in colorful hippie garb, they released a string of hit singles, including "California Dreamin'" and "Monday Monday," and reigned among the hip vanguard that typified the newest breed of groups to follow in the Beatles' wake. But it all came apart in just a few years, as the quartet's intertwining romantic entanglements and chemical excesses strangled their ability to work together. They broke up in 1968 and reunited briefly in 1971 to make one last album per a contractual obligation, but that album flopped, and the Mamas and the Papas became only a fond memory.

Mama Cass Elliot then enjoyed a fairly successful solo career, but while in London for a two-week engagement at the Palladium, she died in 1974, alone in an apartment. A popular legend holds that Cass choked to death on a ham sandwich, but it's not at all true. Instead, a ham sandwich that she hadn't yet touched was on the table next to her bed when she suffered a heart attack. After an autopsy discovered "fatty myocardial degeneration," her official cause of death was ruled as heart failure due to obesity.

At 30, Cass was cremated and her ashes buried at Mount Sinai Memorial Park in North Hollywood, California.

CEMETERY DIRECTIONS: From Highway 134, which is the connector between Highway 101 and I-210, take the Forest Lawn Drive exit. Proceed west for a half-mile and Mount Sinai's entrance is on the left.

GRAVE DIRECTIONS: Go up the hill and, just after the drive bends to the left, the twin Courts of Tanach are on the right. Go up the stairs and enter the first court Cass's marker is in the far left corner on the grass, and it displays her given name, Ellen Naomi Cohen.

Denny disappeared from sight once the group broke up. After John and Michelle divorced, Michelle embarked on an acting career. Meanwhile, John's life went into a tailspin and he spent most of the 1970s under the influence of one drug or another, often getting high with his teenage daughter, MacKenzie, who was a star on the *One Day at a Time* television series. A drug bust finally pushed him into therapy and, once clean and sober, John formed a reunion version of the group with Denny and two new Mamas.

At 65, John died of a heart attack. He now resides at Palm Springs Mortuary and Mausoleum in Cathedral City, California, where his crypt is emblazoned "California Dreamin'."

CEMETERY DIRECTIONS: From I-10, take the Ramon Road exit and proceed south for two miles to Da Vall Drive. Turn left, make a quick right into Palm Springs Mortuary, and park in the office lot to the left.

GRAVE DIRECTIONS: Walk back across the entrance lane, proceed alongside the fountain, then turn at the first left and the next right. John's crypt is on the left, just past the Frink family fountain, four rows from the bottom.

BOB MARLEY
FEBRUARY 6, 1945 – MAY 11, 1981

Even though Bob Marley never had a U.S. hit, he stands as one of the most warmly regarded figures in all of popular music. Within the loose framework of a reggae rhythm that seemed to command listeners to fall into its groove, Bob turned simple lyrics into sharp criticisms, and his outpouring of grief for his beloved but corrupt Jamaican homeland stirred consciences worldwide.

Born to a young black mother and an older white father, Bob grew up in a lush hamlet, high in the mountains of Jamaica. In 1962, at just seventeen, he cut his first single and, throughout the next decade, made a number of recordings for small Jamaican labels with his backing group, the Wailers. But wide commercial success eluded him, and the newly married Bob arrived in the U.S. in 1969 to take a chance on a 9-to-5 routine at a Wilmington, Delaware auto factory.

Bob soon returned to Jamaica. With a fresh focus, he began working with a new producer and record company and, in 1973, released a landmark album, *Catch A Fire*. Unlike Bob's previous releases, this work was packaged and marketed like a rock album and, to complement the strategy, he was astutely promoted to rock audiences, most notably sharing a billing with Bruce Springsteen at a number of New York City shows. Bob's gritty and vibrant blend of rock, blues, and West Indies folk began to catch on. After Eric Clapton covered Bob's "I Shot the Sheriff" in 1974, the transition was complete, and Bob Marley and the Wailers were stars.

As Bob's patterned melodies and endless hooks ramped his success skyward through the 1970s, he also gained credibility as a social leader. But even as a national hero and the King of Reggae, he could not bring change to the tormented social landscape of Jamaica. Bob was a Rastafarian—a member of the religious movement that favors nature, simplicity, marijuana, and, above all, peace—and was committed to peaceful revolution. Unfortunately, Jamaica's government recognized only the sword. In December 1976, two days before he was to give a free "Smile Jamaica" concert aimed at reducing tensions between warring political factions, gunmen attacked him and his entourage. Nobody was killed, though bullets grazed both Bob and his wife, and the incident served only to further galvanize his political outlook. Later works, especially *Exodus* and *Survival*, featured an urgent militant bent.

In 1977, a cancerous growth was found on one of Bob's toes, which he had injured years earlier while playing soccer. In the summer of 1980, it was learned that cancer had invaded his vital organs and, less than a year later, at 36, Bob died at a Miami clinic from brain and lung cancer.

Just steps away from the small stone house in which he was born, Bob lies in a white mausoleum surrounded by a fence splashed with the red, yellow, and green colors of Jamaica. In 1991, the government proclaimed his birthday a national holiday and, every year since, performers have celebrated his memory on a nearby stage. The site is in the tiny village of Nine Mile, 70 miles northwest of Kingston, accessible from the B3 road.

FREDDIE MERCURY

SEPTEMBER 5, 1946 – NOVEMBER 24, 1991

During the infancy and coming of age of "manufactured sound" in the 1970s, the British rock band Queen took great pride in the fact that its music featured no synthesizers. The group instead emphasized electric guitars (albeit heavily mixed) layered over smooth vocal harmonies, while the shrill lead was provided by flamboyant frontman Freddie Mercury.

Freddie had been born Farok Bulsara in the British colony of Zanzibar in Africa, though his Indian family soon moved to Bombay and, when he was thirteen, they settled in England. After obtaining a degree in graphic arts, Freddie flitted about London's eclectic underground during the 1960s, selling clothing and artwork at the Kensington market during the day and singing with a variety of fledgling groups by night.

He eventually joined the group Smile, and in 1971, when fellow songwriter John Deacon joined up, they changed the band's name to Queen. The group found success with a quick streak of well-received singles and in 1975 was catapulted to superstardom by the overwhelming response to their masterpiece album, *A Night at the Opera*. Record executives were initially reluctant to release "Bohemian Rhapsody" as the album's promotional single—with a playing time approaching six minutes, melodramatic élan, and striking tempo changes, it broke the traditional rules about what constituted a commercially viable song—but the band members persisted and, in large part due to Freddie's elaborate vocal arrangements, the song raced up the charts. Further, a short film they cobbled together to help promote the song is credited with kick-starting the music-video age.

Over the next decade, Queen toured worldwide and Freddie became renowned for his odd stage mannerisms and outlandish outfits. During the late 1980s it appeared that Queen had topped out in the studio, and each of the members pursued solo interests. But the band never really disintegrated. Instead, it chugged along in a state of arrested development, existing, it seemed, only to drain concert-goers pocketbooks.

Among other projects, Freddie recorded with Spanish opera star Montserrat Caballe and, at home, he found a passion for the exotic Japanese fish *koi*, which sell for many thousands of dollars each. "Excess is part of my nature. Dullness is a disease," he explained.

In 1991, Queen released a video and Freddie's emaciated and sickly appearance shocked many. Rumors that he had AIDS were routinely denied, but in November a press release confirmed the rumors. Twenty-five hours later it was announced that Freddie had died at his Kensington home of AIDS-related bronchial pneumonia.

At 45, Freddie was cremated at West London Crematorium in Kensal Green, England. Nobody seems to be sure what became of his ashes. Some say they are kept by a lover, while others maintain they were dispersed over Lake Geneva in Montreux, Switzerland, where he owned a cottage.

ROY ORBISON

APRIL 23, 1936 – DECEMBER 6, 1988

Roy was an introverted and subdued performer but, blessed with a clear tenor that soared into an angelic falsetto, his voice was riveting. In dramatic ballads of isolation like "Blue Bayou" and "Crying," Roy's songs received endless radio airplay during the 1960s. Later career forays into rockabilly and then rock and roll were well received by adoring fans as well.

After his wife died in a motorcycle accident and two children perished in a fire, Roy stopped writing songs, and his career ebbed for fifteen years. But in the 1980s it was rejuvenated when contemporary rock artists—musicians he'd influenced—brought a new popularity to his original songs. Roy was inducted into the Rock 'n' Roll Hall of Fame, was featured in a cable-television special, toured regularly again, and had aligned with an all-star cast of musicians who together released a smash album as the Traveling Wilburys. Roy's career was back on track when, at 52, he died of a heart attack.

Roy was buried at Westwood Memorial Park in Los Angeles.

CEMETERY DIRECTIONS: This little cemetery holds numerous celebrities and is peculiarly located behind the office complex at 10850 Wilshire Blvd., just about a half-mile east of I-405.

GRAVE DIRECTIONS: Many folks seem to have a hard time believing or understanding it, but Roy is in an unmarked grave (as is Frank Zappa just 25 feet away). Walk from the office into the central lawn area and count up eight rows to Frank Tuttle's stone. Roy's grave is in the next patch of grass, just left of the water spigot.

GRAM PARSONS

NOVEMBER 5, 1946 – SEPTEMBER 19, 1973

Gram Parsons, born Cecil Ingram Connors III, never hit it big, but has nonetheless become something of a cult figure in musical circles. His groundbreaking style of rock music, a seamless acoustic weave with a decidedly country tilt that he labeled "Cosmic American," was a direct precursor to such bands as the Eagles, and Gram's champions firmly maintain that, "If Gram had lived …"

In 1968, Gram befriended Byrds bassist Chris Hillman. Before he knew it, he was a member of the band and sparring with Roger McGuinn for leadership. He spearheaded their country- influenced *Sweetheart of the Rodeo* album, but immediately after its release, Gram and Chris quit the Byrds and formed their own group, The Flying Burrito Brothers, which met only limited success. In 1972 Gram put out a solo album, *G.P.*, and followed that with *Grievous Angel*, though he never lived to see its release.

A few weeks after completing the *Grievous Angel* sessions, Gram went with some friends to visit California's Joshua Tree National Monument, one of his favorite places. Much of the day was spent at a motel pool drinking, smoking, and injecting a variety of substances. By nightfall, Gram had had enough and went to his room to sleep. A few hours later Gram's friends found him in a particularly deep slumber and a coroner later determined he had died of "drug toxicity, due to multiple drug use." Even in death though, 26-year-old Gram was denied the attention he deserved; coverage of his demise was eclipsed by Jim Croce's death the following day.

After Gram's stepfather was informed of the death, he arranged for Gram's body to be flown to New Orleans for burial, but then, things got weird.

When Phil Kaufman, Gram's manager, learned that Gram had died, he was immediately reminded of a pact he'd made with Gram: After one of them died, "the survivor would take the other guy's body out to Cap Rock (a promontory at Joshua Tree), have a few drinks, and burn it." Once he was sufficiently liquored up, Kaufman decided to make good on his promise and, after having ferreted out the shipping arrangements, he and another friend, Michael Martin, dummied up some paperwork, drove out to the airport in a borrowed hearse, signed the release "Jeremy Nobody," and made off with Gram's remains. The two drunken body-snatchers then drove 150 miles to Joshua Tree and by moonlight dragged the coffin as close to Cap Rock as they could. Kaufman pried open the lid, poured in gasoline, and tossed in a match. As a giant fireball rose from the coffin, the two headed back home.

The story of Gram's hijacked and burnt corpse got more coverage in the newspapers than did his life and death (just as it does here), and there was even speculation that the amateur cremation was "ritualistic." The police, of course, were looking for Kaufman and Martin, and in short order they turned themselves in. Since a corpse has no intrinsic value, the two were charged with misdemeanor theft for stealing the coffin and ordered to pay $708 in damages, and fined an additional $300 each.

Meanwhile, Gram's charred remains were sent back to his stepfather, who had them buried at the Garden of Memories Cemetery in Metairie, Louisiana.

CEMETERY DIRECTIONS: From I-10, take Exit 226 and follow the Clearview Parkway south for two miles to Airline Highway. Turn right and the cemetery is a half-mile ahead on the left.

GRAVE DIRECTIONS: Enter the cemetery, turn at the second right and then again at the next right. After the hairpin left, you'll see a large sculpture of *The Last Supper* in the field on the right. Fifty yards in front of this sculpture are two large hardwood trees. Between these two trees, a small bronze circular marker identifies the resting place of Gram's remains.

Grievous Angel was released in January of 1974 but, despite the publicity surrounding Gram's death, it peaked at only number 195 on the album charts. Later, members of Gram's small but fervent following installed a memorial plaque inscribed "Safe At Home" near Cap Rock.

CARL PERKINS
APRIL 9, 1932 – JANUARY 19, 1998

In 1953 Carl Perkins worked as a baker by day, but his nights were spent performing hillbilly songs at Tennessee honky-tonks in a band with his brothers. After overhearing a boy telling his date not to step on his blue suede shoes, Carl wrote the words on a potato sack. They would become the refrain of his most famous song and, in March 1956, his "Blue Suede Shoes" stomped up the charts. But as the song rose to the top, Carl was involved in a near-fatal traffic accident and, in the hiatus while he recovered, an upcoming artist named Elvis Presley covered "Blue Suede Shoes" and capitalized on the popularity Carl had been building.

His thunder stolen by an unfortunate turn of events and, unable to pen another hit song to regain his momentum, Carl never conquered the world of pop, although his place in music history was assured. Though Carl was inducted into the Rock 'n' Roll Hall of Fame in 1987, he confessed that his biggest thrill was getting a gold record for "Blue Suede Shoes." "After all those days, the dreams came true in a gold record on a piece of wood. It's in my den where I wear it out looking at it everyday."

At 65, Carl died after a series of strokes and was buried at Ridgecrest Cemetery in Jackson, Tennessee.

CEMETERY DIRECTIONS: From I-40, take exit 82A and drive south on Route 45 for a quarter-mile. Make a left onto Ridgecrest Road and the cemetery is a short distance on the right.

GRAVE DIRECTIONS: Enter through the entrance with the brick columns and drive directly to the cemetery's rear. You'll see two mausoleums and there, in the one on the left, approximately in the center and at eye-level, is Carl.

THE RAMONES

After friends Jeffrey Hyman, Douglas Colvin, John Cummings and Tom Erdelyi alternately graduated or flunked out of New York high schools in 1973, they formed a punk-rock band comprising fictitious brothers, the Ramones—Joey, Dee Dee, Johnny and Tommy, respectively. The adopted Ramone surname was borrowed from Paul McCartney who had used it for incognito travel, but any commonality between conventional rock stars and the Ramones ended right there.

The Ramones were musicians strictly in the academic sense; they owned instruments and used them to make sounds. Tommy spent just two weeks mastering the drums before the band played its first gig. Dee Dee freely admitted that he never actually learned the notes on his bass but just "thump(ed) away on one string."

Though the Ramones were the first punk act to score a record deal, they weren't soul-searching lyricists, heartstring-tugging balladeers, or memorable melody makers. In their catalog of almost 200 frenetically paced songs, the average ditty clocked in at 2:19, prompting one wag to comment that the sole purpose of a Ramones song seemed to be to finish it as quickly as humanly possible. They released eighteen albums but only twice grazed the U.S. Top 100, and they never scored a real hit. Nonetheless, the Ramones did something right and their remarkable success can be attributed to the sheer power of persistence.

A few personnel changes notwithstanding, they were a hard-working band and spent twenty grueling years together. In 1989, Dee Dee said, "People always ask why we're still together. It's because we don't have a hit single and we still gotta work for a living." Although they were increasingly relegated to the music fringes, and despite their lack of commercial success, the Ramones never retreated from their punk cause and remained true to their legions of rabid fans. Years into the gig, their cartoon-like distinction continued and they blazed through songs like "I Don't Wanna Be Learned," "Now I Wanna Sniff Some Glue," and "Gimme Gimme Shock Treatment" with the same fiery intensity. In 2002, the Ramones were inducted into the Rock 'n' Roll Hall of Fame.

Jeffrey 'Joey Ramone' Hyman
MAY 19, 1951 – APRIL 15, 2001

From behind a curtain of long and straight black hair, Joey, the wraith-thin frontman, ignited manic audiences with yelped chants like "Hey, Ho, Let's Go!" or the trademark "Gabba Gabba Hey!" for two decades. His grim, leather-clad image was what initially endeared Joey to discontented youth but it was his deadpan, no-nonsense approach that retained the fan base.

When the Ramones finally broke up in 1996, after more than 2,200 pile-driving live shows, Joey continued as an outspoken opponent of censorship. He made select appearances as a headline act and, as reigning king of the music underground, Joey frequently acted as a special host for music events and galas.

The first inkling of a serious illness came in 1998 when chronic ill health forced him to cancel a series of Canadian dates. In March 2001, Joey entered a New York hospital to undergo treatment for acute lymphoma, a cancer that destroys the body's immune defenses. After unsuccessful treatment for the disease, Joey died at 49 in the presence of family and friends in April 2001.

Joey (Jeff Hyman) was buried at New Mount Zion Cemetery, which is a part of Hillside Cemetery, in Lyndhurst, New Jersey. **CEMETERY DIRECTIONS:** From I-280, take Exit 17 and follow Harrison Avenue (Route 508) west for a half-mile to Schuyler Avenue. Turn right on Schuyler and, after a few miles, note a jog in the road and a name-change to Orient Avenue. From there, the cemetery is just another half-mile ahead on the right.

GRAVE DIRECTIONS: Enter the cemetery at the second gate. Drive straight in and, after a hundred yards, you'll see a pair of granite pillars on the right belonging to the New York Social Club. Joey's grave is three rows back and five rows to the right of these pillars.

Douglas 'Dee Dee Ramone' Colvin

SEPTEMBER 18, 1952 – JUNE 5, 2002

A heroin addict and substance abuser for most of his adult life, Dee Dee left the band in 1989, and his departure signaled the end of an era, if not a style. He pursued an ill-fated rap career under the name Dee Dee King, formed a Ramones cover band, and became a painter. Dee Dee died at 49, the same age as Joey. After he was found in his Hollywood home with various drug paraphernalia, including a syringe, scattered about his kitchen, his death was ruled the result of an accidental drug overdose.

Dee Dee (Douglas Colvin) was buried at Hollywood Forever in Hollywood, California.

CEMETERY DIRECTIONS: This cemetery is easy to find at 6000 Santa Monica Blvd., just west of Highway 101.

GRAVE DIRECTIONS: Enter the cemetery, turn immediately left, then stop in front of the Grass mausoleum, which will be on your right at the next intersection. Dee Dee is buried in front of a tree just to the right of the mausoleum.

OTIS REDDING

SEPTEMBER 9, 1941 – DECEMBER 10, 1967

In 1960, Otis Redding recorded a song he'd written entitled "Shout-Bama-Lama." Though he seemed to have the ability and aspirations to be a star, the record was hampered by his reserved demeanor. The next year, Otis drove a few music friends to a studio in Memphis where the friends had booked recording time. At the end of the day, with twenty minutes of pre-paid studio time remaining, they offered it to Otis. With a new self-confidence, he sang another of his original tunes "These Arms of Mine," and it proved to be an R&B hit.

Otis won himself a recording contract and, when his series of releases over the next two years found favor with black record buyers, concert engagements followed. In 1965 he hit full stride with "I've

Been Loving You Too Long," while Aretha Franklin hit gold with his "Respect." After enjoying a hugely successful European tour, then giving a knockout performance alongside Jimi Hendrix at the Monterey Pop Festival in 1967, young music fans in white markets became interested in Otis's sound and it seemed he was breaking out of the strict R&B format. At the end of 1967 he wrote and recorded "Dock of the Bay," which would become his biggest hit, but tragedy struck and Otis never lived to enjoy its success.

Three days after recording "Dock of the Bay," Otis and three of the four members of his touring band, the Bar-Kays, were killed in a late-night plane crash. After a show in Cleveland, they boarded Otis's twin-engine Beechcraft airplane and flew to Madison, Wisconsin. Navigating through thick fog, the pilot became disoriented upon approaching the airport and, three miles from the runway, the plane slammed into Lake Monona, broke through the ice, and sank.

At 26 Otis was entombed in a white marble mausoleum at his Big O Ranch in Round Oak, Georgia.

GRAVE DIRECTIONS: Round Oak is a small, unincorporated village north of Macon and doesn't appear on some Georgia maps. But if you follow Route 11 for fifteen miles south from its intersection with Route 83 in Monticello, you'll see a sign signifying that you've entered Round Oak. Another two miles south, on the left, is Otis Redding Road (though the sign may not be there, as it has a habit of disappearing just a short time after a new one is erected).

Follow Otis Redding Drive for a mile and you'll see the driveway to the Big O ranch on the right. Otis's widow, Zelda, still lives there, and the gate to her private property is often closed. "This is not Graceland, this is my home," she said recently.

A memorial plaque dedicated to Otis and the Bar-Kays can be found on the William T. Evjue Rooftop Garden of Monona Terrace, a Frank Lloyd Wright-designed convention center adjacent to the lake where the musicians died.

In September 2002, a seven-foot-tall bronze statue of Otis was unveiled at the trailhead of the new Ocmulgee Heritage Greenway at Gateway Park in Macon, Georgia. The Ocmulgee River drifts slowly along behind the statue, an appropriate backdrop for a man whose life was washed away, but whose music rolls on.

RANDY RHOADS

DECEMBER 6, 1956 – MARCH 19, 1982

Randy Rhoads was a founding member of Quiet Riot, a heavy metal band rooted in Los Angeles, and in 1981, Randy was named new lead guitarist for Ozzy Osbourne's band during his *Blizzard of Oz* and *Diary of a Madman* period.

While on tour in support of the *Madman* album, Ozzy and his entourage were en route to a show in Orlando when their tour bus driver, Andrew Aycock, stopped at an associate's estate in Leesburg, Florida. He had been at the wheel for ten hours driving from the band's previous engagement in Knoxville, Tennessee.

While members of the band and entourage variously milled around the property or snoozed on the bus, Aycock, who had a pilot's license, took a Beechcraft Bonanza airplane without permission from a hanger on the estate and invited people to join him for a spin. Aycock went up in the airplane with two people and, upon landing without incident, Randy, along with Rachel Youngblood, the group's makeup artist and hairdresser, got in the plane to take a ride with Aycock. During this trip the plane began to fly low to the ground, even below tree level, and three times buzzed the tour bus. On a fourth pass, the plane's left wing struck the bus and the plane hurtled through a pine tree and crashed into a garage, immediately erupting into a fireball.

Ozzy Osbourne, who had been asleep on the bus, initially thought it had been involved in a traffic accident, but the truth was far worse. All three people on the plane were killed instantly.

At 25, Randy was buried at Mountain View Cemetery in San Bernadino, California.

CEMETERY DIRECTIONS: From I-215, take Exit 30 and follow Highway 210 east to Waterman Avenue (Route 18) south. At the second traffic light, turn left onto Highland Avenue and the cemetery is immediately to the left.

GRAVE DIRECTIONS: Enter the cemetery, bear left, and Randy's mausoleum is immediately to the left.

BON SCOTT
JULY 9, 1946 – FEBRUARY 19, 1980

Bon Scott was born in Scotland and lived there until his family moved to Australia when he was in his mid-teens. As a young adult, Bon's was a familiar face drifting around the developing rock-music scene, and in 1974, he was successful in his audition to play drums for a new band that went by the relatively innocuous name of AC/DC.

Bon actually aspired to be the band's frontman, and he seized the opportunity when singer Dave Evans failed to turn up for a show. Bon's incendiary club performance as lead vocalist led to a permanent position, and AC/DC went on to redefine the concept of three-chord, heavy-metal rock. In 1975 their debut album, *High Voltage,* jolted the jaded eardrums of radio listeners and slammed the Billboard charts. Four more albums featuring Bon's thunderous vocals were released by 1979, each one more hotly anticipated than the last, and AC/DC's international rock stardom soared.

Unfortunately for Bon, though, he missed out on the even greater successes that awaited the band over the next decade. In London, after an all-night drinking binge, he died at 33 in a car parked outside a friend's flat. The coroner determined that Bon had polluted his body with too much whiskey, and his official cause of death is listed as "death by misadventure."

Bon was buried near his old stomping grounds at Fremantle Cemetery in Fremantle, Australia. This thriving suburb is located on Australia's west coast, eight miles south of Perth.

STEVIE RAY VAUGHAN
OCTOBER 3, 1954 – AUGUST 27, 1990

Perhaps the leading rock and blues guitarist of his generation, the spellbinding Stevie Ray Vaughan rose from Texas obscurity to meteoric success in the early 1980s by virtue of a technical virtuosity not heard on blues guitar since Jimi Hendrix.

By the age of ten, Stevie was fairly accomplished on the guitar and, at sixteen, left school with his guitar and trademark bandito hat to become a stage fixture in Austin's blues clubs. Stevie's first big break came when David Bowie hired him as lead guitarist for his 1982 *Let's Dance* album, which led to a record deal for Stevie and his band, Double Trouble. In quick succession, *Texas Flood* and

Couldn't Stand the Weather were released, and the following years proved to be a roller-coaster ride for Stevie.

Rabid fans, contemporary guitar heroes, and even jaded music critics hailed the goateed musician as the electric guitar's newest champion. But although his professional status soared, Stevie fell deep into alcoholism and drug addiction and, after an extensive American tour in 1987, he checked himself into a rehab program. Stevie was clean by 1989 and he soon released *In Step*, his fourth album and his most successful to date, which earned a Grammy and went gold within just a few months. Stevie was on top, professionally and personally, and the sky seemed to be the limit.

In the summer of 1990, Stevie and Double Trouble set out on a headlining tour and closed the night's show at the Alpine Valley outdoor amphitheater in East Troy, Wisconsin, with a blazing encore, highlighted by a who's-who of guitarists including Eric Clapton, Buddy Guy, Robert Cray, and Jimmie Vaughan, Stevie's older brother and early mentor. The last song they played was "Sweet Home Chicago."

After the musicians left the stage, Stevie jumped aboard a Bell 206B Jet Ranger, one of four waiting helicopters. The craft took off in fog around 12:40 a.m. but it never arrived in sweet Chicago. Instead, just a couple minutes after taking off, all aboard were killed when the helicopter suffered a "high-energy, high-velocity impact at a shallow angle" with the ground. Occurring on the far side of a nearby hill, the crash wasn't heard by anyone leaving the noisy concert site, and a search was initiated only when a satellite picked up the craft's emergency transmitter signal four hours later. At 7:00

a.m., searchers found the bodies of Stevie, the pilot, and three members of Clapton's entourage. Later that morning, Clapton and Jimmie Vaughan identified the bodies.

At 35, Stevie was buried at Laurel Land Memorial Park in Dallas, Texas.

CEMETERY DIRECTIONS: From I-35E, take Exit 420 and the cemetery is on the east side of the highway.

GRAVE DIRECTIONS: Pull into the parking lot of the funeral home and you'll see two entrances leading to the cemetery—one faces south, the other faces east. Enter through the easterly gate and proceed down that drive, continuing on as straight as possible. There will be a couple of jogs in the road but continue to head east. After a third of a mile you'll come to an intersection and an island. This island, just past Section 38, is called the Vaughan Estate and is where Stevie rests.

SID VICIOUS & NANCY SPUNGEN

Nancy Spungen

FEBRUARY 27, 1958 – OCTOBER 12, 1978

Sid Vicious

MAY 10, 1957 – FEBRUARY 2, 1979

When the Sex Pistols first surfaced on London's 1975 music scene, nobody was quite sure what to make of the band or its heart-attack-paced, anti-love songs. The pack of spiky-cropped, incompetent misfits purported to carry the musical flag for rebellion and anarchy, but it soon became clear that perhaps the only ones less interested in their "music" were the Sex Pistols themselves. In their first interview, frontman Johnny Rotten (his surname earned through the decrepit condition of his teeth) made clear the band wasn't "into music . . . we're into chaos," and he later expanded by declaring that money was their other key interest. The papers realized that the crew of castaways made for good copy and, buoyed by a stream of bizarre news clips, the band prospered.

By 1977, the Sex Pistols were the utter apotheosis of punk rock. In February the band's bassist was replaced by John Ritchie, better known as Sid Vicious, and the Sex Pistols metamorphosed into something else entirely. Little more than a criminally disturbed child possessed by a lust for fame, Sid personified all that the Sex Pistols purported to represent; he was cruel and self-destructive, doggedly pursued a heroin addiction, happily suffered through self-inflicted injuries, and lived his life in a brutally demented haze. But for Sid, sadly, none of this was an act. After Sid's death, Johnny Rotten even confessed that Sid "was nothing more than a coat hanger to fill an empty space on stage."

Remarkably, for a short time anyway, the Sex Pistols seemed to be on the verge of advancing from rock's greatest failure to its greatest success when, nine months after Sid's arrival, their much-anticipated album, *Never Mind The Bullocks—Here's The Sex Pistols,* briefly topped the charts in spite of, or perhaps because of, the fact that many outlets refused to stock it. Despite that accomplishment, the band still managed to self-destruct within another year. After a glorious period of endless turpitude, at their sixth-ever U.S. concert Johnny Rotten declared the group finished.

After the Sex Pistols' 1978 demise, Sid, with groupie-turned-girlfriend Nancy Spungen, circulated as the wandering-soul fun couple of the year. A troubled junkie herself, former go-go dancer Nancy was Sid's most ardent fan, and her tempestuous relationship with him had started a year prior when she traveled to London with the sole intention of "bedding a Sex Pistol." The bedding turned into an extended gothic romance highlighted by drug-crazed dysfunctional debauchery, and after the couple moved into Room 100 in Manhattan's Chelsea Hotel, their relationship turned even stormier.

After two months at the hotel, during which time Nancy worked as a prostitute to support their lifestyle and drug habits, one October morning Sid called the front desk to tell them he had awakened to find his girlfriend dead. When police arrived, they found Nancy, crumpled under the bathroom sink clad in blood-soaked bra and panties, with a single, deep stab wound to her abdomen inflicted by a hunting knife. Still in a drugged haze, Sid was charged with her murder and arrested, but a few days later was released when the band's ex-manager posted a $50,000 bail telegraphed to him by Virgin Records.

Sid stayed in Manhattan upon his release, as his passport had been confiscated, and in December got into a fight at a disco and landed back at Riker's Island prison, where he was put into a seven-week detox program. Released clean and sober from Riker's on February 1, he was greeted that night by some of his junkie friends from the Chelsea. At a friend's room, Sid jumped right back into the

ETERNAL COUPLE

SID VICIOUS &
NANCY SPUNGEN

junk and later went back and collapsed into his bed. His mother Beverly had flown from England to care for her son and, ever fearful that Sid would be arrested in a drug buy on the street, she had bought a supply of heroin for him. He awoke sometime past midnight and, finding the heroin in his mother's purse, he used it and drifted off again—this time permanently. The next morning Beverly found him nude on the floor, "lying there quite peacefully." Sid's mother shook him until she realized "he was very cold and dead." Sid's death at 21 was ruled accidental. But it was not unexpected.

At 20, Nancy was buried at King David Cemetery in Bensalem, Pennsylvania.

CEMETERY DIRECTIONS: From I-95, take Exit 37 and follow Route 132 west for three miles. Turn right onto Richlieu Road and then, at Richlieu Road's intersection with Bristol Road, turn left. The cemetery is a short distance ahead on the left.

GRAVE DIRECTIONS: Turn left into the cemetery at the second entrance, which is a double-wide drive. Stop when this drive intersects the big circular drive and, on the right near the curb, you'll find a Goodman marker. Walk down the concrete path of Goodman and you'll find Nancy's plot at the seventeenth marker on the left.

Sid was cremated, and it's been widely reported that his ashes were either scattered or buried at Nancy's grave. That however seems a bit too romantic, and I'm sure the Spungen family would've protested, considering the circumstances. Besides, in a press conference announcing the Sex Pistols 1996 reunion tour, Johnny Rotten remarked that he "was going to put a funeral urn on the table in his (Sid's) place today but unfortunately his ashes were blown all over Heathrow Airport some time ago. I would have needed a Hoover."

MUDDY WATERS
APRIL 4, 1915 – APRIL 30, 1983

McKinley Morganfield was born to a Mississippi Delta sharecropping family and, as the legend goes, he earned his moniker as a small child for always playing in the mud. But by thirteen Muddy had taken up guitar and developed an interest in blues music.

During a 1941 visit to the Delta region in search of artists to record for the Library of Congress folk-song archives, Alan Lomax found Muddy who, by then, had developed his own jagged bottleneck guitar-playing style. Prompted by Lomax, Muddy moved north to Chicago, where he soon went electric because, "couldn't nobody hear you with an acoustic." That provided the boost that lifted him above his contemporaries; Muddy's earthy, traditional vocals layered over an urgently amplified sound touched off the modern Chicago-blues movement. Into the 1950s, Muddy refined his artistry in releases such as "Hoochie Coochie Man" and the anthemic "Got My Mojo Working," and his style ultimately shaped the development of rock and roll music.

As the 1950s gave way to the '60s, blues of the sort that Muddy performed so definitively became less and less relevant to black listeners, who increasingly involved themselves with soul music and its offshoots. But no matter—by this time, Muddy had been taken up by a new audience, anyway: the young, white middle class that had been born of the folk music revival. The taverns and back halls in which Muddy had performed in the previous decade gave way to college auditoriums, jazz clubs, and festival stages where he was widely accepted by the rock community and accorded the respectful adulation given a founding figure. In the last decade of his life, Muddy made three of his best-selling albums, *Hard Again, I'm Ready,* and *King Bee,* and he frequently performed with such acts as Eric Clapton and the Rolling Stones, who regarded him as their mentor.

Muddy died in his sleep at 68 and was buried at Restvale Cemetery in Worth, Illinois.

CEMETERY DIRECTIONS: From I-294, take the Route 50 exit in Alsip and travel north for a few hundred yards. Turn left on 122nd Street and after a half-mile make a right on Laramie Avenue. The cemetery is a short distance ahead on the left.

GRAVE DIRECTIONS: Enter the cemetery and park your car. Muddy's grave is in Section H to the left of the office, three stones from the drive.

THE WHO

O ne of the most enduring and influential rock groups of all time, the Who, featuring frontman Roger Daltrey, lead guitarist and primary songwriter Pete Townshend, solemn bassist John Entwistle, and wildman drummer Keith Moon, were originally called the Detours but, after discovering that another band of the same name already existed, changed the name to the ever-confusing moniker, the Who.

The group first caught the public's attention around 1965 after becoming a cult act thanks to their energetic live show, which included a nightly onstage destruction of guitars and drum kits that quickly ate up the band's profits. Royalties from early hits such as "Magic Bus" and "I Can't Explain" helped pay the bills, but their real breakout came in 1969 when the Townshend-penned "rock opera" *Tommy*, the story of a handicapped youth who finds salvation through pinball, remained on the charts for over two years. Over the next decade, through *Who's Next, Quadrophenia,* and *Who Are You?,* the foursome crashed its way through a haze of rock and roll excess, emphasizing their art via ear-splittingly loud concerts while punctuating their tours' with hotel room-destroying "Whooliganism."

After Keith died in 1978, the band documented their 1982 "farewell" tour on the live album, *Who's Last,* but the Who didn't really disappear. Pete, Roger, and John pursued solo careers to various degrees of success, and 2002 marked the beginning of their fifth tour as the Who since their "farewell," suggesting that, after 20 years, the Who still hadn't finished saying goodbye.

Keith Moon

AUGUST 23, 1946 – SEPTEMBER 7, 1978

R enowned for his ferocious and frenetic drumming, Keith Moon destroyed more drum kits in his lifetime than most musicians have had the opportunity to play. Though he often did only a mediocre job of timekeeping, he was certainly one of the most exciting drummers from an audience's perspective, and his explosive rolls and frantic style contributed to the outrageous package that was the Who.

Though Keith liked to claim he'd never had drum lessons, he actually had, though the fib wasn't hard to believe, as discipline was certainly not one of his attributes. As one of rock's greatest drummers,

Keith only played when he was with the Who, never practiced and, even after he was famous, never had a drum kit in any place that he lived. Instead, Keith's time away from the band was an endless party, his hedonistic lifestyle perpetually in full swing. His fans revere him for driving a car into a swimming pool, but (sorry) it never happened.

In 1978 Keith was living in Mayfair, London, with his girl-friend, Annette, at Harry Nilsson's pad at 9 Curzon Place—the same flat, Number 12 on the top floor, in which "Mama" Cass Elliot had died four years earlier. Keith had been taking pills that had been prescribed by his doctor to ease alcohol withdrawal. Before going to sleep at about three o'clock one morning, Keith took a handful of the pills. He awoke in a daze a few hours later, had a sizable meal, ingested another bunch of the pills, and returned to bed.

When Annette tried to rouse Keith later that afternoon, he wouldn't be disturbed. The ultimate party animal, the poster-child of recreational drugs and debauchery, had died of an accidental overdose of the prescription drug Heminevrin.

At 32, Keith was cremated at Golder's Green Crematorium in London, and his ashes were scattered there at Section 3P. There is no plaque or memorial; the section is merely a flower-filled field of remembrance.

John Entwistle

OCTOBER 9, 1944 – JUNE 27, 2002

Because the Who has only ever had a single guitarist, Pete Townshend, it was always vital that bassist John Entwistle play loud and complex bass lines to compensate for the absence of a rhythm guitar. The result was that John's fills and counter-melodies, indeed all manner of his bass lines, stood out from the Who's music like no other rock band's, and he became acclaimed as one of rock's premier bassists.

But though John's musical mannerisms stood out, he did not. A tax clerk before joining the Who, he was content to be the quiet one whose calm, anchoring, presence contrasted with his bad-boy band mates' energetic activities. John did, however, contribute a number of songs to the Who catalog, most notably "My Wife" and "Boris the Spider." And, though they were characteristically un-even, John also had a half-dozen solo works to his credit.

The night before the Who were to kick off their 2002 tour, John died at the Hard Rock Hotel and Casino in Las Vegas. Though the cause of his death was determined to have been a heart attack, the coroner also stated that cocaine found in his system was a con-tributing factor.

At 57, John was buried under a simple monument at St. Edwards Church in Stow-on-the-Wold, Gloucester, England, a 1½ hour drive northwest of London.

WOLFMAN JACK

JANUARY 21, 1938 – JULY 1, 1995

Disc jockey Wolfman Jack was the Elvis Presley of rock radio. He fine-tuned and repackaged work originated by black musicians, then became a phenomenon by feeding this music, in his own inimitable style, to a massive white audience hungry for something different and fresh.

During the early 1960s the airwaves were still more or less segregated, so Wolfman (whose real name was Bob Smith) created a shadowy wildman alter ego to play the black rhythm-and-blues records that he so loved. By broadcasting from XERF-AM, a station based just over the border in Mexico that boasted a signal ten times more powerful than any U.S. radio station, the Wolfman soon developed a national following. His trademark throaty voice and rough tongue, peppered with sporadic wolf howls and interjections of black slang, blanketed North America with a flavorsome stew of R&B, jazz, rockabilly, and rock and roll. The restless youth of America immediately embraced Wolfman Jack. Nobody else came close.

The national press eventually took notice, and stories about the Wolfman surfaced in major newspapers and magazines. Todd Rundgren and the Guess Who wrote chart-making songs about him, and his popularity skyrocketed. But the questions lingered: *Who is Wolfman Jack? Where does he come from? What does he look like (is he black or white)?* Only Bob Smith and a few others knew the answers, and they weren't talking.

Finally, though, the cloak was lifted in 1973 when George Lucas, remembering Wolfman from his own youth, wrote him into the screenplay that became his hit film, *American Graffiti*. When *American Graffiti* was released, Wolfman Jack was already firmly enshrined as a part of rock history. But his star certainly shone brighter afterward, and the film transformed him into a media superstar. Wolfman Jack became one of rock and roll's premier spokesmen, engaging in countless personal and television appearances, and even hosting his own television show, *The Midnight Special.*

At 57, Wolfman Jack died of a heart attack and, believe it or not, was buried in the yard of his home in Belvidere, North Carolina.

Belvidere is right in the middle of nowhere. It doesn't appear on some North Carolina maps, but is about fifteen miles west of Elizabeth City and halfway between Albemarle Sound and the Virginia border. If you follow Route 37 north from Route 17, you'll come upon Layden's Supermarket after about nine miles, and that's more or less the town of Belvidere. Follow Route 37 another half-mile north and Wolfman's former residence is on the right. It's easy to determine which house is his—it's the only one with a gravestone in the side yard, and the marker is visible from the road.

As this is private property and a private residence, use discretion if you visit the site.

MAX YASGUR

NOVEMBER 11, 1920 – FEBRUARY 8, 1973

For 30 years, Max Yasgur basked in anonymity as the operator of Yasgur Farms, a wholesale milk business in upstate New York. But in 1969, the Yasgur name leapt overnight to international prominence when Max leased his farmland to a music promoter and the sleepy community of Bethel, New York, was transformed into the site of the world's largest rock festival—Woodstock.

Woodstock is now legendary. Some 500,000 people attended the three-day festival that celebrated peace, love, and, above all, music. But in the eyes of some Bethel residents, the long August weekend was nothing more than an orgy of psychedelic experimentation and group sex played out under the umbrella of loud, god-awful music. They were furious that longhaired, flower children overran their bucolic village, used recreational drugs in the streets, trampled their crops, and brought about enormous traffic jams.

After the event, Max was both blessed and scorned. Masses of thankful hippies applauded his generosity, while neighbors who had previously been his friends rebuked him. Seeking to clear the air between the generations, Max appeared on radio and television and eventually most of the townspeople came around to forgiving him, mindful that he'd probably done more good for the town than harm.

Tragically, not even four years after the festival that made his farm famous, Max died of a heart attack at 52.

He was buried at the Ahavath Israel section of Liberty Street Cemetery in Monticello, New York.

CEMETERY DIRECTIONS: Take Exit 105A off of Route 17 and follow Route 42 South for a quarter-mile. Turn left onto Thompsonville

Road and then, at the next intersection, turn left onto Rock Ridge Drive. Pass back over Route 17 and turn right at the stop sign. After a short distance there will be a series of small cemeteries on the right. Turn right at the third driveway—the one at telephone pole #26-A—and stop halfway before its end.

GRAVE DIRECTIONS: Climb over the three-rail fence on your left and Max's marker is in the third row of stones.

If you'd like to visit the site of either the 1969 or 1994 Woodstock Festivals while you're in the area, directions follow. (The 1999 event, wherein angry concert-goers lit bonfires, looted vendors, and assaulted women, is probably best forgotten.)

DIRECTIONS TO SITE OF 1969 WOODSTOCK: None of the Woodstock concerts actually took place in the town of Woodstock. To get to the 1969 site in Bethel, exit Route 17 at Exit 104 and follow Route 17B west for just over ten miles. Turn right onto Hurd Road and follow it for a mile to its intersection with West Shore Road. On the right-hand corner of this intersection is a large stone marker commemorating the original site.

DIRECTIONS TO SITE OF 1994 WOODSTOCK: The 1994 Woodstock concert took place in Saugerties, New York—some 50 miles east of Bethel. At the intersection of Routes 32 and 212, across from the I-87 southbound toll plaza, is a dirt road, Augusta Savage Road. The 1994 soiree took place in the fields on both sides of this road, and the abandoned water and wash stations that dot the fields are the only clue to these hills' place in rock history.

FRANK ZAPPA
DECEMBER 21, 1940 – DECEMBER 4, 1993

Frank Zappa was one of rock's most committed iconoclasts, blazing new trails in rock music. But Frank was too ambitious to stay within the relative confines of rock, and in his lifetime he embraced everything from doo-wop and heavy metal to big band and orchestral music. Whenever a new pop fad surfaced, he could be counted on to address the craze with a trademark sardonic response. Frank's songs were characterized by bizarre lyrics, and the musical directions he chose turned out to be almost unlistenable at times. But that wasn't really the point. His objective was to push the envelope into the recesses of every musical region, to find out what lay over the horizon, to let the chips fall where they may.

Frank's initial foray into music was as the drummer in his high school marching band, but that ended when he was kicked out for smoking under the bleachers while in uniform. Remarkably, Frank was able to recover from that setback, and in 1966 he and his band, the Mothers of Invention, released *Freak Out,* one of rock's first concept albums. That record was followed up quickly with *Absolutely Free* and *We're Only In It for the Money,* albums that, to some degree, became underground anthems for 1960s counterculture. Over the next 25 years, Frank released 60 more albums and produced several films. Though he developed a substantial catalog of music, his work was uneven—some maintain his first three albums were his best—and Frank was never particularly successful from a commercial standpoint. But again, that never seemed to be the point anyway.

Frank managed to offend numerous political and social groups with biting, satirical, and sometimes lascivious lyrics that left little sacred. He ignored any criticism, but in 1985, when the Parents Music Resource Center recommended voluntary album content labeling, Frank became concerned that artists might be prevented from freely expressing themselves. He went to Capitol Hill to accuse a Senate committee of promoting censorship. Frank compared the proposed warning label tactics to "treating dandruff by decapitation," and, though he seemed victorious in 1985, content labels are de rigueur today.

Frank was rewarded for his innovations by twice being rejected for induction into the Rock 'n' Roll Hall of Fame. On the other hand, after recording two albums with Pierre Boulez and the London Symphony Orchestra, he was honored along with other avantgarde musicians at the 1992 New Music Festival in Frankfurt. Finally, clearer heads prevailed and he was inducted posthumously into the Rock 'n' Hall of Fame in 1995.

In the spring of 1990, Frank was diagnosed with prostate cancer. He held on for almost four more years but succumbed to the disease at 52 and was buried at Westwood Memorial Park in Los Angeles.

CEMETERY DIRECTIONS: Follow Wilshire Boulevard a half-mile east from I-405, turn right onto Glendon Avenue and the cemetery is immediately to the left. Or, you may want to park your car along Wilshire Boulevard and walk to the cemetery behind the office complex at 10850 Wilshire Blvd.

GRAVE DIRECTIONS: From the office, walk into the central lawn area and count up eight rows to the flat, bronze marker of Charles Bassler. Frank rests in the unmarked plot above Bassler.

POPULAR
MUSIC
ICONS

LOUIS ARMSTRONG

AUGUST 4, 1901 – JULY 6, 1971

Most Baby Boomers remember Louis "Satchmo" Armstrong on variety shows as a smiling older uncle warbling his gravelly voice through "What a Wonderful World" and playing a bit of trumpet afterward. But jazz aficionados remember Louis differently and freely refer to him as a genius. According to Tony Bennett (who ought to know), Armstrong "practically invented jazz singing singlehandedly." Further, outside of jazz circles it's largely unknown that, as a young avant-garde musician, Louis' Hot Five and Hot Seven recordings of the 1920s spurred a musical revolution.

Louis' achievements are all the more remarkable given his early life of extreme poverty in a New Orleans slum. But he somehow turned that adversity into opportunity and, while in the Colored Waifs' Home for Boys after a brush with the law, Louis discovered the cornet and began making music. In Joe Oliver, a cornet king playing the new music called jazz, Louis found a mentor and father figure. Sent to join Oliver's Chicago-based Creole Jazz Band in 1922, Louis shortly thereafter made his first recordings, which have since been called "the Rosetta Stone of Jazz."

Before those recordings, jazz musicians modestly limited their solos, but Louis's were longer and bolder, and he started improvising on the chord structure. With his rhythmic fluidity, he also began playing on and around the beat, heralding the swing style that emerged in the 1930s. Louis also pioneered a new style of singing, imitating the horn with his voice and substituting improvised nonsense syllables for the lyrics. With the passing of the big band era, he formed his All Stars, and they became goodwill ambassadors of jazz throughout the world, helping break down racial barriers wherever they played.

Louis never forgot where he came from and recognized that he was blessed twice, first with a sandpapery, distinctive voice and second with keen trumpet skills. Together, his talents helped him reap the rewards that eluded most of the influential creators of his era. The affinity he felt for his trumpet superseded everything else. As he reflected once, "Anything that'll get in the way of blowing my horn, out it goes. The trumpet comes first, before everything, even my wife."

Louis died in his sleep of natural causes and was buried at Flushing Cemetery in Queens, New York.

At the turn of the century, no one paid much notice to the birth of an illegitimate black baby boy in New Orleans and Louis,

never knowing his real birthday, chose to celebrate it as July 4, 1900. A baptismal certificate listing his birth date as Aug. 4, 1901, was finally discovered in 1989, making Louis 69 at his death, not 71, as is generally recorded.

CEMETERY DIRECTIONS: From I-495, take Exit 25 and follow Utopia Parkway north for a half-mile to Pigeon Meadow Road. Turn left on Pigeon Meadow Road and, after a mile, it will intersect with 46th Avenue, where you'll make a right turn into the cemetery.

GRAVE DIRECTIONS: Enter the cemetery and bear left, keeping 46th Avenue on your left. Count the paved drives on your right and park at the fourth one. Section Nine will be in front of you, and Louis's dark brown stone, easily recognizable with a sculptured marble trumpet atop it, is a couple rows off the curb.

CHET ATKINS

JUNE 20, 1924 – JUNE 30, 2001

Known as Mr. Guitar, Chet Atkins was one of the musical architects of the lush Nashville Sound, a style of music featuring string instruments and lots of echo that appealed to older listeners not interested in rock music. Indeed, with his musical innovations, especially his trademark two-finger-and-thumb style of picking, Chet's name inspires the highest of superlatives from a variety of musical circles.

Chet made his recording debut in 1946 and by the time of his death had recorded more than 75 albums of guitar instrumentals.

His own records sold millions, and he played on hundreds of hit records, including "Heartbreak Hotel" and "Wake Up Little Susie." Along the way he produced and guided greats from Roy Orbison to Dolly Parton, and collaborated with a wide range of artists on solo albums from Mark Knopfler to George Benson.

Chet battled prostate and colon cancer in the 1970s, was diagnosed with lung cancer in 1996, and in 1997 he had a tumor removed from his brain. In 2001, the cancer finally won, and Chet died at 77.

He was buried at Harpeth Hills Memory Gardens in Linton, Tennessee.

CEMETERY DIRECTIONS: Linton is a speck of a town about twenty miles southeast of Nashville. From I-40, take Exit 196 and follow McCrory Lane south for four miles to Route 100. Turn right and the cemetery is two miles ahead on the right.

GRAVE DIRECTIONS: Enter the cemetery, bear left around the flower garden, go past the funeral home, then turn right at the second intersection. Just a short distance ahead on the left, Chet's large marker near the road can't be missed.

GENE AUTRY

SEPTEMBER 29, 1907 – OCTOBER 2, 1998

In the early days of Western serials, when the good guys wore white hats and the bad guys wore black, Gene Autry always wore white, rode his horse, Champion, and always had a song to sing. He was best known as "the Singing Cowboy," and while partnered with Roy Rogers, the two actors were the country's best-loved cowboy team.

Gene made 95 movies and hosted his own TV show, which ran for six seasons. He also recorded over 600 songs including his trademark tune, "Back in the Saddle Again," as well as the timeless kiddie recordings "Rudolph the Red-Nosed Reindeer," "Here Comes Santa Claus," and "Peter Cottontail."

He hung up his performing spurs by the early 1960s, then devoted his time to numerous successful business ventures—for many years the Gene Autry name was on *Forbes* magazine's list of the 400 richest Americans.

At 91, Gene died of natural causes and was buried at Forest Lawn Memorial Park in Hollywood Hills, California.

CEMETERY DIRECTIONS: From Highway 134, which is the connector between Highway 101 and I-210, take the Forest Lawn Drive exit. Proceed west for a mile and the park's entrance will be on the left.

GRAVE DIRECTIONS: Enter the cemetery and proceed to the Sheltering Hills section, which is the first big lawn on the right after the information booth. There you'll see a white statue belonging to S.E. Wong and there lies Gene just four rows in front.

FLORENCE BALLARD

JUNE 30, 1943 – FEBRUARY 22, 1976

Stylizing rhythm and blues with a pop flair, the Motown-based Supremes were the number-one American recording group between 1964 and 1967. The vocal trio of Florence Ballard, Diana Ross, and Mary Wilson came from the low-income Brewster housing project in Detroit and rose to international acclaim, enjoying a fantastic rags-to-riches fairy tale. At the height of their fame they sang their blockbuster songs, including "Stop in the Name of Love," to mobs of fans at concert venues worldwide. In those heady days, the girls were featured in fashion magazines, Florence drove a plum-rose Cadillac, and they even had a loaf of bread named after them. The Supremes struck gold.

But in the real world, fairy tales can have unhappy endings, and so it went for Florence, who, in 1967, just as the Supremes reached the peak of their popularity, either quit or was fired from the group, depending upon whose account you believe. Signing away all her rights for only about $100,000, Florence soon lost her home to foreclosure, ballooned to almost 200 pounds, and was living back in the Detroit projects on a $95-per-week stipend from the Aid to Dependent Children program. During that time, she said, "When I go to sleep at night, I have dreams of what it was like when Diana, Mary, and I worked great places like the Copa. Once I had it all. I was Supreme. Now? Now I have nothing."

One evening in February 1976, two months after reconciling with her husband and moving into his home, Florence became alarmed when her hands and feet began to feel numb. She checked into a hospital that night and, at 32, died the next morning of heart failure. Florence now rests at Detroit Memorial Park in Warren, Michigan.

CEMETERY DIRECTIONS: From I-696, take Exit 20 and follow Dequindre Road north for two miles to its intersection with 13 Mile Road. Turn right and the park is a short distance ahead on the right.

GRAVE DIRECTIONS: Florence's marker is inscribed with her given name, Florence Glenda Chapman, and she's in plot Number 564 of Section 14, the lawn immediately on the right, past the flagpole and along the fence.

IRVING BERLIN
MAY 11, 1888 – SEPTEMBER 22, 1989

Irving Berlin set the tone and the tempo for the tunes America played, sang and danced to for much of the 20th century. Interestingly, it was Irving's opinion that there really were only six tunes that existed in the world. Nonetheless, from those six tunes he fashioned a remarkable number of songs (about 1,500) that were by turn romantic, tragic, sentimental, and sophisticated.

His was a classic American success story. His family arrived from Russia penniless when he was five, and three years later his father died. Irving took to selling newspapers to help support his family and this marked the end of his schooling, which totaled less than two years.

Irving married at 24, and his wife died of typhoid fever six months later. To express his grief, he wrote "When I Lost You," which sold more than a million copies. It was like a dam broke when he followed that effort with dozens of standards like "White Christmas," "Always," "Blue Skies," "Puttin' on the Ritz," and "There's No Business Like Show Business." Of course, Irving also wrote America's unofficial national anthem, "God Bless America."

Irving's lack of schooling left him illiterate and, curiously, he could never read or write music; he left it to arrangers to transcribe his melodies. Throughout his long life in the world of music, he never learned to play in any key but F-sharp, and to overcome this limitation he used a specially built piano that had a hand clutch to change keys. It now resides in the Smithsonian Institution.

Irving died in his sleep at 101, at home in Manhattan, just a few miles from the Lower East Side tenement where he had lived while hawking newspapers some 95 years earlier.

He was buried at Woodlawn Cemetery in the Bronx, New York.

CEMETERY DIRECTIONS: Woodlawn is located at 233rd Street and Webster Avenue, immediately off the Bronx River Expressway's 233rd Street exit.

GRAVE DIRECTIONS: Woodlawn Cemetery is enormous, with 350,000 guests on 400 acres. Stop at the booth at the front gate and get a map. Then follow the dashed line painted in the road to its intersection with Prospect Avenue. Turn left on Prospect Avenue and then, at the next intersection (Walnut Avenue), you'll see the mausoleum of a James Hill on the right. Irving's grave is a flat stone just left of the Hill mausoleum.

LEONARD BERNSTEIN
AUGUST 25, 1918 – OCTOBER 14, 1990

K nown as a conductor, composer, pianist, author, and teacher, Leonard Bernstein was the first American musician to achieve worldwide recognition. He entered Harvard at age seventeen, was later a Tanglewood protégé of Koussevitsky, and in 1943 made a sensation when—at 25 years old—he stepped in to conduct the New York Philharmonic at a moment's notice. With his engaging personality and flamboyant conducting style, Leonard Bernstein became a household name and his association with the Philharmonic—he was the orchestra's music director from 1958 to 1969—lasted to the end of his life.

In 1957, his blockbuster musical *West Side Story* debuted, becoming an Academy Award-winning motion picture a few years later. In 1983, Leonard was crowned an honorary member of the Vienna Philharmonic. Recognition and acceptance by the Viennese, where Romanticism had reached its apogee, confirmed his status as a true master and not a flamboyant showman.

At 72, Leonard died of a heart attack. He was buried at Greenwood Cemetery in Brooklyn, New York.

CEMETERY DIRECTIONS: The main entrance to Greenwood is at the intersection of 5th Avenue and 25th Street, and can be reached easily by exiting the Prospect Expressway at either Exit 2 or Exit 3.

GRAVE DIRECTIONS: Enter through the cemetery's elaborate gates, bear left up Battle Avenue, and proceed up the hill. When you get to the intersection of Battle and Fern avenues, park your car and walk up the stairs on the left. Proceed along the stone path to the left of the monument, then turn right at the next path, which is Liberty Path. Fifty feet along Liberty Path, on the right, is the Bernstein plot.

VICTOR BORGE
JANUARY 3, 1909 – DECEMBER 23, 2000

H ailed as a child prodigy in his native Denmark, Victor Borge started his 75-year music career as a classical pianist. But as a talent for making the audience laugh emerged, his act developed into a crazy blend of music and madcap humor, and by his early 20s, Victor was a leading film and stage personality in Scandinavia. His anti-Nazi barbs earned him a spot on Hitler's blacklist, and it was only by chance that he got on the last American passenger ship to leave Northern Europe in 1940.

Stateside, after learning English by watching B movies, he polished his show in venues ranging from nightclubs to concert halls to Carnegie Hall. Victor's act—lauded for the screwball humor he admitted was born of stage fright and tinged with a disdain for the pomposity of many concert musicians—was more remarkable for his seemingly effortless skill as a musician. Able to read and play musical scores backward, forward, and upside down, he appeared with the world's most acclaimed orchestras and averaged 100 performances a year well into his 80s.

Victor Borge died at home in his sleep at 91. He is buried at Putnam Cemetery in Greenwich, Connecticut.

CEMETERY DIRECTIONS: From the Merritt Parkway, take exit 31 and proceed southbound on North Street for three miles. Turn right at the light onto Parsonage Road and the cemetery is a short distance ahead on the right.

GRAVE DIRECTIONS: Enter the cemetery and, just after the office, the road will split into three. Stay on the middle road and, after a hundred yards, stop at the Finney mausoleum on your left. Walk down the grassy slope on your right and you'll see a sculpture of a mermaid atop a boulder. The Borge name is inscribed nowhere on the boulder, but this is the Borge plot.

CAB CALLOWAY
DECEMBER 25, 1907 – NOVEMBER 17, 1994

Involved in show business from an early age, vocalist Cab Calloway worked with a big band, the Missourians, during the 1920s. Although the band consisted of proficient musicians, Cab's flamboyant leadership attracted the most attention; he dressed outlandishly as the eye-catching "man in the zoot suit with the reet pleats," his outfit consisting of a knee-length drape jacket, voluminous trousers, wide-brimmed hat, and a floor-trailing watch chain. Alternately peppering his "singing" with hip phraseology and nonsensical lyrics, including his "hi-de-hi" catch phrase, Cab in a short time became the band's leader. He renamed the act Cab Calloway and his Orchestra, and in 1931 it replaced Duke Ellington's orchestra at the Cotton Club. In that year Cab also recorded "Minnie the Moocher," a song that would remain his theme for his entire life.

With the end of the big band era, Cab reluctantly broke up his orchestra in 1948, but his career didn't end. As far back as 1932 Cab had acted in movies and, once he was free of the band, Cab further promoted himself in that direction, appearing in films such as *The Cincinnati Kid* and *St. Louis Blues*. In the 1950s he toured the world with a production of *Porgy and Bess* as the character Sportin' Life; according to Cab, George Gershwin had modeled the character after him in the first place. In 1980 he reached an entirely new audience when he became known to the college crowd as the "Hi-de-hi-de-hi-de-ho" singer in the movie, *The Blues Brothers*.

Later in his life, when Cab was asked who his heroes were in the music business, he scoffed, "My heroes are the notes, man. You understand what I'm saying? I love the music. The music is my hero."

Cab suffered a stroke in June 1994 and died five months later at 86. He was cremated and his ashes given to his wife, Nuffie, who keeps them in her room at a Delaware retirement home.

KAREN CARPENTER
MARCH 2, 1950 – FEBRUARY 4, 1983

During the 1970s, silky-voiced Karen Carpenter and brother Richard comprised their own soft-rock group, the Carpenters, which proved to be a can't-miss, hit-making association. Their light, airy melodies were in direct contrast to much of the day's gaudy rock. While many of the musicians who ridiculed them have been mostly forgotten, the Carpenters' meticulously crafted singles have stood the test of time.

Early on Karen was a drummer, but it soon became obvious that her talent was in vocals, and she began to focus on singing. Her rich alto would become the hallmark of the Carpenters' sound. Richard described their emerging style as "a choral approach to pop," and they created almost two dozen hit singles including, "Yesterday Once More," "Close to You," and "We've Only Just Begun," the last becoming a popular choice for post-hippie weddings.

By the late 1970s, though, the Carpenters were disintegrating from within; Richard was often strung out on a variety of methamphetamines while Karen was short-tempered and constantly fatigued. Finally, at a November 1978 show in Las Vegas, Richard announced that the Carpenters planned an extended hiatus from touring. In fact, that engagement proved to be their last.

Karen's mysterious fatigue turned out to be caused by self-induced starvation; she suffered from anorexia nervosa. Over the next few years, her attempts to control the disease sent her body on a roller-coaster ride; psychological counseling would help her to gain a healthy amount of weight, but soon she'd be secretly fasting again. In February 1983 it seemed that Karen had finally turned the corner for good; she weighed 110 pounds and seemed to have reached a mental balance, as well. But though her body looked well, it had been malnourished for almost a decade.

One evening, Karen went to a Bob's Big Boy restaurant with her mother and enjoyed a shrimp salad. Upon returning to her mother's home, she complained of being tired and retreated to her old bedroom where she ended up spending the night. The next morning, Karen's mother heard her get out of bed and open her closet door. When Karen failed to come downstairs, her mother went up to the room and found Karen on the floor of her walk-in closet, eyes rolled back, not breathing. At 32, Karen was dead of heart failure.

She rests at Forest Lawn Memorial Park in Cypress, California.

CEMETERY DIRECTIONS: From Highway 91, take Carmenita Road south, turn west onto Lincoln Avenue and Forest Lawn Park is a mile ahead on the right.

GRAVE DIRECTIONS: Go through the main gate, turn right, and drive up to the Ascension Mausoleum. Park in front and enter through the glass doors on the left. Turn left at the first hall, which is the Sanctuary of Compassion, and the beautiful Carpenter crypt is at the end.

When the money started rolling in, Karen and Richard invested some of it in real estate. They bought two apartment buildings in their hometown of Downey, California, and named them Close to You and Only Just Begun. The buildings still retain those names, and you can see them at 8356 Fifth St.

Though neither graduated, Richard and Karen honed their music skills at the University of California in Long Beach. In 1994 the Carpenter Performing Arts Center opened there and it houses a small but interesting Carpenters museum.

PATSY CLINE
SEPTEMBER 8, 1932 – MARCH 5, 1963

After her sophomore year, Virginia Hensley left high school to work the food counter at a Greyhound bus terminal and help support her dirt-poor Appalachian family. At local beer joints "Patsy" entertained as a singer in honky-tonk bands, and in 1954 the newly married Patsy Cline was invited onto the *Town and Country* radio program. The appearance led to her first single, "It Wasn't God Who Made Honky-Tonk Angels," which in turn led to a series of 1957 appearances on the *Arthur Godfrey Talent Show.*

Persuaded to drop her cowgirl attire for a more courtly cocktail dress, Patsy delivered her own heart-stopping rendition of "Walkin' After Midnight" during her first appearance on Godfrey's show. That performance won her a record deal, and by 1960 Patsy was a permanent member of the Grand Ole Opry. She enjoyed success with the chart-topping hit "I Fall to Pieces," but it was "Crazy," a song penned by Willie Nelson, that became Patsy's signature tune. By 1962 Patsy was a certified star, having made landmark appearances in Las Vegas, Hawaii, and at Carnegie Hall.

After a March 1963 concert in Kansas City, Patsy and fellow Opry stars Cowboy Copas and Hawkshaw Hawkins were stranded by a storm that grounded all flights. After almost two days, the weather finally cleared, they boarded their manager's Piper Comanche, and, after a couple hours, stopped for fuel in Dyersburg, Tennessee. But in traveling east, they'd caught up with the same front that had plagued them in Kansas City. Pilot and manager Randy Hughes was emboldened by the uneventful flight he'd just completed and, though he didn't have his instrument-flying certification, he rounded up his passengers and took off eastward again. Caught in a thunderstorm 60 miles out, the plane plunged to earth, and all aboard were lost.

At 30, Patsy was buried at Shenandoah Memorial Park in Winchester, Virginia.

Ten years later, Patsy was elected to the Country Music Hall of Fame, its first female solo artist.

CEMETERY DIRECTIONS: From I-81, take Exit 313A to Route 522 south, and the park is two miles ahead on the right.

GRAVE DIRECTIONS: Turn into the park at the first pair of brick pillars, then turn at the next right, toward the office. Stop after 80 feet and, on the right, you'll see a square, concrete pad; on the left is a stone bench. Patsy's grave is just to the left of this bench. There is also a bell tower erected in her memory at the park.

In 1996, a stone memorial with the names of those lost in the crash was installed at the accident site in Camden, Tennessee. About three miles north of town on Mt. Carmel Road is a sign directing the way to the monument.

NAT KING COLE

MARCH 17, 1919 – FEBRUARY 15, 1965

As is the case of many African American musicians, Nat King Cole's early training came through gospel singing at church and hymns learned on a piano. By sixteen, he was an up-and-comer on the Chicago jazz scene known for his versatility on the piano; outside of his father's church, he'd never sung a note. A couple years later, in 1938, Nat landed in Los Angeles and formed the first of the Nat King Cole trios, soon becoming renowned as a swing pianist.

By 1940 the school-boyish Nat had gained confidence in his own singing, and he developed into an outright crooner; in 1944 his trio had their first major hit with "Straighten Up and Fly Right," and, as it received heavy rotation on the radio, Nat began de-emphasizing his piano. By 1950, thanks in part to the success of his landmark recordings of "The Christmas Song" and "Mona Lisa," his smooth vocal style eclipsed his exemplary piano talents, and Nat emerged as one of the day's most celebrated pop artists.

Not everyone was enamored of Nat's success, though, and the ugly issue of race confronted the crooner. A 1954 concert in Birmingham was ended early by a group of Ku Klux Klan members. Later, as Nat mulled the purchase of a beautiful Hollywood home, an uptight community committee moved to block the sale. Telling Nat they didn't want any undesirables in the neighborhood, he famously replied, "If any move in, I'll let you know." Ultimately, restrictive covenants excluding home sales to Jews and Negroes were removed by the courts.

But in 1957, consistent with the civil rights movement that had begun to roil the nation, the issue reached a boiling point when Nat launched his own television program, *The Nat King Cole Show* on NBC, the first to feature a black host. The show became one of the most popular shows of the time, but not solely for its entertainment value; too, it was a social experiment. Black viewers who were starved for positive television images flocked to the program even as the urbane and elegant Nat was cherished by white viewers. But affiliate Southern stations would not carry the show and, with the deepening racial tensions of the 1950s, it became increasingly difficult to attract corporate sponsors. After Nat outraged some white viewers by touching the arm of a white female guest, the show was cancelled in 1958.

A heavy smoker, Nat's velvet voice and his health deteriorated rapidly in the early 1960s. At 45 he died of lung cancer. At his funeral, Jack Benny offered this epitaph: "Sometimes death is not as tragic as not knowing how to live. This man knew how to live and how to make others glad they were living."

Nat rests at Forest Lawn Memorial Park in Glendale, California.

CEMETERY DIRECTIONS: From Highway 2, exit at San Fernando Road and follow it 1¼ miles north to Glendale Avenue. Make a right and the cemetery entrance is on the right. Stop at the booth for a map of the cemetery's roads, then drive to the Freedom Mausoleum.

GRAVE DIRECTIONS: Walk in the front entrance of the Freedom Mausoleum, proceed down the hall on the right, then turn left into the Sanctuary of Heritage. On the right, along the top row, is Nat's crypt.

In 1991, Natalie Cole won a Grammy for her album *Unforgettable With Love*, a collection in which she covered her father's songs. Millions watched as she sang a touching duet with Nat on kinescope.

JOHN COLTRANE
SEPTEMBER 23, 1926 – JULY 17, 1967

After apprenticeships with the likes of Miles Davis and Dizzy Gillespie, John Coltrane secured his own lofty jazz throne as bandleader, composer, and improviser by the late 1950s. In the early 1960s, he skyrocketed to commercial success with the release of his signature albums *Giant Steps* and *My Favorite Things*, classics

of modern jazz. By the mid-sixties, John was exploring new territories of free jazz and collective improvisation, and even introduced his interest in Eastern music to the scene.

But the ride to success was bumpy and, for a time, it seemed that John's personal troubles would derail his career. Those concerns were realized when Miles Davis, who had already beaten his own heroin addiction, fired John in 1956 for his assorted dependencies. But with the support of his Christian mother and his Muslim wife, John experienced a spiritual awakening the next year and he quit doing drugs. Still, though, John's personal life contrasted with his professional good fortune; in 1959 he lost his front teeth due to the residual effects of his heroin addiction, in 1964 he was agitated by a divorce that was prompted by him twice impregnating pianist Alice McLeod (who would later become his second wife), and, in 1965, John began a struggle to control his weight.

In 1967, John and Alice were living on Long Island with their three children, but John was not well; his weight problem was worse than ever and he was nagged by a constant pain in his side. After a trip to Japan he collapsed on his porch from the pain, which had become unbearably acute. At the hospital it was discovered that a tumor had attached itself to his grossly cirrhotic liver, and three weeks later, John was dead.

At 40, John was buried at Pinelawn Memorial Park in Farmingdale, New York.

CEMETERY DIRECTIONS: Take Exit 39 off I-495, follow Pinelawn Avenue for two miles, and the park is on the left. (Note: In this area there are nine different cemeteries that border each other. Make sure you turn into the correct one.)

GRAVE DIRECTIONS: Enter the park at the main entrance, which is William H. Locke Drive. Turn at the second left after the office onto Walt Whitman Drive, then turn at the second right onto Oak Drive. After a hundred yards, park at the turnout on the right. Across the drive is a brick wall, and John's grave is 24 rows beyond the wall.

PERRY COMO
MAY 18, 1912 – MAY 12, 2001

As a twenty-year-old barber, Italian-American Pierno Como grew tired of cutting the hair of western Pennsylvania coal miners, and instead struck out for Cleveland, where he had an offer to sing with a big band of the day. After the orchestra broke up in 1942, the young and charming Perry showcased his melodic baritone as the host of a regional radio show, *Supper Club*, which attracted recording executives from every label.

Perry began recording, and his watershed came in 1945 when his dreamy rendition of "Till the End of Time" from the film *A Song to Remember* spent ten weeks at the top of the charts, making it the biggest hit of the year. Confessing that his relaxed style was a direct emulation of Bing Crosby, Perry competed with his mentor for recognition as the era's top crooner, and his songs became a mainstay of radio and jukeboxes. But throughout his life, he was never particularly impressed with his own success, and in fact seemed surprised by it. "I don't have a lot to tell the average interviewer. I've done nothing that I can call exciting. I was a barber. After that I've been a singer. That's it."

In 1948, Perry crossed over to the emerging medium of television with the *Chesterfield Supper Club*, one of the earliest variety programs. Perpetually tanned and bedecked in cardigan sweaters, the youthful-looking Perry soon switched networks for his own *Perry Como Show*. Perry later began to indulge in lighter novelty fare, the titles often comprising nonsense words like "Bibbidi-Bobbidi-Boo" and "Hot Diggity Dog Ziggity Boom." These songs cemented Perry's reputation as a king of middle-of-the-road pop. To his credit, Perry openly disdained the lightweight numbers but good-naturedly patronized audiences by continuing to perform them.

By 1960, as rock and rollers crowded out screaming bobby-soxers, the appeal of Perry's breezy songs began to wane. In 1963 he gave up his regular television show and retreated to gala appearances and Christmas specials. But he returned in 1970 with a world tour, and his single "It's Impossible" made it to the top ten. Still, his ultra-mellow stage manner clashed with the day's popular music and he became an obvious target for critics. Perry's resurgence was short-lived.

In 1974, he retired to Florida with his wife of more than 60 years. One Friday afternoon, after sharing ice cream with his daughter and grandson, Perry went for a nap and died of natural causes at 88.

Perry is buried at Riverside Memorial Park in Tequesta, Florida.

CEMETERY DIRECTIONS: The park is located on the northbound side of Highway 1, about 1½ miles north of its intersection with Route 706.

GRAVE DIRECTIONS: Enter the cemetery and turn left at the flagpole. Past the two mausoleum buildings there is a section of upright granite headstones on the right, and that's where you'll find Perry. His stone is nearly at the halfway mark, and not far from the road.

FAMILY TREE

HARRY "BING"
CROSBY

PERRY COMO

"TENNESSEE"
ERNIE FORD

MEL TORME

NAT KING COLE

CROONERS

HARRY "BING" CROSBY

MAY 2, 1901 – OCTOBER 14, 1977

Harry Crosby's lifelong moniker, Bing, was adopted from a popular comic strip he enjoyed as a child, *Bingville Bugle*.

During the 1920s when lung power and projection were important to pop singers, Bing developed a nightclub act with a piano player, and became one of the earliest performers to take advantage of electronic amplification. Relying on a microphone to carry his subtle inflections, Bing's apparent informality and almost conversational, fireside style tugged heartstrings. His croonings were a welcome reprieve for audiences suffering the blues during the Depression and, while World War II raged, his renditions of "Silent Night" and "White Christmas" conveyed the sorrows resulting from the war's separation of loved ones more poignantly than any other pieces of music.

Soon Bing was a box-office attraction, too. He appeared in more than 60 motion pictures, and among his most popular features were his "road" movies with Bob Hope, *The Road to Singapore* and *The Road to Zanzibar*, among others. In 1944 Bing even won an Oscar for his role as a priest in *Going My Way*. Since he was still recording and performing—he recorded some 1,600 songs in his lifetime—Bing was at this time easily the number-one star in show business. By the 1960s, though, Bing's brilliant career wound down as ballads gave way to rock and roll, the tastes of movie audiences changed, and the younger generation moved in.

As one of the best-paid entertainers in the country, Bing was also one of the shrewdest. Over the years he invested his show business fortune and amassed an even greater fortune through a wide range of business interests in everything from frozen orange juice to oil wells, from cattle and race horses to prizefighters, and from professional baseball and hockey teams to banks.

By the 1970s, Bing's health was a bit shaky; a tumor was removed from his lung in 1973, and he was later hospitalized for a month after falling headfirst into an orchestra pit. After a two-week engagement at the London Palladium, Bing, an expert golfer, traveled to Spain to play La Morajela golf course near Madrid. After scoring an 85 and defeating two Spanish pros, Bing sauntered toward the clubhouse and collapsed from a massive heart attack.

Like many of his contemporaries, throughout his professional life Bing conveniently adjusted his date of birth by a few years. He was 76 when buried at Holy Cross Cemetery in Culver City, California, not 72 or 73 as he'd led most to believe.

CEMETERY DIRECTIONS: From I-405, follow Slauson Avenue east for a half-mile and the cemetery is on the left at #5835.

GRAVE DIRECTIONS: Enter the cemetery, turn left and start up the hill. One hundred yards to the left is the Grotto lawn and altar, and four rows from the altar is Bing's grave.

MILES DAVIS

MAY 25, 1926 – SEPTEMBER 28, 1991

Fiercely independent throughout a four-plus decade jazz career, trumpeter Miles Davis followed no one. He came of age in the bebop era but refused to settle into one style. Every few years Miles created a new format, each one instigating a new round of short-lived negative critical reaction. Over the course of his 45 years in jazz, Miles' playing fell into five distinct, sometimes overlapping phases: bebop (1945–1948), cool jazz (1949–1958), hard bop (1952–1963), modal (1958–1968), and electric or fusion (1969–1991).

Generally, Miles definitively declared his new phases with land-mark works including *The Birth of the Cool* in 1949, *Milestones* in 1958, and *Bitches Brew* in 1969. This last work became the standard for the nascent jazz-fusion movement, and was an especially impor-tant milestone because its abrupt commingling of jazz, rock, and funk (not to mention its freaky cover art) crossed over to rock audiences; Miles was "discovered" by a new, far-out generation. In the first five years of the 1970s he leaned toward rock, was overtly influenced by Jimi Hendrix, and even shared a bill with the Grateful Dead.

Although he had created yet another musical genre, Miles left it, and everything he had created before, in 1975 when he dropped out of music and went into retirement for five years. His battles against heroin and alcohol addiction, his unmerciful quest for per-fection, and a relentless touring schedule had taken their tolls on his health, and Miles suffered from ulcers, throat nodes, and bursi-tis. He claimed not to have touched his trumpet even once in those years. But as fusion sputtered in the early 1980s, Miles emerged again to return to an approach that was successful during the 1950s bop years, bravely embracing and reinterpreting popular songs. In Cyndi Lauper's "Time After Time" and Michael Jackson's "Human Nature," Miles reminded audiences that his piercing sound, more than any voice, could touch the soul.

After a variety of health problems, Miles died of respiratory fail-ure at 65 and was buried at Woodlawn Cemetery in the Bronx, New York.

CEMETERY DIRECTIONS: Woodlawn is located at 233rd Street and Webster Avenue immediately off the Bronx River Expressway's 233rd Street exit.

GRAVE DIRECTIONS: Woodlawn Cemetery is enormous with 350,000 guests on 400 acres. If there's someone in the booth at the front gate, stop and get a map. Otherwise, just proceed past the booth and keep the fence on your left. At Robin Avenue turn right, merge onto Knollwood, then turn left onto Heather Avenue. Miles is in the Alpine Section along Heather Avenue. You won't miss his stone adjacent to Duke Ellington's.

JOHN DENVER

DECEMBER 31, 1943 – OCTOBER 12, 1997

A folk-pop balladeer with a breezy voice and an almost childlike love of nature, Henry John Deutschendorf, Jr., better known as John Denver, earned international acclaim as a singer, songwriter, and humanitarian. John's first big break came in 1967 while making the rounds on the lonely folk nightclub scene; Peter, Paul, and Mary took one of his singles, "Leaving on a Jet Plane," and turned it into a number one hit. John's songwriting abilities soon became obvious to music companies, he secured a record deal, and over the next decade was a *Billboard* mainstay for such hits as "Rocky Mountain High," "Country Roads," and "Sunshine on My Shoulders."

With his wholesome good looks, hippie-ish wire-rimmed glasses and aw-shucks disposition, John was a natural star of the television era and there became a fixture, harmonizing with everyone from George Burns to Kermit the Frog to Jacques Cousteau.

John's musical passions provided him the monetary means to pursue another of his passions: flying. By 1997 John was a very experienced pilot and had turned from traditional Cessnas to more esoteric craft, including an experimental, fiberglass aircraft called the Long EZ. This plane had a fuel selection valve located inside the cockpit that allowed the pilot the choice of drawing fuel from either the left or right tanks. However, the valve was located behind the pilot's left shoulder, and the only way to manipulate it was for the pilot to release the flight controls, twist around to the left, and turn the valve with his right hand. Further, in order to twist around, it was necessary for the pilot to brace his right foot, which was very difficult to accomplish without pressing the right rudder pedal all the way to the floor.

On a Sunday afternoon, John practiced touch-and-go landings with his new Long EZ at Monterey Airport in California. After accomplishing a few go-rounds, he went for a spin down the coast. Minutes later, at an altitude of only 500 feet, the engine of his plane started sputtering, starved for fuel. As John reached around to turn the fuel valve, his foot pressed on the right rudder, the plane rolled to the right, and within three seconds it obliterated itself in a full-speed nosedive into the choppy Pacific waters.

What remains could be recovered were cremated, and John's ashes were scattered at his ranch in his adopted hometown of Aspen, Colorado. He was 53.

ARTHUR FIEDLER

DECEMBER 17, 1894 – JULY 10, 1979

In 1885 the founder of the Boston Symphony Orchestra decided the orchestra's activity should extend into the summer with concerts for the masses presented at popular prices. The annual series took off, and this group, consisting of the big orchestra minus about a dozen first-chair players, came to be known as the Pops.

Arthur became conductor of the Boston Pops in 1930 and presided for exactly 50 seasons. Often portrayed as a Mr. Pops in funny costumes, thumbing his nose at "serious" music, he added novelties and lighter pieces from the realm of folk music, Broadway musicals, the popular songbook, and even advertising jingles. Fiedler became a national figure, and under his direction the Boston Pops recorded more than any other orchestra in the world.

Arthur died of natural causes at 84 and was buried in his wife's family plot at Saint Joseph's Cemetery in West Roxbury, Massachusetts.

CEMETERY DIRECTIONS: From I-95, take Exit 20A, follow Route 9 east for 3½ miles, then turn right onto Hammond Street. After a mile, go straight through the traffic circle and Hammond Street becomes Lagrange Street. After another mile, the cemetery is on the right.

GRAVE DIRECTIONS: Enter the cemetery, turn left after the office, then take the next right. Go over two speed bumps and continue straight through the intersections. When the road starts up a hill and bends to the right, stop at the statue on your left. This is the Kenney/Bottomley plot, and it's where you'll find Arthur's marker.

ELLA FITZGERALD
APRIL 25, 1918 – JUNE 16, 1996

Sliding effortlessly from bebop to ballad and employing endlessly inventive vocal improvisations over three full octaves, Ella Fitzgerald thrilled audiences on her way to becoming the preeminent jazz singer of her generation.

A 1938 swing version of the classic nursery rhyme "A-Tisket, A-Tasket" became her first hit recording and made her a national star but, by the forties, Ella had already moved to "scat" singing, a form based on the complex and spontaneous instrumental style of Dizzy Gillespie's band. The war years were spent with various road shows and, in 1955, signing with the Verve record label, she recorded a series of "songbook" albums, each devoted to the work of a particular composer. These recordings are generally regarded as her best work.

In the sixties, Ella attempted to broaden her range into pop recordings, releasing a country album and a record of Christmas music. She returned to jazz in the seventies, but this era marked the decline of her beautiful voice and of her health. She experienced eyesight problems and other ailments, complicated by the diabetes that would require the amputation of her lower legs in 1992.

By the end of her career, Ella had recorded over 2,000 songs, sold some 40 million albums, and won 13 Grammy Awards.

Ella died of complications from diabetes at 79 and is buried at Inglewood Park Cemetery in Inglewood, California.

CEMETERY DIRECTIONS: From I-405, exit at La Tijera Boulevard and head east. After a half-mile turn right onto Centinella Avenue and follow it to Florence Avenue. Turn left and the cemetery is a half-mile on the right at #720.

GRAVE DIRECTIONS: Enter the park and turn right. The Sunset Mission Mausoleum is 200 feet ahead on the right. Walk in the entrance on the front right and proceed down the Sanctuary of El Sereno hall. Go up the stairs and turn left at the top. This is the Sanctuary of Bells, and Ella's crypt is on the right, second row from the bottom.

"TENNESSEE" ERNIE FORD

FEBRUARY 13, 1919 – OCTOBER 17, 1991

Tennessee Ernie Ford has sold more than 60 million records since his first 1949 release, but even more astonishing is that some 40 million of those feature gospel songs, hymns, and spirituals; his first album of inspirational music, entitled simply *Hymns*, remained on the album charts for an unbelievable 277 consecutive weeks. Ernie's voice also graces the classic version of that timeless anthem for the working man, "Sixteen Tons," and his 1955 country hit, "The Ballad of Davy Crockett."

From 1956 to 1965, Tennessee hosted his own television variety show, *The Ford Show*, and with a natural and unaffected charm turned it into a required stop for celebrities. But one simple element separated it from all other shows; he closed each week with a hymn, a spiritual, or a song of faith. For the time, it was a bold statement for a popular entertainer of Tennessee's stature, and the network initially objected. But Tennessee persisted and the audience loved it.

In October of 1991, after attending a state dinner at the White House with President and Mrs. George H.W. Bush, Ernie fell ill while en route to Dulles International Airport. Later, with his sons at his side, he passed away of liver disease at 72.

He was buried at Alto Mesa Cemetery in Palo Alto, California.

CEMETERY DIRECTIONS: From Highway 101, take the exit for San Antonio Road south and, after a quarter mile, turn right onto East Charleston Street. Stay on East Charleston Street—you'll notice after 1½ miles that its name changes to Arastradero Road—then, after another three-fourths of a mile, the cemetery is on the left.

GRAVE DIRECTIONS: Enter the cemetery and, about a hundred yards past the office, the drive splits into a "Y." In the crook of that "Y" is a semicircular lawn with a single small tree in its middle, and Tennessee's cremated remains are buried there. You'll find his marker in the eighth row from the center, at approximately the twelve o'clock position.

ANDY GIBB

MARCH 5, 1958 – MARCH 10, 1988

On the heels of his Bee Gee brothers' *Saturday Night Fever* success, Andy Gibb secured a recording contract. Consequently (for a little while, anyway), Australians dominated the pop music charts, as Andy matched, and then eclipsed, his siblings' star power as a teen heartthrob in his own right.

Andy's success rested on the strength of three quasi-disco singles, "I Just Want to Be Your Everything," "Thicker Than Water," and "Shadow Dancing," but in the fiercely fickle arena of pubescent daydream pinups, his popularity promptly plummeted, and Andy was relegated to hosting *Solid Gold* and guesting on sitcoms like *Punky Brewster*.

By 1986, Andy's life was in free fall; he was divorced, Victoria Principal had ended a romance with him, and cocaine addiction was taking a physical toll. At 30, Andy died in England from myocarditis, an inflammation of the heart muscle caused by viral infection, and he was buried at Forest Lawn Memorial Park in Hollywood Hills, California.

CEMETERY DIRECTIONS: From Highway 134, which is the connector between Highway 101 and I-210, take the Forest Lawn Drive exit. Proceed west for a mile and the park's entrance will be on the left.

GRAVE DIRECTIONS: Get a map at the information booth and proceed to the Courts of Remembrance. Park along Ascension Road, adjacent to the Serenity lawn section, and walk across the grass to the outside crypts on the left. Andy's crypt is in the second row from the bottom, number 2534.

DIZZY GILLESPIE

OCTOBER 21, 1917 – JANUARY 6, 1993

Jazz trumpeter John Birks "Dizzy" Gillespie set new standards for horn players as a prime architect of the 1940s movement from swing to bebop. As an arranger and composer, Dizzy wrote some of the greatest jazz tunes of his era, including "Groovin' High" and "A Night in Tunisia," and later, his interest in Cuban and African music helped introduce that music to a mainstream American audience. But despite his contributions to the art, Dizzy is best remembered for his zany antics; it was no accident that he was nicknamed "Dizzy," a moniker inspired by his "happy clown" personality.

As a kid, Dizzy had first been interested in the trombone, but he gave it up after realizing his arms were too short to play it well. By 1935, eighteen-year-old Dizzy was an up-and-coming jazz figure known for his high-spirited disposition. His antics even got him fired once: In 1941, the equally silly, zoot-suited, bandleader Cab Calloway, never one to appreciate being upstaged, canned Dizzy for his excessive showmanship after Dizzy "just nicked" Calloway's posterior with a knife during a performance. It took ten stitches to close the "nick." (The two jokers later reconciled.)

In 1953 Dizzy's stage appearance, which already featured black horn-rimmed glasses and a beret, was further peculiarized by his instrument itself, its bell bent at a heavenward 45-degree angle. The bend in his horn was originally accidental, caused by another musician falling on his trumpet during an episode of backstage roughhousing. Without another instrument available, Dizzy went onstage with his bent trumpet and was happy to find that he could hit some notes a little softer due to its slightly restricted airway. A trumpet manufacturer began bending Dizzy's trumpet bells upward and that, along with his impossibly bulbous cheeks, became his visual trademark.

In 1956 Dizzy became bandleader for a state department jazz band that made goodwill and diplomatic performances on tours of the Middle East and South America. Upon his return to America, he recorded and toured as a leader of various combos and appeared occasionally in all-star groups with other bebop legends. Dizzy's clean lifestyle and good audience rapport was rewarded, and in his final years he basked in high regard as one of the true elder statesmen of jazz.

After a bout with pancreatic cancer, Dizzy died at 75 and was buried at Flushing Cemetery in Queens, New York.

CEMETERY DIRECTIONS: From I-495, take Exit 25 and follow Utopia Parkway north for a half-mile to Pigeon Meadow Road. Turn left on Pigeon Meadow and, after a mile, it will intersect with 46th Avenue, where you'll make a right turn into the cemetery.

GRAVE DIRECTIONS: Enter the cemetery, bear left and stay left all the way to the back of the cemetery. At Section 30, look for the "Tassa" stone on your left, next to the curb. Dizzy lies 150 feet behind the Tassa stone, four rows from the back fence. His plot is number 1252.

BENNY GOODMAN

MAY 9, 1909 – JUNE 13, 1986

Struggling to raise a family of eleven on sweatshop wages in Chicago's impoverished Jewish ghetto, Benny Goodman's father believed music might be a ticket out of poverty for his eldest sons. He enrolled them in the free music classes that were offered at a local synagogue when Benny was just ten and, as his older brothers were given a tuba and a trombone, little Benny was handed a clarinet. He hardly let go of it for the rest of his life.

Benny dropped from school at fifteen to establish himself as a professional musician and, by seventeen, was a member of the Ben Pollack Orchestra in Los Angeles. The Swing era was an exciting time for music in America. A stepchild of jazz, swing was born around 1930 and was characterized by very large, bass-heavy bands whose musicians took alternating solos, in contrast to group improvisation. The rhythms of big band swing jazz quickened the pulse of a generation determined to jitterbug their way through the Depression, and it initiated a culture of defiant dress and "hipster" attitude. Swing's frenzied followers, "bobbysoxers," answered to no one except their own "King of Swing," who by the mid-1930s, was clearly Benny Goodman.

With clarinet in hand, the tall, apple-cheeked Benny and his various bands were greeted with near pandemonium wherever they played. Through swing, Benny led jazz into the commercial mainstream, was the first major bandleader to put black and white musicians together on stage, and even introduced the common man's music to the sanctity of Carnegie Hall, blowing wide its staid walls with a performance whose live recording later became one of the best-selling jazz albums of all time.

But for all its excitement and spirit, swing jazz faded just as quickly as it had come into prominence and, by the 1940s, big bands had been eclipsed by a new jazz form, bebop. Benny formed a small group that performed selected television engagements and toured throughout the 1950s and '60s and his life story, *The Benny Goodman Story*, became a celluloid box office hit in 1955. Compared to his wildest days as the King of Swing, Benny was no longer in great demand, but there was still a place for his music; Benny's last days were spent as a goodwill ambassador at occasional musical engagements.

Tireless in a quest for impeccable music structure, Benny demanded excellence from band members who, at times, wearied of his meticulous temperament. After Benny's death, one of his pianists remarked, "With him, perfection was always just around the corner. I figured Benny would die in bed practicing that damn clarinet." As it turns out, he wasn't too far off. After rehearsing a Brahms sonata for an upcoming performance at Lincoln Center, Benny lay down on his couch and expired of a heart attack in his sleep.

At 77, Benny was buried at Long Ridge Cemetery in Stamford, Connecticut.

CEMETERY DIRECTIONS: From the center of Stamford, follow Route 104 north for five miles. Turn left onto Erskine Road and the cemetery is a short distance on the left.

GRAVE DIRECTIONS: Benny's grave is in the third row from the back, approximately halfway along the cemetery's length. It's marked with a flat stone and a small bench.

WAYLON JENNINGS
JUNE 15, 1937 – FEBRUARY 13, 2002

With long hair, a black hat, and a bearded, scowling face, Waylon Jennings was one of the first musicians to bring real attitude to country music. By the time he came along in the mid-1960s, country had already had its share of rogues, from Hank Williams to Johnny Cash, but Waylon institutionalized the unapologetic swagger and menacing overtones of "Outlaw" country music and helped sow the seeds for the country megastars who would burst onto the scene two decades later.

Having already formed his own band at age twelve, Waylon dropped out of school two years later (he eventually earned his GED at age 51) to pursue an opportunity as a disc jockey. When he was seventeen, Waylon met rising rock-star Buddy Holly at the radio station and the two became fast friends; Buddy produced Waylon's first record. "Mainly what I learned from Buddy," Waylon said, "was an attitude. He loved music, and he taught me that it shouldn't have any barriers to it."

Buddy later employed Waylon as a bass player, taking him on his 1959 Winter Dance Party tour. In Clear Lake, Iowa, an exhausted Buddy chartered a small plane to get to the next gig and invited Waylon to join him, but Waylon gave his seat to J.P. "Big Bopper" Richardson, who was suffering from the flu. The plane crashed soon after takeoff in the early hours of February 3, 1959, killing everyone aboard—Buddy, the Big Bopper, Ritchie Valens, and the pilot. For years, Waylon was haunted by a joking exchange they'd had just before Buddy left to meet the plane. "Buddy says, 'You're not going on the plane tonight, huh?' I said, 'No.' He said, 'Well, I hope your bus freezes up.' And I said, 'Well, I hope your plane crashes.' I was awful young, and it took me a long time to get over that."

By the mid-sixties, Waylon had cultivated an instantly identifiable country-rockabilly style that featured a thudding, walk-all-over-you bass, a "chicken-pickin'" guitar technique, and rough-edged, plain-spoken lyrics. His rowdy image made him almost as famous as his music and, for a while, he shared a Nashville apartment with Johnny Cash after their respective marriages broke up. The pair lived high on methamphetamines and general destruction, and after Johnny remarried and got sober, Waylon complained that he'd "sold out to religion." Waylon also eventually gave up drugs, but he never gave in to religion. Despite his offstage behavior, he became a sought-after club headliner and recorded more than 60 albums and had dozens of hits, including "Walk On Out Of My Mind" and "Are You Sure Hank Done It This Way?"

In the 1980s, the original country-music legends fell from favor as the genre reverted to slick stylings, but Waylon, along with Willie Nelson, Johnny Cash, and Kris Kristofferson, shrewdly formed a superstar quartet and, as the Highwaymen, the musicians found success anew. But Waylon still remained an outlaw, blowing off his induction into the Country Music Hall of Fame. "It means absolutely nothing," he said, "if you want to know the truth."

Waylon was a lifelong sufferer of diabetes and in 2001 had a foot amputated. At 64, he died of the disease and was buried at the City of Mesa Cemetery in Mesa, Arizona.

CEMETERY DIRECTIONS: Take Exit 52 off of Highway 101 and follow University Drive east for 3½ miles to North Center Street. Turn left and the cemetery is a mile on the left.

GRAVE DIRECTIONS: Inside the cemetery, turn left on Ninth Street and stop at the sixth tree on the left. Waylon has no marker as of this writing, but he lies in the fourth row from the curb, alongside a Gertrude Rice.

SCOTT JOPLIN
NOVEMBER 24, 1868 – APRIL 1, 1917

When Scott Joplin settled in St. Louis in 1890 he was just an anonymous pianist, but by the time he left for New York fifteen years later, he'd singlehandedly developed an entirely new musical genre. Scott created the form known as ragtime by blending European classical styles with African American harmonies and rhythms, and by the turn of the century had published 50 compositions in the vein, including "The Ragtime Dance," "The Easy Winners" and "The Entertainer."

In 1905, Scott settled in Harlem in the hope of elevating his new music to greater popularity. Having already successfully incorporated waltz and habanera dance beats into the style, Scott now sought to develop a ragtime opera. By 1910 his opera *Treemonisha* was complete and he turned it over to Irving Berlin for publication, though Berlin rejected it a few months later. The following spring Irving published a new hit song, "Alexander's Ragtime Band," and Scott was shocked to hear that the master Berlin had stolen the song's verse from a section of his own *Treemonisha*. This prompted Scott to alter that section of the opera so he himself couldn't be accused of plagiarizing Berlin, and to publish the opera himself in the summer of 1911.

Unfortunately, there was no interest in Scott's opera. He was never able to raise any funds for the production of his masterpiece and he died without his *Treemonisha* ever having been performed. As further insult, within a decade after his 1917 death, Scott and his ragtime music were largely forgotten as a new style of jazz stole center stage. But in 1973, several of Scott's "rags" were selected for the soundtrack of a new movie, *The Sting*, and the film's widespread popularity led to renewed interest in Scott's music. Two years later, in 1975, Scott posthumously received his due when his magnum opus *Treemonisha*, after having lain dormant for more than 60 years, received its first professional production. The following year it won a Pulitzer Prize.

By the time Scott was in his mid-40s he was experiencing the physical and mental effects of tertiary syphilis, a disease he had probably contracted almost two decades earlier. Three months before his death from the affliction he was hospitalized, but was soon transferred to a mental institution where he died at 48, on April 1, 1917.

Scott was buried at Saint Michael's Cemetery in Flushing, Queens, New York.

CEMETERY DIRECTIONS: Take either Exit 3 from the Grand Central Parkway or Exit 41 from I-278, and the cemetery entrance is located between these two ramps at 7202 Astoria Blvd.

GRAVE DIRECTIONS: Enter the cemetery and proceed straight past the office. At the second intersection, on the left corner near the curb, is the flat marker for Scott's grave.

PEGGY LEE

MAY 26, 1920 – JANUARY 21, 2002

Norma Deloris Engstrom grew up milking cows on a North Dakota farm and, after singing with the high school glee club, she made her singing debut on a local radio show. The manager there branded her "Peggy Lee," and she soon began singing with the dance bands of the late-1930s. During a gig at a Palm Springs nightspot, Peggy was unable to shout above the clamor of the audience, so she tried to garner attention by lowering her voice; the softer she sang, the more attentive the audience grew, and that soft and cool style, punctuated by seductive purrs, became her trademark.

In 1941 she was invited to join Benny Goodman's band and the next year, after recording "Why Don't You Do Right?" with the group, Peggy catapulted to fame. By 1944 she had embarked on a solo career, and eventually wrote or collaborated on more than 500 songs. Today, it is common for singers to write their own songs, but in the 1940s, when there was a proliferation of music coming out of Tin Pan Alley, Broadway, and Hollywood, it was not; Peggy was among the first to pen and sing her own songs. In the 1950s, Peggy began making featured appearances in movies and was especially praised for her 1955 role opposite Danny Thomas in *The Jazz Singer*. However, Peggy is best remembered for her sultry simplicity and slow finger-snaps in the song "Fever," released in 1958.

Generations of children were introduced to Peggy's talents via the 1955 Disney animated feature, *Lady and the Tramp*. Peggy provided multiple voices for the film, co-wrote six of its songs, and appeared on the soundtrack, including the cartoon's show-stopper, "He's a Tramp." Peggy had retained all the rights and royalties of her *Tramp* work, but her contract—like the contracts of all performers of the day—didn't cover video residuals, since video technology was unknown in 1955. In 1988, after Disney trotted the feature out in video but failed to pay residuals to Peggy, she sued. In 1991, she won her case against Disney in a landmark decision, prompting hundreds of other performers to claim their own video residuals.

In 1985 Peggy was seriously injured in a Las Vegas fall. Later that year she underwent double-bypass heart surgery and, after suffering a stroke and struggling with worsening diabetes in 1999, Peggy was confined to a wheelchair. At 81, Peggy died of a myocardial infarction and was buried at Westwood Memorial Park in Santa Monica, California.

CEMETERY DIRECTIONS: This little cemetery holds numerous celebrities and is peculiarly located behind the office complex at 10850 Wilshire Blvd., just about a half-mile east of I-405.

GRAVE DIRECTIONS: Enter the cemetery, turn left at the office, then walk into the new Garden of Serenity area adjacent to the chapel. Peggy's remains are interred here, and a bench dedicated to her memory is in front of the triple fountains.

WOLFGANG AMADEUS MOZART

JANUARY 25, 1756 – DECEMBER 5, 1791

Mozart was a celebrated child prodigy who at age six delighted Salzburg audiences with his astounding ability to read difficult music perfectly and play an entire tune from memory after hearing it just once. By age ten he had grown even more accomplished, equal in talent to that of his older contemporaries, and, as a teenager, he outstripped them.

Despite his reputation, Mozart could find no suitable post open to him, so in 1769 he set off for Italy and there produced his first large-scale opera seria, including *Mitridate* and *Lucio Silla* all before the age of eighteen. After prolonged stays in Munich and Paris, Mozart ended up in Vienna at 25, where he would remain for the rest of his life, and there had one of the most prolific careers in the history of music.

In the ten years before his premature death, Mozart's music rapidly grew beyond the comprehension of many of his contemporaries. Through dozens of works including symphonies and chamber music of the highest levels of imagination, he exhibited gifts that few could appreciate. Even more remarkable, Mozart produced his three greatest operas, *Figaro*, *Don Giovanni*, and *Cosi fan Tutte*, during the last three years of his life.

Finally, Mozart began work on what was to be his last project, the *Requiem*. This mass had been commissioned by a benefactor unknown to Mozart, and he became obsessed with the project for, in effect, he was writing it for himself. Ill and exhausted, he managed to finish the first two movements before being confined to his bed, suffering from blinding headaches, skin eruptions, and fainting spells. He finally became partially paralyzed and, after last rites were given, died quietly at only 35. Today it's believed that Mozart died either of rheumatic fever or uremia following chronic kidney disease.

For all his musical genius, Mozart was close to destitute at his time of death, received a third-class funeral, and was buried in a pauper's grave at Saint Marx Cemetery in Vienna, Austria. There's a monument there now, but it was erected in 1859 at the approximate location of his grave.

About ten years after Mozart's death, the area where he was buried was dug up to make room for more burials, and the bones from those graves were crushed to reduce their size. After another hundred years, more or less, the Salzburg Mozarteum was presented with an unusual gift: Mozart's skull. Allegedly, a gravedigger rescued the skull during the "reorganization," and his descendants, finally tired of dusting the knick-knack, decided to let others enjoy it, too. It's still on display there, but there's no evidence that it's really the master's.

KATE SMITH
MAY 1, 1909 – JUNE 17, 1986

After achieving success on Broadway and in vaudeville, Kate Smith, "the Songbird of the South" made her radio debut in 1931 and, within a few years, had two shows of her own. *The Kate Smith Hour* was a weekly variety show that featured her perfectly pitched singing and new talent acts (including Abbott & Costello), while her number one daytime radio show, *Kate Smith Speaks,* offered news and homespun commentary that eased an emotionally fraught America through some of its most trying historical times. During World War II, Kate's on-air appeals for war bonds yielded contributions topping $600 million.

Kate was enormously popular; she made more than 15,000 radio broadcasts, received more than twenty million fan letters, and sold countless millions of records—and her trademark song, "When the Moon Comes Over the Mountain," itself sold some six million copies. Kate starred in her own movie, *Hello Everybody!* and in 1950 moved her radio program to TV where it stayed, in various incarnations, until 1962.

But despite her long list of accomplishments, Kate Smith will forever be best remembered as the vibrantly brave and passionate singer who made "God Bless America" an unofficial national anthem. Kate introduced the Irving Berlin song to the country in 1938 and, when it became apparent that it had achieved significance beyond that of just another pop tune, she refused to profit from the song, instead donating the royalties from its performances to the Boy and Girl Scouts of America, an arrangement that remains in place. Once, President Roosevelt quite aptly introduced

Kate to England's King George VI by stating, simply, "This is Kate Smith. Miss Smith is America."

Though, in her life, Kate recorded well over 2,000 songs, fittingly, the last song she ever sang publicly was "God Bless America," on a bicentennial special just a few days before the Fourth of July, 1976.

At 77 Kate died of complications brought on by diabetes, and was buried at Saint Agnes Cemetery in North Elba, New York.

CEMETERY DIRECTIONS: North Elba is a village within the town of Lake Placid. From the junction of routes 73 and 86, proceed east on 73 for almost a mile, and Saint Agnes Cemetery is on the left.

GRAVE DIRECTIONS: Enter the cemetery between the stone pillars and turn left at the "T." You won't miss Kate's mausoleum on the back left lawn.

DUSTY SPRINGFIELD
APRIL 16, 1939 – MARCH 2, 1999

In 1960, the soulful British crooner Dusty Springfield was a third of a folksy vocal trio called the Springfields, and on the strength of her sensuously husky voice, the group topped the charts with several singles, the most recognizable of them being "Silver Thread and Golden Needles."

By 1963, the group parted ways, and Dusty, always experimenting, switched over from a simple folk alto to a sultry and intimate white-soul. With a fresh, raw sound of rare passion, towering beehive hairdo, and panda-eye black mascara, she burst back into the limelight releasing a solo album, *A Girl Called Dusty.* In a short time, Dusty was the newest trailblazer of the fickle fashion and music scene that came to be known as "mod."

In 1969 she recorded what's now considered a landmark album, *Dusty in Memphis,* and though its classic single "Son of a Preacher Man" reached the top ten on both sides of the Atlantic, her commercial fortunes were on the decline. Ten years of whirlwind activity had its physical costs, too; her voice was permanently weakened by repeated bouts of laryngitis, and her health had been compromised by substance abuse.

Weary of fame, Dusty retired to California. Apart from a handful of guest-singing contributions and a half-hearted 1978 comeback that attracted little attention, she was musically dormant throughout the remainder of her life, concentrating instead on gay rights and animal protection organizations.

In 1999 Dusty was scheduled to be inducted into the Rock 'N' Roll Hall of Fame but, ten days before the ceremony, she was felled by breast cancer at 59. She was cremated and her ashes remain with her family.

MEL TORME

SEPTEMBER 13, 1925 – JUNE 6, 1999

A long time ago, on a cold, winter night in a Chicago restaurant, four-year-old Mel Torme was bouncing on his father's knee and singing along with the band when the bandleader invited him on stage. Mel was such a hit that he became a regular with the band and soon, every Monday night in exchange for five dollars and dinner for his family, little Mel belted out tunes. In 1933, when Mel was eight, he became a radio actor playing young boys on such programs as *Little Orphan Annie* and *Jack Armstrong, All-American Boy*, until 1941 when his voice changed. At 15, he sang one of his own compositions, "Lament to Love," during an audition with bandleader Harry James, who recorded Mel's song and turned it into a top-ten hit. Barely out of puberty, Mel was a star.

Before joining the Army during World War II, Mel was cast in the film *Higher and Higher*, which also marked the film debut of another budding star, Frank Sinatra. Later came a couple of musicals and stints as a drummer with a few big bands, including Tommy Dorsey's. In 1945, Mel published the best known of his 250 songs, "The Christmas Song," famous for its signature opening, "Chestnuts roasting on an open fire . . . " The tune would become a holiday classic after Nat King Cole added his smooth flair. Though the song took less than an hour to write, it caught on because "it was a series of random Christmas images and impressions that touch everybody in one way or another," Mel said in 1990. "You should see those royalty checks, even now. Whew!"

During the 1950s, the elegant musical traditions that Mel represented were displaced by rock and roll, and as his recording popularity waned, he moved into jazz. In that genre he also earned distinction, and by the end of the decade, Mel, "the Velvet Fog," had parlayed his mellifluous and perfectly articulated vocals into one of the greatest male jazz forces ever.

When the interest in jazz ebbed during the 1960s, Mel pursued other interests. He became musical advisor for *The Judy Garland Show* and wrote episodes of the television series *Run for Your Life* and *The Virginian*. After publishing a biography of his friend, drummer Buddy Rich, Mel organized a benefit to help cover some of Rich's substantial IRS debt.

By the 1970s, jazz was on the rebound and Mel in particular benefited. During the last twenty years of his career, he performed up to 200 live dates annually and released a steady stream of recordings, including *Top Drawer* and *An Evening with George Shearing and Mel Torme*, both of which won Grammy awards. Younger audiences got to know Mel through his guest appearances on the sitcom *Night Court*.

Mel had a few high-profile marriages and, unfortunately, divorces. In 1949 the Velvet Fog wed actress Candy Toxton but, by 1956, he was hitched to Arlene Miles, a model. In 1966 British actress Janette Scott got the nod, but they were done by 1977. After that third divorce, Mel swore he'd never marry again—until Ali Severson came along ten years later.

Mel suffered a stroke in 1998, and his recovery was complicated when he contracted pneumonia the next month, followed by a gastro-intestinal problem. Finally, with Ali and his five children at his side, Mel died at the UCLA Medical Center from the complications of his ailments at 73.

He was buried at Westwood Memorial Park in Santa Monica, California.

CEMETERY DIRECTIONS: This little cemetery holds numerous celebrities and is peculiarly located behind the office complex at 10850 Wilshire Blvd., which is just about a half-mile east of I-405.

GRAVE DIRECTIONS: Enter the cemetery, turn left, and there on the grass you'll see Mel's distinctive tablet, just a few feet from the crypt wall.

CONWAY TWITTY
SEPTEMBER 1, 1933 – JUNE 5, 1993

At five years old, Harold Lloyd Jenkins was playing the guitar. By ten he had formed his own band called "The Phillips Country Ramblers," and during his teens he played honky-tonk joints throughout his native Mississippi. Harold was an athletic talent, as well. But while contemplating an offer to play baseball for the Philadelphia Phillies he was drafted, instead, and he served in the Army during the Korean War.

After his 1956 discharge, he chose to pursue his musical aspirations and, needing an appropriate stage name, settled on Conway Twitty by combining town names from a map.

Conway's first hit, the rockabilly number "It's Only Make Believe," sold a million copies. The hit was closer to pop than country, and Conway tried unsuccessfully to duplicate that effort with a number

ETERNAL COUPLE

CONWAY TWITTY
& TAMMY WYNETTE

of pop ballads in the years following (though his heartthrob period did see him romp through three teenage B movies, including *Sex Kittens Go to College.*)

Conway returned to his country roots in the mid-1960s and, between 1968 and 1977, his heartfelt singing style led to an incredible 30 successive number one singles. Some of those hits were duets with Loretta Lynn, but it's a feat that remains unmatched by any artist anywhere.

Conway also owned a theme park in Nashville, Twitty City, and, through his purchase of a minor-league baseball team, the Nashville Sounds, he kept his athletic interests close. During his lifetime he had been called Harold and Conway, and sometimes "The Best Friend a Song Ever Had," but the most fitting label may have been *Hatako-Chtokchito-A-Yakni-Toloa*—his name as honorary chief of the Choctaw Indian nation, translated as "Great Man of Music."

After a concert in Branson, Missouri, Conway died of an aneurysm during the trip back to his Nashville home. At 59, he was buried at Sunrise Memorial Park in Gallatin, Tennessee.

CEMETERY DIRECTIONS: This cemetery is on the west side of Route 31E, 1½ miles north of Gallatin center.

GRAVE DIRECTIONS: Enter the park and drive to the mausoleum buildings. Conway's tomb is in the bottom row on the left-hand side of the building furthest to the right, and is inscribed with his given name only.

SARAH VAUGHAN
MARCH 27, 1924 – APRIL 3, 1990

As the daughter of two musicians, Sassy Sarah Vaughan was classically trained and thus tended to treat her voice more as an instrument than as a vehicle for lyrics. Negotiating wide leaps within her full-bodied contralto range and making fluid alterations of timbre from a bell-like clarity to a bluesy growl, she set the improvisational world of jazz on its head and carved for herself a secure role in its history.

Through the 1940s, Sarah recorded with many of the jazz greats of the day, including Dizzy Gillespie and Miles Davis, after which record companies clamored for her rights. She subsequently enjoyed her own recording contracts with numerous labels throughout the remainder of her life. In 1989 she received the Grammy Lifetime Achievement Award and was inducted into the Jazz Hall of Fame in 1990.

At 66, Sarah died of lung cancer and was buried at Glendale Cemetery in Bloomfield, New Jersey.

CEMETERY DIRECTIONS: At Exit 150 off the Garden State Parkway, Glendale Cemetery is just a quarter-mile east along Hoover Avenue.

GRAVE DIRECTIONS: Enter the cemetery, bear left, then make an immediate right so that the Capriglione crypt is on your left. Drive along this road and, at the four-way intersection, you'll see Sarah's grave on the left.

DOTTIE WEST

OCTOBER 11, 1932 – SEPTEMBER 4, 1991

Country-music singer Dottie West earned her first top 40 hit in 1963 with "Let Me Off at the Corner." Demonstrating that it was no fluke, she followed with the hits "Love Is No Excuse" and "Here Comes My Baby," and became the first female country artist to win a Grammy award, leading to an invitation to join the Grand Old Opry.

In 1973, Dottie had a crossover hit with "Country Sunshine," which had originally been written for a Coca-Cola commercial. But she really reached her peak of popularity in the late 1970s when, in duets with Kenny Rogers, she reached the top twenty of the country chart six times. Dottie and Kenny were named Vocal Duo of the Year for two consecutive years by the Country Music Association.

By the mid-eighties, although she remained a popular touring act, Dottie's popularity had slipped, and after three divorces her financial problems had mounted. In 1990, facing foreclosure on her Nashville mansion, she declared bankruptcy and saw her possessions sold at a public auction.

While en route to an Opryland performance, Dottie was involved in a car accident, and she died of her injuries the following week at age 58.

Dottie was buried at Mount View Cemetery in McMinnville, Tennessee.

CEMETERY DIRECTIONS: From the intersection of the Route 70S bypass and Route 56, follow the 70S bypass east for 3/4 mile to North Spring Street. Turn right and the cemetery is a short distance ahead on the left.

GRAVE DIRECTIONS: Enter the cemetery at the second entrance on the left. After a short distance, look to the right for the dark brown, irregularly shaped stone that marks Dottie's grave.

HANK WILLIAMS
SEPTEMBER 17, 1923 – JANUARY 1, 1953

Called the "Hillbilly Shakespeare," Hiram "Hank" Williams wrote simple melodies that mixed the sounds of gospel, blues, and country music, and complemented them with lyrics that evoked powerful emotion. He is often credited with introducing country music to the general public.

As a kid, Hank shined shoes and sold peanuts on the street to bring home a few pennies for his poor Alabama family. But by thirteen, after somehow getting his hands on a guitar and teaching himself to play, he christened himself "the Drifting Cowboy," and within a year had his own band that passed the hat at honky-tonks and square dances.

With the onset of World War II, Hank temporarily shelved his music career in order to work at a shipyard, but by 1944, his Drifting Cowboys had reunited and were regulars on the *Louisiana Hayride* radio show. Hank's version of "Lovesick Blues" went to number one on the 1949 *Billboard* charts, and on the strength of that song, he was invited to perform at the Grand Ole Opry, where he soon became a regular. During the next couple of years, Hank was on top of his game and the hits came in quick succession, including "Cold, Cold Heart," "Hey, Good Lookin'," and "Your Cheatin' Heart."

Despite his success, though, Hank's personal life was a mess and his marriage collapsed due to his womanizing and abusive behavior. As a sufferer of chronic back pain, Hank became addicted to painkillers, and his alcoholism was beyond control, as well. After arriving at gigs too drunk to perform (or not showing up at all) he was finally fired by the Grand Old Opry in August of 1952.

Hank's health deteriorated from the abuse and, at 29, he died en route to a show in Ohio of a "heart attack from excessive drinking."

Hank was buried at Oakwood Annex Cemetery in Montgomery, Alabama.

CEMETERY DIRECTIONS: From I-65, take Exit 172 and follow Herron Street east, which will shortly curve to the left and become Bibb Street. After ¼ mile turn left off of Bibb Street and onto Molton, then right onto Tallapoosa. Tallapoosa will bear to the right and become Jefferson Street, which merges into Upper Wetumpka Road. After continuing for a mile along Upper Wetumpka, you'll see the cemetery on the left.

GRAVE DIRECTIONS: Enter the cemetery and drive to the circle at the top of the hill. You won't miss the two tall monoliths marking the graves of Hank and his first wife, Audrey.

TAMMY WYNETTE
MAY 5, 1942 – APRIL 6, 1998

Tammy Wynette was raised primarily by her grandparents in Mississippi, and by seventeen was married to a sometime bootlegger. The couple lived in a log cabin with no indoor plumbing and Tammy did the cooking in a fireplace. The marriage was short-lived, and after it ended, Tammy supported her three children as a hairdresser—but her dream was to make it as a singer. After ten-hour days in a beauty salon, she'd perform late into the night.

In 1965 she got a break when the *Country Boy Eddie* TV show signed her on as a regular act, and within two years Tammy had a contract with Epic Records. In 1968 she released her defining song. Not only was the song the biggest hit of her career, but 35 years and a fortune in royalties later, "Stand By Your Man" remains the biggest hit ever recorded by any female country singer. But though "Stand By Your Man" was her biggest hit, it certainly wasn't her last; Tammy racked up nineteen more number ones and sold more than 30 million records.

Tammy also collaborated with other country music artists and her most notable partner was fellow country-singer George Jones, whom she married in 1969. (She'd eventually marry five times.) The couple became the king and queen of country music, recorded ten albums together, and enjoyed many chart-topping singles, including "Take Me," and "We Loved It Away." Though their stormy marriage ended in 1975, they continued to record together occasionally.

Much of Tammy's life was spent in relatively poor health, and she had numerous operations for a variety of ailments. One of her long-term afflictions was severe stomach cramping, and for this condition she had been prescribed Versed, a particularly strong sedative. Tammy took the sedative one evening and during her sleep died of a blood clot in the lungs. She was 55. Three years later, the physician who prescribed the drug settled out of court with Tammy's four daughters, who had charged that the Versed contributed to her death.

Tammy was buried at Woodlawn Memorial Park in Nashville, Tennessee.

CEMETERY DIRECTIONS: From I-65, take Exit 79 and follow Armory Drive to Powell Avenue. Turn south on Powell, turn right on Thompson Lane, and Woodlawn is a short distance ahead on the left. Or, from I-40, take Exit 215 and follow the Briley Parkway 6½ miles south. (It will turn into Thompson Lane.) The cemetery will be on the right.

GRAVE DIRECTIONS: Enter the cemetery, turn at the second left, and park in front of the main building. Enter through the double-oak doors and go up the short flight of stairs on your left. Proceed down this corridor, turn right at the second hallway, and go through the glass doors. Tammy's crypt is about three-fourths of the way down this hall, at eye level, on the right.

FAMOUS
PERSONALITIES
& INFAMOUS
NEWSMAKERS

CHARLES ATLAS

OCTOBER 30, 1893 – DECEMBER 24, 1972

A nemic and weak as a youth, Charles Atlas brought body-building into the mainstream. He developed a workout system of pitting muscle against muscle that he called "dynamic tension," and, using this system, built himself up to become "The World's Most Perfectly Developed Man" in the 1920s.

Later he would launch an enormously popular bodybuilding course that featured in its advertising the now-classic image of a 97-pound weakling who loses his girl to a bully at the beach, only to win her back after using the Atlas techniques.

Charles died at 79 of a heart attack and rests at Saint John's Cemetery in Middle Village, New York.

CEMETERY DIRECTIONS: Middle Village is a neighborhood of Queens, New York. From either I-495 or the Interboro Parkway, take Woodhaven Boulevard to Metropolitan Avenue. The cemetery is then just a few blocks west of Woodhaven Boulevard at Metropolitan Avenue and 80th Street.

GRAVE DIRECTIONS: Charles is interred in the enormous mausoleum that sits in the cemetery's center. Drive past the office, turn right, then take the next right and the next left to get to the mausoleum. Drive around to the side and park near the doors to the right of the entrance with a red awning. Enter the bronze doors and go up one flight of stairs. Down the long hall in front of you, the Atlas crypt is about 150 feet away at eye level on the right—Unit 5, Floor 3, Section 1, Crypt 3A.

BONNIE & CLYDE
Clyde Barrow

MARCH 24, 1909 – MAY 23, 1934

Bonnie Parker

OCTOBER 1, 1910 – MAY 23, 1934

O ne hot Texas day in July 1930, a small-time thief named Clyde Barrow visited a friend. While there he happened to meet his friend's neighbor, Bonnie Parker. The two quickly became inseparable, and when Clyde was incarcerated for robbery some months later, Bonnie smuggled a gun into the jail. And so began the infamous saga of Bonnie and Clyde.

Through several books and four movies, their exploits have been romanticized endlessly, taking on bigger-than-life status. But, actually, it's hard to find anything very romantic about Bonnie and Clyde. In short, the Barrow gang, made up of Bonnie, Clyde, and the other outlaws who drifted in and out of their circle, traced a violent path through the south-central United States. Preying not only on "rich" banks, they robbed service stations, hardware stores, and fruit stands as well. As police loops grew tighter and their situation became increasingly desperate, they stepped up their fury and, by the time they were themselves killed in a hail of bullets, twelve innocent people had died.

By November 1932, Bonnie and Clyde were wanted for the murder of two storekeepers and one policeman and, tiring of nickel-and-dime holdups, they robbed their first bank. By March, Clyde's parolee brother, Buck, and his skeptical wife, Blanche, had joined them, and the Barrow gang stepped up their assaults. The law did, too, and the next year was a succession of shootouts staged in dusty, Depression-weary towns. When the smoke cleared, Buck was dead and Blanche was in custody, but Bonnie and Clyde remained on the lam.

In February 1934 Texas authorities had had enough of the duo's crime spree, and they hired bounty-hunter Frank Hamer to end it. In May, Bonnie, Clyde and a new gang member, Henry Methvin, began a stay with Methvin's father, Iverson, at his farm near Gibsland, Louisiana. Hamer, who was hot on their trail, soon pulled into town and, in a secret meeting, hatched a plan with Iverson: In return for a reduced sentence for his son, Iverson would direct Bonnie and Clyde into the crosshairs of an ambush led by Hamer.

While staying with Iverson, Bonnie and Clyde had fallen into a routine. Early each day they drove to the nearby town of Sailes to gather a few supplies, always returning by 10:00 a.m. In setting up an ambush for the outlaws, Iverson's distinctive, beat-up lumber truck was parked along the route to Sailes as if it had broken down, while across the street a half-dozen shooters and an unarmed Iverson concealed themselves in the overhanging moss of the dense woodland. Right on schedule at 9:15 a.m., Bonnie and Clyde ambled up the road, first slowing and then stopping at Iverson's curiously parked truck. Once they were plainly identified, Hamer calmly gave orders to fire, and 167 bullets ended the lives of Bonnie and Clyde.

Inside the car, red-dressed Bonnie's lifeless hand held a bloody pack of cigarettes, Clyde's jaw dangled precariously, and, among the

ETERNAL COUPLE

BONNIE & CLYDE

weapons in the back seat, Hamer found a saxophone. With the bodies still in it, the car was towed to an undertaker in Arcadia, Louisiana.

Contrary to popular myth, Bonnie and Clyde were not buried in the same casket, nor do they share a plot. In fact, they're not even buried in the same cemetery, though both are interred in Dallas, Texas. At 23, Bonnie was buried at Crown Hill Memorial Park, while 25-year-old Clyde was interred alongside his brother Buck at Western Heights Cemetery.

DIRECTIONS TO CEMETERY OF BONNIE: From I-35E, take exit 436 and follow the Northwest Highway (Route 12) east for two miles. Turn left onto Webb Chapel Road and Crown Hill is a half-mile on the right.

DIRECTIONS TO GRAVE OF BONNIE: Enter the cemetery through the green, steel gates and bear left at the first drive. After a hundred feet, stop. Off to the right is a hedgerow, and Bonnie's flat marker can be found against the hedgerow, just a dozen stones from the hedge's end.

DIRECTIONS TO CEMETERY OF CLYDE AND BUCK: These wise guys are buried in a small and defunct old relic of a cemetery on a main thoroughfare, hidden in plain sight. It's interesting that thousands of commuters pass it everyday and it gets nary a glance. From I-35E, take Exit 427 and follow Colorado Boulevard west for three miles to Fort Worth Avenue. Turn right onto Fort Worth Avenue and Western Heights Cemetery is three-fourths of a mile on the left, atop a small knoll.

DIRECTIONS TO GRAVE OF CLYDE AND BUCK: Enter the cemetery (you'll have to hop a short, chain-link fence), walk 75 feet to the left, and just in front of two overgrown bushes is their flat marker.

DIRECTIONS TO THE BONNIE AND CLYDE AMBUSH SITE: A marker was erected where Bonnie and Clyde were killed near Bienville, Louisiana. From I-20, take Exit 61 and follow Route 154 south for 9½ miles, where you'll see a stone tablet marking the site on the right. Bonnie and Clyde were driving north and the police posse hid in the bushes on the east side.

For years, their beige 1934 Ford "death car" was shown at fairs for 25 cents per look. It's now on display, for free, on the connector between the Outlet Mall and the Primm Valley Resort Casino in Primm, Nevada. Primm is about 40 miles south of Las Vegas, along I-15 on the Nevada and California state line.

Henry Methvin received his pardon from Texas as promised, but not from Oklahoma. He was arrested for murder and sentenced to death, though it was later commuted to life, and he was released after serving twelve years. In 1948 Henry was run over by a train.

LIZZIE BORDEN

JULY 19, 1860 – JUNE 1, 1927

One hot afternoon in August 1892 someone savagely murdered Andrew and Abby Borden with an axe in their home but, after more than a century of speculation, nobody can say for certain who really did it. Lizzie, their youngest daughter, was acquitted of the crime following a sensational trial whose high point came when both of the victims' heads were produced as exhibits. She lived the remainder of her life as a recluse, ostracized by a community that believed her to be guilty as charged (a kind of precursor to O.J. Simpson). In any case, she'll not be forgotten as long this familiar jump-rope jingle is still sung by children:

> *Lizzie Borden took an axe and gave her mother forty whacks;*
> *When she saw what she had done, she gave her father forty-one.*

Lizzie died of natural causes at 66 and is buried at Oak Grove Cemetery in Fall River, Massachusetts.

CEMETERY DIRECTIONS: From I-195, take Exit 7 and turn north onto Plymouth Avenue, which will become Robeson Street. After four lights, turn right onto Prospect Street you'll see the cemetery entrance.

GRAVE DIRECTIONS: Enter the cemetery, proceed straight, then bear left at the Turner mausoleum. After you make a left at the four corners, proceed another 75 yards. There on the left you'll see the Borden family plot. The plot holds Lizzie as well as her parents.

The house where the murders took place is at 92 Second St. in Fall River. It's now a museum and, if you dare, a bed and breakfast.

AL CAPONE & ELIOT NESS

Al Capone

JANUARY 17, 1899 – JANUARY 25, 1947

Eliot Ness

APRIL 19, 1903 – MAY 7, 1957

Al Capone, the original "Scarface" (so named because of the three razor slashes across his left cheek), was perhaps the most famous of all mobsters. His life of crime started in Brooklyn and then, in Chicago, he meteorically rose through the syndicate ranks to eventually control the bootleg liquor industry, which brought him an income of some $15 million a year.

In the late 1920s, federal agent Eliot Ness was assigned the duty of bringing down the Capone gang. After assembling a crack squad of ten carefully selected agents, the Untouchables (a nickname referring to the failure of all efforts to bribe them) methodically raided Capone's stills and speakeasies and with new vigor pursued the triggermen in Chicago's gangland-style murders. But despite the Untouchables' dogged determination, Ness was repeatedly frustrated in his attempts to put away the kingpin.

The government's break finally came when agent Eddie O'Hare pointed out that Capone had neglected to pay income taxes—ever. Never before had the government considered pursuing Capone for income tax evasion—such charges seemed too minor for a man who had ordered at least a hundred murders. But this was the dawn of the IRS's far-reaching powers and, in 1931, Capone was found guilty of the charges and sentenced to eleven years in federal prison.

During his initial medical exam in prison, Capone admitted he had contracted syphilis a few years earlier, but insisted he had been cured and declined a spinal tap to determine if he was still infected. After two years Capone was transferred to the newly constructed Alcatraz prison and, after five more unremarkable years, was found one day staring blankly at a wall. Doctors determined that his syphilis was actually in its advanced stages and Capone spent the next year in the hospital ward.

In November 1939, ravaged and demented by the disease, he was judged to be harmlessly insane and was released. The paranoid and kooky Capone retired to an estate near Miami Beach, where he continued his downward spiral. Physically uncoordinated, his speech garbled and confused, Capone fished off his dock for hours at a time, clad in his pajamas. In 1942, his syphilis was successfully treated with penicillin, but not even the new wonder drug could reverse his already severe brain damage.

Capone expired after suffering a brain hemorrhage while in bed.

At 48 he was buried at Mount Carmel Cemetery in Hillside, Illinois.

CEMETERY DIRECTIONS: From I-294, take Route 38 east and the cemetery is immediately to the left.

GRAVE DIRECTIONS: Enter the cemetery at the main entrance, which is the second drive. Inside the cemetery, take an immediate right and stop after a hundred feet. On the right, the tall Capone marker is surrounded by hedges.

Eliot Ness's perseverance in battling Capone assured him a place among the legends of gangland prosecutors. He later became director of public safety in Cleveland but, at just 54, Ness died of a heart attack. He was cremated and for 40 years his ashes were stuck away in a box at his family's home. In 1997, in a special ceremony honoring his contributions to the city, his ashes were scattered in the artificial lake at Cleveland's Lake View Cemetery.

BILLY CARTER

MARCH 29, 1937 – SEPTEMBER 25, 1988

B illy Carter was a gas station proprietor and peanut farmer who was vaulted to national celebrity when his brother Jimmy won the United States presidency in 1976.

Caring little for convention, he proved incapable of handling his sudden fame and became the butt of contemporary jokes for business dealings that were politically embarrassing to his brother, including a Libyan loan fiasco and his short-lived Billy Beer venture. Billy alternately courted and denounced the media, depending on the occasion, but was rather consistently skewered as a buffoon, a boob, and a wacko. In his own defense, with a sister who was a faith healer and a brother who was president, he once observed that he "was probably the only sane member of the family."

At 51 Billy died of pancreatic cancer and was buried at Lebanon Cemetery in Plains, Georgia.

CEMETERY DIRECTIONS: Route 280 is the main road through Plains. From the center of town, follow 280 west for a mile, then turn left onto Old Plains Highway. The cemetery is a half-mile ahead on the right.

GRAVE DIRECTIONS: Make a right onto the first paved drive, then bear left. Stop a short distance on the right when you see a Carter plot (though you're not quite there yet). Another 50 feet behind this Carter plot is a second Carter plot, and it's there you'll find Billy's grave alongside his parents, Lillian and Earl.

JACQUES COUSTEAU

JUNE 11, 1910 – JUNE 25, 1997

Jacques Cousteau, the revered scientist who held no scientific degree, spent most of his life exploring the oceans and discovering their wonders and secrets. Documenting his findings through television programs, he helped to create the nature documentary as a distinct form—but no matter which sea creatures cavorted before the lenses, there was never any question that the star of the show was Captain Cousteau himself. Projecting his image as the leading explorer of the day, he spoke in a highly personal, Gallic-flavored English and, with a dazzling smile, deeply lined face, and red woolen watch cap, became recognizable to people all over the world.

As co-inventor of the "Aqualung," the world's first underwater breathing apparatus, Jacques cleared German mines from French ports during World War II, then formed a series of corporations and nonprofit organizations through which he financed underwater expeditions. In 1953 he gained celebrity with the publication of *The Silent World*, an account of the development and promise of scuba diving, and its documentary film version won him the first of his three Academy Awards.

In the 1960s Cousteau set out to prove that humans, "oceanauts," could live and work on the ocean floor. His three Conshelf experiments competed for public attention with government-financed space programs. Later, Jacques brought the wonders of the Earth's oceans—sharks, whales, dolphins, sunken treasure, and coral reefs—into people's homes through his television series, *The Undersea World of Jacques Cousteau*. He enthralled the world on zigzag voyages from Alaska to Africa to Antarctica aboard his research vessel, *Calypso*. When it became apparent that pollution was degrading the oceans, Jacques turned environmentalist and in 1974 started a nonprofit marine conservation group, the Cousteau Society, which today boasts a membership of more than 300,000.

At 87, Jacques died of a heart attack and was buried in his hometown at the cemetery in Saint Andre-de-Cubzac, France, which is just fifteen miles north of Bordeaux.

JEFFREY DAHMER

MAY 21, 1960 – NOVEMBER 28, 1994

In 1991, Jeffrey Dahmer's gruesome acts of murder, necrophilia, and dismemberment shocked the world. He had lured his victims with promises of beer and money in exchange for posing for nude photographs, but once inside his Milwaukee apartment they were drugged and then stabbed or strangled.

Of the seventeen he's known to have killed, he ate parts of at least five, and stored the remains of several others in his refrigerator. Dahmer told investigators he killed only to ward off loneliness and that he just "didn't want them to leave."

Dahmer was sentenced to fifteen consecutive life terms but served only one. After he'd been in prison only 30 months, he was beaten to death with a broomstick in a prison bathroom by a fellow inmate.

Ten months after his death, Dahmer was finally cremated and his parents, who had divorced, reportedly split the ashes.

Amid fears that someone might create a Jeffrey Dahmer Museum with his gruesome collection of tools, photographs, and his famous refrigerator, in 1996 a group of Milwaukee businessmen bought the motley collection for more than $400,000 and incinerated the lot.

JACK DANIEL

SEPTEMBER 5, 1850 – OCTOBER 10, 1911

The nation's oldest registered distillery and its renowned sipping whiskey take their names from Mr. Jasper Newton (Jack) Daniel. At the age of seven, Jack was hired out to work with a local Lutheran minister, Dan Call, who also happened to own a whiskey still. In 1863, Call's congregation persuaded him to concentrate on uplifting folks through sermons and not spirits, and Call sold his still to his young partner, who was then just thirteen. "Mr. Jack," as he came to be known, continued the tradition of handcrafted whiskey making, and within his lifetime his Tennessee Whiskey become world-famous.

He was known to be kind and generous but he wasn't always patient. Legend has it that once, in a fit of anger, Jack kicked his safe and broke his toe. An infection set in and six years later he died as a result of complications from blood poisoning.

At 61, Jack Daniel was buried at the Lynchburg Cemetery in Lynchburg, Tennessee.

CEMETERY DIRECTIONS: A half-mile south of the distillery on Route 55, turn west onto Elm Street and follow it into the cemetery.

GRAVE DIRECTIONS: Drive straight into the cemetery, then turn right at the first intersection. At the next intersection, Jack's grave is immediately to your right.

BOBBY DARIN

MAY 14, 1936 – DECEMBER 20, 1973

Bobby Darin had an uncommon childhood on two counts. First, he was a sickly child suffering repeated attacks of rheumatic fever, among other health problems, and his physician held out little hope of his reaching age 21. Well, Bobby did manage to survive past that age, long enough to learn, in his 30s, that the woman he'd always believed to be his older sister was actually his mother.

After an otherwise unremarkable childhood, Bobby scratched out a living writing songs and commercial jingles until he vaulted to the status of teen idol upon the 1958 release of "Splish Splash." In an effort to reach a wider audience the next year, he released an album of old favorites that featured a new arrangement of "Mack the Knife." With that release, Bobby's ship came in.

An irresistible showman, Bobby and his flashy dance steps were soon headlining clubs from New York to Las Vegas, and he established himself as one of the most popular and highest-paid night-club performers in the country. As per the standard recipe, film roles, marriages, divorces, and gossip columns followed.

Despite heart ailments that frequently hospitalized him, Bobby performed until the age of 37, when he succumbed to his health problems and died of heart failure. He had requested there be no funeral and that his body be used as a medical cadaver. Bobby's wishes were fulfilled and upon his death his body was donated to UCLA.

JOHN DILLINGER & MELVIN PURVIS

John Dillinger

JUNE 28, 1902 – JULY 22, 1934

Melvin Purvis

OCTOBER 24, 1900 – FEBRUARY 29, 1960

For all the notoriety enjoyed by bank-robber John Dillinger, his life of crime was exceedingly short, and until he went to prison at age twenty for assault, he had no criminal record at all. But it seems that prison soured him, and after his release at 29, he orchestrated the escape of ten of his inmate cronies, and with them established a potent gang. In a seven-month Midwest crime spree, they were responsible for eleven bank robberies and fifteen deaths before their capture in Arizona.

But much to the embarrassment of law enforcement officials, Dillinger quickly escaped from prison using a wooden gun covered with black shoe polish and resumed his violent ways. A foiled Wisconsin ambush killed three more innocents and Dillinger managed to escape the law's grasp yet again. J. Edgar Hoover, then director of the FBI, tagged him as "Public Enemy Number One," thus assuring his status as a kind of folk hero.

Dillinger's capture became the top priority for the agency and especially for Melvin Purvis, head of the FBI's Chicago office. After the Romanian landlady of Dillinger's girlfriend contacted Purvis and agreed to betray Dillinger in return for leniency in her own upcoming deportation hearing, a plan was devised to apprehend him as he and the two women were leaving a Chicago movie theater. As planned, Dillinger walked out of the theater and Purvis lit a cigar to signal the surrounding agents that the man was in fact him. As the agents approached, Dillinger was spooked and pulled a .38-caliber pistol from his belt. But before he could fire a shot he was hit by four bullets, three in his chest and one that entered the back of his neck and exited through his face. When agents arrived at a hospital with the very-dead Dillinger, the hospital refused to allow the gangster inside and he was laid on the lawn to await the coroner.

At 32, Dillinger was buried at Crown Hill Cemetery in Indianapolis, Indiana. For a time after his burial, a guard was posted to prevent souvenir hunters from unearthing the body. Eventually the grave was reopened to contrive a protection of concrete and scrap iron over the coffin.

CEMETERY DIRECTIONS: The cemetery is easy to find at Martin Luther King Boulevard and 38th Street.

GRAVE DIRECTIONS: Enter the cemetery at the funeral home entrance, bear left at the mausoleum, go under the stone bridge, then turn at the next left. Stay on this road for almost a half-mile, then turn right immediately before Section 44. After about 150 feet the Dillinger plot is to the left, visible from the roadway.

After Dillinger's death, law enforcers, led by Purvis, concentrated on capturing or eliminating the remaining members of his gang, and within months most were either behind bars or dead. But Purvis himself got into a stew with his boss, Hoover, and within a year Purvis left the agency.

When he left the FBI, his fellow agents presented him with a nickel-plated Colt .45 and, 25 years later, Purvis may have committed suicide with the weapon. He certainly shot himself to death with it, but it's unclear whether it was intentional or if the gun accidentally went off as he tried to dislodge an odd-sized tracer round from its chamber.

At 59, Purvis was buried at Mount Hope Cemetery in Florence, South Carolina.

CEMETERY DIRECTIONS: From I-95, take Exit 164 and follow route 52 south for four miles to Cherokee Road. Turn left onto Cherokee and the cemetery is immediately on the right.

GRAVE DIRECTIONS: Enter the cemetery, drive past the office, and go to the end of the drive in front of the mausoleum. Turn left, then left again, then make an immediate right and stop. On the left is the tall granite Purvis marker. His epitaph reads "*Saepe Timui Sed Numquam Curri*—Always Be Afraid, Never Run."

DORIS DUKE

NOVEMBER 22, 1912 – OCTOBER 29, 1993

Doris Duke was the only child of American tobacco baron James Duke, and upon his 1925 death, the twelve-year-old Doris inherited the bulk of his $80 million fortune. Christened "the poor little rich girl," Doris was a most reluctant celebrity and avoided the glare of publicity and cameras all her life. That's not to say however, that her life was unengaging.

As a teen, the debutante relished the leisure of austere mansions and, in her twenties, established a reputation for indiscreet affairs. After two failed marriages that produced no children (other than a daughter who died immediately after birth), she developed a case of wanderlust and fraternized with African Massai warriors and witch doctors, studied belly dancing in Turkey, communed with Indian mystics, and worked as a European war correspondent. Through middle age, Doris led a more solitary life and emerged as a leading benefactress, marking a return to a heritage of generous Duke philanthropy.

In her golden years, Doris surrounded herself with a menagerie of characters, and it seems she began to lose her wits. Meeting Chandi Heffner, a Hari Krishna devotee, Doris came to believe that Heffner was the reincarnation of her long-dead infant daughter, and Doris legally adopted the adult Heffner. Three years later, Doris had a change of heart and reversed the adoption. Then, as part of an airplane purchase, Doris accepted two camels, which then resided at (and in) her Newport estate. Around the same time, Doris befriended Imelda Marcos and loaned her $5 million, presumably for shoes.

As Doris had no family or close friends, her alcoholic butler, Bernard Lafferty, took control of her affairs as her age advanced and health declined. Just six months before her death, increasingly frail and disoriented, Doris signed a will naming Lafferty co-executor of her estate and sole trustee of the Doris Duke Foundation, which essentially handed him control of her fortune, then worth more than one billion dollars.

At 80 Doris died of a morphine overdose, was cremated within 24 hours and her ashes scattered in the Pacific Ocean.

After much legal wrangling, Lafferty was ousted as both co-executor of the will and trustee of the foundation. He relinquished his positions for an undisclosed amount of money, retreated from the limelight, and died in 1996. Due to a wealth of speculation surrounding Doris's death, the district attorney launched an investigation but concluded there was no credible evidence to suggest foul play.

Today, The Doris Duke Charitable Foundation continues its philanthropic efforts in support of the arts, environmental causes, and life sciences.

JIM FIXX

APRIL 23, 1932 – JULY 20, 1984

Concerned about a family history of heart disease, Jim Fixx took up jogging at 35 and, after losing 60 pounds and feeling physically and spiritually stronger, he wrote *The Complete Book of Running*. The book spurred the jogging craze of the late seventies and, as a self-styled guru of running, Jim became popular on talk shows and the lecture circuit, spreading the gospel that active people live longer and healthier lives.

After so adamantly extolling the virtues of jogging, Jim dropped dead of a heart attack at 52—while jogging. His death was an all-too-convenient defense for couch potatoes who choose to continue sedentary lifestyles but, after his autopsy, doctors agreed that if Jim had never jogged at all he'd still have died of a heart attack, many years earlier.

Jim was cremated and his ashes entrusted to his family.

At the place where Jim collapsed, a memorial has been erected in his honor. It's on Route 15 in Hardwick, Vermont, just 50 feet north of the Village Motel.

TERRY FOX

JULY 28, 1958 – JUNE 28, 1981

In 1977, 18-year-old Canadian Terry Fox was diagnosed with bone cancer and his right leg was amputated to prevent the spread of the disease. Two years later, Terry resolved to run 5,300 miles across Canada to raise money for cancer research, and in the spring of 1980, with little fanfare, he dipped his artificial leg in the Atlantic Ocean and began his Marathon of Hope. Although it was difficult to garner attention in the beginning, as Terry hobbled painfully westward at the rate of 26 miles a day, enthusiasm for his cause grew. Soon his drama had captured the world's attention.

But Terry never finished his run. After covering 3,339 miles in 143 days, it was learned that the cancer had spread to his lungs and Terry was forced to end his run and return home for treatment. Ten months later, just weeks before his 23rd birthday, this international symbol of hope and courage lost his battle with cancer.

The heroic Canadian was gone, but he inspired an outpouring of national pride, and in that spirit, the Canadian government created the Terry Fox Humanitarian Award Program. Through the annual Terry Fox Run and other fund-raisers, almost $300 million has since been raised in his name.

Terry was buried in his hometown's cemetery in Port Coquitlam, British Columbia.

CEMETERY DIRECTIONS: Follow Shaughnessy Street north from the center of town, turn right onto Prairie Avenue, then left onto Oxford Avenue. The cemetery is a short distance on the right.

GRAVE DIRECTIONS: Walk to the lower area of the cemetery and Terry's knee-high black stone is in the middle toward the back.

RON GOLDMAN & NICOLE BROWN SIMPSON

Ron Goldman

JULY 2, 1968 – JUNE 12, 1994

Nicole Brown Simpson

MAY 19, 1959 – JUNE 12, 1994

In the whole sordid mess of the Simpson murder case, there seems to be only one thing on which everyone agrees: on June 12, 1994, *somebody* brutally stabbed and slashed Nicole Brown Simpson and her sometime-lover Ron Goldman to death at Nicole's posh Brentwood, California, nest.

Nicole was the estranged wife of former football star O.J. Simpson, and soon nearly everyone in America would be pointing at him, convinced for many good reasons that he was the murderer. First of all, O.J. was insanely jealous, thus giving him a motive. Prior to the murders, he had purchased a knife from a cutlery shop that would've caused wounds compatible with those suffered by the victims, and he was never able to locate it later. DNA tests whose margin of error was in the neighborhood of one in a billion linked blood found at the scene to O.J., and blood found on his car and his socks to the victims. Missing gloves and bloody shoe prints were linked to O.J. Furthermore, he never established a verifiable alibi. Instead he jumped from one story to another as they crumbled beneath his inconsistencies. Immediately after the murders took place, O.J. boarded a flight to Chicago.

At this moment, thousands of people are in prison after being tried and convicted of murder, beyond a reasonable doubt, on much less than half of the evidence that was accumulated against O.J. But in October 1995 the millionaire hotshot walked away from his destiny, having been found not guilty.

The next year, the Goldman and Brown families pursued O.J. in a civil suit in which the burden of proof is lower than in criminal proceedings. In a civil case, guilt need only be proven according to a "preponderance of the evidence" rather than "beyond a reasonable doubt." After hearing four months of testimony, including O.J.'s (during the criminal trial he had invoked the fifth amendment, which is not an option in a civil trial), the jury found O.J. liable for the deaths of Ron and Nicole. The Goldman family was awarded $8.5 million in compensatory damages, while another $25 million in punitive damages was to be shared between both families.

Justice was served, except that the money was never paid. O.J. was "broke" and he retreated to Florida where the law does not allow the seizure of future income. Today he lives in a $1.5 million house in Kendall and collects some $20,000 a month from a football pension fund. Between rounds of golf O.J. said, "They can't touch my earnings here. And it'll be a cold day in hell before I pay a penny."

After all the hype and hoopla, all that remains are the graves of the two victims—and a killer who lives free among us.

Ron was 25 at his death and is buried at Valley Oaks Cemetery in Westlake Village, California.

CEMETERY DIRECTIONS FOR RON: From Highway 101, exit at Lindero Canyon Road, head east, and the cemetery is a short distance ahead on the right.

GRAVE DIRECTIONS FOR RON: Drive into the cemetery, turn at the first left, then stop at the pine tree on the right. Ron's grave is beneath the pine tree.

After her death at 35, Nicole was buried at Ascension Cemetery in Lake Forest, California.

CEMETERY DIRECTIONS FOR NICOLE: Lake Forest is a village that doesn't appear on all California maps. It's about ten miles south of Santa Ana on I-5. Take the Lake Forest Drive exit and follow it east for 2½ miles to Trabuco Road, then turn left and the cemetery is half-mile ahead on the left.

GRAVE DIRECTIONS FOR NICOLE: Nicole's grave is directly behind the office, three rows from the hedges.

JOHN GOTTI

OCTOBER 27, 1940 – JUNE 10, 2002

John Gotti quit school in the tenth grade to pursue a career as a professional criminal, and after a decade of relatively tame thievery and robbery, hooked up with the Queens-based Gambino crime family in 1966. He quickly graduated to truck hijackings and assorted murders. In December 1985, Gotti masterminded the murder of mob boss Paul Castellano in the midst of bustling throngs of Christmas shoppers as he exited a Midtown Manhattan restaurant. With Castellano gone, Gotti assumed leadership of the Gambino family but, much to his surprise, his criminal enterprise was driven into the ground less than a decade later.

By the mid-1980s, law-enforcement agencies had finally begun to dismantle the foundations of organized crime with the help of technological advances in listening and tracking, tougher new laws, and a flush of appropriations set aside by the federal sector. Unfortunately for Gotti, his ascent to power coincided with the government's new efforts, and he unwittingly placed himself directly in the cross hairs of prosecutors.

Gotti was the classic gangster, and for the next half-dozen years, the government was obsessed with putting him away. But Gotti beat all the charges during three different trials and, for his habit of coming through criminal prosecutions unscathed, as well as for the air of importance he exuded in his expensive attire and fashionable pinky ring, he earned two monikers, "Teflon Don" and "Dapper Don."

But in 1992 the government showed up in court with a secret weapon: the testimony of Sammy "the Bull" Gravano, Gotti's second-in-command henchman who cut a deal and fingered Gotti as the criminal mastermind. The prosecution also presented tapes in which Gotti was heard ordering mob hits and, this time, his fate was sealed. He was sentenced to life in federal prison without the possibility of parole.

After ten years of living alone in a 6-by-8-foot cell in Marion, Illinois, Gotti died of a cancer that had ravaged his neck and head. At 61, he was laid to rest alongside his son, Frank, at Saint John's Cemetery in Queens, New York.

Twelve-year-old Frank had been killed in March 1980 when he was struck by a car after darting into the street on a minibike. The driver of the vehicle, Gotti's neighbor John Favara, was hustled into a van four months after Frank's death and hasn't been heard from since. How's that for bad luck?

CEMETERY DIRECTIONS: From either I-495 or the Interboro Parkway, take Woodhaven Boulevard to Metropolitan Avenue. Then the cemetery entrance is just west of Woodhaven Boulevard at Metropolitan Avenue and 80th Street.

GRAVE DIRECTIONS: John is interred in the enormous mausoleum that sits in the cemetery's center, which is called the Saint John's Cloister. Drive past the office, turn right, then take the next right and the next left to get to the cloister. You'll have to park along the side, but then return to the front and enter at the entrance with the red awnings. Go up the two short flights of stairs, then turn left and go up the stairs to the next floor. At the top of the stairs, turn right and immediately left. You'll see the wooden-faced crypts of John and his son Frank on the bottom row on the right.

After Gotti was led away in handcuffs in 1992, his son John "Junior" Gotti took over as acting boss of the once-mighty Gambino family, and soon earned a reputation as being numb between the ears. In 1997, after Junior left piles of cash and a handwritten roster of Mafia members lying out for agents to find, tabloids nicknamed him "Dumbfella," and his father remarked that his offspring should not be imprisoned but instead should be "sent to an insane asylum." In 1999 the bumbling gangster was sentenced to 6½ years on a variety of racketeering charges.

After squealing on Gotti, Sammy the Bull did five years of hard time himself, then, courtesy of the Witness Protection Program, he received appearance-altering plastic surgery and settled in Tempe, Arizona as Jimmy Moran. But Jimmy the swimming pool installer soon adopted his old habits as Sammy the hood, and, in 2000, he was arrested on charges of trafficking the designer drug Ecstasy. In September 2002, Jimmy-Sammy was handed a twenty-year prison sentence.

DOUG HENNING
MAY 3, 1947 – FEBRUARY 7, 2000

Doug Henning became fascinated with magic after watching a levitation act on *The Ed Sullivan Show*. At fourteen he placed a classified ad that read, "Magician: Have rabbit, will travel," and was soon performing at parties as "the Great Hendoo." After college Doug applied for a Canadian Council grant, funding usually reserved for more mainstream artists, and after convincing the board that magic was indeed an art form, he used the money to develop a rock-opera magic show that he named *Spellbound*.

The show was a great success in Toronto, so Doug moved it to Broadway in 1974, revamping the staging and costumes and changing the name to *The Magic Show*. Again the show was well received, and soon he was offered his own television program. In December 1975, a tie-dyed and longhaired Doug waved hello from the stage of his inaugural "World of Magic" special. On that program, Doug was careful to point out that, though this was television, there was a live studio audience and no cheap camera tricks or "old-style devices" would be used. Viewers loved it and, annually over the next seven years, were enthralled as Doug recreated Houdini's "water-torture" trick, turned himself into a shark, walked through a brick wall, and made a horse disappear.

Doug's starred in a second Broadway show, *Merlin*, appeared at venues nationwide as the day's best illusionist, and single-handedly revived the public's flagging interest in magic, paving the way for the next generation of magicians. In fact, when Doug changed his direction in 1987, he sold some of his most famous illusions to David Copperfield.

In the late eighties, Doug traded his dedication to illusional magic for a lifetime study of "real magic"—his term for transcendental meditation and levitation. "Illusion magic uses laws of science and nature that are already known," he explained, "but real magic uses laws that haven't yet been discovered." With his friend Maharishi Mahesh Yogi, Doug spent the remainder of his life working toward building a proposed transcendental meditation theme park called

Maharishi Veda Land in India where, he promised, one of the buildings would levitate.

Doug died of liver cancer at 52 and, after cremation, finally achieved "levitation" when his family scattered his ashes.

ABBIE HOFFMAN & JERRY RUBIN

Abbie Hoffman
NOVEMBER 30, 1936 – APRIL 12, 1989

Jerry Rubin
JULY 14, 1938 – NOVEMBER 28, 1994

Abbie Hoffman and Jerry Rubin rose to national prominence as the most vocal members of the Chicago Seven, a group of radicals who nominated a pig for president, among other political stunts, and stood trial on charges of conspiring to disrupt the 1968 Democratic National Convention.

In the famously unruly trial, the defendants chewed jellybeans and screamed insults at the prosecutors. Abbie angered the court by noting that the presiding judge, Julius Hoffman, had the same last name and saying the judge was his "illegitimate father." Jerry showed up at the trial wearing judges' robes that covered a blue Chicago police shirt. Ultimately, the seven were acquitted of the conspiracy.

Jerry and Abbie later founded the Youth International Party, the Yippies, a loose-knit but militant group with a penchant for political theater. The party's stunts included appearing before a congressional committee wearing Revolutionary War costumes and throwing dollar bills onto the floor of the New York Stock Exchange.

In the 1970s Abbie went underground under threat of a long sentence on cocaine charges and Jerry began a prolonged round of self-improvement that included meditation, acupuncture, and hypnotism in his search for a "new consciousness." In 1980, on national television with Barbara Walters, Abbie came out of hiding and, after pleading guilty, served time on lesser charges.

Later in that decade, Jerry abandoned his antiestablishment stance and embraced the capitalistic ideas that he had so vigorously protested. He went to work for a Wall Street firm, promoted networking seminars, and marketed *Wow!*, a nutritional drink. During this time Abbie was again active on the political front and Jerry, ever demonstrating a flair for the public gesture, held a series of "Yippie vs. Yuppie" debates with his old friend.

In 1989 Abbie committed suicide at 52 and was cremated. His ashes were given to a friend who keeps them on the mantle of her New York City apartment.

In 1994, at 56, Jerry met his end after being struck by a car while jaywalking across Wilshire Boulevard in Los Angeles. As one who all his life tweaked authority and defied expectations, it's fitting that what led to his death was one final act of nonconformity.

Jerry was buried at Hillside Memorial Park in Los Angeles.

CEMETERY DIRECTIONS: Hillside Memorial Park is on Centinella Avenue, just east of I-405.

GRAVE DIRECTIONS: Enter the park and make your way to the Mount of Olives section, which is the grassy area on the hill to the left. There you'll see the curb marker for 7-14. Jerry's grave is under a tree at the end of the row directly behind this marking.

JOHN HOLMES
AUGUST 8, 1944 – MARCH 13, 1988

In 1972 two "important" genre-defining films within the dusky realm of pornography were released: *The Devil In Miss Jones* and *Deep Throat*. These hardcore movies may have lent only the smallest amount of legitimacy to porno flicks, but the push was just enough to elevate them from stale and mechanical breeding exhibitions to somewhat professional productions shot in well-lit studios by multiple cameras. The new adult films needed willing actors, and John Holmes stepped up to the plate with bat in hand. The extremely well-endowed, gay-bar stripper found his niche in the burgeoning new business and, as the industry expanded exponentially, so did Holmes' reputation. With his wispy moustache, boyish charm, and bouffant hair, he was ever present, performing with every famous starlet of the age—more than 14,000 women by his own count— and left not one disappointed, or so the legend goes.

As the 1970s drew to a close it seemed as though Holmes had the world at his feet. Private clients, both male and female, paid huge sums for his personal services, he was flown to tropical locations worldwide for film shoots, and he even found himself being courted by mainstream Hollywood celebrities who flirted with the porn industry's newfound hipness. Cult status was confirmed for Holmes with the success of his lewd and long-running celluloid alter ego: Johnny Wadd, the tough, no-nonsense, big gun-carrying private eye.

But within a few years, Holmes had fallen a long way. He had become an incoherent drug addict whose $1,500-a-day habit broke him. He had been blackballed, so to speak, by the porn industry for his unreliability both onscreen and off, and Holmes resorted to petty crime to support his habit. By 1981 he was desperate for a score, and in June set up a friend, the notorious cocaine baron Eddie Nash, to be robbed of drugs, jewelry, and cash.

It didn't take Nash long to figure out who had double-crossed him and, as retribution, Nash forced Holmes to participate in, or at least, witness, the brutally violent murders of those responsible for his robbery. Holmes led Nash and his henchmen to the home of his thieving friends and, after his bloody print was found, Holmes was arrested. Authorities tried to get Holmes to finger Nash, but he wouldn't budge, so Holmes alone went to trial and was acquitted in 1982. Terrified of being murdered himself, for the rest of his life Holmes kept a low profile, moving constantly.

In 1985 Holmes tested positive for AIDS. In February 1988 two detectives appeared at his hospital bed bluffing that they were ready to charge him anew unless he talked, but their timing was a bit late. Holmes was already drifting in and out of consciousness, and he soon died of complications from AIDS at 42.

His last wish was that his body be cremated intact; Holmes was very concerned that his penis would end up pickled in a jar as a sideshow attraction. To that end, his wife supervised his cremation and scattered his ashes over San Francisco Bay.

Remarkably, Holmes' never felt exploited throughout the 2,000 raunchy films he made. "It's like being a carpenter," he once said. "This is my tool and I use it to make a living."

In 1997 Holmes' life was the loose basis for a more mainstream film, *Boogie Nights*. The lead role was played by Mark Wahlberg who, presumably, wore a prosthetic.

HARRY HOUDINI
MARCH 24, 1874 – OCTOBER 31, 1926

After concocting the name "Houdini" from the famous French illusionist Jean Eugene Robert Houdin, the Hungarian-born Ehrich Weiss began his professional life as an entertainer at county fairs before becoming the foremost conjuring magician and escape artist of his day.

In 1894, Houdini met and married a struggling actress named Bess and, with her promotional acumen, Houdini's fledgling magic show grew quickly. He did card manipulations and run-of-the-mill illusions, but when the pair realized that his particularly macabre and dangerous tricks were the real crowd pleasers, Houdini adjusted his act accordingly. First came the Needle Trick, a grisly effect involving the swallowing of needles and thread, followed by their regurgitation with the thread neatly looped through the needles' eyes. By 1898, Houdini was escaping from any pair of handcuffs the audience could produce in his Handcuff Challenge Act, which led to his renown as an escape artist.

In full view of audiences, Houdini was soon escaping from leg irons, straitjackets, and prison cells, and, when those routines became too easy, the drama and difficulty were ratcheted upward. Houdini was thrown into rivers in padlocked crates and locked canvas mailbags, he jumped from bridges in handcuffs, he was buried alive in sealed coffins and, on stage, his Upside-Down Water Torture Cell and Milk Can Escape illusions enthralled audiences, their jaws hanging open in astonishment. For more than two decades Houdini remained in the limelight. He was the first to demonstrate illusions in motion pictures and, in later years, became a relentless exposer of unscrupulous spiritual mediums and a proud debunker of psychic frauds.

In 1926, at 52 years old, Houdini was still packing people in by the thousands, and his reputation was unparalleled. During a tour in the fall of that year, Houdini began experiencing stomach pains, but stubbornly refused to see a doctor. After an appearance at the Princess Theater in Montreal, a college-student J. Gordon Whitehead asked Houdini if the legend that he could sustain punches to his midsection without injury was true. Preoccupied with other conversation, Houdini more or less sidestepped the question, but he should also have sidestepped the blows that were to follow. Without warning, Whitehead pummeled Houdini at least three times in the abdomen, after which Houdini, grimacing in obvious pain, politely excused himself.

He struggled through the next day's show and, after arriving in London, Ontario, for the tour's next stop, a doctor informed Houdini he was suffering from acute appendicitis. But the showbiz veteran refused to cancel that night's sold-out performance, which turned out to be his last. When Houdini's ruptured appendix was removed at three o'clock the next morning, the poison had already entered his bloodstream and he died six days later, on Halloween.

Though the oft-repeated Houdini legend holds that Whitehead's punches were solely responsible for his death, that's not entirely true. It seems Houdini was already suffering from appendicitis and, even if Whitehead had never struck him, Houdini's appendix would have soon ruptured on its own. Nonetheless, his wife Bess was able to collect double indemnity on his life insurance policy claiming that the blows were equivalent to "an accident directly causing the premature death of Harry Houdini."

At Machpelah Cemetery in Queens, New York, Houdini was buried in the very bronze coffin from which he had many times previously escaped. His rather large tombstone originally was topped with an imposing Houdini bust, but it was stolen many years later and never replaced.

CEMETERY DIRECTIONS: From the Interboro Parkway, take Exit 3, turn north onto Cypress Hill Street and Machpelah Cemetery is a few hundred yards to the left. (Note: Cypress Hill Street is not the same as Cypress Avenue.)

GRAVE DIRECTIONS: Enter the cemetery and you won't miss Harry's tomb 50 feet behind the office.

As an ultimate test of spiritualism, Houdini and Bess arranged a series of coded messages by which the first to die would—if possible—communicate with the other. After twelve years of trying to communicate with her deceased husband through the code, Bess finally declared the experiment a failure though, every Halloween since, others have made their own attempts.

HOWARD HUGHES

NOVEMBER 24, 1905 – APRIL 5, 1976

As the only child of millionaire parents, Howard Hughes certainly had a good start in life, but the turning of his silver spoon into platinum was the direct result of personal accomplishments.

The Hughes' family wealth was derived from their Hughes Tool Company, which manufactured a sophisticated rotary bit used by the burgeoning oil industry for drilling through rock. When Howard was orphaned at eighteen, he took over the family business, shrewdly purchased his competitors, and, within a few years, boasted of a $2 million yearly income, quite a comfortable living for today and unheard of in 1928.

Howard later shifted his interest to making Hollywood movies, but he wasn't content as just a silent pocketbook. Instead, he became an independent filmmaker, bought RKO Pictures, and produced a couple dozen films, turning Jean Harlow and Jane Russell into stars and earning an Academy Award for *Two Arabian Knights*. All the while, of course, Howard sampled Hollywood's café society beauties and biggest stars, and became a symbol of Movieland's excesses and eccentricities.

In the midst of his hectic schedule (he was still the CEO of Hughes Tool, too), Howard became intrigued with the still-young field of aviation. In typical bigger-than-life Hughes fashion, not only did he learn to fly, Howard designed his own planes, formed a company that made experimental aircraft, and personally set airspeed records. During World War II, when metal was at a premium, his company built a plane of birch wood, the Spruce Goose (though it only flew once, for a mile with Howard at the controls). In 1938, he flew around the world in 91 hours, a feat for which he earned a Congressional Medal of Honor. (Howard never bothered to pick up the prize. After FDR's death, Harry Truman found the medal in a desk and mailed it to Hughes.)

But after a near-fatal airplane crash in 1946, Howard became addicted to opiates, and from then on began to unravel. By 1950, Howard was in complete seclusion, his comings and goings cloaked in secrecy, and only a few select Mormon nursemaids were allowed to see him. His enormous business enterprise was somehow directed by memo, business meetings were called only when absolutely necessary, and even those were often held in hotel washrooms, Howard in a stall while his associates gathered at the sinks. After 1956, Howard was not seen in public or photographed again for the rest of his life. In 1970, when the FBI investigated the possibility that he'd been murdered and his billions were in the process of being heisted, Howard confirmed through a telephone call that he was just fine, thank you.

In November 1966, clad in blue pajamas, Howard was stretchered off his private train and brought to the Desert Inn Hotel in Las Vegas, where he rented the entire top two floors. As New Year's Eve approached, the management of the hotel demanded that Howard leave to make way for vacationing high rollers, so Howard bought the whole place. Over the next three years, Howard bought five more casinos, including the Sands, where Frank Sinatra was effectively shown the door after Howard cut off his credit. When Howard's complaints about Las Vegas TV station KLAS going off the air after midnight went unanswered, he bought the broadcaster and had his favorite movies shown all night.

Through all of this, Howard *never* left the ninth-floor penthouse suite of his Desert Inn. Almost all of his time was spent sitting naked in a white leather chair in the center of the living room, an area he called the "germ-free zone," watching one film after another, while the windows remained covered by black curtains lest sunlight inadvertently fall on Howard's body. He was protected by guards who never caught a glimpse of their boss, and his staff awaited orders in the parlor around the clock. Due to his germ phobias, Howard slept atop sheets that were covered with a layer of paper towels, and he wrote his aides meticulous memos about how to wrap Kleenex around his eating utensils.

Finally, on Thanksgiving Day 1970, the bundle of neuroses called Howard, with his corkscrewing toenails, greasy, shoulder-length hair, and rotting teeth, was spirited onto a waiting jet and whisked to the Bahamas. The man obsessed with avoiding germs had, ironically, not allowed maids into the suite, and it had become disgustingly filthy and fetid. His aides stayed behind to clean up.

Howard's final years were spent abruptly moving from place to place: the Bahamas, London, Mexico, Panama and, probably, other locations. He would arrive quietly at a luxury hotel after elaborate measures had been undertaken to ensure complete privacy, and he would remain unseen during his stay. By 1976 Howard was a living cadaver: His 6-foot 4-inch frame had shrunk by two inches and had wasted to 100 pounds, his face was gaunt and his dark eyes sunken, and his hair had turned a ghostly gray. As death enveloped him, Howard was boarded onto his jet and flown to Methodist Hospital in Houston for emergency care but, 30,000 feet in the air, Howard expired at 70 of kidney failure. The treasury department, which stood to reap over a billion dollars in estate taxes, required his identity be verified by fingerprints. An autopsy revealed broken hypodermic needles in his arms.

The dead man's legend and legacy were richer than conventional reckoning could calculate. He had parlayed a small fortune from a revolutionary oil-drilling bit into a business empire than made him one of the richest men in the world, his estate estimated at $2 billion. Without an heir or an official will, 400 prospective beneficiaries tried to lay claim, but his assets eventually went to 22 cousins on both sides of his family.

Howard was buried at Glenwood Cemetery in Houston, Texas.

CEMETERY DIRECTIONS: Glenwood Cemetery isn't far from downtown Houston, located at 2525 Washington Ave., and is easily found by accessing the avenue from the exit at either I-10 or I-45, then following the address numbers.

GRAVE DIRECTIONS: Enter the cemetery and turn right beyond the circle and bridge. Stay to the right on this drive and do not inadvertently bear onto any of the left-hand drives. After a couple hundred yards, there is a plot surrounded by an off-green steel fence on the right, which is the Hughes plot.

RAY KROC

OCTOBER 5, 1902 – JANUARY 14, 1984

After a seventeen-year career selling cups to restaurants in the Midwest, high school dropout Ray Kroc felt it was time to get out on his own, so he became the exclusive sales agent for a five-spindle multimixer. In 1953, Dick and Mac McDonald's fast-food emporium in San Bernardino, California, bought eight of the mixing machines from Ray. His curiosity piqued, Ray later explained: "I had to see what kind of an operation was making 40 milkshakes at a time."

When Ray went to see the restaurant the next year, he was entranced by the efficiency of the operation. There was only a very limited, low-priced menu and, though it was a hamburger restaurant, it was not of the popular drive-in variety; people had to get out of their cars to be served. A dyed-in-the-wool capitalist, Ray started dreaming about additional McDonald's stores, each equipped with eight multimixers churning up a steady stream of cash. The following day he pitched the idea of opening several restaurants to the brothers, and when asked, "Who could we get to open them for us?" Ray was ready.

"Well, what about me?" he replied.

Eventually a deal was struck whereby Ray gave the McDonalds a small percentage of the gross, and in 1955, he opened his first McDonald's restaurant in Des Plaines, Illinois. Business proved excellent, and by the time Ray bought the brothers out in 1961 for a paltry $2.7 million, there were 273 locations.

Free to run the business his own way, Ray never changed the fundamental format, but added his own wrinkles. First, from the parking lot to the kitchen floor to the bathrooms, everything was clean. Next, he applied team techniques to the food's preparation. New restaurants were located in swiftly growing suburban areas, where family visits to the local McDonald's became something of a tribal ritual. Finally, millions of dollars were poured into advertising, to the point where consumers were so preconditioned by the McDonald's promotional blanket that, as one industry wag flippantly pointed out, "the hamburger would taste good even if they left the meat out."

In choosing a franchise owner to manage a new outlet, Ray looked for someone who was good with people. "We'd rather get a salesman than a chef," Ray explained. And when it came to training these franchise owners, Ray was unremittingly intense: At his own "Hamburger University," a training course led to a "Bachelor of Hamburgerology with a minor in French fries." Ray's fastidious attention and passion paid off; by 1963 more than 1 billion hamburgers had been sold, and that same year, the 500th restaurant opened. Today there are more than 25,000 McDonald's restaurants in 120 countries.

Ray sensed that a nation of people who ate on the go wanted something different. He changed American business and eating habits by giving them what they wanted or, perhaps what *he* wanted. The ultimate salesman, Ray defined salesmanship as "the gentle art of letting the customer have it *your* way."

Ray served as senior chairman of McDonald's until his death at 81 after a series of strokes.

He was buried at El Camino Memorial Park in La Jolla, California.

CEMETERY DIRECTIONS: From I-805, take the Mira Mesa Boulevard exit and follow it for a quarter-mile east to Scranton Road. Turn right and the road will shortly turn into Carroll Canyon Road. The park is ahead one mile on the left.

GRAVE DIRECTIONS: Enter the cemetery, turn at the first left and go all the way up the hill. Turn left at the "T," follow this drive all the way to its end, and park at the loop. Walk toward the three big bells and turn into the mausoleum on the right. Proceed all the way through the mausoleum, exit the rear door and, once you're back outside, turn right and look up to see Ray's crypt.

LIBERACE

MAY 16, 1919 – FEBRUARY 4, 1987

B est remembered for his extravagant costumes and the trade-mark giant candelabrum atop his piano, Wladziu Valentino Liberace was loved by his audiences for his musical talent and his unique showmanship. Throughout his long and lucrative career—much of it spent in almost ridiculously glitzy costumes consisting of jeweled capes, sequins, bright beads, and even hot pants—the critics found it hard to make fun of him because he always seemed to be having so much fun performing what he called "*Reader's Digest* versions" of familiar classic melodies. Liberace whipped through Chopin's "Minute Waltz" in 37 seconds. Tchaikovsky's 45-minute Piano Concerto No. 1 took him just four minutes. His secret, he said, was "cutting out the dull parts."

But Liberace wasn't without classical credentials: He attended Wisconsin College of Music, followed by a three-year stint in the Chicago Symphony. During a chancy encore after a 1939 recital, he stumbled upon the musical formula that made him famous by breaking with concert tradition and performing the popular novelty song "Three Little Fishes." It drove the audience wild and Liberace later recognized that as the defining moment on his road to rhinestones and Rolls-Royces. In 1952, the *Liberace Television Hour* introduced him to middle America, and for the rest of his career he sold out dozens of shows each year as an American music icon and Las Vegas fixture.

By 1986 though, Liberace had lost significant weight and was in exceedingly poor health. Tabloids soon screamed that he was suffering of AIDS and, as expected, Liberace's camp denied it. But after his death at 67, his death certificate stated that Liberace had died of "cytomegalic virus pneumonia and human immunodeficiency viral disease."

Pictures of his most-recent boyfriend, and of his dog, Wrinkles, were placed in Liberace's casket and, wearing a white tuxedo and full makeup, he was entombed at Forest Lawn Memorial Park in Hollywood Hills, California.

CEMETERY DIRECTIONS: From Highway 134, which is the connector between Highway 101 and I-210, take the Forest Lawn Drive exit. Proceed west for a mile and the park's entrance is on the left.

GRAVE DIRECTIONS: Stop at the booth and after getting a park map, go to the Courts of Remembrance. Walk into the courtyard and you won't miss Liberace's large white tomb against the wall on the right.

BRIAN PICCOLO

OCTOBER 31, 1943 – JUNE 16, 1970

Though he was the nation's leading rusher in college football during the 1964 season, Brian Piccolo was not even drafted by the NFL after his final year at Wake Forest University, as he was deemed too slow and small for the league. Brian instead joined the Chicago Bears as a free agent and spent the next few seasons on the team's practice squad, watching from the sidelines as his roommate Gale Sayers put together consecutive seasons as the team's star running back.

But in 1968, Gale suffered a knee injury and Brian tenderly assisted him through rehab—and played in Gale's starting position for the season's final five games. During the off-season, Gale was cleared to return for the 1969 season and Brian was relegated to his familiar second-string position, but after a starting fullback was injured, Brian was called up again and, in a storybook scenario, started alongside his best friend Gale.

After just one game together, Brian developed breathing problems and doctors soon diagnosed him with embryonal cell cancer. After surgery and chemotherapy it seemed he'd beaten the disease, but it returned the following winter. By summertime the cancer claimed Brian Piccolo at the age of 26.

A movie of his life, *Brian's Song*, was released in 1971, and its touching story of courage and humanity is an enduring tearjerker. The embryonal cell carcinoma that was almost always fatal 30 years ago is now often curable, partly through the generosity of the Brian Piccolo Cancer Research Fund, which was established after his death.

Brian is buried at Saint Mary's Catholic Cemetery in Evergreen Park, Illinois.

CEMETERY DIRECTIONS: Saint Mary's Cemetery is on 87th Street, four miles west of I-94.

GRAVE DIRECTIONS: Enter the cemetery and take the first right turn behind the office so that Section HG is on the right and Section AM is on the left. A hundred feet on the left, stop in front of the Tarantino mausoleum and you'll find Brian's flat stone just to the left of this mausoleum.

BUFORD PUSSER

DECEMBER 12, 1937 – AUGUST 21, 1974

In the early 1970s, the *Walking Tall* true-life movie series lent Hollywood romance to the exploits of a Tennessee sheriff, Buford Pusser. He was canonized as a friend of every honest man and true-grit peacemaker who levied a brand of personal justice against any who might attempt to upset bucolic Southern tradition. Though entertaining, the *Walking Tall* features didn't let the facts get in the way of a good story, and Buford's larger-than-life legend thrived.

Before his career in law enforcement, Buford was discharged from Marine boot camp for an asthma condition, and he followed that stint with a short-lived career as "Buford the Bull" on the Chicago professional wrestling circuit. In 1962 he became the police chief of Adamsville, Tennessee, after his father arranged for Buford to succeed him upon his own retirement. In 1964 he won the seat of McNairy County Sheriff when the favored incumbent was killed in an auto accident before the voting day. It was shortly thereafter that Buford and his trademark Big Stick waged a campaign to rid the county of moonshiners and mobsters. His unorthodox law enforcement practices won him a number of enemies.

In 1967 Buford was called out on a middle-of-the-night emergency that turned out to be bogus and instead, he found himself in an ambush, presumably by folks who were unimpressed by his manner of applying the law. For reasons unexplained, his wife Pauline had accompanied him on the call, and she was killed in a hail of bullets while Buford was lucky to escape with just two bullet holes in his face and jaw. After the attack, Buford redoubled his efforts to clean up the county and sought to avenge his wife's death, but no one was ever brought to trial for the incident. At least one prime suspect shortly wound up dead.

In 1970 Buford stepped down from his post as sheriff, as state law prohibited anyone from holding an elected office for more than three consecutive terms, and he later lost a reelection bid. In 1973, *Walking Tall,* starring Joe Don Baker, was released, and on its heels came a sequel and a song, *The Ballad of Buford Pusser.* Buford's exaggerated exploits soon became bar-talk legend.

On the day it was announced that Buford would star as himself in a third *Walking Tall* movie he was killed in a single-car crash. Just that day, Buford had taken delivery of a new Corvette and, while on his way home, lost control at over 100 m.p.h. He was killed instantly.

Buford was 36 at his death, and was buried next to his wife, Pauline, at the Adamsville War Memorial Park in Adamsville, Tennessee.

CEMETERY DIRECTIONS: The cemetery is located on Route 64 just a short distance west of the Route 22 junction.

GRAVE DIRECTIONS: The Pussers' plot is easy to find, marked by a tall granite slab in the cemetery's northwest corner.

JONBENET RAMSEY
AUGUST 6, 1990 – DECEMBER 26, 1996

JonBenet Ramsey was the six-year-old daughter of John and Patsy Ramsey of Boulder, Colorado. The Ramsey's seemed to be an ideal family: John was a respected and successful businessman while former beauty-queen Patsy maintained the Ramsey social calendar and promoted little JonBenet in toddler beauty pageants.

But in December 1996, everything changed when Patsy awoke to find a ransom note in the kitchen and JonBenet missing. The note demanded $118,000 for JonBenet's safe return and, while police mounted an investigation and searched for the girl, the hysterically distraught Ramseys paced the sidelines and mounted a campaign to raise the ransom money. But in the end, no ransom was necessary. Eight hours after Patsy found the note, John found their daughter dead inside a small basement room that had been overlooked by the swarming cadre of police. JonBenet's mouth was duct-taped closed, a garrote made of white cord and a paintbrush handle was around her neck, and she lay covered by a white blanket. An autopsy determined her death came of asphyxiation by strangulation.

The kidnapping seemed a ruse from the outset and the police, media, and public soon came to believe that either one or both of the Ramseys had killed their daughter. In these post-O.J. Simpson murder case days, the investigation into JonBenet's murder was handled relatively professionally amid much secrecy but, as the legitimate media struggled to fill the information void, the tabloid media took over, covering the JonBenet case from every tawdry angle imaginable.

After polygraph tests, unidentified pubic hairs, inconclusive handwriting samples, countless talk-show debriefings, and finger pointing in every direction, the case remains unsolved. No one has ever been arrested in connection with the murder, and perhaps no one ever will.

JonBenet is buried at the Saint James Episcopal Church Cemetery in Marietta, Georgia.

CEMETERY DIRECTIONS: From I-75, follow the North Marietta Parkway NE west (*Note:* Don't be fooled by the South Marietta Parkway SE) for two miles to Polk Street. Turn right onto Polk Street and the cemetery is a short distance ahead on the left, across from the high school.

GRAVE DIRECTIONS: Drive straight into the cemetery to the end of the paved drive and JonBenet's grave is on the right.

CARL SAGAN
NOVEMBER 9, 1934 – DECEMBER 20, 1996

The scientist Carl Sagan was trained at the University of Chicago in both astronomy and biology, and during the 1950s he began researching the origins of life. By 1962 he was teaching at Harvard University while also working as an astrophysicist at the Smithsonian Observatory, and in 1970 he settled at Cornell University as Professor of Astronomy and the Director for Planetary Studies.

From there, Carl used his natural gift for storytelling to extol the grandeur and mystery of the universe and to stimulate public enthusiasm for space science; the PBS television series, *Cosmos,* which he hosted, became the most-watched series in public-television history. Carl was perhaps the world's greatest popularizer of science and shared his lifelong passion in more than 600 scientific papers in eight books, including the Pulitzer Prize-winning *Dragons of Eden.*

Carl played a leading role in the Mariner, Viking, Voyager, and Galileo expeditions to other planets through his research on topics such as the greenhouse effect on Venus and windblown dust as an explanation for seasonal changes on Mars. He even detoured from space-based considerations to study what might be the long-term environmental consequences of nuclear war on our own Earth. But Carl's unbridled enthusiasm was reserved for searches for intelligent life elsewhere in the universe.

"Are we an exceptionally unlikely accident or is the universe brimming over with intelligence?" he asked as radio telescopes funded by a program close to his heart listened for signs of life in the billions of stars and galaxies.

So far, no response is forthcoming, but Carl offered that, "it says something about the rarity and preciousness of life on this planet. The flip side of not finding life on another planet is appreciating life on Earth."

Carl died of pneumonia at 62 after a two-year battle with a bone-marrow disease, and was buried at Lakeview Cemetery in Ithaca, New York.

CEMETERY DIRECTIONS: On the north side of town, take the Stewart Park exit off Route 13 and head east on East Shore Drive for about a half-mile. Then turn left onto Kline Road, go up the hill and turn left at the stop sign. Take the next left onto Wyckoff Road, then turn left into the cemetery.

GRAVE DIRECTIONS: Enter the cemetery and park in the first paved drive on the right, immediately after the Temple Bethel section. Down the hill on the left is a small chain fence, and on the other side of the fence you'll find the flat stone that marks Carl's grave.

COLONEL SANDERS
SEPTEMBER 9, 1890 – DECEMBER 16, 1980

Harland Sanders grew up in the backwoods of southern Indiana and learned to cook while still a child. His father had died before Harland was three, and by the time he was six it was his responsibility to prepare the meals while his mother worked. After the sixth grade he dropped out of school to supplement the family's meager income, and from his first job he brought home the bacon to the tune of $2 a week. By twelve he had left home to live and work on a farm, and from there he was able to provide the family with a more substantial amount of money. At sixteen Harland volunteered for a one-year stint in the Army during America's intervention in Cuba.

During his adult years, Harland toiled as a streetcar conductor and an insurance agent, a tire salesman and a railroad fireman. He operated an Ohio River steamboat ferry and, after a law correspondence course, he practiced as a justice of the peace. But it was his fate to be the owner of a service station in Corbin, Kentucky.

To augment the station's sparse gas receipts, Harland began cooking for hungry travelers. He didn't actually have a restaurant, so he served folks in his family's dining room. When more people began dropping by for the food than the gasoline, he knew he was on to something. In 1930, he bought the motel across the street and converted it into a 142-seat restaurant, Sanders Court.

Over the next decade, Harland perfected his secret recipe of "eleven herbs and spices" used in the preparation of his Kentucky Fried Chicken, and his Sanders Court restaurant became known for having the best food, and especially the best chicken, for miles around. Business boomed, and the governor even named Harland an honorary Kentucky "Colonel" to recognize his contributions to the state's cuisine.

In the 1950s though, a new interstate highway was built bypassing Corbin, business dried up, and the value of his property plummeted. At 65, the dejected Colonel auctioned everything off and, after paying the bills, found himself penniless and reduced to living on a $105 monthly Social Security check. But remarkably, in the twilight of his life, Harland decided that instead of sitting in a rocking chair feeling sorry for himself while waiting for government checks, he'd start anew.

The Colonel and his wife Claudia hit the road. Traveling around the countryside by car, they visited roadside eateries and cooked batches of chicken for the restaurant owners and their employees. If the reaction to the chicken was favorable, the Colonel entered into a handshake agreement that stipulated a payment to him of a nickel for each chicken the restaurant sold.

By 1964, when he sold his interest in the company for $2 million, the Colonel had more than 600 franchised outlets for his chicken. He stayed on with the new Kentucky Fried Chicken corporation as a spokesman and advisor for the next decade but, in 1975, the relationship strained when he publicly denounced some of KFC's fare, especially its gravy, which he derided as "sludge with a wall-paper taste." Nonetheless, his spectacled caricature today watches over each of the six million people who eat in one of KFC's 12,000 restaurants every day.

Colonel Sanders died of leukemia at 90 and was buried at Cave Hill Cemetery in Louisville, Kentucky.

CEMETERY DIRECTIONS: Take Exit 16 off of I-264, follow Bardstown Road north for 3 3/4 miles, and you'll see the cemetery on the right at the Broadway Street intersection.

GRAVE DIRECTIONS: Enter the cemetery and follow the solid line painted in the middle of the road. At the end of the line, the Sanders plot is on your right.

Also nearby is the Kentucky Fried Chicken Visitor Center, which houses a museum of memorabilia telling the story of the Colonel's life. It's quite interesting and well worth a visit. To get there, take Exit 14 off of I-264, turn south onto Poplar Level Road and, at the first light, turn left onto Sanita Road, which turns into Gardiner Lane. Go past the Colonel Sanders Technical Center and the next building on the left, the one that looks like the White House, is the visitor's center.

EDIE SEDGWICK

APRIL 20, 1943 – NOVEMBER 16, 1971

Who was Edie Sedgwick? She was a strikingly pretty young woman with a genius for self-destruction: daughter of a distinguished, old money family; raised on a 2,000-acre ranch in one of California's most exclusive areas; educated at the finest private schools in the country; fashion icon and muse of decadent glamour; evanescent femme fatale of Andy Warhol's underground movies; a footnote in the pop history of the 1960s and a careless suicide at 28.

In 1964 Edie arrived in New York to seek work as a model and actress. Tall and slim in dresses that ended at her thighs and earrings that hung to her shoulders, she was introduced to pop artist Andy Warhol, who was only too happy to help fulfill her destiny. Edie was the woman of Andy's dreams. Soon her hair was in a boyish cut and tinted silver to match her mentor's, and for the next two years she was his new "Superstar." As Queen of the Underground, Edie, the cast-off debutante, romped through Andy's 8mm movies with titles like *Poor Little Rich Girl* and *Face*. She boogied through fashion and gossip columns, was dubbed a "youthquaker" by *Vogue* magazine, and was seen with all the right people at all the right places. She entertained all the right men; in his haunting *Just Like a Woman*, Bob Dylan wrote that Edie "breaks just like a little girl." And in the midst of the whirlwind, Edie even completed an autobiographical film of her life, *Ciao Manhattan*, which was lauded as "the *Citizen Kane* of the Drug Generation."

It was the high life for Edie and she lived it on coke, heroin, and a mountain of pills—but eventually she lost control and spiraled into psychosis. After a drug bust, a few mental asylums, and shock therapy, all that was left of Edie Sedgwick was a shell of her former self.

At 28 Edie died of "acute barbital intoxication" and was buried at Oak Hill Cemetery in Ballard, California.

After her death, Edie was immortalized in the 1982 bestseller *Edie: An American Biography* by Jean Stein and George Plimpton. Today, the allure of Edie-like luminaries remains undiminished as subsequent generations each discover their own ultimate Superstars.

CEMETERY DIRECTIONS: From Route 154, take Beeline Avenue toward Ballard. Almost two miles down Beeline Avenue, on the left, is the cemetery's entrance. (It's accented by a line of Eucalyptus trees.)

GRAVE DIRECTIONS: Enter the cemetery and proceed down the paved drive that extends to the rear. About 200 feet down this drive, stop. On the lawn to the right count in six rows and you'll find Edie's flat marker, often distinguishable from a distance by the fan memorabilia left upon it.

SAM & MARILYN SHEPPARD

Marilyn Sheppard
AUGUST 20, 1923 – JULY 4, 1954

Sam Sheppard
MARCH 15, 1924 – APRIL 6, 1970

In the early morning hours on the Fourth of July, 1954, a pregnant, 30-year-old Marilyn Sheppard was bludgeoned to death at her home in a quiet Cleveland suburb. Her successful physician husband, Sam Sheppard, was soon arrested and charged with her murder, though he steadfastly maintained his innocence, claiming he'd wrestled with a "bushy-haired stranger," was knocked unconscious, and woke up to find his wife dead.

Sam was convicted of Marilyn's murder in December 1954 and sentenced to life in prison, only to be freed in June 1966 after his saucy attorney, F. Lee Bailey, appealed to the Supreme Court, which ruled the verdict against Sam was unconstitutional because his trial had been a "carnival." In November of 1966, after a retrial, Sam was found not guilty.

We know all of the preceding to be true, but virtually everything else of substance in the Sheppard murder case seems to be either theory, conjecture, half-truth, or outright lie. The case has proved a resilient whodunit and after almost a half-century of speculation the courts finally put the matter to rest in 2002.

Sam Reese Sheppard, the son of Sam and Marilyn, who was seven years old and sleeping upstairs at the time of his mother's murder, had begun a crusade in 1990 to dispel any lingering doubts about his father's innocence. In 2000, Sam, Jr. brought to the courts a "third trial"—a civil suit to declare his father "innocent" rather than merely "not guilty"—and in this trial, because Sam Sheppard was the plaintiff instead of the defendant, the burden of proof was reversed; Sam, Jr. needed to demonstrate his father's innocence by a preponderance of the evidence. In the end the verdict was for the state, unanimous and signed by all eight jurors, and as newspapers across the country put it, Sam Sheppard was found "not innocent," meaning that the evidence suggests he probably committed the murder. In August of 2002, the matter met its absolute finality when the Ohio Supreme Court, in a one-sentence ruling, refused to hear Sam, Jr.'s appeal of the civil-suit verdict.

After 48 years it was all over for everyone. For Sam Sheppard himself, it had been over since April 1970, when he died of liver disease nearly penniless at age 46. Upon his release from prison in 1966, he'd gone back to medicine only to lose his business due to a malpractice suit. As a semi-celebrity with no other real options, the doctor resorted to making appearances as "Killer Sheppard" in professional wrestling matches; his gimmick was that, with his knowledge of anatomy, he could render an opponent helpless.

In the same way that the O.J. Simpson murder trial permeated popular culture in the mid-nineties, the Sheppard case enjoyed its own "heyday" in the sixties. And in 1965, at the height of the case's "popularity," a new television series, *The Fugitive*, later remade into a film of the same name in 1993, caused a sensation with a storyline said to be inspired by the Sheppard case. But upon closer inspection, the correlation is limited, at best. In contrast to the television series, Sam Sheppard never escaped from the law's grasp, he never engaged in a manhunt for the "real" killer, and he never maintained that it was a one-armed man who ran from the crime scene.

After a 1997 exhumation to acquire DNA samples from his corpse, Sam Sheppard was moved from the Columbus, Ohio, cemetery where he had resided to Knollwood Cemetery in Cleveland, Ohio, where he now shares a mausoleum crypt with wife Marilyn.

CEMETERY DIRECTIONS: From I-271, take exit 34 and follow Mayfield Avenue (Route 322) a couple hundred yards east to Som Center Road. Turn right and the cemetery is a short distance ahead on the right.

GRAVE DIRECTIONS: Enter the cemetery and drive all the way to the rear, where you'll see a large mausoleum. Enter the mausoleum and you'll immediately be in a small chapel. Proceed up to the altar and walk down the hall to your right. Turn at the next left, then turn left again, and then, 25 feet to the left, along the second row from the bottom, is the Sheppard crypt.

GENE SISKEL

JANUARY 26, 1946 – FEBRUARY 20, 1999

Gene Siskel was the tall, balding half of the famous *Siskel & Ebert* movie-review team that brought film criticism into the mainstream.

By 1974 Gene had parlayed his lifelong love for movies into a position as the *Chicago Tribune* newspaper's film critic, and in that year, he first teamed on television for a movie-review program with counterpart Roger Ebert, a rival reviewer from the *Chicago Sun-Times*. For a quarter-century, the combative chemistry and classic pairing of opposites lent a fun, one-upmanship quality to the staid arena of film criticism, and their "thumbs up, thumbs down" judgments became a benchmark for the movie industry.

The pair purposely dressed in casual clothes just as most people do when they go to the movies, because, as Siskel explained, "We've always wanted viewers to feel as if they're just eavesdropping on a couple of guys who love movies and are having a spontaneous discussion that'd be ongoing even if they weren't watching."

In May of 1998 Siskel underwent surgery to remove a growth from his brain and returned to the nationally syndicated *Siskel & Ebert* soon afterward. Eight months later he announced he was taking time off for additional recuperation, but Siskel soon died from complications of his brain tumor at 53.

He was buried at Westlawn Memorial Park in Norridge, Illinois.

CEMETERY DIRECTIONS: Westlawn is located on Montrose Avenue, one mile west of Route 43.

GRAVE DIRECTIONS: Enter the cemetery and get a map at the office. In the Memorial section at street marking 22-24, about halfway down, look for Gloria Martin's grave along the curb. Siskel's flat, bronze marker is in the same column as Gloria's, eighteen rows back.

After Siskel's death, an urban legend surfaced, complete with dummied-up newspaper accounts, that he'd requested in his will that he be embalmed with a thumb pointing perpetually up. The scuttlebutt was blatantly contrived and is baseless.

STEVEN STAYNER
APRIL 18, 1965 – SEPTEMBER 16, 1989

In 1973, at seven years old, Steven Stayner was approached by a man who told him that his parents had abandoned him. The kidnapper ordered Steven to call him "Dad," and for the next seven years, secreted in a series of remote California cabins, Steven was psychologically and sexually abused.

After the kidnapper forcibly brought home another victim in 1980, Steven, who by this time was fourteen, recognized what was really happening and he escaped with the other boy in tow. After hitching a ride 40 miles to the nearest police station, Steven tried to explain their plight to the on-duty officer. He started his explanation by saying, "I know my first name is Steven."

The boys' story made news reports around the world and Steven went back home hailed as a hero, while the kidnapper was arrested and ended up doing hard time. Despite what had happened to him, Steven became a fairly ordinary teenager and later married and had two children of his own.

Eight years after the incident, a television mini-series about Steven's drama called *I Know My First Name Is Steven,* was broadcast to much critical acclaim and earned four Emmy nominations.

Tragically, though, the day before the Emmy Awards were held, Steven was killed in a hit-and-run motorcycle accident.

At 24 years old, Steven was buried at Merced District Cemetery in Merced, California.

CEMETERY DIRECTIONS: In Merced, 13th Street runs parallel and just to the west of Route 99. Follow 13th Street to its southern end and the cemetery will be in front of you.

GRAVE DIRECTIONS: Drive to the section of the cemetery that is farthest to the left and the rear. Near a small tree you'll see a sign that denotes this section as the Garden of Peace. Under this sign is the marker for Steven's grave.

Later the Stayners were cast into the limelight again when another publicly shared tragedy beset the family. In 2002, Steven's brother Cary was sentenced to death after a jury found him guilty of murdering three women in Yosemite National Park. The details of the crime were particularly heinous, and Cary was caught only after he struck again, beheading a park naturalist. Included in Cary's defense was the notion that his younger brother's kidnapping had so deeply affected him that it contributed to the decline of his mental health.

HERMAN TARNOWER

MARCH 18, 1910 – MARCH 10, 1980

Herman Tarnower was a respected cardiologist who served the posh enclaves surrounding his Scarsdale, New York, medical office. For many years the doctor had dispensed to his heavier patients a simple, one-page paper that he'd prepared as a primer for paring pounds. The content was not particularly inventive, but it was sound: Cut down on carbohydrates, eat a lot of fruits and vegetables, try to minimize desserts.

In 1978, a writer named Samm Sinclair Baker convinced Dr. Tarnower that his one-page primer constituted the outline of a diet book that they should write together, because such a book would enrich the life of everyone who bought it, not to mention their own pocketbooks. Six months later, *The Complete Scarsdale Medical Diet* hit bookstores and became a bestseller. Shortly, however, only half of its author team was still enjoying its success.

A lifelong bachelor, Herman was very promiscuous and enjoyed casual relationships with the many willing women who were attracted to him. Since 1965 he had been involved with a respected private-school educator named Jean Harris, and though Herman had always been financially generous to her, he was less generous emotionally, and never entirely gave up other women.

Herman was shot and killed in his bedroom one evening, and Jean stood trial for the murder. At the trial, which was marked by a blizzard of media attention, the prosecution charged that Jean had murdered Herman because of her frustration over their relationship; she desired a commitment but he had other distractions—namely, his best-selling diet book and other women. Meanwhile, Jean's defense maintained that, though she had gone to the doctor's house with a gun, she meant only to kill herself in his presence, and as he struggled with her to prevent the suicide, the gun went off and he was killed.

The jury didn't buy Jean's explanation and she was sentenced to prison for fifteen years to life. In 1992, because of a supposed heart condition, then-Governor Mario Cuomo commuted her sentence, and she was released. Ten years later, Jean's heart is still ticking, and she follows a busy national lecture schedule speaking on behalf of an inmates' children's fund and promoting her five books.

Dead at 69, Herman is interred at Mount Hope Cemetery in Hastings-on-Hudson, New York.

CEMETERY DIRECTIONS: From the Sawmill Parkway, turn east onto Jackson Street, go through the traffic light, and enter the cemetery on the left.

GRAVE DIRECTIONS: Drive straight into the cemetery, then take the second right to the Larchmont Temple area. Start up the hill but stop at the "Y." Herman's grave is marked with a stone 50 feet to the right.

DAVE THOMAS
JULY 2, 1932 – JANUARY 8, 2002

In 1956 Dave Thomas was working at a Fort Wayne, Indiana, barbecue restaurant when a bespectacled, white-haired, gentleman stopped in and offered Dave's boss the opportunity to participate in a new chicken franchising deal he was cooking up. The gentleman turned out to be Colonel Harland Sanders, and the franchise was, of course, Kentucky Fried Chicken. But in 1956, neither of those names carried any weight. Still, Dave's boss entered into an agreement with the Colonel and added his chicken to the menu.

Six years later, when four failing Kentucky Fried Chicken outlets in Columbus, Ohio, desperately needed an experienced manager to turn them around, Dave jumped at the opportunity, cutting a deal in which he gained ownership of the locations to boot. In 1968,

FAMILY TREE

DAVE THOMAS

COLONEL
SANDERS

RAY KROC

FAST FOOD
GUYS

just another six years later, Dave sold the revitalized restaurants back to the KFC company and pocketed a cool $1.1 million.

Ever the entrepreneur, Dave a year later opened his first Wendy's Old Fashioned Hamburgers, naming the restaurant after his 8-year-old daughter, Melinda Lou, who had been nicknamed Wendy by her siblings. By lending the KFC restaurant strategies to the burgeoning fast-food hamburger business and always focusing on the customer, Dave grew that single restaurant into a chain of more than 6,000 with sales of over $7 billion.

A shrewd marketer—Wendy's "Where's the beef?" advertising campaign is still a classic—Dave became a household name when he began personally pitching his burgers and fries in television commercials in 1989. At the time, the company was in a difficult period and its earnings had tanked. But the humorous, homespun ads featuring a smiling, portly Dave in a Wendy's apron lent the company a fresh, down-home, unsophisticated image and launched Wendy's to unexpected success.

Dave had been adopted as a child, and in 1990 President George H.W. Bush asked him to be a national advocate for adoption. He accepted the challenge and encouraged people to consider adopting older children, not just babies. In 1992 he established the Dave Thomas Foundation for Adoption, which helps make adoption more affordable. "I know firsthand how important it is for every child to have a home and loving family," he said. "Without a family, I would not be where I am today."

Dave had a carcinoid tumor in his liver for more than a decade, he underwent quadruple heart-bypass surgery in 1996, and began undergoing dialysis for a kidney problem in early 2001. Finally, at 69, Dave's body gave out and he expired of the liver condition.

He was buried at Union Cemetery in Columbus, Ohio.

CEMETERY DIRECTIONS: From Route 315, exit at Broadway Avenue, turn west on Olentangy River Road and the cemetery is immediately on the right.

GRAVE DIRECTIONS: Follow the main drive into the cemetery and you'll see three mausoleum buildings off to the right. Walk in through the middle doors of the building with rust-colored awnings and, immediately inside, look left. There's Dave!

TINY TIM

APRIL 12, 1932 - NOVEMBER 30, 1996

Tiny Tim was the ukulele-strumming crooner who amused millions by trilling "Tiptoe Through the Tulips," a whimsical love ditty he appropriated on behalf of the flower generation. Born Herbert Khaury, the frizzy-haired, goofy-looking, offbeat entertainer built a career on this single hit song, his stratospheric falsetto, and an asexual and childlike stage persona.

Tiny found his fame on Johnny Carson's *Tonight Show*, and his 1969 on-air marriage to Vicki Budinger ("Miss Vicki," as he always called her), whom he met at a promotional event for his book, *Beautiful Thoughts*, drew an audience of 40 million. In later years he found fans within the retro-music crowd and always got an enthusiastic welcome at his off-center appearances, most notably on Howard Stern's radio program where, in fascinating interviews, he divulged numerous eccentricities: He'd never learned to drive; after showering, he dried himself with paper towels; to avoid using public bathrooms, Tiny wore adult diapers when he was away from home; and he applied Oil of Olay lotion to his body eight times a day. Yep, Tiny had his issues.

By 1996, Tiny was on his third marriage (this time to Miss Sue), he was performing some 300 days a year, and he was in terrible health, suffering from a heart condition and diabetes. In September, after he became dizzy and fell from a stage, doctors informed Tiny that, though he might live a few more years, he could also die at any moment and should immediately discontinue performing. For a time, Tiny convalesced, but by November he was appearing at a few gigs. At the Women's Club of Minneapolis, Tiny and his ukulele took the stage but, partway into his signature "Tiptoe Through the Tulips," Tiny was looking shaky. Asked by his concerned Miss Sue if he was feeling alright, Tiny spoke his last words, "No, I'm not."

Tiny often fibbed about his age, but at 64, he was laid to rest, with a ukulele in his casket, at Lakewood Cemetery in Minneapolis, Minnesota.

CEMETERY DIRECTIONS: From I-94, take Exit 231B and follow Hennepin Avenue south for two miles. At that point the road will "T," and the driveway into the cemetery will be in front of you.

GRAVE DIRECTIONS: Enter the cemetery, turn right, and follow the drive to the mausoleum. Enter the mausoleum, turn to the right, and get on the elevator. Take the elevator to the ground floor, then turn left out of the elevator. Proceed to the last alcove on the left and you'll see Tiny's crypt on the left wall.

THE VON TRAPP FAMILY

Georg von Trapp
APRIL 1, 1880 – SEPTEMBER 22, 1947

Maria von Trapp
JANUARY 26, 1905 – MARCH 28, 1987

Baron Georg von Trapp was a distinguished Austrian naval commander, but when the Austro-Hungarian empire collapsed after World War I, his country lost its seacoast, and this captain's naval career promptly ended. After Georg's wife died a few years later, a twenty-year-old Jesuit novitiate named Maria Kutschera joined his household to care for the seven children. A romance blossomed and in 1927 the 47-year-old ex-sailor married Maria the ex-nun. The happy couple would themselves have three children, but in the interim, the banks in Austria crashed and Georg's fortune was wiped out, leaving the von Trapp family destitute.

The von Trapps took the most logical course of action; the musically inclined Maria, all of the children, and their religious mentor, Monsigneur Franz Wasner, polished their singing hobby into a stage act that became the family profession. Though Georg didn't participate in the singing, his stature as a Baron (though a bankrupt one) and a naval commander (without a navy), opened doors, and the von Trapp family was soon performing Gregorian chants and English madrigals all over Europe.

In March 1938 the Nazis goose-stepped into Salzburg and the von Trapps fled Hitler's war machine, leaving their home and material possessions behind, never to return. In contrast to the romanticized version of their story in the *Sound of Music*, the von Trapps did not escape Austria by strolling across the Alps. Instead, they rode a train to Italy and boarded a ship to America without incident.

Stateside, the German-speaking von Trapps struggled to reestablish themselves. The enterprising Maria persisted and the family singing group again found success. For almost two decades the von Trapps spent eight months a year touring America, and every summer ran a music camp at their Vermont farm, until the frenetic pace took its toll; one of Maria's daughter's eloped in 1948 while her eldest daughter suffered a nervous breakdown and was administered electroshock therapy in 1952. Maria was eventually forced to hire non-family members for the singing group and finally, in 1957, when the oldest children were in their 40s, the von Trapps stopped performing.

In 1958 Maria signed away all of the stage and film rights to her book, *The Trapp Family Singers*, for a paltry $9,000, and the story made its Broadway debut as *The Sound of Music* in 1959. The hit musical by Rodgers and Hammerstein enjoyed a run of more than 1,400 performances before it closed, and it's Oscar-winning movie clone starring Julie Andrews as Maria replicated that success after its 1965 premier.

Meanwhile, after a one-year stint as a New Guinea missionary, Maria toiled in the day-to-day operations of the Trapp Family Lodge until she was 80 and then, at 82, died of kidney disease. Georg had died years earlier, in 1947 at age 67. Both Georg and Maria now rest at the Trapp Family Lodge in Stowe, Vermont.

GRAVE DIRECTIONS: From the center of Stowe, take Route 108 north for two miles, then turn left onto Luce Hill Road. Proceed up the hill, after 1½ miles bear left onto Trapp Hill Road, and after another half-mile is the Trapp complex. On your right you'll see a large hotel and a visitor parking area. Once you park your car, you'll be happy to find that the von Trapps have been interred in a garden conveniently located behind the gift shop.

SAM WALTON
MARCH 29, 1918 – APRIL 5, 1992

I n the early 1960s, a franchisee of the Ben Franklin variety store chain presented its executives with an ambitious idea for the operation of a number of new stores. As the concept of discount retailing had just emerged and new discount stores were opening in population centers across the nation, Sam Walton sought to tweak the existing discount concept and open even bigger stores and operate on smaller profit margins in suburban and rural areas. Not surprisingly, in the staid 1960s world of retail, where change occurred glacially, this revolutionary idea bucking every rule of retailing was quickly turned down. Undeterred and confident that large discount stores really could thrive in small towns, Sam went it alone and opened his first Wal-Mart on July 2, 1962.

Now committed to discounting, Sam crusaded to drive costs from the merchandising system and he doggedly drove his prices down and down and down. With his margins cut to the bone, it was imperative that Wal-Mart grow sales at a relentless pace and, boy, did it ever. For the past 40 years, a new Wal-Mart has opened on an average of every four days.

As the chain began to take off, Sam continually managed the growth, and at every turn seemed to make the right decision. As early as 1966 he understood the need to computerize his merchandise controls, and Wal-Mart went on to become the icon of just-in-time inventory. To keep merchandise resupply logistics streamlined, no stores were built more than a day's drive from a distribution center, and today Wal-Mart can fill merchandise orders within two days, compared with a week or more for its rivals. Too, Sam worked hard indoctrinating his employees, whom he always called associates; profit-sharing plans were installed, scholarships were established in the names of associates who crafted particularly useful business improvement ideas, and cheers and songs helped build a team atmosphere.

As Wal-Mart's influence grew, however, Sam was vilified by some, especially beleaguered small-town merchants. A nostalgic national press eulogized the lost graces of small-town America and the blame was put squarely on Sam's shoulders. Sam viewed all these arguments as foolishness though, because *he* had once been a small-town merchant who had seen the future coming and chosen to eat rather than be eaten. Perhaps he did clutter America's countryside, ruin its Main Street, and force a lot of people to change the way they made a living, but he merely hastened such inevitable changes. The consumer had chosen Wal-Mart because it gave America what it really wanted—friendly service, clean and organized stores, enormous selection and, above all, low prices. Capitalism had worked again.

Sam died at 74 of complications due to cancer and was buried at Bentonville Cemetery in Bentonville, Arkansas.

CEMETERY DIRECTIONS: From Highway 71, take Exit 69 and follow Route 72 west for three miles, through the center of Bentonville, to F Street. Turn left on F Street and the cemetery is a short distance ahead on the right.

GRAVE DIRECTIONS: Turn right into the cemetery at the first drive (Lane 10), and the Walton plot can't be missed immediately to your left.

By the way, Sam Walton made a lot of money, and you could've too, if only you'd known. Since Wal-Mart went public in 1970, when its shares were offered for two dollars, it has split eight times and a $1,000 investment made then would now represent 128,000 shares worth a cool $7 million. Sam himself owned 39 percent of the company at his death, and his fortune was split five ways among relatives. Were he still alive and his fortune not divided, his worth would be a whopping 50 percent greater than that of Microsoft founder Bill Gates.

RYAN WHITE

DECEMBER 16, 1971 – APRIL 8, 1990

R yan White was an ordinary Indiana teenager who contracted the AIDS virus through a blood transfusion during an era when public hysteria surrounded the relatively new disease. While his school and community grappled with difficult issues raised by the disease, Ryan helped pierce some of its myths and served as a deterrent to bigotry around the nation. It became hard for people to justify discrimination against AIDS victims once a child's face was put on the disease.

Support for Ryan came from scores of celebrities, and at his death at 18 from a respiratory infection caused by the disease, musician Elton John was at his side. Ryan was buried at the Cicero Cemetery in Cicero, Indiana.

CEMETERY DIRECTIONS: From Route 19, turn west at the traffic light onto Jackson Street. The cemetery is on the left after the lake.

GRAVE DIRECTIONS: Ryan's grave is marked with a six-foot tall monolith on the cemetery's western edge.

NOTABLE
FIGURES
FROM
HISTORY

ALCOHOLICS ANONYMOUS FOUNDERS

Robert 'Dr. Bob' Smith

AUGUST 8, 1879 – NOVEMBER 16, 1950

Bill 'Bill W.' Wilson

NOVEMBER 26, 1895 – JANUARY 24, 1971

At the taste of his first alcoholic drink Bill Wilson was convinced he had found the elixir of life, but after seventeen years of hard drinking, alcohol had served only to destroy his health and career. From the rubble of that wasted life, Wilson overcame alcoholism and founded the Alcoholics Anonymous twelve-step program that has helped millions of others do the same. Influenced by AA, alcoholism has been medically redefined as a chronic disease and, as AA has inspired numerous mirror programs for a host of addictions, Bill is regarded as a profoundly influential social architect.

In 1934, Bill's last drink precipitated an epiphany—a spiritually awakening flash of white light—and the former stockbroker who'd been reduced to an unemployable drunk came to believe that the key to sobriety was a change of heart. Five sober months later, while in Akron, Ohio, on business, Bill was tempted by the sounds and clamor of the hotel bar. Suddenly, at that moment, he realized that the only way he could save himself was to help another alcoholic. Through a series of desperate telephone calls in a strange town far from his home, he was able to find a skeptical drunk named Robert Smith who agreed to meet him that night. One month later, on June 10, 1935, Bob, who happened to be a doctor, had his last drink, and that date is regarded as the official birth of AA, which is based on the idea that an alcoholic can only be helped by another alcoholic.

Dr. Bob (AA members use first names only) immediately began working with alcoholics at Akron hospitals while Bill codified their principles into "Twelve Traditions," an enduring blueprint for the Alcoholics Anonymous fellowship that has no formal or political organization, no governing officers, no rules or regulations, and no fees or dues. The chain reaction of "one drunk helping another" has resulted in mass-produced sobriety, and AA today has more than three million members in 150 countries.

On November 16, 1950, Dr. Bob died of heart failure at 71 and was buried at Mount Peace Cemetery in Akron, Ohio.

CEMETERY DIRECTIONS: From I-77 take Exit 21C and follow Route 59 (Dart Avenue) east for two miles to its intersection with West Market Avenue. Turn left onto West Market, then make a right onto Aqueduct Street at the fourth traffic light and the cemetery will be a short distance ahead on the right.

GRAVE DIRECTIONS: Enter the cemetery at the second drive (the one with the brick columns) and, after 50 feet, stop. Dr. Bob rests 200 feet to the left and six rows from the chain-link fence.

On Jan 24, 1971, Bill died at 75 of emphysema and was buried at South Village Cemetery in East Dorset Vermont.

CEMETERY DIRECTIONS: From the junction of Routes 7 and 7A, follow 7A south for one mile. The cemetery is on the right.

GRAVE DIRECTIONS: Enter the cemetery, turn right, and follow the road up the hill. Fifty feet past the hairpin turn, on the left, are two white footstones marking the graves of Bill and his wife, Lois.

JOHN JAMES AUDUBON
APRIL 26, 1785 – JANUARY 27, 1851

Between 1827 and 1839, John Audubon released his four-volume *Birds of America* folio and its companion, five-volume *Ornithological Biography* text. They were both immediately popular and remain a great achievement of American intellectual history, having been reprinted many times.

While his painted portraits of birds and his writings describing their habits may not wholly satisfy either the critical artist or the meticulous scientist, Audubon's achievement in both areas is considerable and, more importantly, his work instigated a public appreciation for birds and inspired deeper scientific and conservationist interest.

Audubon died at 65 and was buried at Trinity Church Cemetery in Manhattan.

CEMETERY DIRECTIONS: The Trinity Church Cemetery has two different sections, and Audubon is in the section bounded by 153rd and 155th streets on two sides and Broadway and Amsterdam Avenues on the others. It's in the Upper West Side, only a few blocks from the Hudson River.

GRAVE DIRECTIONS: Enter the cemetery at the gate on 155th Street and the tall Audubon spire is directly in front of you.

DANIEL BOONE
NOVEMBER 2, 1734 – SEPTEMBER 26, 1820

Born in a log cabin near present-day Reading, Pennsylvania, Daniel Boone was one of the most famous pioneers in United States history. By 1751 Daniel was getting by in North Carolina as a hunter and trapper, and in 1760 he first ventured into the little-known Cumberland Gap region. Although the location of the pass in the Blue Ridge Mountains had been mapped more than fifteen years earlier, the French and Indian War had discouraged exploration and settlement of the Kentucky wilderness. The British later continued to prohibit western migration (they had no manpower to protect the frontier), but Daniel and many others ignored the crown's ban and crossed the gap to find what lay beyond.

In 1775, the Wilderness Road was built by Daniel and two dozen axmen, and it soon became the primary route to the West. He founded Boonesborough and, during the Revolutionary War, Kentucky was organized as a Virginia county.

Though they may not have been quite as romantic as his legend suggests, Daniel did have numerous encounters with the native people of Kentucky. In 1776, after Shawnee warriors kidnapped his daughter and two others, Daniel made a daring rescue by mounting a surprise nighttime attack. In 1778, after he was himself captured by another band of Shawnee who were planning an attack on Boonesborough, he negotiated a settlement with Chief Blackfish, preventing the onslaught. Admired for his leadership and his woodsman skills, Daniel was later adopted into the tribe as a son of Blackfish.

In 1792, when Kentucky was admitted into the Union as the fifteenth state, litigation questioning settlers' title to their lands arose and Daniel lost all his property due to his lack of clear title. Undaunted, the inveterate pioneer continued west and settled in Missouri. In 1800, Daniel was appointed magistrate of the Femme Osage District in St. Charles County, Missouri and received a large tract of land for his services. But when Missouri was transferred to the United States as part of the Louisiana Purchase, he once again lost all his land.

Daniel spent his remaining years at his son's Missouri home and passed away at 85.

He was buried in Marthasville, Missouri, near his wife, Rebecca, who had died seven years previously.

From there, the story gets muddled. In 1845 a delegation from Kentucky honored their pioneer hero with a monument in the capital city's cemetery (this delegation had had no hand in the federal action that stripped Daniel of his lands 50 years before), and Daniel and Rebecca were exhumed and reinterred in Frankfort. But mistakes happen easily in the grave-switching business, and it seems that someone dug up the wrong body. The grave next to Rebecca's was already occupied when Daniel died, so he was buried at her feet. Daniel's relatives, who were upset that he was being moved at all, didn't inform the diggers of his true location and they allowed Rebecca's bones to be carted off along with someone else's—not Daniel's. In 1983 a forensic anthropologist studied a plaster cast of the skull in the Frankfort grave and concluded that it belonged to "a large black man." Not surprisingly, proponents of the Frankfort locale dismissed the anthropologist's credentials and his findings.

Oh well. Both graves have worthy monuments; Frankfort's is bigger, but rural Marthasville seems more suited to a frontiersman.

DIRECTIONS TO DANIEL'S GRAVE IN FRANKFORT, KENTUCKY: From I-64, take Exit 58, follow Route 60 west for four miles, and the Frankfort Cemetery is on the left. Enter the cemetery and follow the line that's painted on the road. After a short distance, you can't miss his monument on the right.

DIRECTIONS TO DANIEL'S GRAVE IN MARTHASVILLE, MISSOURI: About 30 miles west of St Louis, on Route 94 just west of Dutzow, is a sign on the right that points the way to the grave. On a knoll overlooking Duque Creek, the grave site is quite serene.

JOHN WILKES BOOTH
MAY 10, 1838 – APRIL 26, 1865

The members of John Wilkes Booth's family were touring actors, and John, his father, and his two brothers were firmly established thespians. By 1863, though, the Southern-sympathizing Booth had hatched a preposterous conspiracy to abduct President Lincoln and deliver him to Richmond, then to ransom him in exchange for peace with the South or Confederate prisoners.

Remarkably, Booth was able to enlist at least a half-dozen other conspirators in his kidnapping scheme. It was decided that they would carry out their plot by capturing Lincoln during a planned appearance in March 1865, but the President changed plans at the last minute and the plot was foiled. Just a few weeks later, Robert E. Lee's army surrendered to the Union, and Booth's bunch quickly changed gears, plotting instead to assassinate Lincoln, Vice President Andrew Johnson, and Secretary of State William Seward simultaneously. Booth hoped the resulting chaos and weakness in the government would lead to a comeback for the South.

When Booth learned that Lincoln would be attending a performance at Ford's Theater in Washington on April 14, his plan was set in motion. The conspirators agreed that the three murders would occur at about ten o'clock that evening. At the prescribed time, Booth sneaked into the theater and shot Lincoln in the back of the head at point-blank range. His co-conspirators made no attempt on Johnson's life, but one, David Herold, did manage to stab Seward, wounding him.

After shooting Lincoln, Booth jumped down to the stage shouting, "*Sic semper tyrannis!* (Thus ever to tyrants!) The South is avenged!" He snapped the fibula bone in his left leg during his leap, then limped out the theater's back door to a waiting horse. He fled first to the tavern of sympathizer Mary Surratt, where he met up with Herold, then to the home of another conspirator, Dr. Samuel Mudd, who splinted his leg.

For the next twelve days Booth and Herold traveled south under cover of night until federal authorities caught up with them near Port Royal, Virginia, surrounding them in a tobacco barn. Herold surrendered, but Booth refused to give up and the barn was set afire. In the ensuing confusion Booth was shot through the neck by Sergeant Boston Corbett, though the orders had been to take the assassin alive. Booth died a few hours later at sunrise. According to a popular account Booth repeatedly muttered, "useless, useless," as he lay dying, but some historians now believe that the garbled, barely whispered sounds may have instead been, "Lucy, Lucy," for his betrothed, Lucy Hale. In any event, his final words, supposedly, were, "Tell Mother I died for my country." He was 26.

Booth's remains were sewn up in a horse blanket, wagoned to Belle Plain, then transported aboard the warship *Montauk* to Washington. Though some have maintained that the feds got the wrong man and the corpse was not Booth at all, his body was positively identified by a doctor who knew Booth and was able to confirm an old surgical scar. He also recorded that the corpse's left fibula had been recently broken. The "J.W.B." tattoo on his wrist should have erased any remaining doubts, but skeptics remain.

Booth was buried in a cell of the Old Penitentiary in what is now Fort Lesley J. McNair. Two years later the body was exhumed and reburied in a locked storeroom in Warehouse I at the prison. In 1869, Booth was again exhumed and released to his family, who buried him at Green Mount Cemetery in Baltimore, Maryland, where it's expected he'll remain for a long time to come.

CEMETERY DIRECTIONS: From I-83 take Exit 6 and follow North Avenue east for ¾ mile. (Don't mistake Northern Parkway for North Avenue; they're not the same.) Turn right onto Green Mount Avenue and the cemetery is a short distance ahead on the left.

GRAVE DIRECTIONS: Drive under the stone arch to enter the cemetery and turn immediately right. Follow this drive past the long staircase on the left and, as the drive bends right, the vault of a Richard Hardesty Thompson is on the left. Park here and walk up the cement path between the Hardesty and Sherman vaults. After 75 feet, the Booth plot is on the right marked by a tall obelisk. John's name is engraved into the obelisk, but his grave within the plot is unmarked.

Booth's co-conspirators were eventually captured and, after being tried by a military tribunal, four of them were hanged (including Mary Surratt), and three received life sentences.

CESAR CHAVEZ

MARCH 31, 1927 – APRIL 23, 1993

Migrant farm worker Cesar Chavez captured worldwide attention by leading the battle to unionize the fields and orchards of California. In a life story that mirrored Steinbeck's *Grapes of Wrath,* he poignantly represented the hardship of migrant farm-worker families and founded the United Farm Workers, which sought to end the exploitation of its members. Largely because of his efforts, California in 1975 passed the nation's first collective bargaining act for farm workers.

Cesar's early years were spent on his family's 160-acre farm in Arizona. But after the farm was lost during the Great Depression, the Chavez family, along with thousands of others, picked crops in the arid valleys of California at virtual slave-labor pay rates. In the 1950s Cesar began organizing Mexican-Americans into a political bloc, and by 1965 his fledgling union of 1,700 families had persuaded two growers to raise wages moderately. Cesar's union joined another, less-successful strike alongside a separate group of workers, and that was the beginning of five years of *La Huelga*—"the strike"—in which the frail labor leader became familiar worldwide as he battled the economic powers of California's San Joaquin Valley.

Cesar's style was akin to the methods of Gandhi and Martin Luther King, Jr.: He fasted or invited arrest to call attention to his battle; he organized protest marches; he held lively rallies and organized boycotts. Church groups, college students, and other unionists supported the exploited farm workers and, in 1970, after losing millions of dollars, growers agreed to union contracts.

Though other successful boycotts and unionizations followed, Cesar ultimately failed to realize his dream of forging a nationwide organization, and the 1970 victory was probably the high point in the union's history. When some farm workers started organizing under the Teamster umbrella, their plight ceased to be recognized as a social cause and, by the 1980s, farm-worker unions were essentially non-existent.

At a friend's Arizona home, Cesar died of natural causes in his sleep. His coffin, which was carried four miles to a UFW field office after a funeral mass, had been built by his brother and was so heavy that teams of eight pallbearers rotated every few minutes, while some 25,000 people gathered to say good-bye.

At 66, Cesar was buried at the commune-style headquarters of the former union, now the LaPaz Educational Retreat Center, in Keene, California.

GRAVE DIRECTIONS: Take the Keene exit off of Route 58 and follow Main Street east for a half-mile to a cement drive on the left. Go down the hill and you'll see Cesar's grave in the central courtyard.

WILLIAM "BUFFALO BILL" CODY

FEBRUARY 26, 1846 – JANUARY 10, 1917

The legendary life experiences of Buffalo Bill, some real and others imagined or exaggerated, embody the spirit of the West and fed the national grandiose tradition of frontier life that endures today. Though he certainly led an incredibly interesting and exciting life, over the years his biography has been increasingly romanticized, making it difficult to separate the fact from the fiction. With that, you've reached the interactive part of this book; I'll offer the chronological version of Bill's life that's generally accepted, and you can pencil in or scratch out the "facts" as you see fit.

William Cody was born in Iowa and, while still a child, worked for a wagon-freight company as a mounted messenger and wrangler, crossing the Great Plains several times. After his father died when he was 12, he became a trapper and then a prospector during the Pikes Peak gold rush of 1859. At 14, Bill began working for the Pony Express after the company advertised for "skinny, expert riders willing to risk death daily. Orphans preferred."

During the Civil War he served as a scout for the Union Army in Tennessee and Missouri. In 1867 he became a buffalo hunter supplying meat to the Kansas Pacific Railroad and from that experience gained the moniker "Buffalo Bill." By the next year and until 1872, he was a civilian scout for the Fifth Cavalry, which was fighting the Sioux and Cheyenne Indian tribes. For his efforts Bill was awarded the Congressional Medal of Honor, though it was revoked in 1917 because he had not been in the military.

In 1869 writer Edward Judson, working under the pen name Ned Buntline, began featuring Buffalo Bill in a series of dime novels; while Bill was earning a real-life reputation, he was also becoming a national folk hero in the popular imagination. In 1872 Buntline persuaded Bill to play himself in a stage production, *The Scouts of the Plains*, and Bill proved a natural showman, winning enthusiastic acclaim. Following a falling out with Buntline, Bill remained an actor for eleven more seasons, and began publishing his own Buffalo Bill dime novels. There would eventually be some 1,700 of these frontier tales, the majority written by Prentiss Ingraham.

In 1883, Bill further capitalized on his fame and organized *Buffalo Bill's Wild West Show*, an outdoor extravaganza that dramatized some of the most picturesque elements of frontier life, including Pony Express rides, buffalo hunts, and Indian attacks. Half circus and half history lesson, the show proved an enormous success and toured for 30 years. Though Bill amassed a small fortune from his show business success, it was lost to mismanagement and his weakness for dubious investments and, in the end, even the *Wild West* show became the property of creditors.

Since 1885 Bill had maintained a ranch on an enormous tract outside of Yellowstone Park given him by the State of Wyoming. Today that land is the town of Cody and, as Buffalo Bill is its founding father, you'd expect he'd be buried there. But he's not. At 70 he died of natural causes while in Denver, and his wife Louisa maintained that Bill had indeed desired to be buried near Denver, atop a promontory with spectacular views of both the mountains and plains where he had spent the happiest times of his life. So there Bill rests, in a tomb blasted from solid rock at the summit of Lookout Mountain in Golden, Colorado.

GRAVE DIRECTIONS: From I-70, take Exit 254 and follow Route 40 east. After 1¼ miles, turn left onto Lookout Mountain Road and then, after another 2½ miles, turn left into the Buffalo Bill Memorial Museum. Bill's grave is on private property, and there is a gate there that doesn't open until about nine in the morning. However, people have been known to park outside the gate and visit his grave by strolling up the hill and following the signs.

CHRISTOPHER COLUMBUS

1451 – MAY 20, 1506

There seems to be a sort of movement afoot to discredit Christopher Columbus's discovery of America. Its proponents contend that Native Americans had considered the continent home for who-knows-how-many millennia and, anyway, the Vikings from northern Europe visited North America as early as the eleventh century. Though both contentions are true, the overall argument is tenuous and based on semantics.

Native Americans merely happened to have had migrated to America over the eons; they had no broad understanding of the land mass and, alternately, no knowledge of Europe—and they weren't on track to "discover" it in kind any time soon. The Vikings had found only the cold, rocky, wind-swept coast of what's now Canada and, having enough of that back home in Greenland, they disinterestedly left. On the other hand, Columbus found the lush islands and warm waters of the Caribbean. Though it's true he wasn't the first human to know of its existence, he was certainly the guy who leaked the news of it to Europe's fifteenth-century power club, setting up the endgame for European colonization and migration.

It was Columbus's plan to reach Asia by sailing west across the Atlantic, and therein lies a misconception. It's generally taught that Columbus had difficulty receiving financial backing for his plan because it was believed that the earth was flat. Though that may have been a popular notion among the uneducated masses, it was evident to the informed people of his day, including other sailors and navigators, that the Earth was spherical. The problem was that nobody agreed with Columbus's estimate of the westward distance to Asia; he calculated it to be 2,700 miles, while King Ferdinand's and Queen Isabella's experts insisted it was about 5,000 miles.

In fact, everyone was quite wrong; the westward distance from Spain to Asia would prove about 11,000 miles. But—luckily for Columbus—the Americas were in the way, making his miscalculation more or less irrelevant.

After aiming for Asia, Columbus's three fabled vessels most likely made their first landfall at what is now Watling Island in the Bahamas. A couple months later they headed back to Spain with the good news. Word of his discovery of new Asian lands rapidly spread, and Spain's new hero led dozens of ships and thousands of settlers back to the Caribbean over the next decade. In some of his logs Columbus described the new lands as belonging to a previously unknown continent, but later he retreated to his initial position that they belonged to Asia, and held that conviction to his death.

Of course, Spain was interested in colonizing these new lands, reaping their riches, and populating them with Christians; whether they happened to be part of eastern Asia or an entirely new continent was irrelevant. Columbus appointed himself "Vice King and General Governor of the Islands and Terra Firma of Asia and India," and it seems that, for a while anyway, Spanish royalty went along with it. But though Columbus might've been a pretty good sailor, he was a terribly cruel administrator. Ferdinand and Isabella had specifically instructed Columbus but, ever the renegade, he initiated European imperialism and embarked on a campaign of slavery and genocide, pilfering the natives' gold treasures. In 1500, after Spanish settlers accused him of mismanagement, he was returned to Spain in shackles, stripped of his appointment.

Columbus next promised the king and queen that he had figured out exactly where the strait to India lay, and he finagled a final voyage in 1502. Heading further west of the new Spanish colonies, he searched vainly for a passage along Central America's mosquito coast, but he returned empty-handed in 1504, and was no longer welcome in the royal court. Two years later, Columbus died from some manner of heart disease at 55.

But even in death, Columbus has never been able to stay in one place, and his post-mortem journeys have prompted doubts over his final resting place, with rival tombs claimed by authorities in Seville, Spain, and Santo Domingo, Dominican Republic. He was first interred for three years in Valladolid, Spain, and then in Seville, but in 1542 his son's will had his cadaver transferred to the Cathedral of Santo Domingo. In 1795 the French took over the Dominican Republic and the world's most-active bag of bones was moved to Spanish-controlled Havana. Finally, after Cuba became independent in 1898, Columbus used the last of his frequent-boater miles and was interred at the church of La Cartuja in Seville.

But an 1877 excavation at the Cathedral of Santo Domingo unearthed a lead box inscribed, "Illustrious and distinguished male, don Cristobal Colon," Columbus' given Spanish name. Dominicans suggested that during the move to Havana the wrong body was selected, and maybe they're right. Forensic investigations and DNA analysis have thus far been inconclusive.

GENERAL GEORGE CUSTER

DECEMBER 5, 1839 – JUNE 25, 1876

After graduating last in his West Point class, George Custer surprised his mentors and established a reputation as a hard-fighting (if flamboyant) officer in the Union cavalry. Throughout the Civil War, he led his men in nearly every battle fought by the Army of the Potomac and, by battlefield commission, attained the rank of General.

After the war ended, though, Custer was busted down to the rank of Captain, and as commander of the 7th Calvary was charged with bringing renegade Sioux tribes back to their reservation. One fine summer day, upon discovering an Indian camp along Montana's Little Bighorn River, Custer divided his regiment into three columns in an effort to surround the camp and cut off the Indians' escape route. But unfortunately, the Indians didn't stick to the script and Custer and his column of 267 men were annihilated. He was dead at 36.

Three days later the bodies were given a hasty battlefield burial, and the following year what may have been Custer's remains were disinterred, given a military funeral, and reinterred in the Post Cemetery at the West Point Military Academy in New York.

GRAVE DIRECTIONS: Since September 11, 2001, we've lost some of the privileges we've enjoyed as American citizens, and many will surely never return. One such privilege is our admission to many government and military installations, including West Point Academy. The Academy's visitor's center used to offer a two-hour tour of its grounds, which included a visit to Post Cemetery. But that tour has been discontinued, citing security concerns. A one-hour tour is still offered, but the Post Cemetery visit is not included in that tour. Whether the two-hour tour will ever be offered again is anyone's guess.

So, until further notice, it's impossible to visit Custer's grave unless you have clearance. (I'd wager that it wouldn't hurt if you happened to be a senator's son.) This author visited Custer's grave before September 11, and it really is worth seeing. His stone is emblazoned with a large bronze plaque that details his life accomplishments, and the monument is adorned with enormous buffalo heads on either side. For now, I guess you'll just have to take my word for it.

Still, the visitor center is definitely worth your time. From I-84 take Exit 10S, follow Route 9W south for 15½ miles, then turn at the second West Point exit. Or, from I-287, take Exit 11, follow Route 9W north for 21 miles, then turn at the first West Point exit. In either case, you'll then proceed one mile, bear right at the "Y," and find the visitor center a half-mile ahead on the right.

Finally, the Little Bighorn Battlefield is now a national monument and is also worth a visit the next time you happen to be hanging around Crow Agency, Montana.

CHARLES DARWIN
FEBRUARY 12, 1809 – APRIL 19, 1882

In 1859 Charles Darwin defined his theory of organic evolution in his book *Origin of the Species*, and in one fell swoop became both a well-respected and much-reviled figure. His theory of evolution is considered to be contrary to some biblical teachings and destructive to religion so, with his book's publication, Darwin sparked a controversy that still rages today.

But contrary to popular belief, Darwin was not the first person to propose evolution. In scientific circles it was widely discussed long before Darwin published his theory. Rather, the question was, *how* did evolution occur? Darwin proposed a viable mechanism for evolution (natural selection), and here's how it works: Individuals born with certain beneficial characteristics enjoy an advantage over their peers, and their offspring enjoy the same advantages. Over time, the individuals with the advantageous characteristics do better, live longer, and produce more offspring until eventually, the population looks very different from its original version. In other words, new species arise when the environment favors certain characteristics over others.

What sounds fairly simple was quite controversial, and it remains so today, due in part to the erroneous simplification that natural selection amounts to man being descended from apes. Still, Darwin stood by his theory and spent the remainder of his life defending it, carefully and methodically working over his copious research notes. He never swayed in the doctrine of his theory, and it is accepted today by scientists worldwide.

After months of chest pains and seizures, Darwin died of heart failure at 73.

Westminster Abbey in London functions as neither a cathedral nor a parish church, but is controlled by the royal crown and has been used as the site for the Royal Coronation since 1066. Burial there is one of the rarest and greatest of British honors, and Darwin was so honored; he rests there in the area known as "Scientist's Corner."

His family erected a bronze memorial with a life-sized relief bust near the grave in 1888, but there's also an interesting sequel to this account. His actual burial place is beneath the flagstone in the center of the north aisle, at the precise spot where exists an ornamental iron screen with a gate and a ticket booth. Darwin's grave is at this gate, and every one of the thousands of visitors who file past to pay their admission fee steps on his grave.

THOMAS EDISON
FEBRUARY 11, 1847 – OCTOBER 18, 1931

But for the internal combustion engine and the airplane, it's difficult to name any common Industrial Revolution-era invention for which Thomas Edison cannot claim considerable credit or, more likely, the original patent. Having had just three weeks of public schooling and a few years of home schooling by his mother, Edison patented 1,093 inventions, which, in total, revolutionized the fabric of modern civilization.

At 15, he started work as a telegraph operator, which led to his first inventions: the automatic telegraph and the message printer, which in turn led to his new career as full-time inventor. The vote recorder and stock ticker came quickly, and sale of those patents provided funds for Tom's own invention factory, first in Newark and later in Menlo Park, where a staff of technicians collaborated on "invention to order." The vast New Jersey factory was an antecedent of modern research and development laboratories, and over the course of 50 years, churned out ideas that led to the development or improvement of everything from cement plants to plate glass, typewriters to dry-cell batteries, mimeographs to phonographs, and talking motion pictures. He also made a significant discovery in pure science, the "Edison effect" that led to the electron tube and the underlying technology for radio broadcasting, television, and x-rays.

To research incandescence, Edison Electric Light Company (today's General Electric) was formed, the incandescent light bulb was introduced in 1879, and central municipal power systems under Edison Electric Company soon followed. As consultant to the U.S. Navy during World War I, Tom contributed another 45 inventions, including navigating equipment, ship-to-shore telephones, and defensive systems against U-boats. With Henry Ford and the Firestone Company he developed a process to provide a domestic rubber source, which, in 1930, proved to be his last patent.

At 84 he died from complications of diabetes and is buried behind his home, Glenmont House, in West Orange, New Jersey. The home is now part of the Edison National Historic Site, which also includes the Edison Laboratory Museum where, among other memorabilia, you can peruse some of his 3,400 notebooks containing records of his ideas and research. The Historic Site is easy to find from Interstate 280. If traveling from the west take Exit 9, and if from the east take Exit 10, then follow the signs.

Even more of Edison's Menlo Park laboratory and equipment are preserved at Henry Ford's Greenfield Village Museum in Dearborn, Michigan.

ALBERT EINSTEIN
MARCH 14, 1879 – APRIL 18, 1955

To avoid compulsory military service, the German-born Albert Einstein gained Swiss citizenship and found employment there at a patent office. In 1905, working alone without the benefit of scientific literature or colleagues, he released a series of theoretical physics publications. Particularly astonishing among these was a paper on the theory of relativity, which, if correct, would overturn classical physics and set the scientific community on its head.

Basing his new theory on a reinterpretation of the classical principle of relativity, namely that the laws of physics had to have the same form in any frame of reference, and dismissing the traditional notion that time and space were absolute concepts, "special relativity" suggested instead that both time and space vary with circumstances; it was the speed of light that remained constant in all frames of reference.

Over the next decade, Einstein perfected his general theory of relativity and summed it up with the famous equation, $E=mc^2$. Further, he predicted how a ray of light from a distant star, passing near the sun, would appear to be slightly bent in the direction of the sun. When this prediction was verified by the Royal Society of London, essentially proving relativity and overthrowing Newtonian physics, Einstein earned the international acclaim he deserved.

A confirmed giant of science, Einstein spent the remainder of his life working toward a "grand unified theory of physics" that would integrate the properties of gravity, matter, and energy into a single, universal formula. His quest was unfulfilled however, and continues to elude the best minds still.

In 1932 he accepted a post at Princeton University and in 1940 became a United States citizen. In a letter he later regarded as his life's biggest mistake, Einstein urged President Roosevelt to step up nuclear fission research, and though he played no direct part in the development of the atomic bomb, his name has been inextricably linked to the atomic age.

After the war, Einstein threw himself into political activism and joined other scientists in efforts to prevent the use of atomic weapons, including a proposal for the establishment of a world government system that would provide "the binding authority necessary for world security."

Albert Einstein died at 76 in his sleep. He was cremated the same day and his ashes scattered in New Jersey's Delaware River.

MEDGAR EVERS
JULY 2, 1925 – JUNE 12, 1963

Medgar Evers grew up in the Deep South during the Depression, and as soon as he turned eighteen, like many others of that era, promptly joined the Army. In 1944 he found himself on the beaches of Normandy, but little did he know that the biggest battle of his life was yet to be fought.

In 1954 Medgar decided to make a difference in the growing civil rights movement and in a short while was made Mississippi's first NAACP field secretary. The next years found him organizing voter-registration drives and, at times, boycotts in areas where the local populace was most obstinate. During the early 1960s the increased tempo of desegregation activities in the South created high and constant tensions, and the situation routinely reached the breaking point.

One hot night in 1963, President Kennedy made a broadcast on national television describing a bill he was sending to Congress that later became the Civil Rights Act of 1964. A few hours later, just after midnight, while stepping out of his Oldsmobile with an armload of "Jim Crow Must Go" tee shirts, Medgar was felled by a shotgun blast fired by an assailant who had lurked in the shadows outside his home. Fifteen minutes later, Medgar died at a local hospital.

At 37 he was buried with full military honors at Arlington National Cemetery in Arlington, Virginia.

CEMETERY DIRECTIONS: Arlington National Cemetery is on the west side of the Potomac River in Washington D.C. From any of the major highways you can easily follow the signs to the visitor parking lots.

GRAVE DIRECTIONS: Medgar is buried in Section 36, which is immediately across the drive from the visitor's center. The graves are arranged numerically, and his grave at Number 1431 is easy to locate.

After Medgar's death the shotgun that was used to kill him was found in the bushes nearby, with the owner's fingerprints still fresh on it. Staunch white supremacist Byron De La Beckwith was soon arrested, stating then that, "I didn't kill the nigra, but he's gone and he ain't coming back." Three decades and three trials later, he was convicted of the murder, though the verdict was tainted by what newspapers called an "O.J. jury," comprised of eight minorities, three white women, and one white man.

In 2001, suffering from a variety of health problems, Beckwith died in prison at 80. We don't really care where he's buried.

HENRY FORD
JULY 30, 1863 – APRIL 7, 1947

Henry Ford holds credit for the proliferation of the automobile, for better or for worse, but it's not because be built the first gasoline-powered vehicle (he didn't), nor is it due to his initiation of the assembly line and interchangeable parts. What really matters is that Henry Ford developed mass consumption. Ford's vision helped create a middle class, one marked by urbanization, rising wages, and some free time in which to spend them. If not for his drive to create a mass market for his cars, the American powerhouse economy that emerged, based on the buying power of an enormous middle class more than likely would have developed much less vigorously.

In 1905, when Ford Motor Company had 50 competitors, the conventional wisdom was to build cars for the rich. But Ford recognized that if he were to build an automobile affordable to the common man, and an automotive infrastructure were to develop along with it, the world would beat a path to his door. To that end, Ford streamlined his facilities to produce a simple and reliable car, the Model T. Further, he campaigned in Washington for better roads and pushed for gas stations everywhere.

In 1914 Ford shocked the industrial world by paying his workers a $5-a-day minimum wage that more than doubled the prevailing wage. The *Wall Street Journal* called it an "economic crime," and his competitors expected that he had just expensed himself out of business; they couldn't fathom how low Ford had driven his cost per car and that, by making it feasible for more people to buy cars, his high labor costs were insignificant. Ford figured that if he paid his workers a real living wage, everyone would buy a car. And he was right. Within just two years, sales of the Model T increased to 720,000. People flocked to jobs in Ford's factories—more than 100,000 worked at his gigantic River Rouge plant—and they invariably bought one of his cars. By the time Model T ceased production in 1927, more than 15 million had been sold.

Henry Ford was a complex personality who exhibited a variety of enthusiasms and prejudices. In 1915, adamant that "history is more or less bunk," he chartered an ocean-going "Peace Ship" in an attempt to end World War I by means of "continuous mediation." Three years later, Ford bought the *Dearborn Independent*, and for seven years published a series of attacks on the "International Jew," a mythical figure he blamed for society's ills. "When there is something wrong in this country, you'll find the Jews," he wrote. Anti-immigrant, anti-labor, and anti-liquor, he opposed social and cultural change, decrying Hollywood movies, out-of-home childcare, and new styles in dress and music. Worried that his workers would go crazy with their five bucks a day, he set up a "Sociological Department" to insure that they didn't blow their "wealth" on vices. He introduced European royalty and company executives to peculiar dances like the *mazurka* and the *quadrille* at old-fashioned social outings. He sponsored the reading of quaint essays to "plain folks" on a weekly radio hour, and experimented with soybeans for food and durable goods. Ford also constructed the rural Greenfield Village and its companion Henry Ford Museum, filling them with artifacts from when America was almost wholly countrified.

By the late 1920s, Ford's vertically integrated, automobile-building juggernaut was a model of self-sufficiency, boasting Brazilian rubber plantations and Minnesota iron ore mines. Ford became arrogantly convinced that auto buyers needed Ford more than Ford needed them and, with a similar know-it-all, authoritarian management style, the stage was set for decline. Trusting in what he believed was an unerring instinct for the marketplace, he refused to offer any innovative features, even color, famously adding that "customers could have any color they wanted as long as it's black." He drove out subordinates who bucked his philosophies. Violently opposed to labor organizers, he employed company police to prevent unionization. By 1936 Ford Motor Company was third in sales in the industry and, if World War II hadn't come along and exploited the company's manufacturing prowess in the business of building bombers, tanks, and jeeps, it's entirely possible that Ford's 1932 V-8 engine might have been its last innovation.

A known pacifist, Ford opposed America's entry into World War II, but agreed to build airplane engines for the British in May 1940. After Pearl Harbor was attacked, Ford began a tremendous, all-out manufacturing effort, including the production of B-24 Liberator bombers at the rate of one an hour on a mile-long assembly line. By the end of the war, some 86,000 complete aircraft, 277,000 Willys jeeps, 57,000 airplane engines, and more than a million other fighting vehicles had been built at Ford factories from India to Britain to New Zealand.

Though he would continue to strictly control the company, Ford had turned its presidency over to his son Edsel in 1919. When Edsel died in 1943, Ford resumed the post, but, after a series of strokes, he handed the reins to his grandson.

In 1947, the innovator died in bed at his 1,300-acre Fair Lane mansion. At 83, he was buried at Saint Martha's Episcopal Church in Detroit, Michigan.

CEMETERY DIRECTIONS: From I-96, take Exit 183 and follow Highway 39 south for a mile to Exit 13. Follow Joy Road east for three-fourths of a mile, and the church and cemetery are on the right.

GRAVE DIRECTIONS: Henry's grave is easy to find in the Ford section of the cemetery.

Most of his personal estate, valued at $205 million, went to the Ford Foundation, which had been set up in 1936 as a means of retaining family control of the firm. Today it's one of the world's largest public trusts.

SIGMUND FREUD
MAY 6, 1856 – SEPTEMBER 23, 1939

Though the Austrian doctor Sigmund Freud is known first as an explorer of the psyche, it's also worth noting that he was the first professional to broadly promote cocaine as a tonic, though he was shortly followed by Pope Leo XII, Jules Verne, and Thomas Edison. In 1884, when Freud was a young, obscure neurologist and not yet the pope of psychoanalysis, cocaine had only been researched as a local anesthetic. But Freud found in it a solution for both his depression and his chronic fatigue, and he fell in love with the drug, praising it as a cure for asthma and stomach disorders and recommending it to overcome morphine and alcohol addiction. He was even paid by pharmaceutical giants to endorse their rival brands of cocaine and, when the cocaine-laced health tonic Coca-Cola was sold for the first time in 1886, it was undoubtedly inspired by Freud. Later, he backed away from his earlier claims and acknowledged that repeated use could bring on hallucinations and violent behavior, but the word was out and the damage had already been done.

Ten years later, controversy further dogged Freud's reputation when he developed the cluster of theories he would give the name of "psychoanalysis." His fundamental idea was that all humans are endowed with an unconscious, one in which potent sexual and aggressive drives, and defenses against them, struggle for supremacy. This idea has struck many as a romantic but scientifically unverifiable notion. His contention that the catalog of neurotic ailments to which humans are susceptible is nearly always the work of sexual maladjustments, and that erotic desire starts not in puberty but in infancy, seemed to many at the time nothing less than obscene. His dramatic evocation of a universal Oedipus complex, in which a little boy loves his mother and hates his father, seems to some more like a literary conceit than a thesis worthy of a scientist of the mind.

Freudian theory was built upon the foundations of both medical science and philosophy. As a scientist, Freud was interested in seeing how the human mind affected the body, particularly in cases of paranoia, hysteria, and other mental illnesses. As a theorist, he explored basic truths about how personalities are formed. In 1923 Freud ventured so far as to develop a model of the human mind consisting of three elements—the ego, the id, and the superego.

But the book that made Freud's reputation was his turn-of-the-century work *The Interpretation of Dreams*, an indefinable masterpiece of dream analysis, autobiography, mind theory, and even history. The principle underlying this work is that mental experiences and entities, like physical ones, are part of nature, and there are no mere accidents in mental procedures. The most nonsensical notion, the most casual slip of the tongue, the most fantastic dream, must have a meaning and can be used to demystify our often incomprehensible thoughts and actions.

For good or ill, Sigmund Freud, more than any other explorer of the psyche, shaped the notions of the twentieth century and the methods of contemporary psychoanalysis. The very vehemence and persistence of his detractors are a wry tribute to the staying power of his ideas.

In 1923 Freud was diagnosed with cancer of the jaw, but he continued to smoke heavily, insisting it was the tobacco that gave him his creativity and great capacity to work. By 1938, though, he had undergone 31 operations to remove tumors, and had been fit and refit with an extensive prosthesis to replace half his mouth. In that same year, the Nazis invaded Austria and the dying Freud fled to London, leaving behind virtually all his possessions. By the following summer, the 83-year-old couldn't eat, and he was surrounded by a mosquito net to keep the flies from his open wounds. At Freud's request, his doctor injected him with two lethal doses of morphine, and he was done.

Freud was cremated and his ashes interred in a Greek vase at the Ernest George Mausoleum of Golder Green Crematorium in London.

J. EDGAR HOOVER
JANUARY 1, 1895 – MAY 2, 1972

Two years after earning a law degree from George Washington University, J. Edgar Hoover began working for the Department of Justice and, in 1924, before he was even 30 years old, was named the director of the Federal Bureau of Investigation. Hoover held the prized position for 48 years, through eight different presidential administrations, until his death in 1972. Through politics, publicity, and a strong record in law enforcement bolstered by underhanded manipulations and outright blackmail, Hoover became one of Washington's most powerful figures, taking the free rein of a renegade, all but immune to control by his superiors.

Hoover was, by turns, admired and vilified. His story is enormous and his numerous biographies, some approaching a thousand pages, still fail to capture all of the details of his contributions and crimes. Like many men who are in an all-powerful position for a long period of time, Hoover's strengths and weaknesses were both larger than life.

On the one hand, as America's top policeman, Hoover took a corrupt, inefficient, and dysfunctional organization, top-heavy with political hacks, and whipped it into shape in record time, building the basis of the world's most celebrated arm of law enforcement. Under Hoover's direction, a sense of decorum and professionalism was applied to crime fighting; appointments were based on merits, promotions were made on proven ability, and the round-'em-up, shoot-'em-up traditions were, eventually, abandoned. Hoover also oversaw the application of science to police work; he promoted the creation of police training facilities as well as the National Crime Information Center, its centralized fingerprint cataloging system, and its state-of-the-art laboratories. Hoover monitored and crushed whatever activities he considered to be immoral and dissident (especially when it was in his own best interests); in the 1930s, Hoover's agents rounded up the notorious gangsters and seedy drifters of his "Ten Most Wanted" list; in the war years they arrested German saboteurs and secret agents; in the postwar period, the bureau established itself as the bulwark against communism and, during the turbulent 1960s, the FBI disrupted and eventually destroyed the network of murderous Klansmen who perpetuated rampant racial terrorism. For certain, both during Hoover's tenure and since, the FBI has demonstrated that it is not perfect or infallible, but, in the majority, the organization is an elite, professional, and incorruptible corps that exists to some degree as a result of J. Edgar Hoover's tyrannical determination.

But, of course, there's still the "other hand" to discuss. Hoover's shortcomings as an individual were many and, as would be ex-

pected because the Bureau was his life, these foibles infected his performance as its director. And, many contend, his faults transcended his accomplishments.

A paranoid who held virtually unchecked public power for almost 50 years, he manipulated presidents from Roosevelt to Nixon, and kept extensive files on everyone from Groucho Marx to Bess Truman. Casting aside protections granted by the Constitution, Hoover used federal agents as his exclusive henchmen to destroy personal enemies, either real or imagined, through illegal wiretaps and hidden microphones. Creating the Bureau in his own autocratic image, Hoover did not tolerate dissent or failure, and he directed agents to concentrate on areas that catapulted both his own and the Bureau's public reputations to a fraudulent level of invincibility. Though Hoover was himself a closet homosexual, he was obsessed with the crimes and failings of society's liberal orders and, with straitlaced morality, hypocritically sideswiped any attempts to advance progressive causes. He helped create McCarthyism, blackmailed the Kennedy brothers, forged connections with mobsters, and condoned and planned the systematic harassment of Martin Luther King Jr., retarding the civil rights movement. Indeed, a biographical study of J. Edgar Hoover's life is a contradictory study of observations and speculations blurred by hyperbolized facts and out-and-out lies.

Hoover successfully avoided independent investigations of both his and the FBI's conduct during his tenure. And, upon Hoover's death, Clyde Tolson, who enjoyed triple duty as the FBI's second-ranking officer, Hoover's gay lover, and the primary heir to the Hoover estate, destroyed many of Hoover's personal files, derailing future attempts at sorting out the truths of the Hoover administration. Congress later enacted legislation requiring Senate confirmation of future FBI directors and limiting their power to ten years.

Hoover died of undiagnosed heart disease at 77, while still in the role of FBI director, and was buried at Congressional Cemetery in Washington, D.C.

CEMETERY DIRECTIONS: Congressional Cemetery is located at 1801 "E" Street Southeast. That is, it's located at the intersection of "E" and 18th streets in the southeast quadrant of D.C.

GRAVE DIRECTIONS: Enter the cemetery, drive straight to the chapel, turn left, then turn left again. After 100 feet, stop. On the left, you won't miss his grave.

Upon Tolson's death at 74 in 1975, he was also buried at Congressional Cemetery, just a few yards away from Hoover.

IWO JIMA MARINES

During World War II, the Japanese controlled the tiny South Pacific island of Iwo Jima. But, for its strategic position just 700 miles from Japan's military-industrial complexes, the island became a vital link in the American military's "island-hopping" campaign, and, for an invasion of the Japanese mainland to occur, it was imperative that Iwo Jima be wrested from Japanese control.

The Japanese had buttressed the island with hundreds of machine-gun blockhouses and pillboxes and, in an effort to weaken the Japanese position, the United States Navy and Army Air Force subjected the fortifications to a massive, 74-day bombing campaign. Then, on February 19, 1945, American Marines scrambled from their carriers and waded through ankle-deep volcanic ash to establish a beachhead. Although the beaches had been captured after

only minor resistance, the Japanese later emerged from underground shelters to unleash extensive firepower and wage one of the war's fiercest and bloodiest battles.

Four days after storming the beach, a 40-man American combat patrol reached the top of the island's 550-foot high Mount Suribachi on February 23 and raised there a small United States flag. Later, a larger flag was located, and photographer Joe Rosenthal, recognizing a photographic opportunity, followed its bearer up the hill. As six men struggled on the rugged terrain to raise this larger Stars and Stripes, Rosenthal snapped a picture, perhaps the single most recognizable ever taken, for which he was awarded the Pulitzer Prize.

Although the flag-raising inspired the forces that were still trying to take the island, it could not minimize the heavy casualties suffered and, by March 25, when the clashes finally ended, 5,931 American servicemen lay dead, including three of the six flag-raisers. President Roosevelt ordered the men in the picture be identified, and the three surviving flag-raisers were called home to make public appearances in connection with the Seventh War Loan Drive.

Starting at the bottom of the flagpole and working upward and left, the six men caught on film are: Corporal Harlan Block, PFC Rene Gagnon, PM2/C John Bradley, Sergeant Michael Strank, PFC Franklin Sousley, and PFC Ira Hayes.

Harlan Block

NOVEMBER 6, 1924 – MARCH 1, 1945

Harlan Block graduated from Weslaco High School in 1942 and was drafted into the Marines the following year, where he qualified as a parachutist. After participating in the Bougainville Island campaign, Harlan was among the first of those who stormed Iwo Jima's beaches. His death, at twenty years old, occurred during an attack on the island's Nishi Ridge, just six days after the triumphant stand atop Mount Suribachi. Initially buried in the Marine Cemetery on Iwo Jima, his body was later returned to Texas, and he now rests at the Iwo Jima Monument and Museum in Harlingen. **DIRECTIONS TO HARLAN BLOCK'S GRAVE:** On the north side of Harlingen, take the Primera Road exit off of Route 77 and follow Route 499 east for three miles to a traffic light. Turn left and you won't miss the enormous Iwo Jima Monument and Museum on your right. Harlan is buried in a private plot right next to the monument.

John Bradley

JULY 10, 1923 – JANUARY 11, 1994

After enlisting in the Navy in 1943, John Bradley attended Field Medical School and was assigned to the 28th Marines in 1944. After the appearances in connection with the loan drive, John returned to action and, after being wounded in March 1945, returned home to Wisconsin, where he ran a funeral home until his death at 70 in 1994. John was buried at the Queen of Peace Cemetery in Antigo, Wisconsin.

DIRECTIONS TO JOHN BRADLEY'S GRAVE: In Antigo, Wisconsin, Superior Street is the main road that runs north and south through town. Off of Superior, turn east onto 4th Avenue, then bear right at the hospital. After another hundred yards, turn right onto Park Street, which will lead directly into the cemetery. In the left rear of the cemetery is a large mausoleum, and across the drive from it is the proud Bradley stone.

Rene Gagnon

MARCH 7, 1925 – OCTOBER 12, 1979

Rene Gagnon left high school to work in a textile mill near Manchester, New Hampshire, and was inducted into the Marine Corps Reserve in May 1943. After the loan-drive tour, Rene was sent back overseas and he served in China until his 1946 discharge. He returned to New Hampshire and died unexpectedly at 54. Because Rene hadn't died while on active duty, he didn't meet Arlington National Cemetery burial requirements, and was interred at the Mount Calvary Mausoleum in Manchester. In 1981, two years after his death, a waiver request was approved and he was moved to Arlington.

DIRECTIONS TO RENE GAGNON'S GRAVE: Arlington National Cemetery is located on the west side of the Potomac River in Washington D.C. From any of the major highways, you can easily follow the signs to the visitor parking lots. Once at the cemetery, get a map at the information booth and you can find Rene's marker at Lot 343 in Section 51, which is adjacent to Arlington's own bronze sculpture of that Iwo Jima moment.

Ira Hayes

JANUARY 12, 1923 – JANUARY 24, 1955

Ira Hayes was a Pima Indian on the Gila River Indian Reservation in Arizona, and in 1942 enlisted in the Marines and was assigned to the Parachute Training School. Inordinately shy, he hated the notoriety that the flag raising brought him and even tried to conceal his participation when President Roosevelt ordered the flag-raisers identified. Despite his reluctance, Ira became the best known of the six flag-raisers, as his Native American heritage added a dimension that intrigued an already very interested public. In 1955, suffering from alcoholism at 32, Ira was found dead of exposure near his home. Before he was buried with honors at Arlington National Cemetery, his body lay in state at the Arizona State Capitol and, later, Johnny Cash memorialized him in a song, "The Ballad of Ira Hayes."

DIRECTIONS TO IRA HAYES'S GRAVE: Follow the directions to Arlington as described in Rene Gagnon's profile above and, once there, get a map at the information booth. Ira is buried in Lot 479 of Section 34, which is on the far south of the cemetery, surrounded by Grant and Pershing drives.

Franklin Sousley

SEPTEMBER 19, 1925 – MARCH 21, 1945

After graduating from high school, Kentucky-native Franklin Sousley was drafted into the Marine Corps Reserve in January 1944. Thirteen months later he landed on Iwo Jima, and he was killed on March 21, 1945, during fighting around the island's Kitano Point. He was only nineteen years old. Initially buried in the Marine Cemetery on Iwo Jima, Franklin was later reinterred at Elizaville Cemetery in Elizaville, Kentucky.

DIRECTIONS TO FRANKLIN SOUSLEY'S GRAVE: Elizaville is a community so small that it's not even noted on most Kentucky maps, so if Elizaville isn't on yours, just head for Flemingsburg instead. From the junction of routes 32, 11, and 57 in Flemingsburg, proceed four miles west on Route 32, then turn south on Route 170, where you'll see the cemetery on the left. Enter the cemetery at the second entrance, turn right and then left, and then, on the right, is Franklin's grand monument and grave.

Michael Strank

NOVEMBER 10, 1919 – MARCH 1, 1945

At just 25, Michael Strank was the oldest of the six men in the photograph. A Pennsylvania native, Michael worked for the Civilian Conservation Corps, joined the Marines in 1939, and had participated in campaigns on Wallis, Russell, and Bougainville Islands before storming ashore at Iwo Jima. Just six days after his claim to perpetuity atop Mount Suribachi, Michael was killed by enemy artillery fire on March 1, 1945. Initially buried in the Marine Cemetery on Iwo Jima, he was reinterred in Arlington National Cemetery in 1949.

DIRECTIONS TO MICHAEL STRANK'S GRAVE: Follow the directions to Arlington as described in Rene Gagnon's profile above and, once there, get a map at the information booth. Michael is buried in Lot 7179 of Section 12, down the hill from the Tomb of the Unknown Soldiers.

KENNEDY ASSASSINATIONS

John F. Kennedy
MAY 29, 1917 – NOVEMBER 22, 1963

Robert F. Kennedy
NOVEMBER 20, 1925 – JUNE 6, 1968

Jacqueline Kennedy
JULY 28, 1929 – MAY 19, 1994

The Kennedys are embedded in the American political culture of the past half-century like no other family. The family's stature is partly due to the immense wealth amassed by patriarch Joe Kennedy through his banking and shipbuilding ventures, as well as his participation in liquor smuggling during Prohibition. Power seems to follow money and Joe was no exception; he became the first chairman of the Securities and Exchange Commission, and in 1938 was appointed ambassador to Great Britain. Joe had presidential hopes but, as an outspoken isolationist, that dream died the day the Japanese bombed Pearl Harbor.

After the war, Joe's political aspirations were assumed by his second-oldest son, John Fitzgerald Kennedy. Besides the fact that John came from a wealthy and prominent family, he was an excellent candidate for other reasons; he was Harvard educated, well spoken, good-looking, and his war record was distinguished by brave leadership. As the commander of the Navy torpedo boat PT-109, John had swam his crewmen to safety after their vessel was rammed by a Japanese destroyer.

In 1946 John was elected Democratic congressman from Boston, and in 1952 he easily advanced to the Senate. The following year John married the elegant Jacqueline Bouvier and, while recovering from back surgery in 1956, wrote *Profiles in Courage*, a study of eight bold political leaders. His book won the Pulitzer Prize. If John had been an excellent candidate before, he was now the perfect one, and a legitimate run for the presidency would shortly commence.

With his brother Robert as campaign manager, in 1960 John F. Kennedy beat Republican nominee Richard M. Nixon in a fantastically close election to become the 35th president of the United States. At 43, he was the youngest man and the first Roman Catholic ever elected to the office. President Kennedy's inaugural address set a tone of youthful idealism that raised the nation's hopes: "Ask not what your country can do for you, ask what you can do for your country," he exhorted. With the New Frontier, as his administration called itself, it was apparent that a change had come.

Kennedy's economic programs launched the country on its longest sustained expansion since World War II. He promoted social legislation, including Civil Rights reform, and in forming the Alliance for Progress and the Peace Corps, he brought Americans to the aid of developing nations. In the height of the Cold War period, Kennedy displayed moderation and a firm hand in foreign policy. He accepted responsibility for the Bay of Pigs fiasco and later, at the risk of all-out nuclear war, Kennedy engaged in a showdown with the Soviet Union over its missile installations in Cuba. Attempting to slow the arms race, he negotiated a partial nuclear test-ban treaty with the Soviets in 1963.

Kennedy's wit and charm earned him tremendous popularity and his entire family captivated America. This was Camelot and there was magic in the air. The nation's dashing chief executive gave eloquent speeches while glamorous Jackie sat purposefully beside him in a pillbox hat, hushed and unyieldingly in love. Meanwhile, the first couple's camera-ready children cavorted through the White House; bookish daughter Caroline rode a pony on the lawn, while her energetic, toddler brother, John Jr., played with toy trucks in his daddy's Oval Office.

But just after noontime in Dallas, Texas, on November 22, 1963, the magic ran out. While Abraham Zapruder rolled tape, bullets were fired at the presidential motorcade idling slowly along Elm Street and, at 1:00 p.m. at Parkland Memorial Hospital, John F. Kennedy was pronounced dead at age 46.

John was buried at Arlington National Cemetery in Arlington, Virginia, and within three years, more than fifteen million people had trampled the area of his grave. It was decided that a more suitable site should be constructed, and in 1965 he was moved to a new memorial area nearby. The gravesite consists of a circular walkway paved with irregular stones of Cape Cod granite approaching a small terrace. President Kennedy rests in the elevated terrace, his grave marked with a simple marble tablet. At the head of his grave is a circular stone from which an eternal flame burns at its center.

After its president's assassination, and after its Warren Commission concluded that the assassin, Lee Harvey Oswald, had acted alone, the stunned nation moved slowly forward, albeit with permanent scars. Jackie Kennedy remained in the public eye as John's widow, and a few years later became involved with Robert F. Kennedy's own presidential bid. But on June 5, 1968, tragedy struck again when Bobby was killed. At 12:15 a.m., a Jordanian immigrant named Sirhan Sirhan shot Bobby three times as he walked through the kitchen of the Ambassador Hotel in Los Angeles after a rousing campaign speech. Bobby died 25 hours later and, at 42, was laid to rest a short distance from his brother. His grave at Arlington is marked with a plain white cross.

In October 1968, Jackie became "Jackie O" when she married shipping magnate Aristotle Onassis. The marriage seemed rocky, the couple spent almost all of their time apart, and when Jackie became a widow again in 1975, a weight seemed to be lifted from her shoulders. Just before Aristotle's death, Jackie began working as a book editor, an endeavor she continued for most of the remainder of her life. As Jackie was relentlessly pursued by tabloid photographers, she became a familiar Manhattan sight, camouflaging herself in dark sunglasses and turned-up collar, her signature mane hidden beneath a kerchief. In January 1994 Jackie made public the information that she was being treated for non-Hodgkin's lymphoma, and by May had succumbed to the illness. At 64, Jackie was buried next to John at Arlington.

CEMETERY DIRECTIONS: Arlington National Cemetery is located in Arlington, Virginia, across the Potomac River from Washington. From any of the major highways, follow the signs to its visitor parking lots.

GRAVE DIRECTIONS: John, Jackie, and Bobby are buried together on a knoll just a short distance behind the main gate. There are plenty of signs pointing the way.

John Connally

FEBRUARY 27, 1917 – JUNE 15, 1993

Sitting in the jump seat in front of the Kennedys on that dark day in Dallas were Texas Governor John Connally and his wife, Nellie. Just as the president's Lincoln, its bubbletop off, approached an underpass near the intersection of Elm, Main, and Commerce streets, Nellie turned to the President and said laughingly, "You can't say that Dallas isn't friendly to you today." As he started to reply, a sharp rifle crack filled the air and a bullet crashed into Kennedy's head. John Connally turned to see what the commotion was, and a bullet then caught him in the back. It plowed down into his chest, went through a lung, fractured his right wrist, and lodged in his left thigh. Though Kennedy never knew what hit him, Connally remained conscious until he was anesthetized for surgery. He made a full recovery and later, egocentrically speculated that he was the assassin's real target.

Connally left the governor's post in 1969 and, in 1973, after Spiro Agnew resigned, declared himself a Republican in order to gain an appointment to the newly vacated vice-presidential seat from his friend, Richard M. Nixon. But after a firestorm of protest, the plan was nixed and Connally slinked back to Texas. As it turns out, he may have been more perfectly suited to partner with Nixon than anyone ever guessed; in 1975 he was tried and acquitted in a milk-price bribery scandal, in 1977 he entered into a shady bank partnership with two Arab sheiks and, after he got a bit too acquisitive during Texas' dizzying oil and real-estate heyday, Connally declared bankruptcy in 1987.

At 76, Connally died of pulmonary fibrosis and was buried at the Texas State Cemetery in Austin, Texas.

CEMETERY DIRECTIONS: From I-35, take Exit 234B and turn east onto 7th Street. After a half-mile, turn left onto Navasota Street and the cemetery is a short distance ahead on the right.

GRAVE DIRECTIONS: Connally's elaborate, tall, black monument is easy to find in the stately Republic Hill section.

Lee Harvey Oswald

OCTOBER 18, 1939 – NOVEMBER 24, 1963

It seems apparent that Lee Harvey Oswald shot John F. Kennedy from the sixth floor of the Texas School Book Depository building. Beyond that, however, everything about him is up for grabs. Every conceivable possibility and impossibility concerning his life, whereabouts, motives, connections, and identity has been endlessly debated and examined by an army of government investigators, millions of truth-seeking citizens, and God knows how many conspiracy buffs—some of them flat-out nuts, others just passionate about the truth.

Despite the conclusions of the Warren Report, it *is* very difficult, after even a cursory review of the facts, to accept that Oswald alone killed Kennedy. Every imaginable scenario for complicity and blame has been put forward, and it seems certain that it will never be known exactly what happened and who was, or was not, involved.

There does seem to be very good reason why many are convinced there was at least one accomplice. If Oswald was the lone gunman, sound and film as well as ballistic evidence dictate one or another sequence of events, but, in either of these sequences, unexplainable problems persist: Forensics do not support either sequence of events promoted by "lone gunman" proponents. Supporters of one particular "lone gunman" camp believe that Oswald fired three shots. But if that were true, one of those bullets must have inflicted seven wounds in two bodies—some nearly at right angles to one another—according to ballistic evidence. And, after those gymnastics, the evidence further stipulates that that bullet was the one found in near pristine condition lying atop Kennedy's stretcher—a clear impossibility. Supporters of the other "lone gunman" camp insist that Oswald fired four shots, but this scenario is also unfeasible simply because Oswald couldn't have squeezed four rounds out of his bolt-action rifle in the six seconds of shooting, as exhibited in Zapruder's infamous film—never mind that he would have had to train those shots on a moving target 75 yards away. The forensic evidence of the Kennedy assassination does not support any conceivable sequence of events in which there is only a single gunman. Once the forensic and ballistic evidence is weighed, it seems to have been physically impossible for Oswald to have acted alone.

Jefferson Davis Tippit
SEPTEMBER 18, 1924 – NOVEMBER 22, 1963

In any event, after Oswald fired at Kennedy, he ditched his rifle between some boxes, ran out of the depository building, jumped on a bus and then into a cab, and then walked the remaining few blocks to his rooming house. He left his room after just a few minutes and, at 1:18 p.m., a caller radioed to the Dallas police that one of its own had been gunned down. The fallen policeman was Officer Jefferson Davis Tippit, and his assailant, as you may have guessed, turned out to be Oswald. Apparently, Tippit had stopped to question a suspicious-looking Oswald and, after exchanging a few words, Oswald felled him with revolver shots to the head and chest.

At his funeral, of course, 39-year-old Officer Tippit was afforded all the ceremony that befits one killed in the line of duty and, in light of the circumstances, he was deservedly martyred by the public at large. However, in the eyes of conspiracy theorists, nobody is beyond reproach, and a number of them directly accuse Tippit of being "the other gunman." In these scenarios, Tippit didn't just happen to cross paths with Oswald. Instead, they were discussing their next move minutes after the assassination when Oswald double-crossed Tippit, ostensibly to eliminate a witness. Well, anything's possible, I guess.

Jack Ruby
APRIL 25, 1911 – JANUARY 3, 1967

Two days after Kennedy and Tippit died, Oswald was transferred from police headquarters to the Dallas County jail and a crowd gathered to witness his departure. Oswald was escorted through the basement of the Dallas police building by a black-hatted detective, L. C. Graves, who gripped Oswald's upper arm tightly while a phalanx of police provided the illusion of security. Then, while live television cameras rolled, a strip-club owner, Jack Ruby, emerged from the crowd, stabbed a .38 revolver at Oswald's abdomen, and fired. Two hours later Oswald was dead at 24.

Some call Ruby a hero, while others believe that Ruby, a shady operator who had minor connections to organized crime and the Dallas Police Department, killed Oswald to keep him from revealing a larger conspiracy. During his trial Ruby claimed that his rage at Kennedy's murder was the sole motive for his action but, whatever his motives, he certainly helped propel the cottage business of conspiracy theorists. Ruby was convicted of "murder with malice"

BELOVED
SON AND BROTHER
JACK RUBY
APRIL 25, 1911 — JAN. 3, 1967
תנצב״ה

and sentenced to death in March 1964, but the verdict was overturned in November 1966 on the grounds that he could not have
received a fair trial in Dallas at the time. In January 1967, while
awaiting a second trial, Ruby died of lung cancer at 55.

L.C. Graves

OCTOBER 8, 1918 – FEBRUARY 11, 1995

Some buffs paint a conspiracy of the Kennedy assassination that
even encompasses members of the Dallas police force, and especially L.C. Graves, because of the amateurish protection offered to
Oswald. Graves left the force in 1970 and worked as a bank-fraud
investigator for the next dozen years. Though he had plenty of opportunities, he never cashed in on his link to history. At 76, he died
of cardiac arrest.

DIRECTIONS TO GRAVE OF JEFFERSON DAVIS TIPPIT: He rests at
Laurel Land Memorial Park in Dallas. From I-35E, take Exit 420
and the cemetery is on the east side of the highway. Tippit is buried
in Section 62, a distinguished area reserved for those whose lives
were dedicated to some special service.

DIRECTIONS TO GRAVE OF LEE HARVEY OSWALD: He was buried at
Shannon Rose Hill Memorial Park in Fort Worth, Texas. From I-
820, take Exit 30, follow Lancaster Avenue east for 1½ miles, and
the cemetery is on the left. Enter the cemetery, drive up the road
that runs directly behind the funeral home, and stop at the brown
Shannon mausoleum. Just behind and to the left of this mausoleum, along the road, is a flat marker for Skelton. Oswald lies in
the grass, waiting, just twenty feet behind the Skelton marker. The
inscription on his gravestone reads simply, "Oswald."

DIRECTIONS TO GRAVE OF JACK RUBY: He was buried at Westlawn Memorial Park in Norridge, Illinois. Westlawn is located on Montrose Avenue, a mile west of Route 43. Enter the cemetery, turn at the first left and again at the next right, and then you'll see yellow numbers painted along the road. Stop at "2," and, on the left, eighteen rows back is Ruby's grave.

DIRECTIONS TO GRAVE OF L. C. GRAVES: Buried at Grove Hill Cemetery in Dallas, Texas, his grave is easy to find off of I-30. Take Exit 49B onto Samuell Boulevard and you'll immediately see the cemetery southeast of the highway. Enter the cemetery at the first entrance and park wherever you can. In the section on the left is the Wolff mausoleum, 30 feet in front of which is L.C.'s flat marker.

MARTIN LUTHER KING, JR.

JANUARY 15, 1929 – APRIL 4, 1968

After receiving his doctorate in theology from Boston University, Martin Luther King, Jr. moved to Montgomery, Alabama, in 1955, where he was to be a preacher at a Baptist church. Having grown up in Atlanta he was no stranger to Southern prejudice, but the scale of racial bigotry in Montgomery was so outrageous that Martin's ambitions were refocused, and he dedicated his life to amending those inequities and presenting his race with a fair chance at the American Dream.

By refusing to give up her seat on the bus to a white person, Rosa Parks was the catalyst for a boycott of Montgomery's city buses, organized by Martin, which ended only after the United States Supreme Court ruled that segregation on public transportation is legally and socially unacceptable. Building on that success, achieved through nonviolence, Martin founded the Southern Christian Leadership Conference in 1957 and became a figure with a national platform. The Civil Rights Movement had begun.

In the years following, Martin organized many similar nonviolent protests and the movement reached its zenith when the Civil Rights Act of 1964 was passed. The broad-reaching legislation guaranteed equal rights in all areas of the public domain, and a civil rights commission would ensure that these laws were enforced. Though Martin and his thousands of followers had not struggled in vain, the victory had come at a cost. They had endured high-pressure fire hoses, midnight cross burnings, and backwoods lynchings. But Martin had remained peaceful throughout, and in biblical cadence assured his followers that their fight could be victorious if they did not resort to bloodshed.

At 39, Martin was killed in Memphis, Tennessee. While he stood on the balcony of the Lorraine Motel, a single bullet was fired at him from the bathroom of a flophouse across the parking lot. A fugitive from a Missouri prison, James Earl Ray, was staying in the flophouse and a rifle and a pair of binoculars marked with his fingerprints was found in a bag near there. Arrested in London two months later, Ray never stood trial, but instead pleaded guilty in order to avoid the death penalty. Ballistics tests were never able to prove, or disprove, that the bullet had come from Ray's rifle and, largely on that basis, Ray tried to recant his guilty plea and repeatedly petitioned the court for a trial. However, no court ever recognized his request and, in 1998, he died of hepatitis at 70 and was cremated.

In a magnificent crypt atop a reflecting pool, Martin lies at his own Martin Luther King Jr. National Historic Site, established in Atlanta in 1970.

GRAVE DIRECTIONS: From I-75/85, take Exit 95 and follow either Butler Road or Hilliard Street for one block north to Auburn Avenue. Turn right onto Auburn Avenue and the site is one mile ahead on the right.

MARYJO KOPECHNE

JULY 26, 1940 - JULY 19, 1969

MaryJo Kopechne was the unfortunate passenger in Senator Edward Kennedy's car who drowned after he drove off the side of a bridge. The infamous incident on Martha's Vineyard in Massachusetts will forever be known as "Chappaquiddick." Though the brave and dashing young Kennedy managed to extricate himself from the submerged car and stumble back to his friends, he never explained why he waited nine hours before notifying police of the wreckage from which MaryJo never surfaced.

Kennedy holed up at the family's Hyannis compound for a week and then broke his silence with a televised speech in which he said he had been distraught and confused, wondered if there was a "curse" on the Kennedy family, and asked whether he should continue in the Senate. Despite widespread criticism that the speech raised more questions than it answered and concern that the Kennedy clout had suppressed a bona fide investigation, Kennedy claimed the public overwhelmingly supported his staying in office.

Kennedy's insurance company paid the Kopechne family a $140,000 settlement for the death of their only child, and Kennedy attended the funeral wearing a neck brace that he was never seen wearing again.

At 28, MaryJo was buried at St. Vincent's Cemetery in Larksville, Pennsylvania.

CEMETERY DIRECTIONS: From I-81 take Exit 47 and follow Route 309 north to Route 11 South. After four miles on Route 11, turn right at the traffic light onto Washington Avenue. Proceed straight up the hill for almost two miles and, after the left-hand hairpin turn, the cemetery is on the left.

GRAVE DIRECTIONS: As you enter the cemetery, MaryJo is buried in the first section. Her flat stone is ten rows up the hill next to the Bird plots.

GENERAL DOUGLAS MACARTHUR

JANUARY 26, 1880 – APRIL 5, 1964

Douglas MacArthur was the son of a Union army hero during the Civil War, and he and his father remain the only such pair ever to receive the Congressional Medal of Honor.

After attendance at the West Texas Military Academy, Douglas received an appointment to the United States Military Academy at West Point and graduated first in the Class of 1903. During the next decade he rose steadily in the Army, eventually became its first public-relations officer, and is largely credited with selling the American people on the Selective Service Act of 1917. Upon the entry of the United States into World War I, MacArthur commanded a combat brigade in France and became the war's most decorated American soldier.

While his peers were demoted to their pre-war ranks, MacArthur received a plum new assignment as superintendent of West Point and dragged the moribund academy into the twentieth century, enabling it to produce officers fit to lead the country in the type of modern war he had just experienced firsthand.

In 1923 he took command of the Army's Philippine Department and, in 1930, President Hoover appointed him chief of staff. After only five years, MacArthur was drawn back to the Philippines to head a U.S. military mission charged with preparing the islands

THE MacARTHUR MEMORIAL

for independence. On December 7, 1941, though, an expansionist Japan struck the United States at Pearl Harbor and, without enough time or money to build a force capable of resisting the Japanese, his forces retreated to the Bataan peninsula and struggled to survive while MacArthur himself was ordered to Australia.

MacArthur left his men to face almost-certain destruction, comforted only by the belief that he would later lead an army back to rescue them. For the next three years, his personal quest—"I shall return"—became almost synonymous with the war in the Pacific. Although MacArthur's path through the dense South Pacific island jungles could hardly have been foreseen in the initial war plans, the offensive under his command returned U.S. forces to the Philippines in October of 1944, and MacArthur dramatically waded ashore at Leyte during its liberation. The next year, as supreme commander of the Allied powers, MacArthur presided over the Japanese surrender aboard the *USS Missouri*, which brought an end to World War II.

His place as a leading figure of the twentieth century secure, MacArthur may have made his greatest contribution to history in the next five years as supreme commander of the allied powers in Japan. As its military governor, he implemented policies that purged Japan of its militarism, and through the successful occupation of a devastated Japan, he saw it rebuild, institute a democratic government, and chart a course that has made it one of the world's leading industrial powers.

At the outbreak of the Korean War in July 1950, MacArthur was placed in command of an American-led coalition of United Nations forces, and he reversed their dire military situation with an amphibious assault at the Port of Inchon, where he forced the invading North Koreans to surrender most of their gains. But when Chinese forces began fighting alongside the North Koreans, MacArthur advocated an extension of the war into China, and President Truman relieved him of command on April 11, 1951.

As the last great general of World War II to come home, MacArthur received a hero's welcome and concluded his address to Congress with his citation of an old military song, "Old soldiers never die, they just fade away." True to his word, the old soldier faded from the public eye and quietly lived out the remainder of his years in New York until his death of natural causes at 84.

Douglas MacArthur is buried at his own MacArthur Memorial in Norfolk, Virginia.

GRAVE DIRECTIONS: From I-264, take Exit 10, which is City Hall Avenue, and follow the signs to MacArthur Center, a big shopping mall across the street from the MacArthur Memorial. In the area you might find on-street parking, but it's easiest to park in the south garage of the MacArthur Center and walk to the memorial. Bring your ticket and they'll validate it so you don't have to pay for parking.

The MacArthur Memorial is a National Historic Place that accepts donations and is very much worth whatever you might be able to give. The beautifully landscaped square features a theater, a library, and a museum with nine galleries of exhibits. The General and Mrs. MacArthur lie in the center rotunda.

JOE McCARTHY
NOVEMBER 14, 1909 – MAY 2, 1957

Joe McCarthy was an undistinguished first-term senator from Wisconsin when he found his cause in February 1950. Appearing at a Republican Women's Club meeting in West Virginia,

McCarthy announced that by clandestine effort he had collected a "list of 205 cases of individuals who appear to be either card-carrying members or certainly loyal to the Communist Party" working within the state department.

In spite of the fact that it was not a crime to be a member of the Communist Party, despite McCarthy's refusal to disclose exactly how he had arrived at this list, and, even though McCarthy couldn't nail down the number of infiltrators that existed—in a Salt Lake City speech the following week there were only 57, and on the Senate floor five days later there were 81— the assertion was like gasoline tossed on the smoldering coals of Cold War anxiety.

The furor should have been extinguished in July 1950 when, after McCarthy failed to produce a single name of an actual Communist, the Tydings Senate subcommittee concluded that his campaign was a "hoax and a fraud." But by then, McCarthy's fantastic controversy had gained the momentum of a runaway train, and it certainly wasn't going to be derailed by a mere subcommittee's opinion. Instead, McCarthy rallied anxious supporters with inflammatory speeches and subpoenaed prominent citizens to Washington, where he demanded "the naming of names." Regularly usurping executive and judicial authority, McCarthy cast suspicion on anyone he pleased. To question his character or the motivations of his witch-hunt could result in being blackballed, which was "as good as Red."

His coffers overflowing with donations from frenzied supporters, McCarthy won his 1952 re-election and became chairman of the Permanent Subcommittee on Investigations of Governmental Operations. In 1954, he pressed to convene hearings to investigate the extent of communist espionage activity in the Army. His own Republican party resisted the hearings, as they knew full well that nothing would be found. But Democrats pushed the hearings ahead to allow McCarthy the opportunity to commit political suicide and, with any luck, kill his party.

On April 23, 1954, the hearings began and McCarthy's flagrant disregard for proper investigative procedure and reckless interrogative tactics were quickly exposed to some twenty million television viewers. After 36 days of testimony, the Army was vindicated and Senator McCarthy became immediately irrelevant. In July a resolution accusing McCarthy of conduct "unbecoming a member of the United States Senate" was introduced, and in December 1954 the Senate voted to censure him.

Even before his professional reputation was destroyed there were whisperings that McCarthy suffered from alcoholism, and after his censure, though still a Senator, he stayed home and watched soap operas while drinking continuously. In the summer of 1956 he was hospitalized for detoxification, where he suffered fits of delirium screaming that snakes were attacking him. The treatment helped, but McCarthy soon resumed drinking and his face grew bloated, his body drawn, and his skin yellow.

When he was again admitted to the Navy Medical Center in Bethesda, Maryland, his wife said he was undergoing treatment for an old knee injury, but when he died four days later at 47, the hospital reported it was from "acute hepatitis, origin unknown." It was later acknowledged that McCarthy was being treated in the neurology ward for alcohol abuse, which caused his liver failure.

He is buried at Saint Mary's Church Cemetery in Appleton, Wisconsin.

CEMETERY DIRECTIONS: From routes 41 and 10, take Exit 136 onto Prospect Avenue. Follow Prospect Avenue east for a mile and the cemetery is on the right.

GRAVE DIRECTIONS: Enter the cemetery, go over the bridge and stop after the chapel. Joe's stone is on the right, adjacent to the river.

In the 50 years since McCarthy's hearings, information obtained from the KGB seems to indicate that Communists *did* infiltrate the government. Such revelations however, fall far short of any vindication for McCarthy. It's clear that instead of having any actual knowledge, Joe McCarthy *supposed* there might be infiltration, and after concocting a list of such threats, he trampled over the United States Constitution, smeared hundreds of Americans and profited, for a while anyway, politically and personally from the hysteria he instigated.

HARVEY MILK

MAY 22, 1930 - NOVEMBER 27, 1978

Harvey Milk was a stalwart Republican from Long Island who served in the Navy during the Korean War and came home to find success on Wall Street. But banking bored him, and he slipped into the vibrant gay Greenwich Village milieu. Enraptured by the reports of San Francisco's flourishing gay counterculture, Harvey and his boyfriend headed west in 1972 and opened a camera shop.

To be gay in the 1970s, when many psychiatrists still called homosexuality a mental illness, meant that, to be accepted in conventional society you had to be satisfied with a closeted life and a fake wedding ring. Of course, the political arena was entirely off-limits to "avowed homosexuals."

At the camera shop, Harvey began making waves as he convinced himself that the root cause of the gay predicament was invisibility and that the gay community's political situation needed an overhaul. Instead of being satisfied that members of the gay community had infiltrated the hostile Democratic Party and toiled in quiet anonymity with straight allies, the day had come for the gay community to publicly elect one of its own. Harvey turned his camera shop into a political war room and set out to infiltrate City Hall through the front door.

To secure a seat on the city's administration, Harvey reached out to the gay masses and, in supporting him, they out-ed themselves in an invigorating and once-unthinkable way. In 1977, after three unsuccessful campaigns, he was elected to the San Francisco County Board of Supervisors. It was a watershed event; Harvey Milk had become the first openly gay elected official in the United States.

Though the gay community was ecstatic, not everyone cheered, of course, and death threats multiplied. Scarcely a year after his election, Harvey was killed by Dan White, a former police officer and troubled conservative political rival who had clashed with Harvey over gay issues. White had been a fellow supervisor but left the board and, after Mayor George Moscone denied his request to be reinstated, White became unhinged. He charged into the City Hall offices at midday, shooting and killing both Harvey and Mayor Moscone at their desks.

Harvey was 48. He was cremated and his ashes scattered in San Francisco Bay.

At his trial, Dan White employed the "Twinkie defense," claiming that too much junk food had affected his reasoning abilities. The jury didn't buy it and he was found guilty of voluntary manslaughter. He was sentenced to 92 months for the murders of the two men, and most San Franciscans, both gay and straight, were enraged by the leniency. Demonstrations turned into riots in what became known as "White Night."

After serving 61 months, only two-thirds of an already lenient sentence, White was paroled in January 1984 and, after a year in Los Angeles, he moved back to San Francisco, though Mayor Diane Feinstein publicly asked him not to return. White lived there quietly and without incident until October 21, 1985, when he asphyxiated himself in the garage of his home at age 39.

In 2000, the Board of Supervisors assigned the building that housed Harvey's camera shop the status of Historic Building, and you can visit it at 575 Castro Street. Castro Street runs north-south through the Haight-Ashbury district and Number 575 is just north of Castro Street's intersection with 19th Street.

J. ROBERT OPPENHEIMER

APRIL 22, 1904 – FEBRUARY 18, 1967

In 1939, Niels Bohr brought to the United States the news that German scientists had succeeded at nuclear fission; they'd split the atom. This meant that the Nazis were on their way to developing an atomic bomb and, once President Roosevelt absorbed the terrible implications, he ordered the initiation of a scientific program aimed at developing such a weapon before the enemy did.

Splintered research had been ongoing at Columbia University, the University of Chicago, and at an emerging facility in Oak Ridge, Tennessee, but now there was a new urgency to the atomic project; to realize the objective, no expense would be spared and no sacrifice could be considered too great. The country's top theoretical physicists and a few thousand support staff began working together on the so-called Manhattan Project in Los Alamos, New Mexico. The resident genius, J. Robert Oppenheimer, was appointed technical director.

Under his direction the best minds in physics worked to solve the riddles of the atomic bomb challenge. The efforts of the thousands who contributed to the Manhattan Project were rewarded on July 16, 1945, when the first nuclear detonation occurred at the Trinity Bomb site in the New Mexico desert. As Oppenheimer stood watching the mushroom cloud on that grimly historic day, the gravity of the accomplishment weighed on him, and he later recalled that a phrase of Hindu scripture floated through his mind, "I have become death, the destroyer of worlds."

A few weeks later atomic bombs were detonated over the Japanese cities of Hiroshima and Nagasaki, prompting the unconditional surrender of Japan and the end of World War II.

After the war, Oppenheimer chaired the Advisory Committee to the Atomic Energy Commission and there voiced his opposition to the development of the next generation of atomic bomb, the hydrogen bomb. Later, at the height of the hysterical Communist witch hunts in 1953, Oppenheimer's security clearance was revoked and his advisor role terminated in light of his opposition to new mass-destruction weapons and his increasing support for liberal philosophies.

Oppenheimer served as director of the Institute for Advanced Study at Princeton University for the remainder of his days and died of throat cancer at 62.

He was cremated and his ashes scattered off the Virgin Islands.

KAREN ANN QUINLAN

MARCH 29, 1954 – JUNE 11, 1985

Ten years after lapsing into a coma caused by her ingestion of tranquilizers and alcohol during an evening of partying, Karen Ann Quinlan died at 31.

Back in 1975, Karen's parents had requested that her respirator be disconnected and she be allowed to die with dignity, as there was no chance of recovery from her condition, but doctors refused and in 1976 the matter went to the Supreme Court of New Jersey. Eventually the Court sided with the Quinlans, but in the meantime, a national debate raged around water coolers and over picket fences as ordinary people debated fundamental theological, medical, and legal questions of life and death.

Because of the landmark Quinlan case, new guidelines evolved for "judicious neglect" and the circumstances in which doctors accede to the requests of relatives of terminally ill patients and withhold extraordinary measures to keep them alive. The practice has gained widespread acceptance.

Karen is buried at the Gate of Heaven Cemetery in East Hanover, New Jersey.

CEMETERY DIRECTIONS: From I-287, follow Route 10 east for three miles, then turn north onto Ridgedale Avenue. After another mile, the cemetery is on the right.

GRAVE DIRECTIONS: Enter the cemetery at the first gate and turn right at the "T." Bear left, go halfway around the mausoleum, then follow the drive that extends into the cemetery. You'll pass sections 21, 23, and 30 and then, after the road bends, you'll see Section 29 on the left. In Section 29, two rows from the drive, is Karen's stone.

JULIUS & ETHEL ROSENBERG

Julius Rosenberg
MAY 12, 1918 – JUNE 19, 1953

Ethel Rosenberg
SEPTEMBER 28, 1915 – JUNE 19, 1953

In July of 1950, Ethel and Julius Rosenberg were arrested on charges of espionage on behalf of the Soviet Union. The trial and subsequent conviction of the Rosenbergs in 1951 led to one of the most controversial sentences ever handed down in the United States, as many felt that they were the victims of the era's Communist witch-hunt atmosphere.

Witch-hunt or not, it does seem to have been proven in court, and is generally agreed, that while employed as an engineer by the U.S. Army Signal Corps, Julius stole military technology and passed along atomic secrets through an intermediary to the Soviet vice consul. However, Ethel's prosecution may have been particularly unfair because, though she knew of her husband's role and the role of her brother, David Greenglass, who testified for the prosecution to save his own life, Ethel had not actively spied.

Nonetheless, both Rosenbergs were convicted and sentenced to death under the Espionage Act of 1917 and, despite worldwide pleas that their lives be spared, President Eisenhower refused to commute their sentences.

On a hot June night at the Sing Sing death house in Ossining, New York, in 1953, Julius was led into the death chamber and killed in the electric chair by three shocks of 2,000 volts each. While thousands of people gathered in protest around the country, Ethel was placed in the chair next. The top of her head had been shaved to ensure a good contact with the electrodes, she wore a green print dress with white polka dots, and she was stoic and defiant. It took five jolts before Ethel was declared dead at 8:16 p.m. Julius was 35 and Ethel was 37 at the time of their deaths.

They now lie side by side at Wellwood Cemetery in Farmingdale, New York.

CEMETERY DIRECTIONS: From I-495 on Long Island, take Exit 39 and follow Pinelawn Avenue south for exactly three miles. Wellwood will be on the left. There are a lot of cemeteries in this area, nine different ones bordering each other, so be sure to turn into the correct one.

GRAVE DIRECTIONS: Turn into the first Wellwood entrance, which is North Avenue. Follow North Avenue for a short distance and then, between Akiba and Bialik roads, there will be a marking on the left curb for Walkway F-G. Fifty feet along this walk is the Rosenberg plot.

OSKAR SCHINDLER
APRIL 28, 1908 – OCTOBER 9, 1974

Oskar Schindler grew up the son of a wealthy family in what is now the Czech Republic, but during the deep economic depression that gripped Europe before World War II, the family business was lost and the Schindler family went bankrupt. In 1939 the first German divisions marched into Czechoslovakia and Oskar was inclined to join the Nazi Party. In a short time, Poland fell to the Germans and Oskar immigrated to its city of Krakow in search of opportunity.

In Poland, after developing a rapport with the local Gestapo chiefs, he was recruited by the German Intelligence Agency to collect information about Poles who might not be sympathetic to the Nazi cause. Through the status he acquired in that post, Oskar was able to acquire two factories, previously Jewish-owned, that had recently become "available."

Oskar ran his new pot-making business exactly as his fellow usurping Nazi industrialists did. Employing neighborhood Jews, the cheapest labor he could find, Oskar turned a profit and disregarded the realities that were responsible for his newfound business success.

But soon Oskar had misgivings, and he began to manipulate Nazi officials to prevent his Jewish workers from being carted off to the death camps. Oskar's protection of his Jewish workers became increasingly aggressive but covert until he realized, in 1942, after witnessing a particular raid on a Jewish ghetto, that the Nazis wanted nothing less than the complete extermination of every Jew. While watching innocent people being packed onto trains bound for certain death, something awakened in him. "Beyond this day, no thinking person could fail to see what would happen," he said later. "I was now resolved to do everything in my power to defeat the system."

Soon, Oskar had convinced officials to allow him to house part of the Plazow labor camp in his factory by deeming the detainees "necessary" workers. The old were registered as twenty years younger and the children were registered as adults. Lawyers, doctors, and artists were registered as metal workers and mechanics, all so they might survive.

By the fall of 1944, the Germans were frantically trying to complete their extermination of Poland's Jews before the Russians arrived to liberate them, and it seemed certain that Schindler's Jews' time had run out. But instead of giving them up, Oskar desperately exerted his influence on contacts from Krakow to Warsaw to Berlin in an effort to spare his factory and, most importantly, his workers. And, where no one would have believed it possible, he succeeded. Oskar was granted permission to move the whole of his factory to occupied Bruennlitz, Czechoslovakia, and to take all his workers with him. The 1,098 workers who had been written on Schindler's list of employees avoided the fate of countless others who were sent to the Nazi gas chambers.

In May 1945 it was all over. The Russians moved into Bruennlitz, but in an ironic twist, though Schindler's Jews were now free, Schindler, himself a Nazi, became a fugitive. With his wife and a handful of workers, Schindler fled to Argentina, where he lived until 1958 before returning to Germany. He spent the remaining years of his life dividing his time between Germany and Israel, where he was honored and taken care of by his "*Schindlerjuden*"— Schindler children. Pressed for an explanation of his heroism, Schindler later offered, "I am the conscience of all those who knew something, but did nothing."

In 1962, Schindler was recognized by Yad Vashem, Israel's Holocaust memorial located on the Hill of Remembrance near Mount Herzl on the western outskirts of Jerusalem. Along the avenue of trees where "Righteous Gentiles" are remembered, he was invited to plant a carob tree and, in 1967 when Schindler finally planted the tree, it was adorned with a Talmudic inscription: "Whoever saves a single soul, it is as if he saved the whole world."

In 1993 Steven Spielberg directed an adaptation of Thomas Keneally's award-winning 1982 book, *Schindler's Ark,* into a film that riveted audiences and popularized the story of Oskar Schindler.

Schindler died of liver failure in Hildersheim, Germany, at the age of 66. He was buried in the Catholic section of the Mount Zion Cemetery in Jerusalem. Located atop Mount Zion, the cemetery and grave are easy to locate.

BUGSY SIEGEL

FEBRUARY 28, 1906 – JUNE 20, 1947

Though Benjamin "Bugsy" Siegel didn't invent Las Vegas (and, contrary to popular belief, he didn't even build its first casino), the Las Vegas narrative will be forever linked to the Bugsy Siegel legend.

Beginning around 1920, Bugsy and his childhood pal Meyer Lansky headed a small Brooklyn gang that specialized in shakedowns and bookmaking and, after moving into bootlegging with the help of Lansky's business acumen, they amassed a minor fortune. The lucrative liquor revenue stream dried up when Prohibition was repealed in 1933, and Lansky (who by this time had emerged as the boss) sought to help replace the income by expanding into Nevada, where gambling had been recently legalized.

In 1945, Bugsy, who for the past five years had been establishing a new arm of the Lansky crime syndicate in California, was tapped to develop a casino operation in the dusty, two-track, railroad junction town of Las Vegas. Bugsy tried to buy a couple of existing gambling

joints in the downtown area and, failing that, eventually bought a controlling interest in a venture headed by Billy Wilkerson, who had a vision of a luxurious gaming paradise in the desert six miles outside of town. Wilkerson soon ran out of money and was pushed out, and the Flamingo Hotel and Casino became Bugsy's baby.

Bugsy had estimated that it would cost just over a million dollars to build the lavish facility, but the costs inevitably escalated and Lansky was forced to seek fellow racketeer investors. The price tag topped $6 million before the hotel section was completed, and Lansky's investor buddies were convinced that Bugsy had skimmed money from the construction funds. They voted for a contract on Bugsy's life. However, Lansky recommended that the execution of his childhood friend be stayed until after the casino opened. If Bugsy's desert dream proved as successful as had been promised, there would be ways for him to repay the money. If not, the contract could be fulfilled.

On the day after Christmas 1946, the Flamingo opened and flopped. A tremendous West Coast storm grounded flights that Bugsy had chartered for his Hollywood friends and, because there were yet no rooms to stay in, regular customers who trekked to the gala shortly left. Lansky's cronies again called for Bugsy's execution, but Lansky was convinced that the casino would become profitable and won his old friend another stay. Meanwhile, Bugsy remained ignorant of the ongoing scheme and devoted all of his waking hours to turning the operation around.

The Flamingo Hotel was completed in March 1947, and within two months the business was in the black—but by then it was too late. On a June evening, Bugsy was reading the evening papers on the sofa of his girlfriend's Beverly Hills home when, at about 10:30 p.m., eight bullets flew through the living-room window. Five of them hit their marks, and Bugsy was killed.

Even though his gangland slaying was front-page news, Bugsy's funeral was attended by only five people, all of them relatives. Neither his old buddy Meyer Lansky nor any of his Hollywood acquaintances, not even his girlfriend Virginia Hill, made time for the service.

At 41, Bugsy was buried at Hollywood Forever in Hollywood, California.

CEMETERY DIRECTIONS: This cemetery is easy to find at 6000 Santa Monica Blvd., just west of Highway 101.

GRAVE DIRECTIONS: Enter the cemetery, turn right after the information booth, then make a left and go all the way to the end of the drive, parking in front of the Beth Olam Mausoleum. Walk into the mausoleum and turn right at the second hall, which is labeled "M2." Bugsy's crypt is about halfway down this hall, on the left-hand side, third row from the bottom, Number 3087.

Say what you will about Bugsy Siegel, but he must have done something right. God knows I've seen a lot of celebrity resting places, but his crypt is the first I've ever seen peppered with lipstick impressions.

The Las Vegas that Bugsy knew doesn't really exist anymore, and in 1993 the last of the original Flamingo buildings were torn down. Today, the only homage to Bugsy is a plaque in the garden near the Flamingo's pool.

HARRIET TUBMAN
1820(?) – MARCH 10, 1913

Harriet Tubman's ancestors had been brought from Africa in shackles to slave over the broad farmlands of eastern Maryland, but Harriet escaped to the freedom of Pennsylvania in 1849 after learning that she was to be sold to a slave-owner in the Deep South. Upon reaching Philadelphia, where Harriet later reflected, "I was free, but there was no one to welcome me to the land of freedom," she was directed to the abolitionist William Still, who ran the General Vigilance Committee. Still disclosed to Harriet the existence of the underground railroad, a loose network of safe houses maintained by antislavery sympathizers that constituted a route to freedom in the North. For the next sixteen years, until the Emancipation Proclamation in 1865 freed blacks from indenture, Harriet made at least eighteen trips to the South and led some 300 slaves, including seven members of her family, along the underground railroad, becoming its most celebrated "conductor." By Harriet's own admission, "I never run my train off the track and I never lost a passenger."

Harriet spent two of the Civil War years in South Carolina working for the Union Army as a nurse and helping blacks organize for their impending freedom. After the war, she settled in Auburn, New York, where the state government assisted her in acquiring a home. In 1896, when she was well into her 70s, Harriet acquired additional acreage and established the Harriet Tubman Home for the Aged, which provided shelter and services for the indigent freed blacks.

Harriet's last two years were spent as an in-patient of her own home for the aged, and she died there of pneumonia.

At about 93, Harriet was buried at Fort Hill Cemetery in Auburn, New York.

CEMETERY DIRECTIONS: From I-90, take Exit 40 and follow Route 34 south for nine miles into the center of Auburn. Turn right onto Genesse Street and, after a half-mile, turn left onto Fort Street, which leads directly to the cemetery.

GRAVE DIRECTIONS: Enter the cemetery by turning right immediately before the stone fort building. Follow the drive along the cemetery's chain-link fence perimeter and, a hundred feet after the drive turns hard to the left, look to the left for a big spruce tree. Just in front of the spruce tree, Harriet's gravestone is flanked by a pair of shrubs.

If you're interested, the Harriet Tubman home is now a museum, just 1½ miles further south on Route 34.

THE WRIGHT BROTHERS

Wilbur Wright

APRIL 16, 1867 – MAY 30, 1912

Orville Wright

AUGUST 19, 1871 – JANUARY 30, 1948

In the late 1800s Wilbur and Orville Wright took an interest in flying, which at that time only meant gliding, and within a short time they read all that had been written on the subject. Disagreeing with the manner in which most flying-machine tinkerers were approaching the problem, Wilbur started anew and defined what he felt were the essential elements of a flying machine. To wit, it would need wings to provide lift, a power source for propulsion, and a system of control. Of all the early aviators, Wilbur was the first to recognize that a flying machine must be controlled in all three axes of rotation, now known as pitch, roll, and yaw, and it seems that simple abstraction was his key advantage. This, and their dogged perseverance, led the brothers to build the first successful flying machine.

By 1902 the brothers had built a controllable glider, but to graduate to a self-propelled flying machine they'd need a lightweight internal combustion engine, which did not exist. Undaunted, within a year they had built a four-cylinder, twelve-horsepower engine in their bicycle shop and fitted it with a propeller whose design was based on the same aeronautical principle as their wings. Orville and Wilbur understood that a propeller is essentially a rotating wing.

In the autumn of 1903 the brothers' flying machine was complete. They shipped it to Kitty Hawk, North Carolina, and, after winning a coin toss, Wilbur attempted to fly it. He stalled the engine on takeoff and caused some minor damage, so the next attempt would be Orville's. Three days later, on December 17, 1903, Orville Wright did for twelve seconds what no person had ever done before. He flew.

After two more years of fine tuning their Flyer, they could stay aloft for as long as they liked, or until their fuel ran out, and their 1905 Wright Flyer became the world's first practical airplane. Surprisingly, their airplane was not an immediate commercial success. The Wrights contacted the United States War Department, as well as foreign governments, and offered to sell them a flying machine, but they were turned down time and time again. Government bureaucrats thought they were crackpots, and others thought that if two Ohio bicycle mechanics could build an airplane, they could do it themselves. But the Wrights persisted and finally, in 1908, they sold their first aircraft to the United States government.

Unfortunately, Wilbur never witnessed the tremendous strides made in aviation over the next decades, as he died in 1912 of typhoid fever. He was 45. Orville lived to be 76, expiring of a heart attack while fixing the doorbell at his home in 1948.

Both lifelong bachelors, the brothers are buried together at Woodlawn Cemetery in Dayton, Ohio.

CEMETERY DIRECTIONS: From I-75, take Exit 52 and follow Route 35 east to the Jefferson Street exit. Turn south on Jefferson, which will become Warren Street and then Brown Street. After about a half-mile, turn left onto Woodland Avenue and the cemetery is a short distance ahead.

GRAVE DIRECTIONS: Enter the cemetery, bear left at the "T" and head up the hill. At the first intersection, bear left at the Lowes mausoleum and then turn right at the Staniland mausoleum. Stop at the Phillips mausoleum on the left. The Wrights are in this section, about 50 feet behind Phillips.

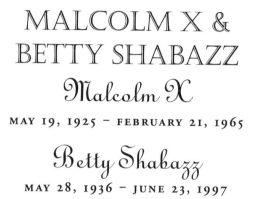

MALCOLM X & BETTY SHABAZZ

Malcolm X

MAY 19, 1925 – FEBRUARY 21, 1965

Betty Shabazz

MAY 28, 1936 – JUNE 23, 1997

Malcolm X's father was an outspoken supporter of black leaders long before "civil rights" became a buzzword. As a result, the family was harassed by vigilante groups and Malcolm's father eventually ended up on streetcar tracks with a crushed skull and a body nearly severed in half, though the death was ruled accidental.

Malcolm was sent to prison for burglary in 1946, and it was there that he converted to the Black Muslim faith, the Nation of Islam. By the time of his 1952 parole, he wholeheartedly embraced the faith's beliefs and tirelessly championed its basic argument that evil is an inherent characteristic of the white man's world. He believed that in order to flourish blacks had to completely separate themselves from white civilization. Malcolm was soon ordained a minister, and in 1956 he met his future wife, Betty, who had also taken the last name "X," as many Nation of Islam followers do—it represents an African family name that can never be known.

Throughout the 1950s and into the early 1960s, Malcolm developed a brilliant platform style and, with bitter eloquence, took the Nation of Islam from an insignificant splinter group to an organization that boasted thousands of official members and an untold number of sympathizers. By far the Nation of Islam's most effective and prominent preacher, Malcolm was in almost constant demand on college campuses, where he derided the civil-rights movement and rejected integration and racial equality, calling instead for black separatism and the taking up of arms against whites. This message was the opposite of the nonviolent approach that activists such as Dr. Martin Luther King, Jr., preached and, as a result of this militant stance, many whites viewed Malcolm with fear and contempt, while many blacks distanced themselves from his tirades.

As Malcolm became increasingly famous, he provoked tension and jealousy among the Nation of Islam leaders. Its founder, Elijah Muhammad, sought to rid himself of the formidable threat to his own power. After Malcolm described John F. Kennedy's assassination as a "case of chickens coming home to roost," Muhammad suspended his protégé from the faith.

In 1964 Malcolm followed a pilgrimage to Mecca with a prolonged period of study in the Middle East, where he was impressed by the sight of people of all races coming together in the name of Islam. He returned to the United States a changed man, proclaimed himself a convert to orthodox Islam, adopted a new name, El-Hajj Malik El-Shabazz, and fostered a new philosophy known as Black Consciousness encouraging blacks to share their racial and cultural heritage.

Malcolm no longer accepted that white people were evil, and he became critical of the now-rival Nation of Islam, condemning its ideas as counterproductive; it was economics, not color, that kept blacks from succeeding, the new Malcolm insisted. Further, Malcolm raised questions about Nation of Islam financial irregularities, and denounced Elijah Muhammad as a fake and an immoral philanderer. As the two sides traded accusations, the conflict escalated into outright violence and death threats were recorded.

While preparing for an address at Harlem's Audubon Ballroom in February 1965, Malcolm X was ambushed and died after being shot more than a dozen times. Though his three assassins had ties to the Nation of Islam, they insisted someone else had paid them. Nonetheless, they were convicted of the murder and sentenced to life in prison.

After her husband's death, Betty Shabazz earned a doctorate in education and traveled widely to speak on civil rights and racial tolerance. In 1994 she spoke publicly about a long-held suspicion that Louis Farrakhan, the current leader of the Nation of Islam, had been behind the assassination of her husband, and a year later, her daughter Qubilah was charged with trying to hire a hit man to kill Farrakhan. Qubilah avoided prosecution by agreeing to accept responsibility for her conduct and completing treatment for alcohol and psychiatric problems, while Betty reconciled with Farrakhan at a fund-raiser for her daughter's defense.

ETERNAL COUPLE

MALCOLM X &
MARTIN LUTHER
KING, JR.

In June 1997, Betty died after being severely burned in a fire started by her twelve-year-old grandson (Qubilah's son), reportedly set because he was unhappy that he had been sent to live with her.

Malcolm X and Betty are buried side by side at Ferncliffe Cemetery in Hartsdale, New York.

CEMETERY DIRECTIONS: From I-87, take Exit 7 in Ardsley and follow Route 9A north for 1¼ miles. Then, at the traffic light, turn right onto Secor Road and the Ferncliffe Cemetery is a short distance ahead on the left.

GRAVE DIRECTIONS: Enter Ferncliffe at the third entrance and bear right. On the left at the top of the paved loop is the Pinewood section. Drive about ¾ of the way around the loop and stop at the rough and narrow path on the left. Four rows from the road and ten rows from the path are the graves of Malcolm X and Betty Shabazz at marker number 150.

ALVIN YORK

DECEMBER 13, 1887 – SEPTEMBER 2, 1964

Alvin York hailed from the backwaters of Tennessee where he and his family scraped out a living and supplemented their dinner table through hunting. In his small world, Alvin was well known as a drinker and gambler and general nuisance, but after an epiphany at 26 he turned his life around. He became a member of the Church of Christ, a teacher in the Sunday school, and leader of the choir.

Three years later, in 1917, the United States joined the war against Germany and Alvin's faith was tested when he received a draft notice. Following the church's teachings, Alvin returned the notice with the words "Dont want to Fight" scrawled across the back. However, his case was denied because his church did not expressly prohibit killing during war, and Alvin reluctantly reported to basic training, where he distinguished himself as an expert marksman.

In the Argonne Forest in October of 1918, Alvin and sixteen other soldiers mistakenly wound up behind enemy lines and surprised a number of German troops eating breakfast. A brief firefight ensued and resulted in the unexpected surrender of a superior German force to the seventeen men. But once the Germans realized that the American contingent was limited, another squad of German machine-gunners on a nearby hill was alerted and opened fire on the Americans, as well as on their own troops, who had just surrendered. Ordered to silence the machine guns, the marksman Alvin picked off at least a dozen of the Germans on the hill, and in short order they, too, chose to surrender. By the time York and his men, now numbering just nine, reached the safety of the American lines they had captured 132 Germans. Word quickly spread that York had single-handedly "captured the whole German army."

Upon returning to America, Sergeant York was issued the Medal of Honor and showered with appearance and endorsement offers. He soon began using his popularity to raise money for a school for underprivileged children and, in 1927, the Alvin C. York Institute was established. It later became a special part of the Tennessee school system.

Alvin's hero status matured to its fullest in the years during World War II, when his story from the previous war was made into a top-grossing movie, *Sergeant York*. Twenty years later, such status mattered little when the Internal Revenue Service pursued him for some $170,000 in back taxes and interest owed from the movie royalty income. Partially paralyzed and almost completely blind from a stroke, Alvin was broke and unable to pay the debt, so the American public rallied behind him and established the York Relief Fund. After $130,000 was raised, President Kennedy called the matter "a national disgrace" and ordered it resolved. The IRS settled for $100,000, and the remainder was placed in a trust for the York family.

In a veteran's hospital, Alvin died at 76 from stroke complications and was buried at Wolf River Cemetery in Pall Mall, Tennessee.

CEMETERY DIRECTIONS: From I-40, follow Route 127 north for 40 miles toward Pall Mall. After a steep and winding downhill drive just before you reach the village, turn right onto Wolf River Loop. Turn left after the second bridge and the cemetery is a short distance ahead on the right.

GRAVE DIRECTIONS: Enter at the second entrance and you'll see Alvin's grave under the American flag, about 50 yards to the right.

HOW TO FIND WHERE SOMEONE IS BURIED

If your personal hero isn't profiled in this book and you'd like to find his or her resting place, don't despair. With persistence you can find just about anyone's grave.

When I first started searching out famous graves, I tried to find them by the most obvious and amateurish means. I ordered copies of death certificates from faraway courthouses, culled old obituaries from microfilm, and painstakingly scoured biographies for clues. But though each course of action held promise at first, no method yielded consistent results: Obituaries often ignore the burial information entirely; Death certificates are written when the ultimate disposition of the body is still unknown; And, though some biographies mention their subjects' resting places, never do they contain the exact burial location. I found a couple books that broached the subject, but they were dated and plagued with errors. Though I was successful in finding a number of cemetery names through one or another of these methods, not once did I obtain concise step-by-step directions to either a cemetery or a grave. It became apparent that I was on my own—and I resolved to develop a fresh technique for locating the graves of the famous.

It seemed clear that the best way to glean the information was from the living. I recognized that every dead person—whether buried, cremated, or shot into space—has left a number of survivors. These run the gamut from friends and relatives to professional associates or even an undertaker—people who have firsthand knowledge of the person's whereabouts. I simply began to seek those people out and ask them.

I became a sort of after-the-fact detective and, though my inquiries could sometimes be a bit uncomfortable for both parties, I quickly developed a rap, a knack, even, for painlessly getting to the bottom of these matters. Preferring to query the family and friends of the deceased only as a last resort, I started my searches by appealing to funeral homes. First I'd determine the town in which the person died and then call funeral homes in that area. In large towns, and even in medium-sized cities, almost without exception I'd learn which funeral home had overseen the deceased's services within two telephone calls. The funerary business is a relatively small and tight-knit industry; any one of the area's funeral operators would be sure to know which of their crosstown competitors had handled a high-profile affair, and they'd direct me accordingly. From my next call I'd often be able to learn the disposition of the remains.

This sounds simple on paper, and sometimes it was, but I also offer this counsel: To locate a grave successfully through telephone inquiries, you'll need a colossal reserve of diplomacy and tact, an ability to think quickly, and a fair amount of nerve. But above all, you must be persistent and continue to chip away at whatever obstacles arise. Here are some of the roadblocks that I most commonly encountered, along with some suggestions for their circumvention:

A funeral home operator refuses to divulge the whereabouts of the deceased. Recognizing their customers' right to privacy, funeral home proprietors sometimes won't disclose what became of a client. When this happens, I call the funeral home again later to tactfully get connected to other people who work there—a sales associate, hearse driver, or chief coffin technician, it really doesn't matter who—and inquire on a more personal basis. It sometimes helps if you have a list of the area's cemeteries close at hand so, if your contact is reluctant to divulge the information, you can keep them on the phone and perhaps have them "tell" you by process of elimination.

You've secured the name of the cemetery, but neither the yellow pages nor the telephone operator have such a listing. Surprisingly, this happens a lot, and it's usually for one of three reasons: Either the cemetery name has been changed, the cemetery has no phone because it's very small, or the cemetery is run by some other administrative agency.

According to the United States Geological Survey, there are some 115,000 cemeteries in the United States. Like every other business (yes, cemeteries are businesses), there has been a lot of consolidation and, sometimes, a number of small adjoining cemeteries are combined into a single large one. The small cemeteries continue to be known by their original names to appease the various denominations but, in a telephone directory, each would no longer have its own listing. In a case like this, call one of the area's larger cemeteries and ask them if they administer the particular branch in which you are interested.

Many small cemeteries do not have their own telephone or a regular person on staff but, nonetheless, I've found a very easy way to contact their caretakers. Call the town hall, the fire department, the police station, or any municipal office, and ask whoever answers the phone if they know who it is that takes care of the cemetery. Someone will know the person who holds that responsibility and, more often than not, they'll even give you his or her home telephone number.

If a cemetery's name clearly identifies it as being affiliated with a particular religious denomination, simply call and inquire through churches or synagogues. You'll find someone who knows something, trust me. Persistence is the key.

A cemetery refuses to divulge the exact location of someone's grave. This is almost unheard-of at small cemeteries, but it's a common obstacle at the large ones, especially those in southern California, where many celebrities are interred. These cemeteries are so vast that it's absolutely impossible to find a grave unless, at the very least, you know in which section or mausoleum the person rests. Again, persistence usually pays off, but at the Forest Lawn Memorial Park chain of cemeteries, where employees are strictly instructed not to give celebrity grave information to the general public, you sometimes need to be cunning and have an extra trick up your sleeve. Modesty aside, I've had my moments.

When I was trying to find the grave of George Burns, I developed a particularly sly maneuver. If I had simply walked into the Forest Lawn office and asked where George was interred, the receptionist would immediately have recognized his name and refused me the information. So instead, I politely asked if she could direct me to the resting place of my dear great-aunt, Mrs. Grace Allen. Of course, my "aunt" was George's wife, the famous Gracie Allen, whom I knew would be resting alongside George. But the manner of my query caught her off guard and she diligently drew a map to the spot.

The cemetery in Fort Worth, Texas, that holds Lee Harvey Oswald has a strict policy against divulging his location, but a clerk dutifully sought out my request for a "Leonard Oswold who died back in the sixties." She returned from the back room about ten minutes later, apologizing for the wait and explaining that she had been unable to find any record of a Leonard Oswold. In fact, the only guest whose name was even close was a Lee Oswald who had died in 1963. "Would you like to check that gravestone?" she asked. "Perhaps there was a misspelling somewhere." I obliged.

If these methods fail and you can't find the location of someone's grave, you'll have to step it up a notch and contact people who were a little closer to your subject. I've had phone conversations with relatives of rock stars, received emails from the agents of sports heroes and actors, and was faxed a hand-drawn map by the editor of a bestselling author. I had a particularly difficult time finding film reviewer Gene Siskel's grave, so I called his employer, the *Chicago Tribune*, on my cell phone from the cemetery. With a bit of diplomacy, I managed to get patched through to one of Gene's colleagues. He had attended Gene's funeral and, while I drove the cemetery's lanes, he described Gene's grave location to the best of his recollection. I easily found it. It's all about creativity and stamina.

Having said all of this, let me remind you that the Internet has changed everything. These days, an online search or a few well-placed, carefully worded emails to Usenet groups and fan clubs can often save a lot of phone calls. If you want to find the grave of a famous person who's not listed in this book, before you do anything else, direct your browser to www.findagrave.com. The sharing of information seems to be a central tenet of Webmaster Jim Tipton's life doctrine and, through the contributions of his thousands of daily visitors, he has built a database of the resting places of many famous deceased. His site is an excellent starting point. Some of its entries offer section and plot numbers or general landmarks that can help you locate a grave, while a few others even boast of Global Positioning System coordinates. But there are no concise directions to the graves—*Where Are They Buried?* is the only comprehensive source for that information. Good luck.

—TOD BENOIT

INDEX